THE CHRIS✝IAN WRITER'S
MARKET GUIDE

2015-16

EVERYTHING YOU NEED
to GET PUBLISHED

JERRY B. JENKINS™

NEW YORK TIMES BESTSELLING NOVELIST & BIOGRAPHER

WESTBOW®
PRESS

An Imprint of Thomas Nelson
visit us at: thomasnelson.com

The Christian Writer's Market Guide 2015–2016: Everything You Need to Get Published

Copyright © 2015 by Jerry B. Jenkins. All rights reserved.

Published in Nashville, Tennessee, by WestBow Press, an imprint of Thomas Nelson. WestBow Press and Thomas Nelson are registered trademarks of HarperCollins Christian Publishing, Inc.

Scripture quotations marked NIV are taken from the Holy Bible, New International Version®. © 1973, 1978, 1984, 2011 by Biblica, Inc.™ Used by permission of Zondervan. All rights reserved worldwide. www.zondervan.com. (Some quotations may be from the previous edition of the NIV®, © 1984.)

Thomas Nelson titles may be purchased in bulk for educational, business, fund-raising, or sales promotional use. For information, please e-mail SpecialMarkets@ThomasNelson.com.

Visit the Jerry Jenkins Writers Guild at www.JerryJenkins.com.

E-mail: marketguide@JerryJenkins.com

Edited by Andy Scheer

ISBN-13:978-1-4041-0305-4

Printed in the United States of America
15 16 17 18 19 RRD 6 5 4 3 2 1

Contents

PART 1: BOOK PUBLISHERS

PART 2: PERIODICAL PUBLISHERS

PART 3: SPECIALTY MARKETS

PART 4: SUPPORT FOR WRITERS

Introduction
The Publishing Landscape

The revolution in the publishing industry remains in full swing, and that is nothing but good news for you, regardless where you find yourself on the writing spectrum. Traditional methods of seeing your writing find its way to the printed or electronic page have broadened dramatically, but no matter where you hope to place your work, it's crucial that you learn and improve so you can separate yourself from the ever-increasing competition.

Besides royalty-paying book publishers and fee-paying periodical markets, opportunities abound if you want to be published electronically, on demand, in a blog, or via self- or subsidy-publishing. Regardless, good writing rises like cream and must be crafted, edited, proofread, honed, and polished.

Some publishers say too many writers clearly don't read their guidelines before submitting. Most carry their guidelines on their websites, so many of these listings include where to find those. Carefully reading guidelines before submitting is a critical step to selling in today's tighter market. *Note:*

- More and more publishers depend almost entirely on e-mail or website contacts.
- Many periodical publishers are assignment-based only, so establish a reputation in your area of expertise before querying those editors to seek assignments.
- Carefully check out agents before signing with them (the agent section has tips on that). Agents have become more important, so we list which writers conferences have agents in attendance.
- Attending conferences is one of the best ways to meet agents, editors, and publishers.
- The "How to Use This Book" section is full of helpful hints and will save you time.
- Start by flipping through the guide to check the supplementary lists, especially to find specific markets for your work.
- If you're new to the guide or to writing for this market, consult the Glossary.
- A common complaint from publishers is receiving material not appropriate for their needs. Editors are looking for writers who understand their unique approach to the marketplace. The guide is designed to help you meet an editor's expectations, distinguish yourself as a professional, and sell what you write.

I wish you Godspeed as you travel the exciting road to publication. You've been assigned a mission for which you might often feel inadequate. Just remember that the writing tasks God has given you could not be written the same by anyone else.

Finally, special thanks to longtime friend Sally Stuart and decades-long colleague Andy Scheer for their work in helping produce the most complete, up-to-date, and helpful guide we have offered in many years. Through their efforts and with the help of my executive assistant Debbie Kaupp, I am proud to be able to present a resource I'm confident you'll find yourself referring to often and will find indispensable.

Jerry B. Jenkins
THE JERRY JENKINS WRITERS GUILD™
PO Box 88288, Black Forest, CO 80908
719.495.7551
Fax: 719.494.1299
E-mail: Marketguide@JerryJenkins.com
Blog: www.JerryJenkins.com
Facebook: facebook.com/jerry.b.jenkins
Twitter: twitter.com/JerryBJenkins

How to Use This Book

The 2015 Christian Writer's Market Guide is designed to make it easier for you to sell your writing. It will serve you well if you use it as a springboard to become thoroughly familiar with those markets best suited to your style and areas of interest and expertise.

Start by getting acquainted with the setup of the guide. The beginnings of chapters 1 and 5 carry comprehensive listings of periodical and book topics. Cross-referencing may be helpful. For example, if you have a novel that deals with doctor-assisted suicide, you might look at the list for adult fiction and the list for controversial issues and look for publishers on both lists.

Read listings carefully to see whether your target market pays, requires an agent, etc. Each book publisher listing carries the following information (as available):

- Name of publisher
- Address, phone and fax numbers, e-mail address, website
- Denomination or affiliation
- Name of editor—This may include the main editor, followed by another editor to whom submissions should be sent. In some cases, several editors are listed with the types of books each is responsible for. (It's always best to submit to a specific person, never just "Sir" or "Madam" or "To Whom It May Concern.")
- Statement of purpose
- List of imprint names
- Number of inspirational/religious titles published per year, followed by formats of books published (hardcover, trade paperbacks, mass-market paperbacks, coffee table books). Note that coffee table books are also represented in the topical listings.
- Number of submissions received annually
- Percentage of books published from first-time authors
- (Usually) whether the publisher accepts, prefers, requires, or doesn't accept manuscripts through agents
- Percentage of books from freelance authors they subsidy publish (if any). This does not refer to percentage paid by author. If percentage of subsidy is over 50 percent, the publisher will be listed in a separate section under "Subsidy Publishers."
- Whether they reprint out-of-print books from other publishers
- Preferred manuscript length in words or pages; "pages" refers to double-spaced manuscript pages; figure approximately 250 words per page.
- Average amount of royalty, if provided, and whether it is based on the retail (cover price) of the book or on the net receipts (wholesale price to bookstores or distributors)
- Average amount paid for advances and whether the publisher pays an advance against royalties. Not all publishers answer this, so if nothing is mentioned, that doesn't necessarily mean none is offered.
- Whether they pay flat fees rather than royalties
- Average number of copies in first printing
- Average length of time between acceptance of a manuscript and publication
- Whether they consider simultaneous submissions. This means you can send a query or proposal or even a complete manuscript simultaneously, as long as you indicate to each that you are doing so.
- Length of time it should take them to respond to a query/proposal or to a complete manuscript (when two lengths of time are given, the first refers to a query and the

latter to a complete manuscript). Give them a one-month grace period beyond that, and then send a polite follow-up letter.

- Whether a publisher "accepts," "prefers," or "requires" manuscripts sent electronically. (Sending hard copies is almost unheard of now.)
- Which Bible version the publisher prefers
- Whether they do print-on-demand publishing
- Availability and cost of writer's guidelines and book catalogs. Most of these will be available online or via e-mail, but if the publisher offers hard copies, ask directly whether there's a charge, postage costs, etc.
- Nonfiction and Fiction sections indicate preference for query letter, book proposal, or complete manuscript, and whether they accept phone, fax, or e-queries. (Most do not.) If they want a query letter, send a letter describing your project. If they want a query letter/proposal, add a chapter-by-chapter synopsis and 2-3 sample chapters.
- Special Needs
- Ethnic Books—Specifies which groups they target
- Also Does—Indicates which publishers also publish booklets, pamphlets, tracts, or e-books
- Photos/Artwork—Indicates whether they accept freelance photos for book covers.
- Tips

At the end of some listings you will find an indication the publisher receives proposals from *www.ChristianManuscriptSubmissions.com* (see website or index) or The Writer's Edge.

In each periodical listing you will find this information (as available) in this format:

- Name of periodical
- Address, phone and fax numbers, e-mail address, website
- Denomination or affiliation
- Name of editor to submit to
- Theme of publication
- Format, frequency of publication, number of pages, and circulation size
- Subscription rate for a one-year subscription. (You might want to subscribe to at least one of your primary markets every year to become acquainted with its focus.)
- Date established, if 2007 or later
- Openness to freelance submissions; percentage of unsolicited freelance submissions accepted versus assigned articles
- Preference for query or complete manuscript also tells whether they want a cover letter with complete manuscripts and whether they accept phone or e-mail queries. If there is no mention of cover letters or phone or e-mail queries, assume they do not accept them.
- Payment schedule, payment on acceptance or publication, and rights purchased. (See glossary for definitions.)
- If a publication does not pay or pays in copies or subscription, that is indicated in bold capital letters.
- If a publication is not copyrighted, you should ask that your copyright notice appear with your published piece so your rights will be protected.
- Preferred word lengths and average number of manuscripts purchased per year (in parentheses)
- Response time—The time they usually take to respond to your query or manuscript submission
- Seasonal and holiday material—should reach them by at least the specified length of time in advance.

- Acceptance of simultaneous submissions and reprints—whether they accept submissions sent simultaneously to several publishers. It's best to send to non-overlapping markets (such as denominational), and be sure to indicate that it is a simultaneous submission. Reprints are pieces you have sold previously but to which you hold the rights (which means you sold only first or one-time rights to the original publisher and the rights reverted to you).
- Whether they accept, prefer, or require submissions electronically. Most prefer them now. Some indicate whether they want submissions as attached files or copied into the message.
- Average kill-fee amount (see glossary)
- Whether they use sidebars (see glossary)
- Their preferred Bible version, if any. See glossary for "Bible versions."
- Whether they accept submissions from children or teens. "Young-Writer Markets" are also found in the topical listings.
- Availability and cost for writer's guidelines, theme lists, and sample copies—most now have guidelines available by e-mail or website.
- Poetry—Name of poetry editor. Average number of poems bought each year. Types of poetry. Number of lines. Payment rate. Maximum number of poems you may submit at one time.
- Fillers—Name of fillers editor. Types of fillers accepted; word length. Payment rate.
- Columns/Departments—Name of column editor. Names of columns in the periodical (information in parentheses gives focus of column); word-length requirements. Payment rate. Be sure to see sample before sending ms or query. Most columns require a query letter first.
- Special Issues or Needs
- Ethnic
- Contest Information. See "Contests" chapter for full list of contests.
- Tips

Adhering closely to the guidelines set out in these listings will mark you as a professional. If your manuscript is completed, be sure the slant fits the publisher you have in mind.

If you have an idea for an article, short story, or book but you have not written it yet, the topical listing will help you decide on a possible slant or approach. If your idea is for an article, do not overlook writing on the same topic for different periodicals listed under that topic. For example, you could write on money management for a general adult magazine, a teen magazine, a women's publication, or a magazine for pastors. Each would require a different slant, but you would get a lot more mileage from that idea.

If you run into words you're not familiar with, check the glossary at the back of the book. If you need someone to evaluate your material or to give it a thorough editing, look up "Editorial Services." That often will make the difference between success or failure in publishing.

If you are a published author, you may be interested in finding an agent. Some agents consider unpublished authors (their listing will indicate that), but even they require you to have a completed manuscript before being considered (see agent list). The list also includes secular agents who handle religious/inspirational material.

Check the "Clubs/Groups" list to find a chapter to join in your area.

Go to the "Conferences" list to find one you might attend this year. Attending a conference every year or two is almost essential to your success.

Do not rely solely on the information provided in this guide. Use it to familiarize yourself with target markets, but then interact personally with an editor to be sure you're providing what they want. It is important to your success that you learn to use writer's guidelines and study book catalogs or sample copies before submitting to any publisher.

PART 1

Book Publishers

1
Topical Listings of Book Publishers

One of the most difficult aspects of marketing your writing is determining which publishers might be interested in your book. This list will help you do that.

If you don't find your area of interest listed, check the table of contents for related topics. Next, secure writer's guidelines (usually on the publisher's Website) and book catalogs from those publishers. Just because a particular publisher is listed under your topic, don't assume it would automatically be interested in your book. You must determine whether your approach will fit the scope of that publisher's mission. It is also helpful to visit a Christian bookstore or a website to peruse the books produced by each publisher you are considering submitting to

---

(a) before a listing indicates the publisher accepts submissions only through agents.

(s) before a listing indicates it's a subsidy publisher.

R — following a listing indicates the publisher reprints out-of-print books from other publishers.

AFRICAN AMERICAN MARKETS
(a) Abingdon Press
(a) Doubleday
    Relig.—R

AMG Publishers—R
Blue Dolphin—R
(s)-Booklocker.com
Bridge Logos—R
Earthen Vessel—R
Ellechor Publishing
Franciscan Media—R
InterVarsity Press—R
Judson Press
Lighthouse/
    Carolinas—R
Moody Publishers
New Hope
Port Yonder Press
Praeger Publishers
(s)-Redemption Press
Tate Publishing—R
Whitaker House—R
White Fire Pub.
Yale Univ. Press—R

APOLOGETICS
(a) Bethany House

(a) Howard Books
(a) Kregel—R
(a) Nelson, Thomas

(s)-Aaron Book
Abingdon Press
(s)-ACW Press—R
Ambassador Intl.
AMG Publishers—R
Ancient Faith—R
BMH Books
(s)-Booklocker.com—R
Bridge Logos
(s)-Brown Books—R
Canticle Books—R
Charisma House—R
Christian Heritage—R
CLC Publications—R
(s)-Creation House—R
Crossway
CSS Publishing
Earthen Vessel—R
Eerdmans Pub.—R
(s)-Essence—R
(s)-Fairway Press—R
(s)-Faith Books &
    More—R
(s)-Grace Acres—R
Grace Publishing—R

Guardian Angel
Hope Publishing—R
InterVarsity Press—R
Lighthouse Pub.—R
Lighthouse Trails—R
Lutheran Univ. Press
Magnus Press—R
NavPress—R
New Leaf
North Wind Publishing
Our Sunday Visitor—R
P&R Publications
Parson Place
Parsons Pub.—R
Pauline Books
Randall House
(s)-Redemption Press
(s)-Salt Works—R
(s)-Signalman—R
Tate Publishing—R
Trail Media
Trinity Foundation—R
Whitaker House—R
White Fire Pub.
(s)-Word Alive—R
(s)-Zoë Life
    Publishing—R

ARCHAEOLOGY
- (a) Baker Academic
- (a) Baker Books
- (a) Doubleday Relig.—R
- (a) HarperOne
- (a) Kregel—R

- (s)-Aaron Book
- Abingdon Press
- (s)-Abuzz Press—R
- AMG Publishers—R
- Blue Dolphin—R
- BMH Books
- (s)-Booklocker.com
- (s)-Brown Books—R
- Christian Writer's Ebook—R
- Comfort Publishing
- Eerdmans Pub.—R
- (s)-Essence—R
- (s)-Fairway Press—R
- Faith Books & More
- Lighthouse Pub.—R
- NavPress—R
- New Leaf
- Pacific Press
- Port Yonder Press
- (s)-Signalman—R
- Tate Publishing—R
- VBC Publishing
- White Fire Pub.
- (s)-Word Alive—R
- Yale Univ. Press—R

ART, FREELANCE
- (s)-Aaron Book
- Abingdon Press
- Abuzz Press
- Ambassador Intl.
- Blue Dolphin
- Bold Vision Books
- Bondfire Books
- Booklocker.com
- Dawn Publications
- Dove Inspirational
- Earthen Vessel
- Eerdmans/Yg Readers
- Ellechor Publishing
- Essence
- Faith Books & More

- Four Craftsmen
- Grace Acres
- Grace Publishing
- Group Publishing
- Guardian Angel
- Halo Publishing
- Ideals Publications
- JourneyForth/BJU
- Judson Press
- Legacy Press
- Lighthouse Pub.
- Lighthouse Trails
- Mystical Rose
- New Leaf
- Parson Place
- Parsons Publications
- Pauline Kids
- Pelican Pub.
- Players Press
- Port Yonder Press
- Rainbow Publishers
- Randall House
- Ravenhawk Books
- (s)-Redemption Press
- Salt Works
- Signaalman Publishing
- Sunpenny Publishing
- Trinity Foundation
- VBC Publishing
- Warner Press

AUTOBIOGRAPHY
- (a) Baker Books
- (a) Doubleday Relig.—R
- (a) HarperOne
- (a) Nelson, Thomas
- (a) WaterBrook Press

- (s)-Aaron Book
- (s)-Abuzz Press—R
- Ambassador Intl.
- Blue Dolphin—R
- Bondfire Books
- (s)-Booklocker.com
- Bridge Logos—R
- (s)-Brown Books—R
- Charisma House—R
- Christian Heritage—R
- Christian Writer's Ebook—R

- CLC Publications—R
- Comfort Publishing
- Creation House
- (s)-Deep River Books
- Earthen Vessel—R
- (s)-Essence—R
- Evergreen Press
- (s)-Fairway Press—R
- Faith Books & More
- Four Craftsmen—R
- (s)-Grace Acres—R
- Kirk House
- Lighthouse Pub.—R
- Lighthouse Trails—R
- Morgan James Pub.—R
- North Wind Publishing
- Pacific Press
- Parson Place
- Port Yonder Press
- (s)-Redemption Press
- (s)-Signalman—R
- Tate Publishing—R
- Trail Media
- Whitaker House—R
- White Fire Pub.
- (s)-Word Alive—R
- (s)-Zoë Life Pub.—R

BIBLE/BIBLICAL STUDIES
- (a) Baker Academic
- (a) Baker Books
- (a) Bethany House
- (a) Cook, David C.
- (a) Doubleday Relig.—R
- (a) Kregel—R
- (a) WaterBrook Press

- (s)-Aaron Book
- Abingdon Press
- (s)-Abuzz Press—R
- Ambassador Intl.
- AMG Publishers—R
- BMH Books
- Bold Vision—R
- Bondfire Books
- (s)-Booklocker.com
- Bridge Logos—R
- (s)-Brown Books—R
- Canticle Books—R

Chalfont House
Christian Writer's
    Ebook—R
CLC Publications—R
Contemporary Drama
CrossLink Publishing
CrossRiver Media
CSS Publishing
(s)-DCTS Publishers
(s)-Deep River Books
Discovery House—R
Earthen Vessel—R
ECS Ministries
Eerdmans Pub.—R
(s)-Essence—R
Evergreen Press
(s)-Fairway Press—R
Faith Books & More
Four Craftsmen—R
Grace Publishing—R
Group Publishing
Hannibal Books
Harrison House
Inkling Books—R
InterVarsity Press—R
JourneyForth/BJU
Lift Every Voice—R
Lighthouse Pub.—R
Lutheran Univ. Press
Magnus Press—R
NavPress—R
New Hope
North Wind Publishing
On My Own Now
Our Sunday Visitor—R
Pacific Press
P&R Publications
Parson Place
Parsons Pub.—R
Pauline Kids
(s)-Redemption Press
(s)-Salt Works—R
(s)-Signalman—R
Tate Publishing—R
Trail Media
Trinity Foundation--R
VBC Publishing
Wesleyan Publishing
Whitaker House—R
(s)-Word Alive—R

Write Integrity Press
Yale Univ. Press—R
(s)-Zoë Life Pub.—R
Zondervan

BIBLE COMMENTARY
(a) Baker Books
(a) B&H Publishing
(a) Cook, David C.
(a) Doubleday
    Relig.—R
(a) Kregel—R
(a) Tyndale House

(s)-Aaron Book
Abingdon Press
(s)-Abuzz Press—R
Ambassador Intl.
AMG Publishers—R
Ancient Faith—R
BMH Books
Bondfire Books
(s)-Booklocker.com
Bridge Logos—R
(s)-Brown Books—R
Christian Writer's
    Ebook—R
CLC Publications—R
CrossLink Publishing
Crossway
CSS Publishing
Earthen Vessel—R
Eerdmans Pub.—R
(s)-Essence—R
(s)-Fairway Press—R
Faith Books & More
Four Craftsmen—R
Grace Publishing—R
Harrison House
Inkling Books—R
InterVarsity Press—R
Lighthouse Pub.—R
Lutheran Univ. Press
NavPress—R
North Wind Publishing
Our Sunday Visitor—R
P&R Publications
(s)-Redemption Press
(s)-Signalman—R
Tate Publishing—R
VBC Publishing

(s)-Word Alive—R
Yale Univ. Press—R
(s)-Zoë Life Pub.—R
Zondervan

BIOGRAPHY
(a) Baker Books
(a) Ballantine
(a) Doubleday
    Relig.—R
(a) HarperOne
(a) Nelson, Thomas
(a) WaterBrook Press

(s)-Aaron Book
(s)-Abuzz Press—R
Ambassador Intl.
Blue Dolphin—R
Bondfire Books
(s)-Booklocker.com
Bridge Logos—R
(s)-Brown Books—R
Charisma House—R
Christian Heritage—R
Christian Writer's
    Ebook—R
CLC Publications—R
Comfort Publishing
Creation House
(s)-Deep River Books
Earthen Vessel—R
Eerdmans Pub.—R
Eerdmans/Yg Readers
(s)-Essence—R
(s)-Fairway Press—R
Faith Books & More
Four Craftsmen—R
Franciscan Media—R
(s)-Grace Acres—R
Grace Publishing—R
Guideposts Books
Hannibal Books
Hope Publishing—R
Inkling Books—R
Kirk House
Lighthouse Pub.—R
Lighthouse Trails—R
New Leaf
North Wind Publishing
On My Own Now
Pacific Press

Parson Place
Pauline Books
Pauline Kids
Port Yonder Press
(s)-Signalman—R
Ravenhawk Books—R
(s)-Redemption Press
Tate Publishing—R
Trail Media
Whitaker House—R
White Fire Pub.
(s)-Word Alive—R
Yale Univ. Press—R
(s)-Zoë Life Pub.—R

BOOKLETS
(s)-Aaron Book
Bold Vision—R
Bondfire Books
Charisma House—R
Christian Writer's
   Ebook—R
Creation House
Earthen Vessel—R
(s)-Essence—R
Evergreen Press
Four Craftsmen—R
(s)-Fruitbearer Pub.
Grace Publishing—R
InterVarsity Press—R
Life Cycle Books—R
Lighthouse Trails—R
North Wind Publishing
Our Sunday Visitor—R
Pacific Press
P&R Publications
Randall House
(s)-Redemption Press
(s)-Salt Works—R
Tate Publishing—R
Trinity Foundation--R
(s)-Word Alive—R

CANADIAN/FOREIGN
(s)-Essence—R
Sunpenny Publishing
(s)-Word Alive—R

CELEBRITY PROFILES
(a) Baker Books

(a) Hay House
(a) Howard Books
(a) Nelson, Thomas

(s)-Aaron Book
(s)-Abuzz Press—R
Bondfire Books
(s)-Booklocker.com
(s)-Brown Books—R
Charisma House—R
Christian Writer's
   Ebook—R
Comfort Publishing
(s)-Deep River Books
Ellechor Publishing
(s)-Essence—R
(s)-Fairway Press—R
Faith Books & More
(s)-Grace Acres—R
Lighthouse Pub.—R
On My Own Now
Ravenhawk Books—R
(s)-Redemption Press
Tate Publishing—R
(s)-Word Alive—R

CHARISMATIC
(a) Nelson, Thomas

(s)-Aaron Book
(s)-Abuzz Press—R
(s)-Booklocker.com
Bridge Logos—R
Canticle Books—R
Charisma House—R
Chosen Books
Comfort Publishing
Creation House
CSS Publishing
(s)-Destiny Image
Eerdmans Pub.—R
(s)-Essence—R
(s)-Fairway Press—R
Faith Books & More
Four Craftsmen—R
(s)-Fruitbearer Pub.
Grace Publishing—R
Harrison House
Lighthouse Pub.—R
Lutheran Univ. Press
Magnus Press—R

Parsons Pub.—R
(s)-Redemption Press
(s)-Salvation
   Publisher—R
Tate Publishing—R
Whitaker House—R
(s)-Word Alive—R
(s)-Zoë Life Pub.—R

CHILDREN'S BOARD BOOKS
Eerdmans/Yg Readers
Faith Books & More
(s)-Halo Publishing—R
Ideals Publications
Morgan James Pub.—R
Pauline Kids
Tate Publishing—R
(s)-Word Alive—R

CHILDREN'S DEVOTIONALS
Bondfire Books
(s)-Essence—R
Group Publishing
Ideals Publications
New Leaf
North Wind Publishing
Pauline Books
Trail Media
Warner Press
(s)-Zoë Life Pub.—R

CHILDREN'S EASY READERS
(a) Baker Books
(a) Cook, David C.
(a) Tyndale House

(s)-Aaron Book
Ancient Faith—R
(s)-Booklocker.com
(s)-Brown Books—R
Charisma House—R
Creation House
Dawn Publications
(s)-Deep River Books
Eerdmans/Yg Readers
(s)-Essence—R
Evergreen Press
(s)-Fairway Press—R

Faith Books & More
Guardian Angel
Ideals Publications
Inkling Books—R
JourneyForth/BJU
Legacy Press
Lift Every Voice—R
Lighthouse Pub.—R
North Wind Publishing
Our Sunday Visitor—R
Pacific Press
Pauline Books
Pauline Kids
Pelican Pub.—R
(s)-Redemption Press
Standard Publishing
Tate Publishing—R
Trail Media
VBC Publishing
Warner Press
(s)-Word Alive—R
(s)-Zoë Life Pub.—R

CHILDREN'S PICTURE BOOKS
(nonfiction)
(a) Baker Books
(a) Bethany House
(a) Cook, David C.
(a) Tyndale House
(a) WaterBrook Press

(s)-Aaron Book
Abingdon Press
(s)-Abuzz Press—R
Ambassador Intl.
Ancient Faith—R
Bridge Logos—R
(s)-Brown Books—R
Creation House
Dove Inspirational—R
Eerdmans Pub.—R
Eerdmans/Yg Readers
(s)-Essence—R
Evergreen Press
Faith Books & More
(s)-Fruitbearer Pub.
Guardian Angel
(s)-Halo Publishing—R
Ideals Publications
Lighthouse Pub.—R

Lighthouse Trails—R
Morgan James Pub.—R
New Leaf
North Wind Publishing
Pauline Books
Pauline Kids
Pelican Pub.—R
ShadeTree Publishing
Standard Publishing
Tate Publishing—R
Trail Media
Warner Press
(s)-Zoë Life Pub.—R

CHRIST
(a) Bethany House
(a) Cook, David C.
(a) Doubleday
    Relig.—R
(a) Nelson, Thomas

(s)-Aaron Book
(s)-Abuzz Press—R
Ambassador Intl.
AMG Publishers—R
Ancient Faith—R
Barbour—R
Blue Dolphin—R
BMH Books
Bondfire Books
(s)-Booklocker.com
(s)-Brown Books—R
Canticle Books—R
Charisma House—R
Christian Heritage—R
Christian Writer's
    Ebook—R
CLC Publications—R
Creation House
CSS Publishing
(s)-Deep River Books
Discovery House—R
Earthen Vessel—R
Eerdmans Pub.—R
Eerdmans/Yg Readers
(s)-Essence—R
(s)-Fairway Press—R
Faith Books & More
(s)-Grace Acres—R
Grace Publishing—R
Guardian Angel

Guideposts Books
JourneyForth/BJU
Lift Every Voice—R
Lighthouse Pub.—R
Lutheran Univ. Press
Magnus Press—R
NavPress—R
New Leaf
North Wind Publishing
Our Sunday Visitor—R
P&R Publications
Parson Place
Pauline Books
Pauline Kids
(s)-Redemption Press
(s)-Salt Works—R
(s)-Signalman—R
Tate Publishing—R
VBC Publishing
Whitaker House—R
White Fire Pub.
(s)-Word Alive—R
(s)-Zoë Life Pub.—R

CHRISTIAN BUSINESS
(a) Cook, David C.
(a) Doubleday
    Relig.—R
(a)Howard Books
(a) Nelson, Thomas
(a) WaterBrook Press

(s)-Aaron Book
(s)-Abuzz Press—R
Ambassador Intl.
BMH Books
Bold Vision—R
Bondfire Books
(s)-Booklocker.com
(s)-Brown Books—R
Charisma House—R
Christian Writer's
    Ebook—R
CLC Publications—R
Comfort Publishing
Creation House
CSS Publishing
(s)-Deep River Books
Eerdmans Pub.—R
Ellechor Publishing
(s)-Essence—R

Evergreen Press
(s)-Fairway Press—R
Faith Books & More
Four Craftsmen—R
(s)-Grace Acres—R
Grace Publishing—R
Hannibal Books
InterVarsity Press—R
JourneyForth/BJU
Kirk House
Lift Every Voice—R
Lighthouse Pub.—R
Lutheran Univ. Press
Morgan James Pub.—R
NavPress—R
New Leaf
North Wind Publishing
Parsons Pub.—R
Ravenhawk Books—R
(s)-Redemption Press
(s)-Salvation
    Publisher—R
(s)-Signalman—R
Tate Publishing—R
Trail Media
VBC Publishing
Whitaker House—R
White Fire Pub.
(s)-Word Alive—R
(s)-Zoë Life Pub.—R

CHRISTIAN EDUCATION

(a) Baker Academic
(a) Baker Books
(a) Cook, David C.
(a) Doubleday
    Relig.—R
(a) Kregel—R

(s)-Aaron Book
(s)-Abuzz Press—R
Ambassador Intl.
Bondfire Books
(s)-Booklocker.com
(s)-Brown Books—R
Christian Heritage—R
Christian Writer's
    Ebook—R
Church Growth Inst.
CLC Publications—R

Contemporary Drama
Crossway
CSS Publishing
(s)-DCTS Publishers
Eerdmans Pub.—R
Ellechor Publishing
(s)-Essence—R
(s)-Fairway Press—R
Faith Books & More
(s)-Grace Acres—R
Grace Publishing—R
(s)-Halo Publishing—R
InterVarsity Press—R
Judson Press
Kirk House
Lift Every Voice—R
Lighthouse Pub.—R
Lutheran Univ. Press
Meriwether
New Leaf
North Wind Publishing
Our Sunday Visitor—R
Pacific Press
Rainbow Publishers
(s)-Redemption Press
Reference Service
(s)-Salvation
    Publisher—R
(s)-Signalman—R
Standard Publishing
Tate Publishing—R
Trail Media
Trinity Foundation--R
VBC Publishing
White Fire Pub.
(s)-Word Alive—R
(s)-Zoë Life Pub.—R

CHRISTIAN HOMESCHOOLING

(a) Baker Books

(s)-Aaron Book
(s)-Abuzz Press—R
AMG Publishers—R
BMH Books
Bondfire Books
(s)-Booklocker.com
(s)-Brown Books—R
Christian Writer's
    Ebook—R

CLC Publications—R
(s)-CrossHouse
CSS Publishing
Eerdmans Pub.—R
(s)-Essence—R
(s)-Fairway Press—R
Faith Books & More
(s)-Fruitbearer Pub.
(s)-Grace Acres—R
Grace Publishing—R
Hannibal Books
Inkling Books—R
Lift Every Voice—R
Lighthouse Pub.—R
Morgan James Pub.—R
New Leaf
North Wind Publishing
Pacific Press
(s)-Redemption Press
(s)-Signalman—R
Standard Publishing
Tate Publishing—R
Trail Media
White Fire Pub.
(s)-Word Alive—R
(s)-Zoë Life Pub.—R

CHRISTIAN LIVING

(a) Baker Books
(a) B&H Publishing
(a) Bethany House
(a) Cook, David C.
(a) Doubleday
    Relig.—R
(a) HarperOne
(a) Howard Books
(a) Multnomah
(a) Nelson, Thomas
(a) Revell
(a) Tyndale House
(a) WaterBrook Press

(s)-Aaron Book
Abingdon Press
(s)-Abuzz Press—R
Ambassador Intl.
Ancient Faith—R
Barbour—R
Bold Vision—R
Bondfire Books
(s)-Booklocker.com

(s)-Brown Books—R
Canticle Books—R
Chalfont House
Charisma House—R
Christian Writer's
    Ebook—R
Cladach Publishing
CLC Publications—R
Comfort Publishing
Creation House
CrossLink Publishing
Crossway
CSS Publishing
(s)-DCTS Publishers
(s)-Deep River Books
(s)-Destiny Image
    (books)
Discovery House—R
Earthen Vessel—R
Eerdmans Pub.—R
Ellechor Publishing
(s)-Essence—R
Evergreen Press
(s)-Fairway Press—R
Faith Books & More
Four Craftsmen—R
Franciscan Media—R
(s)-Grace Acres—R
Grace Publishing—R
Guideposts Books
Hope Publishing—R
Inheritance Press
InterVarsity Press—R
JourneyForth/BJU
Judson Press
Life Cycle Books—R
Lift Every Voice—R
Lighthouse/
    Carolinas—R
Lighthouse Pub.—R
Lighthouse Trails—R
Lutheran Univ. Press
Magnus Press—R
Moody Publishers
Morgan James Pub.—R
NavPress—R
New Hope
New Leaf
North Wind Publishing
OakTara

On My Own Now
Our Sunday Visitor—R
Parsons Pub.—R
Pauline Books
Pauline Kids
(s)-Port Hole
    Public.—R
Randall House
(s)-Redemption Press
(s)-Salvation
    Publisher—R
(s)-Signalman—R
Standard Publishing
Sunpenny Publishing
Tate Publishing—R
Trail Media
Trinity Foundation--R
VBC Publishing
Wesleyan Publishing
Whitaker House—R
White Fire Pub.
(s)-Word Alive—R
Write Integrity Press
(s)-Zoë Life Pub.—R

CHRISTIAN SCHOOL BOOKS
(a) Baker Books

(s)-Aaron Book
(s)-Abuzz Press—R
Bondfire Books
(s)-Booklocker.com
Christian Writer's
    Ebook—R
CSS Publishing
Eerdmans Pub.—R
(s)-Essence—R
(s)-Fairway Press—R
Faith Books & More
(s)-Grace Acres—R
Grace Publishing—R
Inkling Books—R
JourneyForth/BJU
Lighthouse Pub.—R
Our Sunday Visitor—R
Pacific Press
Pauline Kids
(s)-Redemption Press
(s)-Signalman—R
Tate Publishing—R

(s)-Word Alive—R
(s)-Zoë Life Pub.—R

CHRISTMAS BOOKS
Ambassador Intl.
AMG Publishers—R
Ancient Faith—R
Bondfire Books
Chalfont House
Cladach Publishing
Discovery House—R
(s)-Essence—R
Grace Publishing—R
Lighthouse/
    Carolinas—R
North Wind Publishing
Pauline Books
(s)-Redemption Press
(s)-Signalman—R
Trail Media
Warner Press
Whitaker House—R
White Fire Pub.
Write Integrity Press
(s)-Zoë Life Pub.—R

CHURCH GROWTH
(a) Kregel

(s)-Aaron Book
Ambassador Intl.
(s)-Booklocker.com
(s)-Brown Books—R
CLC Publications—R
(s)-CrossHouse
CrossLink Publishing
Crossway
Dove Inspirational—R
(s)-Essence—R
Faith Books & More
(s)-Grace Acres—R
Grace Publishing—R
Guardian Angel
Legacy Press
NavPress—R
New Leaf
North Wind Publishing
P&R Publications
Pauline Kids
Pelican Pub.—R
Randall House

(s)-Redemption Press
(s)-Salt Works—R
(s)-Signalman—R
White Fire Pub.
(s)-Zoë Life Pub.—R

CHURCH HISTORY
(a) Baker Books
(a) B&H Publishing
(a) Doubleday
    Relig.—R
(a) HarperOne
(a) Kregel—R

(s)-Aaron Book
ABC-CLIO
Abingdon Press
(s)-Abuzz Press—R
Ambassador Intl.
Ancient Faith—R
Blue Dolphin—R
Bondfire Books
(s)-Booklocker.com
Christian Heritage—R
Christian Writer's
    Ebook—R
Creation House
(s)-CrossHouse
CrossLink Publishing
Crossway
CSS Publishing
Earthen Vessel—R
Eerdmans Pub.—R
(s)-Essence—R
(s)-Fairway Press—R
Faith Books & More
Franciscan Media—R
Hannibal Books
InterVarsity Press—R
Kirk House
Lighthouse Pub.—R
Loyola Press
Lutheran Univ. Press
NavPress—R
North Wind Publishing
Our Sunday Visitor—R
Pacific Press
Port Yonder Press
Randall House
(s)-Redemption Press
(s)-Signalman—R

Tate Publishing—R
White Fire Pub.
(s)-Word Alive—R
Yale Univ. Press—R
(s)-Zoë Life Pub.—R
Zondervan

CHURCH LIFE
(a) Baker Books
(a) Bethany House
(a) Doubleday
    Relig.—R
(a) HarperOne
(a) Howard Books
(a) Kregel—R
(a) Nelson, Thomas

(s)-Aaron Book
Abingdon Press
(s)-Abuzz Press—R
Ambassador Intl.
Bondfire Books
(s)-Booklocker.com
Charisma House—R
Christian Writer's
    Ebook—R
CLC Publications—R
Creation House
CrossLink Publishing
Crossway
CSS Publishing
(s)-DCTS Publishers
(s)-Deep River Books
Discovery House—R
Earthen Vessel—R
Eerdmans Pub.—R
(s)-Essence—R
(s)-Fairway Press—R
Faith Books & More
(s)-Grace Acres—R
Hannibal Books
Harrison House
Hope Publishing—R
InterVarsity Press—R
Judson Press
Kirk House
Lift Every Voice—R
Lighthouse Pub.—R
Lutheran Univ. Press
NavPress—R
New Hope

North Wind Publishing
Pacific Press
P&R Publications
Parsons Pub.—R
Pauline Books
Pauline Kids
Randall House
(s)-Redemption Press
(s)-Signalman—R
Tate Publishing—R
Wesleyan Publishing
White Fire Pub.
(s)-Word Alive—R
(s)-Zoë Life Pub.—R

CHURCH MANAGEMENT
(a) B&H Publishing
(a) Doubleday
    Relig.—R
(a) Kregel—R

(s)-Aaron Book
Abingdon Press
(s)-Abuzz Press—R
BMH Books
(s)-Booklocker.com
Charisma House—R
Christian Heritage—R
CLC Publications—R
Creation House
CrossLink Publishing
CSS Publishing
Eerdmans Pub.—R
(s)-Essence—R
(s)-Fairway Press—R
Faith Books & More
(s)-Grace Acres—R
Group Publishing
Hannibal Books
Harrison House
Hope Publishing—R
JourneyForth/BJU
Judson Press
Kirk House
Lighthouse Pub.—R
Lutheran Univ. Press
North Wind Publishing
Our Sunday Visitor—R
Parsons Pub.—R
Randall House

(s)-Redemption Press
(s)-Signalman—R
Tate Publishing—R
Wesleyan Publishing
White Fire Pub.
(s)-Word Alive—R
(s)-Zoë Life Pub.—R

CHURCH RENEWAL
(a) Baker Books
(a) Doubleday
    Relig.—R
(a) HarperOne
(a) Howard Books
(a) Kregel—R

(s)-Aaron Book
Abingdon Press
(s)-Abuzz Press—R
BMH Books
Bondfire Books
(s)-Booklocker.com
Bridge Logos—R
Canticle Books—R
Christian Writer's
    Ebook—R
Church Growth Inst.
CLC Publications—R
Creation House
CrossLink Publishing
CSS Publishing
(s)-Deep River Books
(s)-Destiny Image
    (books)
Eerdmans Pub.—R
(s)-Essence—R
(s)-Fairway Press—R
Faith Books & More
Four Craftsmen—R
(s)-Grace Acres—R
Grace Publishing—R
Hannibal Books
Hope Publishing—R
InterVarsity Press—R
Judson Press
Lighthouse Pub.—R
Lutheran Univ. Press
Magnus Press—R
NavPress—R
North Wind Publishing
Pacific Press

Parson Place
Parsons Pub.—R
Randall House
(s)-Redemption Press
(s)-Salvation
    Publisher—R
(s)-Signalman—R
Tate Publishing—R
Wesleyan Publishing
White Fire Pub.
(s)-Word Alive—R
(s)-Zoë Life Pub.—R

CHURCH
TRADITIONS
(a) Baker Books
(a) Doubleday
    Relig.—R
(a) Howard Books
(a) Kregel—R
(a) Nelson, Thomas

(s)-Aaron Book
Abingdon Press
(s)-Abuzz Press—R
Ancient Faith—R
Blue Dolphin—R
(s)-Booklocker.com
Christian Heritage—R
Christian Writer's
    Ebook—R
Creation House
CrossLink Publishing
CSS Publishing
(s)-Deep River Books
Eerdmans Pub.—R
(s)-Essence—R
(s)-Fairway Press—R
Faith Books & More
Franciscan Media—R
Inkling Books—R
InterVarsity Press—R
Lighthouse Pub.—R
Lutheran Univ. Press
NavPress—R
North Wind Publishing
Our Sunday Visitor—R
Pacific Press
Pauline Books
Pauline Kids
Port Yonder Press

Praeger Publishers
(s)-Redemption Press
(s)-Signalman—R
Tate Publishing—R
White Fire Pub.
(s)-Word Alive—R
(s)-Zoë Life Pub.—R

COFFEE TABLE
BOOKS
(s)-Aaron Book
(s)-Abuzz Press—R
Ambassador Intl.
AMG Publishers—R
Blue Dolphin—R
(s)-Brown Books—R
Creation House
(s)-Deep River Books
(s)-Essence—R
(s)-Halo Publishing—R
Kirk House
Lutheran Univ. Press
Players Press
(s)-Redemption Press
(s)-Salt Works—R
(s)-Zoë Life Pub.—R

COMPILATIONS
(a) Doubleday
    Relig.—R
(a) WaterBrook Press

(s)-Aaron Book
Abingdon Press
(s)-Abuzz Press—R
Ancient Faith—R
Blue Dolphin—R
(s)-Booklocker.com
Christian Heritage—R
Christian Writer's
    Ebook—R
Creation House
CrossLink Publishing
CSS Publishing
(s)-Deep River Books
Eerdmans Pub.—R
(s)-Essence—R
(s)-Fairway Press—R
Faith Books & More
Franciscan Media—R
Inkling Books—R

InterVarsity Press—R
Lighthouse Pub.—R
Lutheran Univ. Press
NavPress—R
North Wind Publishing
Our Sunday Visitor—R
Pacific Press
Pauline Books
Pauline Kids
Port Yonder Press
Praeger Publishers
(s)-Redemption Press
(s)-Signalman—R
Tate Publishing—R
White Fire Pub.
(s)-Word Alive—R
(s)-Zoë Life Pub.—R

CONTROVERSIAL ISSUES

(a) Baker Books
(a) Doubleday
    Relig.—R
(a) HarperOne
(a) Hay House
(a) Howard Books
(a) Kregel—R

(s)-Aaron Book
ABC-CLIO
(s)-Abuzz Press—R
Ambassador Intl.
Ancient Faith—R
Blue Dolphin—R
Bondfire Books
(s)-Booklocker.com
Bridge Logos—R
Canticle Books—R
Charisma House—R
Christian Writer's
    Ebook—R
Comfort Publishing
Creation House
(s)-Deep River Books
(s)-Destiny Image
Earthen Vessel—R
Eerdmans Pub.—R
(s)-Essence—R
(s)-Fairway Press—R
Faith Books & More
Four Craftsmen—R

Hannibal Books
Hope Publishing—R
Inkling Books—R
InterVarsity Press—R
Judson Press
Life Cycle Books—R
Lighthouse Pub.—R
Lighthouse Trails—R
Magnus Press—R
MountainView
NavPress—R
OakTara
Ravenhawk Books—R
(s)-Redemption Press
(s)-Salt Works—R
Tate Publishing—R
Trail Media
White Fire Pub.
(s)-Word Alive—R
(s)-Zoë Life Pub.—R

COOKBOOKS

(a) Ballantine
(a) Nelson, Thomas

(s)-Aaron Book
(s)-Abuzz Press—R
Adams Media
Ambassador Intl.
Barbour—R
Blue Dolphin—R
(s)-Booklocker.com
Bridge Logos—R
(s)-Brown Books—R
Charisma House—R
Christian Writer's
    Ebook—R
(s)-CrossHouse
Dove Inspirational—R
(s)-Essence—R
Evergreen Press
(s)-Fairway Press—R
Faith Books & More
Grace Publishing—R
Guardian Angel
(s)-Halo Publishing—R
Hannibal Books
North Wind Publishing
Pacific Press
Pelican Pub.—R
(s)-Redemption Press

(s)-Signalman—R
Sunpenny Publishing
Tate Publishing—R
(s)-Word Alive—R
(s)-Zoë Life Pub.—R

COUNSELING AIDS

(a) Baker Books
(a) Kregel—R
(a) Nelson, Thomas

(s)-Aaron Book
(s)-Abuzz Press—R
Bondfire Books
(s)-Booklocker.com
Bridge Logos—R
(s)-Brown Books—R
Chalfont House
Charisma House—R
Charles Press
Christian Writer's
    Ebook—R
CLC Publications—R
CSS Publishing
(s)-Deep River Books
Eerdmans Pub.—R
(s)-Essence—R
Evergreen Press
(s)-Fairway Press—R
Faith Books & More
Grace Publishing—R
Group Publishing
InterVarsity Press—R
JourneyForth/BJU
Langmarc
Life Cycle Books—R
Lighthouse Pub.—R
Morgan James Pub.—R
North Wind Publishing
OakTara
On My Own Now
P&R Publications
Randall House
(s)-Redemption Press
Reference Service
(s)-Signalman—R
Tate Publishing—R
White Fire Pub.
(s)-Word Alive—R
(s)-Zoë Life Pub.—R

CREATION SCIENCE
  (s)-Aaron Book
  (s)-Abuzz Press—R
  BMH Books
  Bondfire Books
  (s)-Booklocker.com
  Bridge Logos—R
  Charisma House—R
  Christian Writer's
    Ebook—R
  Eerdmans Pub.—R
  (s)-Essence—R
  (s)-Fairway Press—R
  Faith Books & More
  Hope Publishing—R
  Inkling Books—R
  Lighthouse Pub.—R
  New Leaf
  Pacific Press
  Parson Place
  (s)-Redemption Press
  (s)-Salt Works—R
  (s)-Signalman—R
  Tate Publishing—R
  Trail Media
  (s)-Word Alive—R
  (s)-Zoë Life Pub.—R

CULTS/OCCULT
  (a) Baker Books
  (a) HarperOne
  (a) Kregel—R

  (s)-Aaron Book
  ABC-CLIO
  (s)-Abuzz Press—R
  AMG Publishers—R
  Blue Dolphin—R
  (s)-Booklocker.com
  Christian Writer's
    Ebook—R
  Comfort Publishing
  Earthen Vessel—R
  Eerdmans Pub.—R
  (s)-Essence—R
  (s)-Fairway Press—R
  Faith Books & More
  Lighthouse Pub.—R
  Ravenhawk Books—R
  (s)-Redemption Press
  Tate Publishing—R

Whitaker House—R
  (s)-Word Alive—R

CURRENT/SOCIAL
ISSUES
  (a) Baker Academic
  (a) Baker Books
  (a) B&H Publishing
  (a) Bethany House
  (a) Doubleday
    Relig.—R
  (a) HarperOne
  (a) Howard Books
  (a) Kregel—R
  (a) Nelson, Thomas
  (a) Tyndale House

  (s)-Aaron Book
  ABC-CLIO
  (s)-Abuzz Press—R
  Ambassador Intl.
  (s)-Ampelos Press—R
  Ancient Faith—R
  Blue Dolphin—R
  Bondfire Books
  (s)-Booklocker.com
  Bridge Logos—R
  (s)-Brown Books—R
  Charisma House—R
  Christian Writer's
    Ebook—R
  Comfort Publishing
  Conari Press
  Creation House
  (s)-DCTS Publishers
  (s)-Deep River Books
  Earthen Vessel—R
  Eerdmans Pub.—R
  Eerdmans/Yg Readers
  (s)-Essence—R
  (s)-Fairway Press—R
  Faith Books & More
  Hannibal Books
  Inkling Books—R
  InterVarsity Press—R
  JourneyForth/BJU
  Judson Press
  Life Cycle Books—R
  Lighthouse Pub.—R
  Loyola Press
  Lutheran Univ. Press

NavPress—R
  New Hope
  New Leaf
  North Wind Publishing
  On My Own Now
  Pauline Books
  Port Yonder Press
  Ravenhawk Books—R
  (s)-Redemption Press
  (s)-Salt Works—R
  (s)-Signalman—R
  Tate Publishing—R
  Trail Media
  VBC Publishing
  White Fire Pub.
  (s)-Word Alive—R
  Write Integrity Press
  (s)-Zoë Life Pub.—R

CURRICULUM
  (a) Cook, David C.

  (s)-Aaron Book
  (s)-Abuzz Press—R
  Bondfire Books
  CrossLink Publishing
  Eerdmans Pub.—R
  (s)-Fairway Press—R
  Gospel Light
  (s)-Grace Acres—R
  Grace Publishing—R
  Group Publishing
  Hannibal Books
  Inheritance Press
  Lighthouse Pub.—R
  Lighthouse Trails—R
  New Leaf
  (s)-Redemption Press
  (s)-Signalman—R
  Standard Publishing
  Tate Publishing—R
  (s)-Word Alive—R
  (s)-Zoë Life Pub.—R

DATING/SEX
  (a) Ballantine
  (a) Bethany House
  (a) Cook, David C.
  (a) Doubleday
    Relig.—R
  (a) HarperOne

(a) Kregel—R
(a) Nelson, Thomas
(a) WaterBrook Press

(s)-Aaron Book
(s)-Abuzz Press—R
Ambassador Intl.
Barbour—R
Bondfire Books
(s)-Booklocker.com
Bridge Logos—R
Chalfont House
Charisma House—R
Christian Writer's
    Ebook—R
Comfort Publishing
(s)-Deep River Books
(s)-Destiny Image
    (books)
Eerdmans Pub.—R
Ellechor Publishing
(s)-Essence—R
Evergreen Press
(s)-Fairway Press—R
Faith Books & More
Grace Publishing—R
Lift Every Voice—R
Lighthouse Pub.—R
NavPress—R
On My Own Now
P&R Publications
Pauline Books
(s)-Redemption Press
(s)-Signalman—R
Tate Publishing—R
Trail Media
Whitaker House—R
White Fire Pub.
(s)-Word Alive—R
(s)-Zoë Life Pub.—R

DEATH/DYING

(a) Baker Books
(a) Cook, David C.
(a) Doubleday
    Relig.—R
(a) HarperOne
(a) Kregel—R
(a) Nelson, Thomas
(a) WaterBrook Press

(s)-Aaron Book
Abingdon Press
ABC-CLIO
(s)-Abuzz Press—R
Ambassador Intl.
Ancient Faith—R
Blue Dolphin—R
Bondfire Books
(s)-Booklocker.com
Bridge Logos—R
(s)-Brown Books—R
Charisma House—R
Christian Writer's
    Ebook—R
Comfort Publishing
Creation House
CSS Publishing
(s)-Deep River Books
Discovery House—R
Eerdmans Pub.—R
Ellechor Publishing
(s)-Essence—R
Evergreen Press
(s)-Fairway Press—R
Faith Books & More
Grace Publishing—R
Guardian Angel
(s)-Halo Publishing—R
Hope Publishing—R
Life Cycle Books—R
Lift Every Voice—R
Lighthouse Pub.—R
Loyola Press
Lutheran Univ. Press
NavPress—R
North Wind Publishing
Pacific Press
P&R Publications
Pauline Books
(s)-Redemption Press
(s)-Signalman—R
Tate Publishing—R
Trail Media
Whitaker House—R
White Fire Pub.
(s)-Word Alive—R
(s)-Zoë Life Pub.—R

DEVOTIONAL BOOKS

(a) Baker Books

(a) Bethany House
(a) Cook, David C.
(a) Doubleday
    Relig.—R
(a) HarperOne
(a) Howard Books
(a) Kregel—R
(a) Nelson, Thomas
(a) Tyndale House
(a) WaterBrook Press

(s)-Aaron Book
Abingdon Press
(s)-Abuzz Press—R
Ambassador Intl.
(s)-Ampelos Press—R
Ancient Faith—R
Barbour—R
Bold Vision—R
Bondfire Books
(s)-Booklocker.com
(s)-Brown Books—R
Chalfont House
Charisma House—R
Christian Heritage—R
Christian Writer's
    Ebook—R
CLC Publications—R
Contemporary Drama
Creation House
CrossLink Publishing
CrossRiver Media
CSS Publishing
(s)-Deep River Books
Discovery House—R
Eerdmans Pub.—R
Ellechor Publishing
(s)-Essence—R
Evergreen Press
(s)-Fairway Press—R
Faith Books & More
Four Craftsmen—R
Franciscan Media—R
(s)-Fruitbearer Pub.
Grace Publishing—R
Group Publishing
Guideposts Books
Hannibal Books
Harrison Hous
Inheritance Press
Inkling Books—R

Judson Press
Legacy Press
Lift Every Voice—R
Lighthouse/
    Carolinas—R
Lighthouse Pub.—R
MOPS Intl.
Morgan James Pub.—R
NavPress—R
New Hope
New Leaf
North Wind Publishing
OakTara
On My Own Now
P&R Publications
Parson Place
Pauline Books
(s)-Redemption Press
(s)-Salt Works—R
(s)-Salvation
    Publisher—R
(s)-Signalman—R
Standard Publishing
Tate Publishing—R
Trail Media
VBC Publishing
Warner Press
Wesleyan Publishing
Whitaker House—R
White Fire Pub.
(s)-Word Alive—R
(s)-Zoë Life Pub.—R

DISCIPLESHIP
(a) Baker Books
(a) B&H Publishing
(a) Bethany House
(a) Cook, David C.
(a) Doubleday
    Relig.—R
(a) HarperOne
(a) Howard Books
(a) Kregel—R
(a) Nelson, Thomas
(a) WaterBrook Press

(s)-Aaron Book
Abingdon Press
(s)-Abuzz Press—R
Ambassador Intl.
AMG Publishers—R

Barbour—R
BMH Books
Bold Vision—R
Bondfire Books
(s)-Booklocker.com
Bridge Logos—R
(s)-Brown Books—R
Charisma House—R
Christian Heritage—R
Christian Writer's
    Ebook—R
CLC Publications—R
Comfort Publishing
Creation House
CrossRiver Media
Crossway
CSS Publishing
(s)-DCTS Publishers
(s)-Deep River Books
(s)-Destiny Image
    (books)
Discovery House—R
Earthen Vessel—R
Eerdmans Pub.—R
(s)-Essence—R
Evergreen Press
(s)-Fairway Press—R
Faith Books & More
(s)-Grace Acres—R
Grace Publishing—R
Group Publishing
Harrison House
Inheritance Press
Inkling Books—R
InterVarsity Press—R
JourneyForth/BJU
Judson Press
Lift Every Voice—R
Lighthouse Pub.—R
Lutheran Univ. Press
Moody Publishers
Morgan James Pub.—R
NavPress—R
New Hope
New Leaf
North Wind Publishing
On My Own Now
Pacific Press
P&R Publications
Parson Place

Parsons Pub.—R
Pauline Books
Randall House
(s)-Redemption Press
(s)-Salt Works—R
(s)-Salvation
    Publisher—R
(s)-Signalman—R
Standard Publishing
Tate Publishing—R
Trail Media
White Fire Pub.
(s)-Word Alive—R
(s)-Zoë Life Pub.—R

DIVORCE
(a) Baker Books
(a) Bethany House
(a) Cook, David C.
(a) Kregel—R
(a) Nelson, Thomas
(a) WaterBrook Press

(s)-Aaron Book
(s)-Abuzz Press—R
Ambassador Intl.
AMG Publishers—R
Bondfire Books
(s)-Booklocker.com
Bridge Logos—R
(s)-Brown Books—R
Charisma House—R
Christian Writer's
    Ebook—R
Comfort Publishing
Creation House
CSS Publishing
(s)-Deep River Books
Discovery House—R
Earthen Vessel—R
Eerdmans Pub.—R
Ellechor Publishing
(s)-Essence—R
(s)-Fairway Press—R
Faith Books & More
Grace Publishing—R
Guideposts Books
(s)-Halo Publishing—R
InterVarsity Press—R
Lighthouse/
    Carolinas—R

Lighthouse Pub.—R
Pacific Press
P&R Publications
Pauline Books
(s)-Redemption Press
(s)-Signalman—R
Tate Publishing—R
Trail Media
White Fire Pub.
(s)-Word Alive—R
(s)-Zoë Life Pub.—R

DOCTRINAL
(a) Baker Books
(a) Bethany House
(a) Doubleday
   Relig.—R
(a) Kregel—R
(a) Tyndale House

(s)-Aaron Book
(s)-Abuzz Press—R
AMG Publishers—R
Ancient Faith—R
(s)-Booklocker.com
(s)-Brown Books—R
Canticle Books—R
Christian Heritage—R
Christian Writer's
   Ebook—R
CLC Publications—R
Creation House
CrossLink Publishing
Crossway
(s)-DCTS Publishers
Earthen Vessel—R
Eerdmans Pub.—R
(s)-Essence—R
(s)-Fairway Press—R
Faith Books & More
InterVarsity Press—R
Lighthouse Pub.—R
Lutheran Univ. Press
Pacific Press
Parsons Pub.—R
Randall House
(s)-Redemption Press
(s)-Signalman—R
Tate Publishing—R
Trinity Foundation--R
VBC Publishing

(s)-Word Alive—R
(s)-Zoë Life Pub.—R

DRAMA
(a) Kregel—Rl

(s)-Aaron Book
(s)-Abuzz Press—R
Contemporary Drama
Earthen Vessel—R
(s)-Fairway Press—R
Faith Books & More
Guardian Angel
(s)-Halo Publishing—R
Lighthouse Pub.—R
Meriwether
North Wind Publishing
Ravenhawk Books—R
(s)-Redemption Press
(s)-Salt Works—R
(s)-Signalman—R
Tate Publishing—R
(s)-Word Alive—R

E-BOOKS
(a) Tyndale House

Ambassador Intl.
AMG Publishers—R
Ancient Faith—R
Aneko
Blue Dolphin—R
Bold Vision—R
Bondfire Books
(s)-Booklocker.com
Chalfont House
Christian Writer's
   Ebook—R
CLC Publications—R
Comfort Publishing
CrossLink Publishing
CSS Publishing
Earthen Vessel—R
Faith Books & More
Four Craftsmen—R
(s)-Grace Acres—R
Grace Publishing—R
Guardian Angel
InterVarsity Press—R
Lighthouse/
   Carolinas—R

Lighthouse Pub.—R
NavPress—R
New Leaf
OakTara
Parsons Pub.—R
Pauline Books
(s)-Redemption Press
(s)-Salt Works—R
(s)-Signalman—R
Sunpenny Publishing
Trail Media
(s)-Westbow Press
Whitaker House—R
White Fire Pub.
White Rose
(s)-Word Alive—R
(s)-Zoë Life Pub.—R

ECONOMICS
(a) Baker Books

(s)-Aaron Book
ABC-CLIO
(s)-Abuzz Press—R
(s)-Booklocker.com
(s)-Brown Books—R
Christian Writer's
   Ebook—R
Creation House
(s)-Deep River Books
Eerdmans Pub.—R
(s)-Essence—R
Evergreen Press
(s)-Fairway Press—R
Faith Books & More
Four Craftsmen—R
Lighthouse Pub.—R
New Hope
New Leaf
Praeger Publishers
(s)-Salvation
   Publisher—R
(s)-Signalman—R
Tate Publishing—R
Trinity Foundation--R
(s)-Word Alive—R
(s)-Zoë Life Pub.—R

ENCOURAGEMENT
(a) Doubleday
   Relig.—R

(a) Howard Books
(a) WaterBrook Press

(s)-Aaron Book
(s)-Abuzz Press—R
AMG Publishers—R
Bold Vision—R
Bondfire Books
(s)-Booklocker.com
(s)-Brown Books—R
Charisma House—R
CLC Publications—R
Comfort Publishing
Creation House
CrossLink Publishing
CSS Publishing
Discovery House—R
Earthen Vessel—R
Eerdmans Pub.—R
Ellechor Publishing
(s)-Essence—R
(s)-Fairway Press—R
Faith Books & More
(s)-Grace Acres—R
Guardian Angel
JourneyForth/BJU
Lift Every Voice—R
Lighthouse Pub.—R
NavPress—R
New Hope
North Wind Publishing
OakTara
On My Own Now
Parson Place
Parsons Pub.—R
Players Press
(s)-Port Hole
    Public.—R
Randall House
(s)-Redemption Press
(s)-Salvation
    Publisher—R
(s)-Signalman—R
Tate Publishing—R
Trail Media
VBC Publishing
Whitaker House—R
White Fire Pub.
(s)-Word Alive—R
Write Integrity Press
(s)-Zoë Life Pub.—R

ENVIRONMENTAL ISSUES
(a) Baker Books
(a) Doubleday
    Relig.—R

(s)-Aaron Book
ABC-CLIO
(s)-Abuzz Press—R
Blue Dolphin—R
(s)-Booklocker.com
Christian Writer's
    Ebook—R
Cladach Publishing
Dawn Publications
(s)-Deep River Books
Eerdmans Pub.—R
Eerdmans/Yg Readers
(s)-Essence—R
(s)-Fairway Press—R
Faith Books & More
InterVarsity Press—R
Judson Press
Lighthouse Pub.—R
New Leaf
Port Yonder Press
Praeger Publishers
Ravenhawk Books—R
(s)-Redemption Press
(s)-Signalman—R
Sunpenny Publishing
Tate Publishing—R
(s)-Word Alive—R

ESCHATOLOGY
(a) Baker Books
(a) Kregel—R
(a) Nelson, Thomas

(s)-Aaron Book
(s)-Abuzz Press—R
Ambassador Intl.
Ancient Faith—R
Blue Dolphin—R
BMH Books
(s)-Booklocker.com
Bridge Logos—R
Charisma House—R
Christian Heritage—R
Christian Writer's
    Ebook—R

CLC Publications—R
Creation House
CSS Publishing
(s)-DCTS Publishers
Earthen Vessel—R
Eerdmans Pub.—R
(s)-Essence—R
(s)-Fairway Press—R
Faith Books & More
(s)-Grace Acres—R
Kirk House
Lighthouse Pub.—R
Lighthouse Trails—R
Lutheran Univ. Press
Nelson, Thomas
Pacific Press
Parson Place
(s)-Redemption Press
(s)-Signalman—R
(s)-Strong Tower—R
Tate Publishing—R
VBC Publishing
(s)-Word Alive—R
(s)-Zoë Life Pub.—R

ETHICS
(a) Baker Books
(a) Howard Books
(a) Kregel—R

(s)-Aaron Book
(s)-Abuzz Press—R
Ancient Faith—R
Blue Dolphin—R
Bondfire Books
(s)-Booklocker.com
Christian Heritage—R
Christian Writer's
    Ebook—R
CLC Publications—R
Creation House
CrossLink Publishing
Crossway
(s)-Deep River Books
Earthen Vessel—R
Eerdmans Pub.—R
(s)-Essence—R
(s)-Fairway Press—R
Faith Books & More
Four Craftsmen—R
Franciscan Media—R

(s)-Grace Acres—R
Guardian Angel
Hannibal Books
Inkling Books—R
InterVarsity Press—R
Kirk House
Life Cycle Books—R
Lift Every Voice—R
Lighthouse Pub.—R
Lutheran Univ. Press
North Wind Publishing
Our Sunday Visitor—R
Pacific Press
Paragon House
Parsons Pub.—R
Pauline Books
Port Yonder Press
Randall House
Ravenhawk Books—R
(s)-Redemption Press
(s)-Salt Works—R
(s)-Signalman—R
Tate Publishing—R
Trinity Foundation--R
White Fire Pub.
(s)-Word Alive—R
Yale Univ. Press—R
(s)-Zoë Life Pub.—R

ETHNIC/CULTURAL
(a) Baker Books
(a) Doubleday
     Relig.—R
(a) HarperOne
(a) Howard Books
(a) Kregel—R

(s)-Aaron Book
ABC-CLIO
Abingdon Press
(s)-Abuzz Press—R
Blue Dolphin—R
(s)-Booklocker.com
Bridge Logos—R
Christian Writer's
     Ebook—R
Creation House
(s)-Deep River Books
Discovery House—R
Eerdmans Pub.—R
Eerdmans/Yg Readers

(s)-Essence—R
(s)-Fairway Press—R
Faith Books & More
Franciscan Media—R
Guardian Angel
InterVarsity Press—R
Judson Press
Kirk House
Lift Every Voice—R
Lighthouse Pub.—R
Lutheran Univ. Press
Moody Publishers
NavPress—R
New Hope
North Wind Publishing
Pacific Press
Port Yonder Press
Praeger Publishers
(s)-Redemption Press
(s)-Signalman—R
Standard Publishing
Sunpenny Publishing
Tate Publishing—R
Whitaker House—R
White Fire Pub.
(s)-Word Alive—R
Yale Univ. Press—R
(s)-Zoë Life Pub.—R
Zondervan

EVANGELISM/ WITNESSING
(a) Baker Books
(a) Cook, David C.
(a) Kregel—R
(a) Nelson, Thomas
(a) Tyndale House

(s)-Aaron Book
(s)-Abuzz Press—R
Ancient Faith—R
BMH Books
Bold Vision—R
Bondfire Books
(s)-Booklocker.com
Bridge Logos—R
Charisma House—R
Christian Heritage—R
Christian Writer's
     Ebook—R
Church Growth Inst.

CLC Publications—R
Creation House
(s)-CrossHouse
CrossLink Publishing
Crossway
CSS Publishing
(s)-DCTS Publishers
(s)-Deep River Books
Discovery House—R
Earthen Vessel—R
Eerdmans Pub.—R
(s)-Essence—R
Evergreen Press
(s)-Fairway Press—R
Faith Books & More
(s)-Grace Acres—R
InterVarsity Press—R
Judson Press
Lift Every Voice—R
Lighthouse Pub.—R
Lutheran Univ. Press
Moody Publishers
Morgan James Pub.—R
NavPress—R
New Hope
North Wind Publishing
Pacific Press
P&R Publications
Parson Place
Pauline Books
Randall House
(s)-Redemption Press
(s)-Salt Works—R
(s)-Signalman—R
Tate Publishing—R
VBC Publishing
Wesleyan Publishing
Whitaker House—R
White Fire Pub.
(s)-Word Alive—R
Write Integrity Press
(s)-Zoë Life Pub.—R

EXEGESIS
(a) Baker Books
(a) Doubleday
     Relig.—R
(a) Kregel—R

(s)-Aaron Book
Abingdon Press

(s)-Abuzz Press—R
Ambassador Intl.
AMG Publishers—R
BMH Books
Bondfire Books
(s)-Booklocker.com
Canticle Books—R
Christian Writer's
   Ebook—R
CLC Publications—R
CSS Publishing
(s)-Deep River Books
Earthen Vessel—R
Eerdmans Pub.—R
(s)-Essence—R
(s)-Fairway Press—R
Faith Books & More
(s)-Grace Acres—R
InterVarsity Press—R
Lighthouse Pub.—R
Lutheran Univ. Press
(s)-Redemption Press
(s)-Salt Works—R
(s)-Signalman—R
Tate Publishing—R
VBC Publishing
(s)-Word Alive—R
(s)-Zoë Life Pub.—R

EXPOSÉS
(a) Baker Bookss

(s)-Aaron Book
(s)-Abuzz Press—R
(s)-Booklocker.com
Christian Writer's
   Ebook—R
Eerdmans Pub.—R
(s)-Fairway Press—R
Faith Books & More
Lighthouse Pub.—R
Lighthouse Trails—R
Ravenhawk Books—R
(s)-Redemption Press
(s)-Salt Works—R
(s)-Signalman—R
(s)-Word Alive—R
(s)-Zoë Life Pub.—R

FAITH
(a) Baker Books

(a) B&H Publishing
(a) Bethany House
(a) Doubleday
   Relig.—R
(a) HarperOne
(a) Howard Books
(a) Kregel—R
(a) Nelson, Thomas
(a) Tyndale House
(a) WaterBrook Press

(s)-Aaron Book
Abingdon Press
(s)-Abuzz Press—R
Ambassador Intl.
AMG Publishers—R
Ancient Faith—R
Barbour—R
Bold Vision—R
Bondfire Books
(s)-Booklocker.com
Bridge Logos—R
(s)-Brown Books—R
Charisma House—R
Christian Heritage—R
Christian Writer's
   Ebook—R
CLC Publications—R
Comfort Publishing
Creation House
CrossLink Publishing
CrossRiver Media
Crossway
(s)-DCTS Publishers
(s)-Deep River Books
(s)-Destiny Image
   (books)
Discovery House—R
Earthen Vessel—R
Ellechor Publishing
Eerdmans Pub.—R
Eerdmans/Yg Readers
(s)-Essence—R
Evergreen Press
(s)-Fairway Press—R
Faith Books & More
(s)-Fruitbearer Pub.
(s)-Grace Acres—R
Grace Publishing—R
Group Publishing
Guardian Angel

Guideposts Books
(s)-Halo Publishing—R
Harrison House
Inheritance Press
InterVarsity Press—R
JourneyForth/BJU
Judson Press
Lift Every Voice—R
Lighthouse/
   Carolinas—R
Lighthouse Pub.—R
Loyola Press
Lutheran Univ. Press
Magnus Press—R
Morgan James Pub.—R
NavPress—R
New Hope
North Wind Publishing
OakTara
On My Own Now
Pacific Press
Parson Place
Parsons Pub.—R
Pauline Books
Randall House
(s)-Redemption Press
(s)-Salt Works—R
(s)-Salvation
   Publisher—R
(s)-Signalman—R
Tate Publishing—R
Trail Media
VBC Publishing
Wesleyan Publishing
Whitaker House—R
White Fire Pub.
(s)-Word Alive—R
Write Integrity Press
(s)-Zoë Life Pub.—R

FAMILY LIFE
(a) Baker Books
(a) B&H Publishing
(a) Bethany House
(a) Cook, David C.
(a) HarperOne
(a) Howard Books
(a) Kregel—R
(a) Nelson, Thomas
(a) Tyndale House

(a) WaterBrook Press

(s)-Aaron Book
Abingdon Press
(s)-Abuzz Press—R
Ambassador Intl.
AMG Publishers—R
Ancient Faith—R
Barbour—R
Bold Vision—R
Bondfire Books
(s)-Booklocker.com
Bridge Logos—R
(s)-Brown Books—R
Charisma House—R
Christian Writer's
    Ebook—R
CLC Publications—R
Comfort Publishing
Conari Press
Creation House
CrossLink Publishing
CrossRiver Media
Crossway
(s)-DCTS Publishers
(s)-Deep River Books
(s)-Destiny Image
    (books)
Discovery House—R
Dove Inspirational—R
Eerdmans Pub.—R
Eerdmans/Yg Readers
Ellechor Publishing
(s)-Essence—R
Evergreen Press
(s)-Fairway Press—R
Faith Books & More
Franciscan Media—R
(s)-Grace Acres—R
Grace Publishing—R
Guardian Angel
Guideposts Books
(s)-Halo Publishing—R
Hannibal Books
Hope Publishing—R
InterVarsity Press—R
JourneyForth/BJU
Judson Press
Langmarc
Legacy Press
Life Cycle Books—R

Lift Every Voice—R
Lighthouse/
    Carolinas—R
Lighthouse Pub.—R
Loyola Press
MOPS Intl.
Morgan James Pub.—R
MountainView
NavPress—R
New Hope
New Leaf
North Wind Publishing
Our Sunday Visitor—R
Pacific Press
P&R Publications
Parsons Pub.—R
Pauline Books
Pelican Pub.—R
(s)-Port Hole
    Public.—R
Randall House
(s)-Redemption Press
(s)-Salvation
    Publisher—R
(s)-Signalman—R
Tate Publishing—R
Trail Media
VBC Publishing
Whitaker House—R
White Fire Pub.
(s)-Word Alive—R
Write Integrity Press
(s)-Zoë Life Pub.—R

FICTION: ADULT/ GENERAL

(a) Ballantine
(a) HarperOne
(a) Howard Books
(a) Kregel—R
(a) Multnomah
(a) Nelson, Fiction,
    Thomas

(s)-Aaron Book
(s)-Abuzz Press—R
Ambassador Intl.
Barking Rain Press—R
Blue Dolphin—R
Bold Vision—R
Bondfire Books

(s)-Brown Books—R
Charisma House—R
Cladach Publishing
Comfort Publishing
Creation House
Earthen Vessel—R
(s)-Essence—R
Evergreen Press
Grace Publishing—R
(s)-Halo Publishing—R
Lighthouse/
    Carolinas—R
Lighthouse Pub.—R
Lighthouse Trails—R
Love Inspired
Mantle Rock
Morgan James Pub.—R
MountainView
New Leaf
OakTara
Parable Book Group
Parson Place
Port Yonder Press
Ravenhawk Books—R
(s)-Redemption Press
(s)-Signalman—R
White Fire Pub.
Write Integrity Press

FICTION: ADULT/RELIGIOUS

(a) Baker Books
(a) Ballantine
(a) B&H Publishing
(a) Barbour—R
(a) Bethany House
(a) Doubleday
    Relig.—R
(a) HarperOne
(a) Howard Books
(a) Kregel—R
(a) Multnomah
(a) Nelson, Fiction,
    Thomas
(a) Revell
(a) WaterBrook Press

(s)-Aaron Book
(s)-Abuzz Press—R
Adams Media
Ambassador Intl.

Barking Rain Press—R
Blue Dolphin—R
Bold Vision—R
Bondfire Books
(s)-Booklocker.com
Bridge Logos—R
(s)-Brown Books—R
Chalfont House
Charisma House—R
Christian Writer's
   Ebook—R
Cladach Publishing
Comfort Publishing
Creation House
(s)-CrossHouse
CrossLink Publishing
(s)-Deep River Books
(s)-Destiny Image
   (books)
Earthen Vessel—R
Eerdmans Pub.—R
Ellechor Publishing
(s)-Essence—R
Evergreen Press
(s)-Fairway Press—R
Faith Books & More
(s)-Fruitbearer Pub.
Grace Publishing—R
Guideposts Books
(s)-Halo Publishing—R
Hannibal Books
Lift Every Voice—R
Lighthouse/
   Carolinas—R
Lighthouse Pub.—R
Lighthouse Trails—R
Love Inspired
Mantle Rock
Moody Publishers
Morgan James Pub.—R
MountainView
NavPress—R
New Leaf
OakTara
Pacific Press
Parson Place
(s)-Port Hole
   Public.—R
Prism Book Group
(s)-Redemption Press

(s)-Salt Works—R
(s)-Signalman—R
Sunpenny Publishing
Tate Publishing—R
Trail Media
Whitaker House—R
White Fire Pub.
White Rose
(s)-Word Alive—R
Write Integrity Press
(s)-Zoë Life Pub.—R

FICTION: ADVENTURE
(a) Baker Books
(a) Barbour—R
(a) Howard Books
(a) Multnomah
(a) WaterBrook Press

(s)-Aaron Book
(s)-Abuzz Press—R
AMG Publishers—R
Barking Rain Press—R
Bondfire Books
(s)-Booklocker.com
Bridge Logos—R
(s)-Brown Books—R
Chalfont House
Charisma House—R
Christian Writer's
   Ebook—R
Comfort Publishing
Creation House
(s)-Deep River Books
Earthen Vessel—R
Eerdmans/Yg Readers
Ellechor Publishing
(s)-Essence—R
Evergreen Press
(s)-Fairway Press—R
Faith Books & More
Grace Publishing—R
(s)-Halo Publishing—R
JourneyForth/BJU
Lift Every Voice—R
Lighthouse/
   Carolinas—R
Lighthouse Pub.—R
Mantle Rock
Morgan James Pub.—R

MountainView
New Leaf
OakTara
P&R Publications
Parson Place
Pauline Kids
(s)-Port Hole
   Public.—R
Port Yonder Press
Ravenhawk Books—R
(s)-Redemption Press
(s)-Salt Works—R
(s)-Signalman—R
Sunpenny Publishing
Tate Publishing—R
White Fire Pub.
Write Integrity Press
(s)-Zoë Life Pub.—R

FICTION: ALLEGORY
(a) Baker Books
(a) Barbour—R
(a) Howard Books
(a) Multnomah

(s)-Aaron Book
(s)-Abuzz Press—R
Ambassador Intl.
AMG Publishers—R
Bondfire Books
(s)-Booklocker.com
Bridge Logos—R
(s)-Brown Books—R
Chalfont House
Charisma House—R
Christian Writer's
   Ebook—R
Creation House
(s)-Deep River Books
(s)-Destiny Image
   (books)
(s)-Essence—R
Evergreen Press
(s)-Fairway Press—R
Faith Books & More
Grace Publishing—R
Lighthouse Pub.—R
Parable Book Group
(s)-Port Hole
   Public.—R
(s)-Redemption Press

(s)-Salt Works—R
(s)-Signalman—R
Tate Publishing—R
White Fire Pub.
(s)-Zoë Life Pub.—R

FICTION: BIBLICAL
(a) Baker Books
(a) Howard Books
(a) Multnomah
(a) Nelson, Fiction,
      Thomas
(a) WaterBrook Press

(s)-Aaron Book
Abingdon Press
(s)-Abuzz Press—R
Ambassador Intl.
AMG Publishers—R
Barking Rain Press—R
Bondfire Books
(s)-Booklocker.com
Bridge Logos—R
(s)-Brown Books—R
Chalfont House
Charisma House—R
Christian Writer's
      Ebook—R
Creation House
(s)-Deep River Books
(s)-Destiny Image
      (books)
Earthen Vessel—R
Eerdmans Pub.—R
Eerdmans/Yg Readers
(s)-Essence—R
Evergreen Press
(s)-Fairway Press—R
Faith Books & More
Grace Publishing—R
Guideposts Books
Hannibal Books
Ideals Publications
Lift Every Voice—R
Lighthouse Pub.—R
Lighthouse Trails—R
Mantle Rock
Moody Publishers
Morgan James Pub.—R
NavPress—R
OakTara

Olivia Kimbrell Press
Pacific Press
P&R Publications
(s)-Port Hole
      Public.—R
(s)-Redemption Press
(s)-Salt Works—R
(s)-Signalman—R
Tate Publishing—R
Trail Media
White Fire Pub.
Write Integrity Press
(s)-Zoë Life Pub.—R

FICTION: CHICK LIT
(a) Multnomah
(a) Nelson, Fiction,
      Thomas
(a) WaterBrook Press

(s)-Aaron Book
(s)-Abuzz Press—R
Barking Rain Press—R
Bondfire Books
(s)-Booklocker.com
(s)-Brown Books—R
Chalfont House
Charisma House—R
Christian Writer's
      Ebook—R
Creation House
(s)-Deep River Books
Ellechor Publishing
(s)-Essence—R
Faith Books & More
Lighthouse/
      Carolinas—R
Lighthouse Pub.—R
Love Inspired Suspense
Mantle Rock
Morgan James Pub.—R
OakTara
Parable Book Group
(s)-Port Hole
      Public.—R
Ravenhawk Books—R
(s)-Redemption Press
Write Integrity Press
(s)-Zoë Life Pub.—R

FICTION: CHILDREN'S PICTURE BOOK
Ancient Faith—R
Eerdmans/Yg Readers
Ideals Publications

FICTION: CONTEMPORARY
(a) Avon Inspire
(a) Baker Books
(a) Ballantine
(a) B&H Publishing
(a) Barbour—R
(a) Bethany House
(a) Howard Books
(a) Kregel—R
(a) Multnomah
(a) Nelson, Fiction,
      Thomas
(a) Revell
(a) Tyndale House
(a) WaterBrook Press

(s)-Aaron Book
(s)-Abuzz Press—R
AMG Publishers—R
Barking Rain Press—R
Bondfire Books
(s)-Booklocker.com
(s)-Brown Books—R
Chalfont House
Charisma House—R
Christian Writer's
      Ebook—R
Creation House
(s)-Deep River Books
Desert Breeze Pub.
(s)-Destiny Image
      (books)
Earthen Vessel—R
Eerdmans/Yg Readers
Ellechor Publishing
(s)-Essence—R
(s)-Fairway Press—R
Faith Books & More
Grace Publishing—R
JourneyForth/BJU
Lift Every Voice—R
Lighthouse/
      Carolinas—R

Lighthouse Pub.—R
Love Inspired
Mantle Rock
Moody Publishers
Morgan James Pub.—R
MountainView
NavPress—R
New Leaf
OakTara
Parable Book Group
Parson Place
Pauline Kids
(s)-Port Hole
    Public.—R
Port Yonder Press
Prism Book Group
Ravenhawk Books—R
(s)-Redemption Press
(s)-Salt Works—R
(s)-Signalman—R
Sunpenny Publishing
Tate Publishing—R
White Fire Pub.
Write Integrity Press
(s)-Zoë Life Pub.—R

FICTION: COZY MYSTERIES

(s)-Abuzz Press—R
Barking Rain Press—R
Bondfire Books
Chalfont House
Comfort Publishing
Ellechor Publishing
(s)-Essence—R
Grace Publishing—R
Lighthouse/
    Carolinas—R
Mantle Rock
OakTara
Parable Book Group
(s)-Signalman—R
Write Integrity Press
(s)-Zoë Life Pub.—R

FICTION: ETHNIC

(a) Baker Books
(a) Ballantine
(a) Multnomah

(s)-Aaron Book

(s)-Abuzz Press—R
(s)-Booklocker.com
Chalfont House
Charisma House—R
Christian Writer's
    Ebook—R
(s)-Deep River Books
Eerdmans/Yg Readers
Ellechor Publishing
(s)-Essence—R
Evergreen Press
(s)-Fairway Press—R
Faith Books & More
Lift Every Voice—R
Lighthouse Pub.—R
Mantle Rock
OakTara
Parable Book Group
Port Yonder Press
(s)-Redemption Press
(s)-Signalman—R
Sunpenny Publishing
Tate Publishing—R
Whitaker House—R
White Fire Pub.
(s)-Zoë Life Pub.—R

FICTION: FABLES/PARABLES

(a) HarperOne

(s)-Aaron Book
(s)-Abuzz Press—R
Barking Rain Press—R
(s)-Booklocker.com
(s)-Brown Books—R
Chalfont House
(s)-Deep River Books
Eerdmans/Yg Readers
(s)-Essence—R
Faith Books & More
Lighthouse Pub.—R
Parson Place
Pauline Kids
(s)-Redemption Press
(s)-Salt Works—R
(s)-Signalman—R
Tate Publishing—R
(s)-Zoë Life Pub.—R

FICTION: FANTASY

(a) Ballantine
(a) Barbour—R
(a) Multnomah
(a) WaterBrook Press

(s)-Aaron Book
(s)-Abuzz Press—R
AMG Publishers—R
Barking Rain Press—R
Bondfire Books
(s)-Booklocker.com
Chalfont House
Charisma House—R
Christian Writer's
    Ebook—R
Comfort Publishing
Creation House
(s)-Deep River Books
Desert Breeze Pub.
(s)-Destiny Image
    (books)
Eerdmans Pub.—R
(s)-Enclave Pub.—R
(s)-Essence—R
(s)-Fairway Press—R
Faith Books & More
Grace Publishing—R
Lighthouse/
    Carolinas—R
Lighthouse Pub.—R
MountainView
OakTara
Olivia Kimbrell Press
P&R Publications
Parable Book Group
(s)-Port Hole
    Public.—R
Port Yonder Press
Ravenhawk Books—R
(s)-Redemption Press
(s)-Signalman—R
Tate Publishing—R
White Fire Pub.
(s)-Zoë Life Pub.—R

FICTION: FRONTIER

(a) Baker Books
(a) Bethany House
(a) Multnomah

(a) Nelson, Fiction,
   Thomas

(s)-Aaron Book
(s)-Abuzz Press—R
Barking Rain Press—R
(s)-Booklocker.com
(s)-Brown Books—R
Charisma House—R
Christian Writer's
   Ebook—R
Cladach Publishing
(s)-Deep River Books
(s)-Essence—R
(s)-Fairway Press—R
Faith Books & More
Guardian Angel
JourneyForth/BJU
Lighthouse/
   Carolinas—R
Lighthouse Pub.—R
Mantle Rock
MountainView
OakTara
Parable Book Group
Parson Place
(s)-Port Hole
   Public.—R
Ravenhawk Books—R
(s)-Redemption Press
(s)-Signalman—R
Tate Publishing—R
Trail Media
(s)-Zoë Life Pub.—R

**FICTION: FRONTIER/
ROMANCE**
(a) Baker Books
(a) Barbour—R
(a) Bethany House
(a) Multnomah
(a) Nelson, Fiction,
   Thomas

(s)-Aaron Book
(s)-Abuzz Press—R
Ambassador Intl.
Barking Rain Press—R
Bondfire Books
(s)-Booklocker.com
(s)-Brown Books—R

Chalfont House
Charisma House—R
Christian Writer's
   Ebook—R
(s)-Deep River Books
Desert Breeze Pub.
(s)-Essence—R
(s)-Fairway Press—R
Faith Books & More
Lighthouse/
   Carolinas—R
Lighthouse Pub.—R
Mantle Rock
MountainView
OakTara
Parable Book Group
Parson Place
(s)-Port Hole
   Public.—R
Ravenhawk Books—R
Redbud Press
(s)-Redemption Press
(s)-Redemption Press
(s)-Signalman—R
Tate Publishing—R
Whitaker House—R
White Rose
(s)-Zoë Life Pub.—R

**FICTION:
HISTORICAL**
(a) Avon Inspire
(a) Baker Books
(a) Ballantine
(a) B&H Publishing
(a) Bethany House
(a) Howard Books
(a) Kregel—R
(a) Multnomah
(a) Nelson, Fiction,
   Thomas
(a) Revell
(a) WaterBrook Press

(s)-Aaron Book
Abingdon Press
(s)-Abuzz Press—R
Ambassador Intl.
Barking Rain Press—R
Blue Dolphin—R
Bold Vision—R

Bondfire Books
(s)-Booklocker.com
Bridge Logos—R
(s)-Brown Books—R
Charisma House—R
Christian Writer's
   Ebook—R
Comfort Publishing
(s)-Deep River Books
Earthen Vessel—R
Eerdmans Pub.—R
Eerdmans/Yg Readers
(s)-Essence—R
(s)-Fairway Press—R
Faith Books & More
Grace Publishing—R
Hannibal Books
JourneyForth/BJU
Lift Every Voice—R
Lighthouse/
   Carolinas—R
Lighthouse Pub.—R
Mantle Rock
Moody Publishers
Morgan James Pub.—R
MountainView
NavPress—R
OakTara
Parable Book Group
Parson Place
Pauline Kids
(s)-Port Hole
   Public.—R
Port Yonder Press
Prism Book Group
Ravenhawk Books—R
(s)-Redemption Press
(s)-Salt Works—R
(s)-Signalman—R
Sunpenny Publishing
Tate Publishing—R
Trail Media
White Fire Pub.
(s)-Zoë Life Pub.—R

**FICTION: HISTORICAL/
ROMANCE**
(a) Baker Books
(a) B&H Publishing
(a) Bethany House

(a) Barbour—R
(a) Multnomah
(a) Nelson, Fiction,
　　Thomas
(a) Tyndale House
(a) WaterBrook Press

(s)-Aaron Book
Abingdon Press
(s)-Abuzz Press—R
Ambassador Intl.Bold
　　Vision—R
Barking Rain Press—R
Bondfire Books
(s)-Booklocker.com
(s)-Brown Books—R
Chalfont House
Charisma House—R
Christian Writer's
　　Ebook—R
Comfort Publishing
(s)-Deep River Books
Desert Breeze Pub.
(s)-Essence—R
(s)-Fairway Press—R
Faith Books & More
Hannibal Books
Lift Every Voice—R
Lighthouse/
　　Carolinas—R
Lighthouse Pub.—R
Mantle Rock
Morgan James Pub.—R
MountainView
OakTara
Parable Book Group
Parson Place
(s)-Port Hole
　　Public.—R
Ravenhawk Books—R
Redbud Press
(s)-Redemption Press
(s)-Signalman—R
Tate Publishing—R
Whitaker House—R
White Fire Pub.
White Rose
(s)-Zoë Life Pub.—R

FICTION: HUMOR
(a) Baker Books

(a) Ballantine
(a) Multnomah

(s)-Aaron Book
(s)-Abuzz Press—R
Barking Rain Press—R
Bondfire Books
(s)-Booklocker.com
Chalfont House
Charisma House—R
Christian Writer's
　　Ebook—R
Creation House
(s)-Deep River Books
Eerdmans/Yg Readers
(s)-Essence—R
Evergreen Press
(s)-Fairway Press—R
Faith Books & More
Grace Publishing—R
(s)-Halo Publishing—R
JourneyForth/BJU
Lighthouse/
　　Carolinas—R
Lighthouse Pub.—R
Mantle Rock
MountainView
OakTara
Parson Place
(s)-Port Hole
　　Public.—R
Prism Book Group
Ravenhawk Books—R
(s)-Redemption Press
(s)-Salt Works—R
(s)-Signalman—R
Sunpenny Publishing
Tate Publishing—R
White Fire Pub.
Write Integrity Press
(s)-Zoë Life Pub.—R

FICTION: JUVENILE
(Ages 8-12)
(a) Baker Books
(a) Barbour—R
(a) Kregel—R
(a) Tyndale House

(s)-Aaron Book
(s)-Abuzz Press—R

Ambassador Intl.
AMG Publishers—R
Blue Dolphin—R
Bold Vision—R
(s)-Booklocker.com
(s)-Brown Books—R
Chalfont House
Charisma House—R
Comfort Publishing
Creation House
(s)-CrossHouse
(s)-Deep River Books
Eerdmans Pub.—R
Eerdmans/Yg Readers
(s)-Essence—R
Evergreen Press
(s)-Fairway Press—R
Faith Books & More
(s)-Fruitbearer Pub.
Guardian Angel
(s)-Halo Publishing—R
JourneyForth/BJU
Lift Every Voice—R
Lighthouse Pub.—R
Moody Publishers
Morgan James Pub.—R
OakTara
Pacific Press
P&R Publications
Parson Place
Pauline Kids
(s)-Port Hole
　　Public.—R
(s)-Redemption Press
(s)-Salt Works—R
(s)-Signalman—R
Standard Publishing
Tate Publishing—R
Warner Press
(s)-Word Alive—R
Write Integrity Press
(s)-Zoë Life Pub.—R

FICTION: LITERARY
(a) Baker Books
(a) Ballantine
(a) Bethany House
(a) HarperOne
(a) Multnomah

(a) Nelson, Fiction,
   Thomas
(a) WaterBrook Press

(s)-Aaron Book
(s)-Abuzz Press—R
Ambassador Intl.
AMG Publishers—R
Barking Rain Press—R
Blue Dolphin—R
Bondfire Books
(s)-Booklocker.com
(s)-Brown Books—R
Chalfont House
Charisma House—R
Christian Writer's
   Ebook—R
Cladach Publishing
(s)-Deep River Books
Eerdmans Pub.—R
Eerdmans/Yg Readers
(s)-Essence—R
(s)-Fairway Press—R
Faith Books & More
Grace Publishing—R
JourneyForth/BJU
Lighthouse/
   Carolinas—R
Lighthouse Pub.—R
Mantle Rock
Moody Publishers
NavPress—R
OakTara
(s)-Port Hole
   Public.—R
Port Yonder Press
Ravenhawk Books—R
(s)-Redemption Press
(s)-Salt Works—R
(s)-Signalman—R
Sunpenny Publishing
Tate Publishing—R
White Fire Pub.
(s)-Zoë Life Pub.—R

FICTION: MYSTERY/
ROMANCE
(a) Baker Books
(a) Ballantine
(a) B&H Publishing
(a) Barbour—R

(a) Bethany House
(a) Howard Books
(a) Kregel—R
(a) Multnomah
(a) Nelson, Fiction,
   Thomas
(a) Summerside Press

(s)-Aaron Book
(s)-Abuzz Press—R
Ambassador Intl.
Barking Rain Press—R
Bold Vision—R
Bondfire Books
(s)-Booklocker.com
(s)-Brown Books—R
Chalfont House
Charisma House—R
Christian Writer's
   Ebook—R
Comfort Publishing
(s)-Deep River Books
Desert Breeze Pub.
Ellechor Publishing
(s)-Essence—R
(s)-Fairway Press—R
Faith Books & More
Grace Publishing—R
Guideposts Books
Lift Every Voice—R
Lighthouse/
   Carolinas—R
Lighthouse Pub.—R
Love Inspired Suspense
Mantle Rock
Morgan James Pub.—R
MountainView
OakTara
Parable Book Group
Parson Place
(s)-Port Hole
   Public.—R
(s)-Redemption Press
(s)-Signalman—R
Tate Publishing—R
White Fire Pub.
White Rose
Write Integrity Press
(s)-Zoë Life Pub.—R

FICTION: MYSTERY/
SUSPENSE
(a) Baker Books
(a) Ballantine
(a) B&H Publishing
(a) Bethany House
(a) Howard Books
(a) Kregel—R
(a) Multnomah
(a) Revell
(a) Tyndale House

(s)-Aaron Book
(s)-Abuzz Press—R
Ambassador Intl.
Barking Rain Press—R
Blue Dolphin—R
Bold Vision—R
(s)-Booklocker.com
(s)-Brown Books—R
Chalfont House
Charisma House—R
Christian Writer's
   Ebook—R
Comfort Publishing
Creation House
(s)-Deep River Books
Desert Breeze Pub.
Ellechor Publishing
(s)-Essence—R
(s)-Fairway Press—R
Faith Books & More
Grace Publishing—R
Guideposts Books
JourneyForth/BJU
Lift Every Voice—R
Lighthouse/
   Carolinas—R
Lighthouse Pub.—R
Love Inspired Suspense
Mantle Rock
Moody Publishers
Morgan James Pub.—R
MountainView
New Leaf
OakTara
Olivia Kimbrell Press
Parable Book Group
Parson Place
Pauline Kids

(s)-Port Hole
   Public.—R
Port Yonder Press
Prism Book Group
Ravenhawk Books—R
(s)-Redemption Press
(s)-Salt Works—R
(s)-Signalman—R
Sunpenny Publishing
Tate Publishing—R
White Fire Pub.
Write Integrity Press
(s)-Zoë Life Pub.—R

FICTION: NEW ADULT
(s)-Abuzz Press—R
Chalfont House
Earthen Vessel—R
Ellechor Publishing
Grace Publishing—R
Lighthouse/
   Carolinas—R
OakTara
Parable Book Group
Port Yonder Press
(s)-Redemption Press
(s)-Signalman—R
White Fire Pub.

FICTION: NOVELLAS
(a) Baker Books
(a) Barbour—R

(s)-Aaron Book
(s)-Abuzz Press—R
Ambassador Intl.
Bondfire Books
Barking Rain Press—R
(s)-Booklocker.com
Chalfont House
Christian Writer's
   Ebook—R
(s)-Essence—R
(s)-Fairway Press—R
Faith Books & More
(s)-Halo Publishing—R
Lighthouse/
   Carolinas—R
Lighthouse Pub.—R
MountainView
OakTara

Parable Book Group
Port Yonder Press
(s)-Redemption Press
(s)-Salt Works—R
White Fire Pub.
(s)-Zoë Life Pub.—R

FICTION: PLAYS
CSS Publishing
Earthen Vessel—R
(s)-Essence—R
(s)-Fairway Press—R
Guardian Angel
Meriwether
Players Press
(s)-Redemption Press
(s)-Salt Works—R

FICTION: ROMANCE
(a) Baker Books
(a) Ballantine
(a) Barbour—R
(a) Bethany House
(a) Multnomah
(a) Nelson, Fiction,
   Thomas
(a) Summerside Press
(a) Tyndale House
(a) WaterBrook Press

(s)-Aaron Book
(s)-Abuzz Press—R
Ambassador Intl.
Barking Rain Press—R
Bondfire Books
(s)-Booklocker.com
(s)-Brown Books—R
Chalfont House
Charisma House—R
Christian Writer's
   Ebook—R
Comfort Publishing
Creation House
(s)-Deep River Books
(s)-Essence—R
(s)-Fairway Press—R
Faith Books & More
Hannibal Books
Lift Every Voice—R
Lighthouse/
   Carolinas—R

Lighthouse Pub.—R
Love Inspired
Love Inspired Suspense
Mantle Rock
Morgan James Pub.—R
MountainView
OakTara
Olivia Kimbrell Press
Parable Book Group
Parson Place
(s)-Port Hole
   Public.—R
Prism Book Group
Redbud Press
(s)-Redemption Press
Sunpenny Publishing
Tate Publishing—R
Whitaker House—R
White Fire Pub.
White Rose
Write Integrity Press
(s)-Zoë Life Pub.—R

FICTION: SCIENCE FICTION
(a) WaterBrook Press

(s)-Aaron Book
(s)-Abuzz Press—R
Barking Rain Press—R
Bondfire Books
(s)-Booklocker.com
Chalfont House
Charisma House—R
Christian Writer's
   Ebook—R
Comfort Publishing
Creation House
(s)-Deep River Books
Desert Breeze Pub.
(s)-Enclave Pub.—R
(s)-Essence—R
Evergreen Press
(s)-Fairway Press—R
Faith Books & More
Lighthouse/
   Carolinas—R
Lighthouse Pub.—R
MountainView
OakTara
Olivia Kimbrell Press

Parable Book Group
(s)-Port Hole
   Public.—R
Port Yonder Press
(s)-Redemption Press
(s)-Signalman—R
Sunpenny Publishing
Tate Publishing—R
White Fire Pub.
(s)-Zoë Life Pub.—R

FICTION: SHORT STORY COLLECTIONS
(a) Baker Books
(a) Ballantine

(s)-Aaron Book
(s)-Abuzz Press—R
Barking Rain Press—R
Bondfire Books
(s)-Booklocker.com
Chalfont House
Christian Writer's
   Ebook—R
Comfort Publishing
(s)-Deep River Books
Earthen Vessel—R
Eerdmans Pub.—R
(s)-Essence—R
(s)-Fairway Press—R
Faith Books & More
MountainView
OakTara
Parson Place
Pauline Kids
(s)-Port Hole
   Public.—R
(s)-Salt Works—R
(s)-Signalman—R
Tate Publishing—R
Trail Media
White Rose
(s)-Zoë Life Pub.—R

FICTION: SPECULATIVE
(a) Baker Books
(a) Multnomah

(s)-Aaron Book
(s)-Abuzz Press—R

AMG Publishers—R
(s)-Booklocker.com
Chalfont House
Charisma House—R
Christian Writer's
   Ebook—R
(s)-Deep River Books
(s)-Enclave Pub.—R
(s)-Essence—R
Faith Books & More
Lighthouse/
   Carolinas—R
Lighthouse Pub.—R
MountainView
OakTara
Olivia Kimbrell Press
Parable Book Group
(s)-Port Hole
   Public.—R
Port Yonder Press
(s)-Redemption Press
(s)-Salt Works—R
(s)-Signalman—R
Tate Publishing—R
White Fire Pub.
(s)-Zoë Life Pub.—R

FICTION: TEEN/ YOUNG ADULT
(a) Baker Books
(a) Barbour—R
(a) Kregel—R
(a) Multnomah
(a) Nelson, Fiction,
   Thomas
(a) WaterBrook Press

(s)-Aaron Book
(s)-Abuzz Press—R
Ambassador Intl.
AMG Publishers—R
Barking Rain Press—R
Blue Dolphin—R
Bold Vision—R
Bondfire Books
(s)-Booklocker.com
Chalfont House
Charisma House—R
Christian Writer's
   Ebook—R
Comfort Publishing

Creation House
(s)-Deep River Books
Eerdmans Pub.—R
Eerdmans/Yg Readers
(s)-Essence—R
(s)-Fairway Press—R
Faith Books & More
(s)-Fruitbearer Pub.
Grace Publishing—R
JourneyForth/BJU
Kirk House
Legacy Press
Lift Every Voice—R
Lighthouse/
   Carolinas—R
Lighthouse Pub.—R
Lighthouse Trails—R
Moody Publishers
Morgan James Pub.—R
MountainView
NavPress—R
OakTara
P&R Publications
Parable Book Group
Parson Place
Prism Book Group
Ravenhawk Books—R
(s)-Redemption Press
(s)-Signalman—R
Tate Publishing—R
Trail Media
Warner Press
Watershed Books
Write Integrity Press
(s)-Word Alive—R
(s)-Zoë Life Pub.—R

FICTION: WESTERNS
(a) Baker Books
(a) Multnomah

(s)-Aaron Book
(s)-Abuzz Press—R
Ambassador Intl.
Barking Rain Press—R
(s)-Booklocker.com
(s)-Brown Books—R
Chalfont House
Charisma House—R
Christian Writer's
   Ebook—R

(s)-Deep River Books
Desert Breeze Pub.
(s)-Essence—R
(s)-Fairway Press—R
Faith Books & More
Grace Publishing—R
JourneyForth/BJU
Lighthouse Pub.—R
Mantle Rock
MountainView
OakTara
Parable Book Group
Parson Place
Prism Book Group
Ravenhawk Books—R
(s)-Redemption Press
(s)-Salt Works—R
(s)-Signalman—R
Tate Publishing—R
Trail Media
Whitaker House—R
Write Integrity Press
(s)-Zoë Life Pub.—R

FORGIVENESS
(a) B&H Publishing
(a) Doubleday
    Relig.—R
(a) HarperOne
(a) Howard Books
(a) Kregel—R
(a) Nelson, Thomas

(s)-Aaron Book
Abingdon Press
(s)-Abuzz Press—R
Ambassador Intl.
AMG Publishers—R
Ancient Faith—R
Barbour—R
Blue Dolphin—R
Bold Vision—R
Bondfire Books
(s)-Booklocker.com
Bridge Logos—R
(s)-Brown Books—R
Charisma House—R
Christian Writer's
    Ebook—R
Cladach Publishing
CLC Publications—R

Comfort Publishing
Creation House
CrossLink Publishing
CrossRiver Media
Crossway
CSS Publishing
(s)-DCTS Publishers
(s)-Deep River Books
(s)-Destiny Image
    (books)
Discovery House—R
Earthen Vessel—R
Eerdmans Pub.—R
Eerdmans/Yg Readers
Ellechor Publishing
(s)-Essence—R
(s)-Fairway Press—R
Faith Books & More
(s)-Grace Acres—R
Grace Publishing—R
Guardian Angel
(s)-Halo Publishing—R
InterVarsity Press—R
JourneyForth/BJU
Judson Press
Lift Every Voice—R
Lighthouse Pub.—R
Lutheran Univ. Press
Morgan James Pub.—R
NavPress—R
New Hope
North Wind Publishing
OakTara
On My Own Now
Pacific Press
Parson Place
Parsons Pub.—R
Pauline Books
(s)-Redemption Press
(s)-Salt Works—R
(s)-Salvation
    Publisher—R
(s)-Signalman—R
Tate Publishing—R
VBC Publishing
Whitaker House—R
White Fire Pub.
(s)-Word Alive—R
Write Integrity Press
(s)-Zoë Life Pub.—R

GAMES/CRAFTS
(a) Baker Books

(s)-Booklocker.com
Contemporary Drama
(s)-Essence—R
(s)-Fairway Press—R
Faith Books & More
Guardian Angel
Legacy Press
Lighthouse Pub.—R
Players Press
Rainbow Publishers
(s)-Redemption Press
Standard Publishing
Tate Publishing—R
Warner Press
(s)-Zoë Life Pub.—R

GIFT BOOKS
(a) Howard Books

(s)-Aaron Book
(s)-Abuzz Press—R
Bold Vision—R
Bridge Logos—R
(s)-Brown Books—R
Charisma House—R
Creation House
Eerdmans Pub.—R
(s)-Essence—R
Faith Books & More
(s)-Fruitbearer Pub.
Grace Publishing—R
Lighthouse Pub.—R
Ravenhawk Books—R
(s)-Redemption Press
(s)-Salt Works—R
(s)-Signalman—R
(s)-Zoë Life Pub.—R

GRANDPARENTING
(a) Bethany House
(a) Howard Books
(a) Nelson, Thomas

(s)-Aaron Book
Abingdon Press
(s)-Abuzz Press—R
Blue Dolphin—R
Bold Vision—R
Bondfire Books

(s)-Booklocker.com
Bridge Logos—R
(s)-Brown Books—R
Cladach Publishing
CLC Publications—R
Comfort Publishing
Creation House
Discovery House—R
Eerdmans Pub.—R
(s)-Essence—R
Faith Books & More
Grace Publishing—R
Lighthouse Pub.—R
New Hope
OakTara
North Wind Publishing
Parson Place
Pauline Books
(s)-Redemption Press
(s)-Salvation
    Publisher—R
(s)-Signalman—R
VBC Publishing
Write Integrity Press
(s)-Zoë Life Pub.—R

GRIEF

(a) Bethany House
(a) Howard Books

(s)-Aaron Book
ABC-CLIO
(s)-Abuzz Press—R
Ambassador Intl.
Ancient Faith—R
Blue Dolphin—R
BMH Books
Bold Vision—R
Bondfire Books
(s)-Booklocker.com
Charisma House—R
CLC Publications—R
Comfort Publishing
Creation House
Discovery House—R
Earthen Vessel—R
Eerdmans Pub.—R
Ellechor Publishing
(s)-Essence—R
Faith Books & More
Franciscan Media—R

Grace Publishing—R
Lift Every Voice—R
Lighthouse Pub.—R
Morgan James Pub.—R
NavPress—R
North Wind Publishing
Pauline Books
(s)-Port Hole
    Public.—R
Ravenhawk Books—R
(s)-Redemption Press
(s)-Salvation
    Publisher—R
(s)-Signalman—R
White Fire Pub.
(s)-Zoë Life Pub.—R

GROUP STUDY BOOKS

(a) Baker Books

(s)-Aaron Book
Abingdon Press
(s)-Abuzz Press—R
Ambassador Intl.
AMG Publishers—R
BMH Books
Bondfire Books
(s)-Booklocker.com
Bridge Logos—R
Chalfont House
Christian Writer's
    Ebook—R
CLC Publications—R
(s)-CrossHouse
CrossLink Publishing
CSS Publishing
(s)-Deep River Books
Discovery House—R
Eerdmans Pub.—R
(s)-Essence—R
Evergreen Press
(s)-Fairway Press—R
(s)-Grace Acres—R
Grace Publishing—R
Hannibal Books
InterVarsity Press—R
Judson Press
Lighthouse/
    Carolinas—R
Lighthouse Pub.—R

Morgan James Pub.—R
New Hope
North Wind Publishing
Pacific Press
Parson Place
Randall House
(s)-Redemption Press
(s)-Salt Works—R
(s)-Signalman—R
Tate Publishing—R
Trail Media
(s)-Word Alive—R
(s)-Zoë Life Pub.—R

HEALING

(a) Baker Books
(a) Cook, David C.
(a) Hay House
(a) Nelson, Thomas

(s)-Aaron Book
(s)-Abuzz Press—R
Blue Dolphin—R
(s)-Booklocker.com
Bridge Logos—R
(s)-Brown Books—R
Canticle Books—R
Charisma House—R
Christian Heritage—R
Christian Writer's
    Ebook—R
Comfort Publishing
Creation House
CSS Publishing
(s)-Deep River Books
(s)-Destiny Image
    (books)
Eerdmans Pub.—R
(s)-Essence—R
(s)-Fairway Press—R
Faith Books & More
Harrison House
Hope Publishing—R
Lighthouse Pub.—R
Loyola Press
Lutheran Univ. Press
Magnus Press—R
NavPress—R
North Wind Publishing
Pacific Press
Parson Place

Parsons Pub.—R
Pauline Books
(s)-Redemption Press
(s)-Salvation
    Publisher—R
(s)-Signalman—R
Tate Publishing—R
Whitaker House—R
White Fire Pub.
(s)-Word Alive—R
(s)-Zoë Life Pub.—R

HEALTH
(a) Baker Books
(a) Ballantine
(a) Hay House
(a) Nelson, Thomas

(s)-Aaron Book
ABC-CLIO
(s)-Abuzz Press—R
Blue Dolphin—R
(s)-Booklocker.com
(s)-Brown Books—R
Canticle Books—R
Charisma House—R
Charles Press
Christian Writer's
    Ebook—R
Cladach Publishing
Comfort Publishing
Creation House
(s)-Deep River Books
(s)-Destiny Image
    (books)
Eerdmans Pub., Wm. B.
(s)-Essence—R
Evergreen Press
(s)-Fairway Press—R
Faith Books & More
Franciscan Media—R
Grace Publishing—R
Guardian Angel
Hope Publishing—R
Langmarc
Life Cycle Books—R
Lighthouse Pub.—R
Loyola Press
Magnus Press—R
Morgan James Pub.—R
MountainView

New Hope
OakTara
Olivia Kimbrell Press
Pacific Press
Parsons Pub.—R
Pauline Books
(s)-Redemption Press
(s)-Salvation
    Publisher—R
(s)-Signalman—R
Sunpenny Publishing
Tate Publishing—R
VBC Publishing
Whitaker House—R
(s)-Word Alive—R
(s)-Zoë Life Pub.—R

HISPANIC MARKETS
(a) Doubleday
    Relig.—R

Abingdon Press
AMG Publishers—R
B&H Publishing
(s)-Booklocker.com
Bridge Logos—R
Charisma House—R
CLC Publications—R
Earthen Vessel—R
Eerdmans/Yg Readers
InterVarsity Press—R
Judson Press
Pacific Press
Port Yonder Press
Praeger Publishers
(s)-Redemption Press
(s)-Signalman—R
Tate Publishing—R
Tyndale Español
Whitaker House—R
White Fire Pub.

HISTORICAL
(a) Baker Academic
(a) Baker Books
(a) Doubleday
    Relig.—R
(a) HarperOne
(a) Kregel—R
(a) Nelson, Thomas

(s)-Aaron Book
ABC-CLIO
(s)-Abuzz Press—R
Blue Dolphin—R
(s)-Booklocker.com
Bridge Logos—R
(s)-Brown Books—R
Christian Heritage—R
Christian Writer's
    Ebook—R
Comfort Publishing
Creation House
Eerdmans Pub.—R
Eerdmans/Yg Readers
(s)-Essence—R
(s)-Fairway Press—R
Faith Books & More
Inkling Books—R
InterVarsity Press—R
Kirk House
Lift Every Voice—R
Lighthouse/
    Carolinas—R
Lighthouse Pub.—R
Loyola Press
Lutheran Univ. Press
(s)-Redemption Press
(s)-Salt Works—R
(s)-Signalman—R
Sunpenny Publishing
Tate Publishing—R
White Fire Pub.
(s)-Word Alive—R
(s)-Zoë Life Pub.—R

HOLIDAY/SEASONAL
(a) Cook, David C.
(a) HarperOne
(a) Howard Books

(s)-Aaron Book
(s)-Aaron Book
Abingdon Press
(s)-Abuzz Press—R
AMG Publishers—R
Barbour—R
Bondfire Books
(s)-Booklocker.com
Charisma House—R
Christian Writer's
    Ebook—R

CSS Publishing
(s)-Deep River Books
(s)-Essence—R
Evergreen Press
(s)-Fairway Press—R
Faith Books & More
Grace Publishing—R
Guardian Angel
Guideposts Books
Judson Press
Lighthouse/
   Carolinas—R
Lighthouse Pub.—R
Meriwether
New Hope
OakTara
Pauline Books
Ravenhawk Books—R
(s)-Redemption Press
(s)-Salt Works—R
(s)-Signalman—R
Standard Publishing
Tate Publishing—R
Trail Media
Warner Press
White Fire Pub.
(s)-Word Alive—R
Write Integrity Press

HOLINESS

(a) Bethany House
(a) Howard Books

(s)-Aaron Book
(s)-Abuzz Press—R
Ambassador Intl.
Ancient Faith—R
Bondfire Books
(s)-Booklocker.com
Bridge Logos—R
(s)-Brown Books—R
Charisma House—R
Christian Heritage—R
Creation House
Earthen Vessel—R
Eerdmans Pub.—R
(s)-Essence—R
Faith Books & More
(s)-Grace Acres—R
InterVarsity Press—R
Lighthouse Pub.—R

NavPress—R
Parson Place
Parsons Pub.—R
Pauline Books
(s)-Redemption Press
(s)-Salt Works—R
(s)-Salvation
   Publisher—R
(s)-Signalman—R
Tate Publishing—R
Wesleyan Publishing
Whitaker House—R
White Fire Pub.
Write Integrity Press

HOLY SPIRIT

(a) Kregel—R
(a) Nelson, Thomas

(s)-Aaron Book
(s)-Abuzz Press—R
AMG Publishers—R
Ancient Faith—R
Blue Dolphin—R
Bondfire Books
(s)-Booklocker.com
Bridge Logos—R
Canticle Books—R
Charisma House—R
Christian Heritage—R
Christian Writer's
   Ebook—R
CLC Publications—R
Comfort Publishing
Creation House
CrossRiver Media
CSS Publishing
(s)-Deep River Books
(s)-Destiny Image
   (books)
Discovery House—R
Earthen Vessel—R
Eerdmans Pub.—R
(s)-Essence—R
(s)-Fairway Press—R
Faith Books & More
Four Craftsmen—R
Grace Publishing—R
Harrison House
InterVarsity Press—R
Lift Every Voice—R

Lighthouse Pub.—R
Lutheran Univ. Press
Magnus Press—R
Morgan James Pub.—R
NavPress—R
Pacific Press
Parson Place
Parsons Pub.—R
Pauline Books
(s)-Redemption Press
(s)-Salvation
   Publisher—R
(s)-Signalman—R
Tate Publishing—R
VBC Publishing
Whitaker House—R
White Fire Pub.
(s)-Word Alive—R
Write Integrity Press
(s)-Zoë Life Pub.—R

HOMESCHOOLING RESOURCES

(a) Baker Books

(s)-Aaron Book
(s)-Aaron Book
(s)-Abuzz Press—R
AMG Publishers—R
Bondfire Books
(s)-Booklocker.com
Christian Writer's
   Ebook—R
(s)-CrossHouse
Eerdmans Pub.—R
(s)-Essence—R
(s)-Fairway Press—R
Faith Books & More
(s)-Grace Acres—R
Grace Publishing—R
Guardian Angel
Hannibal Books
JourneyForth/BJU
Lighthouse Pub.—R
Lighthouse Trails—R
New Leaf
(s)-Redemption Press
(s)-Salt Works—R
(s)-Signalman—R
Tate Publishing—R
Trail Media

(s)-Word Alive—R
(s)-Zoë Life Pub.—R

HOMILETICS
(a) Baker Books
(a) Kregel—R

(s)-Aaron Book
Abingdon Press
(s)-Abuzz Press—R
Bondfire Books
(s)-Booklocker.com
Christian Writer's
   Ebook—R
CLC Publications—R
CSS Publishing
(s)-DCTS Publishers
(s)-Deep River Books
Earthen Vessel—R
Eerdmans Pub.—R
(s)-Essence—R
(s)-Fairway Press—R
Faith Books & More
Judson Press
Lighthouse Pub.—R
Lutheran Univ. Press
NavPress—R
(s)-Redemption Press
(s)-Salt Works—R
(s)-Signalman—R
Tate Publishing—R
VBC Publishing
(s)-Word Alive—R
(s)-Zoë Life Pub.—R

HOW-TO
(a) Baker Books
(a) Baker Books
(a) Ballantine
(a) Howard Books
(a) Nelson, Thomas
(a) Revell

(s)-Aaron Book
(s)-Abuzz Press—R
Adams Media
Bondfire Books
(s)-Booklocker.com
Bridge Logos—R
Christian Writer's
   Ebook—R

Church Growth Inst.
(s)-Deep River Books
(s)-Essence—R
Evergreen Press
(s)-Fairway Press—R
Faith Books & More
Gospel Light
Guardian Angel
(s)-Halo Publishing—R
Inkling Books—R
Kirk House
Lighthouse Pub.—R
Meriwether
Morgan James Pub.—R
MountainView
OakTara
Our Sunday Visitor—R
Pacific Press
Parson Place
Players Press
Pauline Books
(s)-Redemption Press
(s)-Salt Works—R
(s)-Salvation
   Publisher—R
(s)-Signalman—R
Standard Publishing
Tate Publishing—R
VBC Publishing
(s)-Word Alive—R
(s)-Zoë Life Pub.—R

HUMOR
(a) Baker Books
(a) Ballantine
(a) Cook, David C.
(a) Nelson, Thomas

(s)-Aaron Book
(s)-Abuzz Press—R
Barbour—R
Bold Vision—R
Bondfire Books
(s)-Booklocker.com
Bridge Logos—R
Christian Writer's
   Ebook—R
Comfort Publishing
Creation House
(s)-Deep River Books
Eerdmans/Yg Readers

(s)-Essence—R
Evergreen Press
(s)-Fairway Press—R
Faith Books & More
Grace Publishing—R
Guideposts Books
Kirk House
Lighthouse/
   Carolinas—R
Lighthouse Pub.—R
Loyola Press
Meriwether
MOPS Intl.
Morgan James Pub.—R
NavPress—R
North Wind Publishing
On My Own Now
Pacific Press
Parson Place
Pauline Books
(s)-Redemption Press
(s)-Salt Works—R
(s)-Salvation
   Publisher—R
(s)-Signalman—R
Tate Publishing—R
Trail Media
White Fire Pub.
(s)-Word Alive—R
(s)-Zoë Life Pub.—R

INSPIRATIONAL
(a) Baker Books
(a) Bethany House
(a) Doubleday
   Relig.—R
(a) Hay House
(a) Howard Books
(a) Nelson, Thomas
(a) Tyndale House
(a) WaterBrook Press

(s)-Aaron Book
Abingdon Press
(s)-Abuzz Press—R
Adams Media
Ambassador Intl.
AMG Publishers—R
Barbour—R
Bold Vision—R
Bondfire Books

(s)-Booklocker.com
Bridge Logos—R
(s)-Brown Books—R
Canticle Books—R
Chalfont House
Charisma House—R
Christian Writer's
    Ebook—R
CLC Publications—R
Comfort Publishing
Creation House
(s)-CrossHouse
CrossLink Publishing
CrossRiver Media
Crossway
CSS Publishing
(s)-DCTS Publishers
(s)-Deep River Books
(s)-Destiny Image
    (books)
Discovery House—R
Dove Inspirational—R
Eerdmans/Yg Readers
Ellechor Publishing
(s)-Essence—R
Evergreen Press
(s)-Fairway Press—R
Faith Books & More
Franciscan Media—R
(s)-Fruitbearer Pub.
Grace Publishing—R
Guardian Angel
Harrison House
Hope Publishing—R
JourneyForth/BJU
Judson Press
Kirk House
Langmarc
Lighthouse/
    Carolinas—R
Lighthouse Pub.—R
Loyola Press
Lutheran Univ. Press
Magnus Press—R
Morgan James Pub.—R
MountainView
NavPress—R
New Leaf
North Wind Publishing
OakTara

On My Own Now
Pacific Press
Parson Place
Parsons Pub.—R
Pauline Books
Pelican Pub.—R
(s)-Port Hole
    Public.—R
Pauline Books
Ravenhawk Books—R
(s)-Redemption Press
(s)-Salt Works—R
(s)-Salvation
    Publisher—R
(s)-Signalman—R
Sunpenny Publishing
Tate Publishing—R
VBC Publishing
Wesleyan Publishing
Whitaker House—R
White Fire Pub.
(s)-Word Alive—R
Write Integrity Press
(s)-Zoë Life Pub.—R

LAY COUNSELING
Bondfire Books
Four Craftsmen—R
North Wind Publishing
Randall House
(s)-Redemption Press
(s)-Signalman—R
(s)-Zoë Life Pub.—R

LEADERSHIP
(a) Baker Books
(a) B&H Publishing
(a) Bethany House
(a) Cook, David C.
(a) Kregel—R
(a) Nelson, Thomas
(a) WaterBrook Press

(s)-Aaron Book
Abingdon Press
(s)-Abuzz Press—R
AMG Publishers—R
BMH Books
Bold Vision—R
Bondfire Books
(s)-Booklocker.com

Bridge Logos—R
Charisma House—R
Christian Writer's
    Ebook—R
Church Growth Inst.
CLC Publications—R
Creation House
CrossLink Publishing
CSS Publishing
(s)-DCTS Publishers
(s)-Deep River Books
Eerdmans Pub.—R
Ellechor Publishing
(s)-Essence—R
Evergreen Press
(s)-Fairway Press—R
Faith Books & More
(s)-Grace Acres—R
Grace Publishing—R
Group Publishing
Guardian Angel
Harrison House
InterVarsity Press—R
Judson Press
Kirk House
Lift Every Voice—R
Lighthouse Pub.—R
Lutheran Univ. Press
Morgan James Pub.—R
NavPress—R
New Hope
New Leaf
North Wind Publishing
Parson Place
Parsons Pub.—R
Randall House
Ravenhawk Books—R
(s)-Redemption Press
(s)-Salt Works—R
(s)-Salvation
    Publisher—R
(s)-Signalman—R
Standard Publishing
Tate Publishing—R
Trail Media
VBC Publishing
Wesleyan Publishing
Whitaker House—R
White Fire Pub.
(s)-Word Alive—R

(s)-Zoë Life Pub.—R

LIFESTYLE
(s)-Abuzz Press—R
Ambassador Intl.
Bold Vision—R
Bondfire Books
Comfort Publishing
CrossLink Publishing
Ellechor Publishing
(s)-Halo Publishing—R
Lighthouse/
   Carolinas—R
Morgan James Pub.—R
NavPress—R
New Leaf
North Wind Publishing
Parsons Pub.—R
(s)-Redemption Press
(s)-Signalman—R
White Fire Pub.
Write Integrity Press
(s)-Zoë Life Pub.—R

LITURGICAL STUDIES
(a) Baker Books
(a) Doubleday
   Relig.—R

(s)-Aaron Book
(s)-Abuzz Press—R
American Cath.
   Press—R
Ancient Faith—R
Blue Dolphin—R
Bondfire Books
(s)-Booklocker.com
Christian Heritage—R
Christian Writer's
   Ebook—R
CrossLink Publishing
CSS Publishing
Eerdmans Pub.—R
(s)-Fairway Press—R
Faith Books & More
Group Publishing
InterVarsity Press—R
Lighthouse Pub.—R
Lutheran Univ. Press
Parson Place

Ravenhawk Books—R
(s)-Redemption Press
(s)-Salt Works—R
(s)-Signalman—R
Tate Publishing—R
Trail Media
White Fire Pub.
(s)-Word Alive—R
(s)-Zoë Life Pub.—R

MARRIAGE
(a) Baker Books
(a) B&H Publishing
(a) Bethany House
(a) Cook, David C.
(a) Doubleday
   Relig.—R
(a) HarperOne
(a) Howard Books
(a) Kregel—R
(a) Nelson, Thomas
(a) Revell
(a) Tyndale House
(a) WaterBrook Press

(s)-Aaron Book
(s)-Abuzz Press—R
Ambassador Intl.
AMG Publishers—R
Ancient Faith—R
Barbour—R
Blue Dolphin—R
Bondfire Books
(s)-Booklocker.com
(s)-Brown Books—R
Charisma House—R
Christian Writer's
   Ebook—R
CLC Publications—R
Comfort Publishing
Creation House
(s)-CrossHouse
CrossLink Publishing
Crossway
CSS Publishing
(s)-Deep River Books
(s)-Destiny Image
   (books)
Discovery House—R
Eerdmans Pub.—R
(s)-Essence—R

Evergreen Press
(s)-Fairway Press—R
Faith Books & More
Franciscan Media—R
(s)-Grace Acres—R
Grace Publishing—R
Guideposts Books
(s)-Halo Publishing—R
Hannibal Books
Hope Publishing—R
InterVarsity Press—R
JourneyForth/BJU
Judson Press
Lift Every Voice—R
Lighthouse/
   Carolinas—R
Lighthouse Pub.—R
Loyola Press
MOPS Intl.
Morgan James Pub.—R
NavPress—R
New Hope
New Leaf
OakTara
Pacific Press
Parson Place
Parsons Pub.—R
Pauline Books
Randall House
(s)-Redemption Press
(s)-Signalman—R
Standard Publishing
Tate Publishing—R
Trail Media
VBC Publishing
Whitaker House—R
White Fire Pub.
(s)-Word Alive—R
Write Integrity Press
(s)-Zoë Life Pub.—R

MEMOIRS
(a) Baker Books
(a) Ballantine
(a) Doubleday
   Relig.—R
(a) HarperOne
(a) Nelson, Thomas

(s)-Aaron Book
(s)-Abuzz Press—R

Ambassador Intl.
Ancient Faith—R
Bondfire Books
(s)-Booklocker.com
(s)-Brown Books—R
Christian Heritage—R
Christian Writer's
    Ebook—R
Cladach Publishing
Creation House
(s)-Deep River Books
Earthen Vessel—R
(s)-Essence—R
(s)-Fairway Press—R
Faith Books & More
Four Craftsmen—R
Franciscan Media—R
(s)-Fruitbearer Pub.
(s)-Grace Acres—R
Guideposts Books
(s)-Halo Publishing—R
Inheritance Press
Lighthouse Pub.—R
Lighthouse Trails—R
Morgan James Pub.—R
On My Own Now
Pacific Press
Port Yonder Press
(s)-Redemption Press
(s)-Salvation
    Publisher—R
(s)-Signalman—R
Sunpenny Publishing
Tate Publishing—R
Trail Media
Whitaker House—R
White Fire Pub.
(s)-Word Alive—R
(s)-Zoë Life Pub.—R

MEN'S BOOKS

(a) Baker Books
(a) B&H Publishing
(a) Bethany House
(a) Doubleday
    Relig.—R
(a) Howard Books
(a) Kregel—R
(a) Nelson, Thomas
(a) WaterBrook Press

(s)-Aaron Book
(s)-Abuzz Press—R
Ambassador Intl.
AMG Publishers—R
Barbour—R
Blue Dolphin—R
BMH Books
Bondfire Books
(s)-Booklocker.com
Bridge Logos—R
Charisma House—R
Christian Writer's
    Ebook—R
CLC Publications—R
Comfort Publishing
Creation House
CrossLink Publishing
Crossway
(s)-Deep River Books
Discovery House—R
Earthen Vessel—R
Eerdmans Pub.—R
Ellechor Publishing
(s)-Essence—R
Evergreen Press
(s)-Fairway Press—R
Faith Books & More
Franciscan Media—R
Grace Publishing—R
(s)-Halo Publishing—R
Inkling Books—R
InterVarsity Press—R
Lift Every Voice—R
Lighthouse/
    Carolinas—R
Lighthouse Pub.—R
Loyola Press
NavPress—R
New Leaf
OakTara
Pacific Press
Parson Place
Parsons Pub.—R
Pauline Books
Randall House
Ravenhawk Books—R
(s)-Redemption Press
(s)-Signalman—R
Tate Publishing—R
Trail Media

VBC Publishing
Whitaker House—R
White Fire Pub.
(s)-Word Alive—R
(s)-Zoë Life Pub.—R

MINIBOOKS

Bold Vision—R
Charisma House—R
Earthen Vessel—R
Four Craftsmen—R
Grace Publishing—R
Harrison House
Legacy Press
Lighthouse Pub.—R
(s)-Redemption Press
(s)-Salt Works—R
Tate Publishing—R
Trail Media

MIRACLES

(a) Baker Books
(a) HarperOne

(s)-Aaron Book
(s)-Abuzz Press—R
AMG Publishers—R
Ancient Faith—R
Blue Dolphin—R
Bondfire Books
(s)-Booklocker.com
Charisma House—R
Christian Heritage—R
Christian Writer's
    Ebook—R
Comfort Publishing
Creation House
CSS Publishing
(s)-Deep River Books
(s)-Destiny Image
    (books)
(s)-Essence—R
Evergreen Press
(s)-Fairway Press—R
Faith Books & More
Four Craftsmen—R
Guideposts Books
Harrison House
Lighthouse Pub.—R
Loyola Press
North Wind Publishing

On My Own Now
Pacific Press
Parson Place
Parsons Pub.—R
Pauline Books
(s)-Redemption Press
(s)-Salvation
    Publisher—R
(s)-Signalman—R
Tate Publishing—R
Whitaker House—R
White Fire Pub.
(s)-Word Alive—R
(s)-Zoë Life Pub.—R

MISSIONS/ MISSIONARY
(a) Baker Books

(s)-Aaron Book
(s)-Abuzz Press—R
AMG Publishers—R
(s)-Ampelos Press—R
Bondfire Books
(s)-Booklocker.com
(s)-Brown Books—R
Charisma House—R
Christian Heritage—R
Christian Writer's
    Ebook—R
CLC Publications—R
Comfort Publishing
Creation House
(s)-CrossHouse
CSS Publishing
(s)-Deep River Books
Earthen Vessel—R
Eerdmans Pub.—R
(s)-Essence—R
Evergreen Press
(s)-Fairway Press—R
Faith Books & More
Four Craftsmen—R
(s)-Grace Acres—R
Group Publishing
Hannibal Books
Hope Publishing—R
InterVarsity Press—R
Lift Every Voice—R
Lighthouse Pub.—R
Lighthouse Trails—R

Lutheran Univ. Press
NavPress—R
North Wind Publishing
OakTara
Pacific Press
P&R Publications
Parson Place
Parsons Pub.—R
Port Yonder Press
Randall House
(s)-Redemption Press
(s)-Salt Works—R
(s)-Signalman—R
Tate Publishing—R
Trail Media
VBC Publishing
White Fire Pub.
(s)-Word Alive—R
Write Integrity Press
(s)-Zoë Life Pub.—R

MONEY MANAGEMENT
(a) Baker Books
(a) Cook, David C.
(a) Nelson, Thomas
(a) WaterBrook Press

(s)-Aaron Book
(s)-Abuzz Press—R
Ambassador Intl.
Barbour—R
BMH Books
Bondfire Books
(s)-Booklocker.com
Charisma House—R
Christian Writer's
    Ebook—R
Creation House
CrossLink Publishing
(s)-Deep River Books
Eerdmans Pub.—R
Ellechor Publishing
(s)-Essence—R
Evergreen Press
(s)-Fairway Press—R
Faith Books & More
Four Craftsmen—R
Grace Publishing—R
Hannibal Books
JourneyForth/BJU

Judson Press
Lift Every Voice—R
Lighthouse Pub.—R
Moody Publishers
Morgan James Pub.—R
MountainView
NavPress—R
New Hope
New Leaf
North Wind Publishing
Pacific Press
Parson Place
Ravenhawk Books—R
(s)-Redemption Press
Reference Service
(s)-Salvation
    Publisher—R
(s)-Signalman—R
Tate Publishing—R
VBC Publishing
Whitaker House—R
(s)-Word Alive—R
(s)-Zoë Life Pub.—R

MUSIC-RELATED BOOKS
(a) Baker Books

(s)-Aaron Book
American Cath.
    Press—R
Blue Dolphin—R
BMH Books
(s)-Booklocker.com
Christian Writer's
    Ebook—R
Contemporary Drama
(s)-Deep River Books
(s)-Destiny Image
    (books)
Eerdmans Pub.—R
(s)-Essence—R
(s)-Fairway Press—R
Faith Books & More
Guardian Angel
Lighthouse Pub.—R
Lutheran Univ. Press
North Wind Publishing
Players Press
(s)-Redemption Press
Standard Publishing

Tate Publishing—R
(s)-Word Alive—R
(s)-Zoë Life Pub.—R

NOVELTY BOOKS FOR KIDS

(a) Baker Books

(s)-Fairway Press—R
Guardian Angel
Legacy Press
Lift Every Voice—R
(s)-Redemption Press
(s)-Salt Works—R
Standard Publishing
Tate Publishing—R
(s)-Word Alive—R
(s)-Zoë Life Pub.—R

PAMPHLETS

Christian Writer's
  Ebook—R
(s)-Essence—R
(s)-Fruitbearer Pub.
Lift Every Voice—R
Our Sunday Visitor—R
(s)-Redemption Press
(s)-Salt Works—R
Trinity Foundation—R

PARENTING

(a) Baker Books
(a) Ballantine
(a) B&H Publishing
(a) Bethany House
(a) Cook, David C.
(a) Howard Books
(a) Kregel—R
(a) Nelson, Thomas
(a) Revell
(a) Tyndale House
(a) WaterBrook Press

(s)-Aaron Book
(s)-Abuzz Press—R
Adams Media
Ambassador Intl.
Ancient Faith—R
Barbour—R
Bondfire Books
(s)-Booklocker.com

(s)-Brown Books—R
Chalfont House
Charles Press
Christian Writer's
  Ebook—R
CLC Publications—R
Comfort Publishing
Conari Press
Creation House
CrossLink Publishing
Crossway
(s)-Deep River Books
(s)-Destiny Image
  (books)
Discovery House—R
Eerdmans Pub.—R
(s)-Essence—R
Evergreen Press
(s)-Fairway Press—R
Faith Books & More
Four Craftsmen—R
Franciscan Media—R
(s)-Grace Acres—R
Grace Publishing—R
Group Publishing
(s)-Halo Publishing—R
Harrison House
InterVarsity Press—R
JourneyForth/BJU
Langmarc
Lift Every Voice—R
Lighthouse/
  Carolinas—R
Lighthouse Pub.—R
MOPS Intl.
NavPress—R
New Hope
New Leaf
OakTara
Our Sunday Visitor—R
Pacific Press
P&R Publications
Pauline Books
(s)-Port Hole
  Public.—R
Randall House
(s)-Redemption Press
(s)-Salt Works—R
(s)-Signalman—R

Standard Publishing
Sunpenny Publishing
Tate Publishing—R
Trail Media
VBC Publishing
Whitaker House—R
White Fire Pub.
(s)-Word Alive—R
Write Integrity Press
(s)-Zoë Life Pub.—R

PASTORS' HELPS

(a) Baker Academic
(a) Baker Books
(a) B&H Publishing
(a) Kregel—R

(s)-Aaron Book
(s)-Abuzz Press—R
Ambassador Intl.
(s)-Booklocker.com
Bridge Logos—R
Christian Writer's
  Ebook—R
Church Growth Inst.
CLC Publications—R
Creation House
CrossLink Publishing
CSS Publishing
(s)-DCTS Publishers
(s)-Deep River Books
Earthen Vessel—R
Eerdmans Pub.—R
(s)-Essence—R
(s)-Fairway Press—R
Faith Books & More
Grace Publishing—R
Group Publishing
Lighthouse Pub.—R
Lutheran Univ. Press
NavPress—R
Parsons Pub.—R
Pauline Books
Randall House
(s)-Redemption Press
(s)-Signalman—R
Standard Publishing
Tate Publishing—R
VBC Publishing
Wesleyan Publishing

(s)-Word Alive—R
(s)-Zoë Life Pub.—R
Zondervan

PERSONAL EXPERIENCE

(a) Baker Books
(a) HarperOne
(a) Kregel—R
(a) Nelson, Thomas

(s)-Aaron Book
(s)-Abuzz Press—R
AMG Publishers—R
(s)-Ampelos Press—R
Bondfire Books
(s)-Booklocker.com
Bridge Logos—R
Canticle Books—R
Charisma House—R
Christian Writer's
    Ebook—R
Comfort Publishing
Creation House
CrossLink Publishing
CrossRiver Media
(s)-DCTS Publishers
(s)-Deep River Books
Ellechor Publishing
(s)-Essence—R
(s)-Fairway Press—R
Faith Books & More
Four Craftsmen—R
(s)-Fruitbearer Pub.
Guideposts Books
(s)-Halo Publishing—R
Hannibal Books
Lighthouse Pub.—R
Lighthouse Trails—R
North Wind Publishing
On My Own Now
Pacific Press
Parsons Pub.—R
Ravenhawk Books—R
(s)-Redemption Press
(s)-Salvation
    Publisher—R
(s)-Signalman—R
Tate Publishing—R
Trail Media

White Fire Pub.
(s)-Word Alive—R

PERSONAL GROWTH

(a) Baker Books
(a) B&H Publishing
(a) Bethany House
(a) HarperOne
(a) Hay House
(a) Howard Books
(a) Kregel—R
(a) Nelson, Thomas
(a) Tyndale House
(a) WaterBrook Press

(s)-Aaron Book
(s)-Abuzz Press—R
Ambassador Intl.
AMG Publishers—R
Ancient Faith—R
Barbour—R
Blue Dolphin—R
BMH Books
Bold Vision—R
Bondfire Books
(s)-Booklocker.com
Bridge Logos—R
Canticle Books—R
Charisma House—R
Christian Writer's
    Ebook—R
Comfort Publishing
Conari Press
Creation House
CrossLink Publishing
CrossRiver Media
(s)-DCTS Publishers
(s)-Deep River Books
(s)-Destiny Image
    (books)
Discovery House—R
Ellechor Publishing
(s)-Essence—R
Evergreen Press
(s)-Fairway Press—R
Faith Books & More
Four Craftsmen—R
Franciscan Media—R
Grace Publishing—R
Guideposts Books

(s)-Halo Publishing—R
Hannibal Books
InterVarsity Press—R
JourneyForth/BJU
Lift Every Voice—R
Lighthouse/
    Carolinas—R
Lighthouse Pub.—R
Morgan James Pub.—R
NavPress—R
New Hope
North Wind Publishing
OakTara
On My Own Now
Pacific Press
Parson Place
Parsons Pub.—R
Pauline Books
Ravenhawk Books—R
(s)-Redemption Press
(s)-Signalman—R
Tate Publishing—R
Trail Media
Whitaker House—R
White Fire Pub.
(s)-Word Alive—R
Write Integrity Press

PERSONAL RENEWAL

(a) Baker Books
(a) HarperOne
(a) Howard Books
(a) Kregel—R
(a) Tyndale House

(s)-Aaron Book
(s)-Abuzz Press—R
Barbour—R
BMH Books
Bondfire Books
(s)-Booklocker.com
Bridge Logos—R
Canticle Books—R
Charisma House—R
Christian Writer's
    Ebook—R
Comfort Publishing
Conari Press
Creation House
CrossLink Publishing

(s)-DCTS Publishers
(s)-Deep River Books
(s)-Destiny Image
    (books)
Earthen Vessel—R
Ellechor Publishing
(s)-Essence—R
Evergreen Press
(s)-Fairway Press—R
Faith Books & More
Grace Publishing—R
(s)-Halo Publishing—R
Hannibal Books
Kirk House
Lift Every Voice—R
Lighthouse/
    Carolinas—R
Lighthouse Pub.—R
NavPress—R
New Hope
North Wind Publishing
OakTara
On My Own Now
Pacific Press
Parsons Pub.—R
Ravenhawk Books—R
(s)-Redemption Press
(s)-Signalman—R
Tate Publishing—R
Trail Media
Whitaker House—R
White Fire Pub.
(s)-Word Alive—R
(s)-Zoë Life Pub.—R

PHILOSOPHY
(a) Baker Books
(a) Doubleday
    Relig.—R
(a) HarperOne
(a) Kregel—R

(s)-Aaron Book
(s)-Abuzz Press—R
Bondfire Books
(s)-Booklocker.com
Charles Press
Christian Writer's
    Ebook—R
Creation House

(s)-Deep River Books
Eerdmans Pub.—R
(s)-Essence—R
(s)-Fairway Press—R
Faith Books & More
Inkling Books—R
InterVarsity Press—R
Lighthouse Pub.—R
Lutheran Univ. Press
Paragon House
(s)-Port Hole
    Public.—R
Port Yonder Press
(s)-Redemption Press
(s)-Salt Works—R
(s)-Signalman—R
Tate Publishing—R
Trinity Foundation--R
White Fire Pub.
(s)-Word Alive—R
Yale Univ. Press—R
(s)-Zoë Life Pub.—R

PHOTOGRAPHS (FOR COVERS)
Abingdon Press
Abuzz Press
Ambassador Intl.
AMG Publishers
Ancient Faith
Blue Dolphin
Bold Vision
Booklocker.com
Bridge Logos
Charisma House
Church Growth Inst.
CLC Publications
Comfort Publishing
Creation House
CrossHouse
CrossLink Publishing
Earthen Vessel
Ellechor Publishing
Essence
Faith Books & More
Four Craftsmen
Fruitbearer Pub.
Guardian Angel
Life Sentence
    Publishing

Lift Every Voice
Lighthouse/Carolinas
Lighthouse Pub.
Lutheran Univ. Press
Morgan James Pub.
MountainView
Mystical Rose
New Hope
North Wind Publishers
Our Sunday Visitor
Parson Place
Parsons Publishers
Pauline Kids
Players Press
Ravenhawk Books
Salt Works
Signalman
Sunpenny Publishing
Tate Publishing
Trinity Foundation
Whitaker House
White Fire Pub.
Zoë Life Pub.

POETRY
(s)-Aaron Book
(s)-Abuzz Press—R
Bondfire Books
(s)-Booklocker.com
Christian Writer's
    Ebook—R
Creation House
Earthen Vessel—R
Eerdmans Pub.—R
Eerdmans/Yg Readers
(s)-Essence—R
(s)-Fairway Press—R
Faith Books & More
(s)-Halo Publishing—R
Lighthouse Pub.—R
(s)-Port Hole
    Public.—R
Port Yonder Press
(s)-Redemption Press
Tate Publishing—R
(s)-Word Alive—R
Yale Univ. Press—R
(s)-Zoë Life Pub.—R

POLITICS
(a) Baker Books
(a) Doubleday
    Relig.—R
(a) HarperOne
(a) Howard Books
(a) Nelson, Thomas

(s)-Aaron Book
ABC-CLIO
(s)-Abuzz Press—R
Bondfire Books
(s)-Booklocker.com
Christian Writer's
    Ebook—R
Creation House
(s)-Deep River Books
Eerdmans Pub.—R
(s)-Essence—R
(s)-Fairway Press—R
Faith Books & More
Inkling Books—R
Lighthouse Pub.—R
Praeger Publishers
Ravenhawk Books—R
(s)-Redemption Press
(s)-Salt Works—R
(s)-Signalman—R
Tate Publishing—R
White Fire Pub.
(s)-Word Alive—R
Yale Univ. Press—R
(s)-Zoë Life Pub.—R

POPULAR CULTURE
ABC-CLIO
(s)-Abuzz Press—R
Bondfire Books
Comfort Publishing
Discovery House—R
(s)-Essence—R
Lighthouse/
    Carolinas—R
Pauline Books
Port Yonder Press
(s)-Redemption Press
(s)-Signalman—R
White Fire Pub.
(s)-Zoë Life Pub.—R

POSTMODERNISM
ABC-CLIO
(s)-Abuzz Press—R
Ambassador Intl.
Earthen Vessel—R
(s)-Essence—R
Port Yonder Press
(s)-Redemption Press
(s)-Signalman—R
White Fire Pub.
(s)-Zoë Life Pub.—R

PRAYER
(a) Baker Books
(a) Bethany House
(a) Cook, David C.
(a) Doubleday
    Relig.—R
(a) HarperOne
(a) Howard Books
(a) Kregel—R
(a) Nelson, Thomas
(a) Tyndale House
(a) WaterBrook Press

(s)-Aaron Book
Abingdon Press
(s)-Abuzz Press—R
Ambassador Intl.
AMG Publishers—R
(s)-Ampelos Press—R
Ancient Faith—R
Barbour—R
Blue Dolphin—R
BMH Books
Bold Vision—R
Bondfire Books
(s)-Booklocker.com
Bridge Logos—R
Charisma House—R
Christian Heritage—R
Christian Writer's
    Ebook—R
CLC Publications—R
Creation House
(s)-CrossHouse
CrossLink Publishing
CrossRiver Media
Crossway
CSS Publishing

(s)-DCTS Publishers
(s)-Deep River Books
(s)-Destiny Image
    (books)
Discovery House—R
Earthen Vessel—R
Eerdmans Pub.—R
Eerdmans/Yg Readers
(s)-Essence—R
Evergreen Press
(s)-Fairway Press—R
Faith Books & More
Four Craftsmen—R
Franciscan Media—R
(s)-Fruitbearer Pub.
Grace Publishing—R
Guideposts Books
(s)-Halo Publishing—R
Harrison House
Hope Publishing—R
InterVarsity Press—R
JourneyForth/BJU
Legacy Press
Lift Every Voice—R
Lighthouse/
    Carolinas—R
Lighthouse Pub.—R
Loyola Press
Lutheran Univ. Press
Moody Publishers
NavPress—R
North Wind Publishing
On My Own Now
Our Sunday Visitor—R
Pacific Press
Parsons Pub.—R
Pauline Books
Pauline Kids
(s)-Port Hole
    Public.—R
PrayerShop Pub.—R
(s)-Redemption Press
(s)-Salvation
    Publisher—R
(s)-Signalman—R
Standard Publishing
Tate Publishing—R
VBC Publishing
Wesleyan Publishing
Whitaker House—R

White Fire Pub.
(s)-Word Alive—R
Write Integrity Press
(s)-Zoë Life Pub.—R

PRINT-ON-DEMAND
(s)-Aaron Book
(s)-Abuzz Press—R
Ambassador Intl.
AMG Publishers—R
Ancient Faith—R
Blue Dolphin—R
Bold Vision—R
(s)-Booklocker.com
Bridge Logos—R
Christian Writer's
    Ebook—R
CLC Publications—R
CrossLink Publishing
CSS Publishing
Earthen Vessel—R
Evergreen Press
Faith Books & More
Four Craftsmen—R
Grace Publishing—R
Hannibal Books
Inkling Books—R
Lighthouse/
    Carolinas—R
Lighthouse Pub.—R
North Wind Publishing
OakTara
Parsons Pub.—R
Players Press
Ravenhawk Books—R
(s)-Redemption Press
(s)-Salvation
    Publisher—R
(s)-Signalman—R
(s)-Strong Tower—R
VBC Publishing
Whitaker House—R
(s)-Word Alive—R
Write Integrity Press

PROPHECY
(a) Baker Books
(a) Kregel—R

(s)-Aaron Book

(s)-Abuzz Press—R
Ambassador Intl.
AMG Publishers—R
Blue Dolphin—R
BMH Books
Bondfire Books
(s)-Booklocker.com
Bridge Logos—R
Charisma House—R
Christian Writer's
    Ebook—R
Comfort Publishing
Creation House
CSS Publishing
(s)-Deep River Books
(s)-Destiny Image
    (books)
Eerdmans Pub.—R
(s)-Essence—R
(s)-Fairway Press—R
Faith Books & More
Four Craftsmen—R
Harrison House
Lighthouse Pub.—R
Lutheran Univ. Press
Pacific Press
Parson Place
Parsons Pub.—R
Ravenhawk Books—R
(s)-Redemption Press
(s)-Salvation
    Publisher—R
(s)-Signalman—R
Tate Publishing—R
Whitaker House—R
White Fire Pub.
(s)-Word Alive—R
(s)-Zoë Life Pub.—R

PSYCHOLOGY
(a) Baker Academic
(a) Kregel—R
(a) Tyndale House

(s)-Aaron Book
ABC-CLIO
(s)-Abuzz Press—R
Adams Media
Blue Dolphin—R
Bondfire Books

(s)-Booklocker.com
Charles Press
Christian Writer's
    Ebook—R
Comfort Publishing
Creation House
(s)-Deep River Books
Eerdmans Pub.—R
(s)-Essence—R
Evergreen Press
(s)-Fairway Press—R
Faith Books & More
Hope Publishing—R
InterVarsity Press—R
Lighthouse Pub.—R
MountainView
On My Own Now
Paragon House
Port Yonder Press
(s)-Redemption Press
(s)-Signalman—R
Tate Publishing—R
White Fire Pub.
(s)-Word Alive—R
Yale Univ. Press—R
(s)-Zoë Life Pub.—R

RACISM
(a) Baker Books
(a) Howard Books

(s)-Aaron Book
ABC-CLIO
(s)-Abuzz Press—R
Blue Dolphin—R
(s)-Booklocker.com
Charisma House—R
Christian Writer's
    Ebook—R
(s)-DCTS Publishers
(s)-Deep River Books
Eerdmans Pub.—R
(s)-Essence—R
(s)-Fairway Press—R
Faith Books & More
Hope Publishing—R
InterVarsity Press—R
Judson Press
Kirk House
Lift Every Voice—R

Lighthouse Pub.—R
New Hope
Port Yonder Press
(s)-Redemption Press
(s)-Salt Works—R
Tate Publishing—R
White Fire Pub.
(s)-Word Alive—R
(s)-Zoë Life Pub.—R

RECOVERY
(a) Baker Books
(a) HarperOne
(a) Howard Books
(a) Tyndale House
(a) WaterBrook Press

(s)-Aaron Book
ABC-CLIO
(s)-Abuzz Press—R
Ambassador Intl.
Blue Dolphin—R
Bondfire Books
(s)-Booklocker.com
(s)-Brown Books—R
Charisma House—R
Christian Writer's
    Ebook—R
Comfort Publishing
Creation House
CSS Publishing
(s)-Deep River Books
Earthen Vessel—R
Eerdmans Pub.—R
(s)-Essence—R
Evergreen Press
(s)-Fairway Press—R
Faith Books & More
Grace Publishing—R
(s)-Halo Publishing—R
Hannibal Books
Hope Publishing—R
Langmarc
Lighthouse Pub.—R
NavPress—R
Parsons Pub.—R
Randall House
(s)-Redemption Press
(s)-Signalman—R
Tate Publishing—R

VBC Publishing
(s)-Word Alive—R
Write Integrity Press
(s)-Zoë Life Pub.—R

REFERENCE
(a) Baker Academic
(a) Baker Books
(a) Bethany House
(a) Cook, David C.
(a) Doubleday
    Relig.—R
(a) HarperOne
(a) Kregel—R
(a) Tyndale House

(s)-Aaron Book
ABC-CLIO
Abingdon Press
(s)-Abuzz Press—R
Barbour—R
BMH Books
Bondfire Books
(s)-Booklocker.com
Bridge Logos—R
Charles Press
Christian Heritage—R
Christian Writer's
    Ebook—R
Creation House
Eerdmans Pub.—R
Ellechor Publishing
(s)-Essence—R
(s)-Fairway Press—R
Faith Books & More
Guardian Angel
Hope Publishing—R
InterVarsity Press—R
Life Cycle Books—R
Lighthouse Pub.—R
Our Sunday Visitor—R
Paragon House
(s)-Redemption Press
Reference Service
(s)-Signalman—R
Tate Publishing—R
VBC Publishing
White Fire Pub.
(s)-Word Alive—R
(s)-Zoë Life Pub.—R

Zondervan

RELATIONSHIPS
(a) Bethany House
(a) Howard Books
(a) Kregel—R
(a) Nelson, Thomas

(s)-Aaron Book
(s)-Abuzz Press—R
Adams Media
Ambassador Intl.
Barbour—R
Blue Dolphin—R
Bold Vision—R
Bondfire Books
(s)-Booklocker.com
Bridge Logos—R
(s)-Brown Books—R
Charisma House—R
Church Growth Inst.
Cladach Publishing
CLC Publications—R
Comfort Publishing
Creation House
(s)-CrossHouse
CrossLink Publishing
Crossway
Discovery House—R
Eerdmans Pub.—R
Ellechor Publishing
(s)-Essence—R
Evergreen Press
Faith Books & More
Four Craftsmen—R
Grace Publishing—R
(s)-Halo Publishing—R
Hannibal Books
InterVarsity Press—R
Judson Press
Lift Every Voice—R
Lighthouse/
    Carolinas—R
Lighthouse Pub.—R
MOPS Intl.
NavPress—R
New Hope
New Leaf
OakTara
On My Own Now

P&R Publications
Parsons Pub.—R
Pauline Books
(s)-Port Hole
    Public.—R
Randall House
Ravenhawk Books—R
(s)-Redemption Press
(s)-Salt Works—R
(s)-Signalman—R
Tate Publishing—R
Trail Media
White Fire Pub.
Write Integrity Press
(s)-Zoë Life Pub.—R

RELIGION
(a) Baker Academic
(a) Baker Books
(a) Ballantine
(a) B&H Publishing
(a) Doubleday
    Relig.—R
(a) HarperOne
(a) Nelson, Thomas
(a) Revell
(a) Tyndale House
(a) WaterBrook Press

(s)-Aaron Book
ABC-CLIO
Abingdon Press
(s)-Abuzz Press—R
Ambassador Intl.
American Cath.
    Press—R
Ancient Faith—R
Blue Dolphin—R
Bold Vision—R
Bondfire Books
(s)-Booklocker.com
(s)-Brown Books—R
Charisma House—R
Charles Press
Christian Heritage—R
Christian Writer's
    Ebook—R
Church Growth Inst.
Comfort Publishing
Creation House

CrossLink Publishing
CSS Publishing
(s)-Deep River Books
Earthen Vessel—R
Eerdmans Pub.—R
Eerdmans/Yg Readers
(s)-Essence—R
(s)-Fairway Press—R
Faith Books & More
(s)-Grace Acres—R
Grace Publishing—R
(s)-Halo Publishing—R
Harrison House
InterVarsity Press—R
Kirk House
Life Cycle Books—R
Lighthouse Pub.—R
Loyola Press
Lutheran Univ. Press
NavPress—R
New Leaf
North Wind Publishing
Our Sunday Visitor—R
Pacific Press
Pauline Books
Praeger Publishers
(s)-Redemption Press
(s)-Salt Works—R
(s)-Signalman—R
Tate Publishing—R
Whitaker House—R
White Fire Pub.
(s)-Word Alive—R
Yale Univ. Press—R
(s)-Zoë Life Pub.—R

RELIGIOUS TOLERANCE
(a) Baker Books
(a) Howard Books

(s)-Aaron Book
ABC-CLIO
(s)-Abuzz Press—R
Blue Dolphin—R
Bondfire Books
(s)-Booklocker.com
Charisma House—R
Christian Writer's
    Ebook—R

Creation House
(s)-Deep River Books
Eerdmans Pub.—R
(s)-Essence—R
(s)-Fairway Press—R
Faith Books & More
Four Craftsmen—R
Judson Press
Lighthouse Pub.—R
North Wind Publishing
On My Own Now
Paragon House
Port Yonder Press
(s)-Signalman—R
Tate Publishing—R
(s)-Word Alive—R
Yale Univ. Press—R
(s)-Zoë Life Pub.—R

RETIREMENT
(a) Baker Books

(s)-Aaron Book
(s)-Abuzz Press—R
Bold Vision—R
Bondfire Books
(s)-Booklocker.com
Charisma House—R
Christian Writer's
    Ebook—R
Eerdmans Pub.—R
(s)-Essence—R
(s)-Fairway Press—R
Faith Books & More
Grace Publishing—R
Kirk House
Lighthouse/
    Carolinas—R
Lighthouse Pub.—R
(s)-Redemption Press
(s)-Signalman—R
Tate Publishing—R
(s)-Word Alive—R
(s)-Zoë Life Pub.—R

SCHOLARLY
(a) Baker Academic
(a) Baker Books
(a) Cook, David C.

(a) Doubleday
 Relig.—R
(a) Kregel—R

(s)-Aaron Book
ABC-CLIO
Abingdon Press
(s)-Abuzz Press—R
Bondfire Books
(s)-Booklocker.com
Christian Heritage—R
Christian Writer's
 Ebook—R
(s)-Deep River Books
Earthen Vessel—R
Eerdmans Pub.—R
(s)-Essence—R
(s)-Fairway Press—R
Faith Books & More
(s)-Grace Acres—R
Guardian Angel
Inkling Books—R
InterVarsity Press—R
Life Cycle Books—R
Lighthouse Pub.—R
Lutheran Univ. Press
Paragon House
Parsons Pub.—R
Port Yonder Press
(s)-Redemption Press
(s)-Signalman—R
Tate Publishing—R
Trinity Foundation--R
VBC Publishing
White Fire Pub.
(s)-Word Alive—R
Yale Univ. Press—R
(s)-Zoë Life Pub.—R
Zondervan

SCIENCE
(a) Baker Books
(a) Doubleday
 Relig.—R

(s)-Aaron Book
(s)-Abuzz Press—R
Blue Dolphin—R
(s)-Booklocker.com
Christian Writer's
 Ebook—R

Earthen Vessel—R
Eerdmans Pub.—R
(s)-Essence—R
(s)-Fairway Press—R
Faith Books & More
Guardian Angel
Inkling Books—R
InterVarsity Press—R
Lighthouse Pub.—R
New Leaf
Port Yonder Press
(s)-Salt Works—R
(s)-Signalman—R
Tate Publishing—R
White Fire Pub.
(s)-Word Alive—R
Yale Univ. Press—R
(s)-Zoë Life Pub.—R

SELF-HELP
(a) Baker Books
(a) Ballantine
(a) HarperOne
(a) Hay House
(a) Howard Books
(a) Nelson, Thomas
(a) Revell
(a) Tyndale House
(a) WaterBrook Press

(s)-Aaron Book
(s)-Abuzz Press—R
Adams Media
Blue Dolphin—R
Bold Vision—R
Bondfire Books
(s)-Booklocker.com
Bridge Logos—R
(s)-Brown Books—R
Charisma House—R
Charles Press
Christian Writer's
 Ebook—R
Comfort Publishing
Creation House
CrossRiver Media
(s)-DCTS Publishers
(s)-Deep River Books
Discovery House—R
Ellechor Publishing

(s)-Essence—R
Evergreen Press
(s)-Fairway Press—R
Faith Books & More
Franciscan Media—R
Grace Publishing—R
Guideposts Books
(s)-Halo Publishing—R
Langmarc
Lighthouse Pub.—R
Morgan James Pub.—R
MountainView
North Wind Publishing
OakTara
On My Own Now
Pauline Books
(s)-Redemption Press
(s)-Salvation
 Publisher—R
(s)-Signalman—R
Tate Publishing—R
Trail Media
VBC Publishing
(s)-Word Alive—R
(s)-Zoë Life Pub.—R

SENIOR ADULT CONCERNS
(a) Baker Books
(a) Cook, David C.

(s)-Aaron Book
(s)-Abuzz Press—R
Bondfire Books
(s)-Booklocker.com
Charisma House—R
Charles Press
Christian Writer's
 Ebook—R
(s)-Deep River Books
Eerdmans Pub.—R
(s)-Essence—R
Evergreen Press
(s)-Fairway Press—R
Faith Books & More
Grace Publishing—R
Langmarc
Lighthouse/
 Carolinas—R
Lighthouse Pub.—R

New Hope
North Wind Publishing
(s)-Redemption Press
(s)-Signalman—R
Tate Publishing—R
(s)-Word Alive—R
Write Integrity Press
(s)-Zoë Life Pub.—R

SERMONS
(a) Baker Books
(a) Kregel—R

(s)-Aaron Book
Abingdon Press
(s)-Abuzz Press—R
Ambassador Intl.
Bondfire Books
(s)-Booklocker.com
Christian Writer's
    Ebook—R
Church Growth Inst.
CrossLink Publishing
CSS Publishing
(s)-DCTS Publishers
(s)-Deep River Books
Earthen Vessel—R
Eerdmans Pub.—R
(s)-Essence—R
(s)-Fairway Press—R
Faith Books & More
Group Publishing
Judson Press
Lighthouse Pub.—R
MountainView
NavPress—R
Pacific Press
(s)-Redemption Press
(s)-Salt Works—R
(s)-Salvation
    Publisher—R
(s)-Signalman—R
Tate Publishing—R
(s)-Word Alive—R
(s)-Zoë Life Pub.—R

SINGLES' ISSUES
(a) Baker Books
(a) Bethany House
(a) Cook, David C.

(a) Kregel—R
(s)-Aaron Book
(s)-Abuzz Press—R
Ambassador Intl.
Barbour—R
Bondfire Books
(s)-Booklocker.com
Charisma House—R
Christian Writer's
    Ebook—R
Creation House
(s)-Deep River Books
Earthen Vessel—R
Eerdmans Pub.—R
(s)-Essence—R
Evergreen Press
(s)-Fairway Press—R
Faith Books & More
(s)-Fruitbearer Pub.
Grace Publishing—R
InterVarsity Press—R
Judson Press
Lift Every Voice—R
Lighthouse/
    Carolinas—R
Lighthouse Pub.—R
NavPress—R
New Hope
On My Own Now
Pacific Press
P&R Publications
Pauline Books
(s)-Redemption Press
(s)-Salt Works—R
(s)-Signalman—R
Tate Publishing—R
Trail Media
VBC Publishing
Whitaker House—R
White Fire Pub.
(s)-Word Alive—R
Write Integrity Press
(s)-Zoë Life Pub.—R

SMALL-GROUP RESOURCES
Bold Vision—R
Bondfire Books
Discovery House—R

Ellechor Publishing
(s)-Essence—R
Franciscan Media—R
(s)-Grace Acres—R
Grace Publishing—R
Morgan James Pub.—R
NavPress—R
North Wind Publishing
Randall House
(s)-Redemption Press
(s)-Signalman—R
(s)-Zoë Life Pub.—R

SOCIAL JUSTICE ISSUES
(a) Baker Books
(a) FaithWords
(a) HarperOne
(a) Howard Books
(a) Nelson, Thomas

(s)-Aaron Book
ABC-CLIO
(s)-Abuzz Press—R
(s)-Ampelos Press—R
Bondfire Books
(s)-Booklocker.com
Charisma House—R
Christian Writer's
    Ebook—R
Comfort Publishing
(s)-DCTS Publishers
(s)-Deep River Books
(s)-Destiny Image
    (books)
Discovery House—R
Eerdmans Pub.—R
Eerdmans/Yg Readers
(s)-Essence—R
(s)-Fairway Press—R
Faith Books & More
Hope Publishing—R
Inkling Books—R
InterVarsity Press—R
Judson Press
Life Cycle Books—R
Lift Every Voice—R
Lighthouse Pub.—R
NavPress—R
New Hope

North Wind Publishing
On My Own Now
Our Sunday Visitor—R
Pauline Books
Port Yonder Press
Ravenhawk Books—R
(s)-Redemption Press
(s)-Signalman—R
Tate Publishing—R
Trail Media
Whitaker House—R
(s)-Word Alive—R
(s)-Zoë Life Pub.—R

SOCIOLOGY
(a) Baker Books

(s)-Aaron Book
ABC-CLIO
(s)-Abuzz Press—R
Blue Dolphin—R
Bondfire Books
(s)-Booklocker.com
Charisma House—R
Charles Press
Christian Writer's
    Ebook—R
(s)-Deep River Books
Eerdmans Pub.—R
(s)-Essence—R
(s)-Fairway Press—R
Faith Books & More
InterVarsity Press—R
Life Cycle Books—R
Lighthouse Pub.—R
North Wind Publishing
On My Own Now
Port Yonder Press
(s)-Redemption Press
(s)-Signalman—R
Tate Publishing—R
Trail Media
White Fire Pub.
(s)-Word Alive—R
Yale Univ. Press—R
(s)-Zoë Life Pub.—R

SPIRITUAL GIFTS
(a) Baker Books
(a) B&H Publishing

(a) Howard Books
(a) Kregel—R
(a) Nelson, Thomas

(s)-Aaron Book
(s)-Abuzz Press—R
Ambassador Intl.
AMG Publishers—R
Blue Dolphin—R
(s)-Booklocker.com
Bridge Logos—R
(s)-Brown Books—R
Canticle Books—R
Charisma House—R
Christian Writer's
    Ebook—R
Church Growth Inst.
Comfort Publishing
Creation House
(s)-CrossHouse
CrossLink Publishing
CSS Publishing
(s)-Deep River Books
(s)-Destiny Image
    (books)
Discovery House—R
Earthen Vessel—R
Eerdmans Pub.—R
(s)-Essence—R
(s)-Fairway Press—R
Faith Books & More
(s)-Grace Acres—R
Grace Publishing—R
Group Publishing
Guardian Angel
(s)-Halo Publishing—R
Harrison House
InterVarsity Press—R
Lift Every Voice—R
Lighthouse Pub.—R
Lutheran Univ. Press
Magnus Press—R
NavPress—R
New Hope
Pacific Press
Parson Place
Parsons Pub.—R
(s)-Redemption Press
(s)-Salvation
    Publisher—R

(s)-Signalman—R
Tate Publishing—R
Whitaker House—R
White Fire Pub.
(s)-Word Alive—R
Write Integrity Press
(s)-Zoë Life Pub.—R

SPIRITUALITY
(a) Baker Books
(a) Ballantine
(a) Bethany House
(a) Doubleday
    Relig.—R
(a) HarperOne
(a) Hay House
(a) Howard Books
(a) Kregel—R
(a) Nelson, Thomas
(a) Tyndale House
(a) WaterBrook Press

(s)-Aaron Book
Abingdon Press
(s)-Abuzz Press—R
AMG Publishers—R
Ancient Faith—R
Blue Dolphin—R
Bondfire Books
(s)-Booklocker.com
Bridge Logos—R
(s)-Brown Books—R
Canticle Books—R
Charisma House—R
Christian Heritage—R
Christian Writer's
    Ebook—R
Comfort Publishing
Conari Press
Creation House
CrossLink Publishing
Crossway
CSS Publishing
(s)-Deep River Books
(s)-Destiny Image
    (books)
Discovery House—R
Eerdmans Pub.—R
Eerdmans/Yg Readers
(s)-Essence—R

Evergreen Press
(s)-Fairway Press—R
Faith Books & More
Franciscan Media—R
(s)-Grace Acres—R
Grace Publishing—R
Guardian Angel
(s)-Halo Publishing—R
InterVarsity Press—R
Kirk House
Lighthouse/
    Carolinas—R
Lighthouse Pub.—R
Loyola Press
Lutheran Univ. Press
Magnus Press—R
NavPress—R
New Hope
On My Own Now
Pacific Press
Paragon House
Parsons Pub.—R
Pauline Books
Ravenhawk Books—R
(s)-Redemption Press
(s)-Salt Works—R
(s)-Signalman—R
Sunpenny Publishing
Tate Publishing—R
Whitaker House—R
White Fire Pub.
(s)-Word Alive—R
Write Integrity Press
(s)-Zoë Life Pub.—R

SPIRITUAL LIFE

(a) B&H Publishing
(a) Bethany House
(a) HarperOne
(a) Howard Books
(a) Kregel—R
(a) Nelson, Thomas
(a) WaterBrook Press

(s)-Aaron Book
Abingdon Press
(s)-Abuzz Press—R
Ambassador Intl.
AMG Publishers—R
Ancient Faith—R

Barbour—R
Blue Dolphin—R
BMH Books
Bold Vision—R
Bondfire Books
(s)-Booklocker.com
Bridge Logos—R
(s)-Brown Books—R
Canticle Books—R
Charisma House—R
Christian Writer's
    Ebook—R
Church Growth Inst.
CLC Publications—R
Comfort Publishing
Creation House
(s)-CrossHouse
CrossLink Publishing
CrossRiver Media
Crossway
CSS Publishing
(s)-Deep River Books
(s)-Destiny Image
    (books)
Discovery House—R
Earthen Vessel—R
Eerdmans Pub.—R
Ellechor Publishing
(s)-Essence—R
Evergreen Press
(s)-Fairway Press—R
Faith Books & More
Four Craftsmen—R
(s)-Grace Acres—R
Grace Publishing—R
Guardian Angel
(s)-Halo Publishing—R
Harrison House
Inheritance Press
InterVarsity Press—R
JourneyForth/BJU
Judson Press
Lift Every Voice—R
Lighthouse/
    Carolinas—R
Lighthouse Pub.—R
Morgan James Pub.—R
NavPress—R
New Hope
New Leaf

OakTara
On My Own Now
Parsons Pub.—R
Pauline Books
(s)-Port Hole
    Public.—R
Randall House
(s)-Redemption Press
(s)-Salvation
    Publisher—R
(s)-Signalman—R
Tate Publishing—R
Trail Media
Wesleyan Publishing
Whitaker House—R
White Fire Pub.
(s)-Word Alive—R
Write Integrity Press
(s)-Zoë Life Pub.—R

SPIRITUAL WARFARE

(a) Baker Books
(a) B&H Publishing
(a) Nelson, Thomas

(s)-Aaron Book
(s)-Abuzz Press—R
AMG Publishers—R
Ancient Faith—R
(s)-Booklocker.com
Bridge Logos—R
(s)-Brown Books—R
Charisma House—R
Christian Writer's
    Ebook—R
Comfort Publishing
Creation House
CrossLink Publishing
CrossRiver Media
(s)-Destiny Image
    (books)
Earthen Vessel—R
Eerdmans Pub.—R
(s)-Essence—R
Evergreen Press
(s)-Fairway Press—R
Faith Books & More
Four Craftsmen—R
(s)-Grace Acres—R
Grace Publishing—R

Harrison House
Lighthouse Pub.—R
Morgan James Pub.—R
NavPress—R
New Hope
On My Own Now
Parson Place
Parsons Pub.—R
(s)-Redemption Press
(s)-Salvation
   Publisher—R
(s)-Signalman—R
Tate Publishing—R
VBC Publishing
Whitaker House—R
White Fire Pub.
(s)-Word Alive—R
Write Integrity Press
(s)-Zoë Life Pub.—R

SPORTS/RECREATION
(a) Baker Books
(a) Ballantine

(s)-Aaron Book
(s)-Abuzz Press—R
(s)-Booklocker.com
(s)-Brown Books—R
Charisma House—R
Christian Writer's
   Ebook—R
Comfort Publishing
(s)-Deep River Books
Earthen Vessel—R
(s)-Essence—R
Evergreen Press
(s)-Fairway Press—R
Faith Books & More
Guardian Angel
(s)-Halo Publishing—R
Judson Press
Lighthouse Pub.—R
North Wind Publishing
Ravenhawk Books—R
Reference Service
(s)-Redemption Press
(s)-Signalman—R
Sunpenny Publishing
Tate Publishing—R
(s)-Word Alive—R

(s)-Zoë Life Pub.—R

STEWARDSHIP
(a) Baker Books
(a) Bethany House
(a) Kregel—R

(s)-Aaron Book
(s)-Abuzz Press—R
Ambassador Intl.
BMH Books
(s)-Booklocker.com
(s)-Brown Books—R
Christian Writer's
   Ebook—R
Church Growth Inst.
Creation House
CrossLink Publishing
CSS Publishing
(s)-Deep River Books
Discovery House—R
Eerdmans Pub.—R
(s)-Essence—R
Evergreen Press
(s)-Fairway Press—R
Faith Books & More
(s)-Grace Acres—R
Hope Publishing—R
InterVarsity Press—R
Judson Press
Kirk House
Lift Every Voice—R
Lighthouse Pub.—R
Lutheran Univ. Press
Morgan James Pub.—R
NavPress—R
New Hope
On My Own Now
Our Sunday Visitor—R
Pacific Press
Parson Place
Parsons Pub.—R
Pauline Books
Randall House
(s)-Redemption Press
(s)-Salvation
   Publisher—R
(s)-Signalman—R
Tate Publishing—R
VBC Publishing

Whitaker House—R
White Fire Pub.
(s)-Word Alive—R
(s)-Zoë Life Pub.—R

THEOLOGY
(a) Baker Books
(a) Bethany House
(a) Cook, David C.
(a) Doubleday Relig.—R
(a) HarperOne
(a) Kregel—R
(a) Multnomah
(a) Nelson, Thomas
(a) Tyndale House

(s)-Aaron Book
Abingdon Press
(s)-Abuzz Press—R
Ambassador Intl.
American Cath.
   Press—R
AMG Publishers—R
Ancient Faith—R
Blue Dolphin—R
BMH Books
Bondfire Books
(s)-Booklocker.com
(s)-Brown Books—R
Canticle Books—R
Christian Heritage—R
Christian Writer's
   Ebook—R
CLC Publications—R
Creation House
CrossLink Publishing
Crossway
CSS Publishing
(s)-Deep River Books
Discovery House—R
Earthen Vessel—R
Eerdmans Pub.—R
(s)-Essence—R
(s)-Fairway Press—R
Faith Books & More
(s)-Grace Acres—R
Inkling Books—R
InterVarsity Press—R
Kirk House
Lift Every Voice—R

Lighthouse Pub.—R
Lighthouse Trails—R
Lutheran Univ. Press
Magnus Press—R
Meriwether
NavPress—R
Pacific Press
Parsons Pub.—R
Randall House
Ravenhawk Books—R
(s)-Redemption Press
(s)-Signalman—R
Tate Publishing—R
Trinity Foundation—R
VBC Publishing
Wesleyan Publishing
White Fire Pub.
(s)-Word Alive—R
(s)-Zoë Life Pub.—R
Zondervan

TIME MANAGEMENT
(a) Baker Books
(a) Cook, David C.
(a) Nelson, Thomas

(s)-Aaron Book
(s)-Abuzz Press—R
Barbour—R
(s)-Booklocker.com
(s)-Brown Books—R
Charisma House—R
Christian Writer's
    Ebook—R
(s)-CrossHouse
(s)-DCTS Publishers
(s)-Deep River Books
Ellechor Publishing
(s)-Essence—R
Evergreen Press
(s)-Fairway Press—R
Faith Books & More
(s)-Grace Acres—R
Grace Publishing—R
Judson Press
Kirk House
Lighthouse Pub.—R
Morgan James Pub.—R
NavPress—R
New Hope

On My Own Now
Parsons Pub.—R
(s)-Redemption Press
(s)-Salvation
    Publisher—R
(s)-Signalman—R
Tate Publishing—R
VBC Publishing
(s)-Word Alive—R
(s)-Zoë Life Pub.—R
Zoë Life Publishing

TRACTS
Christian Writer's
    Ebook—R
Crossway
(s)-Essence—R
(s)-Fruitbearer Pub.
Life Cycle Books—R
Trinity Foundation—R
(s)-Word Alive—R

TRAVEL
(a) Baker Books
(a) Ballantine

(s)-Aaron Book
(s)-Abuzz Press—R
(s)-Booklocker.com
(s)-Brown Books—R
Christian Heritage—R
Christian Writer's
    Ebook—R
Cladach Publishing
(s)-Essence—R
(s)-Fairway Press—R
Faith Books & More
Hope Publishing—R
Lighthouse Pub.—R
New Leaf
(s)-Redemption Press
(s)-Signalman—R
Sunpenny Publishing
Tate Publishing—R
Trail Media
White Fire Pub.
(s)-Word Alive—R
(s)-Zoë Life Pub.—R

TWEEN BOOKS
(s)-Aaron Book
(s)-Abuzz Press—R
AMG Publishers—R
Barbour—R
Bold Vision—R
Bondfire Books
(s)-Booklocker.com
Comfort Publishing
Eerdmans Pub.—R
(s)-Essence—R
Faith Books & More
(s)-Fruitbearer Pub.
Legacy Press
Lighthouse Pub.—R
Pauline Books
(s)-Redemption Press
(s)-Signalman—R
Tate Publishing—R
Trail Media
(s)-Zoë Life Pub.—R

WOMEN'S ISSUES
(a) Baker Academic
(a) Baker Books
(a) Ballantine
(a) B&H Publishing
(a) Bethany House
(a) Cook, David C.
(a) Doubleday Relig.—R
(a) HarperOne
(a) Howard Books
(a) Kregel—R
(a) Nelson, Thomas

(s)-Aaron Book
ABC-CLIO
(s)-Abuzz Press—R
Adams Media
Ambassador Intl.
AMG Publishers—R
Barbour—R
Blue Dolphin—R
BMH Books
Bold Vision—R
Bondfire Books
(s)-Booklocker.com
Bridge Logos—R
(s)-Brown Books—R
Charisma House—R

Christian Writer's
  Ebook—R
Cladach Publishing
CLC Publications—R
Comfort Publishing
Creation House
(s)-CrossHouse
CrossRiver Media
Crossway
(s)-Deep River Books
Discovery House—R
Earthen Vessel—R
Eerdmans Pub.—R
Ellechor Publishing
(s)-Essence—R
Evergreen Press
(s)-Fairway Press—R
Faith Books & More
Franciscan Media—R
(s)-Fruitbearer Pub.
Grace Publishing—R
Group Publishing
(s)-Halo Publishing—R
Hope Publishing—R
Inkling Books—R
InterVarsity Press—R
JourneyForth/BJU
Judson Press
Kirk House
Langmarc
Life Cycle Books—R
Lift Every Voice—R
Lighthouse/
  Carolinas—R
Lighthouse Pub.—R
Loyola Press
Moody Publishers
Morgan James Pub.—R
NavPress—R
Nelson, Thomas
New Hope
North Wind Publishing
OakTara
On My Own Now
Parson Place
Parsons Pub.—R
Pauline Books
(s)-Port Hole
  Public.—R
Praeger Publishers

Ravenhawk Books—R
(s)-Redemption Press
Reference Service
(s)-Signalman—R
Sunpenny Publishing
Tate Publishing—R
Trail Media
VBC Publishing
Whitaker House—R
White Fire Pub.
(s)-Word Alive—R
Write Integrity Press
(s)-Zoë Life Pub.—R

WORLD ISSUES
(a) Baker Books
(a) Doubleday Relig.—R
(a) HarperOne
(a) Kregel—R
(a) Tyndale House

(s)-Aaron Book
ABC-CLIO
(s)-Abuzz Press—R
(s)-Ampelos Press—R
Blue Dolphin—R
(s)-Booklocker.com
Bridge Logos—R
Charisma House—R
Christian Writer's
  Ebook—R
Comfort Publishing
Creation House
(s)-Deep River Books
Earthen Vessel—R
Eerdmans Pub.—R
Eerdmans/Yg Readers
(s)-Essence—R
(s)-Fairway Press—R
Faith Books & More
(s)-Halo Publishing—R
InterVarsity Press—R
Kirk House
Lift Every Voice—R
Lighthouse Pub.—R
NavPress—R
New Hope
Port Yonder Press
Ravenhawk Books—R
(s)-Redemption Press

(s)-Salt Works—R
(s)-Signalman—R
Tate Publishing—R
Trail Media
VBC Publishing
Whitaker House—R
White Fire Pub.
(s)-Word Alive—R
(s)-Zoë Life Pub.—R

WORSHIP
(a) B&H Publishing
(a) Bethany House
(a) Cook, David C.
(a) Kregel—R
(a) Nelson, Thomas

(s)-Aaron Book
Abingdon Press
(s)-Abuzz Press—R
Ambassador Intl.
AMG Publishers—R
Barbour—R
BMH Books
Bondfire Books
(s)-Booklocker.com
Bridge Logos—R
Charisma House—R
Christian Heritage—R
Christian Writer's
  Ebook—R
CLC Publications—R
Creation House
CrossLink Publishing
Crossway
CSS Publishing
(s)-Deep River Books
Earthen Vessel—R
Eerdmans Pub.—R
(s)-Essence—R
(s)-Fairway Press—R
Faith Books & More
(s)-Grace Acres—R
(s)-Halo Publishing—R
Harrison House
InterVarsity Press—R
JourneyForth/BJU
Judson Press
Lift Every Voice—R
Lighthouse Pub.—R

Lutheran Univ. Press
NavPress—R
New Hope
North Wind Publishing
Pacific Press
Parsons Pub.—R
(s)-Redemption Press
(s)-Salt Works—R
(s)-Signalman—R
Tate Publishing—R
VBC Publishing
White Fire Pub.
(s)-Word Alive—R

WORSHIP RESOURCES

(a) Baker Books
(a) B&H Publishing
(a) Kregel—R

(s)-Aaron Book
Abingdon Press
(s)-Abuzz Press—R
American Cath.
    Press—R
Bondfire Books
(s)-Booklocker.com
Christian Writer's
    Ebook—R
CLC Publications—R
CrossLink Publishing
CSS Publishing
(s)-DCTS Publishers
(s)-Deep River Books
Eerdmans Pub.—R
(s)-Essence—R
(s)-Fairway Press—R
Faith Books & More
Grace Publishing—R
Group Publishing
InterVarsity Press—R
Judson Press
Lighthouse Pub.—R
Lutheran Univ. Press
Meriwether
NavPress—R
North Wind Publishing
Our Sunday Visitor—R
Parsons Pub.—R
(s)-Redemption Press

(s)-Salt Works—R
(s)-Signalman—R
Standard Publishing
Tate Publishing—R
(s)-Word Alive—R
(s)-Zoë Life Pub.—R

WRITING HOW-TO

(s)-Aaron Book
(s)-Abuzz Press—R
Bold Vision—R
Bondfire Books
(s)-Booklocker.com
Christian Writer's
    Ebook—R
CrossLink Publishing
(s)-Deep River Books
Ellechor Publishing
(s)-Essence—R
Evergreen Press
(s)-Fairway Press—R
Faith Books & More
Grace Publishing—R
Kendall Neff Publishing
Lighthouse Pub.—R
Morgan James Pub.—R
OakTara
Parson Place
Parsons Pub.—R
(s)-Redemption Press
ShadeTree Publishing
(s)-Signalman—R
Tate Publishing—R
(s)-Word Alive—R
Write Integrity Press
(s)-Zoë Life Pub.—R

YOUTH BOOKS
(Nonfiction)
Note: Listing denotes
books for 8- to 12-year-
olds, junior highs, or senior
highs. If all three, it will
say "all." If no age group is
listed, none was specified.
(a) Baker Books
(a) WaterBrook Press
    (All)

**(s)-Aaron Book (8-12/
    Jr. High)**
(s)-Abuzz Press—R
(All)
Ambassador Intl. (8-12)
AMG Publishers—R
(All)
Ancient Faith—R (All)
Barbour—R (8-12/Jr.
    High)
Bondfire Books
(s)-Booklocker.com (All)
(s)-Brown Books—R
(All)
Christian Writer's
    Ebook—R (All)
Comfort Publishing
(All)
Contemporary Drama
(s)-Creation House—R
(All)
(s)-CrossHouse (All)
Dawn Publications (Jr.
    High)
(s)-Deep River Books
(All)
Eerdmans/Yg Readers
(All)
Ellechor Publishing
(s)-Essence—R (All)
Evergreen Press
(s)-Faith Books &
    More—R (All)
Guardian Angel (8-12)
(s)-Halo Publishing—R
(All)
Legacy Press (8-12)
Life Cycle Books—R
(8-12)
Lighthouse Pub.—R
(All)
Lighthouse Trails—R
(All)
Meriwether (Jr./Sr.
    High)
Moody Publishers
NavPress—R (Sr. High)
New Leaf (All)
On My Own Now (Sr.
    High)

Pacific Press
P&R Publications (All)
Parsons Pub.—R
Pauline Kids (All)
Ravenhawk Books—R
   (Jr./Sr. High)
(s)-Redemption Press
   (All)
(s)-Signalman—R (All)
Tate Publishing—R
   (All)
Trail Media (All)
Warner Press (All)
(s)-Word Alive—R
   (All)
(s)-Zoë Life Pub.—R

YOUTH PROGRAMS
(a) Baker Books
(a) Kregel—R

(s)-Abuzz Press—R
Christian Writer's
   Ebook—R
Church Growth Inst.
Contemporary Drama
CrossLink Publishing
(s)-Fairway Press—R
Group Publishing
(s)-Redemption Press
(s)-Signalman—R
Standard Publishing
Tate Publishing—R
(s)-Zoë Life Pub.—R

Writer's Helps

A Writer's Foundations

Grace - letting
go of old hurts,
indebtedness.

Help me see
Steve as well
Brother in Christ.

To live, increasingly
closer to God.

Should not be conflict
between loving God +
loving others.

Coveting?
Motivation?
Place?

Where to Begin

by Jerry B. Jenkins

BEGINNING WRITERS are told to write what they know. Now may be the season of life to write your family history, keep up with correspondence, or pen poetry. You might enjoy creating a family newsletter or keeping your home Web page updated.

Those are worthy goals. Prior to my mother's death, I helped her put together anthologies of my father's poetry and publish them for our family and friends. These are treasures. I also wrote and published a history of my now late hundred-year-old grandmother-in-law.

I did these projects as labors of love after I was a widely published author, but it strikes me that such projects — and many other types — would have been ideal for someone just starting out. You want to be a writer, people tell you that you have a knack, but how do you break in? And before that great day comes when you actually sell a piece of your work, how do you do the work of a writer? By writing.

Does your church have a newsletter? You can bet that whoever is putting it together would love to have more material to work with. Interview anyone in your church with an interesting history or story. Your byline appearing in print will be your only pay, but you will be exercising muscles you'll need in your writing career.

Is there a community flyer that circulates in your neighborhood, or a free paper that is mostly advertising? Many of these contain fillers and general-interest articles their publishers get free from various sources. Find out who publishes that flyer and see if that publisher would like some local news to really make it sing. Again, you may be donating your time and work, but you are getting started.

Do you belong to a group, organization, or club that needs a newsletter— online or otherwise? Volunteer to handle it; write all the pieces yourself. Someday you may look back and fret over how amateurish the writing seems, and you may wish you'd had an editor. But you will have gained invaluable experience.

Most of the published writers I know have some background in journalism. If you're having trouble starting, or breaking into print, you might want to find an evening course and study newspaper writing, news reporting, or feature writing. One semester could unlock a door for you.

I studied journalism in high school and college, and worked in the field for many years. Journalism teaches you to get to the point and write quickly. You also learn to write regardless the distractions. Some need solitude to focus and write. I find that the case when I'm working on a book, because, while I have never been diagnosed with ADD, I do find myself unendingly curious about mail, visitors, phone calls, e-mail, what's on the radio or TV. I need to get away to what I call my cave to have any hope of making my deadlines.

But when it comes to newspaper or magazine writing, strangely, it's the opposite. I seemed to be able to write even with activity all around me. I believe that's because of my roots in journalism.

When I started in the newspaper business, I worked in a large room filled with sets of four metal desks shoved together. Everyone worked against a backdrop of clacking typewriters, Teletype machines, and ringing phones. People walked about, talking and laughing, sometimes wrestling, and throwing crumpled up paper.

The closer it came to deadline time, the fewer the people who played and gabbed and the more frantic the writing pace. In a strange way, it was great fun. That's how we worked. We had no choice.

Occasionally somebody who had just graduated from journalism school would holler, "Could you please be quiet? I'm writing!" We'd laugh and throw things at them, whereupon they would complain to the big boss — who would also laugh and throw things.

It helps to learn to write in a boiler-room atmosphere. Do that and you can write anywhere.

What Not To Write

One of the most common mistakes new writers make is trying to start their career with a book. That's like starting your education in graduate school.

Start small. Write for the joy of it, to see your name in print, even if you're giving your work away. You need to work countless clichés out of your system, tone writing muscles, and learn both the business and the craft.

Approach magazines, e-zines, and newspapers, and get experience writing articles before tackling your book. See what your stuff looks like in print; become your own toughest critic.

Learn everything there is to know about how to submit your material, then start small.

Learn everything there is to know about how to submit your material, then start small. Write for local publications, and when you have scored some clips, try regional magazines, then national. You'll stub your toe occasionally, but you'll learn. You'd be surprised at how many submissions magazine editors get from people who don't even know to double-space their work and use a readable 12-point, serif typestyle.

An even larger issue is trying to write on issues beyond your grasp, like writing a memoir when you're only in your twenties. While your story may be huge and significant, you'll need years of mature reflection before you can make sense of it and present it so it will have a real impact on readers.

Even if you're a mature thinker already, are you far enough along with your writing skills to do justice to the topic? I have been a church-going Christian all my life and attended Bible college right out of high school, but even today I wouldn't dream of trying to tackle theological and biblical subjects on my own.

A little knowledge can be dangerous. Either make thorough use of interviews with experts in the area you wish to write about, or stick to what you really know.

Take the Plunge

Would-be writers often read a book and decide they could have done better. That's a start. Don't talk about what you would have done differently; do it. Start with your own characters, and come up with something fresh and believable. If you think you can write better than the bestsellers, who's to say you can't?

All the big names were beginners once. Editors are looking for writers, regardless whether they've been published before. Yes, the competition is fiercer than it's ever been, and yes, someone with an already-established name has an edge. But more than anything, an editor wants to say, "I've discovered the next talent."

Adapted by permission from Writing for the Soul *by Jerry B. Jenkins.*

Key Traits of Professional Writers

Dennis E. Hensley

NO WRITER WRITES IN A VACUUM. We write from firsthand experience or from things experienced through books, movies, magazines, newspapers, or conversations. If you have limited life experience, you will need to do a great deal of researching, interviewing, and probing before you can write convincingly.

If you have traveled extensively, read widely, worked with a vast range of people groups, and held numerous jobs, you likely already have a sense of how the world works and what people are interested in. Regardless, craftsmanship supersedes street savvy. Professional writing requires patience, discipline, training, practice, and determination.

To understand what editors consider the most valuable traits in a writer, let's review the makeup of a working professional writer.

A good manager of time. To editors, the word deadline means what it says: "Go past this line and your manuscript is dead." Completing assignments on time is a hallmark of a professional.

Someone with people skills. Writers spend a lot of time alone at the keyboard, but they still need the ability to deal with people. Nonfiction writers conduct interviews, negotiate deals, establish contacts, and promote their books. The image of the hermit writer is a myth. Contemporary writers need to understand what makes people tick.

A person of integrity. Writers must be fair and honest, even when reporting something they don't like. If you have strong feelings against abortion, but your research requires you to interview a physician who performs abortions, you must not misquote or misrepresent the physician. You must not overplay or underplay something newsworthy because of your feelings. Nonfiction writing is exactly what it says: that which is not fiction.

Someone with a sense of humor. In the writing business if you cannot laugh, you cannot survive. Sometimes your feature newspaper article will be bumped from the front page because of a more important breaking news event. Your favorite editor may move to a different publishing house in the middle of your project, forcing you to work with someone new. Such events are more the norm than a surprise. Keep smiling. Overall, the good times outweigh the bad — usually.

An individual with a nose for news. Periodical editors depend on nonfiction writers to continuously seek article ideas. You need to be talking to people, reading, exploring new concepts, and looking under rocks. Editors seldom come to nonfiction writers with assignments. They rely on experienced writers to be up to speed on new topics worthy of publication.

A self-starter. You will have to set your own schedule and stick to it.

Someone with oral and written communication skills. Nonfiction writers have to conduct interviews, secure quotes from experts, and pitch ideas to editors and publishers. In short, talking comes before writing. Writers need the gift of gab. Writers also need command of the written language, a good vocabulary, excellent mechanical skills, and a good sense of narrative drive. Say it well and write it well.

Someone with versatility. A single-skilled writer rarely succeeds on a large scale. Can you write articles, conduct interviews, research, report, and review media? The more you can write, the more you will be called upon to write. Diversify, expand your range of literary expressions, and advance your communication talents.

Someone who knows people. Nonfiction writers keep their ears open, listening to factory workers, school teachers, ministers, union leaders, politicians, business executives, artists, soldiers, dancers, cab drivers, beauticians, and farmers. Writers probe, seek leads on newsworthy events, discover fascinating topics to investigate. Your network of contacts must be wide, extensive, and diverse.

An efficient writer. Editors are impressed with a writer who can squeeze the most out of an idea. From a basic concept comes research, interviews, sidebars, revelatory experiments, and breakthrough data. Develop a reputation as the go-to person for uncovering what is what about any new subject.

Someone creative. Readers get bored quickly, so editors are desperate for new ideas, unusual topics, innovative writing. Don't review a Chinese restaurant; explain how they get that fortune inside the cookie. Don't write a business piece on an Army surplus store; profile one of its customers living in a fortress waiting for World War III. Create a reason for people to seek out your books and log onto your blog. Be offbeat, exploratory, and nontraditional.

Create a reason for people to seek out your books and log onto your blog. Be offbeat, exploratory, and nontraditional.

A person of endurance. Writing a nonfiction book is not a sprint. It's a marathon. Many a would-be author has gotten to the midway point and called it quits. Your best intentions aren't worth a hill of beans. Only a completed manuscript — solidly researched, well written, and carefully proofread — will land you a shot at future book deals. Do it all or don't do any of it.

Someone with a proven track record. Get writing credits and experience anywhere you can. Become a columnist for your town's newspaper. Sell a short devotion to a religious publication or a vignette to a Sunday school take-home paper or write a book review for a literary quarterly. Never disdain a periodical's circulation size or payment rate. Each publication gives you credibility. As Major League baseball teams discover their next stars by sending scouts to high school, college, and amateur leagues, editors at large-circulation magazines or major book publishing houses scan periodicals in search of the next star writer.

An individual who is intellectually divergent. As important as book learning in a writer's development is knowledge gained from the School of Hard Knocks. Larry Weeden, editor at Focus on the Family, tells writers, "Don't send me a manuscript until I can smell the gunpowder on it." Unless a writer has been in the battle, his manuscript won't have a sense of realism. Climb a mountain, go skydiving, work in the church nursery, donate blood to the Red Cross, or do a ride-along one night in a squad car. Live life before you write about it.

Used by permission of the Jerry Jenkins Writers Guild.

The Calling of the Christian Writer

by Les Stobbe

LIKE EVERY CHRISTIAN, THE WRITER'S FIRST CALLING is to build a vibrant relationship with his Lord and Savior. That is the apostle's prayer for the Ephesians when he writes, "I pray that out of his glorious riches he may strengthen you with power through his Spirit in your inner being, so that Christ may dwell in your hearts through faith" (3:16-17).

Another facet of our calling is to "prepare your minds for action; be self-controlled; set your hope fully on the grace to be given you when Jesus Christ is revealed" (1 Peter 1:13). Paul writes, "Offer your bodies as living sacrifices, holy and pleasing to God — this is your spiritual act of worship" (Romans 12:1). This calls for establishing priorities in your life in Christ and in your service for Him as a writer.

Your calling as a Christian writer may have manifested itself by an interest in writing very early, or you may have discovered you loved writing in high school or college. God calls some to writing as they become old enough to reflect on life's experiences. One's gifts may be revealed at any stage of life.

I was in my early 20s when, as first aid man in a mine in northern British Columbia, I spent a week seeking God's will for my life — and God impressed on me that I was to focus on proclaiming the gospel. A month later, I landed in the hospital after a mountain climbing accident. There I saw an ad in a Christian magazine that shouted, "You can write!" Intrigued, since I had done a bit of writing for my high school paper, I sent for the beginner's correspondence course for Christian writers. I completed it while convalescing as a dispatcher with the B. C. Forest Service. That seven-lesson course launched me on a career as a writer that has so far spanned nearly 50 years. God's calling became focused through an advertisement. That may also be your experience.

Jerry B. Jenkins felt a definite call to full-time Christian work when he was a teenager at a summer Bible camp. Though he enjoyed writing, he assumed that this call meant he should be a pastor or missionary, neither of which he felt gifted for. "I was stunned and thrilled," he says, "to soon discover that God often calls us to that for which He has already gifted us."

Since offering our bodies as living sacrifices is pleasing to God, then writing becomes our 'spiritual act of worship.'

God's calling to every Christian writer is to worship Him. Prayer facilitates that worship, opening to the control of the Holy Spirit areas of our lives that we have reserved as off limits even to God. Since offering our bodies as living sacrifices is pleasing to God, then writing becomes our "spiritual act of worship" (Romans 12:1). When we're intimately related to Christ as Savior and Lord, everything we do expresses our worship of our great God.

Used by permission of the Jerry Jenkins Writers Guild.

Five Ps for the Christian Writer

by Les Stobbe

Purpose

While the reasons we write may vary significantly over the years, purpose helps fuel determination — and determination leads to completion of correspondence course lessons and the writing and marketing of articles, poems, fillers, and photo essays. Your overall purpose may be to glorify God, and that ought to naturally express itself in purposeful preparation for excellence.

If your purpose is only to express yourself, you may soon run short of significant material. If your purpose is only to provide extra income, you may find that slow to develop. But if your purpose is to serve the needs of your readers — the "cup of cold water" kind of writing — you may achieve significant success while also glorifying God. Take time right now to write down your purpose in light of what you've already learned.

Practical

As a good steward of the time God gives you, be alert to practical ways to apply the writing and marketing techniques available. One may be a simple news release announcing the arrival of a new pastor, but another may be an article on the many ministries of an international organization. Creativity will be revealed in all facets of article structure, word use, imagery, and life application.

Persuasive

Read one of Paul's New Testament letters strictly from the perspective of a persuasive presentation of truth. In fact, one of his letters (not included in Scripture but referred to there) was so persuasive that the Corinthian church effectively tackled sinful attitudes and behavior. Read the sayings of Jesus in John's Gospel. Mentally listen to the cadence of His voice as He rebutted the accusations of His enemies. Now transfer that insight to the writing of Billy Graham, Philip Yancey, Becky Pippert, or Lee Strobel. Remember, they were once beginning writers. This course will help you develop your persuasion skills.

Precise

A properly trained horse can be controlled with just two words: giddap and whoa. While you will learn the significance of complex sentences and varying sentence length, you'll also discover that precise writing communicates simply and powerfully.

Professional

Don't let the word professional scare you. Dr. Sherwood Wirt, founding editor of Decision magazine and initiator of numerous writers conferences, constantly reminded participants that they were professional writers once they had made one sale. But income is not the only standard. Cultivate a truly professional attitude; become, a writer who takes pride in his or her work because it is being done excellently to the glory of God. Professionalism extends beyond the quality of your writing to all your relationships with writers and editors.

Used by permission of the Jerry Jenkins Writers Guild.

Establish Your Priorities

by Les Stobbe

You may have children to care for, and they might not consider your writing preoccupation valid. But don't we all somehow find time to do the things we really want to do, regardless the other worthy activities crowding our lives? Through the centuries, writers have demonstrated ways to establish priorities that involve the whole family. Try initiating family conferences where you can freely discuss such issues.

What should you consider in establishing priorities?

The inner life

Mark records a telling moment in the life of Jesus: "Very early in the morning, while it was still dark, Jesus got up, left the house and went off to a solitary place, where he prayed" (1:35). Another time He went up a mountain to pray (see Matthew 14:23). Even though He kept reminding His listeners that He came from the Father, that He was one with the Father, and that He did only what the Father asked Him to do, He also withdrew for prayer time, for the inner refreshment that communing with the Father gave Him.

Writing in the Sept./Oct 2001 *Discipleship Journal* about his own prayer life, Timothy Jones confesses:

> Years earlier I had learned, with a mixture of surprise and delight, to do more than read the Bible. I also learned to pray it. Now, I began to realize that another way into the church's wealth was to appropriate the prayers of earlier generations.

Becoming intimately acquainted with what God is saying to us through the Scriptures requires making Bible study a priority. Becoming part of a small-group Bible study adds a variety of understanding, practical application, and a strengthening of our sense of accountability to God's Word through community.

If you become a writer who has made Scripture study and prayer a priority, you will find your inner well filled to overflowing with the water of life. If you don't develop those disciplines, you'll be drawing on a well that quickly runs dry.

Reading

Wise is the writer who sets as a priority the reading of excellent writing. Writers are readers. Good writers are good readers. Great writers are great readers. The classics, as well as more-recent quality works, not only provide illustrations of stimulating writing, but they also fill the soul and mind with great ideas and rich insights. More than 300 years ago, Francis Bacon wrote:

> Reading maketh a full man; conference a ready man; and writing an exact man. And therefore, if a man ... read a little, he had need have much cunning, to seem to know what he doth not.

One of today's leading Christian writers, Philip Yancey, devoted an entire book, *Soul Survivor,* to explaining how great writers fed his soul and mind and nurtured him in ways the church did not. In addition, he came to value the gospel story in new ways as he read Tolstoy and Dostoyevsky. Here's what he says about the spiritual nurturing they provided:

At the exact same time, I was living in the West surrounded by Christians, saturated with religious literature and frankly unable to make sense of most of it. These two Russian novelists, whom no one would accuse of being balanced or even psychologically healthy, helped restore to me a sense of balance. As Robert Coles had found that novelists knew more about human behavior than all of his psychological teachers, I found that they also knew more theology than most theologians. At a crucial stage in my pilgrimage they became my spiritual guides in coming to terms with a problem that vexes every thoughtful Christian — or follower of any religion, for that matter — namely the huge gap between life as it should be and life as it is, between the theory of faith and its practice.

Time

Writers face the same time issues as any hobbyist — but for Christian writers, getting in front of the keyboard is not a hobby. You are called to ministry, to worship, and that's expressed through your writing. Family members often have a tough time accepting that. Some may consider it a time waster, an addiction; others, a search for glory. So your task is to help them recognize the importance of your writing time. That may mean establishing times when you can't be interrupted except for emergencies — or writing when family members are not around.

The late Calvin Miller, author of both creative books and preaching texts, confessed he often awoke at night with an idea and would rush to his typewriter for several hours of work. Some mothers of young children, despite their exhaustion, write for an hour or two before the children awaken. Others are night owls and work late. One pastor took two weeks each summer to write all day, with his wife bringing him meals and encouragement. During the winter, his secretary edited his material as he continued fine-tuning it.

Establish a specific time every week, even every day, to write.

Jerry B. Jenkins, a self-proclaimed morning person, for years could do his own book writing only between 9:00 p.m. and midnight, when his wife and young family were asleep. He rose early to drive to work, and he tenaciously maintained the time from when he got home in the afternoon until nine as family time — no writing, and no work from the office. "It wasn't easy," he says, "but if you feel called to write and yet must maintain your other priorities, you do what you have to do."

Establish a specific time every week, even every day, to write. If you write two pages a day, five days a week, you'll write 10 pages a week and 520 pages a year. That's two books' worth!

Used by permission of the Jerry Jenkins Writers Guild.

Making Time to Write
by Dennis E. Hensley

IF YOU HAD THREE MONTHS OFF to work on your book, all expenses paid, could you get a lot done? That is less a fantasy than you might imagine.

Say each day you work at your regular job 8 hours and sleep 8 hours. That leaves 8 hours to use as you wish. Suppose you used 6 of those to eat, watch TV, shower, read the newspaper, help your kids with homework, take out the garbage, wash dishes, and do your daily devotions. The other 2 hours you reserve for your writing. That might mean writing before the family gets up, while the kids are napping, or after the family has gone to bed.

Assuming you leave weekends free to spend time with your family, by investing just 2 hours per day Monday through Friday writing, the result is 10 hours per week. That's 40 hours — or a full work week — each month. In a year you will log 480 hours, or one dozen 40-hour workweeks. Three months' worth. Amazing. There is time in your schedule to write a full-length book

Become More Disciplined

Many never get around to writing because they are always sailing to a mythical placed called One Day Isle. "One day I'll set up a home office," or "One day I'll take a class on writing," or "One day I'll pound out the outline of my book." They never get to it because they fill their time playing video games, watching television, sending text messages, and daydreaming about what success would be like.

Real writers write.

You can learn to use your time effectively. Let's take steps now to make you more productive:

Start With Prayer

Seek God's direction, assistance, wisdom, and affirmation in all you set out to accomplish. Be open to the leading of the Holy Spirit as you serve the Lord through your career as a writer.

Set Goals

Make them specific and achievable. Dream big, but break big projects into smaller, more manageable ones. Challenge yourself to do more of what you feel most proud of having achieved last year. If you read two books on how to improve your writing, set a goal to read five such books this year. If a one-day writers workshop was beneficial last year, determine to attend a four-day writers conference this year.

Establish Priorities

While you're learning and establishing yourself as a writer, consider stepping down from many of the volunteer activities you've taken on. You may feel guilty at first, but to succeed, your writing must take precedence over other responsibilities for a while. Consider a year's sabbatical. Notify people that you'll be stepping down from neighborhood association duties, assistant coaching for your child's sports team, and organizing the greeters at church. You may decide to return to these responsibilities in the future, but for now your writing needs a chance to reach its potential. Don't consider it abandoning your other tasks; you're just rotating ministries, putting your writing first while you learn and grow. Teaching Sunday school can impact a few dozen lives, but a successful book can multiply that impact by thousands.

Learn to Say No

If you do your writing at home, people won't think you have a real job. They'll ask you to babysit, run errands, become a member of a bowling team, bake cookies for the hospital fundraiser, and drive them to an appointment. Your answer must be, "I'd like to, but I'm working." If you don't want to have to explain that you're writing, just say you have another commitment and leave it at that. The more frequently you say no, the less frequently people will request your time. If you feel guilty about not caving in to requests for favors, remember what author and editor Lin Johnson says: "Saying no to other things is saying yes to God's call for you to write."

Don't Wait for the Muse

Occasionally writers have ah-ha! moments of inspiration. But most of the time it's just plain hard work to churn out pages. Establish a writing routine and then go to work. Proofread what you wrote the day before. Read your dialogue aloud to see if it sounds natural. Use the internet to research a topic you plan to write about. Create momentum. Be a writer!

Establish Deadlines

Parkinson's Law states that a project expands to fill the time allotted. Set deadlines for when you'll have the first draft of a chapter completed, when you'll have your column ready to email to your editor, and when you'll send in your registration for that writers conference. Mark your calendar, stick to your schedule, and hold yourself accountable. Strive for results.

Organize Your Work Area

Create a space where your computer, printer, reference materials, filing cabinet, and supplies are easily accessible. Keep it organized so you can always work at peak efficiency.

Reduce interruptions. Close the door. Don't check email. Assemble your supplies, then stay in the chair and write.

Reduce interruptions. Switch your phones to voicemail. Close the door. Don't check email during writing time. Look at snail mail when you're on break. Advise your family and friends of your work hours and tell them not to interrupt except for an emergency. Assemble your supplies. Grab your beverage of choice, then stay in the chair and write.

Find an Accountability Partner

Establish a relationship with another writer you can meet with every few weeks for prayer and career assessment. Have that person hold you accountable for projects you have pledged to finish. Having to report to someone will motivate you. Wanting to be a writer doesn't make you a writer. Writing makes you a writer.

Used by permission of the Jerry Jenkins Writers Guild.

Creating a Writing Environment
by Les Stobbe

Do you long for a quiet retreat house in the woods of Maine or the mountains of Colorado in which to write? Someday you might enjoy that. But most writers, especially just starting out, find that space to write is at a premium. Jerry B. Jenkins first wrote on the couch in his living room, with his typewriter on a chair before him. Later he used a spare bedroom until a new baby came along, and then he wrote in the basement, a tiny space heater rattling to keep pace with the cold.

Here's how Ethel Herr, author of both fiction and nonfiction books and An Introduction to Christian Writing, describes her writing environment:

> I remember ... my own big old dining room table. I picture it in at least four different houses, cluttered with papers and books and a decrepit manual typewriter. I had to clean up the mess every time I prepared a meal for my family. Before my husband returned from work, I stashed away all the evidence of my labors so I could greet him with an orderly house at day's end. On this table and under these circumstances, all my articles and poems of several years were born. My first book was written at this table.

Today's writer has an incredible advantage over how Ethel got started. Much of what she did on her dinner table can be done on the computer without ever leaving the keyboard. Click on File, then on Save As, and presto, your "dining room table" is cleared of freshly written material.

The computer also makes small spaces work as writing environments. A prolific author, the late Nancy Bayless lived on a boat with her husband in a southern California harbor, her work space a triangular "cupboard." Using a laptop, she spent hours writing poetry and prose.

So what do you need to provide copy for today's newspapers, magazines, and book publishers?

A Basic Computer and Software

Publishers today require copy in electronic format. But you need not buy the newest, fastest computer. Even a machine that's three or four years old is fine for most writers. Just make sure your software can read and save documents in the Microsoft Word .doc format publishers require. If you don't already have Word, your options include low-cost programs designed to substitute for Word, and even free "open-source" software.

Make sure your computer can read and save documents in the .doc format publishers require.

A Printer

You can get basic laser printers that will produce black-and-white copy for under $100. The greatest cost comes in replacement toner cartridges, so compare the price of different brands' cartridges before you buy, including the availability of generic replacements.

A Scanner

Prices for scanners have dropped enough to be easily obtainable. While many writers get along without a scanner, scanning from a book or magazine is faster than entering the material via the keyboard.

Data Back-Up

No matter how new or sophisticated your computer, failures can occur — destroying all the information for your writing projects. So professional writers create regular backup files for critical information. (To protect against small-scale computer problems, set your word-processor to automatically save open documents every few minutes.) Technology will change, but options for insuring against a computer crash include copying files to an inexpensive flash drive or an external hard drive. Having backups on such a device enabled one professional writer to save all his current work when a fire destroyed his home.

> *No matter how new your computer, failures can occur. So professional writers create regular backup files.*

A Comfortable Desk and Chair

Don't jeopardize your back or risk carpal tunnel syndrome. Invest in a desk that lets you place the keyboard at a comfortable elevation and your monitor at eye level. A chair that lets you adjust both height and back support is worth its weight in gold.

Used by permission of the Jerry Jenkins Writers Guild.

Reading for Style

by Les Stobbe

Have you read the Gospels for style recently? What sets Mark apart? He wrote crisply, with action verbs. The apostle Peter loved action, and Mark reflected his attitude. He was the true bottom line communicator, and you can imagine him saying in interviews, "Just give me the facts." He uses two verses to cover an incident that Luke described in 15 verses. That's why we go to Luke for the caring attitude of a physician. He loved stories and parables. People come alive in Luke, and Jesus is shown as deeply human. Luke's style is more relaxed.

John's style shows a philosophical bent. He provided wonderful details of Jesus' exchanges, His debates with the Pharisees and Sadducees. He was out to win over the reader, so his style is more persuasive than that of the other Gospel writers. No wonder the Gospel of John is so often used as an evangelistic tool. Reading a Gospel of John left on a Chicago bus brought a man to faith and into the bookstore at the Moody Bible Institute for more literature.

What about the apostle Paul? Ever read his letters for the style of writing? Reading Romans, you'd think he was a theologian. But reading the Corinthian letters, you'd swear he was a pastor. Get into Galatians and he becomes an apologist. In Ephesians he presents a treatise on the church, and in Philippians he delivers a personal letter of encouragement. As a highly educated apostle, he was able, under the guidance of the Holy Spirit, to adapt his style to the life situation he was addressing.

Analyze sentence structure, the use of verbs, and how the writer uses various forms of imagery.

Now read some contemporary best-selling writers for style. Borrow from the library three or four of the past year's nonfiction best-sellers and study how each author addresses the reader in the opening paragraph of the first chapter. Analyze sentence structure, the use of verbs, and how the writer uses various sorts of imagery. Look at the flow of thought, how the writers get the reader from point A to point B in attempting to tell a story or prove a point. What kind of transitions do they use? Style is built word by word, image by image, by sentence construction and paragraph design.

Concerning the content of their writing, what kinds of stories do these writers use? How transparent are they about their own failures?

Finally, take time to work through books on writing style, like *Championship Writing: 50 Ways to Improve Your Writing*, by Paula LaRoque, published by Marion Street Press. *The Elements of Style* is a classic. Also consider studying the chapter on style in *On Writing Well*, by William K. Zinsser.

Four Attractive Writing Approaches
by Les Stobbe

Simple and direct

If you're just getting into writing, maybe even wondering if writing is really for you, start with a simple and direct style. Avoid long, complex sentences. Instead, express your ideas clearly as though you were interacting with your reader eyeball to eyeball. Here's a sample lead from an article on how a church was dealing with one of its attendees, an ex-convict, killing a member:

> With a deep, clear voice and an overhead screen highlighting his key points, Pastor Jim Johnson preached about faith last Sunday at the Lighthouse Free Methodist church in Lynnwood.

Writing in *Discipleship Journal*, Timothy Jones opened an article with:

> There was a time in my Christian life when I had little interest in "book" prayers. I felt little attraction to (or patience with) patterning my own praying after another's. I could manage to find the words on my own just fine, thank you. Anything else smacked of needless formality.

Discovery

Today's readers tend to reject anything that smacks of authoritarianism. They want to think for themselves. They are especially repelled by absolute truth. And yet we Christian writers believe there is absolute truth. So how do you go eyeball to eyeball with them? The discovery approach has proved its worth time and again.

In the discovery approach, your focus is on the reader, not on the important truth you want to express. You are, in effect, putting your arm around the reader and saying, "Let's see if what I've found matches what you're looking for."

Consider the lead sentences from Timothy Jones's article above. He disarmed readers with, "There was a time in my Christian life ... ." Then he confessed how he felt, which may well match what the reader is feeling. The third sentence admitted an arrogant attitude — no plastic Christian here. And for all Baby Boomers, he admitted to thinking, *Anything else smacked of needless formality.* There was no telling the readers what they should think or do — just what he found after he became willing to get over his prejudices. Readers likely said to themselves, *I like this guy. He's honest, up front about his own weaknesses and prejudices, so I'll stick with him a little longer.*

In an article that appeared in *Christian Reader* on the importance of being willing to serve the Lord in areas of ministry that aren't often applauded, Rose Buschman made eye contact with her reader by opening her article with:

> Recently my husband and I were weeding some foundation plantings round the entrance to our church. It was a very hot Saturday afternoon and I had to frequently duck into the shade to get a break from the blazing sun. "This is what I call donkey work," I said while sweat trickled down my cheeks.

Humorous

One of the most difficult styles to master is the humorous style of a Patsy Clairmont, Barbara Johnson, or Dave Barry. They seem to have a native wit, but they spent years developing an effective humorous style. Just when you think you're reading something serious, they slip in a comparison that evokes a chuckle. Phil Callaway, whose columns on family life in *Servant* magazine of Prairie Bible College reveal his humorous bent (or should I say a side-angle way of looking at life), writes about flying home after a job interview. His wife was raising questions, but he was determined to take the job.

> As I walked to a nearby restroom, I practiced my acceptance speech .... Entering a tiny stall, I latched the door behind me. Suddenly the place began to shake. Lights flickered. Doors rattled. Walls shook. For the first time in my life, I was in an earthquake. Now I don't know if you've thought much about dying, or if you've thought about where you would most like to die, but if you're anything like me, your list does not include an airport washroom.
>
> As the rattling stopped, a man in the cubicle next to me said loudly, "Did I do that?" I was speechless. Unlatching the door, I ran quickly from the room, hoping to hold my wife before being encased in rubble. I'll kiss her, I thought, and let her feel the earth move one last time!
>
> Later we learned that the quake had registered 5.0 on Mr. Richter's scale. Believe me, it registered much higher on mine.

Notice how humor depends on the surprise — the juxtaposition of practicing an acceptance speech versus the reality of an earthquake threatening death by entombment. The idea of his kiss letting his wife feel the earth move. The scientific size of the earthquake versus the impact on his life, which he revealed in the next paragraph, explaining that he ultimately turned down the opportunity.

Meditative/Reflective

Much Christian writing tends to a meditative, reflective style. Devotional writing, always popular, provides the best examples of this, though we may also see it in newspaper columns reflecting on people or current events. Writing in *Discipleship Journal* about a "Journey to Compassion," Doug Prensner reflects:

> The Lord had still more lessons for me. At one of my lowest points, our house was vandalized and burglarized while we were away on vacation. Liquid drain cleaner was poured on most of the carpets upstairs — to name just one evidence of the destruction. I was frustrated, for I could clearly remember asking the Lord to protect our home before we left town.

You'll notice this writer uses the past tense, a feature of the reflective writer. But meditative writing works with active verbs as well, though that requires a deliberate reshaping of the way a person would normally write.

Find and Capture Big Ideas
by Les Stobbe

WRITERS MUST BECOME HUNTERS AND GATHERERS, always looking for topics to benefit readers and details to enliven their writing. An interior decorator entering a room immediately notices what must be done. As a writer, you must train yourself to observe your environment for ideas to develop into news stories, articles, and even books.

A writer of a column for preteen boys learned to look at his son in a whole new way. He observed his interactions with his sister, with neighborhood children, at church, and with people on outings. Regardless your assignment or project, keep your eyes and ears open.

- Keep that notebook, tablet, or smart phone near you.
- Really notice flowers, bushes, trees, and animal life. One writer gained enough from observing life on her property to write four books of meditations on the land.
- Listen to people in social settings, on public transportation, in airports and depots. Conversations can trigger ideas for a dozen articles, and noticing how people express themselves will breathe life into your written dialogue.
- Ask leading questions like: "Who had the greatest influence on you as a teen? What is the most important thing you've learned about people? Where would you want to go on vacation if money were no object? What do you especially like about your job?" Besides making you a better conversationalist, the answers can lead to fascinating article ideas.
- Listen to sermons with notebook or tablet in hand. A sermon may trigger an article idea or simply enhance a point in something you're writing.
- Be alert to ideas on TV, radio, newspapers, magazines, and websites. One writer heard an interview with a refugee on national television and quickly contacted the network for the script. She followed leads to where that refugee was living and pursued writing a book with him.

Used by permission of the Jerry Jenkins Writers Guild.

Opportunity Unlimited

by Les Stobbe

Many beginning writers focus so strongly on their goal of writing a nonfiction book or novel, they miss opportunities popping up almost daily to minister to people through their writing.

Church newsletters: Start by writing announcements. Learn to be exact and include all the details. Then progress to writing news articles about people and events.

Local newspapers: Local newspaper editors have insatiable appetites for news and human interest stories. A church opening its homes to several boys who were orphan refugees from Sudan resulted in numerous newspaper articles.

The smaller the paper's circulation, the better your chances of writing for them as you begin. Columns, opinion pieces that accompany the editorial page, and letters to the editor all provide opportunities for Christian writers.

Christian newspapers: Many areas of the world have regional Christian newspapers. Most of them are on extremely tight budgets and pay little if anything, but they also need news stories, personality features, and meditations. They may be minor league in some eyes, but they provide an important Christian service to readers and a training ground for new writers.

Christian education take-home papers: Most must fill eight pages 52 weeks of the year and use a lot of articles by freelance writers. Circulation may surprise you — they can have major impact in tens of thousands of people's lives.

Magazines: Check all the periodical listings in *The Christian Writer's Market Guide* complete with descriptions of what each is looking for. Your local library will have what is called LMP (*Literary Market Place*), with listings of newspapers and magazines, names of editors, and addresses. Check publication websites for their writers guidelines.

Check all the periodical listings, complete with descriptions of what each is looking for.

Websites: Help your church webmaster by writing interesting articles about what's going on with your congregation's ministries. Likewise the Christian organizations with which you re acquainted. Offer them an article about their ministry or the involvement of someone from your area.

Church drama: Many churches perform their own skits and dramas and are looking for material. Study the basics of script writing and try your hand at writing for your local congregation.

You have entered the world of the Christian writer! Grab hold of the opportunities.

2

Alphabetical Listings of Book Publishers

If you do not find the publishers you are looking for, check the General Index. It is critical that you read and follow a publisher's guidelines exactly. In most cases their guidelines are available on their website, and a direct link is indicated in their listing. Check out any publisher thoroughly before signing a contract.

(*) before a listing indicates unconfirmed or no information update.
(+) before a listing indicates it's a new listing

+AAEDON PUBLISHING COMPANY, Acquisitions, PO Box 223, Hartford CT 06141. Query first. Nonfiction 140,00-200,000 wds. Responds in 6 wks. Guidelines at www.aadeon.com/submissions.html.
   Tips: "Currently we are considering proposals relative to the cultural and moral makeup of society in the U.S. and its impact on Christianity."

+ABC-CLIO, 130 Cremona Dr., Santa Barbara, CA 93117. (805)968-1911. E-mail: achiffolo@abc-clio.com. Website: www.abc-clio.com. Company blog: http://abcclio. blogspot.com. Anthony Chiffolo, ed. Dir., print. We provide authoritative, scholarly information about headline issues or controversies for general readers. Imprints: ABC-CLIO, Greenwood, Praeger. Publishes 16 titles/yr.; hardcover, digital. Accepts submissions through agents or authors. No subsidy. Does print-on-demand. No reprints. Prefers 80,000 wds.; 196 pgs. Royalty 6-10% on net; same for e-books; advance $500-750. Average first print run 500. Publication in 7-8 mos. Considers simultaneous submissions. Reports in 2 mos. Catalog and guidelines on Website.
   NonfictionBook proposal/sample chapters. Accepts e-mail & snail mail queries. Looking for thesis-driven manuscripts written by scholars for a lay readership.
   Ethnic market: Black, hispanic.
   Tips: "Most open to a thesis-driven manuscript focusing on 'headline' issues."

ABINGDON PRESS, 201 Eighth Ave. S., PO Box 801, Nashville TN 37202. (615) 749-6000. E-mail: [first initial and last name]@umpublishing.org. Website: www. abingdonpress.com. United Methodist Publishing House/Cokesbury. Mary C. Dean, ed-in-chief. Editors: Ramona Richards, fiction; Ron Kidd, study resources; Michael Stephens, Bible reference; Kathryn Armistead, theology; Constance Stella, leadership; Lil Copan, Christian living. Books and church supplies directed primarily to a mainline religious market. Publishes 120 titles/yr.; hardcover, trade paperbacks. Receives 2,000 submissions annually. Less than 5% of books from first-time authors. Accepts mss through agents only for fiction and Christian living. No reprints. **Royalty 7.5% on net.** Average first printing 2,500-4,000. Publication within 18 mos. Requires requested ms electronically. Prefers Common English Bible or a variety of which CEB is one. Guidelines on website: http://www.abingdonpress.com/submissions.html; free catalog.
   Nonfiction: Proposal/3 chapters; no phone/fax/e-query.
   Fiction: Solicited or agented material only.
   Ethnic Books: African American, Hispanic, Native American, Korean.

Music: See guidelines on website.

Tips: "We develop and produce materials to help more people in more places come to know and love God through Jesus Christ and to choose to serve God and neighbor."

This publisher serviced by ChristianManuscriptSubmissions.com.

+ACTA PUBLICATIONS, 4848 N. Clark St., Chicago IL 60640. Toll free: (800) 397-2282. E-mail: acta@actapublications.com. Website: www.actapublications.com. Submit to: Acquisitions Ed. Accepts simultaneous submissions & unsolicited mss. No electronic submissions. Send a cover letter, table of contents, introduction, and one chapter. Guidelines at www.actapublications.com/about/acta_submission_guidelines.

ADAMS MEDIA CORP., 57 Littlefield St., Avon MA 02322. (508) 427-7100. Toll-free fax (800) 872-5628. Website: www.adamsmedia.com. Division of F + W Publications. Jill Alexander, sr. ed.; submit to Paula Munier. Publishes 250 titles/yr. Receives 6,500 submissions annually. 40% of books from first-time authors. Accepts mss through agents or authors. Royalty; variable advance; or outright purchase. Publication within 12-18 mos. Considers simultaneous submissions. Responds in 3 mos. to queries. No mss accepted by e-mail. Guidelines at www.adamsmedia.com/call-for-submissions; catalog for 9 x 12 SAE/5 stamps.

    Nonfiction: Query first by mail; no phone/fax/e-query.

    Tips: General publisher that does some inspirational books.

AMBASSADOR INTERNATIONAL, 427 Wade Hampton Blvd., Greenville SC 29609. (864) 235-2434. Fax (864)235-2491. E-mail: publisher@emeraldhouse.com. Website: www.ambassador-international.com. Company blog: www.ambassodor-international.com/blog. Sam Lowry, pub. Dedicated to spreading the gospel of Christ and empowering Christians through the written word. Publishes 50 titles/yr.; hardcover, trade paperbacks, coffee table books, digital. Receives 750 submissions annually. 50% of books from first-time authors. Accepts mss through agents or authors. Subsidy publishes 40-50%; does print-on-demand. Reprints books. Prefers 144+ pgs. Royalty 15-20% of net; 25% for e-books; no advance. Average first printing 2,000. Publication within 6-8 mos. Considers simultaneous submissions. Responds within 30 days. Prefers KJV, NIV, ESV, NKJV, NASB. Guidelines at http://ambassador-international.com/get-published/submission-guidelines; catalog online only.

    Nonfiction: E-mail proposal/3 chapters; phone/fax/e-query OK.

    Fiction: For teens, new adults, and adults. E-mail proposal/3 chapters; phone/fax/e-query OK.

    Special Needs: Business, finance, biographies, novels, inspirational, devotional, topical, Bible studies.

    Also Does: DVDs.

    Photos/Artwork: Accepts freelance photos for book covers; open to queries from freelance artists.

    Tips: "We're most open to a book which has a clearly defined market and the author's total commitment to the project. We do well with first-time authors. We have full international coverage. Many of our titles sell globally."

*AMERICAN CATHOLIC PRESS, 16565 State St., South Holland IL 60473-2025. (708) 331-5485. Fax (708) 331-5484. E-mail: acp@acpress.org. Website: www.acpress.org or www.leafletmissal.com. Catholic worship resources. Father Michael Gilligan, ed. dir. Publishes 4 titles/yr.; hardcover. Receives 10 submissions annually. Reprints books. Pays $25-100 for outright purchases only. Average first printing 3,000.

Publication within 1 yr. No simultaneous submissions. Responds in 2 mos. Prefers NAS. Guidelines at http://www.americancatholicpress.org/faq.html#faq5 (scroll down to #5); catalog for SASE.

Nonfiction: Query first; no phone/fax/e-query.

Tips: "We publish only materials on the Roman Catholic liturgy. Especially interested in new music for church services. No poetry or fiction."

*AMG PUBLISHERS, 6815 Shallowford Rd., Chattanooga TN 37421. Toll-free (800) 266-4977. (423) 648-2255. Toll-free fax (800) 265-6690. (423) 894-9511. E-mail: ricks@amgpublishers.com, or through website: www.amgpublishers.com. Company blog: https://www.facebook.com/AMGPublishers and https://twitter.com/AMGPublishers AMG International (nondenominational). Rick Steele, product development & acquisitions; Trevor Overcash, operations and editorial production mgr. "God's Word to you is our highest calling." We are unique in that proceeds from our sales are funneled into world missions through our parent organization, AMG International. More info about AMG International ministries can be found at www.amginternational.org. Imprints: Living Ink Books; God and Country Press. Publishes 15-20 titles/yr.; trade paperbacks, coffee table books, digital. Receives 1,500 submissions annually. 25% of books from first-time authors. Accepts mss through agents or authors. No subsidy. Does print-on-demand. Reprints books. Prefers 40,000-60,000 wds. (128-224 pgs.) for Bible studies; 70,000- 120,000 wds. (224-400 pgs.) for fiction; 60,000-100,000 wds. (208-400 pgs.) for trade nonfiction. **Royalty 10-20% of net; 30-40% for e-books; average advance $2,500.** Average first printing 3,500. Publication within 12-18 mos. Accepts simultaneous submissions. Prefers accepted ms by e-mail. Responds in 1-4 mos. Prefers NASB 95, NKJV, ESV, or NIV 2011. Guidelines by e-mail/website at http://www.amgpublishers.com/main/pdf/Prospective_Author_Guidelines.pdf; catalog for 9 x 12 SAE/5 stamps.

Nonfiction: Query letter first; accepts e-queries.

Fiction: Query letter only first; e-query preferred. For children & teens. "We specialize in middle reader and YA fantasy/speculative."

Special Needs: Bible studies, devotionals, and reference..

Also Does: Bible software, Bible audio cassettes, CD-ROMs.

Ethnic market: Black & Hispanic.

Photos: Open to submissions of freelance photos.

Tips: "Most open to an interactive workbook Bible study geared for small groups that effectively taps into a largely female audience. We are currently placing priority on books with strong bibliocentric focus."
This publisher serviced by ChristianManuscriptSubmissions.com and The Writer's Edge.

+ANCIENT FAITH PUBLISHING, (formerly Conciliar Press), Chesterton, IN. E-mail for adult submissions: khyde@ancient faith.com (for children's submissions: jmeyer@ancientfaith.com). Website: www.store.ancientfaith.com. Antiochian Orthodox Christian Archdiocese of N.A. Katherine Hyde, adult acquisitions; Jane Meyer, children's acquisitions. Publishes 8-18 adult titles/yr.; 2-4 children's titles/yr. Receives 100 submissions annually. 20% of books from first-time authors. Accepts ms through agents or authors. Reprints books. Prefers 40,000-80,000 wds. **Pays royalty; no or small advance.** Average first printing 2,000. Accepts simultaneous submissions. E-mail submissions only. Responds in 103 mos. Prefers NKJV. Catalog & guidelines on Website: http://store.ancientfaith.com/submission-guidelines.

Nonfiction: Only Eastern Orthodox content/authors. E-query only.

Children's Books: E-query only. Send full ms for picture books under 2,000 wds.

Accepts Eastern Orthodox material from Eastern Orthodox authors only.

Photos: Accepts freelance photos for book covers.

Tips: "Please explore our Website before submitting and carefully follow posted guidelines. We reserve the right not to respond to inappropriate submissions."

+ANEKO PRESS, 203 E. Birch St., PO Box 652, Abbotsford WI 54405. (855) 489-7839. Website: anekopress.com/FAQ. Company blog: anekopress.com/bloggers. Jeremiah Zeist, pres. Imprint of Life Sentence Publishing. Publisher for missionaries and ministries. Publishes and distributes books and e-books in the U.S. And around the world. Their ministry printing program is used by ministries which give away books for free. Also sends books to prisons. Open to submissions; see Website.

AVON INSPIRE, HarperCollins, 10 E. 53rd St., New York NY 10022. (212) 207-7000. Website: www.harpercollins.com. Cynthia DiTiberio, ed. Inspirational women's fiction. Publishes 8-10 titles/yr. Agented submissions only.

   Fiction: Historical & contemporary; Amish

BAKER ACADEMIC, 6030 E. Fulton Rd., Ada MI 49301. (616) 676-9185. Fax (616) 676-9573. E-mail: submissions@bakeracademic.com. Website: www.bakeracademic.com. Imprint of Baker Publishing Group. Jim Kinney, ed. dir. Publishes religious academic books and professional books for students and church leaders. Publishes 50 titles/yr.; hardcover, trade paperbacks. 10% of books from first-time authors. Accepts mss through agents, submission services, or editor's personal contacts at writers' conferences. **Royalty; advance.** Publication within 1 yr. Guidelines on website: http://bakerpublishinggroup.com/contact/submission-policy; catalog on website.

   Nonfiction: No unsolicited queries.

   This publisher serviced by ChristianManuscriptSubmissions.com.

BAKER BOOKS, of Baker Publishing Group, 6030 E. Fulton Rd., Ada MI 49301. (616) 676-9185. Fax (616) 676-2315. Website: www.bakerbooks.com. Publishes ministry and Christian living for the church. Publishes hardcover, trade paperbacks. No unsolicited proposals. Catalog found on website. Guidelines at: http://bakerpublishinggroup.com/contact/submission-policy. Submit only through an agent. Acquired Regal Books in 2014.

+BAKER'S PLAYS. Not currently accepting unsolicited mss. Check out this publisher's guidelines at: http://www.samuelfrench.com/submissions, for current submissions status.

BALLANTINE PUBLISHING GROUP, 1745 Broadway, 18th Fl., New York NY 10019. (212) 782-9000. Website: www.randomhouse.com. A Division of Random House. Not accepting submissions of query, proposals, or manuscripts at this time.

B&H PUBLISHING GROUP, One Lifeway Plaza, MSN 188, Nashville TN 37234. E-mail: Manuscript Submission@lifeway.com. Website: www.bhpublishinggroup.com. Twitter: @BHpub. Facebook: www.facebook.com/bhpublishing. B&H Publishing Group, a division of LifeWay Christian Resources, is a team of mission-minded people with a passion for taking God's Word to the world. Because we believe Every Word Matters, we seek to provide innovative, intentional content that is grounded in biblical truth. Imprints: B&H Books, B&H Academic, Holman Bible Publishers, Holman Reference, Broadman ChurchSupplies, B&H Español. Send submissions to:

ManuscriptSubmissions@lifeway.com. Publishes 90-100 titles/yr.; hardcover, trade paperback. Receives 3,000 submissions annually. 10% of books from first-time authors. **Royalty on net; advance.** Publication within 18 mos. Considers simultaneous submissions. Responds in 2-3 mos. Prefers HCSB. Guidelines at: http://www.bhpublishing-group.com/consumer-faq/#3.

> **Nonfiction:** Query first; no phone/fax query.
> **Fiction:** Query first; no phone/fax query.
> **Also Does:** Licensing, Kindle Reader, some audio.
> **Blog:** blog.bhpublishinggroup.com/
> **Tips:** "Follow guidelines when submitting. Be informed that the market in general is very crowded with the book you might want to write. Do the research before submitting."
> This publisher serviced by ChristianManuscriptSubmissions.com and The Writer's Edge.

BANTAM BOOKS. See Doubleday Religious on p. 92.

BARBOUR PUBLISHING INC., 1810 Barbour Dr., PO Box 719, Uhrichsville OH 44683. (740) 922-6045. Fax (740) 922-8065. Mission statement: To publish and distribute inspirational products offering exceptional value and biblical encouragement to the masses. E-mail: submissions@barbourbooks.com. Requires e-mail submissions. Accepts proposals only through agents. Publishes 300+ titles/yr.; fiction, nonfiction, Bible reference, devotions, gift books, Christian classics, children's titles; hardcover, flexibound, trade paperbacks, mass market paperbacks. Considers simultaneous submissions & reprints. Responds only if interested. Writers' guidelines at: www.barbourbooks.com/pages/writersguide.aspx.

> This publisher serviced by The Writer's Edge.

BARKING RAIN PRESS, 1PO Box 822674, Vancouver WA 98682. (208) 352-0396. Fax (208) 246-3962. E-mail: publisher@barkingrainpress.org. Website: www.barkingrainpress.org. Ti Locke, ed. dir. Imprints: Barking Rain Press, Virtual Tales, Nitis Books. Publishes complete novels or novellas of at least 20,000 words to sell through the BRP website and other partner sites in print and eBook formats. We will also consider the following: short story collections (anthologies) with a strong central theme, written by a single author; reprints of previously published works that are out-of-print, so long as the author owns both the worldwide electronic rights and print rights. Publishes 12-14 bks./yr. Receives 100+ ms/yr. 60% first-time authors. Accepts bks. submitted by agents and unsolicited mss from authors. Hardcover, trade paperbacks, digital, reprints. Prefers 20,000-100,000 wds. **Royalty 50-60%. Advance for established authors.** Exclusively POD services & e-books. Publication within 12 mos. No simultaneous submissions. Responds 30-60 days. Catalog on website. Guidelines at: http://www.barkingrainpress.org/submissions.

> **Fiction:** Only book proposal w/4 chapters. Open submissions: January, May, September. Electronic submissions only. Sign up for reminder list on website.
> **Special Needs:** Non-erotic romance, YA, speculative fiction.
> **Tips:** Well written, good plot and story arc, no POV issues (head-hopping). Barking Rain Press is a nonprofit publisher. Our mission is to help new authors and midlist authors further their writing careers. Freelance openings posted on website.

+BAYLOR UNIVERSITY PRESS, One Bear Place 97363, Waco TX 76798-7363.

(254) 710-3164. E-mail: Carey_Newman@baylor.edu. Carey Newman, press dir. Requires e-mail submissions. Guidelines at: www.baylorpress.com/en/Publish_With_Us.

+BEACON HILL PRESS, PO Box 419527, Kansas City MO 64141. E-mail: crm@ nph.com. Rene' McFarland, submissions ed. E-mail her for detailed submissions guidelines. General guidelines at: http://www.nph.com/nphweb/html/bhol/FAQ.jsp?faqsect ion=NA&faqsection2=BHOL&faqId=1170&nid=lcol.

BETHANY HOUSE PUBLISHERS, a division of Baker Publishing Group, 6030 E. Fulton Rd., Ada MI 49301. Website: www.bethanyhouse.com. Offering inspiration and encouragement to readers through story and spiritual insight, Bethany House titles help Christians apply biblical truth in all areas of life. Publishes approx. 80 titles/yr.; hardcover, trade paperbacks. 10% of books from first-time authors. Accepts mss through agents only. **Negotiable royalty on net; negotiable advance.** Publication within 18 mos. Considers simultaneous submissions. Catalog available on website.

> **Nonfiction:** "Seeking well-planned and developed books in the following categories: personal growth, deeper-life spirituality, contemporary issues, women's issues, reference, applied theology, and inspirational."
>
> **Fiction:** See website for fiction guidelines.
>
> **Tips:** "We do not accept unsolicited queries or proposals."

BLUE DOLPHIN PUBLISHING, INC., 13340-D Grass Valley Ave., Grass Valley CA 95945. (530) 477-1503. Fax (530) 477-8342. E-mail: Bdolphin@bluedolphinpublishing. com. Website: www.bluedolphinpublishing.com. Paul M. Clemens, pub. Imprints: Pelican Pond (fiction & poetry), Papillon (juvenile), and Symposium (nonfiction). Specializes in publishing books on comparative spiritual traditions, lay and transpersonal psychology, self-help, health, healing, and whatever helps people grow in their social awareness and conscious evolution. Publishes 10-15 titles/yr. (includes print-on-demand); hardcover, trade paperbacks, coffee-table books, and digital. Receives 2,000 submissions annually. 75% of books from first-time authors. Accepts submissions through agents or authors. No subsidy. Does print-on-demand. Accepts reprints. Prefers about 60,000 wds. or 200 pgs. **Royalty 10-15% of net; 25% for e-books; no advance.** Average first printing 300-3,000. Publication in 6-12 mos. Considers simultaneous submissions. Responds in 3-6 mos., if interested. Prefers NAB (no KJV). Guidelines on Website: www.bluedolphinpublishing. com/msguide.htm; catalog for 8.5 x 11 SAE/2 stamps.

> **Nonfiction:** Proposal/sample chapters or complete ms; accepts e-queries and snail-mail queries. "Looking for books that will increase people's spiritual and social awareness. We will consider all topics."
>
> **Fiction:** Query letter only first; then proposal/sample chapters. Pelican Pond Imprint. For teens and adults; no children's board books or picture books.
>
> **Also Does:** E-books.
>
> **Special needs:** Manuscripts by "enlightened" people.
>
> **Photos/Artwork:** Accepts freelance photos for book covers; open to queries from freelance artists.
>
> **Tips:** "Looking for mature writers whose focus is to help people lead better lives. Our authors are generally professionals who write for others—not just for themselves. We look for topics that would appeal to the general market, are interesting, different, and will aid in the growth and development of humanity. See website before submitting."
>
> **Note:** This publisher also publishes books on a range of topics, including cross-cultural spirituality. They also may offer a co-publishing arrangement, not necessarily a royalty deal.

BMH BOOKS, PO Box 544, Winona Lake IN 46590. Toll free: (800) 348-2756. (574) 372-3098. Fax (574) 268-5384. E-mail: lcgates@bmhbooks.com. Website: www. BMHbooks.com. Fellowship of Grace Brethren Churches. Liz Cutler Gates, ed./pub. Trinitarian theology; dispensational eschatology; emphasis on exegesis. Publishes 3-5 titles/yr.; hardcover, trade paperbacks. Receives 30 submissions annually. 50% of books from first-time authors. Accepts mss through agents or authors. Seldom reprints books. Prefers 50,000-75,000 wds. or 128-256 pgs. **Royalty 8-10% on retail; rarely pays an advance.** Also doing some subsidy publishing. Average first printing 2,000. Publication within 1 yr. Prefers not to consider simultaneous submissions. Responds in 3 mos. Prefers KJV or NIV. No longer accepts unsolicited mss. Requires accepted mss by e-mail. Guidelines at: http://bmhbooks.com/faqs; free catalog.

   Nonfiction: Proposal/2 chapters; no phone/fax query; e-query OK. "Most open to a small-group study book or text for Bible college/Bible institute."
   Tips: "Most open to biblically based, timeless discipleship material."

BOLD VISION BOOKS, PO Box 2011, Friendswood TX 77549-2011. phone/fax: (832) 569-4282. E-mail: kaeporter@gmail.com. Website: www.boldvisionbooks.com. George Porter, pub; Karen Porter, sr. ed. We are small enough to give you personal service, and we are big enough to get your book into the marketplace. Imprint: Optasia Books (subsidy imprint). Publishes 12 titles/yr.; trade paperbacks, mass-market paperbacks, digital. Receives 100 submissions annually 85% of books from first-time authors. Accepts submissions from agents or authors. Subsidy only through Optasia Books. Does print-on-demand. Reprints books. Prefers 40,000 wds. or 280 pgs. **Royalty 25-50% on net; no advance.** Publication within 6 mos. Considers simultaneous submissions. Responds 1-3 mos. No preference on version. Digital catalog & guidelines at: http://www.boldvisionbooks.com/Submission_Guidelines.html.

   Nonfiction: Compelling stories of life change and spiritual growth. Query letter only first. Accept e-mail queries. Require mss by e-mail.
   Fiction: For teens & adults. Query letter only first. Looking for strong story skills with compelling characters who experience life change.
   Photos/Artwork: Accepts freelance photos for book covers; open to queries from freelance artists.
   Special needs: Well-written, compelling books on Christian living. Looking for fresh voices and clear concepts.
   Also does: Booklets & mini-books.
   Tips: "Show us that you have a clear, concise handle on your project. What is the book about? Who is the audience? What is the benefit to the reader? Your best opportunity with BVB is strong writing and a powerful takeaway message. Bold Vision Books exists to bring personal publishing solutions to authors with strong, fresh expressions of faith and purpose. To be noticed by our editors, write in crisp, tight, and authoritative language and offer answers that lead to transformation."

BONDFIRE BOOKS, Parent Co. Alive Communications, 7680 Goddard St., Ste. 220, Colorado Springs CO 80920. (719) 260-7080. Fax: (719) 260-8223. E-mail: submissions@bondfirebooks.com. Website: www.bondfirebooks.com. Chief Kindler, ed. Bondfire Books is an e-publisher focused on kindling thought and action through Christian and inspirational content while maximizing digital prospects for authors. Publish 50+/yr. Receives 5,000 proposals/yr. 10% first-time authors. Accepts books submitted by agents. Digital. Reprints books. Preferred book length 150,000 wds. **Royalty 50% based on net. E-books 50%. No advance.** Avg. time to publication 2 mos. Considers simultaneous submissions. Responds 4-6 wks. (If you don't hear by 6 wks., you can assume they are not interested.) Catalog on website. Guidelines at: http://www.bondfirebooks.com/submission.

Nonfiction: Proposal with 2 chap. E-mail queries. Requires mss by e-mail.
Fiction: Teens/adults. Query letter ONLY. Proposal with 2 chap.
Artwork: Open to queries from freelance artists.
Special Needs: Memoir, fiction, nonfiction, tie-ins to news events. News makers. Out of print with rts. reverted, in print works with available electronic rights.
Tips: "Publishers and agents are being much more selective with what they say yes to. And yet amidst increased competition, the cream always rises to the top. The great books get noticed and picked up." Contemporary fiction or big nonfiction book tied to a news maker. Primarily interested in working with authors with established platforms and audiences.

+BOYDS MILLS PRESS, 815 Church St., Honesdale PA 18431. Toll free: (800) 490-5111. (570) 253-1164. Website: www.boydsmillspress.com. High quality fiction and nonfiction for young readers.

BRAZOS PRESS, 6030 E. Fulton Rd., Ada MI 49301. (616) 676-9185. Fax (616) 676-2315. Website: www.brazospress.com. Imprint of Baker Publishing Group. Publishes thoughtful, theologically grounded books on subjects of importance to the church and the world. Publishes hardcover, trade paperbacks. Guidelines & catalog on website: http://bakerpublishinggroup.com/brazospress/contact/submitting-a-proposal.

BRIDGE LOGOS, 17750 N.W. 115th Ave., Bldg. 200, Ste. 220, Alachua FL 32615. (386) 462-2525. Fax (586) 462-2535. E-mail: editorial@bridgelogos.com or phildebrand@bridgelogos.com. Website: www.bridgelogos.com. Peggy Hildebrand, acq. ed. Publishes classics, books by Spirit-filled authors, and inspirational books that appeal to the general evangelical market. Imprint: Synergy. Publishes 40 titles/yr.; hardcover, trade paperbacks, mass-market paperbacks. Receives 200+ submissions annually. 30% of books from first-time authors. Accepts mss through agents or authors. Subsidy publishes to 5%; does very little print-on-demand. Reprints books. Prefers 250 pgs. **Royalty 10% on net; rarely pays $500 advance.** Average first printing 4,000-5,000. Publication within 6-12 mos. Considers simultaneous submissions. Responds in 6 wks. Prefers accepted mss by e-mail; free catalog. Guidelines at: www.bridgelogosfoundation.com/Manuscript-Submission.html.

Nonfiction: Proposal/3-5 chapters; no phone/fax query; e-query OK. "Most open to evangelism, spiritual growth, self-help, and education." Charges a $50 manuscript submission/evaluation fee.
Fiction: Proposal/3-5 chapters; no phone/fax query; e-query OK.
Special Needs: Reference, biography, current issues, controversial issues, church renewal, women's issues, and Bible commentary. Also teen, preteen, and kids' books.
Ethnic Books: African American & Hispanic.
Photos: Accepts freelance photos for book covers.
Tips: "Looking for well-written, timely books that are aimed at the needs of people and that glorify God. Have a great message, a well-written manuscript, and a specific plan and willingness to market your book. Looking for previously published authors with an active ministry who are experts on their subject."

+CAMBRIDGE SCHOLARS PUBLISHING, Cambridge Scholars Publishing, Lady Stephenson Library, Newcastle upon Tyne, NE6 2PA, United Kingdom. E-mail:

camilla.harding@cambridge.org. Camilla Harding, commissioning ed. Proposal includes overview, sample chapter, and academic profile. Responds in 4-6 wks. Guidelines at: www.c-s-p.org/submission_guidelines.htm.

+CAMBRIDGE UNIVERSITY PRESS, 32 Avenue of the Americas, New York NY 10013-2473. (212) 337-5000. E-mail: editorial@cambridge.org, or newyork@cambridge.org. Check out this publishers' guidelines at: www.cambridge.org/us/knowledge/streams/item2271285/?site_locale=en_US.

CANTICLE BOOKS, 1647 Shire Ave., Oceanside CA 92057. (760) 806-3743. Fax (760) 806-3689. E-mail: magnuspress@cox.net. Website: www.magnuspress.com. Imprint of Magnus Press. Warren Angel, ed. dir. To publish biblical studies by Catholic authors that are written for the average person and that minister life to Christ's Church. Publishes 2 titles/yr.; trade paperbacks. Receives 60 submissions annually. 50% of books from first-time authors. Accepts mss through agents or authors. Reprints books. Prefers 100-375 pgs. **Graduated royalty on retail; no advance.** Average first printing 2,500. Publication within 1 yr. Considers simultaneous submissions. Accepts requested ms on disk. Responds in 1-4 wks. Guidelines at: www.magnuspress.com/SubmissionGuidelinesCB.html also by mail/e-mail; free catalog.

> **Nonfiction:** Query or proposal/2-3 chapters; fax query OK. "Looking for spirituality, thematic biblical studies, unique inspirational books."
> **Tips:** "Our writers need solid knowledge of the Bible and a mature spirituality that reflects a profound relationship with Jesus Christ. Most open to well-researched, popularly written biblical studies geared to Catholics, or personal experience books that share/emphasize a person's relationship with Christ."

+CAREPOINT PUBLISHING, PO Box 870490, Stone Mountain GA 30087. (800) 378-9584 (if outside GA). (404) 625-9217. E-mail: info@carepointministries.com. We are currently seeking only those mss that fit into one of two categories: (1) Care group resources (about running a care ministry for people facing a specific life challenge, such as pornography/sex addition, abortion grief, physical disability, sex abuse, and the like). Or, (2) Fiction novellas, 15,000-25,00 wds., through Five Loaves Press/Way-Out Books. See details on guidelines at: www.carepointministry.com/writers.html.

+CAREY LIBRARY, WILLIAM. E-mail: submissions@WCLBooks.com. Website: www.missionbooks.org. Publishes scholarly & professional books, or educational books. Responds in 3-6 mos. Send a maximum 2-page query letter initially. No unsolicited mss, graphics, or images (will not be returned). Guidelines at: https://missionbooks.org/submissions.

+CARSON-DELLOSA CHRISTIAN EDUCATION, PO Box 35665, Greensboro NC 27425-5665. E-mail samples and resume to: freelancesamples@carsondellosa.com. Samples of supplemental educational materials (not returnable). Details and guidelines at: http://www.carsondellosa.com/cd2/default.aspx?HolderName=freelancers.

+CASCADIA PUBLISHING HOUSE (formerly Pandora Press U.S.), 126 Klingerman Rd., Telford PA 18969. E-mail: editor@CascadiaPublishingHouse.com. Michael A. King, pub./ed. Query only by mail or e-mail. Guidelines at: www.cascadia-publishinghouse.com/submit.htm.

+CASTLE GATE PRESS, E-mail: submissions@castlegatepress.com. Website: www.castlegatepress.com. Traditional Christian publisher accepting fiction; no nonfiction. Suzanne Hartman, ed. Dir. Accepts submissions from agents or authors. For adults, new adults, young adults. Length: 70,000-100,000 wds. **Royalty 50%.** Submit a query with

1-page, single spaced synopsis, and the first 50 pages, double-spaced. Likes speculative fiction or at least of touch of speculative. Also does novellas. Submit to e-mail.

+CATHOLIC BOOK PUBLISHING, 77 West End Rd., Totowa NJ 07572. (973) 890-2400. Fax (973) 890-2410. E-mail: info@catholicbookpublishing.com. Anthony Buono, ed. Publishes mainly liturgical books, Bibles, Missals, and prayerbooks. Prefers query; no phone/fax/e-query. No simultaneous submissions or submissions from agents. Outright purchases; no royalties or advances. Responds in 2-3 mos. Publication in 12-15 mos. Guidelines at: http://www.catholicbookpublishing.com/faq.php#manuscript.

+CATHOLIC UNIVERSITY OF AMERICA PRESS, 240 Leahy Hall, 620 Michigan Ave. NE, Washington DC 20064. Trevor Lipscombe, dir. Mailed proposal only. Publishes in the fields of history (ecclesiastical & secular), language and litera-ture, philosophy, political theory, and theology. Guidelines at: http://cuapress.cua.edu/resources/EditorialPolicyProcedures.cfm. Photos: Accepts freelance photos for book covers.

CHALFONT HOUSE, PO Box 84, Dumfries VA 22026. (800) 728-9893. Phone & fax: (800) 728-9893. E-mail: info@chalfonthouse.com. Website: www.chalfonthouse.com. Lynellen Perry, pres. Imprint: HopeSprings Books. We are focused on publish-ing quality books that don't shy away from tough topics. Publishes 12 titles/yr.; trade paperbacks, digital. Receives 50 submissions annually. 75% of books from first-time authors. Accepts books submitted by agents or authors. No subsidy. Does print-on-demand. No reprints. Prefers 70,000-95,000 wds. **Royalty based on net; $10 advance. E-books based on net.** Publication within 12 mos. Considers simultaneous submis-sions. Guidelines on website: http://www.chalfonthouse.com/authorq.html.

> **Nonfiction:** Complete ms.; e-query OK. Accepts mss by e-mail.
>
> **Fiction:** For children, teens, new adults, adults. Complete mss. e-query.
>
> **Tips:** "In fiction, a good story is key. We look for characters who draw you in and keep you reading. We're open to discussion of topics that are often considered 'off limits,' and we enjoy transformational and reality-based fiction, because we understand that Christians aren't perfect and we don't expect fictional Christians to be either. In nonfiction, you need to have a fairly established platform, or at least a good idea of how to develop one already in place. There needs to be something unique about your proposal that sets your work apart from the other similar books out there already.

+CHALICE PRESS. Send e-query only initially to submissions@chalicepress.com. Check out this publisher's guidelines at: www.chalicepress.com/AuthorGuidelines.aspx.

CHARISMA HOUSE, 600 Rinehart Rd., Lake Mary FL 32746. (407) 333-0600. No phone calls. Fax (407) 333-7100. E-mail: creationhouse@charismamedia.com or charis-mahouse@charismamedia.com. Website: www.charismamedia.com. Communications. Submit to Acquisitions Assistant. To inspire and equip people to live a Spirit-led life and walk in the divine purpose for which they were called. This house has 8 imprints, which are listed with descriptions/details. Publishes 150 titles/yr.; hardcover, trade paper-backs, mass-market paperbacks. Receives 1,500 submissions annually. 65% of books from first-time authors. Not currently accepting unsolicited mss from new authors, agents, or published authors. Reprints books. Prefers 55,000 wds. **Royalty on net or outright purchase; advance.** Average first printing 7,500. Publication within 9 mos. Considers simultaneous submissions. Accepts requested ms on disk or on website. Responds in 4-8 wks. Guidelines by mail/e-mail/website: http://charismahouse.com/index.php/submit-book-proposal; free catalog.

Nonfiction: Proposal or complete ms; by mail or e-query OK; no phone query. Book proposal application on website. "Open to any books that are well written and glorify Jesus Christ."

Fiction: Proposal or complete ms; by mail or e-query OK; no phone query. Book proposal application on website. "For all ages. Fiction must have a biblical worldview and point the reader to Christ."

Photos: Accepts freelance photos for book covers.

Charisma House: Books on Christian living, mainly from a Charismatic/Pentecostal perspective. Topics: Christian living, work of the Holy Spirit, prophecy, prayer, Scripture, adventures in evangelism and missions, popular theology.

Siloam: Books about living in good health—body, mind, and spirit.

Topics: alternative medicine; diet and nutrition; and physical, emotional, and psychological wellness. We prefer manuscripts from certified doctors, nutritionists, trainers, and other medical professionals. Proof of credentials may be required.

Frontline: Books on contemporary political and social issues from a Christian perspective.

Creation House: Co-publishing imprint for a wide variety of Christian books. Author is required to buy a quantity of books from the first press run. This is not self-publishing or print-on-demand.

Realms: Christian fiction in the supernatural, speculative genre. Full-length adult novels, 80,000-120,000 wds. Will also consider historical or biblical fiction if supernatural element is substantial.

Excel: Publishes books that are targeted toward success in the workplace and businesses.

Casa Creación: Publishes and translates books into Spanish. (800) 987-8432. E-mail: casacreacion@charismamedia.com. Website: www.casacreacion.com.

Publicaciones Casa: Publishes the same as Creation House and is for people who like to co-publish in Spanish. Contact info same as Casa Creacion. This publisher services by ChristianManuscriptSubmissions.com and The Writer's Edge.

THE CHARLES PRESS, PUBLISHERS, 230 N. 21st St., Ste. 202, Philadelphia PA 19103-1095. (215) 561-2786. Fax: (215) 600-1248. E-mail: submissions@charles-presspub.com. Website: www.charlespresspub.com. Lauren Metzler, pub. (lauren@charlespresspub.com). Accepts submissions from Agents or authors. Accepts simultaneous submissions. Query first. Responds in 4-14 wks. Guidelines at: http://www.charlespresspub.com/submissions.html; catalog.

Nonfiction: Submit a letter of inquiry first; no fax submissions. No attachments.

+CHELSEA HOUSE, Infobase Publishing, 132 W. 31st St., 17th Fl., New York NY 10001. E-mail: editorial@factsonfile.com. Submit to Editorial Director. Infobase is parent company. Publishes curriculum-based nonfiction books for middle school and high school. Chelsea Clubhouse is their elementary imprint; presents easy-to-read, full-color books for grades 2 through 5. Guidelines at: www.infobasepublishing.com/ContactUS.aspx?Page=AuthorSubmission.

CHICKEN SOUP FOR THE SOUL BOOKS. See listing in Periodicals section.

CHOSEN BOOKS, Division of Baker Publishing Group, 3985 Bradwater St., Fairfax VA 22031-3702. (952) 829-2550. E-mail: jcampbell@chosenbooks.com. Website: http://

bakerpublishinggroup.com/chosen. Jane Campbell, editorial dir. Charismatic; Spirit-filled–life titles and a few thematic narratives. No autobiographies. No unsolicited mss, but will respond to e-mail queries. Credentials and platform vital. Guidelines at: http://bakerpublishinggroup.com/contact/submission-policy

This publisher is serviced by The Writer's Edge.

+CHRISTIAN FOCUS PUBLICATIONS, Geanies House, Fearn, Tain, Ross-shire IV20 1TW, Scotland, UK. Tel: 01862 871011. Fax: 01862 871699. E-mail: info@christianfocus.com. Includes 3 adult imprints: (1) Christian Focus contains popular works including biographies, commentaries, basic doctrine, and Christian living. (2) Mentor focuses on books written at a level suitable for Bible college and seminary students, pastors, and other serious readers; the imprint includes commentaries, doctrinal studies, examination of current issues, and church history. (3) Christian Heritage contains classic writings from the past. Also has a children's line. Submit to: submissions@christianfocus.com. Guidelines at: www.christianfocus.com/feedback/log/-/-.

CHRISTIAN HERITAGE SOCIETY, PO Box 519, Baldwin Place NY 10505. Phone/fax (914) 962-3287. E-mail: gtkurian@aol.com. George Kurian, ed. Publishes 6 titles/yr.; hardcover, trade paperbacks. Receives 100 submissions annually. 50% of books from first-time authors. Prefers mss through agents. No subsidy. Reprints books. Prefers 120,000 wds. Royalty 10-15% on net; no advance. Average first printing 10,000. Publication within 1 yr. Considers simultaneous submissions. Responds in 3 mos. Guidelines by mail; free catalog

> **Nonfiction:** Query; e-query OK. "Looking for Christian history, reference books, memoirs, devotionals, and evangelism."

CHURCHGROWTH.ORG, PO Box 763, Forest VA 24551-0763. (434) 525-0022. Fax (434) 525-0608. E-mail: info@churchgrowth.org. Website: www.ChurchGrowth.org. Ephesians Four Ministries. Cindy G. Spear, operations mngr. Providing timeless tools for Chriatian growth. Publishes 3 titles/yr.; trade paperbacks/other. Receives 20 submissions annually. 7% of books from first-time authors. No mss through agents. Prefers 64-160 pgs. **Royalties vary; 6% on retail or outright purchase; no advance.** Average first printing 100. Publication within 1 yr. Considers simultaneous submissions. Responds in 3 mos. Requires requested ms on disk or by e-mail. Guidelines at: www.churchgrowth.org. No printed catalog; full product listing on website.

> **Nonfiction:** Query; no phone/fax query; e-query OK. "We prefer our writers to be experienced in what they write about."
>
> **Special Needs:** New or unique ministries (how-to). Self-discovery and evaluation tools, such as our Spiritual Gifts Inventory and Spiritual Growth Survey, Friendship Skills Assessment.
>
> **Photos:** Rarely use freelance photos.
>
> **Tips:** "Currently concentrating on own Team Ministry/Spiritual Gifts resources and updating bestsellers. Accept very few unsolicited submissions. Most open to ministry how-to manuals for ministry leaders—something unique with a special niche. Must be practical and different from anything else on the same subject—or must be a topic/slant few others have published. May consider evaluation tools as mentioned above. No devotionals, life testimonies, commentaries, or studies on books of the Bible."

+CISTERCIAN PUBLICATIONS. E-mail: dutton@ohio.edu. Marsha L. Dutton, executive dir. Prefers a proposal. All submissions must be accompanied by a Summary

Form—available on the Website. Guidelines at: www.cistercianpublications.org/manuscript.html.

CLADACH PUBLISHING, PO Box 336144, Greeley CO 80633. (970) 371-9530. E-mail: office@cladach.com. Website: www.cladach.com. Company blog: http://cladach.wordpress.com. Independent, small Christian press. Catherine Lawton, pub/ed. (cathyl@cladach.com); Christina Slike, asst. ed. We are family owned and small enough to be entrepreneurial, to take risks on new authors and ideas. . Categories: memoirs, fiction, relationships, God in creation. Publishes 3 titles/yr.; trade paperbacks and digital. Receives 100s submissions annually. 65% of books from first-time authors. Accepts submissions through agents or authors. No subsidy, print-on-demand, or reprints. Prefers 192-272 pgs. **Royalty 5-15% on net; e-book royalty varies; $100 advance.** Average first printing 750. Publication within 9 mos. Considers simultaneous submissions. Responds in 3-6 mos. Prefers NIV, NRSV. Guidelines at: www.cladach.com/ForAuthors.html; catalog Website.

Nonfiction: Query letter only first (we're very selective); e-query OK.

Fiction: For adults. Query letter only first (1-2 pgs.); e-query OK (copied into message). For adults. "Prefers gripping stories depicting inner struggles and real-life issues; well crafted. Interested in frontier fiction set in Colorado."

Special needs: Nature writings, memoirs, and fiction.

Tips: "Read some of our titles to learn our editorial style and treatment of the topics/genres we publish. We will no longer accept unsolicited queries/proposals. We simply do not have time to read and reply to the volume of queries we receive. We will only consider queries from authors we meet at writers conferences, or when introduced through our present authors or through mutual acquaintances." Unsolicited mss are returned unopened.

+CLARKE & CO., JAMES, PO Box 60, Cambridge, CB1 2NT, United Kingdom. Fax: +44 (0)1223-366951. E-mail: publishing@jamesclarke.co.uk. Submit to Editorial by fax or e-mail. Only publishes scholarly books of nonfiction. Publishes 12 titles/yr. Include the New Proposal Form (on Website) with your proposal. Check out this publisher's guidelines at: www.jamesclarke.co/author_guidelines.php?osCsid=8273fad889796b48c7430351069f2a4a.

CLC PUBLICATIONS, 701 Pensylvania Ave., Fort Washington PA 19034. (215) 542-1242. Fax: (215) 542-7580E-mail: submissions@clcpublications.com. Website: www.clcpublications.com. Company blog: https://facebook.com/CLCPublications. CLC Ministries Intl. Erika Cobb, mng. ed.; Sherif Gendy, submissions/acquisitions coordinator. We are an evangelical publishing company that is committed to maintaining sound biblical truths, and seeks to publish works that align with this purpose and mission. The purpose of CLC is to make evangelical Christian literature available to all nations so that people may come to faith and maturity in the Lord Jesus Christ. Publishes 16 titles/yr.; hardcover, trade paperbacks, mass-market paperbacks, digital. Receives 120 submissions annually. 50% of books from first-time authors. Prefer/accepts mss through agents. No subsidy. Does print-on-demand. Reprints books. Prefers under 45,000 wds. or 150 pgs. **Royalty 12-16% of net; 14% for e-books; pays an average advance of $1,500.** Average first printing 2,000. Publication within 1 yr. Considers simultaneous submissions. Requires accepted mss on disk or by e-mail. Prefers NKJV. Guidelines by e-mail/website: www.clcpublications.com/shop/writer_guide.php; catalog free on request.deeper life.

Nonfiction: Query letter only first; proposal/2-3 chapters; or complete ms; e-query OK. Books for the deeper life.

Photos: Accepts freelance photos for book covers.

Special Needs: Looking for evangelism, discipleship, missions, parenting, marriage, biblical theology, redemptive history, Christ in all of scripture, Christians worldwide,biblical principals for running private business, prayer, family, Bible study.

Ethnic: Hispanic & black.

Tips: "We are most open to manuscripts that approach a given topic (parenting, marriage, discipleship, Evangelism, Mission, etc.) in a fresh and unique ways are of particular interest to us."

+COLLEGE PRESS PUBLISHING, PO Box 1132, 2111 N. Main St., Ste. C, Joplin MO 64801. Toll free: (800) 289-3300. Fax: (417) 623-1929. Requires a query or proposal first. Responds in 2-3 mos. Open to Bible studies, topical studies (biblically based), apologetic studies, and Sunday/Bible school curriculum (adult electives). Guidelines at: www.collegepress.com/storefront/node/239.

COMFORT PUBLISHING, 296 Church St. N, Concord NC 28027, PO Box 6265, Concord NC 28025. (704) 782-2353. Fax (704) 782-2393. Pamilla S. Tolen, President/Book Division (ptolen@comfortpublishing.com); Kristy Huddle, Director of Acquisitions & Author Relations (khuddle@comfortpublishing.com). Website: www. comfortpublishing.com. Comfort Publishing Services, LLC. Submit to Kristy Huddle by e-mail; no mailed submissions. To promote Christian literature in a manner that is easy to read and understand, with a message that either teaches a principle or supports the truth of Christian faith. Nonfiction, self-help, true stories. Publishes 10 titles/yr.; hardcover, trade paperbacks, digital. Receives 3,000 submissions annually. 65% of books from first-time authors. Prefers mss through agents; will accept from authors. No subsidy or print-on-demand. No reprints. Requires at least 80,000 wds. **Royalty 8-15% on retail; some advances; e-books 50% of net.** Average first printing 2,500. Publication within 12 mos. Considers simultaneous submissions. Responds in 18 mos. Accepts requested mss by e-mail. Guidelines by mail/e-mail/website: www.comfortpublishing. com/content/ComfortPublishing/SubmitManuscript/tabid/63/Default.aspx; digital catalog. Accepts freelance photos. Prefers NKJV.

Nonfiction: Proposal/3 chapters, or complete ms; e-query preferred.

Fiction: For teens & adults. Submit complete ms.

Special Needs: Adventure, romance, mystery romance, suspense, teen/YA fiction, adult. Not currently accepting children's picture books or poetry.

Also Does: E-books.

Photos: Accepts freelance photos for book covers.

Tips: "Desire to break away from traditional Christian literature. Readers are looking for more modern stories that deal with current dilemmas. Through our books we want to provide entertainment but also present books that represent good moral judgment within the Christian experience.

CONARI PRESS, 665 Third St., Ste. 400, San Francisco CA 94107. E-mail: submissions@rwwbooks.com. Website: www.redwheelweiser.com. An imprint of Red Wheel/Weiser, LLC. Ms. Pat Bryce, acq. ed. Inspire, literally to breathe life into. That's what Conari Press books aim to do — inspire all walks of life, mind, body, and spirit; inspire creativity, laughter, gratitude, good food, good health, and all good things in life. We publish wellness and recovery books, particularly 12-step books, books on health and eating, books especially for women, and books on spirituality, personal growth, parenting, and social issues. Books on spirituality, personal growth, parenting, and social issues.

Publishes 30 titles/yr. Responds in up to 3 mos. Guidelines and catalog on website: http://redwheelweiser.com/p.php?id=8. Incomplete topical listings.

CONCILIAR PRESS (see Ancient Faith Publishing)

CONCORDIA PUBLISHING HOUSE, 3558 S. Jefferson Ave., St. Louis MO 63118-3968. (314) 268-1080. E-mail: ed.engelbrecht@cph.org. Website: www.cph. org. Lutheran Church/Missouri Synod. Publication within 2 yrs. Responds in 6 wks. Guidelines at: http://www.cph.org/t-topic-proacabooks-manuscript.aspx.

Nonfiction: Proposal/sample chapters.

Tips: "Freelance submissions for academic publications in biblical studies are welcome. Prospective authors should consult the peer review guidelines on the website for an author prospectus and submission guidelines."

This publisher serviced by The Writer's Edge.

+CONQUEST PUBLISHERS, PO Box 611, Bladensburg MD 20710. (240) 342-3293. E-mail: Acquisitions@conquestpublishers.com. Website: www.conquestpublishers.com. Publishes nonfiction, fiction, and poetry. No reprints. Proposal by e-mail only; no complete mss. Responds in 3-4 wks. Royalties 30% of list price. Guidelines at: http://www.conquestpublishers.com/publish_with_us.

CONTEMPORARY DRAMA SERVICE, Meriwether Publishing Ltd., 885 Elkton Dr., Colorado Springs CO 80907. E-mail: editor@meriwether.com. Website: www. ChristianPlaysandMusicals.com. Publishes Christian plays for mainline churches. Also supplemental textbooks on theatrical subjects. Prefers comedy but does publish some serious works. Accepts full-length or one-act plays—comedy or musical. General and Christian. Publishes 30 plays/yr. Responds in 4-6 wks. See the Meriwether Publishing listing or website for additional details. Guidelines at: https://www.christianplaysandmusicals.com/guidelines.aspx.

DAVID C. COOK, 4050 Lee Vance View, Colorado Springs CO 80918. (719) 536-0100. Fax (719) 536-3269. Website: www.davidccook.com. Not accepting unsolicited proposals or manuscripts at this time. However, will consider proposals submitted through literary agents, as well as proposals submitted in response to select invitations extended at writers' conferences. Any unsolicited manuscripts or proposals will be returned to sender without review. We suggest for help, you go to: www.christianmanuscriptsubmissions.com.

CROSSLINK PUBLISHING, PO Box 1232, Rapid City SD 57709. Toll-free (888) 697-4851. Toll-free fax (800) 934-6762. E-mail: publisher@crosslinkpublishing.com. Website: www.crosslinkpublishing.com. CrossLink Ministries. Rick Bates, mng. ed. As a small publisher, they are very author focused, their processes are nimble, and they pride themselves on having the most transparent and participative publishing process in the industry. Imprint: New Harbor Press. Publishes 35 titles/yr.; trade paperbacks. Receives 530 submissions annually. 85% of books from first-time authors. Accepts submissions through agents. No subsidy; does print-on-demand. No reprints. Prefers 12,000-60,000 wds. **Royalty 10% of retail; 20% for E-books; no advance.** Average first printing 2,000. Publication within 4 mos. Considers simultaneous submissions. Responds within 7 days. No Bible version preferred. No catalog; guidelines on Website: www.crosslink.org/publishing.php. Requires ms submission on website.

Nonfiction: Complete ms; e-query OK.

Fiction: For adults. Complete ms.

Special Needs: Bible studies, devotional, inspirational, meditations, and spiritual growth areas.

Photos: Accepts freelance photos for book covers.

Tips: "We are particularly interested in providing books that help Christians succeed in their daily walk (inspirational, devotional, small groups, etc.)." This publisher serviced by The Writer's Edge.

+CROSSRIVER MEDIA GROUP, PO Box 187, Brewster KS 67732. (785)269-4730. E-mail: info@crossrivermedia.com. Website: www.crossrivermedia.com. Tamara Clymer, fiction ed.; Debra L. Butterfield, nonfiction ed. Imprints: CrossRiver; CrossRiver Kids. Publishes 5 title/yr.; trade paperbacks & digital. Receives 60 submissions annually. 75% of books from first-time authors. Prefers/accepts submissions through agents. No subsidy. Does print-on-demand. No reprints. **Royalty negotiable; no advance.** Average first printing 200. Publication within 18 mos. Considers simultaneous submissions. Two submissions periods with deadlines of June 30 and December 31. Response sent within two months after deadline. Free catalog; digital copy on Website. Nonfiction only.

+CROSSROAD PUBLISHING. E-mail: submissions@crossroadpublishing.com. Website: www.crossroadpublishing.com. Open to unsolicited proposals; e-mail submissions only. Responds in 6-8 wks. Accepts submissions from agents or authors. Accepts simultaneous submissions. **Pays royalties; no advance.** Guidelines at: http://www.crossroadpublishing.com/crossroad/static/for-authors.

CROSSWAY, 1300 Crescent St., Wheaton IL 60187. (630) 682-4300. Fax (630) 682-4785. E-mail: submissions@crossway.org. Website: www.crossway.org. Company blog: www.crossway.org/blog. A publishing ministry of Good News Publishers. Justin Taylor, sr. vp for book publishing; submit to Jill Carter, editorial administrator, or www.submissions.org. Publishes books that combine the truth of God's Word with a passion to live it out, with unique and compelling Christian content. Publishes 80 titles/yr.; hardcover, trade paperbacks. Receives 1,000 submissions annually. 2% of books from first-time authors. Accepts mss through agents or authors. No subsidy, no reprints, no print-on-demand. Prefers 25,000 wds. & up. **Royalty on net; 25% for e-books; advance varies.** Average first printing 7,500. Publication within 18 mos. No simultaneous submissions. Responds in 6-8 wks. Prefers ESV. Guidelines at: http://www.crossway.org/contact/submissions; free catalog.

Nonfiction: Query letter only first. Accepts e-mail and snail mail queries

Also Does: Tracts (Good News Publishers).

This publisher serviced by ChristianManuscriptSubmissions.com and The Writer's Edge.

CSS PUBLISHING GROUP INC., 5450 N. Dixie Hwy., Lima OH 45807-9559. (419) 227-1818. Fax (419) 228-9184. E-mail: david@csspub.com. Website: www.csspub.com. Missy Cotrell, mng. ed. Serves the needs of pastors, worship leaders, and parish program planners in the broad Christian mainline of the American church. Imprints: Fairway Press (subsidy—see separate listing); B.O.D. (Books On Demand); FaithWalk Publishing. Publishes 15 titles/yr.; trade paperbacks, digital. Receives 500-1,000 submissions annually. 50% of books from first-time authors. Subsidy publishes 50-60% through Fairway Press; does print-on-demand. Reprints books. Prefers 100-125 pgs. **No royalty or advance.** Average first printing 1,000. Publication within 12-24 mos. Considers simultaneous submissions. Responds in 3 wks. to 3 mos.; final decision within 12 mos. Requires requested ms on disk and in hard copy. Prefers NRSV. Guidelines by e-mail/website: https://store.csspub.com/page.php?Custom%20Pages=10; no catalog.

Nonfiction: Query or proposal/3 chapters; phone/e-query OK; complete ms for short works. "Looking for pastoral resources for ministry; lectionary sermons. Our material is practical in nature."

Fiction: Complete ms. Easy-to-perform dramas and pageants for all age groups. "Our drama interest primarily includes Advent, Christmas, Epiphany, Lent, and Easter. We do not publish long plays." Subsidy-only for fiction.

Tips: "We're looking for authors who will help with the marketing of their books."

DAWN PUBLICATIONS, 12402 Bitney Springs Rd., Nevada City CA 95959. (530) 274-7775. Fax (530) 274-7778. E-mail: submission@dawnpub.com. Website: www. dawnpub.com. Muffy Weaver, acq. ed. Dedicated to inspiring in children a sense of appreciation for all of life on earth; creative nonfiction. Publishes 6 titles/yr.; hardcover, trade paperbacks. Most publications are picture books, but they do some chapter books for middle school readers. Receives 2,500 submissions annually. 35% of titles are by new authors. Accepts mss through agents or authors. Submit by mail or e-mail. No reprints. **Royalty on net; pays an advance.** Publication within 1-2 yrs. Considers simultaneous submissions. Responds in 2 mos. Guidelines/catalog on website: www.dawnpub.com/submission-guidelines.

Nonfiction: Complete manuscript by mail or e-mail.

Artwork: Open to queries from freelance artists (send sample c/o Muffy Weaver).

Tips: "Most open to creative nonfiction. We look for nature awareness and appreciation titles that promote a relationship with the natural world and specific habitats, usually through inspiring treatment and nonfiction."

DESERT BREEZE PUBLISHING, E-mail: submissions@desertbreezepublishing. com. Website: www.desertbreezepublishing.com. Gail Delaney, ed. Publishes romance fiction in a variety of sub-genres, and women's fiction, with or without romance. Also Christian romance and Christian women's fiction; and a variety of YA and new adult fiction. Novellas 25,000-35,000 (prefers 30,000); super books over 100,000 wds. Prefers 55,000-80,000 wds. Will accepts queries or series. No simultaneous submissions; accepts reprints. Release 9-12 titles/mo. Guidelines at: http://www.desertbreezepublishing.com/submissions; catalog online.

Fiction: See guidelines. Now accepting women's fiction with either secondary or no romantic elements required.

Special Needs: Seeking single-title works in all sub-genres. Will consider series. See guidelines for other specific genres.

Tips: "If you have questions about the guidelines, e-mail us at submissionsquestions@desertbreezepublishing.com."

DISCOVERY HOUSE PUBLISHERS, PO Box 3566, Grand Rapids MI 49501. Toll-free (800) 653-8333. (616) 942-9218. Fax (616) 974-2224. E-mail: dhptc@rbc. org. Website: www.dhp.org. Our Daily Bread Ministries. Carol Holquist, pub.; Andrew Rogers, acq. ed. Publishes nonfiction books that feed the soul with the word of God. Publishes 14 titles/yr.; hardcover, trade paperbacks, mass-market paperbacks, digital. Receives 300 submissions annually. 10% of books from first-time authors. Accepts mss through agents or authors. No subsidy or print-on-demand. Reprints books. **Royalty 10-15% on net; no advance.** Publication within 12-18 mos. Considers simultaneous submissions. Responds in 4-6 wks. Guidelines at: https://dhp.org/author-guidelines (FAQ#4); free catalog.

Nonfiction: Proposal/sample chapters; accepts e-mail & snail mail queries. If by e-mail, "Attn: Ms Review Editor" in subject line.

This publisher serviced by ChristianManuscriptSubmissions.com and The Writer's Edge.

+DISCUS PUBLISHING. Currently closed to submissions, but plans to reopen soon. Check guidelines for current status: www.diskuspublishing.com/submission.htm.

DOUBLEDAY RELIGIOUS PUBLISHING, 1745 Broadway, New York NY 10019. (212) 782-9000. Fax (212) 782-8338. Website: www.randomhouse.com. Imprint of Random House, Inc. Imprints: Image, Galilee, New Jerusalem Bible, Three Leaves Press, Anchor Bible Commentaries, Anchor Bible Reference Library. Publishes 45-50 titles/yr.; hardcover, trade paperbacks. Receives 1,500 submissions annually. 10% of books from first-time authors. Requires mss through agents. Reprints books. **Royalty 7.5-15% on retail; pays an advance.** Average first printing varies. Publication within 8 mos. Considers simultaneous submissions. Responds in 4 mos. No disk. Guidelines at: www.randomhouse.biz/manuscripts ; catalog for 9 x 12 SASE/3 stamps.

Nonfiction: Agented submissions only. Proposal/3 chapters; no phone query.

Fiction: Religious fiction. Agented submissions only.

Ethnic Books: African American; Hispanic.

Tips: "Most open to a book that has a big and well-defined audience. Have a clear proposal, lucid thesis, and specified audience.

This publisher serviced by ChristianManuscriptSubmissions.com.

+DOULOS RESOURCES, PO Box 69485, Oro Valley AZ 85737. (901) 201-4612. Fax: (801) 605-4612. E-mail: info@doulosresources.org. Website: www.doulosresources.org. Requires an e-mail or e-query first to submissions@doulosresources.org. No attachments. Guidelines at: http://www.doulosresources.org/about/about/submissions.html.

DOVE INSPIRATIONAL PRESS, 1000 Burmaster St., Gretna LA 70053. (504) 368-1175. Fax (504) 368-1195. E-mail: editorial@pelicanpub.com. Website: www.pelicanpub.com. Nina Kooij, ed-in-chief. To publish books of quality and permanence that enrich the lives of those who read them. Imprint of Pelican Pub.—R . Publishes 1 title/yr.; hardcover, trade paperbacks. Receives 250 submissions annually. No books from first-time authors. Accepts mss through agents or authors. Reprints books. Prefers 200+ pgs. **Royalty; some advances.** Publication within 9-18 mos. No simultaneous submissions. Responds in 1 mo. on queries. Requires accepted ms on disk. Prefers KJV. Guidelines at: http://www.pelicanpub.com/viewer.php?region=92.

Nonfiction: Proposal/2 chapters; no phone/fax/e-query.

Fiction: Children's picture books only.

Artwork: Open to queries from freelance artists.

+DOVER PUBLICATIONS, 31 E. 2nd St., Mineola NY 11501-3852. Fax: (516) 742-6953. No e-mail submissions. Check out this publisher's guidelines at: http://www.doverpublications.com/faq/contacting-dover#EDITSUB.

EARTHEN VESSEL PUBLISHING, 9 Sunny Oaks Dr., San Raphael CA 94903. (415) 302-1199. E-mail: kentphilpott@comcast.net. Website: www.earthenvesseljournal.com Evangelical/Baptist/ABC & SBC dually aligned. Kent & Katie Philpott, eds. We focus on presenting the message of Jesus to non-Christians, and the Scripture to Christians. Imprint: Siloam Springs Press. Publishes 4 titles/yr.; trade paperback & digital. Receives 30 submissions annually. 50% of books from first-time authors. No subsidy; does print-on-demand. Accepts mss through agents or authors. Reprints books. Prefers 100-300 pgs. **Royalty 50% of retail price; e-books 50%; no advance.**

Average first printing varies. Publication time varies. Considers simultaneous submissions. Response time varies. Any version. Guidelines by e-mail; no catalog.

Nonfiction: Proposal/sample chapters; accepts e-mail or snail-mail queries.

Fiction: Proposal/sample chapters. For children, teens, new adults, and adults.

Special Needs: Edgy topics that appeal to youngish non-Christians.

Also does: E-books & mini-books.

Photos/Artwork: Accepts freelance photos for book covers; open to queries from freelance artists.

Tips: "Well-written and edited work is best. Not able to do major rewriting or editing. Lean toward, but not exclusively, Reformed thought. Our goal is to present the gospel to unbelievers and the Scriptures to believers. We are small and can do very little, but we look forward to working with the print-on-demand format."

+ECS MINISTRIES, PO Box 1028, Dubuque IA 52004-1028. (563) 585-2070. Fax: (563) 585-1660. E-mail: ecsorders@ecsministries.org. Website: www.ecsministries.org. Contact: Mark Wainwright. ECS Ministries is the largest publisher of correspondence Bible study courses, with around 1.4 million distributed each year across the world.

EERDMANS BOOKS FOR YOUNG READERS, 2140 Oak Industrial Dr. N.E., Grand Rapids MI 49505. Toll-free (800) 253-7521. (616) 459-4591. Fax (616) 742-6117. E-mail: youngreaders@eerdmans.com or info@eerdmans.com. Website: www.eerdmans.com/youngreaders. Company blog: www.eerdword.wordpress.com. Wm. B. Eerdmans Publishing. Kathleen Merz, mng. ed. Strives to publish books that are honest, wise, and hopeful—books that will stand the test of time. Publishes 2-5 titles/yr.; hardcover, trade paperbacks, digital. Receives 2,000-3,000 submissions annually. 10% of books from first-time authors. Accepts mss through agents or authors. No subsidy or print-on-demand. Picture books 1,000 wds.; middle-grade books 15,000 wds.; yg. adult 35,000 wds. **Royalty 5-7% on retail; 7-9% on net; advance varies.** Average first printing varies. Publication within 1 year for novels, 2-3 years for picture books. Considers simultaneous submissions. Responds in 3-4 mos., if interested. Free catalog; guidelines by e-mail or on Website: http://www.eerdmans.com/Pages/YoungReaders/EBYR-Guidelines.aspx.

Fiction: For children and teens. Proposal/3 chapters for book length; complete ms for picture books. No e-mail or fax submissions.

Looking for: Stories that celebrate diversity, stories of historical significance, and stories that relate to contemporary social issues are of interest to us at this time.

Also does: Board games.

Artwork: Please do not send illustrations with picture-book manuscripts unless you are a professional illustrator. When submitting artwork, send color copies, not originals. Send illustrations sample to art director.

Tips: "We are always looking for well-written picture books and novels for young readers. Make sure that your submission is a unique, well-crafted story, and take a look at our current list of titles to get a sense of whether yours would be a good fit for us."

*WM. B. EERDMANS PUBLISHING CO., 2140 Oak Industrial Dr. N.E., Grand Rapids MI 49505. Toll-free (800) 253-7521. (616) 459-4591. Fax (616) 459-6540. E-mail: info@eerdmans.com. Website: www.eerdmans.com. Protestant/Academic/Theological. Jon Pott, ed-in-chief. Imprint: Eerdmans Books for Young Readers (see separate listing). Publishes 120-130 titles/yr.; hardcover, trade paperbacks. Receives 3,000-4,000 submissions annually. 10% of books from first-time authors. Accepts mss through agents or authors. Reprints books. **Royalty; occasional advance.** Average first printing 4,000. Publication within 1 yr. Considers simultaneous submissions. Responds in 4 wks. to query; several months for mss. Guidelines by mail/website (www.eerdmans. com/submit.htm); free catalog.

> **Nonfiction:** Proposal/2-3 chapters; no fax/e-query. "Looking for religious approaches to contemporary issues, spiritual growth, scholarly works."
> **Fiction:** Proposal/chapter; no fax/e-query. For all ages. "We are looking for adult novels with high literary merit."
> **Tips:** "Most open to material with general appeal, but well-researched, cutting-edge material that bridges the gap between evangelical and mainline worlds. Please include e-mail and/or SASE for a response."

+ELDRIDGE CHRISTIAN PLAYS AND MUSICALS. E-mail: NewWorks@ histage.com. Open to plays or musical suitable for performance by community theaters and junior and senior high schools. Minimum running time: 30 minutes. Let them know if it's a simultaneous submission. Requires e-mail submissions. **Royalty 50%, 10% of copy sales; paid 2X/yr.** Responds in 8 wks. Guidelines at: http://www.histage. com/guidelines.pdf.

+ELLECHOR PUBLISHING HOUSE, LLC, 2373 NW 185th Ave., #510, Hillsboro OR 97124. (559)744-3553. E-mail: rcarter@ellechorpublishing.com. Website: www. ellechorpublishinghouse.com. Veronika Walker, managing ed.; Sharon Jenkins, acq. ed. Imprints: Ellechor Publishing House, Ellechor eBooks & Co. Publishes 15 title/yr. Receives 250 submissions annually. 90% of books from first-time authors. Accepts submissions through agents. No subsidy or POD. Publishes trade paperbacks & digital. No reprints. Prefers 65,000 wds. or 280 pgs. **Royalty 10-30% on net; 30-50% for ebooks; no advance.** Average first printing 1,200. Publication within one year. Considers simultaneous submissions. Free catalog on request. Prefers KJV. Guidelines on Website.

> **Nonfiction:** Complete ms.
> **Fiction:** For teens, new adults, and adults. Complete ms.
> **Photos/Artwork:** Accepts photos for book covers; open to queries from freelance artists.
> **Contest:** An annual Avant-Gard Manuscript Award for unpublished fiction. Entry details on Website.
> **Tips:** "Looking for Christian romantic mystery, and Christian business."

+EMMAUS ROAD PUBLISHING. Not currently accepting submissions. Check guidelines at: http://www.emmausroad.org/SubmissionGuidelines.aspx.

EVERGREEN PRESS, 5601-D Nevius Rd., Mobile AL 36619.(251) 861-2525. Fax: (251) 287-2222. E-mail: jeff@evergreen777.com. Website: www.evergreenpress.com. Genesis Communications. Jeff Banashak, pres.; Brian Banashak & Kathy Banashak, ed-in-chief. Publishes books that empower people for breakthrough living by being practical, biblical, and engaging. Imprints: Evergreen Press, Gazelle Press, Axiom Press (print-on-demand). Publishes 30 titles/yr. Receives 250 submissions annually. 40% of books from first-time authors. Accepts mss through agents or authors. Subsidy publishes 35%. Does print-on-demand. Prefers 96-160 pgs. **Royalty on net; no advance.** Average first printing 4,000. Publication within 6 mos. Considers simultaneous submissions. Requires requested ms on disk or by e-mail. Responds in 4-6 wks. Guidelines at: www.evergreenpress.com/new-guidelines.htm; free catalog.

> **Nonfiction:** Complete ms; fax/e-query OK. Submission form on website.
> **Fiction:** For all ages. Complete ms; phone/fax/e-query OK. Submission form on website.

Special Needs: Business, finance, personal growth, women's issues, family/ parenting, relationships, prayer, humor, and angels.
Also Does: Booklets.
Tips: "Most open to books with a specific market (targeted, not general) that the author is qualified to write for and that is relevant to today's believers and seekers. Author must also be open to editorial direction."

+FACTS ON FILE. Infobase Publishing, 132 W. 31st St., 17th Fl., New York NY 10001. E-mail: editorial@factsonfile.com. Submit to Editorial Director. Infobase is parent company. Publishes curriculum-based nonfiction books for middle school and high school. Chelsea Clubhouse if their elementary imprint; presents easy-to-read, full-color books for grades 2 through 5. Guidelines at: www.infobasepublishing.com/ContactUS. aspx?Page=AuthorSubmission.

+FAITH ALIVE CHRISTIAN RESOURCES, 1700 - 28th St. SE, Grand Rapids MI 49508-1407. E-mail: rvanderhart@crcna.org. Ruth Vanderhart, mng. ed. Publishes educational curricula for children, teens, and adults; Bible studies; church leadership and training materials; books. Mailed or e-mailed submissions. Responds in 1 mo. Check out this publisher's guidelines at: www.faithaliveresources.org/Pages/About/ Submission_Guidelines.aspx.

+FAITHWALK PUBLISHING, 5450 N. Dixie Hwy., Lima OH 45807. (419) 227-1818. Fax: (419) 228-9184. E-mail: submissions@faithwalkpub.com. Send a short e-mail initially, no attachments. Responds only if interested. Guidelines at: www.faith-walkpub.com/contentdetail.php?contentID=12.

FAITHWORDS/HACHETTE BOOK GROUP, 10 Cadillac Dr., Ste. 220, Brentwood TN 37027. (615) 221-0996, ext. 221. Fax (615) 221-0962. Website: www. faithwords.com. Hachette Book Group USA. Not able to consider unsolicited manuscripts or unsolicited queries.
    This publisher serviced by ChristianManuscriptSubmissions.com.

+FATHER'S PRESS, Pleasant Hill, MO. (816) 987-0045. E-mail: mike@fatherspress. com. Mike Smitley, ed. Publishes contemporary and historical fiction; and nonfiction. Accepts mss only through authors (no agents). E-mail submissions. Guidelines at: http://fatherspress.com/?page_id=2380
    Also does: E-books.

FOCUS ON THE FAMILY BOOK PUBLISHING AND RESOURCE DEVEL-OPMENT, (street address not required), Colorado Springs CO 80995. (719) 531-3400. Fax (719) 531-3448. E-mail through website: www.focusonthefamily.com. Not currently accepting unsolicited submissions. Check guidelines for current status: http:// family.custhelp.com/app/answers/detail/a_id/487/session/L3RpbWUvMTM5MDc2 NDkzNS9zaWQveHNPeUFtTGw%3D; no catalog.
    This publisher serviced by ChristianManuscriptSubmissions.com and The Writer's Edge.

+FORDHAM UNIVERSITY PRESS, 2546 Belmost Ave., University Box L, Bronx NY 10458. Fredric Nachbaur, dir. Publishes scholarly books in the humanities and social sciences, as ell as trade books of interest to the general public. Accepts hard copy proposals; no e-mail submissions. Responds in 6 wks. Guidelines at: http://fordham-press.com/index.php/resources?id=1.

+FORTRESS PRESS, PO Box 1209, Minneapolis MN 55440-1209. Online submissions form. Publishes academic topics: Bible, theology, and Christian history. Guidelines at: http://fortresspress.com/contactus/submitfp.jsp.

+FORWARD MOVEMENT, 412 Sycamore St., Cincinnati OH 45202-4110. Toll free: (800) 543-1813. E-mail: editorial@forwardmovement.org. Episcopal Church. Submit through e-mail. Responds in 4-6 wks.Check out this publisher's guidelines at: http://www.forwardmovement.org/Pages/About/Writers_Guidelines.aspx.

+FOUR CRAFTSMEN PUBLISHING, PO Box U, 1293 W. Apache Ln., Lakeside AZ 85929-0585. (928) 367-2076. Fax: (928) 367-5223. E-mail: info@fourcraftsmen. com. Martin Jackson, ed. Believes the truth of scripture in real life, and seeks to publish material the big houses may overlook. Publishes 2 title/yr.; hardcovers, trade paperbacks. Receives 2 submissions annually. 100% of books from first-time authors. Accepts submissions through agents. Subsidy publishes 5%. Does print-on-demand. Reprints books. Prefers 40,000-80,000 wds. **Royalty 10-50% of retail; no advance.** Average first printing 500. Publication within 3 mos. No simultaneous submissions. Reports within 2 wks. Prefers NASU, NKJV, CEB. Free catalog; guidelines at: www.fourcraftsmen. com/author%20info.htm.

> **Nonfiction:** Book proposal/sample chapters. Accepts snail mail or e-mail queries.
> **Also does:** Booklets, Mini-books.
> **Photos/Artwork:** Accepts freelance photos for book covers; open to queries from freelance artists.
> **Special needs:** "Looking for: ministering to victims of idols on the heart; explanation of idols on the heart; and testimony, which need not be dramatic, but deal with heart issues."
> **Tips:** "Most open to to realistic dependence on the grace of God, so that Jesus is glorified. Please do not shy away from the Bible, but avoid long quotations and quotations from others' works still in copyright."

FRANCISCAN MEDIA (formerly St. Anthony Messenger Press) 28 West Liberty Street, Cincinnati OH 45202. Toll-free (800) 488-0488; (513) 241-5615 (ext. 162). Fax (513) 241-0399. Website: www.FranciscanMedia.org. Submit to Mary Carol McKendzia, Directors of Product Development, at MCKendzia@FranciscanMedia. org. Book proposal form on Website. Seeks mss that inform and inspire adult Catholic Christians, that identify trends surfacing in the Catholic world, and that help Catholics and those who want to be Catholic, understand their faith better. Publishes 20-30 titles/ yr; trade paperbacks (mostly). Receives 450 submissions annually. 5% of books from first-time authors. Accepts mss through agents or authors. Reprints books (seldom). Prefers 25,000-50,000 wds or 100-250 pgs. **Royalty 10-14% on net; advance $1,000-3,000.** Average first printing 4,000. Publication within 18 mos. Discourages simultaneous submissions. Accepts requested mss by e-mail. Responds in 60 days. Prefers NRSV. Catalog for 9 x 12 SAE/4 stamps. Nonfiction: proposal/outline/1-2 chapters; fax/e-query OK. Publishes for those who want to connect to the world around them in the context of the Catholic faith and for those who minister to adult Catholics in the parish and in religious institutions and schools. Catalog.FranciscanMedia.org/ FranciscanMediaBooks. Guidelines at: http://www.americancatholic.org/ContactUS/ FranciscanMediaBooksGuidelines.aspx.

> **Nonfiction:** proposal/outline/1-2 chapters; fax/e-query OK.
> This publisher serviced by The Writer's Edge.

+FRIENDS UNITED PRESS, 101 Quaker Hill Dr., Richmond IN 47374. (765)

962-7573. Fax: (765) 966-1293. E-mail: friendspress@fum.org. Open to Quaker/ Friends history, theology, biography, spirituality, peace and justice. Proposal by mail or e-mail; responds in 3-6 mos. Publishes 2-5 bks./yr. **Royalty 7 1/2%; no advance.** Guidelines at: http://shop.fum.org/category_s/38.htm.

+GEORGETOWN UNIVERSITY PRESS, 3240 Prospect St. NW, Ste. 250, Washington DC 20007. (202) 687-5889. Fax: (202) 687-6340. E-mail: gls@george-town.edu, or gupress@georgetown.edu. Website: www.georgetown.edu. Glen Saltzman, editorial & production mngr. Submissions form on Website. Check out this publisher's guidelines at: http://press.georgetown.edu/georgetown/our-authors/guidelines.

*GOSPEL LIGHT, 1957 Eastman Ave., Ventura CA 93003. Toll-free (800) 4-GOSPEL. (805) 644-9721, ext. 1223. Website: www.gospellight.com. Submit to: The Editor. Accepts proposals for Sunday school and Vacation Bible School curriculum and related resources for children from birth through the preteen years; also teacher resources.

>   **Also Does:** Sometimes has openings for readers of new curriculum projects. See website for how to apply.
>   **Tips:** "All our curriculum is written and field-tested by experienced teachers; most of our writers are on staff."
>   This publisher serviced by ChristianManuscriptSubmissions.com.

GRACE PUBLISHING, PO Box 1233, Broken Arrow OK 74013-1233. (918) 346-7960. E-mail: editorial@grace-publishing.com. Website: www.grace-publishing.com. Submit to Acquisitions. Founded with the intent to develop and distribute—with integrity and excellence—biblically-based resources that challenge, encourage, teach, equip, and entertain Christians young and old in their personal journeys. Publishes 5-10 titles/yr.; trade paperbacks, digital. Receives 250 submissions/yr. 50% first-time authors. Accepts submission through agents or authors. Does print-on-demand. Reprints books. Preferred book length 40,000 wds; 160 pages. **Royalty 12-15% on net; e-books 25%; no advance.** Outright purchase varies. First run varies. Publication within 6 mos. Considers simultaneous submissions. Responds to freelance submissions in 16 wks. Guidelines at: Grace Publishing – http://grace-publishing.com/manuscript-submission; no catalog. Preferred Bible version NIV.

>   **Nonfiction:** Query letter only first. Proposal with 3 sample chapters. Complete manuscript. Accepts E-mail or snail mail queries.
>   **Fiction:** For teens, new adults, adults. Query letter only first. Book proposal with 3 sample chapters. Complete manuscript by e-mail.
>   **Also does:** Booklets, mini books, pamphlets,
>   **Artwork:** Open to queries from freelance artists.
>   **Tips:** "Well written with a unique approach. Our intent is to make Christian authors and their works easily accessible to the Christian body around the world in every form of media possible; to develop and distribute—with integrity and excellence—biblically-based resources that challenge, encourage, teach, equip, and entertain Christians young and old in their personal journeys."

GROUP PUBLISHING INC., Attn: Submissions, 1515 Cascade Ave., Loveland CO 80538. Toll-free (800) 447-1070. (970) 669-3836. Fax (970) 292-4374. E-mail: PuorgBus@group.com. Website: www.group.com. Nondenominational. We create experiences that help people grow in relationship with Jesus and each other. Imprint: Group Books. To equip churches to help children, youth, and adults grow in their relationship with Jesus. Publishes 60 titles/yr.; trade paperbacks, digital. Receives 200+ submissions annually. 50% of books from first-time authors. Accepts mss through agents or authors. No subsidy. Does print-on-demand. No reprints. Prefers 128-250 pgs. **Outright purchases of $25-3,000 or royalty of 8-10% of net; advance $3,000.** Average first printing 5,000. Publication within 12-18 mos. Considers simultaneous submissions. Responds in up to 3 mos. Prefers NLT. Guidelines at: http://www.group.com/customer-support/submissions; no catalog.

   Nonfiction: Proposal/sample chapters; e-query & snail-mail query OK. "Looking for practical ministry tools for youth workers, C.E. directors, and teachers with an emphasis on active learning."

   Artwork: Open to queries from freelance artists.

   Tips: "Most open to a practical resource that will help church leaders change lives; innovative, active/interactive learning. Tell our readers something they don't already know, in a way that they've not seen before."

   This publisher serviced by The Writer's Edge.

GUARDIAN ANGEL PUBLISHING INC., 12430 Tesson Ferry Rd., #186, St. Louis MO 63128. (314) 276-8482. E-mail: editorial_staff@guardianangelpublishing.com. Website: www.guardianangelpublishing.com. Lynda S. Burch, pub. Goal is to inspire children to learn and grow and develop character skills to instill a Christian and healthy attitude of learning, caring, and sharing. Imprints: Wings of Faith, Angel to Angel, Angelic Harmony, Littlest Angels, Academic Wings, Guardian Angel Animals & Pets, Spanish Editions, Guardian Angel Health & Hygiene. Publishes 60-75 titles/yr.; trade paperbacks, some hardcover. Receives 600-800 submissions annually. 15% of books from first-time authors. No subsidy; does print-on-demand. Prefers 500-5,000 wds. or 32 pgs. **Royalty 30-50%; no advance.** Average first printing 50-100. Print books are wholesale and worldwide distributed; e-books are sold through many distribution networks. Publication within 24 mos. No simultaneous submissions. Responds in 1 wk.-1 mo. Accepted mss by e-mail only. Guidelines at: http://www.guardianangel-publishing.com/submissions.htm; catalog as e-book PDF. Submissions are only open June 1 to August 31, 2015.

   Nonfiction: Complete ms; no phone/fax query; e-query OK. "Looking for all kinds of kids' books."

   Fiction: Complete ms; no phone/fax query; e-query OK.

   Also Does: E-books.

   Photos/Artwork: Accepts freelance photos for book covers; open to queries from freelance artists.

   Contest: Sponsors children's writing contest for schools.

   Tips: "Most open to books that teach children to read and love books; to learn or grow from books, and educational."

GUIDEPOSTS BOOKS, 110 William St., Rm. 901, New York NY 10038. (212) 251-8100. E-mail: bookeditors@guideposts.org. Website: www.guideposts.org. "Discovering God's presence in our everyday lives." Keren Baltzer, Tarice Gray, nonfiction eds.; Jessica Barnes, Jon Woodhams, Susan Downs, fiction eds. Guidelines at: www.guideposts.org

   Nonfiction: Inspirational memoir and Christian living.

   Fiction: Contemporary women's fiction focusing on faith, family, and friendships.

   Tips: Extremely limited acquisitions. Accepts mss through agents only. Publishes 20-30 titles/yr.

HANNIBAL BOOKS, 313 S. 11th Street, Suite A, Garland TX 75040. Toll-free (800) 747-0738. Toll-free fax (888) 252-3022. E-mail: hannibalbooks@earthlink.net.

Website: www.hannibalbooks.com. KLMK Communications Inc. Louis Moore, pub. Evangelical Christian publisher specializing in missions, marriage and family, critical issues, and Bible-study curriculum. Not currently accepting new book-proposal submissions.

HARBOURLIGHT BOOKS, PO Box 1738, Aztec NM 87410. E-mail: inquiry@ harbourlightbooks.com. Website: www.pelicanbookgroup.com. Division of Pelican Ventures, LLC. Nicola Martinez, editor-in-chief. Christian fiction 25,000-80,000 wds. Limited-edition hardback, trade paperbacks, and e-book. **Royalty 40% on download; 7% on print.** Pays nominal advance. Accepts unagented submissions. Responds to queries in 30 days, full ms in 90 days. Considers reprints but accepts few. E-mail submissions only; see website for submission form and procedure: http://pelicanbookgroup. com/ec/index.php?main_page=page&id=55&zenid=06f25d411f1d61bfa008693b5b2 46c4.

Fiction: Query via submission form on website. Interested in series ideas.

*HARPERONE, 353 Sacramento St., #500, San Francisco CA 94111-3653. (415) 477-4400. Fax (415) 477-4444. E-mail: hcsanfrancisco@harpercollins.com. Website: www.harpercollins.com. Religious division of HarperCollins. Strives to be the preeminent publisher of the most important books across the full spectrum of religion and spiritual literature, adding to the wealth of the world's wisdom by respecting all traditions and favoring none; emphasis on quality Christian spirituality nonfiction. Publishes 75 titles/yr.; hardcover, trade paperbacks. Receives 10,000 submissions annually. 5% of books from first-time authors. Requires mss through agents. No reprints. Prefers 160-256 pgs. **Royalty 7.5-15% on retail; advance $20,000-100,000.** Average first printing 10,000. Publication within 18 mos. Considers simultaneous submissions. Responds in 3 mos. Requires requested ms on disk. Guidelines at: http://corporate. harpercollins.com/us/for-authors/submit-a-manuscript; catalog.

Nonfiction: Proposal and one sample chapter; fax query OK
Fiction: Does not publish, as a rule.
Tips: "Agented proposals only."

HARRISON HOUSE PUBLISHERS, Box 35035, Tulsa OK 74153. Toll-free (800) 888-4126. (918) 523-5400. Website: www.harrisonhouse.com. Evangelical/charismatic. Guidelines at: http://www.harrisonhouse.com/client/client_pages/publishing.cfm; no catalog. Not currently accepting any proposals or manuscripts.

This publisher serviced by ChristianManuscriptSubmissions.com.

HARVEST HOUSE PUBLISHERS, 990 Owen Loop North, Eugene, OR 97402-9173. Toll-free (800) 547-897. Website: http://harvesthousepublishers.com. No longer accepting unsolicited submissions. Requires submissions through agents.

This publisher serviced by C484hristianManuscriptSubmissions.com.

HAY HOUSE INC., PO Box 5100, Carlsbad CA 92018-5100. (760) 431-7695. E-mail: editorial@hayhouse.com. Website: www.hayhouse.com. Alex Freemon, submissions ed. Books to help heal the planet. Accepts submissions only through agents.

+HEALTH COMMUNICATIONS, Attention Editorial Committee, 3201 SW 15th St., Deerfield Beach FL 33442. Toll free: (800) 441-5569. (954) 360-0909. Fax: (954) 360-0034. E-mail: editorial@hcibooks.com. Accepts submission through agents or authors. Responds in up to 6 mos. Accepts proposals by e-mail. Check out this publisher's guidelines at: http://www.hcibooks.com/t-submission_guidelines.aspx.

+HEART OF WISDOM PUBLISHING, 200 Coble Rd., Shelbyville TN 37160. Website: www.heartofwisdom.com. Home school resources.

+HEARTSONG PRESENTS/MYSTERIES. Accepts submissions through agents only. Check out this publisher's guidelines at: http://www.barbourbooks.com/pages/contactus_FAQ.aspx?Tab=ContactUs#16 (scroll down).

+HEARTSPRING PUBLISHING, 2111 N. Main St., Joplin MO 64801. Toll free: (800) 289-3300. Fax: (417) 623-1929. Imprint of College Press. Check this publisher's guidelines at: http://www.collegepress.com/storefront/authors.

+HIDDEN BROOK PRESS, 109 Bayshore Rd., Brighton ON Canada K0K 1H0. (905) 376-9106. E-mail: writers@hiddenbrookpress.com. Author is responsible for having the ms edited before submitting. Guidelines at: http://www.hiddenbrookpress.com/HBP.html (scroll to bottom).

HOPE PUBLISHING HOUSE, PO Box 60008, Pasadena CA 91106. (626) 792-6123. Fax (626) 792-2121. E-mail: hopepublishinghouse@gmail.com. Website: www.hope-pub.com. Southern California Ecumenical Council. Faith A. Sand, pub. Produces thinking books that challenge the faith community to be serious about their pilgrimage of faith. Imprint: New Paradigm Books. Publishes 6 titles/yr. Receives 40 submissions annually. 30% of books from first-time authors. No mss through agents. Reprints books. Prefers 200 pgs. **Royalty 10% on net; no advance.** Average first printing 3,000. Publication within 6 mos. No simultaneous submissions. Accepts mss by disk or e-mail. Responds in 3 mos. Prefers NRSV. Guidelines at: www.hope-pub.com; catalog for 7 x 10 SAE/4 stamps.

    Nonfiction: Query only first; no phone/fax query; e-query OK.

    Tips: "Most open to a well-written manuscript, with correct grammar, that is provocative, original, challenging, and informative."

+HOURGLASS BOOKS, 387 Northgate Rd., Lindenhurst IL 60047. E-mail: editor@hourglassbooks.org. Website: www.hourglassbooks.org. Publishes anthologies of short stories around a common theme; literary fiction only. E-mail submissions, copied into message. Accepts simultaneous submissions & reprints. Shared royalties for anthologies. Guidelines at: www.hourglassbooks.org/submissions.html.

HOWARD BOOKS, 2 216 Centreville Dr., Ste. 303, Brentwood TN 37027-3226. (615) 873-2080. E-mail through website: http://imprints.simonandschuster.biz/howard. Does not accept, review, or return unsolicited mss, except through agents.

    This publisher serviced by ChristianManuscriptSubmissions.com and The Writer's Edge.

IDEALS PUBLICATIONS, 2630 Elm Hill Pike, Ste. 100, Nashville TN 37214. (615) 781-1451. E-mail: kwest@guideposts.org. Website: www.idealsbooks.com. A Guideposts Company. Kristi West, ed. Share a book with a child and share a moment of love. Imprints: Ideals Children's Books, CandyCane Press, Williamson Books. Publishes 20-25 new children's titles/yr under various imprints; hardcover, trade paperbacks, digital. Receives 300-500 unsolicited submissions annually. 1% of books from first-time authors. Accepts submissions through agents or authors. No subsidy or print-on-demand. No reprints. Prefers 800 words or less. Response time for submissions ranges from 3 to 6 months. Considers simultaneous submissions. Reports on submissions in 6 mos. Queries not accepted. Manuscripts for Ideals Children's Books (picture books) should be 800-1,000 words. Manuscripts for CandyCane Press (board books) should be no more than 250 words. E-mail submissions not accepted. Ideals Publications reviews uplifting, optimistic, and inspirational poetry and prose for possible use in our Easter and Christmas magazine. Guidelines at: http://www.idealsbooks.com/info/author_guidelines.

Nonfiction: Complete ms. Looking for holiday, inspirational, family, and values themes.

Fiction: For children. Complete ms.

Artwork: Open to queries from freelance artists.

Tip: "Become familiar with the types of books we are already publishing so that your manuscript fits within our niche."

INHERITANCE PRESS, LLC, PO Box 950477, Lake Mary FL 32795. (407) 474-0483. E-mail: submissions@inheritancepress.com. Website: www.inheritancepress.com. Independent publisher. Monique Donahue, ed. No advance. Responds in 60 days. Guidelines at: http://inheritancepress.com/submissions. Incomplete topical listings.

Nonfiction: Proposal by mail or e-mail; no phone query.

INKLING BOOKS, 582 Homewood Dr., Auburn AL 36830. (334) 369-9613. E-mail: editor@inklingbooks.com. Website: www.InklingBooks.com. Michael W. Perry, pub. Publishes 6 titles/yr.; hardcover, trade paperbacks. No mss through agents. Reprints books. Prefers 150-400 pgs. No advance. Print-on-demand. Publication within 2 mos. Guidelines at: www.InklingBooks.com; no catalog. Not currently accepting submissions.

INTERVARSITY PRESS, Box 1400, Downers Grove IL 60515-1426. Receptionist: (630) 734-4000. Fax (630) 734-4200. E-mail: email@ivpress.com. Website: www.ivpress.com. InterVarsity Christian Fellowship. Andrew T. LePeau, ed. dir.; submit to General Book Editor or Academic Editor. IVP books are characterized by a thoughtful, biblical approach to the Christian life that transforms the hearts, souls, and minds of readers in the university, church, and the world, on topics ranging from spiritual disciplines to apologetics, to current issues, to theology. Imprints: IVP Academic (Dan Reid, ed.), IVP Connect (Cindy Bunch, ed.), IVP Books (Al Hsu, ed.). Publishes 110-120 titles/yr.; hardcover, trade paperbacks, mass-market paperbacks. Receives 1,300 submissions annually. 15% of books from first-time authors. Accepts mss through agents or authors. Reprints books. Prefers 50,000 wds. or 200 pgs. Negotiable royalty on retail or outright purchase; negotiable advance. Average first printing 5,000. Publication within 12 mos. Considers simultaneous submissions. Responds in 3 mos. Prefers NIV, NRSV. Accepts e-mail submissions after acceptance. Guidelines at: http://www.ivpress.com/submissions; catalog for 9 x 12 SAE/5 stamps.

Nonfiction: Query only first, with detailed letter according to submissions guidelines, then proposal with 2 chapters; no phone/fax/e-query.

Ethnic Books: Especially looking for ethnic writers (African American, Hispanic, Asian American).

Also Does: e-books.

Blogs: www.ivpress.com/blogs/andyunedited

Tips: "Most open to books written by pastors (though not collections of sermons) or other church staff, by professors, by leaders in Christian organizations. Authors need to bring resources for publicizing and selling their own books, such as a website, an organization they are part of that will promote their books, speaking engagements, well-known people they know personally who will endorse and promote their book, writing articles for national publication, etc."

This publisher serviced by ChristianManuscriptSubmissions.com and The Writer's Edge.

*JOURNEYFORTH/BJU PRESS, 1700 Wade Hampton Blvd., Greenville SC 29614. (864) 370-1800, ext. 4350. Fax (864) 298-0268. E-mail to: journeyforth@bju. edu. Website: www.bjupress.com or www.journeyforth.com. Nancy Lohr, acquisitions ed. Our goal is to publish engaging books for children with a biblical worldview as well as Bible studies and Christian-living titles for teens and adults. Publishes 8-12 titles/ yr.; trade paperbacks. Receives 400 submissions annually (50 Christian living/350 youth novels). 10% of books from first-time authors. Accepts mss through agents or authors. **Royalty.** Average first printing varies. Publication within 12-18 mos. Considers simultaneous submissions but not multiple submissions. Accepts submissions by US mail or e-mail. Responds in 8-12 wks. Requires KJV. Guidelines at: http://www.bjupress.com/ books/freelance.php, by mail, or by e-mail; free catalog.

> **Nonfiction:** Proposal/3-5 chapters; e-query OK.
>
> **Fiction:** Proposal/5 chapters or complete ms. For children & teens. "Fiction must have a Christian worldview."
>
> **Artwork:** Open to queries from freelance artists.
>
> **Tips:** "The pre-college, homeschool market welcomes print-rich, well-written novels. No picture books, please, but compelling novels for early readers are always good for us, as are biographies on the lives of Christian heroes and statesmen. We focus on books for all ages that will help to both develop skill with the written word as well as discernment as a believer; we complement the educational goals of BJU Press, our K-12 textbook division."
>
> This publisher serviced by The Writer's Edge.

JUDSON PRESS, PO Box 851, Valley Forge PA 19482-0851. Toll-free (800) 458-3766. Fax (610) 768-2107. E-mail: acquisitions@judsonpress.com. Website: www. judsonpress.com. American Baptist Churches USA/American Baptist Home Mission Societies. Linda Johnson-LeBlanc, ed. We are theologically moderate, historically Baptist, and in ministry to empower, enrich, and equip disciples of Jesus and leaders in Christ's church. Publishes 10-12 titles/yr.; hardcover, trade paperbacks. Receives 800 submissions annually. 25% of books from first-time authors. Accepts mss through agents or authors. No subsidy; rarely does print-on-demand or reprints. Prefers 100-200 pgs. or 30,000-75,000 wds. **Royalty 10-15% on net; some work-for-hire agreements or outright purchases; occasional advance $300.** Average first printing 3,000. Publication within 18 mos. Considers simultaneous submissions. Requires accepted submissions on disk or by e-mail. Responds in 4-6 mos. Prefers NRSV or CEB. Guidelines at: http://www.judsonpress.com/contact_us_manuscript_submissions.cfm; catalog online.

> **Nonfiction:** Query or proposal/2 chapters; e-query OK. Practical books for today's church and leaders.
>
> **Ethnic Books:** African American, Asian North American, and Hispanic.
>
> **Tips:** "Most open to practical books that are unique and compelling, for a clearly defined niche audience. Theologically and socially we are a moderate publisher. And we like to see a detailed marketing plan from an author committed to partnering with us."
>
> This publisher serviced by The Writer's Edge.

+KENDALL NEFF PUBLISHING, PO Box 22, Talladega AL 35160. (256)368-1559. E-mail: publr@KendallNeff.com. Website: www.KendallNeff.com. Tana N. Thompson, Ph.D., pub. A Christian-based company dedicated to bringing glory to God. Publishes less than 10 titles/yr.; hardcover & trade paperbacks. No print-on-demand or reprints. Traditional publisher; no self-publishing services.

Also does: Greeting cards, gifts, and specialty products.

Tips: "We are especially looking for products (stories, gift, and specialty products) to add to a new platform at www.LoveUnleashed.us. Send inquiries to publisher for product ideas, affiliate marketing opportunities, custom artwork outlet, etc."

+JESSICA KINGSLEY PUBLISHERS, 400 Market St., Ste. 400, Philadelphia PA 19106. E-mail: hello@jkp.com. Book proposal form on the Website. Submit through e-mail. Check guidelines at: http://www.jkp.com/jkp/forauthors.php.

KIRK HOUSE PUBLISHERS, PO Box 390759, Minneapolis MN 55439. (952) 835-1828. Toll-free (888) 696-1828. Fax (952) 835-2613. E-mail: publisher@kirk-house.com. Website: www.kirkhouse.com. Leonard Flachman, pub. Imprints: Lutheran University Press, Quill House Publishers. Publishes 10-15 titles/yr.; hardcover, trade paperbacks, coffee table books. Receives hundreds of submissions annually. 95% of books from first-time authors. No mss through agents. No reprints. **Royalty 10-15% on net; no advance.** Average first printing 500-3,000. Publication within 6 mos. No simultaneous submissions. Initial inquiry only via e-mail. Requires hard copy and electronic submission. Responds in 2-3 wks. Guidelines by e-mail/website ("Submissions")..

Nonfiction: Inquiries and author bio.

Tips: "Our catalog is eclectic; send a query. Our imprint, Quill House Publishers, accepts adult fiction."

+KNIGHT GEORGE PUBLISHING HOUSE, 3310 Warringham Ave., Waterford MI 48329. E-mail: authors@knightgeorge.com. Publishes Christian educational materials. Submit by mail or e-mail. Click on "Authors Submission Tool." Check out this publisher's guidelines at: www.knightgeorge.com.

KREGEL PUBLICATIONS, 2450 Oak Industrial Dr. NE, Grand Rapids MI 49505. (616) 451-4775. Fax (616) 451-9330. E-mail: kregelbooks@kregel.com. Website: www. kregel.com. Blog: www.kregel.com/news. Evangelical/conservative. Does not accept unsoliciated material for review. Guidelines at: http://www.kregel.com/ME2/dirmod. asp?sid=A12DB34B70B34EA28EA748A96CD5AEFE&type=gen&mod=Core+Pag es&gid=407071182FF54073997E4A2312FC25D9.

This publisher serviced by ChristianManuscriptSubmissions.com and The Writer's Edge.

LANGMARC PUBLISHING, PO Box 90488, Austin TX 78709-0488. (512) 394-0989. Fax (512) 394-0829. E-mail: langmarc@booksails.com. Website: www.langmarc. com. Lutheran. Lois Qualben, pub. Focuses on spiritual growth of readers. Publishes 3-5 titles/yr.; hardcover, trade paperbacks. Receives 230 submissions annually. 60% of books from first-time authors. Accepts mss through agents or authors. No reprints. Prefers 150-300 pgs. **Royalty 10-14% on net; no advance.** Average first printing varies. Publication usually within 18 mos. Considers simultaneous submissions. Responds in 3 mos. Requires requested ms on disk. Prefers NIV. Guidelines at: www.langmarc.com ("Guidelines for Nonfiction Authors"); free catalog.

Nonfiction: Proposal/3 chapters; no phone query. "Most open to inspirational books."

+LARSON PUBLICATIONS, Acquisitions, 4936 NYS Route 414, Burdett, NY 14818. Mail queries only. Responds in 8+ wks. Guidelines at: http://www.larsonpubli-cations.com/submission-guidelines.php.

LEGACY PRESS, PO Box 261129, San Diego CA 92196. (858) 277-1167. Fax:

(858) 277-4743. E-mail: john.gregory@rainbowpublishers.com. Website: www. Rainbowpublishers.com. Rainbow Publishers. John Gregory, ed. We are an established, well-respected publisher of Christian education materials, devotions, and fiction for ages 1-12. Imprint: Rainbow Publishers (see separate listing). Publishes 12-18 titles/yr.; mass-market paperbacks. Receives 208 submissions annually. 1% of books from first-time authors. Accepts submissions through agent or authors. No subsidy, print-on-demand, or reprints. Prefers 26,000 wds. or 200 pgs. **Pay $500-$1,000 for outright purchase.** Average first printing 1,500. Publication within 1 yr. Considers simultaneous submissions. Responds in 2-8 wks. Prefers NIV. Guidelines at: http://www.rainbowpublishers.com/submissions.aspx; no catalog.

Nonfiction: Proposal/3-5 chapters; no e-queries.

Fiction: For children. Proposal/3 chapters. For ages 2-12 only.

Special Needs: Bible school activities ages 1 to 12, children's inspirational books, Christian fiction action-adventure.

Artwork: Open to queries from freelance artists.

Tips: "We prefer children's activities be included between chapters. Propose at least a 3-book series."

+LIFE CHANGING MEDIA. Publishes books in four categories: emotional, financial, physical, and spiritual health. Send a 500-word synopsis for review. **Pays royalties.** Guidelines at: http://www.lifechangingmedia.net/submission.htm.

*LIFE CYCLE BOOKS, 1085 Bellamy Rd. N #20, Toronto ON M1H 3C7 Canada. (416) 690-5860. E-mail: paulb@lifecyclebooks.com. Website: www.lifecyclebooks.com. Paul Broughton, gen. mngr.; submit to Attention: The Editor. Toll-free (866) 880-5860. Toll-free fax (866) 260-8172. Specializes in pro-life material. Publishes 6 titles/yr.; trade paperbacks. Receives 100+ submissions annually. No mss through agents. 50% of books from first-time authors. Reprints books. **Royalty 8-10% of net (advance $250-1,000; outright purchase of brochure material, $250+.** Subsidy publishes 10%. Publication within 3 mos. to 1yr. No simultaneous submissions. Responds in 3-5 wks. Guidelines at: http://www.lifecyclebooks.com/store/usa/faq/#12. Catalog on website.

Nonfiction: Query or complete ms. "Our emphasis is on pro-life and pro-family titles."

Tips: "We are most involved in publishing leaflets of about 1,500 wds., and we welcome submissions of manuscripts of this length." No fiction or poetry.

LIGHTHOUSE PUBLISHING OF THE CAROLINAS, 2333 Barton Oaks Dr., Raleigh NC 27614. E-mail: lighthousepublishingcarolinas@gmail.com. Websites: http://lighthousepublishingofthecarolinas.com; candlightfiction.com; guidlinglightfiction.com; heritagebeaconfiction.com; www.fireflysouthernfiction.com; sonrisedevotionals.com; brimstonefiction.com. Company blog: http://lighthousepublishing ofthecarolinas.com/category/readerconnect. LPC is an approved ACFW, royalty-paying publisher of e-books and print-on-demand (POD) paperbacks. Eddie Jones, founder/CEO; for editors of each imprint see that Website (above). Imprints: Candlelight Romance, Guiding Light Women's Fiction, Heritage Beacon Fiction, Firefly Southern Fiction, Brimstone Fiction, SonRise Devotionals, Straight Street Books. Publishes 40+ titles/yr.; trade paperbacks, digital. Receives 300+ submissions annually. 40% of books from first-time authors. Prefers/accepts submissions through agents. No subsidy. Does print-on-demand. Reprints books. Length varies; with POD, the fewer words the better. **Royalty about 40% of net; e-books the same; no advance (subject to change).** Publication within 12 mos. Considers simultaneous submissions. Reports within 3 months. No catalog; guidelines at: http://lighthousepublishingofthecarolinas.com/submissions or by e-mail.

Nonfiction: Query letter only first; e-query OK.

Fiction: For teens, new adults, adults. Query letter only first.

Photos: Accepts freelance photos for book covers.

More about this publisher: We take chances on niche books, debut authors, and established authors who understand that the book publishing industry is changing — fast. We care less about pedigree and more about story, message, and an author's ability to market their book online. We pay royalties monthly and have over 100 titles in print. If you can accept that your book might never see the inside of a bookstore but may sell thousands and put thousands in your pocket, then LPC might be a good fit for you.

Tips: "You've heard the question: "How do I make an editor sit up and beg for my manuscript?" Know who your main character is, what she wants, and how she will be transformed. Hint: the character that changes the most during the story is your lead character. Be prepared to answer the question: "How would you like your reader to feel at the end of the story and what do you want readers to learn?" See imprint submission guidelines for more tips on what our editors want.

LIGHTHOUSE TRAILS PUBLISHING LLC, PO Box 908, Eureka MT 59917. (406) 889-3610. Fax (406) 889-3633. E-mail: editors@lighthousetrails.com. Website: www.lighthousetrails.com. Blog: www.lighthousetrailsresearch.com/blog. David Dombrowski, acq. ed. We publish books that bring clarity and light to areas of spiritual darkness or deception, and we seek to preserve the integrity of God's Word in all our books. Publishes 4 titles/yr. Receives 50-75 submissions annually. 30% of books from first-time authors. Accepts mss through agents or authors. No subsidy or print-on-demand. Reprints books. Prefers 160-300 pgs. **Royalty 12-17% of net or 20% of retail.** Publication within 9-12 mos. Considers simultaneous submissions. Prefers accepted ms on disk or by e-mail; OK to mail or e-mail proposal. Responds in 8 wks. Prefers KJV. Guidelines at: http://www.lighthousetrails.com/authorguidelines.htm; free catalog by mail.

Nonfiction: Proposal/2 chapters; no phone/fax query; e-query OK.

Fiction: Proposal/2-3 chapters. For all ages. "We are looking for a fiction book or fiction series that would include elements from our nonfiction books exposing the emerging church and mystical/New Age spirituality; Bible prophecy/eschatological."

Special Needs: Will look at autobiographies or biographies about people who have courageously endured through overwhelming circumstances (Holocaust survivors, child-abuse survivors, etc.) with a definite emphasis on the Lord's grace and faithfulness and his Word.

Artwork: Open to queries from freelance artists.

Tips: "No poetry at this time. Any book we consider will not only challenge the more scholarly reader, but also be able to reach those who may have less experience and comprehension. Our books will include human interest and personal experience scenarios as a means of getting the point across. Read a couple of our books to better understand the style of writing we are looking for. Also check our research website for an in-depth look at who we are (www.lighthousetrailsresearch.com). We also have a doctrinal statement on our website that helps to define us."

+LITURGICAL PRESS, 2950 St. John's Rd, PO Box 7500, Collegeville MN 56321-7500. Submit to: Publisher at submissions@litpress.org. Download Project Summary

Form and guidelines for manuscript style and submission on their Website. Guidelines at: http://www.litpress.org/Authors/manuscript.html.

+LITURGICAL TRAINING PUBLICATIONS, 3949 S. Racine Ave., Chicago IL 60609-2523. (773) 579-4900. Fax (773) 579-4929. Deanna Keefe, publication mngr. Website: www.ltp.org.

LOVE INSPIRED, 233 Broadway, Ste. 1001, New York NY 10279-0001. (212) 553-4200. Fax (212) 277-8969. E-mail: giselle_regus@harlequin.ca. Website: www. harlequin.com. Harlequin Enterprises. Submit to any of the following: Melissa Endlich, sr. ed.; Shanan Smith, assoc. ed.; Giselle Regus, asst. ed. Contemporary inspirational romances that feature characters facing the many challenges of life and live in today's world. Imprints: Love Inspired, Love Inspired Historical, Love Inspired Suspense. Publishes 168 titles/yr.; mass-market paperbacks. Receives 500-1,000 submissions annually. 15% of books from first-time authors. Accepts mss through agents or authors. No reprints. Prefers 55,000-60,000 wds. **Royalty on retail; competitive advance.** Publication within 12-24 mos. Requires ms on disk/hard copy. Responds in 3 mos. Prefers KJV. Guidelines by mail/website: http://www.harlequin.com/articlepage. html?articleId=538&chapter=0; no catalog.

> **Fiction:** Query letter or 3 chapters and up to 5-page synopsis; no phone/ fax/e-query.
> **Tips:** "We want character-driven romance with an author voice that inspires." This publisher serviced by ChristianManuscriptSubmissions.com.

LOYOLA PRESS, 3441 N. Ashland Ave., Chicago IL 60657. (773) 281-1818. Toll-free (800) 621-1008. Fax (773) 281-0152. E-mail: editorial@loyolapress.com. Website: www.loyolabooks.org. Catholic. Joseph Durepos, acq. ed. (durepos@loyolapress.com). Publishes religion books for the general trade; Catholic readers; Catholic spirituality and tradition. Publishes 20-30 titles/yr.; hardcover, trade paperbacks. Receives 500 submissions annually. Accepts mss through agents or authors. Prefers 25,000-75,000 wds. or 150-300 pgs. **Standard royalty; reasonable advance.** Average first printing 7,500-10,000. Considers simultaneous submissions and first-time authors without agents. Responds in 3 mos. Prefers NRSV (Catholic Edition). Guidelines/catalog on website at: http://www.loyolapress.com/assets/pdf/AuthorGuidelines.pdf.

> **Nonfiction:** E-query first; proposal/sample chapters; no phone query.
> **Tips:** "Looking for books and authors that help make Catholic faith relevant and offer practical tools for the well-lived spiritual life."
> This publisher serviced by The Writer's Edge.

*LUTHERAN UNIVERSITY PRESS, PO Box 390759, Minneapolis MN 55439. (952) 835-1828. Toll-free (888) 696-1828. Fax (952) 835-2613. E-mail: publisher@ lutheranupress.org. Website: www.lutheranupress.org. Leonard Flachman, pub.; Karen Walhof, ed. Proposal of 15 pages, max. Publishes 8-10 titles/yr.; hardcover, trade paperbacks, coffee table books. Receives dozens of submissions annually. Subsidy publishes 25%. No print-on-demand or reprints. **Royalty 10-15% of net; no advance.** Average first printing 500-2,000. Publication within 6 mos. No simultaneous submissions. Responds in 3 wks. Guidelines by e-mail/website at: http://www.lutheranupress.org/ submissions.php; free catalog by mail.

> **Nonfiction:** Proposal/sample chapters in electronic format or by mail.
> **Photos:** Accepts freelance photos for book covers.
> **Tips:** "We accept manuscripts only from faculty (and faculty emeritus) of Lutheran colleges, universities, seminaries, and Lutheran faculty from other institutions."

+LUTHERAN VOICES, PO Box 1209, Minneapolis MN 55440-1209. Quality accessible books by Lutheran authors that inform, teach, inspire, and renew. Grounded in Lutheran theology and practice, the books will cover a wide range of subjects and themes of interest to ELCA members and the wider Christian community. Check out this publisher's guidelines at: http://www.augsburgfortress.org/company/submit.jsp.

+LUTTERWORTH PRESS, PO Box 60, Cambridge CB1 2NT, United Kingdom. E-mail: publishing@lutterworth.com. Fax: +44 (0)1223-366951. Not currently accepting children's books. Publishes scholarly or reference books. Proposal by mail. "New Book Proposal Form" on Website. Publishes 50 title/yr. Guidelines at: http://www.lutterworth.com/author_guidelines.php?osCsid=6edb17b02f39728e4bd8642d13dfdaff.

MAGNUS PRESS, 1647 Shire Ave., Oceanside CA 92057. (760) 806-3743. Fax (760) 806-3689. E-mail: magnuspress@cox.net. Website: www.magnuspress.com. Warren Angel, ed. dir. All books must reflect a strong belief in Christ, solid biblical understanding, and the author's ability to relate to the average person. Imprint: Canticle Books. Publishes 3 titles/yr.; trade paperbacks. Receives 60 submissions annually. 50% of books from first-time authors. Accepts mss through agents or authors. Reprints books. Prefers 105-300 pgs. **Graduated royalty on retail; no advance.** Average first printing 2,500. Publication within 1 yr. Considers simultaneous submissions. Accepts requested ms on disk. Responds in 1 mo. Guidelines by mail/e-mail/website: http://www.magnuspress.com/SubmissionGuidlinesMP.html; free catalog by mail.

> **Nonfiction:** Query or proposal/3 chapters; fax query OK. "Looking for spirituality, thematic biblical studies, unique inspirational/devotional books, e.g., *Adventures of an Alaskan Preacher.*"
>
> **Tips:** "Our writers need solid knowledge of the Bible and a mature spirituality that reflects a profound relationship with Jesus Christ. Most open to a popularly written biblical study that addresses a real concern/issue in the church at large today; or a unique inspirational book. Study the market; know what we do and don't publish."

+MANTLE ROCK PUBLISHING COMPANY, 2879 Palma Rd., Benton KY 42025. (270) 493-1560. E-mails: kattanderson4@gmail.com (submit to) or jkcret1@bellsouth.net. Website: www.mantlerockpublishing.com. Jerry and Katherine Cretsinger, pubs. Estab. 2012. Open to historical and contemporary novels (and novellas) of most genres (no sci-fi). No children's chapter books at this time. Accepting a few YA, which includes tweens. Traditional royalty publisher of Christian books. Novellas 15,000-69,000 wds.; novels 50,000-80,000 wds. ;historical novels 60,000-110,000 wds. Send e-proposal with 3 sample chapters; for complete ms only. Guidelines on Website.

MARCHER LORD PRESS (see Enclave Publishing in Subsidy Publishers.)

+MASTER BOOKS, PO Box 726, Green Forest AR 72638. Toll free: (800) 999-3777. Fax: (870) 438-5120. E-mail: nlp@newleafpress.net. An imprint of New Leaf Press. Produces creation-based resources for all ages. Check out this publisher's guidelines at: www.masterbooks.net.

+MERCER UNIVERSITY PRESS, 1400 Coleman Ave., Macon GA 31207. (478) 301-2880. Fax: (478) 301-2585. Submit to Editor-in-chief. Open to scholarly works in religious studies, esp. Bible studies; philosophy, Southern Culture, esp. history of the South; and literary fiction. Send a proposal. Responds in 3-4 mos. Publication in a year. Guidelines at: http://www.mupress.org/client/client_pages/authors/submissions.cfm.

MERIWETHER PUBLISHING LTD., 885 Elkton Dr., Colorado Springs CO 80907. (719) 594-4422. Fax (719) 594-9916. E-mail: editor@meriwether.com. Website: www.ChristianPlaysandMusicals.com. Nondenominational. Arthur L. Zapel, exec. ed.; submit to Rhonda Wray, assoc. ed. Publishes 30-45 plays & books/yr. Primarily a publisher of plays for Christian and general markets; must be acceptable for use in a wide variety of Christian denominations. Imprint: Contemporary Drama Service. Publishes 3 bks./25 plays/yr. Receives 1,200 submissions annually (mostly plays). 75% of submissions from first-time authors. Accepts mss through agents or authors. No reprints. Prefers 225 pgs. **Royalty 10% of net or retail; no advance.** Average first printing of books 1,500-2,500, plays 500. Publication within 6 mos. Considers simultaneous submissions. No e-mail submissions. Responds in up to 3 mos. Any Bible version. Guidelines at: www.ChristianPlaysandMusicals.com; catalog for 9 x 12 SASE.

> **Nonfiction:** Table of contents/1 chapter; fax/e-query OK. "Looking for creative worship books, i.e., drama, using the arts in worship, how-to books with ideas for Christian education." Submit books to Meriwether.
> **Fiction:** Complete ms for plays. Plays only, for all ages. Always looking for Christmas and Easter plays (1 hr. maximum). Submit plays to Contemporary Drama.
> **Special Needs:** Religious drama—or religious plays—mainstream theology. We prefer plays that can be staged during a worship service.
> **Tips:** "Our books are on drama or any creative, artistic area that can be a part of worship. Writers should familiarize themselves with our catalog before submitting to ensure that their manuscript fits with the list we've already published." Contemporary Drama Service wants easy-to-stage comedies, skits, one-act plays, large-cast musicals, and full-length comedies for schools (junior high through college), and churches (including chancel dramas for Christmas and Easter). Most open to anything drama-related. "Study our catalog so you'll know what we publish and what would fit our list."

+MONARCH BOOKS, Wilkinson House, Jordan Hill Rd., Oxford OX2 8DR, United Kingdom. Proposals by mail or e-mail. Supports Christian families, individuals, and communities in their devotional and spiritual lives. Books for children & adults. If not response in 3 months, consider it a rejection. Guidelines at: www.lionhudson.com.

MOODY PUBLISHERS, 820 N. LaSalle Blvd., Chicago IL 60610. Fax (312) 329-2144. Email: acquisitions@moody.edu. Website: www.moodypublishers.com/. Moody Publishers exists to help our readers know, love, and serve Jesus Christ. Publishes 60-70 titles per year; hardcover, trade paperbacks, mass-market paperbacks, e-books. Receives 3,500 submissions annually; 10% of books from first-time authors. Does not accept unsolicited manuscripts in any category unless submitted via: literary agent; an author who has published with us; a Moody Bible Institute employee; a personal contact at a writers conference. **Royalty paid on net; advances begin at $500.** Average first printing 10,000. Publication within 1 year. Responds in 1-2 mos. Prefers NAS, ESV, NKJV, NIV (1984). Please do not call our offices with manuscript ideas. Rather, for submissions meeting the criteria detailed above, have your query sent to: Acquisitions Coordinator, Moody Publishers, 820 North LaSalle Blvd., Chicago, IL 60610. Responds in 1 month. Guidelines at: www.moodypublishers.com/pub_main.aspx?id=46381. Catalog for 9 x 12 SAE/$2.38 postage (mark "Media Mail").

> **Nonfiction Categories & Audiences:** Academic & Bible reference; spiritual growth; Millennials (18- to 30-year-olds); women; urban; family & relationships
> **Fiction:** "We are looking for stories that glorify God both in content and style. Featured categories include mystery, contemporary, historical, young adult.

Ethnic Books: African American.

Tips: "Most open to books where the writer is a recognized expert with a platform to promote the book."

This publisher serviced by ChristianManuscriptSubmissions.com and The Writer's Edge.

MOPS INTERNATIONAL, 2370 S. Trenton Way, Denver CO 80231-3822. (303) 733-5353. Fax (303) 733-5770. E-mail: info@MOPS.org. Website: www.MOPS.org Jean Blackmer, pub. mngr.; Carla Foote, dir. of media. Publishes books dealing with the needs and interests of mothers with young children, who may or may not be Christians. Publishes 2-3 titles/yr. Guidelines at: http://www.mops.org/writers-guidelines. Catalog on website.

Nonfiction: Query or proposal/3 chapters; by mail, fax, or e-mail.

Tips: "Review existing titles on our website to avoid duplication."

+MORE THAN NOVELLAS.COM. E-mail: lizdelayne@hotmail.com. Liz DeLayne, ed. Publishes family-friendly fiction. E-mail submission as an attachment. Guidelines at: http://www.morethannovellas.com.

MORGAN JAMES PUBLISHING, 5 Penn Plaza, 23rd Floor, New York City NY 10001. (212) 655-5470. Fax (516) 908-4496. Morgan James, LLC. E-mail: terry@ morganjamespublishing.com. Website: www.morganjamespublishing.com. W. Terry Whalin, acq. ed. Imprints: Guerrilla Marketing Press, Koehler Books (fiction), Morgan James Faith, Morgan James Kids, Sports Professor. Religious titles/yr 45-50. Receives 5,000 proposals/yr. 10-15% first-time authors. Accept books submitted by agents. Reprints books. Preferred book length 40-60,000 wds. or 200 pgs. **Royalty 20-30% of net. 50% on e-books. Offer an advance.** Avg. first printing 1800-2200. Publication 4 months. Consider simultaneous submissions. Guidelines at: http://morganjames-publishing.com/submit.Catalog free on request. Writer's guidelines by e-mail. Accept freelance photos for covers.

Nonfiction: Query letter, proposal with 3 sample chapters, or complete mss. Accept e-mail queries. Require mss by e-mail.

Fiction: Accept for children, teens, adults. Query letter, proposal with 3 sample chapters, or complete manuscript.

MULTNOMAH BOOKS, 12265 Oracle Blvd., Ste. 200, Colorado Springs CO 80921. (719) 590-4999. Fax (719) 590-8977. E-mail: info@waterbrookmultnomah.com. Website: www.waterbrookmultnomah.com. Part of WaterBrook Multnomah, a division of Random House Inc. Laura Barker, ed. dir. Imprint information listed below. Publishes 75 titles/yr.; hardcover, trade paperbacks. **Royalty on net; advance.** Multnomah is currently not accepting unsolicited manuscripts, proposals, or queries; no proposals for biographies, poetry, or children's books. Queries will be accepted through literary agents and at writers' conferences at which a Multnomah representative is present. Guidelines at: http://waterbrookmultnomah.com/submissions; catalog on website.Multnomah Books: Christian living and popular theology books.

Multnomah Books: Christian living and popular theology books.

Multnomah Fiction: Well-crafted fiction that uses truth to change lives.

This publisher serviced by The Writer's Edge.

MY HEALTHY CHURCH, 1445 N. Boonville Ave., Springfield MO 65802. Toll-free (800) 641-4310. (417) 831-8000. E-mail: newproducts@myhealthychurch.com. Website: www.myhealthychurch.com. Assemblies of God/Pentecostal. Steve Blount, VP publishing. We do not accept unsolicited manuscripts unless represented by a professional literary agent. For a listing of the unsolicited manuscripts we are accepting, please visit the website. Responds in 60-90 days. Guidelines at: http://myhealthychurch.com/store/startcat.cfm?cat=tWRITGUID.

NAVPRESS, 3820 N. 30th St., Colorado Springs, CO 80904. E-mail: editorial.submissions@navpress.com. Website: www.navpress.com. An alliance with Tyndale House. To advance the calling of The Navigators by bringing biblically rooted, culturally relevant, and highly practical products to people who want to know and love Christ more deeply. Imprint: TH1NK. Publishes 45 titles/yr. Hardcover, trade paperbacks, digital. Reprints books. **Royalties; advance.** Publication in 12-18 mos. Considers simultaneous submissions. Responds in 6-12 wks. Catalog free on request. Guidelines at: Need books for TH1NK, 16- to 21-yr-olds, inc. Bible studies, nonfiction, YA fiction.

> **Nonfiction:** proposal with 2-3 chap. E-mail queries OK. Require mss by e-mail.
> **Fiction:** Teen/YA fiction. No adult at this time. Proposal with 2-3 sample chap.
> **Special Needs:** Transforming, life-changing nonfiction and Bible studies, as well as YA fiction.
> This publisher serviced by The Writer's Edge.

THOMAS NELSON & ZONDERVAN FICTION, the combined division under HarperCollins Christian Publishers, PO Box 141000, Nashville TN 37215. (615) 889-9000. Website: www.harpercollinschristian.com. Thomas Nelson Inc. Ami McConnell, sr. acq. ed.; Amanda Bostic, acq. ed. Zondervan: Sue Browers, exec. ed.; Becky Philpott, assist. acq. ed. Fiction from a Christian worldview. Publishes fewer than 100 titles/yr.; hardcover, trade. Requires mss through agents; does not accept unsolicited manuscripts. Guidelines at: http://www.harpercollinschristian.com/write-for-us; catalog available online at www.harpercollinschristian.com/media/.

> This publisher serviced by The Writer's Edge.

THOMAS NELSON PUBLISHERS, PO Box 141000, Nashville TN 37214-1000. (615) 889-9000. Fax (615) 902-2745. Website: www.thomasnelson.com. Does not accept or review any unsolicited queries, proposals, or manuscripts. Guidelines at: http://www.harpercollinschristian.com/write-for-us.

> This publisher serviced by ChristianManuscriptSubmissions.com and The Writer's Edge.

TOMMY NELSON. See Thomas Nelson Publishers above.

+NEW CANAAN PUBLISHING. No longer reviewing unsolicited manuscripts.

NEW HOPE PUBLISHERS, PO Box 12065, Birmingham AL 35202-2065. (205) 991-8100. Fax (205) 991-4015. Website: www.newhopedigital.com. Division of WMU. Imprints: Fiction (contemporary issues); New Hope Impact (missional community, social, personal-commitment, church-growth, and leadership issues); New Hope Arise (inspiring women, changing lives); New Hope Grow (Bible-study & teaching resources). Publishes 24-28 titles/yr.; hardcover, trade paperbacks. No unsolicited queries, proposals, or manuscripts. Guidelines at: http://www.newhopedigital.com/contact/ (scroll down).

> This publisher serviced by ChristianManuscriptSubmissions.com and The Writer's Edge.

NEW LEAF PUBLISHING GROUP, PO Box 726, Green Forest AR 72638-0726. (870) 438-5288. Fax (870) 438-5120. E-mail: submissions@newleafpress.net. Craig Froman, acq. ed. The world's largest creation-based publisher. To impact eternity, reaching hearts across the world to know Him and make Him known as our Savior. Imprints: New Leaf Press, Master Books. Publishes 30-35 titles/yr.; hardcover, trade paperbacks, occasionally high-end gift titles, digital. Receives 1,000 submissions annually. 10% of books from first-time authors. Accepts mss through agents or authors. Requires e-mail submission; no mail. Author's Proposal Document on Website. No subsidy, print-on-demand, or reprints. No length preference. **Variable royalty on net; no advance.** Average first printing varies. Publication within 8 mos. Considers simultaneous submissions. Responds within 90 days, or isn't interested. Requires accepted ms by e-mail. Guidelines by mail/e-mail/website: http://www.nlpg.com/submissions; free catalog by mail.

Nonfiction: Must complete Author's Proposal form; no phone/fax query; e-query OK. Accepts mss by e-mail. "Looking for books for the homeschool market, especially grades 1-8."

Special Needs: Stewardship of the earth; ancient man technology, inventions, etc.; educational products for grades K-12.

Tips: "Accepts submissions only with Author's Proposal form available by e-mail or on our website."

This publisher serviced by The Writer's Edge.

+NEW YORK UNIVERSITY PRESS, 838 Broadway, 3rd Fl., New York NY 10003-4812. (212) 998-2575. Fax: (212) 995-3833. E-mail: jennifer.hammer@nyu.edu. Jennifr Hammer, sr. ed. Religion. Mail hard copy of the proposal. Guidelines at: http://nyupress.org/for-authors.aspx (scroll down).

+NORTHWESTERN PUBLISHING HOUSE, 1250 N. 113th St., Milwaukee WI 53226. (800) 662-6022. Check out this publisher at: www.nph.net.

+NORTH WIND PUBLISHING, PO Box 3655, Brewer ME 0441. (207)922-8435. E-mail: info@northwindpublishing.com. Website: www.northwindpublishing.com. Protestant. Janet Robbins, pub. Publishes 2 titles/yr.; trade paperbacks & digital. Receives 10 submissions annually. 50% of books from first-time authors. Accepts submissions through agents. No subsidy. Does print-on-demand. No reprints. **No advance.** Publication within 6-12 mos. Considers simultaneous submissions. Catalog online; no guidelines.

Nonfiction: Query letter only first; e-mail or snail-mail queries. Then book proposal/sample chapters.

Photos: Accepts freelance photos for book covers.

+NYREEPRESS LITERARY GROUP, PO Box 164882, Fort Worth TX 76161. (972) 793-3736. E-mail: submissions@nyreepress.com. Website: www.nyreepress.com. Kennisha Hill, ed. Go to Website for their 3-step process for submitting. They require that you use the submission form on their Website. Not included in topical listings.

OAKTARA PUBLISHERS, 2206 N. Main St., Ste. 343, Wheaton IL 60187. E-mail: rtucker@oaktara.com. Website: www.oaktara.com. Ramona Tucker, ed. dir. OakTara, a traditional publisher, was founded in 2007 by two veterans of the publishing world to step into the marketplace gap to provide writers with a mind-stretching, heart-transforming-life-inspiring fiction and nonfiction that is different, vibrant, and relevant. Publishes 75 titles/yr. Receives over 20,000 submissions annually. 60% 0f books from first-time authors. Accepts submissions by agents. No subsidy. Does print-on-demand. Publishes trade paperbacks & digital. No reprints. Prefers 60,00-80,000 wds.; 160-300 pgs. **Royalty 25% on net; e-books 25%; no advance.** Publication within 9-12 mos. No simultaneous submissions. Reports in 16 wks. Guidelines at: http://www.oaktara.com/writersguidelines; free catalog.

Nonfiction: Complete ms. Accepts e-mail queries.

Fiction: Complete ms. For children, teens, new adults and adults. Genres: romance, historical romance, contemporary romance, dystopian, fantasy, frontier romance, western romance, and mystery/suspense.

Tips: "Looking for mind-stretching, heart-transforming, life-inspiring fiction and nonfiction. Fresh and from authors with passion. Most open to a thoughtful, fresh nonfiction or fiction book that doesn't simply supply 'the average read' but goes beyond a 'typical plot' to provide reflection for the reader and a potential for life change."

This publisher serviced by The Writer's Edge.

+OLIVIA KIMBRELL PRESS, PO Box 4393, Winchester KY 40392-4393. (859) 577-1071. E-mail: admin@oliviakimbrellpress.com. Website: www.oliviskimbrellpress. com. G. B. Williams, ed. Specializing in true to life, meaningful Christian fiction or nonfiction titles intended to uplift the heart and engage the mind. Primary focus on "Roman Road" small group guides or reader's guides to accompany nonfiction, or fiction stories of suspense, intrigue, or family sagas with an inspirational or romantic theme. Imprint Sign of the Whale™ specializes in biblical and/or Christian fiction primarily with speculative fiction, science fiction, fantasy, or other futuristic and/or supernatural themes. House of Bread™ imprint specializes in biblical and/or traditional foods, clean foods, fasting, feasts, and healthy, nutritious information presented in an educational and entertaining manner. Incomplete topical listings. Guidelines on Website (click on "submissions guidelines.")

+ONE WORLD/BALLANTINE BOOKS. Not accepting submissions of queries, proposals or manuscripts at this time. Check out this publisher's guidelines at: http:// www.randomhouse.biz/manuscripts.

ON MY OWN NOW MINISTRIES (formerly The Quilldriver), 1000 N. Dover Dr., Rogers AR 72756. Phone/fax (479) 774-5699. E-mail: donna@onmyownnow.com. Website: www.onmyownnow.com. Donna Lee Schillinger, pub. Inspirational nonfiction directed at young adults (17-25). Imprint: Two-Faced Books. Publishes 3 titles/ yr. Receives 12 submissions annually. 67% of books from first-time authors. No mss through agents. Would consider reprinting books. Prefers 200 pgs. **Royalties; $500 advance.** Average first printing 2,000. Publication within 18 mos. Considers simultaneous submissions. Responds in 8 wks. Prefers NIV. Guidelines by e-mail; catalog for #10 SAE/1 stamp.

    Nonfiction: Query first; or proposal/2 chapters; e-query OK.

    Tips: "Most open to books that are hip and biblically sound—must resonate with young adults."

+OREGON CATHOLIC PRESS, OCP Music submissions, 5536 NE Hassalo, Portland OR 97213. Accepts no more than 3 compositions for review from an individual in any 6 month period. Guidelines at: http://www.ocp.org/about/music_submissions.

OUR SUNDAY VISITOR INC., 200 Noll Plaza, Huntington IN 46750-4303. (260) 356-8400. Toll-free (800) 348-2440. Fax (260) 356-8472. E-mail: booksed@osv.com. Website: www.osv.com. To assist Catholics to be more aware and secure in their faith and capable of relating their faith to others. Submit to Acquisitions Editor, Book Dept. Submit proposal first. Publishes 30-40 titles/yr.; hardcover, trade paperbacks. Receives 500+ submissions annually. 10% of books from first-time authors. Prefers not to work through agents. Reprints books. **Royalty 10-12% of net; average advance $1,500.** Average first printing 5,000. Publication within 1-2 yrs. Accepts simultaneous submissions (tell them). Responds in 6-8 wks. Requires requested ms on disk. Guidelines at: https://www.osv.com/More/WritersGuidelines.aspx, catalog for 9 x 12 SASE.

Nonfiction: Proposal/2 chapters; e-query OK. "Most open to devotional books (not first person), church history, heritage and saints, the parish, prayer, and family."

Also Does: Pamphlets, booklets.

Photos: Occasionally accepts freelance photos for book covers.

Tips: "All books published must relate to the Catholic Church; unique books aimed at our audience. Give as much background information as possible on author qualification, why the topic was chosen, and unique aspects of the project. Follow our guidelines. We are expanding our religious education product line and programs."

PACIFIC PRESS PUBLISHING ASSN., PO Box 5353, Nampa ID 83653-5353. (208) 465-2500. Fax (208) 465-2531. E-mail: booksubmissions@pacificpress.com. Website: www.pacificpress.com. Seventh-day Adventist. Submit to: Book Acquisitions Editor. Books of interest and importance to Seventh-day Adventists and other Christians of all ages. Publishes 35-40 titles/yr.; hardcover, trade paperbacks. Receives 500 submissions annually. Prefers e-mail submissions; accepts mailed. 5% of books from first-time authors. Accepts mss through agents or authors. No reprints. Prefers 40,000-90,000 wds; 128-320 pgs.. or 160-400 pgs. **Royalty 12-16% of net; advance $1,500.** Average first printing 5,000. Publication within 6 mos. Considers simultaneous submissions. Responds in 1-3 wks. Requires requested ms on disk or by e-mail. Guidelines at: http://www.pacificpress.com/index.php?pgName=newsSubGuides; no catalog.

Nonfiction: Query only; e-query OK.

Fiction: Query only; almost none accepted; mainly biblical. Children's books: "Must be on a uniquely Seventh-day Adventist topic. No talking animals or fantasy."

Ethnic Books: Hispanic.

Also Does: Booklets.

Tips: "Most open to spirituality, inspirational, and Christian living. Our website has the most up-to-date information, including samples of recent publications. For more information, see www.adventistbookcenter.com. Do not send full manuscript unless we request it after reviewing your proposal."

+PAGE PUBLISHING, 1 Penn Plaza, Ste. 6289, New York NY 10119. E-mail: contact@pagepublishing.com. Website: www.pagepublishing.com. Published print and digital editions. **Royalty 70%.** Publication in up to 6 mos. Not clear whether this is a traditional or subsidy publisher.

+PALGRAVE MACMILLIAN, 175 Fifth Ave., New York NY 10010. (646) 307-5151. E-mail: proposals@palgrave.com. A global academic publisher for scholarship, research and professional learning. We publish monographs, journals, reference works and professional titles, online and in print. With a focus on humanities and social sciences, Palgrave Macmillan offers authors and readers the very best in academic content whilst also supporting the community with innovative new formats and tools. Proposal form on Website. Guidelines at: http://www.palgrave.com/page/submit-a-proposal.

P&R PUBLISHING CO., 1102 Marble Hill Rd., Phillipsburg NJ 08865. (908) 454-0505. Fax (908) 859-2390. E-mail: editorial@prpbooks.com. Website: www.prpbooks.com. Company blog: http://prpbooks.com/blog. Aaron Gottier, editorial project mngr; Amanda Martin, developmental ed. Devoted to stating, defending, and furthering the gospel in the modern world. Publishes 45 titles/yr.; hardcover and trade paperbacks. Receives 400 submissions annually. Fewer than 10% of books from first-time authors. Accepts mss through agents. Reprints books. Prefers 140-240 pgs. **Royalty 10-15% of**

net; advance. Average first printing 3,500. Publication within 10-12 mos. Considers simultaneous submissions. Responds in 1-4 mos. Guidelines at: http://www.prpbooks. com/submission_form.php?session=cfccdfe3bc9e1be39f8960c14422c9a1.

Nonfiction: Proposal/2-3 chapters. E-mail only.

Fiction: Proposal/2-3 chapters. E-mail only. For children or teens.

Tips: "Direct biblical/Reformed content. Clear, engaging, and insightful applications of Reformed theology to life. Offer us fully developed proposals and polished sample chapters. Check our website to see the categories we publish."*

PARAGON HOUSE, 3600 Labore Rd., Ste. 1, St. Paul MN 55110-4144. (651) 644-3087. Fax (651) 644-0997. E-mail: submissions@paragonhouse.com. Website: www. paragonhouse.com. Gordon Anderson, acq. ed. Serious nonfiction and texts with an emphasis on religion, philosophy, and society. Imprints: Omega, Vision of ... Publishes 8-10 titles/yr.; hardcover, trade paperbacks, e-books. Receives 1,200 submissions annually. 20% of books from first-time authors. Accepts mss through agents or authors. Prefers average 250 pgs. **Royalty 7-10% of net; royalties paid as earned twice a year.** Average first printing1,500-3,000. Publication within 12-18 mos. Considers few simultaneous submissions. Accepts e-submissions (attached file). Responds in 1-2 mos. Guidelines at: http://www.paragonhouse.com/pages.php?pageid=15. Catalog on Website.

Nonfiction: Query; proposal/2-3 chapters or complete ms; no phone/fax query. Endorsements are helpful. "Looking for scholarly overviews of topics in religion and society; textbooks in philosophy; and ecumenical subjects."

PARSON PLACE PRESS LLC, Box 8277, Mobile AL 36689-0277. (251) 643-6985. E-mail: info@parsonplacepress.com. Website: www.parsonplacepress.com. Michael L. White, mng. ed. Devoted to giving both Christian authors and Christian readers a fair deal. Publishes 2-5 titles/yr.; hardcover, trade paperbacks, e-books. Receives about 25 submissions annually. 80% of books from first-time authors. Accepts mss through agents or authors. Does print-on-demand. Prefers 100-220 pgs. **Royalty on net; no advance.** Average first printing 50. Publication within 3 mos. No simultaneous submissions. Responds in 4-6 wks. Requested mss by e-mail (attached file). Prefers NKJV or NASB. Guidelines at: http://www.parsonplacepress.com/guide.html; electronic catalog on website.

Nonfiction: Proposal/2 chapters; e-query OK. Christian topic/content only.

Fiction: Proposal/2 chapters; e-query OK. For middle school through adult.

Special Needs: In nonfiction: end-times prophecy, evangelism, and Bible studies. In fiction: mystery, romance, historical.

Photos/Artwork: Accepts freelance photos for book covers; open to queries from freelance artists.

Tips: "Most open to conservative, biblically based content that ministers to Christians. Write intelligently, clearly, sincerely, and engagingly."

PARSONS PUBLISHING HOUSE, PO Box 488, Stafford VA 22555. (850) 867-3061. E-mail: info@parsonspublishinghouse.com. Website: www.parsonspublishing-house.com. We have a mandate to assist authors in releasing their voice to their world to impact it for Jesus Christ. Diane Parsons, chief ed. Exists to partner with authors to release their voice into their world. Imprint: PPH Books. Publishes 6-12 titles/yr.; hardcover, trade paperbacks. Receives 50-75 submissions annually. 75% of books from first-time authors. No mss through agents; accepts from authors. No subsidy. Does print-on-demand. Reprints books. Prefers 35,000-60,000 wds,; 160-200 pgs. **Royalty 10% on net; 10% for e-books; no advance.** Average first printing 1,000. Publication within 7 mos. Considers simultaneous submissions. Responds in 60 days. No preferred version. No catalog; guidelines at: http://www.parsonspublishinghouse.com.

Nonfiction: Book proposal/sample chapters; e-query OK.

Fiction: Query; proposal/3 chapters; e-query OK. For teens & adults.

Ethnic Books: Hispanic.

Special needs: Always need books about our victory in Christ.

Photos/Artwork: Accepts freelance photos for book covers; open to queries from freelance artists.

Tips: "Most open to a book that is about victory, and is positive about the saving grace of Christ and his delivering power."

PAULINE BOOKS & MEDIA, Daughters of St. Paul, 50 Saint Pauls Ave., Jamaica Plain MA 02130-3491. (617) 522-8911. E-mail: editorial@paulinemedia.com. Website: www.pauline.org. Catholic/Daughters of St. Paul. Christina Wegendt, FSP, and Sr. Sean Mayer, FSP, acq. eds.; Submit to Brittany Schlorff, ed. asst. Responds to the hopes and needs of their readers with the Word of God and in the spirit of St. Paul, utilizing all available forms of media so others can find and develop faith in Jesus within the current culture. Publishes 20 titles/yr.; hardcover & trade paperbacks. Receives 350-400 submissions annually. 10% of books from first-time authors. Accepts mss through agents or authors. No subsidy or print-on-demand. Reprints books. Prefers 10,000-60,000 wds. **Royalty 5-10% on net; offers an advance.** Average first printing 2,000-5,000. Publication within 24 mos. Considers simultaneous submissions. Responds in 2-3 mos. Prefers requested ms by e-mail. Prefers NRSV. Guidelines at: http://www.pauline.org/Publishing/Submit-a-Manuscript; free catalog by mail.

Nonfiction: Proposal/2 chapters; complete ms; e-query or snail mail queries.

Fiction: Book proposal/sample chapters. See entry for Pauline Kids and Teens; no adult fiction. Does children's board books, children's fiction picture books, juvenile (8-12 yrs.), and teen/YA fiction.

Ethnic books: Spanish language for children only.

Special Needs: "Spirituality (prayer/holiness of life/seasonal titles), faith formation (religious instruction/catechesis), family life (marriage/parenting issues), biographies of the saints, prayer books. Of particular interest is our faith and culture line, which includes titles that show how Christ is present and may be more fully embraced and proclaimed within our media culture."

Tips: "Most open to books that help readers discover hope. Submissions are evaluated on adherence to gospel values, harmony with the Catholic tradition, relevance of topic, and quality of writing."

This publisher serviced by The Writer's Edge.

PAULINE KIDS AND TEEN, 50 St. Paul's Ave., Boston MA 02130. (617) 522-8911. Fax (617) 524-9805. E-mail: editorial@paulinemedia.com. Website: www.pauline.org. Pauline Books & Media/Catholic. Marilyn Monge, FSP, and Jaymie Stuart Wolfe, eds. Seeks to provide wholesome and entertaining reading that can help children and teens develop strong Christian values. Publishes 20-25 titles/yr.; hardcover, trade paperbacks. Receives 300-450 submissions annually. 10% of books from first-time authors. Accepts mss through agents or authors. Reprints books. **Royalty 5-10% on net; pays an advance.** Average first printing 2,000-5,000. Publication within 18 mos. Considers simultaneous submissions. Responds in 2-3 mos. Prefers accepted ms by e-mail. Prefers NRSV. Guidelines at: http://www.pauline.org/Publishing/Submit-a-Manuscript; free catalog by mail.

Nonfiction/Fiction: Proposal/2 chapters for easy-to-read, middle-grade readers, and teen; complete ms for board and picture books; e-query OK.

Special Needs: Easy-to-read fiction, middle-grade nonfiction.

Photos/Artwork: Accepts freelance photos for book covers; open to queries from freelance artists. Send illustration queries to Sr. Mary Joseph Peterson, Design Dept., Pauline Books & Media, 50 St. Paul's Ave., Jamaica Plain MA 02130.

+PAULIST PRESS, 997 Macarthur Blvd., Mahwah NJ 07430-9990. Website includes separate guidelines in four different categories: academic, childrn's, popular, and professionsal or clergy books. Guidelines at: http://www.paulistpress.com/Pages/Center/auth_res_0.aspx.

+PELICAN BOOK GROUP, PO Box 1738, Aztec NM 87410. Website: http://pelicanbookgroup.com. Company blog: http://pelicanbookgroup.blogspot.com. Nicola Martinez, ed.-in-chief. Imprints: White Rose Publishing (see separate listing), Harbourlight Books (see separate listing), Watershed Books, Pure Amore. Publishes 52+ titles/yr. Accepts submissions through agents. No subsidy. Does print-on-demand. Prefers 10,000-80,000 wds. **Pays royalties & advance.** No simultaneous submissions. Reports in 120 days. Guidelines on Website.

   Fiction: E-mail query. For teens, new adults and adults

   Tips: "We're looking for well-written stories that remain true to the Gospel. Write your best book, and see if it fits our guidelines, then query us via our submission form on the Website."

PELICAN PUBLISHING CO. INC., 1000 Burmaster St., Gretna LA 70053. (504) 368-1175. Fax (504) 368-1195. E-mail: editorial@pelicanpub.com. Website: www.pelicanpub.com. Nina Kooij, ed-in-chief. To publish books of quality and permanence that enrich the lives of those who read them. Imprints: Firebird Press, Jackson Square Press, Dove Inspirational Press (see separate listing). Publishes 1 title/yr.; hardcover, trade paperbacks. Receives 250 submissions annually. No books from first-time authors. Accepts mss through agents or authors. Reprints books. Prefers 200+ pgs. **Royalty; pays some advances.** Publication within 9-18 mos. No simultaneous submissions. Responds in 1 mo. on queries. Requires accepted ms on disk. Prefers KJV. Guidelines at: http://www.pelicanpub.com/viewer.php?region=92.

   Nonfiction: Proposal/2 chapters; no phone/fax/e-query. Children's picture books to 1,100 wds. (send complete ms); middle readers about Louisiana (ages 8-12) at least 25,000 wds.; cookbooks at least 200 recipes.

   Fiction: Complete ms. Children's picture books only. For ages 5-8 only.

   Artwork: Open to queries from freelance artists.

   Tips: "On inspirational titles we need a high-profile author who already has an established speaking circuit so books can be sold at these appearances."

PLAYERS PRESS INC., PO Box 1132, Studio City CA 91614-0132. (818) 789-4980. E-mail: playerspress@att.net. Website: www.ppeps.com. (New website is under construction.) Robert W. Gordon, ed. To create is to live life's purpose. Publishes mostly dramatic works; prides themselves on high-quality titles. Imprints: Players Press, Brown Son Fergusson, Phantom Publications, and Showcase. Publishes 1-6 religious titles/yr.; hardcover, trade paperbacks, acting editions, workbooks, paperbacks, coffee table books. Receives 50-80 religious submissions annually. 90% of books from first-time authors. Accepts mss through agents or authors. No subsidy publishing. Does print-on-demand with older titles. Sometimes reprints quality theater titles and costume books. Variable length. **Royalty 10% on net; pays advances on some titles.** Average first printing 1,000-10,000. Publication within 12 mos. No simultaneous submissions. No submissions by e-mail. Responds in 1-3 wks. on query; 3-12 mos. on ms. Guidelines by mail; catalog for 9 x 12 SAE/11 stamps or $4.50.

Nonfiction/Plays: Query letter only; no phone/fax/e-query. "Always looking for plays and musicals, books on theater, film, and/or television. Good plays; all categories. For all ages." Likes religious, romantic, comic, and/or children's plays. New classic translations and musicals are important to them.

Contests: Sometimes sponsors a contest.

Photos/Artwork: Accepts freelance photos for book and play covers; open to queries from freelance artists.

Tips: "Most open to plays, musicals, books on theater, film, television, and supporting areas: cameras, lighting, costumes, etc."

PORT YONDER PRESS, 6332—33rd Ave. Dr., Shellsburg IA 52332. (319) 436-3015. E-mail: contact@portyonderpress.com. Website: www.PortYonderPress.com. Chila Woychik, mng. ed. Imprints: SharksFinn, SkySail, Sea Beast, and Port Yonder Books. Crossover publisher of both Christian and general market books. We want only the very best from those who claim to follow God, and we want it said in a way that draws rather then repels readers. Publishes 1-3 religious titles/yr.; hardcover, trade paperbacks. Receives 500 submissions annually. 20% of books from first-time authors. Accepts mss through agents or authors. No subsidy. Does print-on-demand. No reprints. Prefers 40,000-90,000 wds.; 250 pgs. **Royalty 40-50% on net; average $50 advance.** Average first print run 100. Publication within 12-18 mos. Considers simultaneous submissions. Responds in 1-3 mos. Any Bible version. Guidelines at: http://www.portyonderpress.com/submission-guidelines.html; no catalog.

Nonfiction: Query letter only first; e-query OK.

Fiction: For new adults, adults. Literary. Query letter only first.

Special need: Crossover-books for a wide audience: both faith and non-faith.

Artwork: Open to queries from freelance artists.

Tips: "We are most interested in Christians and writing which addresses universal themes, takes a broad view of the global scene, and is strong in literary merit. We disdain the judging of others. We want to see gut-level honesty and soul-level beauty. We prefer oblique biblical concepts over Bible verses and sermonizing."

PRAEGER PUBLISHERS, 130 Cremona Dr., Santa Barbara CA 93117. (805) 968-1911. E-mail: achiffolo@abc-clio.com. Website: www.abc-clio.com. Imprint of ABC-CLIO. Anthony Chiffolo, acq. ed. Primary market is public and university libraries worldwide; no bookstore distribution. Publishes 5-10 titles/yr. in religion; hardcover and e-book; nonfiction only. Receives 50-100 submissions annually. Accepts mss through agents or authors. No subsidy or reprints. Minimum length: 100,000 wds. **Variable royalty on net; pays minor advances.** Average first printing 450. Publication within 12-18 mos. Considers simultaneous submissions. Responds in 2-4 mos. Guidelines at: www.abc-clio.com; catalog on website.

Nonfiction: Thorough book proposal/1-3 chapters or all chapters available; e-query preferred.

Special Needs: Religion and society/culture; religious controversies/issues; paranormal; neuro-religion.

Ethnic Books: African American religion; Native American religion; Hispanic/Latino religion; Asian American religion.

Tips: "Most open to books on 'headline' issues and controversies; books on 'religion and culture' are needed; must be written for general, nonspecialist readership. No monographs/no dissertations. No self-help or how-to books. No scriptural studies or Bible scholarship. No fiction or poetry."

+PRAYERSHOP PUBLISHING, 3525 S. 3rd Place, Terre Haute IN 47802. (812)238-5504. Fax (812)235-6646. E-mail: jong@harvestprayer.com. Website: www. prayershoppublishing.com. Jonathan Graf, pub. Our ministry is to disciple people in prayer and grow praying churches. We only do resources that will move an individual or church deeper in prayer. Publishes 4-6 title/yr.; trade paperbacks, mass-market paperbacks. Receives 10-15 submissions annually. 15% of books from first-time authors. Accepts mss through agents or authors. Subsidy publishes 5%. Reprints books. Prefers 30,000-50,000 wds.; 128-144 pgs. **Royalty 10-15% of net; same for e-books.** No advance. Average first printing 3,500. Publication in up to 9 mos. Considers simultaneous submissions. Reports in 6-8 wks. Prefers NIV. Catalog on Website; guidelines by e-mail or on Website.

Nonfiction: Book proposal/sample chapters. E-mail & snail-mail queries OK. Books on prayer only.

Looking for: We prefer very practical books on prayer—ones that show how to pray or provide guides to help people learn to pray.

Tips: "Needs to be very practical and loaded with excellent personal illustrations. With first time authors, they have the best shot is they have a regular speaking ministry and plan to purchase a quantity at the start. While we do not require it of our authors, we obviously will not do a book if we do not think we can sell it, and it is tough, almost impossible these days, with first time authors to get their books into distributors and bookstores."

+PRISM BOOK GROUP. Joan Alley, owner/ed.-in-chief, (contact@prismbookgroup.com); Jacqueline Hopper, acq. ed., jhopper@prismbookgroup.com. Website: www.prismbookgroup.com. Publishes the best in quality fiction, with lines featuring romance, Christian romance, Christian fiction, young adult tiles, and more. Imprints: Inspired (Christian Romance Line), Illuminate (Christian fiction line). Small, independent publisher, opened in 2011. Traditional publisher, no subsidy. Publishes 20-40 titles annually. **Royalties paid quarterly.** Publishes in e-book format; print-on-demand trade paperbacks.

Tips: Our books offer clean and compelling reads for the discerning reader. You won't encounter graphic language or scenes between our pages, but you will find great stories, intense plots, and captivating characters.

+PURE AMORE, PO Box 1738, Aztec NM 87410. Email: customer@pelicanbookgroup.com Website: pelicanbookgroup.com. Division of Pelican Ventures, LLC. Nicola Martinez, editor-in-chief. Contemporary Christian romance. 40,000-45,000 wds. **Pays advance plus royalties.** Accepts unagented submissions. Responds to queries in 30 days, full ms in 120 days. No reprints. E-mail submissions only; see website for form and procedure

Fiction: Query via submission form on website. Pelican Pure Amore romances are sweet in tone and in conflict. These stories are the emotionally-driven tales of youthful Christians who are striving to live their faith in a world where Christ-centered choices may not fully be understood. Plots should not contain overly hard-hitting or controversial subjects but should be hope-filled, enjoyable reads that don't come with a lot of excess baggage. Stories should be written in an active, engaging style that leaves the reader satisfied and smiling. Plots should focus on the love between a man and a woman who both hold God at the center of their lives and who have never been married. The hero and heroine will exhibit traditional Christian values but also should be three-dimensional and therefore exhibit flaws as well as virtues.

Fiction guidelines: (1) Neither the hero nor heroine can have been married before. No divorced, separated, or widowed protagonists. (2) Both Hero and Heroine should be Christians throughout. While Pure Amore may feature subplots that include the hero or heroine rediscovering or growing to a deeper faith, these are not stories centered on conversion. Therefore, both Hero and Heroine must be Christian at the onset. (3) Either the hero or heroine, or both, must be a virgin. That means they must be a physical virgin as opposed to being a "rededicated" virgin, and this fact must be addressed naturally within the context of the story. (4) These are stories of Christians living Christian lives. Characters should adhere to mainline Christianity, but should not be preachy or didactic. The Christian element and/or lesson should be inherent to the characterizations and so should come through in the protagonists' natural actions/reactions to events and people around them. (5) Heroes and heroines must be between the ages of 21 and 33, inclusive. (6) All titles must be between 40,000 and 45,000 words. No exceptions.

Tips: "Pure Amore romances emphasize the beauty in chastity, so physical interactions such as kissing or hugging should focus on the characters' emotions rather than heightened sexual desire, and scenes of physical intimacy should be integral to the plot and/or emotional development of the character or relationship."

+QUIET WATERS PUBLICATIONS, PO Box 34, Bolivar MO 65613-0034. (417) 429-0834. E-mail: qwp@usa.net. Check out this publisher's guidelines at: www.quiet-waterspub.com.

+QUINTESSENTIAL BOOKS, PO Box 8755, Kansas City MO 84114. (816) 561-1555. Fax: (816) 561-4109. Publishes nonfiction and fiction. Publishes 5-10 titles/yr. Prefers 60,000-70,000 wds. Accepts reprints and simultaneous submissions. Responds in 3-5 mos. Publication within 18 mos. Guidelines at: http://www.quintessentialbooks. com/guidelines.html.

RAINBOW PUBLISHERS, PO Box 261129, San Diego CA 92196. (858) 277-1167. Fax: (858) 277-4743. E-mail: john.gregory@rainbowpublishers.com. Website: www. Rainbowpublishers.com. Legacy Press. John Gregory, ed. We are an established, well-respected publisher of Christian education materials, devotions, and fiction for ages 1-12. Imprint: Rainbow Publishers (see separate listing). Publishes 12-18 titles/yr.; mass-market paperbacks. Receives 208 submissions annually. 1% of books from first-time authors. Accepts submissions through agent or authors. No subsidy, print-on-demand, or reprints. Prefers 26,000 wds. or 200 pgs. **Pay $500-$1,000 for outright purchase.** Average first printing 1,500. Publication within 1 yr. Considers simultaneous submissions. Responds in 2-8 wks. Prefers NIV. Guidelines at: http://www.rainbowpublishers.com/submissions. aspx; no catalog

Nonfiction: Proposal/3-5 chapters; no e-queries.

Fiction: For children. Proposal/3 chapters. For ages 2-12 only.

Special Needs: Bible school activities ages 1 to 12, children's inspirational books, Christian fiction action-adventure.

Artwork: Open to queries from freelance artists.

Tips: "We prefer children's activities be included between chapters. Propose at least a 3-book series."

RANDALL HOUSE PUBLICATIONS, PO Box 17306., Nashville TN 37217. Toll-free (800) 877-7030. (615) 361-1221. Fax (615) 367-0535. E-mail: michelle. orr@randallhouse.com. Website: www.randallhouse.com. Free Will Baptist. Michelle Orr, sr. acq. ed. Publishes Sunday school and Christian education materials to make Christ known, from a conservative perspective. Publishes 10-15 titles/yr.; hardcover, trade paperbacks, digital. Receives 300-500 submissions annually. 40% of books from first-time authors. Accepts mss through agents or authors. No subsidy or reprints. Prefers 40,000 wds. **Royalty 12-18% on net; pays an advance.** Average first printing 5,000. Publication within 18 mos. Considers simultaneous submissions. Accepts requested mss by e-mail. Responds in 10-12 wks. Guidelines at: http://www.randall-house.com/root/downloads/BookProposalGuide_9-09.pdf; no catalog.

> **Nonfiction:** Query; e-query or mailed query OK; proposal/2 chapters. Must fill out book proposal form they provide.
>
> **Artwork:** Open to queries from freelance artists (andrea.young@randallhouse. com).
>
> **Tips:** "We are expanding our book division with a conservative perspective. We have a very conservative view as a publisher."
>
> This publisher serviced by ChristianManuscriptSubmissions.com.

RAVENHAWK BOOKS, 7739 E. Broadway Blvd., #95, Tucson AZ 85710. E-mail: ravenhawk6dof@yahoo.com. Website: www.6dofsolutions.com. Blog: see website. The 6DOF Group. Karl Lasky, pub.; Hans B. Shepherd, Jr., submissions ed. Publishes variable number of titles/yr.; hardcover, trade paperbacks. Receives 1,000-1,500 submissions annually. 70% of books from first-time authors. Print-on-demand. Reprints books. **Royalty 40-50% on gross profits after production costs; no advance.** Average first printing 2,500. Publication in up to 18 mos. Considers simultaneous submissions. Responds in 6 wks., if interested. Guidelines at: www.6dofsolutions.com. Catalog on website.Nonfiction: Query first; e-query OK. "Looking for profitable books from talented writers."

> **Nonfiction:** Query first; e-query OK. "Looking for profitable books from talented writers."
>
> **Fiction:** Query first. For all ages. Unsolicited full mss returned unopened.
>
> **Special Needs:** Looking for books from young authors, 16-22 years old.
>
> **Photos/Artwork:** Accepts freelance photos for book covers; open to queries from freelance artists.
>
> **Tips:** "Most open to crisp, creative, entertaining writing that also informs and educates. Writing, as any creative art, is a gift from God. Not everyone has the innate talent to do it well. We are author-oriented. We don't play games with the numbers."

REFERENCE SERVICE PRESS, 2310 Homestead Rd., Ste. C1 #219, Los Altos CA 94024. (650) 871-3170. Fax (650) 861-3171. E-mail: info@rspfunding.com. Website: www.rspfunding.com. R. David Weber, ed. Books related to financial aid and Christian higher education. Publishes 1 title/yr.; hardcover, trade paperbacks. Receives 3-5 submissions annually. Most books from first-time authors. No reprints. **Royalty 10% of net; usually no advance.** Publication within 5 mos. May consider simultaneous submissions. No guidelines; free catalog for 2 stamps.

> **Nonfiction:** Proposal/several chapters.
>
> **Special Needs:** Financial aid directories for Christian college students.

+REFORMATION TRUST PUBLISHING, 421 Ligonier Ct., Sanford FL 32771.

Toll free: (800) 435-4343. (407) 333-4244. Check out this publisher at: www.reformationtrust.com.

+REDBUD PRESS, 340 S. Lemon Ave. #1639, Walnut CA 91789. E-mail: info@redbudpress.com. Website: http://redbudpress.com. Lacy Williams, mng. ed. Submit to: Erin Taylor Young (erin@redbudpress.com). Uses innovative marketing and adaptive strategies to help published authors connect with readers who want more romance from voices they love. Imprints: Hometown Romance and Timeless. Publishes 16-24 titles/yr. 10% of books from first-time authors. Accepts submissions from agents. Does print-on-demand in trade paperback and digital. Hometown Romance: 45,000-65,000 wds.; Timeless: 45,000-110,000 wds. Royalties paid monthly. Pay rate for E-books. **No advance.** Publication within 9 mos. Considers simultaneous submissions. Responds in 2 mos. Guidelines and catalog on Website.

Fiction: Open to frontier romance, historical romance, and romance. Query letter only first. Published authors send a proposal/3 sample chapters. Debut authors send a proposal/complete ms.

Timeless imprint: Features previously published books that they bring back to the market for a new generation of readers. Primary consideration is the power of a memorable story. The romance thread needs to be very strong, but that doesn't mean the book has to fit squarely into the romance genre. A bent toward romantic suspense or historical, etc, would not exclude a great story from consideration.

Hometown Romance imprint: Story needs to be original, memorable, and of exceptional craftsmanship, with a strong sense of setting and community. While stories can be contemporary or historical, the romance must be the primary focus. Slots for debut authors are extremely limited.

+RESOURCE PUBLICATIONS, 160 E. Virginia St. #290, San Jose CA 95112-5878. (408) 286-8504. Fax: (408) 287-8748. Helen St. Paul, acquisitions ed. Provides imaginative resources that help lay and ordained pastoral leaders and volunteers in their ministries; pastoral and faith-based resources for personal growth and use by educators and other help professions. Three major markets: Religious ministry and education; public/private educators; and helping professions. Publishes 10-16 titles/yr. Royalty 8% of net; no advance. Author Data Questionnaire on Website. Guidelines at: http://www.rpinet.com/Pub_with_RPI.pdf.

REVELL BOOKS, 6030 E. Fulton Rd., Ada MI 49301. (616) 676-9185. Fax (616) 676-2315. Website: www.revellbooks.com. Imprint of Baker Publishing Group. Publishes inspirational fiction and nonfiction for the broadest Christian market. Catalog on website. No unsolicited proposals. Submit only through an agent, Authonomy.com, The Writer's Edge Service, or ChristianManuscriptSubmissions.com. Guidelines at: http://bakerpublishinggroup.com/contact/submission-policy.

+SAINT CATHERINE OF SIENA PRESS, 4812 N. Park Ave., Indianapolis IN 46205. (888) 232-1492. Check out this publisher at: www.saintcatherineofsienapress.com.

+SCEPTER PUBLISHERS, PO Box 1391, New Rochelle, NY 10802. Toll free: (800)322-8773. (212) 354-0670. Fax: (646) 417-7707. E-mail: info@scepterpublishers.org. Nathan Davis, ed. Send a 1-2 page proposal with cover letter by mail or e-mail. Guidelines at: http://www.scepterpublishers.org/contact/ (scroll down).

+SMYTH & HELWYS PUBLISHING, 6316 Peake Rd., Macon GA 31210-3960. (478) 757-0564. Fax: (478) 757-1305. E-mail: proposal@helwys.com. Submit hard copy of complete proposal, plus 2-4 sample chapters. Responds in several mos. Guidelines at: http://www.helwys.com/submit-a-manuscript.

STANDARD PUBLISHING, 8805 Governor's Hill Dr., Ste. 400, Cincinnati OH 45249. (513) 931-4050. Fax (513) 931-0950. Website: www.standardpub.com. CFM Religion Publishing Group LLC. Provides true-to-the-Bible resources that inspire, educate, and motivate Christians to a growing relationship with Jesus Christ. Accepts mss through agents or authors. Hardcover & trade paperbacks. No reprints. **Royalty or outright purchase; advance.** No simultaneous submissions. Responds in 3-6 mos. Prefers NIV/KJV. Guidelines at: http://www.standardpub.com/Pages/About/For_Writers.aspx.

> **Nonfiction:** Query only; e-query OK.
> **Fiction:** Query only; e-query OK. Children's picture or board books; juvenile novels.
> **Special Needs:** Adult and youth ministry resources; children's ministry resources. This publisher serviced by ChristianManuscriptSubmissions.com and The Writer's Edge.

ST. ANTHONY MESSENGER PRESS (see Franciscan Media)

SUMMERSIDE PRESS/GUIDEPOSTS, 16 E. 34th St., 12th Floor, New York NY 10016. (212) 251-8100. E-mail: info@summersidepress.com. Website: www.summersidepress.com . Rachel Meisel, ed. dir. Inspirational romance fiction series. Accepts mss through agents only. Publishes 12 titles/yr. Prefers 80,000-100,000 wds. Guidelines on website ("Submissions").

> **Fiction:** Agents send paragraph overview plus a 2-3 page synopsis and 3 sample chapters by e-mail (attached files).

SUNPENNY PUBLISHING, Sunpenny Limited, Urbanització Tossal Gross, 90-1, La Font d'en Carròs, 46717, Valencia Communidad, Spain. Based in England & Spain. E-mail: Sunpenny group@gmail.com. Website: www.sunpenny.com. Interested in travel, sailing and boating books, adventure, historical novels, inspirational romance, women's fiction. Mainstream and literary fiction, courage and overcoming, gift & coffee-table books; also books for children & young teens, and are opening up to commercial nonfiction. Jo Holloway, ed. Submit a 1-2 pg. synopsis Publishes 15-20 titles/yr.; hardcover, trade paperbacks, mass-market paperbacks, electronic originals (e-books). 50% of books from first-time authors. Accepts mss through agents or authors. **Royalty on sliding scale beginning at 15% of margin.** Considers simultaneous submissions. Responds in 1-2 wks. to queries; 1-2 mos. to proposals; 2-3 mos. to manuscripts. Guidelines at: http://www.sunpenny.com/#!submissions; catalog on website.

> **Nonfiction:** Query, proposal, or complete ms.
> **Fiction:** Query, proposal, or complete ms. Children's, general fiction, romance, and Christian/inspirational books.
> **Photos/Artwork:** Accepts freelance photos for book covers; open to queries from freelance artists.

TATE PUBLISHING & ENTERPRISES LLC, Tate Publishing—Executive Office Bldg., 127 E. Trade Center Ter., Mustang OK 73064-4421. Toll-free (888) 361-9473. Fax (405) 376-4401. E-mail: publish@tatepublishing.com. Website: www.tatepublishing.com. Dr. Richard Tate, founder and chairman of the board. Owns and operates a state-of-the-art book manufacturing printing plant facility. Hardcover, trade paperbacks, e-books, CD's, DVD's and mass-market paperbacks. All work is done by professional in-house staff of over 500 full-time employees. Tate is a traditional publisher and absorbs 100% of the cost of production, manufacturing, marketing, and distribution of the few works that are selected. No production work is outsourced for any project. Receives 60,000-75,000 unsolicited contacts annually and only a single digit percentage are actually published. 60% of books from first-time authors. Accepts mss through agents. Authors are not required to purchase their books and there are no minimum purchase requirements for authors. Some first-time unpublished authors may be asked to contribute a refundable $3,990.00 retainer if they cannot provide legitimate marketing and publicist staff and must use Tate Publishing marketing and publicist staff assigned to their book. The retainer is refunded to the author once the book sells 1,000 copies in distribution and advances are then considered on future submissions. Not print-on-demand. Reprints books. Prefers 115,000 wds. **Royalty 15-40% of net; negotiable author cash advances and no refundable retainer if the author meets minimum requirements.** Average first print budget is 5,000. Publication within 90 days is an option if certain criteria met. Considers simultaneous submissions. Responds in 3-6 wks. Accepts submissions by e-mail or US mail. Any Bible version. Guidelines by mail/e-mail/website; free catalog.

Nonfiction: Proposal with synopsis & any number of chapters, or complete ms; phone/fax/e-query OK. Any topic. "Looking for books by authors who know how to work with our marketing and publicist staff to sell books."

Fiction: Proposal with synopsis & any number of chapters or complete ms; phone/fax/e-query OK. For all ages. Any genre.

Ethnic Books: For all ethnic markets.

Artwork: Has full-time artists on staff; open to queries from freelance artists.

+TAU-PUBLISHING, 4727 N. 12th St., Phoenix AZ 85014. (602) 625-6183. Fax: (602) 651-1875. E-mail through Website. Imprint of Vesuvius Press, Inc. Prefers e-mail submission. Guidelines at: http://www.tau-publishing.org/showPage.aspx?pageID=276.

TRAIL MEDIA, PO Box 1265, Valley Center CA 92082. (760) 212-6519. E-mail: submissions@ChisholmTrailMedia.com. Website: www.ChisholmTrailMedia.com. Dana S. Chisholm, pub. Publishes 20 mss/yr. Receives 100 mss/yr. 100% first-time authors. Does mss through agents. No subsidy. Paperbacks, Digital. **Royalty negotiable.** Publication within 6 mos. Will consider simultaneous submissions. Guidelines at: http://chisholmtrailmedia.com/Submission-Guidelines.htm.

Nonfiction: Submit proposal with one chapter. E-mail queries only.

Fiction: Adult, children, teen. Most interested in YA, children's illustrated, historical fiction, adult/general. Query letter first by e-mail.

Tips: We are a new publishing house specifically established to help new authors refine their work and publish, with professional editors and graphic artists, no up-front fees. We are looking for nonfiction inspirational life experiences, YA fiction, children's illustrated books, and Americana (getting back to the founders' intent). The industry is flooded with self-publishing options, or authors can submit to big publishing houses and face rejection after rejection. Trail Media is called to meet writers in the gap.

THE TRINITY FOUNDATION, PO Box 68, Unicoi TN 37692. (423) 743-0199. Fax (423) 743-2005. E-mail: tjtrinityfound@aol.com. Website: www.trinityfoundation.org. Thomas W. Juodaitis, pres. To promote the logical system of truth found in the Bible. Publishes 3-5 titles/yr.; hardcover, trade paperbacks, digital. Receives 10 submissions annually. 5% of books from first-time authors. Accepts mss through agents. Reprints books. Subsidy publishes 5-10%. No print-on-demand. Prefers 100-200 pgs.

Outright purchases up to $2,000; free books; no advance. Average first printing 1,000-2,000. Publication within 6 mos. No simultaneous submissions. Responds within a week. Prefers KJV or NKJV. Guidelines by e-mail or at: www.trinityfoundation.org; catalog on website.

> **Nonfiction:** Book proposal/sample chapters. Open to Calvinist/Clarkian books, Christian philosophy, economics, and politics. Accepts snail mail or e-mail queries.
> **Also Does:** Pamphlets, booklets, tracts.
> **Photos/Artwork:** Accepts freelance photos for book covers; open to queries from freelance artists.
> **Contest:** Christian Worldview Essay Contest for ages 17-23 based on a book they publish. Details on Website.
> **Tips:** "Most open to doctrinal books that conform to the Westminster Confession of Faith; nonfiction, biblical, and well-reasoned books, theologically sound, clearly written, and well organized. Must be biblical."

+TROITSA BOOKS, 400 Oser Ave., Ste. 1600, Hauppauge NY 11788-3619. (631) 231-7269. Fax: (631) 231-8175. e-mail: nova.main@novapublishers.com. Religious imprint of Nova Science Publishers. Book Idea Form on Website. Check out this publisher's guidelines at: https://www.novapublishers.com/catalog/index.php?page=for_authors.

TYNDALE ESPAÑOL, 351 Executive Dr., Carol Stream IL 60188. (630) 784-5272. Fax (630) 344-0943. E-mail: andresschwartz@tyndale.com. Website: www.tyndale.com. Andres Schwartz, publisher—Spanish division of Tyndale House Publishers. Guidelines on website.

TYNDALE HOUSE PUBLISHERS, INC., 351 Executive Dr., Carol Stream IL 60188. Toll-free (800) 323-9400. (630) 668-8300. Toll-free fax (800) 684-0247. E-mail through website: www.tyndale.com. Submit to Manuscript Review Committee. Practical Christian books for home and family. Imprints: Tyndale Español (Spanish imprint). Publishes 150-200 titles/yr.; hardcover, trade paperbacks. 5% of books from first-time authors. Requires mss through agents. Average first printing 5,000-10,000. Publication within 9 mos. Considers simultaneous submissions. Responds in 3-6 mos. Prefers NLT. Unable to accept manuscript proposals from anyone except literary agents or writers who work has already been published. Guidelines/catalog on website (under "Site Map"/"Authors"/"Manuscript Policy").

> **Nonfiction:** Query from agents or published authors only; no phone/fax query. No unsolicited mss (they will not be acknowledged or returned).
> **Fiction:** Novels 75,000-100,000 wds. All must have an evangelical Christian message."
> **Also Does:** E-books.
> This publisher serviced by ChristianManuscriptSubmissions.com and The Writer's Edge.

+UNIVERSITY OF ARKANSAS PRESS, McIlroy House, 105 N. McIlroy Ave., Fayetteville AR 72701. toll free: (800) 626-0090. Website: www.uapress.com. Full guidelines at: https://uark.submittable.com/submit/33040.

WARNER PRESS INC., 1201 E. 5th St., Anderson IN 46012. Fax (765) 640-8005. Website: www.warnerpress.org. Joe Allison, ed. (jallison@warnerpress.org), intergenerational discipleship resources and Bible electives. Read more at his blog: www.newlifetogether.org. Karen Rhodes, ed. (krhodes@warnerpress.org), church and ministry resources. Robin Fogle, ed. (rfogle@warnerpress.org0, children's resources, greeting cards and teaching resources. Our purpose is to equip the Church with creative products and solutions combined with exceptional service to glorify God, advance His Kingdom, and give hope for future generations. Hardcover, paperback, and e-books. Receives 100+ submissions annually. Accepts mss through agents or authors. **Royalty & advance based on the author and type of book.** Publication within 12 mos. Considers simultaneous submissions. Responds in 6-8 wks. Prefers KJV or NIV. Guidelines at: http://www.warnerpress.org/custom.aspx?id=3; no catalog.

Nonfiction: Complete ms; fax/e-query OK. Accepts e-mail submissions. We are currently accepting mss for adult Bible studies (personal and small group) and personal spiritual growth, as well as short instructional booklets (32-64 pgs.) dealing with various aspects of ministry and leadership.

Artwork: Send to Curtis Corzine, Creative Art Director (curtis@warnerpress.org).

WATERBROOK PRESS, 12265 Oracle Blvd., Ste. 200, Colorado Springs CO 80921. (719) 590-4999. Fax (719) 590-8977. E-mail: info@waterbrookmultnomah.com. Website: www.waterbrookmultnomah.com. Part of WaterBrook Multnomah, a division of Random House Inc. Laura Barker, ed. dir. Publishes 75 titles/yr.; hardcover, trade paperbacks. **Royalty on net; advance.** WaterBrook is currently not accepting unsolicited manuscripts, proposals, or queries; no proposals for biographies or poetry. Queries will be accepted though literary agents and at writers conferences at which a WaterBrook representative is present. Guidelines at: http://waterbrookmultnomah.com/submissions; catalog on website.

Nonfiction/Fiction: Agented submissions only.

This publisher serviced by The Writer's Edge.

WATERSHED BOOKS, PO Box 1738, Aztec NM 87410. E-mail: customer@pelicanbookgroup.com. Website: www.pelicanbookgroup.com. Division of Pelican Ventures, LLC. Nicola Martinez, editor-in-chief. Christian fiction 25,000-60,000 wds. Limited-edition hardback, trade paperbacks, and e-book. Royalty 40% on download; 7% on print. Pays nominal advance. Accepts unagented submissions. Responds to queries in 30 days, full ms in 90 days. Considers reprints but accepts few. E-mail submissions only; see website for submission form and procedure.

Fiction: Query via submission form on website. Interested in series ideas. Submissions must be Young Adult fiction that features young adult characters.

WESLEYAN PUBLISHING HOUSE, PO Box 50434, Indianapolis IN 46250-0434. (317) 774-7900. E-mail: wph@wesleyan.org. Website: www.wesleyan.org/wph. The Wesleyan Church. No longer accepting unsolicited submissions.

WHITAKER HOUSE, 1030 Hunt Valley Cir., New Kensington PA 15068. (724) 334-7000. Fax: (724) 334-1200. E-mail: publisher@whitakerhouse.com. Website: www.whitakerhouse.com. Whitaker Corp. Tom Cox, mng. ed. A family-owned and operated company, we are dedicated to spreading the good news of Christ and His message all over the world for over 40 years. Imprints: Banner Publishing, Resolute Books. Publishes 70 titles/yr.; hardcover, trade paperbacks, mass-market paperbacks, digital. Receives 50-100 submissions annually. 15-20% of books from first-time authors. Prefers mss through agents. Subsidy publishes 5-10%. Does print-on-demand. Reprints books. Prefers 40,000-70,000 wds.; 96-336 pgs. **Royalty 6-20% on net; e-books 25%; variable advances.** Average first printing 5,000. Publication within 4-6 mos. Considers simultaneous submissions. Responds in 4-6 mos. Guidelines at: http://www.whitakerhouse.com/downloads/WhitakerManuscriptSubmissionGuidelines.pdf; no catalog.

Nonfiction/Fiction: Query letter only first; e-mail & snail-mail query OK.
Fiction: For Adults. Query letter only first. Especially want inspirational romance and Amish fiction.
Special Needs: Christian nonfiction for a general audience, Charismatic titles.
Ethnic Books: Black, Hispanic.
Photos: Accepts freelance photos for book covers.
Tips: "Looking for quality nonfiction and fiction by authors with a national marketing platform. Most open to high-quality, well-thought-out, compelling pieces of work. Review the guidelines and submit details as thoroughly as possible for publication consideration."

WHITE FIRE PUBLISHING, 13607 Bedford Rd. NE, Cumberland MD 21502. (866) 245-2211. E-mail: info@whitefire-publishing.com. Website: www.whitefire-publishing.com. Roseanna White (r.white@whitefire-publishing.com), fiction acquisitions; Dina Sleiman (d.sleiman@whitefire-publishing.com,) fiction acquisitions; Wendy Chorot, non-fiction acquisitions. Publishes 7-12 titles/yr.; trade paperbacks & digital. Receives 100 submissions annually. 25% of books from first-time authors. Accepts mss through agents or authors. No subsidy. Does print-on-demand. Prefers 50,000-115,000 wds. **Royalty 10-50% on retail. E-books 50% on net. Offers advance.** Average first run 1,000. Publication in 12 months. Considers simultaneous submissions. Responds to proposals within 3-6 months. Catalog and guidelines on website: http://whitefire-publishing.com/wordpress/sample-page/what-were-looking-for.
   Nonfiction: New adults & adults. Query letter only first; book proposal/sample chapters. Query by e-mail. Narrative nonfiction. Must meet our motto of "Where Spirit Meets the Page." Send to Wendy Chorot, Nonfiction Editor at w.chorot@whitefire-publishing.com.
   Fiction: Query letter only first; book proposal/sample chapters. Query by e-mail. Accepts fiction for teens and adults. Likes historical, especially with exotic settings and with romance threads.
   Photos: Accepts freelance photos for book covers; open to queries from freelance artists.
   Tips: "We love books with strong hooks and unmistakable voice, where the author's passion for his or her story or topic comes shining through from page 1. For a good idea of whether a manuscript fill fit our line, it's a good idea to familiarize oneself with our other titles."

WHITE ROSE PUBLISHING, PO Box 1738, Aztec NM 87410. E-mail: customer@pelicanbookgroup.com. Website: http://pelicanbookgroup.com. An imprint of Pelican Book Group. Nicola Martinez, ed.-in-chief. Christian romance 10,000-80,000 wds. Limited-edition hardback, trade paperbacks, and digital. **Royalty 40% on download; 7% on print. Pays nominal advance.** Accepts unagented submissions. Responds to queries in 30 days, full ms in 90 days. Considers reprints but accepts few. E-mail submissions only; guidelines at: http://pelicanbookgroup.com/ec/index.php?main_page=page&id=55&zenid=25dcd651c49b295c26aa5682d1a3d3d6.
   Fiction: Query via submission form on website. Interested in series ideas. Submissions must be Christian romance.

+WILSHIRE BOOK CO, 9731 Variel Ave., Chatsworth CA 91311-4315. Prefers 30,000 words for adult allegories; 60,000 wds. for nonfiction works. No e-mail submissions. Publishes adult allegories that teach principles of psychological/spiritual growth. Guidelines at: http://www.mpowers.com/becomepublished.html.

+WIPF AND STOCK PUBLISHERS 199 W 8th Ave., Ste. 3, Eugene, OR 97401-2960. (541) 344-1528. Fax: (541) 344-1506. E-mail: Proposal@wipfandstock.com. Send proposal by e-mail; attached file. Proposal form on Website. Responds in 4-6 wks. Check guidelines at: http://wipfandstock.com/submitting-a-proposal?hl=

WORTHY PUBLISHING GROUP, 134 Franklin Road, Ste 200, Brentwood TN 37027. (615) 932-7600. Website: http://www.worthypublishing.com. Imprints: Worthy Publishing, Freeman-Smith, Ellie Claire. Publishes 36 titles/yr. Requires submission by agents. Hardcover, trade paperbacks, digital. **Offers advance.** Guidelines on website. Unsolicited mss returned unopened.

    Fiction: Adult.

WRITE INTEGRITY PRESS, 130 Prominence Point Pkwy., #130-330, Canton GA 30114. (678) 493-9330. E-mail: editor@writeintegrity.com. Websites: www.WriteIntegrity.com and www.PixNPens.com. "We view our authors as family—we team together to support, promote, and pray for one another." Tracy Ruckman, pub. Imprints: Write Integrity Press (WIP), Pix-N-Pens Publishing (PNP), and TMP Books (TMP). WIP publishes 6-8 titles/yr.; PNP 3-5; and TMP 10+. Receives 200+ proposals/yr. 75% from first-time authors. Subsidy publishes 10% through TMP. Accepts books submitted by agents. Does print-on-demand. Trade paperbacks, digital. No reprints. **Royalty 50% on net; no advance.** Publication in 6-8 mos. Responds in 2 mos. Guidelines on website: http://www.writeintegrity.com (click on "submissions").

    Nonfiction: Book proposal with sample chapters. Accepts e-mail queries.

    Fiction: For children, teens and adults. Book proposal/sample chapters. Strong preference for contemporary fiction, mystery/suspense, others that don't fit a formula. We don't publish traditional historical novels, but we are open to novels set from the 1940s to present.

    Contest: Hosts different writing contests each year. Check Website for updates.

    Tips: "Be professional. Be courteous. Have a website and social media presence. Write Integrity Press publishes clean, wholesome entertainment. Pix-N-Pens Publishing is our evangelical imprint, and each book will carry a strong gospel message."

WRITE NOW PUBLICATIONS, PO Box 110390, Nashville TN 37222. Toll-free (800) 21-WRITE. E-mail: RegAForder@aol.com. Website: www.writenowpublications.com. Reg A. Forder, exec. ed. To train and develop quality Christian writers; books on writing and speaking for writers and speakers. Royalty division of ACW Press. Publishes 1-2 titles/yr.; trade paperbacks. Receives 6 submissions annually. 0% from first-time authors. Accepts mss through agents or authors. Reprints books. **Royalty 10% of net.** Average first printing 2,000. Publication within 12 mos. Considers simultaneous submissions. Requires requested ms on disk. Guidelines at: www.writenowpublications.com; no catalog.

    Nonfiction: Writing how-to only. Query letter only; e-query OK.

YALE UNIVERSITY PRESS, 302 Temple St., New Haven CT 06511. (203) 432-6807. Fax (203) 436-1064. E-mail: jennifer.banks@yale.edu. Website: www.yalebooks.com. Jennifer Banks, exec. ed. By publishing serious works that contribute to a global understanding of human affairs, Yale University Press aids in the discovery and dissemination of light and truth, *lux et veritas,* which is a central purpose of Yale University. The publications of the Press are books and other materials that further scholarly investigation, advance interdisciplinary inquiry, stimulate public debate, educate both within and outside the classroom, and enhance cultural life. In its commitment to increasing the range and vigor of intellectual pursuits within the university and elsewhere, Yale University Press continually extends its horizons to embody university publishing at its best. Publishes 30 religious titles/yr.; hardcover, trade paperbacks, digital. Receives 1,000 submissions annually. 10% of books from first-time authors. Accepts mss through agents or authors. Does print-on-demand. Reprints books. **Royalty 15-25% of net; advance $0-100,000.** Publication within 1 yr. Considers simultaneous submissions. Requires requested ms on hard copy; no e-mail submissions. Responds in 2 mos. Guidelines at: http://www.yalebooks.com/yupbooks/submissions.asp; catalog on website.

Nonfiction: Proposal/sample chapters; accepts snail mail queries. "Excellent and salable scholarly books."

Contest: Yale Series of Young Poets; Yale Drama Series.

+YOUTH SPECIALTIES, 3530 E. 28th St., Ste. 100, Minneapolis MN 55406. Website: ys@youthspecialites.com. Youth Specialties publishes books, curricula, and other products. Send proposal by e-mail with attached file to: publishing@youth specialties.com. Check this publisher's guidelines at: http://youthspecialties.com/aboutus/writeforus.

ZONDERKIDZ, 5300 Patterson S.E., Grand Rapids MI 49530-0002. (616) 698-6900. Fax (616) 698-3578. E-mail: zpub@zondervan.com. Website: www.zonderkidz.com. Zondervan/ HarperCollins. Children's book line of Zondervan; ages 12 & under. Not currently accepting proposals. Guidelines at: http://zondervan.com/about/manuscripts.

This publisher serviced by ChristianManuscriptSubmissions.com.

ZONDERVAN, General Trade Books; Academic and Professional Books, 5300 Patterson S.E., Grand Rapids MI 49530-0002. (616) 698-6900. Manuscript submission line: (616) 698-3447. E-mail through website: www.zondervan.com. HarperCollins Publishers. Mission is to be the leading Christian communications company meeting the needs of people with resources that glorify Jesus Christ and promote biblical principles. Publishes 120 trade titles/yr.; hardcover, trade paperbacks, mass-market paperbacks. No subsidy or reprints. **Royalty 12-14% of net; variable advance.** Publication within 12-18 mos. Requires requested ms by e-mail. Prefers NIV. Guidelines at: http://zondervan.com/about/manuscripts; catalog online.

Nonfiction: Submissions only by e-mail and only certain types of mss. See website for e-mail address and submission guidelines.

Fiction: No fiction at this time; refer to website for updates.

Special Needs: Currently accepting unsolicited book proposals in academic, reference, or ministry resources only (see guidelines).

Children's Lines: ZonderKidz and Faithgirlz (not currently accepting new products).

Ethnic Books: Vida Publishers division: Spanish and Portuguese.

Tips: "Almost no unsolicited manuscripts are published. Book proposals should be single-spaced with one-inch margins on all sides."

This publisher serviced by ChristianManuscriptSubmissions.com and The Writer's Edge.

3

Subsidy Publishers

A subsidy publisher requires that the author pay for any part of the publishing costs. They may call themselves by a variety of names, such as book packager, cooperative publisher, self-publisher, or simply someone who helps authors get their books printed. Print-on-demand (POD) businesses print books in quantities as few as one at a time and usually much faster than traditional publishers. Custom publishers develop new authors to eventually work with royalty publishers.

To my knowledge the following subsidy publishers are legitimate (as opposed to simply being out to take your money and offering little in return), but I cannot guarantee that. Any time you pay for any part of the production of your book, you are entering into a nontraditional relationship. Some subsidy publishers do some royalty publishing, so you could approach them as a royalty publisher. They are likely to offer you a subsidy deal, so if you are interested only in a royalty arrangement, indicate that in your cover letter.

Some subsidy publishers will publish any book, as long as the author is willing to pay for it. Others are as selective about what they publish as a royalty publisher would be. As subsidy publishers become more selective, the professional quality of subsidy books is improving.

It has been my experience that for every complaint I get about a publisher, several other authors sing the praises of the same publisher. All I can do is give a brief overview of what to expect from a subsidy publisher and what terms should raise a red flag.

If you are unsuccessful placing your book with a royalty publisher but feel strongly about seeing it published, a subsidy publisher can make printing your book easier and often less expensive than doing it yourself. Having it produced as a e-book is also an option.

Get more than one bid to determine whether the terms you are being offered are competitive. A legitimate subsidy publisher will provide a list of former clients as references. Get a catalog of the publisher's books to check the quality of their work, the covers, bindings, etc. See if their books are available through Amazon.com or similar online services. Get answers before committing yourself. Also have someone in the book publishing industry review your contract before you sign it. Some experts listed in the Editorial Services section of this book do review contracts. The listings that follow include printers who could help you complete the printing process yourself.

The more copies of a book printed, the lower the cost per copy. But never let a publisher talk you into more copies than you think is reasonable. Also, some subsidy publishers will do as much promotion as a royalty publisher; others do none at all. If the publisher is not doing promotion and you don't have any means of distribution, you may prefer print-on-demand so you don't end up with a garage full of books you can't sell.

Definitions of different types of publishers:

Commercial/Mainstream/Traditional Publisher: One who takes all the risks and pays all the costs of producing and promoting your book (see previous book section).

Vanity Publisher: Prints at the author's expense. Will print any book the author is willing to pay for. May offer marketing help, warehousing, editing, or promotion of some sort at the author's expense.

Subsidy Publisher: Shares the cost of printing and binding a book. Often more selective, but the completed books belong to the publisher, not the author. Author may buy books from the publisher and may also collect a royalty for books the publisher sells.

Self-Publishing: Author pays all the costs of publishing the book and is responsible for all the marketing, distribution, promotion, etc. Author may select a service package that defines the cost and services. The books belong to the author and he/she keeps all the income from sales. Following this section, I include the names and addresses of Christian book distributors. Some will consider distributing a subsidy-published book. You may want to contact them to determine their interest before you sign a contract with a subsidy publisher. For more help on self-publishing, go to: www.bookmarket. com/index.html.

(*) before a listing indicates unconfirmed information or no information update.
+ A plus sign means it is a new listing

+AARON BOOK PUBLISHING, 1104 Bristol Caverns Hwy., Bristol TN 37620. (423) 212-1208. E-mail: info@aaronbookpublishing.com. Website: www. AaronBookPublishing.com. Lidany Rouse, acq. ed. Professional self-publishing, print-on-demand. Book covers, formatting, editing, printing, and marketing products. **100% royalty from net sales.** Considers simultaneous submissions. Hardcover, paperback, coffee table books. Prefers mss by e-mail. Guidelines on website.

Nonfiction/Fiction: Query first; proposal/2-3 chapters; e-query.

Special Needs: Books of good content. Strong characters, great story line.

Artwork: Open to queries from freelance artists.

Tips: Open to almost any topic. Guidelines at: http://www. aaronbookpublishing.com/Publishing%20Services.htm.

ABUZZ PRESS, 5726 Cortez Rd. W. #349, Bradenton FL 34210. Fax: (305) 768-0261. E-mail: angela@booklocker.com. Website: www.AbuzzPress.com. Angela Hoy, pub. Parent Co.: Booklocker.com. Abuzz Press is for authors who are serious about selling books. We offer fast and free print and electronic book publication and distribution. Publishes a variable number of book annually; trade paperbacks. Receives 200 submissions/yr. 50% of books from first-time authors. No submissions from agents. No subsidy. Does print-on-demand. Reprints books. Prefers 48-1,050 pgs. **Royalty 25-40% on net; e-books 25%-35%. Will consider purchasing all rights to a book on a case-by-case basis.** No advance. Considers simultaneous submissions. Responds in one week. Catalog & guidelines on Website.

Nonfiction: Query letter only first; book proposal/sample chapters; complete ms.; e-query OK.

Fiction: Complete ms.; e-query OK. For children, teens, and new adults.

Photos: Accepts freelance photos for book covers.

Also does: Computer games.

ACW PRESS, American Christian Writers, PO Box 110390, Nashville TN 37222. Toll-free (800) 21-WRITE. E-mail: Jim@JamesWatkins.com. Website: www.acwpress. com. Reg A. Forder, owner; James Watkins, editorial advisor. A self-publishing book packager. Imprint: Write Now Publications (see separate listing). Publishes 40 titles/ yr.; hardcover, trade paperbacks, mass-market paperbacks, coffee table books. Reprints books. Subsidy publishes 95%; does print-on-demand. Average first printing 200+. Publication within 2-4 mos. Responds within 8 hrs. Request estimate by sending number of words in ms to Jim@JamesWatkins.com. Not in topical listings; will consider any nonfiction, fiction, or poetry. Guidelines on website.

Nonfiction/Fiction/Poetry: All types considered.

Tips: "We offer a high-quality publishing alternative to help Christian authors get their material into print. High standards, high quality. If authors have a built-in audience, they have the best chance to make self-publishing a success." Has a marketing program available to authors.

This publisher serviced by ChristianManuscriptSubmissions.com.

AMPELOS PRESS, 951 Anders Rd., Lansdale PA 19446. Phone/fax: (484) 991-8581. E-mail: mbagnull@aol.com. Website: http://writehisanswer.com/ampelospress. Marlene Bagnull, acq. ed. Especially interested in helping authors independntly publish books about missions and the needs of children such as The Place of the Mourning Doves—Reaching Out to Romanian Orphans and The Quest of the Kenyan Pastor. Publishes 2-3 titles/yr.; trade paperback, digital. Not actively soliciting ms. 50% of books from first-time authors. Does print-on-demand & e-books. No reprints. Prefers 60,000 wds. No minimum purchase required. **Author receives 100% royalty.** Publication in 6 mos. Responds in 2 mos. No catalog or guidelines.

Nonfiction: Query letter only first; e-query OK Requires ms via e-mail.

Fiction: Query letter only first. For adults.

+ASHBERRY LANE PUBLISHING, PO Box 665, Gaston OR 97119. (503)860-5069. E-mail: christina@ashberrylane.com. Website: www.ashberrylane.com. Company blog: http://ashberrylane.com/category/latest-news. Christian Tarabochia, acq. ed.; Sherrie Ashcraft, co-owner. Publishes Heartfelt Tales of Faith—stories that point to God, but might not fit with the larger CBA houses. Publishes 12 title/yr.; trade paperback, digital. Receives 70 submissions annually. 50% of books from first-time author. No print-on-demand. Reprints books. Preferred book length: YA fiction 45,000-70,000 wds.; middle grade fiction 25,000-45,000 wds.; novel 85,000-100,000 wds. No retail sales team. Publishes & distributes e-books. **Royalty 50%. Royalties paid twice a yr.** Publication in 3-6 mos. Responds in 1-2 mos. Catalog free on request; guidelines on Website.

Nonfiction: E-mail query. Prefers submission by e-mail.

Fiction: For all ages. Proposal/sample chapters.

Legendary editor
Dave Lambert advises,
"Learn to see your fiction
as your reader will," in
Three Things Readers Expect
page 442

BK ROYSTON PUBLISHING LLC, PO Box 4321, Jeffersonville IN 47131. (502) 802-5385. E-mail: bkroystonpublishing@gmail.com. Website: www.bkroystonpublishing.com. Julia A. Royston, CEO. The focus of the BK Royston Publishing LLC are books that inform, inspire, and entertain. Imprints: Everyday Miracles, Frontline Worshipper, How Hot Is Your Love Life, 30 Lessons That the Student Taught the Teacher, Yield, All New Season in Word. Publishes 5-10 titles/yr. Receives 20 mss/yr. 95% first-time authors. Prefers books submitted by agents. SUBSIDY PUBLISHES 10%. Print-on-demand. Hardcover, trade, mass-market, digital. **Royalty 30-50% based on net.** Pays for e-books. First printing 50. Publishes in 4-8 mos. Considers simultaneous submissions. Responds in 1 mo. Guideline by e-mail. Accepts freelance photos for covers. Open to queries from freelance artists. Prefers KJV. Guidelines at: http://bkroystonpublishing.com/2014/01/15/calling-all-writers-bk-royston-publishing-is-accepting-submissions.

Nonfiction: Query letter only first. Accepts phone queries and e-mail queries. Mss by e-mail.

Fiction: All genres. Query letter only first.

Tips: Desires Christian fiction books.

BOOKLOCKER.COM INC., 5726 Cortez Road W. #349, Bradenton FL 34210. (305) 768-0261. E-mail: angela@booklocker.com. Website & blog: www.booklocker.com. Angela Hoy, pub. We break even on set-up fees and earn profits on book sales. Every BookLocker author receives a free copy of *90+ Days of Promoting Your Book Online: Your Book's Daily Marketing Plan.* Publishes 50 titles/yr.; hardcover, trade paperbacks, coffe table books, digital. Receives 1,000+ submissions annually. 50% of books from first-time authors. Charges for service packages. No mss through agents. Subsidy publishes 100%; does print-on-demand & e-books. Book length varies. **Royalty 15-35% on retail (15% on wholesale orders; 35% on booklocker.com orders; 50-70% for e-books); no advance.** Publication in 30 days. Considers simultaneous submissions. Publication in 4 wks., usually. Responds in 3 business days. Bible version is author's choice. Guidelines on website: https://secure.booklocker.com/authors/new/info.php; free catalog on request.

Nonfiction: Complete ms; e-query OK. Requires submission by e-mail. "We're open to all unique ideas."

Fiction: Complete ms; e-query OK. All genres for all ages.

Ethnic Books: Publishes for all ethnic groups.

Looking for: Booklocker will consider all genres, and prefers to work with good writers who are serious about selling books.

Photos/Artwork: Uses stock photos or author-supplied photos/artwork.

Tips: "Low up-front fees, fast publication (usually within a month), friendly service, and direct contact with the owners. No third-world customer service reps. All authors work with the publisher one-on-one. Since BookLocker does not accept every manuscript, we are able to give each author individual attention."

Six Tips for a Great Author Photo page 153

+BOOK PUBLISHERS NETWORK, PO Box 2256, Bothel WA 98041. Toll free: (877) 483-3040. (425) 483-3040. Fax: (425) 483-3098. Guidelines at: www.bookpublishersnetwork.com.

+BOOKS JUST BOOKS.COM, 93 Lake Ave., Tuckahoe NY 10707. Toll free: (800) 621-2556. Guidelines at:www.booksjustbooks.com.

+BOOKSTAND PUBLISHING, 305 Vineyard Town Center #302, Morgan Hill CA 95037. Toll free: (866) 793-9365. (408) 852-1832. E-mail: support@bookstand-publishing.com. Guidelines at:www.bookstandpublishing.com.

BROWN BOOKS PUBLISHING GROUP, 16250 Knoll Trail Dr., Ste. 205, Dallas TX 75248. (972) 381-0009. E-mail: publishing@brownbooks.com. Website: www.brownbooks.com. Chesle Blair, Brown Christian Press Division; Derek Royal, ed. Dir. We are a relationship publisher and work with our authors from beginning to end in the journey of publishing. Imprints: Personal Profiles, The P3 Press. Imprints: Brown Books, Brown Christian Press, Brown Books Kids, Texas Press. Publishes 25 religious titles/yr.; hardcover, trade paperbacks, mass-market paperbacks, coffee table books, digital. Receives 50+ submissions annually. 75% of books from first-time authors. Subsidy publishes 100%. Does not do print-on-demand. Reprints books. Does not require minimum purchase. Has a retail sales team. Publishes & distribute e-books. **Royalty 100%.** Authors retain rights to their work. Average first printing 3,000-5,000. Publication in 6 mos. Responds in 2-6 wks. No catalog; guidelines at: http://www.brownbooks.com/submit_a_manuscript.php.

   Nonfiction: Complete ms; e-query preferred.

   Fiction: Complete ms; e-query OK. For all ages.

   Tips: "We publish all genres with an emphasis on business, self-help, children's, and general Christian topics."

CARPENTER'S SON PUBLISHING, 307 Verde Meadow Drive, Franklin TN 37067. (615) 472-1128. E-mail: larry@christianbookservices.com. Website: www.carpenterssonpublishing.com. Parent Co: Christian Book Services, LLC. Imprint: Carpenter's Son Publishing. Larry Carpenter, pres./CEO, ed. Publishes 100 mss/yr. Receives 300 mss/yr. 90% first-time authors. Accepts books submitted by agents. 100% subsidy. Print-on-demand. Hardcover, trade, mass-market, digital. Does reprint. All sizes mss. **Author receives 63% of net revenue.** Avg. first print 1,000-10,000. Publication within 9 mos. Considers simultaneous submissions. Responds in 1 week. Ads: charge $350 for half-page ad/$600 for full-page ad. Guidelines by mail/e-mail/website: https://sites.google.com/site/carpenterssonpublishing. Accepts freelance photo for book cover. Accepts all topics. Open to queries from freelance artists.

   Nonfiction: Complete mss. Phone/e-mail queries. Accepts mss by e-mail.

   Fiction: Complete mss. Phone/e-mail queries. Accepts mss by e-mail.

   This publisher serviced by ChristianManuscriptSubmissions.com.

+CHRISTIAN BOOK SERVICES, LLC, 307 Verde Meadow Dr., Franklin TN 37067. Phone/fax (615) 472-1128. E-mail: larry@christianbookservices.com. Website: www.christianbookservices.com. Larry Carpenter, acq. ed. We give authors control over the editorial and creative process, but mirror the quality and experience of traditional publishing. Imprints: Carpenter's Son Publishing, Clovercraft Publishing. Publishes about 100 titles/yr.; hardcover, trade paperbacks, coffee-table books, digital. Receives 200 submissions annually. 75% of books from first-time authors. Does print-on-demand & e-books. Distributes e-books through Kindle, The Nook, and Apple. Prefers 40,000-100,000 for adult books (144-500 pgs.); 900-3,000 wds. for children's books (32-96 pgs.). No minimum purchase required. Has a retail sales team. **Author gets 63% of the sales proceeds. Royalty paid monthly.** Publication within 6 months. Responds in 2 wks. Catalog free on request; guidelines by mail, e-mail, or Website.

Nonfiction: Complete ms; e-mail & phone queries OK. Requires submission by e-mail.

Fiction: For all ages. Complete ms.

Also does: Audio books.

+CHRISTIAN SERVICES NETWORK. (619) 445-1873. Check this publisher's guidelines at: http://www.csnbooks.com.

CHRISTIAN SMALL PUBLISHERS ASSOCIATION (CSPA), PO Box 481022, Charlotte NC 28269. (704) 277-7194. Fax: (704) 717-2928. Email: cspa@christian-publishers.net. Website: www.christianpublishers.net. . CSPA is an organization for small publishers producing materials for the Christian marketplace. We help small publishers (including those who self-publish) market their books.

+CHRISTIAN WRITER'S EBOOK NET, PO Box 446, Ft. Duchesne UT 84026. (435) 772-3429. E-mail: editor@writersebook.com or through website: www.writersebook.com. Nondenominational/evangelical Christian. Linda Kay Stewart Whitsitt, ed-in-chief (linda@webtechdg.com); M. P. Whitsitt, asst. ed. (MP@webtechdg.com); Terry Gordon Whitsitt, asst. to ed. (terry@webtechdg.com). Gives first-time authors the opportunity to bring their God-given writing talent to the Christian market. Publishes 25 titles/yr. Receives 150 submissions annually. 95% of books from first-time authors. Accepts mss through authors. Reprints books. Prefers 60+ pgs. **Royalty 35-50%; no advance.** E-books only for Kindle and other e-reader formats. Publication within 6 mos. Considers simultaneous submissions. Electronic queries and submissions only; mss need to be in electronic form (MS Word, WordPerfect, ASCII, etc.) to be published; send by e-mail (preferred). No mail submissions accepted without contact by e-mail first. Responds in 1-2 mos. Guidelines at: www.writersebook.com/publishing.

Nonfiction/Fiction: E-query only. Any topic or genre.

Also Does: Booklets, pamphlets, tracts. E-books.

Tips: "Make sure your work is polished and ready for print. The books we publish are sold in our online store at Amazon and Ebay. If you are not sure what an e-book is, check out our website's FAQ page."

+CLM PUBLISHING, Bldg. D Ste. 5, Countryside Village Shopping, Grand Cayman, Cayman Islands KY1 1108. (718) 705-0368. E-mail: clmeditor@gmail.com. Website: www.clmpublishing.com. Karen Chin, ed. Prefers book proposal. Guidelines on Website.

CREATION HOUSE, 600 Rinehart Rd., Lake Mary FL 32746-4872. (407) 333-0600. Fax (407) 333-7100. E-mail: creationhouse@charismamedia.com. Website: www.creationhouse.com. Charisma Media. Submit to Acquisitions Editor. To inspire and equip people to live a Spirit-led life and to walk in the divine purpose for which they were created. Publishes 125 titles/yr.; hardcover, trade paperbacks, mass-market paperbacks, coffee table books. Receives 1,500 submissions annually. 80% of books from first-time authors. Accepts mss through agents. Reprints books. Prefers 25,000+ wds. or 100-200 pgs. **Royalty 12-15% of net; no advance.** Average first printing 2,000. Publication within 2-4 mos. Considers simultaneous submissions. Responds in 10-12 wks. Open to submissions on disk or by e-mail. Guidelines at: http://www.creation-house.com/index.php/proposal-application-form; free catalog.

Nonfiction: Proposal/complete ms; no phone/fax query; e-query OK. "Open to any books that are well written and glorify Jesus Christ."

Fiction: Proposal/complete ms; no phone/fax query; e-query OK. For all ages. "Fiction must have a biblical worldview and point the reader to Christ."

Photos: Accepts freelance photos for book covers.

Tips: "We use the term 'co-publishing' to describe a hybrid between conventional royalty publishing and self- or subsidy publishing, utilizing the best of both worlds. We produce a high-quality book for our own inventory, market it, distribute it, and pay the author a royalty on every copy sold. In return, the author agrees to buy, at a deep discount, a portion of the first print run."

+CREATIVE ENTERPRISES STUDIO, PO Box 224, Fort Worth TX 76095. (817)312-7393. Fax: (817) 685-7393. E-mail: AcreativeShop@aol.com. Website: CreativeEnterprisesStudio.com. Mary Hollingsworth, pub. & mng. dir. With 30 years' experience, CES is the best alternative to traditional publishing and self-publishing, offering first-class, custom publishing services from manuscript through printed books to help Christian authors powerfully glorify God in print. Publishes 10-12 titles/yr.; hardcover, trade paperbacks, mass-market paperback, coffee table books, digital. Receives 50-60 submissions annually. 70% of books from first-time authors. Offers print-on-demand. Reprints books. Length is author's choice. No retail sales team. Publishes e-books; posts them on Amazon. **Author keeps all profits.** Publication in 6 mos. Responds in 2-3 wks. No catalog or guidelines.

Nonfiction: Query letter only first. E-queries OK. Requires submission of mss through e-mail.

Fiction: For all ages. Query letter only first.

Also does: Audio books, book video trailers, e-books.

CREDO HOUSE PUBLISHERS, 3148 Plainfield Ave. NE, Ste. 111, Grand Rapids MI 49525-3285. (616) 363-2686. E-mail: publish@credocommunications.net. Website: www.credohousepublishers.com. A division of Credo Communications LLC. Timothy J. Beals, submissions/acquisitions ed. Exists to "bring words to life" by working with Christian ministry leaders and organizations to develop life-changing books, Bible-related products, and other Christian resources. Publishes 10-15 titles/yr.; hardcover, trade paperbacks, mass-market paperbacks, coffee-table books, digital. Receives 50-60 submissions annually. 30-40% from first-time authors. Does print-on-demand & e-books. Reprints books. Prefers 50,000-60,000 wds.; 180-240 pgs. No minimum purchase required. **Royalties paid annually.** Reports in 1-2 wks. No catalog; guidelines at: http://www.credocommunications.net/services/writing-and-editing.

Nonfiction: Proposal/sample chapters; e-queries OK. Prefers e-mail submissions.

Fiction: For all ages. Proposal/sample chapters.

*CROSSHOUSE PUBLISHING, 2844 S. FM 549, Suite A, Rockwall TX 75032. Toll-free (877) 212-0933. Fax (877) 212-0933. E-mail: sales@crosshousepublishing.org or through website: www.crosshousepublishing.org. Self-publishing branch of KLMK Communications. Dr. Katie Welch, pub. To achieve excellence in Christian self-publishing without sacrificing personal interest and care for customers. Publishes hardcover, trade paperbacks. No mss through agents. Subsidy publisher. **Royalty 25% on net; no advance.** Publication within 3 mos. Guidelines at: www.crosshousepublishing.org..

Nonfiction/Fiction: Accepts fiction for all ages.

Photos: Accepts freelance photos for book covers.

Tips: "We provide authors the opportunity to have their books distributed through a wide array of Christian and general bookstores. We aspire to offer the marketplace superior Christian literature that will impact readers' lives."

DCTS PUBLISHING, PO Box 40216, Santa Barbara CA 93140. (805) 570-3168. E-mail: dennis@dctspub.com. Website: www.dctspub.com. "For authors who want quality low-cost publishing, we will partner with you in producing a fantastic marketable book that will sell anywhere in the world. Please contact me for more details." Dennis Stephen Hamilton, ed. Books are designed to enrich the mind, encourage the heart, and empower the spirit. Publishes 5 titles/yr. Receives 25 submissions annually. 35% of books from first-time authors. No mss through agents. Subsidy publishes 70%. No reprints. Prefers 100-300 pgs. **Royalty 17% of retail; no advance.** Average first printing 3,500. Publication within 6-8 mos. No simultaneous submissions. Prefers KJV. Guidelines at: www.dctspub.com; free catalog/brochure.

Nonfiction: Query or proposal/2-3 chapters; e-query OK.

+DEEPER REVELATION BOOKS, PO Box 4260, Cleveland TN 37320-4260. (423) 478-2843. Fax: (423) 479-2980. Check this publisher's guidelines at: http://www. deeperrevelationbooks.org/authors/publish.htm.

DEEP RIVER BOOKS, 26306 Metolius Meadows Dr., Camp Sherman OR 97730. (541) 549-1139. E-mail: bill@deepriverbooks.com, nancie@deepriverbooks.com. Website: www.deepriverbooks.com. Bill and Nancie Carmichael, pubs. Partnering with new authors. Publishes 35 titles/yr.; hardback, trade paperbacks, coffee table books. Receives hundreds of submissions annually. 90% of books from first-time authors. Accepts mss through agents. No reprints. Prefers 45,000+ wds. or 192-400 pgs. **Royalty 12-18% of net; no advance.** Custom publisher; see website for details. Average first printing 2,500+. Publication within 9-12 mos. Considers simultaneous submissions. Requires accepted ms by e-mail. Responds in 2 mos. Guidelines at: http://www.deepriverbooks.com/about-deepriver-authors/how-to-become-a-deep-river-author.html.

Nonfiction: Query first by e-mail only; proposal/2-3 chapters.

Fiction: Query first by e-mail only; proposal/2-3 chapters. For all ages. "Anything Christian or inspirational that is well written, especially from new authors."

Tips: "Go to our website first, and read how we partner with new authors. Then, if you feel Deep River Books would be a good fit for you, e-mail your proposal." This publisher serviced by ChristianManuscriptSubmissions.com.

+DEO VOLENTE PUBLISHING, PO Box 119, Humboldt TN 38343. Contact: Larry Byars. Publisher's guidelines at: http://www.deovolente.net/WriterGuide.html.

DESTINY IMAGE PUBLISHERS, PO Box 310, Shippensburg PA 17257. Toll-free (800) 722-6774.(717) 532-3040. Fax (717) 532-9291. E-mail: manuscripts@norimediagroup.com. Website: www.destinyimage.com. Mykela Krieg, exec. acq. asst. To help people grow deeper in their relationship with God and others. Accepts mss through agents or authors. Prefers 40,000-60,000 wds. Responds in 8-12 wks. Publication within 12 mos. Considers simultaneous submissions. Requires e-mail submission (attached file). Download their Book Proposal Form. Guidelines at: http://www.destinyimage.com/submit-your-manuscript

Tips: "Most open to books on the deeper life, or of charismatic interest."

+ELDERBERRY PRESS, 1393 Old Homestead Dr., Oakland OR 97462-9690.)541) 459-6043. E-mail: editor@elderberrypress.com. Check out this publisher's guidelines at: http://www.elderberrypress.com/publishing_services.

+ENCLAVE PUBLISHING, (formerly Marcher Lord Press), 5025 N. Central Ave. #635, Phoenix AZ 85012. (602) 336-8910. E-mail: acquisitions@enclavepublishing. com. Website: www.enclavepublishing.com. Steve Laube, submissions/acquisitions ed. Enclave is the premier publisher of Christian fantasy and science fiction. Publishes 10-12 titles/yr.; trade paperbacks, digital. Receives 500 submissions annually. 50% of books from first-time authors. Does print-on-demand and e-books. Reprints books. Prefers 100,000 wds. No minimum purchase requirement. Has a retail sales team. **Royalties paid quarterly.** Publication within 9-12 mos. Reports within 45 days. No catalog; guidelines on Website.

Fiction: For adults. Proposal/sample chapters.

ESSENCE PUBLISHING CO. INC., 20 Hanna Ct., Belleville ON K)l 1L0, Canada. Toll-free (800) 238-6376, ext. 7110. (613) 962-2360. Fax (613) 962-3055. E-mail: info@essence-publishing.com. Website: www.essence-publishing.com. Sherrill Brunton, publishing mgr., (s.brunton@essence-publishing.com). Provides affordable, short-run book publishing to mainly the Christian community; dedicated to furthering the work of Christ through the written word. Imprints: Essence Publishing, Guardian Books, Epic Press. (Epic Press is reserved for non-Christian books such as biographies, cookbooks, text books, history books, etc.). Publishes 150 titles/yr.; hardcover, trade paperbacks, mass-market paperbacks, coffee table books. Receives 250+ submissions annually. 75% of books from first-time authors. Accepts mss from agents or authors. Subsidy publishes 100%. Does print-on-demand. Reprints books. Any length. Completes books in other languages. **Royalty 50% from bookstore and e-books, no advance.** Average first printing 500-1,000. Publication within 3 mos. Considers simultaneous submissions. Responds in 2 wks. Prefers requested ms on disk or by e-mail. Bible version is author's choice. Free publishing guide by mail/e-mail. Guidelines at: www.essence-publishing.com; catalog online (www.essencebookstore.com); and international distribution available. E-books available with listings on Kindle, Apple, and KOBO.

Nonfiction: Complete ms; phone/fax/e-query OK. Accepts all topics.

Fiction: Complete ms. All genres for all ages. Including full-color children's picture books.

Also Does: Pamphlets, booklets, tracts, and posters.

Photos/Artwork: Accepts freelance photos for book covers; open to queries from freelance artists.

+EVERFAITH PRESS, 2373 NW 185th Ave. #510, Hillsboro OR 97124. (559) 744-3553. E-mail: getpublished@everfaithpress.com. Website: www.everfaithpress. com. Rochelle Carter, pub. Christian self-publishing press. For details on their publishing services, go to: http://www.everfaithpress.com/publishing-services.

FAIRWAY PRESS, subsidy division for CSS Publishing Company, 5450 N. Dixie Hwy., Lima OH 45807-9559. Toll-free (800) 241-4056. (419) 227-1818. Fax: (417) 228-9184. E-mail: david@csspub.com or through website: www.fairwaypress.com. David Runk, ed.; submit to Missy Cotrell, acq. ed. Publishes 10-15 titles/yr.; trade paperback, digital. Receives 100-150 submissions annually. 80% of books from first-time authors. Reprints books. Subsidy publishes 100%. **Royalty to 50%; no advance.** Average first printing 500-1,000. Publication within 6-9 mos. Considers simultaneous submissions. Responds in up to 1 mo. Prefers requested ms on disk; no e-mail submissions. Prefers NRSV. Guidelines at: www.fairwaypress.com; catalog for 9 x 12 SAE.

Nonfiction: Complete ms; phone/fax/e-query OK. All types. "Looking for manuscripts with a Christian theme, and seasonal material."

Fiction: Complete ms. For adults, teens, or children; all types. No longer producing anything in full color or with four-color illustrations.

FAITH BOOKS & MORE, 3255 Lawrenceville-Suwanee Rd., Ste. P250, Suwanee GA 30024. (678) 232-6156. E-mail: publishing@faithbooksandmore.com. Website: www.faithbooksandmore.com. 100% custom publishing. Nicole Smith, mng. ed. Imprints: Faith Books & More; Friends of Faith, Corporate Connoisseur, or custom imprint for author branding. Publishes 100 titles/yr; hardcover, trade paperbacks, and e-books. Receives 200 submissions annually. 90% of books from first-time authors. Accepts mss through agents or authors. Subsidy publishes 50%; does print-on-demand and offset. Reprints books. Any length; no less than 4 pages. **Royalty; no advance.** Publication within 2 mos. Considers simultaneous submissions. Responds in 1 mo. Prefers NKJV or NIV. Guidelines by e-mail/website; no catalog.

    Nonfiction: Complete ms; phone/e-query OK. Any topic.

    Fiction: Complete ms; phone/e-query OK. Any genre, for all ages.

    Photos/Artwork: Accepts freelance photos for book covers; considers queries from freelance artists

FRUITBEARER PUBLISHING LLC, PO Box 777, Georgetown DE 19947. (302) 856-6649. Fax (302) 856-7742. E-mail: cfa@candyabbott.com or through website: www.fruitbearer.com. Candy Abbott, mng. partner. Offers editing services and advice for self-publishers. Publishes 5-10 titles/yr.; hardcover, picture books. Receives 10-20 submissions annually. 90% of books from first-time authors. Subsidy publishes100%. No reprints. Average first printing 500-5,000. Publication within 1-6 mos. Responds in 3 mos. Guidelines by mail/e-mail/website: www.fruitbearer.com; brochure for #10 SAE/1 stamp.

    Nonfiction: Proposal/2 chapters; phone/fax/e-query OK.

    Fiction: For all ages.

    Also Does: Pamphlets, booklets, tracts.

    Photos: Accepts freelance photos for book covers.

    Tips: "Accepting limited submissions."

GRACE ACRES PRESS, PO Box 22, Larkspur CO 80118. (303) 681-9995. Fax (303) 681-2176. E-mail: info@GraceAcresPress.com. Website: www.GraceAcresPress. com. Grace Acres, Inc. Anne R. Fenske, ed./pub. Conservative, evangelical, dispensational nonfiction materials for spiritual growth that will last over time. Publishes 2-6 titles/yr.; hardcover, trade paperbacks. Receives 50 submissions annually. 99% of books from first-time authors. Does print-on-demand; publishes and distributes e-books. Reprints books. Requires minimum purchase of 500 bks. Has a retail sales team. **All royalty to the author; paid twice a year.** Publication in 2-6 mos. Responds in 2-6 mos. Average first printing 1,500-2,500. Considers simultaneous submissions. Guidelines at www.graceacrespress.com; free catalog.

    Nonfiction: Query letter only first; accepts phone, fax, e-query. Requires accepted mss by e-mail.

    Artwork: Open to queries from freelance artists.

    Tips: "Most open to a book with a built-in audience/buyer; i.e., speaker, textbook."

HALO PUBLISHING INTL., 1031 Cherry Spring, AP 726, Houston TX 77038. (216) 255-6756. E-mail: lisa@halopublishing.com. Website: www.halopublishing.com. Company blog: http://halopublishig.blogspot.mx. Jodie Greenberg, acq. ed. Publishes unique subject-matter. Imprints: Hola Publishing, Bric Book Co. Halo is dedicated to serving authors around the world and providing the highest level of professional publishing services. Our offices in USA and Mexico specialize in designing, producing, publishing, and marketing books for independent authors. Publishes 60 titles/yr.; hardcover, trade paperbacks, coffee table books, digital. Receives 300 submissions annually. 95% of books from first-time authors. Does print-on-demand & e-books. Reprints books. No minimum purchase required. **Royalty 95%; paid in 30 days.** Publication in 60 days. Responds in 2 wks. Guidelines by e-mail; no catalog.

Nonfiction: Complete ms; phone/e-query OK.

Fiction: Compete ms; phone/e-query OK. For all ages.

Artwork: Open to queries from freelance artists.

HEALTHY LIFE PRESS, 2603 Drake Drive, Orlando FL 32810. E-mail: HealthyLifePress@aol.com. Website: www.HealthyLifePress.com. Blog: www.davebiebel.com. Evangelical, nondenominational. David Biebel, pub. Imprint: Healthy Life Press. We see health as a verb ... a dynamic sum of one's wellness in all areas at any given time. Helping people toward greater is our goal. Helping previously unpublished authors with something important to contribute to this field to market brings significant satisfaction to us. Keeping worthy books that fit our focus in print is also important to us. Publishes 6-10 titles/yr. Receives 20 mss/yr. 80% first-time authors. Accepts books submitted by agent. Subsidy publisher. 60% subsidy. Print-on-demand exclusively. Trade, mass-market, digital. Does reprint out-of-print books. Prefers 120-220 pgs. **Royalty of 50% based on net. E-books 50% of net. Outright purchase option.** Author purchase: 50-60% off retail (plus S&H), depending on contract terms. Print-on-demand, shipped direct from distributor. Publishes in 6-8 mos. Responds in 1 month. Catalog free on request. Guidelines on website. Accepts freelance photos for book covers. Always looking for books in the interface of the Christian faith and health, as viewed from a holistic perspective (physical, emotional, relational, spiritual).

Nonfiction: Book proposal/3 sample chapters.; requires ms by e-mail.

Fiction: For all ages. Prefers romance, mystery, allegory. Proposal/3 sample chapters.

Tips: "Well-written, edited, and ready for design manuscripts on a topic within our purview that the author is passionate about, and about which he/she is able to provide a new, different, unique, original perspective."

+HIGHER LIFE PUBLISHING AND MARKETING, 400 Fontana Cir., Bldg. 1, Ste. 105, Oviedo FL 32765. (407) 563-4806. E-mail: info@ahigherlife.com. Website: www.ahigherlife.com. Estab. 2006. Recognized in the industry. Full-service publishing (books, e-books, mobile apps), marketing strategy, and services, trade sales distribution, curriculum development, author development, and coaching. Open to unpublished authors and new clients. Handles religious/inspirational novels and nonfiction for all ages, picture books, crossover books. Open to simultaneous submissions; responds in 2 wks. Guidelines on Website.

+HOLY FIRE PUBLISHING, 205 St. James Ave., Goose Creek SC 29445. (843) 285-3130. Attn: COO Vanessa Hensel, MS-274. Guidelines at: www.christianpublish.com.

+INFINITY PUBLISHING, 1090 New Dehaven St., Ste. 100, West Conshohocken PA 19428. (610) 941-9999. Fax: (610) 941-9959. Guidelines at: www.infinitypublishing.com.

LIFE SENTENCE PUBLISHING, 203 E. Birch St., PO Box 652, Abbotsford WI 54405. (715) 223-3013. Fax: (715) 316-0204. E-mail: info@lifesentencepublishing.com. Website: www.lifesentencepublishing.com. Company blog: lifesentencepublishing.blogspot.com. Jeremiah Zeiset, acq. ed. Imprints: Life Sentence Publishing, and

ANEKO Press (see separate listing). Our niche is working with those in ministry, and have a special ministry pricing for books used in ministry. Publishes 36 titles/yr.; hardcover, trade paperbacks, mass-market paperbacks, digital. Receives 100 submissions annually. 40% first-time authors. Accepts books submitted by agents. 50% subsidy. Does print-on-demand. Reprints books. Prefers 50,000 wds or 150 pgs. **Royalty 25-40% of net; same for e-books. No advance.** Average first printing 1,000 offset or 50 POD. Publishes within 6 mo. Considers simultaneous submissions. Responds in 3 wks. Charges for catalog. Guidelines at: http://www.lifesentencepublishing.com/submissions.

Nonfiction: Complete ms.

Fiction: For all ages. Complete ms. "Fiction is fine, provided the main goal is to share the Gospel or help a Christian in their walk with the Lord."

Looking for: Our publishing niche is for those in ministry, either here in the US or abroad. If the Lord has called you to ministry, we'd be honored to review your manuscript for potential publication.

Photos: Accepts freelance photos for book covers.

Tips: "Have a main goal of sharing the Gospel or helping Christians in their walk with the Lord."

+MANTLE ROCK PUBLISHING, 2879 Palma Rd., Benton KY 42025. (270) 343-1560. E-mail: kac@bellsouth.net. Website: www.mantlerockpublishing.com. Kathy Cretsinger, ed.

represent authors of different fiction genres. At this time we do not accept children's picture books, paranormal, or nonfiction."

MARKETINGNEWAUTHORS.COM, 22910 E. Eisenhower Pkwy., Ann Arbor MI 48108. (734) 975-0028. Fax (734) 973-9475. E-mail: info@marketingnewauthors.com. Website: www.MarketingNewAuthors.com. Company blog: manasunriser.blogspot.com. Imprint of Robbie Dean Press. To primarily serve authors who wish to self-publish. Dr. Fairy C. Hayes-Scott, owner; Elizabeth Cobbs, ed. MANA provides customized layouts that fit the style of the writer and provides one of the highest royalty pay back of 70%. Publishes 2-3 titles/yr.; hardcover, trade paperbacks, mass-market paperbacks, coffee table books. Receives 2-3 submissions annually. 100% of books from first-time authors. Does print-on-demand; publishes & distributes e-books. Reprints books. Length flexible. No required minimum purchase. **Royalty 70%; paid within a month of receipt.** Publication within 6 mos. Considers simultaneous submissions. Responds in 1 mo. No catalog; guidelines by e-mail/website: http://www.marketingnewauthors.com/selfpub.html.

Nonfiction: Complete ms; phone, fax, e-queries OK. Prefers submissions by e-mail.

Fiction: For all ages. Complete ms.

Contest: The MANA Passion for Poetry Contest, held annually.

MYSTICAL ROSE, PO Box 13, Warrenton VA 20188. (540) 364-2841. Fax 1-888-965-7955. E-mail: query@mysticalroseinspirations.com. Website: www.mysticalroseinspirations.com. Blog: www.mysticalroseinspirations.com/blog-preludes-to-peace.html. Tamara Amos/CEO, ed. Mystical Rose specializes in presenting fresh perspectives and new solutions that pertain to our present time and culture using inspirational, humorous, and creative methodology. Accepts books submitted by agents or authors. Subsidy publisher. Print-on-demand. Hardcover, trade, mass-market, coffee table books, digital. Reprints out-of-print books. Considers simultaneous submissions. Responds in 1 mo. Guidelines at: www.mysticalroseinspirations.com.

Nonfiction: Proposal with 2 sample chapters. E-mail queries. Accepts mss by e-mail.

Fiction: Proposal with 2 sample chapters. We are looking for fresh voices that bring new perspectives to modern issues, convey wisdom without being preachy, and use creative, humorous, inspiring, and entertaining methods. We are also looking for fiction pertaining to ADD/ADHD and learning disabilities.

Photos/Artwork: Accepts freelance photos for covers. Open to queries from freelance artists.

Also Does: Educational materials, greeting cards, inspirational, and humorous merchandise.

Tips: "Multidimensional educational resources, right-brained educational resources; books and resources pertaining to ADD/ADHD; insightful books that are well written and entertaining.

+NORDSKOG PUBLISHING, 4562 Westinghouse St., Ste. E, Ventura CA 93003. (805) 642-2070. Fax: (805) 642-1862. Seeks to publish the best in sound theological and applied Christian faith books; nonfiction and fiction. Now a subsidy publisher. Guidelines at: http://www.nordskogpublishing.com/publishing-guidelines.shtml.

PORT HOLE PUBLICATIONS, 179 Laurel St., Ste. D, Florence OR 97439. (541) 999-5725. E-mail: info@ellentraylor.com. Website: www.portholepublications.com. Nondenominational. Ellen Traylor, pub. We are CBA suppliers, founded and owned by bestselling CBA author, Ellen Gunderson Traylor, who understands and sympathizes with writers' hearts and dreams. Imprint: Lear-to-Grow Books. Publishes a variable number of titles/yr.; hardcover, trade paperbacks, mass-market paperbacks, coffee table books, digital. Receives 20-30 submissions annually. 90% of books from first-time authors. Reprints books. No minimum purchase required. Has a retail sales team. Publishes & distributes e-books. **Offers a standard royalty contract. Royalties paid semi-annually.** Publication within 15 months. Responds immediately. No catalog; guidelines by e-mail/website: http://www.portholepublications.com/pages/submission.php.

Nonfiction: Proposal/sample chapters. Phone/e-mail queries OK. Prefers ms via e-mail.

Fiction: For all ages. Proposal/sample chapters.

Tips: "We are a general publisher with several Christian content books; all books are "family friendly" or have a moral thrust consistent with Christianity."

+REDEMPTION PRESS, 1730 Railroad St., Enumclaw WA 98022. (360) 226-3488. E-mail: info@redemption-press.com. Website: www.redemption-press.com. Athena Dean Holtz, pub.; Michael Fleiss, Submissions ed.; Inger Logelin, Sr. ed.; Brittany Osborn, In-house ed.; Valerie McKay & Brenda Anderson, Acquisitions eds. Imprints: Redemption Press, Zelos Books, and Mountain View Press (General Market). Receives 400-500 submissions annually. 50-60% of books from first-time authors. Offers print-on-demand. Publishes hardcover, trade paperbacks, mass-market paperbacks, coffee-table books, and digital. Reprints books. Prefers 20,000-150,000 wds. or 108-600 pgs. Offers a la carte services. Sales team direct to consumers. For package costs, go to: www.redemption-press.com/services/publishing. Pays 100% of print book revenues (net revenue from sales, less cost to print = profit to author). **Royalties paid quarterly.** Offers a wide variety of publishing services. Offers discounted payment plans. Publication within 3-4 mos. Responds within 7 days. Guidelines on Website; no catalog.

Nonfiction: Send complete ms. Prefers e-mail queries. Accepts phone queries. Any appropriate topics.

Fiction: For all ages. Send complete ms. Accepts phone queries. Any genre.

E-Books: Publishes & distributes e-books. Pays 90% of net e-book revenues to the author.

Artwork: Accepts submissions from freelance artists.

Tips: "We have created a different business model where we put the author in charge, while giving expert advice and guidance on producing and promoting a quality product—offering personal service, realistic expectations, and no hype— we under promise and over deliver."

+REVIVAL WAVES OF GLORY BOOKS & PUBLISHING, PO Box 596, Litchfield IL 62056. (217) 851-0361. E-mail: bill.vincent@yahoo.com. Website: www. revivalwavesofgloryministries.com. Bill Vincent, pub. Does both traditional and self-publishing. Submit complete ms by e-mail.

*THE SALT WORKS, PO Box 37, Roseville CA 95678. (916) 784-0500. Fax (916) 773-7421. E-mail: books@publishersdesign.com. Website: www.publishersdesign. com. Division of Publishers Design Group Inc. Robert Brekke, pub.; submit to Project Manager. Seeks to demonstrate through books that God is sovereign, just, and merciful in all he does. Imprint: Salty's Books (children's—see separate listing), PDG, Humpback Books. Publishes 7-10 titles/yr.; hardcover, trade paperbacks, coffee table books. Receives 100+ submissions annually. 90% of Christian books from first-time authors. No mss through agents. Subsidy publishes 95%. Offset and print-on-demand. Reprints books. Prefers 95,000-150,000 wds. **Rarely pays royalty of 7-12% on net; occasional advance.** Average first printing 1,500-5,000. Publication within 4-12 mos. Considers simultaneous submissions. Responds within 45 days. Prefers ESV/NASB/ NKJV/NIV (in that order). Prospects must study publisher's website labeled "Custom Publishing" along with all five case studies before contacting. After preliminary screening, prospect will be sent a project questionnaire and a project assessment will be performed for projects with strong concepts. Guidelines at: http://www.publishersdesign. com/submissions.php.

Nonfiction: E-query only first; after query & phone meeting, send proposal. Unsolicited mss returned unopened.

Fiction: E-query only first; after query & phone meeting, send proposal. Unsolicited mss returned unopened. For adults and children. "Looking for titles that help believers in exploring and facing common issues surrounding God's sovereignty, his grace and forgiveness, their own sin and idolatry, and the areas where pop culture has influenced the church. Characters are blatantly human."

Special Needs: Looking for titles that communicate a biblical Christian worldview without promoting overly simplistic, idealistic, or theoretical solutions to life's biggest questions; books that honestly show no timidity in addressing our humanness. Looking for manuscripts that demonstrate that society's problems are rooted in the personal and spiritual, not in the political, educational, moral, and financial realms.

Also Does: Board games and other specialty products: fitness products, art projects and products, interactive projects for children. Specializes in projects designed to build a person or organization into a brand in the marketplace. See publisher's "MarketByPublishing.com" division for details.

Photos/Artwork: Rarely accepts freelance photos for book covers; open to queries from freelance artists.

Tips: "Most open to books that look at the Christian experience through a realistic biblical and Reformed perspective. Books that address the Christian's real problems as a 'heart' problem—not a theological problem; not from a victim mind-set, not a mental or logical one; not from a perspective of merely needing another program, pep talk, or the latest rehash of formulas for victorious living. Books that show the author understands that unless God changes the heart and brings a person to repentance, there are no real and lasting answers. This publisher serviced by ChristianManuscriptSubmissions.com.

+SALTY'S BOOKS, PO Box 37, Roseville CA 95678. (916) 784-0500. Fax (916) 773-7421. E-mail: books@publishersdesign.com. Website: www.publishersdesign.com. Division of Publishers Design Group Inc. Guidelines at: http://www.publishersdesign.com/submissions.php.

*SALVATION PUBLISHER AND MARKETING GROUP, PO Box 40860, Santa Barbara CA 93140. (805) 682-0316. Fax (call first). E-mail: opalmaedailey@aol.com. Wisdom Today Ministries. Opal Mae Dailey, ed-in-chief. We encourage, inspire, and educate; author has the choice to be involved as much or little as desired—which gives the opportunity to control income; personal coaching and collective marketing available. Publishes 5-7 titles/yr.; hardcover, trade paperbacks, mass-market paperbacks. 60% of books from first-time authors. No mss through agents. Subsidy publishes 80%; does print-on-demand. Reprints books. Prefers 96-224 pgs. Average first printing 1,000. Publication within 3-4 mos. No simultaneous submissions. Accepts requested ms on disk or by e-mail (not attachments). Responds in 1 mo. Prefers KJV. Guidelines (also by e-mail).

Nonfiction: Query only first; phone/fax/e-query OK.

Tips: "Turning taped messages into book form for pastors is a specialty. We do not accept any manuscript that we would be ashamed to put our name on."

+SIGNALMAN PUBLISHING, 3700 Commerce Blvd., Kissimmee FL 34741. Toll free: (888)907-4423. E-mail: info@signalmanpblishing.com. Website: www.signalman-publishing.com. Company blog: www.signalmanpublishing.com/blog. John McClure, ed. Imprints: Trinity Grace Press. Publishes 12 titles/yr.; trade paperbacks & digital. Receives 50 submissions/yr. 25% of books from first-time authors. Accepts submissions through agents. Subsidy publishes 80%. Does print-on-demand. Reprints books. Prefers 40,000 wds. **Royalty 20% & up; E-book royalty 40%; no advance.** Publication within 3 mos. Considers simultaneous submissions. Reports within 2 wks. No catalog or guidelines.

Nonfiction: Complete ms. Accepts e-mail and snail mail queries.

Fiction: For children, teens, new adults, and adults. Complete ms.

Photos/Artwork: Accepts freelance photos for book covers; accepts queries from freelance artists.

+SONFIRE MEDIA, 974 E. Stuart Dr., Ste. D, PMB 232, Galax VA 24333. (276) 221-4141. Guidelines at: http://www.sonfiremedia.com/submit.html.

STONEHOUSE INK, (208)608-8325. Fax: (208) 441-6024. E-mail: stonehouse-press@hotmail.com. Website: Http://stonehouseink.net. Clean-fiction imprint of Ampelon Press (www.ampelonpublishing.com). Aaron Patterson, ed./pub. Specializing in thrillers, mystery, young adult, paranormal, and out-of-print titles. Find on Facebook and Twitter @StoneHouseInk.

STRONG TOWER PUBLISHING, PO Box 973, Milesburg PA 16863. E-mail: strongtowerpubs@aol.com. Website: www.strongtowerpublishing.com. Heidi L. Nigro, pub. Specializes in eschatology and books that challenge readers to think more deeply about their faith and scriptural truths; must be biblically responsible, doctrinally defensible, and consistent with their statement of faith. Publishes 1-2 titles/yr.; trade paperbacks. 50% of books from first-time authors. No mss through agents. Reprints books. Print-on-demand 100%. **Royalty 25% of net; no advance.** Average first printing 50. Publication within 3-4 mos. Guidelines/information/prices on website: http://www. strongtowerpublishing.com/editorialservice.html.

Nonfiction: Query. Eschatology.

Tips: "We recommend that all first-time authors have their manuscripts professionally edited. We will consider putting first-time authors into print, but by invitation only. That invitation comes only after the manuscript has been thoroughly evaluated and we have discussed the pros and cons of our unique on-demand publishing model with the author.

+TEACH SERVICES, INC., 8300 Hwy. 41, Unit 107, PO Box 954, Ringgold GA 30736. (800) 367-1844. E-mail: Publishing@teachservices.com. Website: www.teach-services.com. Contact: Timothy Hullquist. Check out this publisher's guidelines at: http://www.teachservices.com/publishing-with-us.

+TRAFFORD PUBLISHING, 1663 Liberty Dr., Bloomington IN 47403. Toll free: (888) 232-4444. Guidelines at: www.trafford.com.

TRUTH BOOK PUBLISHERS, 824 Bills Rd., Franklin IL 62638. (217) 675-2191. E-mail: truthbookpublishers@yahoo.com. Website: www.truthbookpublishers.com. JaNell Lyle, ed. We all have something to offer to the body and we hope to be a tool for that purpose. Publishes 50 titles/yr.; hardcover, trade paperbacks, mass-market paperbacks, digital. Receives 75 submissions annually. 65% of books from first-time authors. Does print-on-demand & e-books. Distributes e-books. Reprints books. Prefers 150-200 pgs. Requires minimum purchase of 25 copies. Average first run 100-500. Publication within 1 mo. Responds in 10 days. Catalog on request; guidelines by e-mail or Website: www.truthbookpublishers.com.

Nonfiction: Query letter only first. Accepts phone & e-mail queries.

Fiction: For all ages. Query letter only first.

Tips: "We are missionary minded and desire to help the body of Christ mature."

WESTBOW PRESS, 1663 Liberty Dr., Bloomington IN 47403. Toll-free (866) 928-1240. Website: www.westbowpress.com. Subsidy division of Thomas Nelson Publishers. Kevin A. Gray, news media contact. Estab. 2009. A Christian self-publishing company that provides author services to help them fulfill their dream of becoming a published author. Fill out online form to receive information on their publishing program. Guidelines at: http://www.westbowpress.com/WhyWestBowPress/Default.aspx.

WORD ALIVE PRESS, 131 Cordite Rd., Winnipeg MB R3W 1S1, Canada. Toll-free (866) 967-3782. (204) 777-7100. Toll-free fax (800) 352-9272. (204) 669-0947. E-mail: publishing@wordalivepress.ca. Website: www.wordalivepress.ca. Company blog: http://wordalivepress.ca/blogs. Publishes 100-120 titles/yr.; hardcover, trade paperbacks, mass-market paperbacks, coffee table books, digital. Requires purchase of 100-400 bks. No sales team. URL for package costs: http://wordalivepress.ca/services. Publishes & distributes e-books. Receives 100-150 submissions annually. Does print-on-demand & reprints. **Royalties paid quarterly.** No catalog; guidelines and price list available by mail, e-mail or Website: http://www.wordalivepress.ca/gettingstarted.html.

Nonfiction: Complete ms. Accepts phone, fax, e-queries. Prefers submissions by e-mail.

Fiction: Complete ms. All genres, for all ages.

Contest: Our free publishing contest open for submissions from Canadian Christian writers in spring. Check our website for full details.

ZOË LIFE PUBLISHING, PO Box 871066, Canton MI 48187. (88) 400-4922. E-mail: info@zoelifepub.com. Website: www.zoelifepub.com. Zoë Life Christian Communications. Sabrina Adams, ed. We were called to change the world and glorify God, one book at a time through the power of the written word. Imprints: Pen of a Ready Writer, Titus, Business Builders. Publishes 40 titles/yr.; hardcover, trade paperbacks, mass-market paperbacks, coffee table books, digital. Receives 120 submissions/yr. 50% of books from first-time authors. No print-on-demand. Reprints books. Prefers 40,000 wds. Authors charged for service packages. No minimum purchase required. Publishes e-books. Royalty is 50% of distribution price. Accepts mss through authors or agents. Subsidy publishes 50%. Length open. **Royalty 10-25% of net; usually no advance.** Average first printing 3,000. Publication within 12 mos. Responds in 7 days. Open on Bible version. Not included in topical listings. Guidelines by e-mail/snail mail/website: http://www.zoelifepub.com/Pages/submission.html (click on "FAQ"); no catalog.

> **Nonfiction:** Complete ms; phone/fax/e-query OK.
> **Fiction:** Proposal/ 3 chapters or complete ms; phone/fax/e-query OK. For all ages; all genres. Complete mss for picture books.
> **Photos:** Accepts freelance photos for book covers.

SUPPLIERS TO SELF-PUBLISHING AUTHORS

BOOK COVER & INTERIOR DESIGN SERVICES, PO Box 1382, Running Springs CA 92382. (909) 939-0311. E-mail: info@lionsgatebookdesign.com. Website: www.lionsgatebookdesign.com. Call/e-mail. Has 35 yrs exp. in prof. graphic design, art direction, and advertising. Works with new and seasoned authors, providing personal attention and custom design. Book cover packages range from $395-$650. Custom interior designs compliment book cover designs and range from $3-$5/pg. See portfolios on website. Free consultation.

BOOK PROMOTION & MARKETING MATERIALS, PO Box 1382, Running Springs CA 92382. (909) 939-0311. E-mail: info@lionsgatebookdesign.com. Portfolio: www.lionsgatebookdesign.com. Call/e-mail. Has 35 yrs exp. in prof. graphic design, art direction, and advertising for national accounts. Products designed, printed, and delivered include bookmarks, postcards, promotional business cards, posters, banners, retractable signs for book signings, conferences, and events, and more. Logo design and website design are also available. Free consultation.

Note: Please see Chapter 11: Editorial Services for your editorial needs.

4

Distributors

CHRISTIAN BOOK/MUSIC/GIFT DISTRIBUTORS

AMAZON ADVANTAGE PROGRAM, Go to Amazon.com, scroll down to "Features & Services," click on "Selling with Amazon," and on the drop-down menu, click on "Advantage Program" in left-hand column. This is the site to contact if you want Amazon to distribute your book.

*B. BROUGHTON CO., LTD., 322 Consumers Rd., North York ON M2J 1P8, Canada. Toll-free (800) 268-4449 (Canada only). (416) 690-4777. Fax (416) 690-5357. E-mail: sales@bbroughton.com. Website: www.bbroughton.com. Brian Broughton, owner. Canadian distributor. Distributes books, DVDs, gifts, greeting cards. Does not distribute self-published books.

CBA MAILING LISTS OF CHRISTIAN BOOKSTORES, 9240 Explorer Dr., Ste. 200, Colorado Springs CO 80920. (719) 265-9895. Fax (719) 272-3510. E-mail: info@cbaonline.org. Website: www.cbaonline.org. Contact: info@cbaonline.org. Available for rental. Three different lists available, including nonmember stores, 4,700 addresses ($249); member stores, 1,275 addresses ($599); or a combined list of all stores, 5,800 addresses ($699). Prices and numbers available subject to change. Call toll-free (800) 252-1950 for full details.

CHRISTIAN BOOK DISTRIBUTORS, PO Box 7000, Peabody MA 01961-7000. Toll-free (800) 247-4784. (978) 977-5000. Fax (978) 977-5010. E-mail through website: www.christianbooks.com. Does not distribute self-published books.

MCBETH CORP., Fulfillment and Distribution Headquarters, PO Box 400, Chambersburg PA 17201. Toll-free (800) 876-5112. (717) 263-5600. Fax (717) 263-5909. E-mail: mcbethcorp@supernet.com. Distributes Christian gifts, boxed cards, and napkins.

*QUALITY BOOKS, 1003 W. Pines Rd., Oregon IL 61061. Toll-free (800) 323-4241. (815) 732-4450. Fax (815) 732-4499. E-mail: publisher.relations@quality-books.com. Website: www.qualitybooks.com. Distributes small press books, audios, DVDs, CD-ROMs, and Blu-ray to public libraries. Distributes self-published books; asks for 1 copy of your book.

*WORD ALIVE, INC., 131 Cordite Rd., Winnipeg MB R3W 1S1, Canada. Toll-free (800) 665-1468. (204) 667-1400. Toll-free fax (800) 352-9272. (204) 669-0947. E-mail: orderdesk@wordalive.ca. Website: www.wordalive.ca. Distributor of Christian books and products into the Canadian market. Contact: Rosa Peters. Contact by e-mail.

BONUS SECTION

Writer's Helps

Basic Skills

Keys to Professional Formatting

YOU'VE WRITTEN THE STORY OF YOUR HEART, and now you're ready to share it with the world. All you have to do is send it off with a prayer, right? Wrong. Properly formatting your manuscript can make the difference between a sale and a rejection, no matter how well written it is.

Why? What's the big deal about formatting? One word: professionalism.

Appearance matters, and following publishing standards makes an editor's job easier. Your submission will be just one of hundreds on an editor's read list. A glance can tell an editor where you stand as a professional writer.

Even if you opt for independent book publishing, formatting your manuscript professionally enables your editor to concentrate on your words.

Manuscript Preparation

Ever try to read a page that uses several different fonts, different type sizes, more than one color, *italics*, **bold,** ALL CAPS, and <u>underlining</u>? Amateurs think this somehow dresses up a manuscript and makes it more attractive. But the fact is, such gimmicks annoy editors and detract from your message, the core of your writing.

Font: Times New Roman, 12-Point, Black

For most word-processing programs, Times New Roman 12-point is the default setting, and it is the only style you'll need. If it isn't set as the default, select it. It's easily readable, and for editors, that's crucial. For the same reason, use only black type. Fun as it might be to experiment with different colors and sizes, copy that's easy on an editor's eyes marks you as a professional.

Double-Spaced

With few exceptions (like cover letters, query letters, and proposals), everything you submit should be double-spaced. The original rationale was that it left room on the paper for the editor to edit between the lines. Today, while most editing is done on screen, it's still the format editors prefer for readability.

Set your word-processing program's line spacing to double, and do not hit Enter twice at the end of each line. Let the computer do the double-spacing for you, freeing you to focus on what you're writing.

Single Space Between Sentences

Press the spacebar only once to separate the end of one sentence from the beginning of the next. This is the standard of the publishing industry. If you're in the habit of hitting that spacebar twice after each sentence, retraining yourself may take time.

If your manuscript is finished and contains two spaces between sentences throughout, your computer can help. In your Find and Replace feature, type two spaces in the Find What box. In the Replace With box, type a single space. Hit Replace All and Voila! You now have a single space between each sentence.

Paragraph Indents

Don't insert an extra line space between paragraphs. Instead, set your computer to indent the first line of each new paragraph 0.5". (The occasional exception comes in fiction, where an extra line of space — sometimes with a few centered asterisks

— indicates a change of location or passage of time.) Your word-processing software may have as its default some extra space between paragraphs. Reset those values to zero.

Margins

Adequate white space around the edges of your manuscript makes it easy to read — and easy for you or your editor to make notes on printouts. The standard margin settings for most word-processing software are an inch top and bottom, and an inch-and-a-quarter on the sides. Make sure your margins are set to that standard.

Ragged Right

Although most book and magazine publishers print text that aligns evenly on the left and right margins, known as *justified text,* this isn't what you'll use for your manuscript. Instead, create text that looks like what you see in this lesson. Most computer toolbars have buttons that will format text as follows: *aligned left, centered, aligned right,* or *justified* (both left and right margins aligned). Select the *Center* icon for titles, then the *Align left* icon for everything else.

Special Features

Headers and footers. Inserting your last name and the title on each page will help your editor identify your manuscript should the pages of the printout get separated. Your computer will do this for you automatically when you use the Header and Footer feature.

In the small dashed box that appears for the Header, type your last name, forward slash, and your title (Jones/True Forgiveness). When you close that feature, this information will appear at the top of every page.

Page numbers. Page numbers should appear in the upper right corner of each page. Click Insert on the toolbar, select Page Numbers, select Top of page (Header) under Position and Right under Alignment.

Spell Check: Use With Caution

Most word-processing programs automatically correct misspelled words or underline them in red. Spell check will also ask about fixing some correct

---

Formatting Terms

Font. A style of lettering. Common fonts include Times New Roman (used for most professional writing), Courier (like a typewriter), and Arial (sans serif). Do not use sans serif type.

Point size. A measurement for fonts. The larger the size, the larger the letters. 72 points equal one inch. For professional writing use 12-point type.

Boldface. A darker version of a font. Use it primarily for subheads.

Italic. A slanted version of a font. Use it for foreign words and terms, to distinguish key terms, and for book, magazine, and film titles — but only rarely for emphasis. Large blocks of italic type are hard to read.

Centered. Used primarily to type the title at the beginning of a manuscript or chapter.

Justified. Evenly aligned on both sides. The text of most books is *justified,* but material submitted for publication should be aligned only on the left side.

Flush-left, ragged right. The text is aligned at the left margin, but not the right. This is the preferred format for manuscripts, proposals, and correspondence.

Double-spaced. Use this word-processor setting for all material you submit for publication. When revising printouts of your work, the space between lines gives room for comments and editing.

Single-spaced. Use this setting for query letters to editors and agents and to type the author information at the top of the first page, and unless otherwise instructed, for the lessons you submit to your mentor.

Uppercase (capital letters). *The Chicago Manual of Style* and *Christian Writer's Manual of Style* offer guidance on when to capitalize a term. Never use all capitals for emphasis.

words it doesn't recognize. It will also miss correctly spelled words that aren't what you meant to type. (Now instead of not. Or they're instead of their or there.) So don't depend solely on spell check. Print your manuscript, then read it aloud as you proofread. Or have someone else read it for you.

Grammar Check

Similarly, don't trust grammar check to catch all your mistakes or to provide accurate corrections. False alarms abound. There's no substitute for understanding the basics of English grammar. If you're weak in this area, find a simple grammar book that explains the essentials. When your grammar check points out what may be an error, compare it against your handbook. If your computer doesn't check spelling and grammar automatically, select Spelling and Grammar Check on the toolbar. You will still want to print out a copy to manually check it.

More Essentials

Italics. Use only:
- To differentiate thoughts from dialogue. Dialogue is quoted.
- To identify specific words or terms, especially those in a foreign language.
- To set apart the name of a newspaper, magazine, or book (*Washington Post, Christianity Today, Left Behind*), a TV series (*Jeopardy!*), or a ship (*U.S.S. Midway*).
- To emphasize a word or phrase. (For example, "You *did* get that, didn't you?") Limit your use of italics for emphasis, as it becomes distracting. Careful word choice should make the emphasis clear.

Boldface. Use this darker version of the standard typeface only to create a subhead to identify a new section in a book manuscript. Never use boldface (especially **ALL-CAPITALIZED)** for emphasis within a sentence. Also, do not use it or larger type for a title in your manuscripts. .

Capitalization and numbers. Besides beginning sentences and proper nouns with a capital letter, the choice to capitalize certain words is a matter of a publisher's style. For book authors, the key resource is the *Chicago Manual of Style,* which can be purchased in book form or by subscription to the online version. To find whether to capitalize religious terms (capitalize Bible, lowercase biblical) or deity (Him or him), refer to *The Christian Writer's Manual of Style*

Your Author Photo

With a digital camera, you can produce a photo suitable for publication. Just make sure you — or whoever shoots the picture — follow these tips.
- Dress appropriately. Remember, you're a professional.
- Stand in open shade, not facing the sun. This prevents harsh shadows or glare. If the camera has a "fill flash" option, try it.
- Stand before a plain background or, better yet, in the open away from any background. Avoid the "tree-growing-from-your-head" or "pattern-of-bricks" syndrome.
- Step away from a wall. The flash will cast a shadow behind you. Stand six to eight feet from any wall, inside or out (and make sure it's plain and not the same color as what you're wearing).
- Take a head-and-shoulders shot. Unless the publication asks for an "environmental portrait" that shows you at work, have the person taking the picture turn the camera sideways and zoom in on your head and shoulders. If the camera has a "portrait" setting, use it.
- Don't settle for the first try. Try several poses, with multiple shots of each. Select the best one to send as an attached .jpg file.
- Rename the file you send with your first and last name.

by Robert Hudson or *The Little Style Guide to Great Christian Writing and Publishing* by Leonard G. Goss and Carolyn Stanford Goss.

Whichever capitalization style you use, be consistent. Often publishers prefer one style over another, and if you are consistent they can more easily make the changes.

Likewise be consistent whether you use a numeral to indicate a number between 10 and 100 or spell out numbers between ten and one hundred. Use the Chicago Manual as your guide.

Quotation Marks

Lines of dialogue, or when you cite another's spoken or written words, should be placed within quotation marks. "Writers need to know this," says writing mentor Joyce K. Ellis. Note that a comma, not a period, occurs before the end quotation mark when attribution ("says writing mentor Joyce K. Ellis") follows. When no attribution follows, end punctuation (period, exclamation point, or question mark) is placed inside the end quotation mark, in most cases.

A word about "said": Despite what your high school English teacher taught, don't search your thesaurus for synonyms for *said*. In dialogue you may rarely need to have a speaker shout, mutter, or whisper. But make those the exception. *Replied* and *exclaimed* are archaic, and asked is redundant if a line of dialogue ends with a question mark. *Responded* and *retorted* and *answered* are superfluous, and *stated* is just plain awkward. If a character says something in response, we know he has answered. "*Said* is still the best word to use for *said*," says Jerry Jenkins.

Use a single quotation mark for a quote within a quote: "Jesus spoke these things, and lifting up His eyes to heaven, He said, 'Father, the hour has come.'"

Manuscript Formatting

Besides these basics, a few other formatting particulars apply to the electronic file of the manuscript you'll submit to an agent or editor.

Cover page. Using single spacing, in the upper left corner type your name and contact information. Space down to the middle of the page. Using centered text, type the title of your book. Centered and double spaced below that, place your name. (If you are writing under a pen name, include both your real name and your pen name.) Centered and double-spaced below that, give the word count, rounded to the nearest thousand words.

RIVEN

Jerry B. Jenkins

110,000 words

Copyright notice. It is not legally necessary to include a copyright notice on a manuscript. Further, some agents and editors view the insertion of a copyright notice as the mark of an amateur. If adding a copyright notice gives you peace of mind, you may add it below the word count or in the footer. Type the word Copyright or the © symbol (typing a C in parentheses should result in ©), the year, and your name. When you put the copyright notice in the footer, use a smaller size font (8- or 10-point) and center it. This sufficiently demonstrates your ownership of the work; there's no need to register it with the U.S. Copyright Office.

Header information. Beginning with the next page, the header of each page of your novel manuscript should contain:

- Your last name.
- The book's title (or a key word or phrase from it).
- The page number.

Jenkins/Riven   2

Your word-processing program will insert this information automatically, including the page number, on each following page. The page numbers should run successively throughout the entire manuscript, not begin renumbering with each chapter.

Chapters and titles. Use the "Insert" and "Page Break" commands so each chapter begins at the top of a new page. Center numbers and type chapter titles centered, with all caps.

Electronic File Do's and Don'ts

Whatever word-processing software you use, publishers expect submissions as Microsoft Word documents. (Each file name is followed by *.doc* or *.docx*.) If you use a program other than Word, use the "Save As" function to create a *.doc* file. Editors can sometimes open files saved in other document formats; other times they see only gibberish. If you don't know what format your word-processing program creates — or don't know how to save a file to a *.doc* format — ask a computer-savvy friend to coach you.

Via Email

Usually you'll send your *.doc* file manuscript to an editor or agent via email as an attachment. This is also how you'll send your author publicity photo if your editor asks for one. If you're uncertain how to attach files to an email, again your computer friend can coach you.

Emails and Professionalism

Avoid confusion about who is sending the message by establishing an email account just for your writing. The simpler, the better. (*BeckyJones@ISP.com* looks more professional than *GodsFaithfulWriterinCincinnati@ISP.com* or *FuzzyPinkBunnySlippers@ISP. com*.) Free email accounts are available from many companies, such as Yahoo, Google, and MSN. Maintain a professional tone throughout the text of your email. Do not use abbreviations such as "LOL."

File Names

Editors work with files from many contributors. Before emailing a file, rename it for the editor's convenience. Keep it simple: Use your last name, followed by the title of your submission. For example, writer Becky Jones will name her file *Jones True Forgiveness*. Sending an agent at Acme Literary a file named *Acme nonfiction manuscript.doc* won't identify the submission clearly. Do the same if you're asked to send an electronic version of your author photo (usually a *.jpg* file). Use only your first and last name: *Becky Jones.jpg*, not *My summer picture.jpg* or *IMG_0016.jpg*.

Manuscript Formatting Checklist

Use this checklist before submitting your manuscript:

_____ Font: Times New Roman, 12-point, black

_____ Double-spaced (no extra space between paragraphs); Flush-left, ragged right (not justified)

_____ Margins: 1" top and bottom, 1¼" sides

_____ Consistent spacing: indents; only one space after end punctuation; no extra spaces between words or letters

_____ Italics used sparingly for emphasis and to differentiate thoughts from dialogue.

_____ Italics used for titles of books, newspapers, and magazines

_____ No punctuation overuse: too many commas, dashes, exclamation points, etc.

_____ No bold-faced text or underlining

_____ Numbers treated according to *The Chicago Manual of Style*

_____ Key information in the right places on the cover page

_____ Header information and page number

_____ Adheres to the publisher's or agent's submission guidelines

Resources

The Chicago Manual of Style (available in both book and online versions)

The Christian Writer's Manual of Style by Robert Hudson

The Little Style Guide to Great Christian Writing and Publishing by Leonard G. Goss and Carolyn Stanford Goss

The Elements of Style by William Strunk, Jr. and E. B. White

English grammar handbook of your choice

The Write Way: The S.P.E.L.L. Guide to Real-Life Writing by Richard Lederer and Richard Dowis

Online grammar helps: *Purdue Owl, GrammarGirl*

Used by permission of the Jerry Jenkins Writers Guild.

Where to Find Ideas

by Les Stobbe

A MAJOR ADVANTAGE WE CHRISTIAN WRITERS ENJOY is our power source: the Holy Spirit. This Holy Spirit lives in everyone who has been born again by faith in Christ. He's the genius behind every genuinely good idea, every inspired big idea, that pops up in your mind. Pray, ask for wisdom and good ideas. Bruce Wilkinson writes in *The Prayer of Jabez:*

> That's the catch — if you don't ask for His blessing, you forfeit those that come to you only when you ask. In the same way that a father is honored to have a child beg for his blessing, your Father is delighted to respond generously when His blessing is what you covet most.

Where might you find these big ideas inspired by the Holy Spirit?

In Yourself

Where might you find these big ideas inspired by the Holy Spirit?

- *During Scripture reading and meditation.* Ever had the ah-ha moment when the Holy Spirit clearly gave you a new insight? Some ideas grow on you — like the writer who meditated on the names of God for years and turned that study into speaking material, articles, and book topics.
- *During journaling.* Not everything you record in your journal is worthy of the light of day. Some is private. But if you daily ask the Holy Spirit for His presence and help, outstanding insights will arise, worthy of further consideration.
- *In preparation for leading a class at any age level.* Insights about God and how He works will come out of the woodwork when you're preparing to teach others. For one writer, a lesson in Matthew led to an article on "Who is the greatest?" for a sports magazine.
- *Lessons learned from life.* For example, insights gained from Hebrews 2:14-15 that drove away the fear of death after terrorist attacks, could result in a great article.
- *Your dreams or aspirations.* Always wanted to fly? When you finally take flying lessons, analogies to the spiritual life will abound.

Your Family

While there may be times when your family doesn't appreciate an article that showcases them, you can still glean ideas from them that, properly researched, will benefit others

- You watch a family member practice playing a musical instrument. Suddenly you recognize an analogy to the perseverance needed in prayer.
- You see the faith of a grandmother transmitted through four generations and decide to do a series of interviews on the impact of long-term faith in a family.
- You watch your husband or father helping a child build and fly a kite and begin research on father-son relationships.
- You see your father care for your mother, who has Alzheimer's, and you're inspired to research and write on the impact of senility on a family.

- A rebellious teen turns back to the faith of his family and becomes a productive Christian. You start to study the trigger points in turning around rebellious teens.
- Your mother does needlepoint or quilting in a group, leading to an article on the role of craft making in building community.

Your Church

Churches are full of excellent ideas.

- Teens report on their short-term missions trip, and you begin to wonder about the long-term impact of such service.
- You write down a thought expressed by the pastor and suddenly realize it's the germ of an article on walking with God in troubled times.
- Your pastor has been in place for 20 or more years. You could write an article on the importance of longevity in the pastorate, with your pastor as the major source of information, expanded through personal interviews.
- You hear several testimonies in a prayer meeting. Consider using them as a starting point for an inspirational article on how God moves people to ccept by faith the atoning death and resurrection of His Son.
- A musician who plays on Sunday morning has an extremely varied musical life outside the church. A personality profile could be interesting for the church newsletter.

Your Community

Many people exist in a community without really living in it. It's where they sleep, eat, shop, and get their hair done. But there's a world of ideas out there beyond your church if you get involved as a volunteer — or just keep your eyes and ears open.

- The ministerial association helps establish a halfway house for people released from prison.
- A Christian entrepreneur becomes the city's website guru.
- A principal celebrates 25 years as a teacher and administrator, so you get an interview on the changes he has seen in education.
- A Special Olympics is held in your community, and you discover a poignant story of a volunteer who devotes her life to the disabled.

Local and National Media

Newspapers, radio, and television exist to inform and entertain. They're a never-ending source of big ideas. Local media often present great human interest stories right in your backyard, stories that can be expanded into features.

Used by permission of the Jerry Jenkins Writers Guild.

Is Your Idea Worth Writing?

by Les Stobbe

IT'S ONE THING TO STUMBLE ONTO A BIG IDEA, another to frame it in a context that makes it significant to a large number of readers. Ask yourself:

1. Is this idea truly significant?

2. Is this a fresh idea or something already well covered?

3. If already well covered, what's a unique angle I might tackle?

4. How many people would be genuinely interested in this idea/theme?

5. Who is my target reader?

6. What's the positive angle/slant that would give my reader the most information/encouragement/motivation/action opportunities?

7. What might be wrong with developing this idea? Might my family or someone at church be legitimately offended? If it is a genuinely important topic, can I take a less controversial approach?

8. Might my approach arouse animosity to the cause of Christ?

9. Do I have enough stories to go with this idea?

10. Will it still be timely a year or more from now?

11. Will this fit the magazine I want to write for?

12. Do I have the experience to back up the idea so it won't come off as half-baked?

Used by permission of the Jerry Jenkins Writers Guild.

Focus Your Idea

1. From broad to narrow

You've heard a talk on witnessing for Christ, so you decide to do an article for your denominational publication. You receive a rejection. Are they opposed to witnessing? Probably not, but perhaps you weren't focused enough. Rather than writing on the broad subject of sharing one's faith, you might have scored by focusing on becoming a contagious Christian, or witnessing as a teen, or on reaching those who have rejected church.

2. From vague to sharp

You're concerned that many people in your church are aging, yet nothing seems to be done for them. Instead of a general lament, do an article on a church that runs an arts program for seniors that includes painting, poetry readings, and woodcarving.

3. From distant to close-up

Instead of a general article on beautifying the neighborhood through flowers, write an article about perennial borders. Rather than a general article about how God answers prayer, tell the story of "When God answered my prayer."

What's Newsworthy: The Elements of News

by Les Stobbe

JOURNALISTS AND THEIR EDITORS use a number of characteristics to determine news-worthiness. Terms may differ with varying publications, but all cover the following basic elements:

1. **Significant,** with great impact on readers (war, elections, epidemics, natural disasters, lifesaving health breakthroughs)

2. **Unique and of human interest** (often written as a news feature)

3. **Prominence of subject** (the famous and infamous, or at least well-known in the community)

4. **Conflict** (of countries, people, humans against nature, etc.)

5. **Consequence** (result or follow-up of earlier stories of major impact)

6. **Proximity** (either the event or subject is physically close enough to matter to readers, or they have something else in common)

7. **Timely** (the event just happened and is printed in the next possible edition)

8. **Evergreen** (story is ongoing, with enough happening periodically to interest readers; can also refer to features and articles that are always of interest)

News stories usually have at least three and often more of these elements. The more elements, the more newsworthy the idea.

Getting Started in Interviewing
by Les Stobbe

EACH INTERVIEW SUBJECT requires a somewhat different approach to pre-interview research. Interviewing your grandmother will take relatively little research — and you're usually operating from a more easily gained basis of trust. Let's consider some categories of interview subjects.

Friends or Family Members

It's important to establish confidence that you know what you're doing. If it's a grandparent, have your mother or father talk casually to the person about the course of instruction you're taking. Talk to the grandparent yourself about some elements of your course and what you hope to achieve. Let Grandma or Grandpa develop a sense of pride in what you're trying to achieve.

If you plan to interview a parent or grandparent who has immigrated, study his or her native country and see what questions it sparks in your mind. Determine the cultural background, the event that may have propelled the family out of the country, and conditions in your country when they arrived. Your library, the internet, and other relatives can be important sources.

Members of Your Church

If you're interviewing a Sunday school teacher, talk to the department head or Sunday school superintendent first. If you're interviewing the pastor, ask the church secretary for a résumé that he probably has on file. If he's part of a denomination, talk to the district superintendent about his perspective on your pastor and his work. When interviewing a member with a unique achievement, such as a short-term mission trip, acquaint yourself with the area in which the person served. Study any literature available from a missions pastor or chair of the missions committee.

Community People

If the person you want to interview is part of the community leadership, your local newspaper may have information. Look for previous articles, especially if he or she is an elected official. Don't be bashful about getting into what's called the newspaper's morgue (the library or archives). If your subject is involved in a specialized hobby, learn some of its basic terminology before the interview.

Visiting Speakers or Musicians

Speakers and musicians have assistants, agents, and/or publicists helping them either fend off or meet the press. The easiest way to get started is to contact them for a press kit, which usually contains a photo. The kit may suggest other sources for information, such as newspaper, magazine, and web articles.

Authors will be represented by a publicity person at their publisher. The publicist will be happy to supply a copy of the author's newest book and a press kit — and often a list of suggested interview questions.

Many of today's authors, speakers, and musicians maintain websites rich in background information. That's also true of sports personalities, whose publicity managers have a lot of data about their stars — though probably not about their Christian testimony. At the very least, find out how to spell and pronounce your subject's name and title, and learn what he or she is best known for doing or creating.

Jerry Jenkins, whose early writing career was marked by several as-told-to autobiographies with sports stars, made it a point to make friends with a team's publicist. "I didn't want to waste a star's time by asking him for details that filled a file cabinet in someone's office. I immersed myself in that information first, and during the interview I didn't ask for detail; I asked for personal memories. Rather than asking Nolan Ryan, 'When did you throw your first no-hitter,' I was able to ask, 'Did you think you had lost it when that line drive nearly got through the infield in the seventh inning?'"

Developing an Angle

You'll get little help from your interview subject if you don't have a good idea of what you're looking for; this is called the angle. Consider what unique aspect of the person's life would provide entertainment and information for your reader. To try to talk about everything the person knows, without an angle, would be disastrous. A young journalist landed an interview with Billy Graham by making clear that he wanted to focus on the famous evangelist's pioneering work in Christian radio and television.

If you have already contacted a newspaper or magazine editor about your interview idea, discuss the angle with the editor. He or she will help you determine an angle for that publication. Questions to ask yourself:

• What makes this person newsworthy?
• If the person has a book or record, what's the theme of it?
• If this person were going to speak at my church or a community banquet, what would be his or her subject?
• What's unique about this person?
• How is this person using his or her God-given gifts?
• Has this person had some dramatic experience?
• Does this person have the capacity to make readers laugh, cry, rejoice, or become angry?
• What controversy, if any, has this person been involved in?
• How will this person's experiences best help my publication's readers?
• How can I show that this VIP is human after all?

When you get into an interview, you may find yourself stumbling onto a new angle that's even more promising. Explore it with your subject. It may develop into a second article for a different publication.

That's why it's important not to feel you need to have every question listed before you start. That can give the interviewee the impression that you're looking for something specific and that you think you know what he or she might say. Rather, list three or four general areas you want to cover and make the interview a conversation. Let each succeeding question derive from the answers.

You may be interviewing a community old-timer about what farming was like when he was growing up. A chance remark reveals he became an environmental activist and put some of his land into a conservancy to prevent people from building on it. If you have a prescribed list of questions, you may miss his answer and keep reading from your list. But if this is really a conversation, you can chase that gem and mine a whole separate article from it.

Or suppose you're talking to a retired pastor who became a land developer and you discover he's also an avid woodcarver. That could make a fascinating article for a craft magazine.

Conducting an Interview

by Les Stobbe

FOR A CHRISTIAN WRITER, the most important step in approaching an interview is prayer. I have experienced amazing openings as a result of prayer.

Writing is largely a solitary pursuit. We lock ourselves away in our offices, turn on our favorite playlist, and cut ourselves off from this world. This comes with a price. Writing requires focus, dedication, passion, and a dream that those who aren't writers cannot fully understand. While family and friends may offer tremendous support, they struggle to relate to the frustrations that come from hours alone at the keyboard.

Setting the appointment for the interview will normally be easy with your friends, may involve more calls for a person in your church or community, and may require prolonged effort with a nationally known speaker, author, musician, actor or actress, or sports personality.

For anyone outside your community, you will most likely do the interview by telephone. Amazingly, many authors and speakers can be reached directly — once you have a phone number from a friend, agent, or publicity representative. Be prepared to suggest the reason and angle for the interview, as well as how much time you'll need, though 30 to 45 minutes is likely all you'll get.

If you can say you are under assignment from a newspaper or magazine, it should help you get a response or phone number from the agent or publicist, especially if you send a copy of the publication. If you're able to drop a name of a mutual friend, that may help open the door. Even then, however, several phone calls may be necessary. Since speakers and musicians are on

Record Every Word

UNLESS YOU'RE EFFICIENT AT SHORTHAND, you will find an audio recorder most valuable. For people new to being interviewed, it's important that your machine not intimidate them. Use inexpensive lapel microphones for both you and your subject (an inexpensive Y-clip allows you to run two out of one jack). Those small investments result in great fidelity, making it easier for you or someone else to transcribe the interview.

Clipping the mike on their blouse or shirt keeps it out of their line of sight and it is soon forgotten. Assure them you're recording not for broadcast or for anyone else's hearing, but just for your own research. Don't be afraid to cough or misspeak while recording so they know you're not self-conscious about being recorded. The less obtrusive you can make your recorder, the better.

It takes time to transcribe the interview, but you'll save time and expense if you do it yourself. Do it while it's fresh in your memory and you can skip several minutes of stuff you know you won't use in your article. Employing a keyboarder can be helpful, but you wouldn't want them to decide what to include or leave out. Also, someone unfamiliar with the topic may hear key words wrong, so type them incorrectly.

Caution: If you record a telephone interview, ethics (as well as the law in many states) require that you ask your subject for permission.

Even if you do record, write down key points and good quotes, because recorders have been known to malfunction. One new writer was so excited about interviewing a favorite Christian musician that she didn't write down a word of the interview. She had great eye contact, asked pertinent questions, and ended up with nothing but memories when she later tried to transcribe the session.

Always carry an extra set of batteries, just as you would carry two pens. Better, use an extension cord plugged into an electrical outlet.

the road a lot, you'll probably have to set up an appointment with an assistant so your subject can call you when he or she has time.

When you've done your research, prepared your questions, and have an interview scheduled, pray again, asking for wisdom. As you begin the interview, be ready to digress from your questions if you discover an interesting new insight, experience, or passion. Be prepared to gently push the envelope if you discover the subject is not coming clean or being forthright in an area of special interest to you. Comments like "I sense this is a sensitive area with you; can you help me understand ..." may break down the resistance.

When I discovered in an interview that Dale Evans Rogers had been married three times before she met Roy, my probing revealed a reluctance to name her second husband because she thought it might hurt him. Yet the depth of her rebellion against God — and the corresponding repentance and growth that came from it — could not be portrayed without showing how that had affected all her relationships.

Don't let a subject's celebrity status overwhelm you. You will fail to get a solid interview.

Don't let a subject's celebrity status overwhelm you and make you fawn over him or her. You will only gain disapproval and fail to get a solid interview. Well-known people have enough fans, and it puts them off if someone who is supposed to be a professional acts like a groupie. Sure, it's exciting and you can't wait to tell your friends how interesting the person was. But hold that in abeyance. Postpone expressing your excitement until your job is done.

Gathering personal information about your subject should be part of your pre-interview research, but if you were unable to collect it in advance, be sure to get it at the start of the interview. A form listing all the information you need will help you to fill in the blanks. Make sure you have an email or street address so you can let the person check your facts — unless the periodical for which you're writing has a policy of not letting the subject see the pre-published article. Many publications won't let subjects see the article because interviewees often want to change an uncomfortable admission. More than once, people I've written about were startled when they saw in print what they had said.

A good policy is always to double check any technical or statistical information or anything you found confusing. You can always let the subject see or hear selected parts of your article that need fact-checking, rather than the entire piece.

Professional interviewers make the subject feel at ease, honor the subject's time by being prepared, thank him or her for participating, and write a factually correct article. Follow up with a thank you note. Once you complete the interview, assess if you should change the angle before you start writing. You may need to market the article to a different publication because of the new slant.

Not every publication prints Q&A articles. So consider writing an article built with a blend of direct quotes (the person's exact words), indirect quotes (paraphrases), and facts from your research. Good interview articles can change lives. Take the time to do them right!

Used by permission of the Jerry Jenkins Writers Guild.

Structural Self-Editing

by Les Stobbe

EFFECTIVE ARTICLES DISPLAY THREE TRAITS: unity, coherence, and emphasis.

Unity

If you don't feel satisfied with an article (as a reader or a writer), it may be because you have a vague sense that it lacks the same kind of unity we feel from God. We're made in the image of God. With that in mind as you read your own writing, ask yourself:

a. Is my thesis clear all the way through, or did I digress?
b. Have I maintained a consistent point of view? Am I writing as the expert or as the investigator? Am I writing in the first person or third?
c. Is my tense consistent, or do I switch between past and present tense without good reason?
d. What mood does my article create? Is it uplifting, sad, triumphant, hopeful?

Coherence

Coherence is largely achieved through transitional words, phrases, and sentences. They provide the framework that helps an article hang together. Ask yourself:

a. Are there transitional words from sentence to sentence?
b. Are there transitional words, phrases, or clauses tying paragraphs together?
c. Are there examples of illogical development that will make readers stop in their tracks?

Like anything else, transitions can be overdone. Some of the best style guides and manuals urge avoiding hackneyed transitional phrases, especially when the context is clear without them. Here's an example of overdone transitioning between sentences:

On the other hand, like anything else, this can, *of course,* be overdone. The truth is that some of the best style guides and manuals urge avoiding hackneyed transitional phrases, *for instance,* especially

---

Why Use Story

WHAT MAKES AN ARTICLE, a sermon, or a book life changing? Is it the fortuitous coming together of special idea, prepared audience, transcendent moment, and moving of the Holy Spirit? Or could it be that the use of story was also a major contributor?

When a lawyer asked Jesus, "Who is my neighbor?" Jesus did not give him a quick description, as we twenty-first century Christians probably would.

Instead, Jesus launched into the story of the Good Samaritan (Luke 10:29-30). Then He asked, "And which of these three do you think proved to be a neighbor to the man who fell into the robber's hands?" No contest, according to the lawyer: "The one who had mercy on him" (verse 37).

A story like that is a time bomb. Its emotion causes it to stick in the mind and heart, exploding when life experience matches its truth and it becomes instantly applicable by the Holy Spirit. It touches us not only at the level of understanding but also awakens God-given and Holy Spirit-sharpened sensitivities to the needs of others. It motivates us to do something, having left such a powerful imprint on our mind and feelings that we can't escape our responsibility.

when the context is clear without them. *Let's turn our attention now to* an example of overdone ...

Emphasis

On pages 137–38 of *An Introduction to Christian Writing*, Ethel Herr provides "Ten Tools to Increase Emphasis." Many beginning writers use words in italics, underlining, and bold type or exclamation points to emphasize their key ideas.

Those devices often serve only to distract. According to Ethel, a colorful style uses powerful nouns and verbs and achieves far more, as do poignant statements, proper arrangement of words in sentences, quotes and dialogue, anecdotes, and discovery techniques.

It's also been shown that putting quote marks around words we fear the reader won't "understand" is not only not "helpful," but is also "condescending" and subtly "insulting" to the reader.

Used by permission of the Jerry Jenkins Writers Guild.

Taking the Path to Publication
by Jerry B. Jenkins

Do YOUR HOMEWORK. Know what your target market is looking for. Occasionally you'll hear back from a magazine or a publisher that your idea didn't ring a bell. But that's not a rejection. That's a business transaction. You did a bit of work, solicited their interest, they passed. You move on.

Now, if you had written the entire article or even whole book before determining even an inkling of interest on the part of the editor, you probably deserved a rejection.

Even if you're brand new to the writing game, save yourself mountains of fruit-less work by trying to get an editor on board with you early. If you're new, she'll likely express only speculative interest ("Yes, it sounds interesting, and we'll be happy to give it a look, provided you . . .").

It's what comes after that provided you that becomes your marching orders. Does she want it longer than you proposed? Shorter? In first person rather than third? Does she have suggestions for other angles, other people to interview?

To the best of your ability, do everything she suggests. You have a green light on spec, which is nearly as rare as a sale. And while she can still reject your submission, by proving yourself able to work with an editor, you're nearly forcing the editor to stick with you — even if your writing is light-years from where it should be some day. She may ask for rewrites, bring a seasoned writer alongside, or assign you one of her best copyeditors.

By showing you have a thick skin, you can take input, and you recognize a piece of published work is not a solo, but rather a duet between writer and editor, you've given yourself the best chance at a sale. And you've avoided rejection.

Veterans will tell you not to take rejections personally. That's a laugh. If you're like me, your very soul is on that page. The reason we want to avoid rejection letters is that no one wants to be rejected.

Our goal as writers should be to write better than we, our spouses, our parents, or our editors dreamed possible. That's my wish for you, and that's why I'm trying to stuff this book with practical tips and proven strategy.

Now that you're ready to dive in, let's debunk a few myths. I'll be blunt and let you in on a few things I wish I'd learned early in my career.

Writing Is Hard Work

Don't agree so quickly. Wait till you've been dragged across the bumpy road toward publication a few times. For now, admit that you suspect you're something special. For you, writing will be a breeze. Editors will clamor for your work. You foresee a bidding war over your next book. Is that Reader's Digest on the phone? Not so fast.

I was talking with an editor friend the other day, a veteran of many writers confer-ences, who has seen all levels of competency. "It's rare that you find a first-timer who really gets it," she said. What first-timers don't get is that writing is not a hobby, a spare-time activity, or something to play at. It's work.

It's a calling, like it or not.

For me, writing is as exhausting as physical labor. After writing (and publishing) more than 180 books, that still surprises me. Sometimes, on deadline, I'll sit at the keyboard for six, eight, ten hours or more. When I'm finished, I'm as spent as if I've been ditch-digging all day. It doesn't seem that physically taxing, but it is. I guess it's the fact that you must be constantly thinking in order to write.

Creativity will cost you, wear you out. Don't ever get the idea writing is easy. If it is, you're not working hard enough. The stuff that comes easy takes the most rewriting. And the stuff that comes hard reads the easiest.

Writing Takes Specialized Skills

A psychologist friend once asked if I would have lunch with him and give him a few tips. "I'm thinking about doing a little freelance writing in my spare time," he said.

"That's interesting," I said, "because I've been thinking about doing a little psychological counseling in my spare time."

"I didn't know you were trained for that."

"Gotcha," I said.

When you hang out your shingle as a writer, be prepared for such unintended slights. People tell me all the time that they have a book in them, if they only had the time to write. That would be like my saying I have a sermon in me, if only I had the time to prepare it.

Writing is rarely accorded the same respect as other professions, but if people want to tell themselves they could be the one-in-a-thousand writer who could sell a manuscript to a book publisher, if they could only find the time, fine.

It's Not You Against the World

Don't think of writing as competitive. This is tough. Nearly impossible. We all compare ourselves to our peers, worrying who's winning, who's publishing more, selling more, earning more, enjoying more visibility. You might think, That's easy for you to say, now that you've arrived. Maybe. But anyone who has succeeded was once an unknown beginner.

I decided a long time ago that I could only be the best writer I could be. I had to stop worrying about where my writing put me in the pecking order. I have no control over the success of a project in the marketplace. And if my book sells a hundred times more than another writer's, that doesn't make me a better writer.

My goals are internal. If I succeed in being the best I can be — maximizing my potential, taking no shortcuts — and this success makes me the thousandth best writer in my field, am I not ahead of the writer who is number one and yet still not doing his best work? Stop comparing.

What matters is where you are on your journey, striving to be the best you can be.

The world is full of wonderful writers. There are apprentices, journeymen, craftsmen, and bestselling authors. Sometimes the bestselling author is a master craftsman, sometimes not. What matters is where you are on your journey, striving to be the best you can be.

I need to grow and learn. I read everything I can find on the craft of writing. My goal is to write better this week than last, this year than last. Where that places me on the spectrum of writers is irrelevant. That's all about ego, and worrying about it won't make me a better writer.

A little secret: Once you've come to grips with the comparison gremlins, you can actually be happy for another writer who succeeds (rejoice with those who rejoice).

Even 'Sacred' Writing Can Be Edited

The words you choose, regardless how completely you have surrendered yourself and your work to God, are not sacred. Only Scripture is God-breathed. However, the *result* of your writing might very well be sacred.

I split hairs for a reason. *Sacred* can mean "untouchable," and it can mean "godly." If you regard your writing as sacred in the sense of "untouchable" (*God gave me these words, so don't edit them*), they had better be divinely perfect, or God gets a bad rap.

Frankly, writers who make this claim—and it happens often—are immediately branded as amateurs. An inside joke among editors in inspirational publishing is that God is the worst literary agent ever.

> *If you really believe your writing is beyond improvement, you're deluding yourself.*

If you really believe your writing is beyond reproach, beyond question, beyond improvement, then you've made it an idol or you're deluding yourself. We've all been there. It hurts to give an editor free rein to shred the work we'd prefer to believe was dictated by God Himself. Are we giving the editor a break, or protecting ourselves from criticism, when we inform her that God has already ordained every word?

Doing your best writing is only step one. I never think of submitting a piece of writing that I think I can still improve. The emphasis there is on *I*. I'm not saying *no one* can make it better. Fresh eyes are always valuable, but avoid the temptation to tell an editor, "I'm sure this needs more work, but here it is." Submit the absolute best work you can do, and then be open to input. It's a duet, never a solo.

Editors Are Sometimes Wrong

At the risk of seeming contradictory, I must also advise that you not automatically agree with every suggestion your editor makes. Any humble editor would agree that editing is largely subjective. Often, an editor has a better idea of what works than you do. And editors should better understand their readers.

They're usually right, but not always. Sometimes you must plead your case. To avoid being labeled belligerent, choose your fights carefully.

Speak your mind kindly. Your editor, I hope, will do the same.

It's okay to ask an editor to explain herself. But ultimately, you need to submit both your words and your will. If you're publishing a book at your own expense, in the end this is your call. Otherwise, someone else is assigned to make the call.

The editor exists to satisfy readers. Putting the reader first may mean putting you, the writer, second. That's the way it is. Live with it and learn to put your priorities on the same plane as the editor's.

Learn *The Elements of Style*

While I espouse wide reading in the area of writing, few single books can make an immediate, significant improvement in a writer like Strunk and White's *The Elements of Style*. It's a small volume worth reading annually, and it contains advice on everything from clear writing to punctuation to avoiding needless words. I've never seen so much information packed into one thin book.

Ignore Writer's Block

I quarrel with anyone claiming she can't write because of writer's block. The answer to writer's block is Nike's motto: Just do it.

We all get stuck, but that's when the fun and creative flow we enjoyed yesterday becomes a job today. We still have to sit there and do our work.

If I were a factory worker or an executive, I wouldn't be able to call in and plead worker's block. Imagine what I'd hear from my boss.

Some days, you won't have the inspiration, and your muse will be on strike. But if you don't write today, you're going to pay for it tomorrow. As your own boss, you can allow yourself the freedom to take a day off, as long as you understand the consequences.

Old Rules Still Apply

The Internet and e-mail make life easier for everybody. I'm old enough to remember buying manuscript boxes and packing up my precious babies to ship to publishers. Today, like everyone else, I attach my manuscript files to e-mails and transmit them in seconds.

But be sure to use the same level of professionalism when sending electronic documents. I'm appalled at how sloppy people are on the Internet and in e-mail. Punctuation and spelling go out the window, and it often appears that people are making up words as they go along.

Your prospects for publication may depend on how you come across. Leave nothing to chance.

Just for the sake of discipline and reputation, I try to make sure that anything I write, even a brief note. is spelled and punctuated correctly.

In many cases, especially when you're communicating with editors and publishers, your prospects for publication may depend on how you come across. Leave nothing to chance.

Many websites are hungry for content. Competition is fierce, and the pay is often poor. But with so many online sources—many tied to print publications—any writer should be able to find a place to publish. Research to find sites that match your interests, and then submit story ideas.

Once you've scored with such a website, use those articles as clips with prospective magazine or newspaper editors.

Read About the Craft

Subscribe to a writer's magazine. Read books on writing. In the inspirational market, two volumes are no-brainers: *The Christian Writer's Market Guide* and *The Christian Writer's Manual of Style.*

There are significant differences in guidelines within Christian publishing. If you've been a person of faith for any length of time, you know that each denomination and publication and publishing house has its own list of preferences and taboos. Disregarding or not knowing these is the quickest path to a rejection.

PART 2

Periodical Publishers

5

Topical Listings of Periodicals

As soon as you have an article or story idea, look up that topic in the following topical listings (see Table of Contents for a full list of topics). Study the appropriate periodicals in the primary/alphabetical listings (as well as their writer's guidelines and sample copies) and select those that are most likely targets for the piece you are writing.

Most ideas can be written for more than one periodical if you slant them to the needs of different audiences. Have a target periodical and audience in mind before you start writing. Each topic is divided by age group/audience.

If the magazine requires a query letter, write that first, and then follow their suggestions if they give you a go-ahead to write the article.

R – Takes Reprints; $ - Indicates a paying market

APOLOGETICS
ADULT/GENERAL
American Chr. Voice—R
Believers Bay—R
$-Bible Advocate—R
$-Brink, The—R
CBN.com—R
$-Celebrate Life
$-Christianity Today—R
Christian Online
Christian Ranchman
$-Christian Research
$-Christian
    Standard—R
$-Columbia
$-Drama Ministry—R
$-Faith Today
$-Homeschooling
    Today—R
$-Indian Life—R
$-In Touch
Leaves—R
$-Lookout
$-Mature Living
Movieguide
$-Our Sunday
    Visitor—R
Perspectives
Priscilla Papers
$-Seek—R
$-War Cry—R

CHILDREN
$-Guide—R
$-Sparkle—R

DAILY DEVOTIONALS
$-Brink Magazine—R
Penned from the
    Heart—R

PASTORS/LEADERS
$-Christian Century—R
$-Enrichment—R
$-Outreach—R
$-Small Groups.
    com—R

TEEN/YOUNG ADULT
$-Direction
$Young Salvationist—R

WOMEN
$-Mother's Heart
Virtuous Woman—R

ARTS/
ENTERTAINMENT
ADULT/GENERAL
American Chr. Voice—R
Believers Bay—R
$-Faith Today
Genuine Motivation—R
$-Indian Life—R

$-Prairie Messenger—R
Storyteller—R
$-War Cry—R

PASTORS/LEADERS
$-Brink Magazine—R

TEEN/YOUNG ADULT
Genuine Motivation—R
Sisterhood
$-TC Magazine
$Young Salvationist—R

BEAUTY/FASHION
ADULT/GENERAL
Believers Bay—R
Genuine Motivation—R

CHILDREN
$-Guide—R
$-Sparkle—R

TEEN/YOUNG ADULT
Genuine Motivation—R
Single!—R
Sisterhood

WOMEN
Halo Magazine—R
Treasure—R
Virtuous Woman

BIBLE STUDIES
ADULT/GENERAL
$-Alive Now
American Chr. Voice—R
$-Arlington Catholic
Believers Bay—R
CBN.com—R
Christian Journal—R
Christian Online
Christian Ranchman
$-Christian Research
$-Christian
    Standard—R
Church Herald &
    Holiness
$-Columbia
$-Dreamseeker—R
Eternal Ink—R
$-Gem, The—R
Highway News—R
$-Homeschooling
    Today—R
$-In Touch
Leaves—R
$-Lutheran Journal—R
$-Lutheran Witness
$-Mature Living
Mature Years
Our Sunday Visitor
Perspectives
$-Point—R
Priscilla Papers
$-Purpose—R
$-St. Anthony
    Messenger
$-Seek—R

CHRISTIAN EDUCA-
TION/LIBRARY
$-Catechist
$-Group Magazine
PASTORS/LEADERS
$-SmallGroups.com—R

TEEN/YOUNG ADULT
Single!—R

WOMEN
Halo Magazine—R
$-Mother's Heart

Treasure—R
Virtuous Woman

BOOK EXCERPTS
ADULT/GENERAL
$-Alive Now
American Chr. Voice—R
Believers Bay—R
CBN.com—R
$-Charisma
$-Catholic Digest
$-Chicken Soup Bks—R
$-Christianity Today—R
$-Christian Retailing
$-Columbia
$-Covenant
    Companion—R
$-Faith Today
Genuine Motivation—R
$-Homeschooling
    Today—R
$-Indian Life—R
New Heart—R
$-Point—R
$-Power for Living—R
$-Prairie Messenger—R
Priscilla Papers
$-Prism
$-United Church
    Observer
$-U.S. Catholic
$-War Cry—R

CHRISTIAN EDUCA-
TION/LIBRARY
$-Journal/Adventist
    Ed.—R
PASTORS/LEADERS
$-Christian Century—R
$-L Magazine—R
$-Ministry Today
$-Outreach—R

TEEN/YOUNG ADULT
$-Boundless.org—R
Genuine Motivation—R
Single!—R

WOMEN
Share
Virtuous Woman

WRITERS
$-Freelance Writer's
    Report—R
$-Writer

BOOK REVIEWS
ADULT/GENERAL
$-Abilities
$-America
American Chr. Voice—R
$-Arlington Catholic
Believers Bay—R
$-Brink, The—R
byFaith
CBN.com—R
$-Charisma
$-Christian Courier—R
$-Christian Herald
$-Christianity Today—R
Christian Journal—R
Christian Ranchman
$-Christian Research
$-Christian Retailing
$ChristianWeek
$-City Light News
$-Cresset, The
Eternal Ink—R
$-Eureka Street
$-Faith & Friends—R
$-Faith Today
Genuine Motivation—R
$-Homeschooling
    Today—R
$-Home Times—R
$-Image
$-Indian Life—R
MovieGuide—R
New Frontier
Our Sunday Visitor
Penwood Review
Perspectives
$-Prairie Messenger—R
Priscilla Papers
$-Prism
$-Testimony—R
Time of Singing—R
$-U.S. Catholic
$-War Cry—R
$-Weavings
$-World & I

CHRISTIAN EDUCA-TION/LIBRARY
$-Journal/Adventist
    Ed.—R

MISSIONS
$-Operation
    Reveille—R

PASTORS/LEADERS
$-Christian Century—R
$-Enrichment—R
$-Leadership—R
$-L Magazine—R
$-Ministry Today
$-Reformed Worship
Sharing the Practice—R

TEEN/YOUNG ADULT
$-Devo'zine
$-Direction
Genuine Motivation—R
Single!—R
$Young Salvationist—R

WOMEN
Dabbling Mum
Halo Magazine—R
$-Mother's Heart
Share
Virtuous Woman

WRITERS
$-Christian
    Communicator—R
$-Fellowscript—R
$-Writer

CANADIAN/ FOREIGN MARKETS
ADULT/GENERAL
$-Abilities
$Anglican Journal
$-Canada Lutheran—R
Canadian Lutheran
$-Canadian Mennonite
$-Christian Courier—R
$-Christian Herald
$ChristianWeek
$-City Light News
$-Common Ground—R

Converge Magazine
$-Eureka Street
$-Faith & Friends—R
$-Faith Today
$-Indian Life—R
$-Living Light—R
$-Messenger
$-Prairie Messenger—R
$-Testimony—R
$-United Church
    Observer

DAILY DEVOTIONALS
$-Rejoice!

PASTORS/LEADERS
Technologies for
    Worship

WRITERS
$-Fellowscript—R

CELEBRITY PIECES
ADULT/GENERAL
American Chr. Voice—R
$-Angels on Earth
$-Arlington Catholic
Believers Bay—R
$-Brink Magazine—R
$-Catholic Digest
CBN.com—R
$-Celebrate Life
$-Christian Herald
Christian Journal—R
Christian Online
Christian Ranchman
$-City Light News
Genuine Motivation—R
$-Good News, The –R
$-Good News, Etc.—R
$-Guideposts—R
$-Home Times—R
$-In Touch
$-Living Light
    News—R
Movieguide
Our Sunday Visitor
$-Power for Living—R
$-Prism

$-St. Anthony
    Messenger
$-Vibrant Life—R
$-War Cry—R

PASTORS/LEADERS
$-Ministry Today

TEEN/YOUNG ADULT
Genuine Motivation—R
Single!—R
$-TC Magazine
$Young Salvationist—R

WOMEN
Virtuous Woman—R

WRITERS
Writer's Chronicle

CHRISTIAN BUSINESS
ADULT/GENERAL
American Chr. Voice—R
$-Angels on Earth
Believers Bay—R
$-Brink Magazine—R
$-CBA Retailers
CBN.com—R
$-Christian Courier—R
Christian Journal—R
Christian News NW—R
Christian Online
Christian Ranchman
$-Christian Retailing
$ChristianWeek
$-City Light News
$-Faith Today
$-Gem, The—R
Genuine Motivation—R
$-Guideposts—R
$-Home Times—R
$-In Touch
Joyful Living—R
$-Lookout
Our Sunday Visitor
$-Power for Living—R
$-Prism
$-Purpose—R
$-St. Anthony
    Messenger

PASTORS/LEADERS
$-InSite—R

TEEN/YOUNG ADULT
Genuine Motivation—R

WOMEN
Dabbling Mum
Halo Magazine—R
Virtuous Woman

CHRISTIAN EDUCATION
ADULT/GENERAL
$-America
$-Arlington Catholic
Believers Bay—R
$-Celebrate Life
$-Christian Courier—R
$-Christian Examiner
$-Christian Home &
　School
Christian Journal—R
$-Christianity Today—R
Christian Online
Christian Ranchman
$-Christian Retailing
$-Christian
　Standard—R
$-ChristianWeek
$-City Light News
$-Columbia
$-Cresset, The
Eternal Ink—R
$-Faith Today
$-Gem, The—R
Genuine Motivation—R
$-Good News, Etc.—R
$-Homeschooling
　Today—R
$-Home Times—R
Joyful Living—R
$-Lookout
$-Lutheran Witness
Movieguide
Our Sunday Visitor
$-ParentLife
Penned from the
　Heart—R
Perspectives

$-Presbyterians Today
$-Prism
$-Purpose—R
$-St. Anthony
　Messenger
$-Seek—R
$-Testimony—R

CHILDREN
$-Guide—R
$-Juniorway

CHRISTIAN EDUCATION/LIBRARY
$-Catechist
$-Journal/Adventist
　Ed.—R
$-Today's Catholic
　Teacher

PASTORS/LEADERS
$-Christian Century—R
$-Enrichment—R
$-L Magazine—R
$-Ministry Today
$-SmallGroups.com—R
$-YouthWorker

TEEN/YOUNG ADULT
Genuine Motivation—R
$-Insight
$Young Salvationist—R

WOMEN
Right to the Heart—R
Share

CHRISTIAN LIVING
ADULT/GENERAL
$-Alive Now
$-America
American Chr. Voice—R
$-Angels on Earth
$-Arlington Catholic
Believers Bay—R
$-Bible Advocate—R
$-Brink Magazine—R
Canada Lutheran
$-Catholic Digest
$-Catholic New York
CBN.com—R

$-Celebrate Life
$-CGA World
$-Charisma
$-Chicken Soup Bks—R
$-Christian Courier—R
$-Christian Examiner
$-Christian Home &
　School
$-Christianity Today—R
Christian Journal—R
Christian Online
Christian Ranchman
$-Christian Research
$-Christian
　Standard—R
$-ChristianWeek
Church Herald &
　Holiness
$-City Light News
$-Columbia
$-Covenant
　Companion—R
$-Dreamseeker—R
Eternal Ink—R
$-Evangel—R
$-Faith & Friends—R
$-Faith Today
Fit Christian—R
$-Gem, The—R
$-Gems of Truth
Genuine Motivation—R
$-Good News, The –R
$-Good News, Etc.—R
$-Guideposts—R
Highway News—R
$-Holiness Today
$-Homeschooling
　Today—R
$-Home Times—R
$-Indian Life—R
$-In Touch
Joyful Living—R
Keys to Living—R
Leaves—R
$-Light & Life
$-Liguorian
$-Live—R
$-Lookout
$-Lutheran Digest—R
$-Lutheran Journal—R

$-Lutheran Witness
$-Mature Living
Mature Years
Men of the Cross
New Heart—R
Our Sunday Visitor
$-ParentLife
Penned from the
    Heart—R
Pentecostal Evangel
Perspectives
$-Point—R
$-Power for Living—R
$-Presbyterians Today
$-Psychology for
    Living—R
$-Purpose—R
$-St. Anthony
    Messenger
$-Seek—R
$-Testimony—R
$-United Church
    Observer
$-U.S. Catholic
$-Vibrant Life—R
$-Vision—R
$-War Cry—R
$-Wesleyan Life

CHILDREN
$-Cadet Quest—R
$-Focus/Clubhouse Jr.
$-Guide—R
$-Juniorway
$-Pockets—R

DAILY DEVOTIONALS
$-Brink Magazine—R
Penned from the
    Heart—R

PASTORS/LEADERS
$-Christian Century—R
$-Net Results

TEEN/YOUNG ADULT
$-Boundless.org—R
$-Cadet Quest—R
$-Devo'zine
$-Direction

Genuine Motivation—R
$-Insight—R
Single!—R
$-TC Magazine

WOMEN
Halo Magazine—R
$-Hello, Darling—R
$-Mother's Heart
Right to the Heart—R
Share
Virtuous Woman
Women of the Cross

CHURCH GROWTH
ADULT/GENERAL
$-America
American Chr. Voice—R
Believers Bay—R
$-Christian Examiner
Christian Journal—R
Christian Online
$-Christian
    Standard—R
$-ChristianWeek
$-Columbia
$-EFCA Today
$-Evangel—R
$-Faith Today
$-Gem, The—R
Genuine Motivation—R
$-Good News, Etc.—R
$-Holiness Today
$-In Touch
$-Liguorian
$-Lookout
$-Mature Living
Our Sunday Visitor
Penned from the
    Heart—R
$-Presbyterians Today
$-Purpose—R
$-St. Anthony
    Messenger
$-Seek—R
$-Testimony—R
$-Wesleyan Life

MISSIONS
$-Operation
    Reveille—R

PASTORS/LEADERS
$-Christian Century—R
$-Enrichment—R
$-Growth Points—R
$-Leadership—R
$-Ministry Today
$-Net Results
$-Outreach—R

TEEN/YOUNG ADULT
$-Direction
Genuine Motivation—R

WOMEN
Share

CHURCH HISTORY
ADULT/GENERAL
$-America
American Chr. Voice—R
Believers Bay—R
$-Catholic Digest
$-Catholic Sentinel
CBN.com—R
$Christian History
Christian Online
$-Christian
    Standard—R
$-City Light News
$-Columbia
$-Cresset, The
$-Faith Today
Genuine Motivation—R
$-Holiness Today
$-Homeschooling
    Today—R
$-In Touch
Leaves—R
$-Leben—R
$-Liguorian
$-Lookout
$-Lutheran Journal—R
$-Lutheran Witness
Movieguide
Our Sunday Visitor
$-Prairie Messenger—R

$-Presbyterians Today
Priscilla Papers
$-Purpose—R
$-St. Anthony
  Messenger
$-U.S. Catholic
$-Wesleyan Life

CHRISTIAN EDUCA-
TION/LIBRARY
$-Catechist

DAILY DEVOTIONALS
Penned from the
  Heart—R

MISSIONS
$-Operation
  Reveille—R

PASTORS/LEADERS
$-Christian Century—R
$-Enrichment—R
$-Leadership—R
$-Parish Liturgy

TEEN/YOUNG ADULT
Genuine Motivation—R

WOMEN
Halo Magazine—R
Share

CHURCH LIFE
ADULT/GENERAL
$-America
Believers Bay—R
$-Bible Advocate—R
Canada Lutheran
$-Catholic Digest
$-Catholic Sentinel
CBN.com—R
$-Christian Home &
  School
$-Christianity Today—R
Christian Journal—R
Christian Online
$-Christian
  Standard—R
$-ChristianWeek
$-Columbia

Christian News NW—R
$-Covenant
  Companion—R
$-Dreamseeker—R
$-EFCA Today
Encompass
Eternal Ink—R
$-Evangel—R
$-Faith Today
$-Gem, The—R
$-Good News, The –R
$-Good News, Etc.—R
$-Holiness Today
$-Home Times—R
$-In Touch
Leaves—R
$-Light & Life
$-Liguorian
$-Lookout
$-Lutheran Journal—R
$-Lutheran Witness
Our Sunday Visitor
Penned from the
  Heart—R
Pentecostal Evangel
$-Presbyterians Today
Priscilla Papers
$-Purpose—R
$-St. Anthony
  Messenger
$-Seek—R
$-Testimony—R
$-U.S. Catholic
$-Wesleyan Life

DAILY DEVOTIONALS
Penned from the
  Heart—R

PASTORS/LEADERS
$-Christian Century—R
$-Enrichment—R
$-Leadership—R
$-Ministry Today
$-Net Results
$-Parish Liturgy
$-Priest
$-YouthWorker

TEEN/YOUNG ADULT
$-Direction
Single!—R

WOMEN
Share

CHURCH
MANAGEMENT
ADULT/GENERAL
$-America
Believers Bay—R
Canada Lutheran
Christian Journal—R
Christian News NW—R
Christian Online
$-Christian
  Standard—R
$-ChristianWeek
$-Covenant
  Companion—R
$-EFCA Today
$-Faith Today
$-Gem, The—R
$-Lookout
Our Sunday Visitor
Priscilla Papers
$-Purpose—R
$-St. Anthony
  Messenger

DAILY DEVOTIONALS
Penned from the
  Heart—R

PASTORS/LEADERS
$-Enrichment—R
$-Growth Points—R
$-Leadership—R
$-Ministry Today
$-Net Results
$-Outreach—R
Sharing the Practice—R

WOMEN
Share

CHURCH
OUTREACH
ADULT/GENERAL
$-America

Believers Bay—R
$-Bible Advocate—R
Canada Lutheran
$-Catholic Sentinel
CBN.com—R
$-Christian Home &
    School
Christian Journal—R
Christian Online
$-Christian Research
$-Christian
    Standard—R
$-ChristianWeek
$-City Light News
$-Columbia
$-Covenant
    Companion—R
$-EFCA Today
Eternal Ink—R
$-Evangel—R
$-Faith & Friends—R
$-Faith Today
$-Gem, The—R
$-Good News, The –R
$-Good News, Etc.—R
$-Holiness Today
$-Home Times—R
$-In Touch
$-Light & Life
$-Lookout
$-Lutheran Witness
Our Sunday Visitor
$-Point—R
$-Presbyterians Today
Priscilla Papers
$-Prism
$-Purpose—R
$-St. Anthony
    Messenger
$-Seek—R
$-Testimony—R
$-Wesleyan Life

CHRISTIAN EDUCA-
TION/LIBRARY
$-Group Magazine
$-Journal/Adventist
    Ed.—R

PASTORS/LEADERS
$-Christian Century—R
$-Enrichment—R
$-Growth Points—R
$-Leadership—R
$-Ministry Today
$-Net Results
$-Outreach—R
$-Small Groups.
    com—R
$-YouthWorker

TEEN/YOUNG ADULT
$-Direction
$-Insight—R

WOMEN
Share

CHURCH TRADITIONS
ADULT/GENERAL
$-America
American Chr. Voice—R
Believers Bay—R
$-Brink Magazine—R
Canada Lutheran
$-Catholic Digest
CBN.com—R
$-Celebrate Life
$-CGA World
$-Christian Examiner
$Christian History
Christian Online
$-Christian Research
$-Christian
    Standard—R
$-Columbia
$-Cresset, The
Encompass
$-Faith Today
$-Gem, The—R
$-Holiness Today
$-Homeschooling
    Today—R
Leaves—R
$-Light & Life
$-Liguorian
$-Lutheran Journal—R
$-Lutheran Witness

Our Sunday Visitor
Perspectives
$-Presbyterians Today
Priscilla Papers
$-Purpose—R
$-St. Anthony
    Messenger
$-Testimony—R
$-U.S. Catholic

CHILDREN
$-Cadet Quest—R
$-Focus/Clubhouse Jr.
$-Guide—R
$-Juniorway
$-Pockets—R

DAILY DEVOTIONALS
$-Brink Magazine—R
Penned from the
    Heart—R

PASTORS/LEADERS
$-Christian Century—R
$-Net Results

TEEN/YOUNG ADULT
$-Boundless.org—R
$-Cadet Quest—R
$-Devo'zine
$-Direction
Genuine Motivation—R
$-Insight—R
Single!—R
$-TC Magazine

WOMEN
Halo Magazine—R
$-Hello, Darling—R
$-Mother's Heart
Right to the Heart—R
Share
Virtuous Woman
Women of the Cross

CONTROVERSIAL ISSUES
ADULT/GENERAL
American Chr. Voice—R
Believers Bay—R
$-Bible Advocate—R

$-Brink Magazine—R
Canada Lutheran
CBN.com—R
$-Celebrate Life
$-Christian Courier—R
$-Christian Examiner
$-Christian Home &
   School
$-Christianity Today—R
Christian Online
$-Christian
   Standard—R
$-ChristianWeek
$-City Light
   News
$-Columbia
$-Creative Nonfiction
$-Dreamseeker—R
$-EFCA Today
Encompass
$-Eureka Street
$-Faith Today
Genuine Motivation—R
$-Good News, The –R
$-Good News, Etc.—R
$-Homeschooling
   Today—R
$-Home Times—R
$-Indian Life—R
$-In Touch
$-Light & Life
$-Lookout
Movieguide
$-Now What?—R
Our Sunday Visitor
Perspectives
$-Prairie Messenger—R
Priscilla Papers
$-Prism
$-Psychology for
   Living—R
$-Purpose—R
$-St. Anthony
   Messenger
$-U.S. Catholic
$-War Cry—R
$-World & I

CHILDREN
$-Animal Trails—R

Skipping Stones—R

*CHRISTIAN EDUCA-
TION/LIBRARY*
$-YouthWalk

MISSIONS
$-Operation
   Reveille—R

PASTORS/LEADERS
$-Christian Century—R
$-Enrichment—R
$-InSite—R
$-L Magazine—R
$-Ministry Today
$-Outreach—R
Sharing the Practice—R

TEEN/YOUNG ADULT
$-Animal Trails—R
$-Boundless.org—R
Genuine Motivation—R
Single!—R
$-TC Magazine
$Young Salvationist—R

CRAFTS
ADULT/GENERAL
Believers Bay—R
$-CGA World
Christian Online
$-Indian Life—R
$-ParentLife
$-World & I

CHILDREN
$-Cadet Quest—R
Focus/Clubhouse
$-Focus/Clubhouse Jr.
$-Guide—R
$-Juniorway
$-Pockets—R
$-SHINE brightly—R
$-Sparkle—R
*CHRISTIAN EDUCA-
TION/LIBRARY*
$-Catechist

TEEN/YOUNG ADULT
$-Cadet Quest—R

WOMEN
$-Hello, Darling—R
$-Mother's Heart
Virtuous Woman

CREATION SCIENCE
ADULT/GENERAL
American Chr. Voice—R
Answers Magazine
Believers Bay—R
$-Bible Advocate—R
CBN.com—R
$-Christian Courier—R
$-Christian Examiner
Christian Journal—R
$-Christian Research
Creation Illust.
$-Good News, The –R
$-Homeschooling
   Today—R
$-Home Times—R
$-Light & Life
$-Lookout
$-St. Anthony
   Messenger

CHILDREN
$-Animal Trails—R
$-Guide—R
$-Nature Friend—R

*CHRISTIAN EDUCA-
TION/LIBRARY*
$-Journal/Adventist
   Ed.—R

TEEN/YOUNG ADULT
$-Animal Trails—R

WOMEN
$-Mother's Heart

CULTS/OCCULT
ADULT/GENERAL
American Chr. Voice—R
Believers Bay—R
CBN.com—R
$-Christian Examiner
$-Christian Research
$-Creative Nonfiction
$-Indian Life—R

$-In Touch
$-Light & Life
$-Lookout
New Heart—R

CHILDREN
$-Guide—R

PASTORS/LEADERS
$-Ministry Today

TEEN/YOUNG ADULT
$-TC Magazine

CURRENT/SOCIAL ISSUES
ADULT/GENERAL
American Chr. Voice—R
$-Arlington Catholic
Believers Bay—R
$-Bible Advocate—R
$-Brink Magazine—R
Canada Lutheran
$-Catholic New York
CBN.com—R
$-Christian Courier—R
$-Christian Examiner
$-Christian Home &
   School
$-Christianity Today—R
Christian News NW—R
Christian Online
Christian Ranchman
$-Christian Research
$-Christian
   Standard—R
$-ChristianWeek
$-City Light News
$-Columbia
$-Covenant
   Companion—R
$-Creative Nonfiction
$-Cresset, The
$-Disaster News
$-Dreamseeker—R
Encompass
$-Eureka Street
$-Faith Today
$-Gem, The—R
Genuine Motivation—R

$-Good News, The –R
$-Good News, Etc.—R
$-Homeschooling
   Today—R
$-Home Times—R
$-Indian Life—R
$-In Touch
$-Light & Life
$-Liguorian
$-Lookout
$-Lutheran Witness
Movieguide
New Heart—R
$-Now What?—R
Our Sunday Visitor
$-ParentLife
Perspectives
$-Point—R
Priscilla Papers
$-Prism
$-Psychology for
   Living—R
$-St. Anthony
   Messenger
$-Seek—R
$-U.S. Catholic
$-War Cry—R
$-World & I

CHILDREN
$-Guide—R
$-Juniorway
$-SHINE brightly—R
Skipping Stones—R
$-Sparkle—R

**CHRISTIAN EDUCA-
TION/LIBRARY**
$-Brink Magazine—R
$-Group Magazine
Penned from the Heart
MISSIONS
$-Operation
   Reveille—R

PASTORS/LEADERS
$-Christian Century—R
$-Enrichment—R
$-InSite—R
$-Leadership—R
$-Ministry Today

$-Outreach—R

TEEN/YOUNG ADULT
$-Devo'zine
$-Direction
Genuine Motivation—R
$-Insight—R
$-TC Magazine
$Young Salvationist—R

WOMEN
$-FullFill
$-Mother's Heart
Virtuous Woman

DEATH/DYING
ADULT/GENERAL
$-America
American Chr. Voice—R
$-Arlington Catholic
Believers Bay—R
$-Bible Advocate—R
$-Brink Magazine—R
CBN.com—R
$-Celebrate Life
$-Chicken Soup Bks—R
$-Christianity Today—R
Christian Journal—R
Christian Online
Christian Ranchman
$-ChristianWeek
$-Columbia
$-Creative Nonfiction
$-Faith Today
$-Gem, The—R
Genuine Motivation—R
$-Good News, Etc.—R
$-Guideposts—R
$-Indian Life—R
$-In Touch
Joyful Living—R
$-Light & Life
$-Liguorian
$-Lookout
$-Mature Living
New Heart—R
$-Now What?—R
Our Sunday Visitor
$-ParentLife
$-Point—R

$-Prairie Messenger—R
$-Presbyterians Today
$-Psychology for
   Living—R
$-St. Anthony
   Messenger
$-Seek—R
$-Testimony—R
$-U.S. Catholic

CHILDREN
$-Guide—R
Skipping Stones—R

DAILY DEVOTIONALS
Penned from the Heart

PASTORS/LEADERS
$-Christian Century—R
$-Enrichment—R
$-InSite—R
$-Leadership—R
$-L Magazine—R
Sharing the Practice—R

TEEN/YOUNG ADULT
Genuine Motivation—R

WOMEN
Virtuous Woman

DEPRESSION
ADULT/GENERAL
American Chr. Voice—R
Believers Bay—R
$-Bible Advocate—R
Christian Journal—R
$-Faith Today
Genuine Motivation—R
$-Indian Life—R
Joyful Living—R
$-Mature Living
$-Now What?—R
$-U.S. Catholic
$-War Cry—R

TEEN/YOUNG ADULT
Single!—R

WOMEN
$-Brink Magazine—R

$-Mother's Heart
Virtuous Woman

DEVOTIONALS/ MEDITATIONS
ADULT/GENERAL
$-Adoptee Search—R
$-Alive Now
$-America
American Chr. Voice—R
$-Arlington Catholic
Believers Bay—R
CBN.com—R
$-Chicken Soup Bks—R
$-Christian Home &
   School
Christian Journal—R
Christian Online
Christian Ranchman
$-Columbia
$-Covenant
   Companion—R
Eternal Ink—R
$-Evangel—R
$-Faith & Friends—R
$-Forward Day By Day
$-Gem, The—R
Genuine Motivation—R
$-God's Word for Today
Highway News—R
$-In Touch
Keys to Living—R
Leaves—R
$-Liguorian
$-Lutheran Digest—R
$-Mature Living
New Heart—R
$-ParentLife
Penned from the
   Heart—R
Pentecostal Evangel
Perspectives
$-Quiet Hour
$-Rejoice!
$-St. Anthony
   Messenger
$-Sports Spectrum
$-These Days
$-Upper Room
$-Vision—R

$-Weavings
$-Wesleyan Life
WorshipMinistry
   Devotions.com

CHILDREN
$-Animal Trails—R
Keys for Kids
$-Pockets—R

CHRISTIAN EDUCA- TION/LIBRARY
$-Group Magazine

DAILY DEVOTIONALS
$-Brink Magazine—R
Christian Devotions
Daily Dev. for Deaf
$-Everyday with the
   Word
Light from the Word
Mustard Seed
Penned from the Heart
$-Quiet Hour
$-Rejoice!
Secret Place
$-Upper Room
Word in Season

PASTORS/LEADERS
$-Ministry Today

TEEN/YOUNG ADULT
$-Animal Trails—R
$-Devo'zine
Single!—R
$-Take Five Plus—R

WOMEN
Dabbling Mum
Halo Magazine—R
$-Mother's Heart
Virtuous Woman

WRITERS
$-Fellowscript—R
$-Shades of Romance

DISCIPLESHIP
ADULT/GENERAL
$-Alive Now

American Chr. Voice—R
$-Arlington Catholic
Believers Bay—R
$-Bible Advocate—R
Canada Lutheran
CBN.com—R
Christian Journal—R
Christian Online
Christian Ranchman
$-Christian Research
$-Christian
   Standard—R
$-ChristianWeek
$-Columbia
$-Covenant
   Companion—R
$-Decision
$-EFCA Today
Eternal Ink—R
$-Evangel—R
$-Faith & Friends—R
$-Faith Today
$-Gem, The—R
Genuine Motivation—R
Highway News—R
$-Homeschooling
   Today—R
$-In Touch
$-Light & Life
$-Liguorian
$-Lookout
$-Mature Living
Men of the Cross
Movieguide
Penned from the Heart
Perspectives
$-St. Anthony
   Messenger
$-Seek—R
$-War Cry—R
$-Wesleyan Life

CHILDREN
   $-Guide—R

CHRISTIAN EDUCA-
TION/LIBRARY
   $-Group Magazine

DAILY DEVOTIONALS
   $-Brink Magazine—R
   Penned from the
     Heart—R

PASTORS/LEADERS
   $-Christian Century—R
   $-Enrichment—R
   $-Growth Points—R
   $-InSite—R
   $-Leadership—R
   $-Net Results
   $-SmallGroups.com—R

TEEN/YOUNG ADULT
   $-Boundless.org—R
   $-Devo'zine
   $-Direction
   $-Insight
   Single!—R
   $-TC Magazine
   $Young Salvationist—R

WOMEN
   $-Mother's Heart
   Virtuous Woman
   Women of the Cross

DIVORCE
ADULT/GENERAL
   American Chr. Voice—R
   $-Angels on Earth
   $-Arlington Catholic
   Believers Bay—R
   $-Bible Advocate—R
   $-Catholic Digest
   CBN.com—R
   $-Christian Examiner
   Christian Online
   Christian Ranchman
   $-ChristianWeek
   $-Columbia
   $-Faith Today
   $-Family Smart—R
   $-Gem, The—R
   $-Good News, Etc.—R
   $-Guideposts—R
   $-Home Times—R
   $-Indian Life—R
   $-In Touch

$-Light & Life
$-Lookout
$-Mature Living
New Heart—R
$-Now What?—R
Our Sunday Visitor
$-ParentLife
Perspectives
Priscilla Papers
$-Psychology for
   Living—R
$-St. Anthony
   Messenger
$-Seek—R
Storyteller—R
$-U.S. Catholic
$-World & I
CHILDREN
   $-Guide—R

PASTORS/LEADERS
   $-Christian Century—R

TEEN/YOUNG ADULT
   $-Boundless.org—R
   $-Direction

WOMEN
   Virtuous Woman

DOCTRINAL
ADULT/GENERAL
   American Chr. Voice—R
   Believers Bay—R
   $-Bible Advocate—R
   CBN.com—R
   Christian Online
   $-Christian Research
   $-Christian
     Standard—R
   Eternal Ink—R
   $-In Touch
   Leaves—R
   $-Mature Living
   Movieguide
   Our Sunday Visitor
   Perspectives
   $-Prairie Messenger—R
   Priscilla Papers
   $-St. Anthony
     Messenger

$-U.S. Catholic
$-Wesleyan Life

CHILDREN
$-Guide—R

PASTORS/LEADERS
L Magazine

TEEN/YOUNG ADULT
$-Direction
$Young Salvationist—R

DVD REVIEWS
ADULT/GENERAL
Believers Bay—R
Genuine Motivation—R
$-Homeschooling
    Today—R

TEEN/YOUNG ADULT
Single!—R

WOMEN
$-Brink Magazine—R
$-Mother's Heart
Virtuous Woman

ECONOMICS
ADULT/GENERAL
$-America
American Chr. Voice—R
Believers Bay—R
$-CBA Retailers
CBN.com—R
Christian Online
Christian Ranchman
$-Christian Retailing
$-ChristianWeek
$-City Light News
$-Creative Nonfiction
$-Faith Today
Genuine Motivation—R
$-Homeschooling
    Today—R
$-Home Times—R
$-In Touch
$-Light & Life
Movieguide
Our Sunday Visitor

Perspectives
$-St. Anthony
    Messenger
$-World & I

ENCOURAGMENT
ADULT/GENERAL
$-Adoptee Search—R
American Chr. Voice—R
Believers Bay—R
$-Brink Magazine—R
$-Catholic Digest
CBN.com—R
$-Christian Home &
    School
Christian Journal—R
Christian Online
Christian Ranchman
$-Christian
    Standard—R
$-City Light News
Eternal Ink—R
$-Evangel—R
$-Faith & Friends—R
Gems of Truth
Genuine Motivation—R
Highway News—R
$-Homeschooling
    Today—R
$-Home Times—R
$-In Touch
Joyful Living—R
Keys to Living—R
$-Light & Life
$-Liguorian
$-Lookout
$-Lutheran Digest—R
Men of the Cross
New Heart—R
$-ParentLife
Penned from the Heart
$-Point—R
$-Seek—R
Storyteller—R
$-Vision—R
$-Wesleyan Life

CHILDREN
$-SHINE brightly—R
Skipping Stones—R

DAILY DEVOTIONALS
$-Brink Magazine—R
Penned from the
    Heart—R

TEEN/YOUNG ADULT
$-Boundless.org—R
$-Direction
Genuine Motivation—R
$-Insight
Single!—R

WOMEN
Halo Magazine—R
$-Mother's Heart
Virtuous Woman
Women of the Cross

WRITERS
$-Fellowscript—R

ENVIRONMENTAL
ISSUES
ADULT/GENERAL
$-America
American Chr. Voice—R
Believers Bay—R
$-Bible Advocate—R
$-Brink Magazine—R
$-Christian Courier—R
Christian Online
$-ChristianWeek
$-Common Ground—R
$-Covenant
    Companion—R
Creation Illust.
$-Creative Nonfiction
$-Disaster News
$-Faith Today
Genuine Motivation—R
$-Indian Life—R
$-In Touch
$-Light & Life
$-Liguorian
$-Lookout
Our Sunday Visitor
$-ParentLife
Perspectives
$-Prism
$-Ruminate

$-St. Anthony
   Messenger
$-Seek—R
$-U.S. Catholic
$-World & I

CHILDREN
$-Animal Trails—R
$-Guide—R
$-Pockets—R
Skipping Stones—R

PASTORS/LEADERS
$-Christian Century—R
$-InSite—R

TEEN/YOUNG ADULT
$-Animal Trails—R
$-Devo'zine

WOMEN
Share

ESSAYS
ADULT/GENERAL
$-America
American Chr. Voice—R
$-Arlington Catholic
Believers Bay—R
$-Catholic Digest
$-Chicken Soup Bks—R
$-Christian Courier—R
$-Christianity Today—R
Christian Online
$-Columbia
$-Covenant
   Companion—R
$-Creative Nonfiction
Eternal Ink—R
$-Faith Today
$-Gem, The—R
Genuine Motivation—R
$-Indian Life—R
$-In Touch
$-Liguorian
$-Lutheran Digest—R
Our Sunday Visitor
Penwood Review
$-Prism
$-Ruminate

$-St. Anthony
   Messenger
$-Seek—R
Storyteller—R
Studio—R
$-U.S. Catholic
$-World & I

CHILDREN
$-Nature Friend—R
Skipping Stones—R

**CHRISTIAN EDUCA-
TION/LIBRARY**
$-Journal/Adventist
   Ed.—R

PASTORS/LEADERS
$-Christian Century—R
$-Priest
$-YouthWorker

TEEN/YOUNG ADULT
Genuine Motivation—R
Single!—R
$-TC Magazine

WOMEN
Dabbling Mum

WRITERS
$-Christian
   Communicator—R
$-Writer
Writer's Chronicle
Writer's Digest

ETHICS
ADULT/GENERAL
$-America
American Chr. Voice—R
$-Angels on Earth
Believers Bay—R
$-Brink Magazine—R
$-Catholic Digest
CBN.com—R
$-Celebrate Life
$-Christian Courier—R
$-Christian Examiner
Christian Online
Christian Ranchman

$-Christian Research
$-Christian
   Standard—R
$-ChristianWeek
$-Columbia
$-Creative Nonfiction
$-Cresset, The
$-Eureka Street
$-Good News, Etc.—R
$-Faith Today
Genuine Motivation—R
$-In Touch
$-Light & Life
$-Liguorian
$-Lookout
Movieguide
New Heart—R
Our Sunday Visitor
Perspectives
$-Prairie Messenger—R
Priscilla Papers
$-Prism
$-St. Anthony
   Messenger
$-Seek—R
$-World & I

CHILDREN
Skipping Stones—R

DAILY DEVOTIONALS
$-Brink Magazine—R
Penned from the
   Heart—R

PASTORS/LEADERS
$-Christian Century—R
$-Enrichment—R
L Magazine
$-Ministry Today
Sharing the Practice—R

TEEN/YOUNG ADULT
$-Devo'zine
$-Direction
Genuine Motivation—R
Single!—R

WOMEN
Halo Magazine—R

ETHNIC/CULTURAL ISSUES
ADULT/GENERAL
$-Adoptee Search—R
$-America
American Chr. Voice—R
$-Arlington Catholic
   Believers Bay—R
$-Brink Magazine—R
Canada Lutheran
$-Catholic Digest
$-CBA Retailers
CBN.com—R
$-Celebrate Life
$-Christian Courier—R
$-Christian Home &
   School
Christian News NW—R
Christian Online
$-ChristianWeek
$-Columbia
$-Commonweal
$-Creative Nonfiction
$-EFCA Today
Encompass
$-Eureka Street
$-Faith Today
$-Gem, The—R
Genuine Motivation—R
$-Good News, The –R
$-Good News, Etc.—R
$-Indian Life—R
$-In Touch
$-Light & Life
$-Lookout
Movieguide
Our Sunday Visitor
$-ParentLife
Penned from the
   Heart—R
$-Prairie Messenger—R
Priscilla Papers
$-Prism
$-St. Anthony
   Messenger
$-Seek—R
$-Wesleyan Life
$-World & I

CHILDREN
$-Guide—R
Skipping Stones—R

DAILY DEVOTIONALS
$-Brink Magazine—R
Penned from the Heart

MISSIONS
$-Operation
   Reveille—R

PASTORS/LEADERS
$-Christian Century—R
$-Enrichment—R
$-Ministry Today
$-Net Results
Sharing the Practice—R

TEEN/YOUNG ADULT
$-Devo'zine
Genuine Motivation—R
Single!—R
$Young Salvationist—R

EVANGELISM/ WITNESSING
ADULT/GENERAL
$-Adoptee Search—R
$-America
American Chr. Voice—R
Believers Bay—R
$-Bible Advocate—R
$-Brink Magazine—R
CBN.com—R
$-Christian Home &
   School
$-Christianity Today—R
Christian Journal—R
Christian Online
Christian Ranchman
$-Christian Research
$-Christian
   Standard—R
$-Columbia
$-Decision
Eternal Ink—R
$-Evangel—R
$-Faith Today
$-Gem, The—R
Genuine Motivation—R

$-Good News, Etc.—R
Highway News—R
$-In Touch
Leaves—R
$-Light & Life
$-Lookout
$-Lutheran Journal—R
$-Mature Living
New Heart—R
Our Sunday Visitor
$-ParentLife
Penned from the
   Heart—R
$-Point—R
$-Power for Living—R
$-St. Anthony
   Messenger
$-Seek—R
$-Testimony—R
$-War Cry—R
$-Wesleyan Life

CHILDREN
$-Focus/Clubhouse Jr.
$-Guide—R
$-Juniorway

CHRISTIAN EDUCATION/LIBRARY
$-Group Magazine

DAILY DEVOTIONALS
$-Brink Magazine—R
Penned from the
   Heart—R

MISSIONS
$-Operation
   Reveille—R

PASTORS/LEADERS
$-Cook Partners
$-Enrichment—R
$-Growth Points—R
$-Leadership—R
$-Ministry Today
$-Outreach—R
Sharing the Practice—R
$-SmallGroups.com—R

TEEN/YOUNG ADULT
$-Devo'zine
Genuine Motivation—R
$-Insight
Single!—R
$-TC Magazine
$Young Salvationist—R

WOMEN
Share

EXEGESIS
ADULT/GENERAL
$-Alive Now
Believers Bay—R
$-Bible Advocate—R
CBN.com—R
Christian Ranchman
$-Christian
    Standard—R
$-In Touch
Our Sunday Visitor
Perspectives
Priscilla Papers
$-St. Anthony
    Messenger
$-U.S. Catholic
$-Wesleyan Life

PASTORS/LEADERS
$-Enrichment—R

FAITH
ADULT/GENERAL
$-Adoptee Search—R
$-America
American Chr. Voice—R
Believers Bay—R
$-Bible Advocate—R
$-Brink Magazine—R
byFaith
Canada Lutheran
$-Catholic Digest
CBN.com—R
$-Christian Courier—R
$-Christian Home &
    School
$-Christianity Today—R
Christian Journal—R
Christian Online

$-Christian Research
$-Christian Retailing
$-Christian
    Standard—R
$-ChristianWeek
$-City Light News
Church Herald &
    Holiness
$-Columbia
$-Covenant
    Companion—R
Eternal Ink—R
$-Faith & Friends—R
$-Faith Today
$-Gem, The—R
Genuine Motivation—R
$-Good News, The –R
Highway News—R
$-Home Times—R
$-In Touch
Leaves—R
$-Light & Life
$-Liguorian
$-Live—R
$-Lookout
$-Lutheran Digest—R
$-Lutheran Journal—R
$-Mature Living
New Heart—R
Our Sunday Visitor
$-ParentLife
Penned from the
    Heart—R
$-Point—R
$-Prairie Messenger—R
Priscilla Papers
$-Psychology for
    Living—R
$-Purpose—R
$-St. Anthony
    Messenger
$-Seek—R
SW Kansas Faith
$-Testimony—R
$-United Church
    Observer
$-War Cry—R
$-Weavings
$-Wesleyan Life
$-World & I

CHILDREN
$-Animal Trails—R
$-Focus/Clubhouse Jr.
$-Guide—R
$-Juniorway
$-Our Little Friend
$-Primary Treasure
$-SHINE brightly—R

DAILY DEVOTIONALS
$-Brink Magazine—R
Penned from the
    Heart—R

PASTORS/LEADERS
$-Ministry Today
$-SmallGroups.com—R

TEEN/YOUNG ADULT
$-Animal Trails—R
$-Boundless.org—R
$-Devo'zine
$-Direction
Genuine Motivation—R
$-Insight
Single!—R
$-TC Magazine

WOMEN
Halo Magazine—R
$-Mother's Heart
Virtuous Woman
Women of the Cross

FAMILY LIFE
ADULT/GENERAL
$-Abilities
$-Adoptee Search—R
$-America
American Chr. Voice—R
$-Angels on Earth
$-Arlington Catholic
Believers Bay—R
$-Bible Advocate—R
$-Brink Magazine—R
byFaith
Canada Lutheran
$-Catholic Digest
CBN.com—R
$-Chicken Soup Bks—R
$-Christian Courier—R

$-Christian Home &
    School
Christian Journal—R
Christian Online
Christian Ranchman
$-ChristianWeek
Church Herald &
    Holiness
$-City Light News
$-Columbia
$-Covenant
    Companion—R
$-Creative Nonfiction
Eternal Ink—R
$-Faith & Friends—R
$-Family Smart—R
$-Gem, The—R
$-Good News, The –R
$-Good News, Etc.—R
$-Guideposts—R
Highway News—R
$-Homeschooling
    Today—R
$-Home Times—R
$-Indian Life—R
$-In Touch
Joyful Living—R
Keys to Living—R
$-Liguorian
$-Live—R
$-Living Light—R
$-Lookout
$-Lutheran Digest—R
$-Lutheran Witness
$-Mature Living
$-Mature Years—R
Men of the Cross
Our Sunday Visitor
$-ParentLife
Penned from the
    Heart—R
Pentecostal Evangel
$-Point—R
$-Power for Living—R
$-Prairie Messenger—R
Priscilla Papers
$-Psychology for
    Living—R
$-Purpose—R

$-St. Anthony
    Messenger
$-Seek—R
SW Kansas Faith
$-Testimony—R
$-Thriving Family
$-United Church
    Observer
$-Vibrant Life—R
$-Vision—R
$-Wesleyan Life
$-World & I

CHILDREN
Focus/Clubhouse
$-Focus/Clubhouse Jr.
$-Guide—R
$-Juniorway
$-Pockets—R
$-SHINE brightly—R

DAILY DEVOTIONALS
Penned from the
    Heart—R

PASTORS/LEADERS
$-Enrichment—R
$-InSite—R
$-Ministry Today

TEEN/YOUNG ADULT
$-Boundless.org—R
$-Direction
$-Insight
Single!—R
$-TC Magazine
$Young Salvationist—R

WOMEN
Dabbling Mum
$-Hello, Darling—R
$-Mother's Heart
Share
Virtuous Woman
Women of the Cross

FEATURE ARTICLES
ADULT/GENERAL
American Chr. Voice—R
Believers Bay—R
Canada Lutheran

Christian Journal—R
Christian News NW—R
$-Columbia
$-EFCA Today
Eternal Ink—R
$-Faith Today
$-Indian Life—R
$-Mature Living
Studio—R
$-War Cry—R

CHILDREN
$-Animal Trails—R
$-SHINE brightly—R
$-Sparkle—R

CHRISTIAN EDUCA-
TION/LIBRARY
$-Group Magazine
$-Seek—R

TEEN/YOUNG ADULT
$-Animal Trails—R
Single!—R
$Young Salvationist—R

WOMEN
$-Brink Magazine—R
Halo Magazine—R
$-Mother's Heart

FILLERS:
ANECDOTES
ADULT/GENERAL
$-Alive Now
American Chr. Voice—R
$-Angels on Earth
Believers Bay—R
$-Catholic Digest
Christian Journal—R
Christian Ranchman
Church Herald &
    Holiness
$-City Light News
$-Gem, The—R
$-Homeschooling
    Today—R
$-Home Times—R
$-Indian Life—R
$-Lutheran Digest—R
$-Mature Years—R

Movieguide
Pentecostal Evangel
$-Purpose—R
$-St. Anthony
   Messenger
$-War Cry—R

CHILDREN
Skipping Stones—R

PASTORS/LEADERS
$-Enrichment—R
$-Leadership—R

TEEN/YOUNG ADULT
Genuine Motivation—R

WOMEN
Halo Magazine—R
$-Mother's Heart
Right to the Heart—R
Virtuous Woman

WRITERS
$-Christian
   Communicator—R
$-Fellowscript—R
New Writer's Mag

FILLERS:
CARTOONS
ADULT/GENERAL
American Chr. Voice—R
$-Angels on Earth
Believers Bay—R
$-Catholic Digest
$-Christian Herald
Christian Journal—R
Christian Ranchman
$-Christian
   Standard—R
$-City Light News
$-Eureka Street
$-Evangel—R
$-Faith & Friends—R
$-Gem, The—R
$-Homeschooling
   Today—R
$-Home Times—R
$-Indian Life—R

Joyful Living—R
$-Lutheran Digest—R
$-Mature Years—R
Movieguide
New Heart—R
$-Power for Living—R
$-Presbyterians Today
$-St. Anthony
   Messenger
$-United Church
   Observer
$-War Cry—R

CHILDREN
$-Animal Trails—R
$-Guide—R
Skipping Stones—R

CHRISTIAN EDUCA-
TION/LIBRARY
$-Journal/Adventist
   Ed.—R
$-YouthWalk

PASTORS/LEADERS
$-Christian Century—R
$-Enrichment—R
$-Leadership—R
$-Priest
$-SmallGroups.com—R

TEEN/YOUNG ADULT
$-Animal Trails—R

WRITERS
New Writer's Mag.
$-Writer

FILLERS: FACTS
ADULT/GENERAL
American Chr. Voice—R
Believers Bay—R
$-Catholic Digest
$-Christian Herald
Christian Ranchman
$-City Light News
$-Gem, The—R
$-Homeschooling
   Today—R
$-Home Times—R
$-Indian Life—R

$-Lutheran Digest—R
$-Lutheran Journal—R
Movieguide
Pentecostal Evangel
$-St. Anthony
   Messenger
$-War Cry—R

CHILDREN
$-Animal Trails—R
$-Nature Friend—R
$-SHINE brightly—R

CHRISTIAN EDUCA-
TION/LIBRARY
$-YouthWalk

MISSIONS
$-Operation
   Reveille—R

PASTORS/LEADERS
$-Enrichment—R

TEEN/YOUNG ADULT
$-Animal Trails—R

WOMEN
Halo Magazine—R
$-Mother's Heart
Virtuous Woman

WRITERS
New Writer's Mag.

FILLERS: GAMES
ADULT/GENERAL
American Chr. Voice—R
Believers Bay—R
$-CGA World
$-Christian Herald
Christian Ranchman
$-Faith & Friends—R
$-Family Smart—R
$-Gem, The—R
Joyful Living—R
$-Lutheran Journal—R
Movieguide

CHILDREN
$-Cadet Quest—R

$-Guide—R
$-Pockets—R
$-SHINE brightly—R

TEEN/YOUNG ADULT
$-Cadet Quest—R

FILLERS: IDEAS
ADULT/GENERAL
American Chr. Voice—R
Believers Bay—R
$-Brink, The—R
$-CGA World
$-Christian Home &
    School
Christian Ranchman
$-Family Smart—R
$-Gem, The—R
$-Homeschooling
    Today—R
$-Home Times—R
Movieguide
$-Seek—R

CHILDREN
$-Animal Trails—R
$-SHINE brightly—R

PASTORS/LEADERS
$-Small Groups.
    com—R

TEEN/YOUNG ADULT
$-Animal Trails—R

WOMEN
$-Mother's Heart
Right to the Heart—R
Virtuous Woman

FILLERS: JOKES
ADULT/GENERAL
American Chr. Voice—R
Believers Bay—R
$-Catholic Digest
Christian Journal—R
Christian Ranchman
$-City Light News
$-Faith & Friends—R
$-Gem, The—R
$-Home Times—R

$-Indian Life—R
Joyful Living—R
$-Lutheran Digest—R
$-Mature Years—R
Movieguide
New Heart—R
$-St. Anthony
    Messenger

CHILDREN
$-SHINE brightly—R

WOMEN
Virtuous Woman

FILLERS: KID QUOTES
ADULT/GENERAL
American Chr. Voice—R
Believers Bay—R
Christian Journal—R
$-Family Smart—R
Halo Magazine—R
$-Home Times—R
$-Indian Life—R
$-Mother's Heart
Movieguide

FILLERS: NEWSBREAKS
ADULT/GENERAL
American Chr. Voice—R
Believers Bay—R
$-Brink, The—R
Christian Journal—R
Christian Ranchman
$-City Light News
$-Gem, The—R
$-Home Times—R
Movieguide
$-War Cry—R

CHILDREN
$-Animal Trails—R
TEEN/YOUNG ADULT
$-Animal Trails—R

MISSIONS
$-Operation
    Reveille—R

WRITERS
New Writer's Mag.

FILLERS: PARTY IDEAS
ADULT/GENERAL
American Chr. Voice—R
Believers Bay—R
Christian Ranchman
Movieguide

CHILDREN
$-SHINE brightly—R

WOMEN
Right to the Heart—R
Virtuous Woman

FILLERS: PRAYERS
ADULT/GENERAL
$-Alive Now
American Chr. Voice—R
$-Angels on Earth
Believers Bay—R
$-CGA World
$-Christian Herald
Christian Journal—R
Christian Online
Christian Ranchman
Eternal Ink—R
$-Gem, The—R
$-Homeschooling
    Today—R
$-Home Times—R
Movieguide
$-War Cry—R

CHILDREN
$-SHINE brightly—R

DAILY DEVOTIONALS
Word in Season

WOMEN
Halo Magazine—R
Right to the Heart—R
Virtuous Woman

FILLERS: PROSE
ADULT/GENERAL
American Chr. Voice—R

Believers Bay—R
Christian Online
Christian Ranchman
$-Decision
$-Gem, The—R
$-Homeschooling
   Today—R
$-Indian Life—R
Movieguide
Pentecostal Evangel
$-Purpose—R
$-War Cry—R

WRITERS
$-Freelance Writer's
   Report—R
$-Writer

FILLERS: QUIZZES
ADULT/GENERAL
American Chr. Voice—R
Believers Bay—R
$-Brink, The—R
Christian Online
Christian Ranchman
Church Herald &
   Holiness
$-Faith & Friends—R
$-Gem, The—R
$-Homeschooling
   Today—R
$-Lutheran Journal—R
Movieguide

CHILDREN
Focus/Clubhouse
$-Guide—R
$-Nature Friend—R
$-SHINE brightly—R
Skipping Stones—R

*CHRISTIAN EDUCA-
TION/LIBRARY*
$-Ministry Today

WOMEN
Virtuous Woman

FILLERS: QUOTES
ADULT/GENERAL
$-Alive Now

American Chr. Voice—R
Believers Bay—R
$-Catholic Digest
$-Christian Herald
Christian Journal—R
Christian Ranchman
$-Faith & Friends—R
$-Homeschooling
   Today—R
$-Home Times—R
$-Indian Life—R
$-Lutheran Journal—R
Movieguide
$-St. Anthony
   Messenger
$-Seek—R

CHILDREN
$-Animal Trails—R
Skipping Stones—R

TEEN/YOUNG ADULT
$-Animal Trails—R

WOMEN
Halo Magazine—R
Right to the Heart—R
WRITERS
$-Fellowscript—R

FILLERS: SERMON
ILLUSTRATIONS
PASTORS/LEADERS
Believers Bay—R

FILLERS: SHORT
HUMOR
ADULT/GENERAL
American Chr. Voice—R
$-Angels on Earth
Believers Bay—R
Christian Journal—R
Christian Online
Christian Ranchman
$-City Light News
Eternal Ink—R
$-Gem, The—R
$-Homeschooling
   Today—R
$-Home Times—R
$-Indian Life—R

Joyful Living—R
$-Leben—R
$-Lutheran Digest—R
$-Mature Years—R
$-Mother's Heart
Movieguide
New Heart—R
$-Presbyterians Today
$-Seek—R

CHILDREN
$-Animal Trails—R
$-SHINE brightly—R

PASTORS/LEADERS
$-Enrichment—R
$-Leadership—R

TEEN/YOUNG ADULT
$-Animal Trails—R

WRITERS
$-Christian
   Communicator—R
$-Fellowscript—R
New Writer's Mag

FILLERS: TIPS
ADULT/GENERAL
American Chr. Voice—R
Believers Bay—R
Christian Ranchman
$-Homeschooling
   Today—R
$-Home Times—R
Joyful Living—R
Movieguide
$-War Cry—R

PASTORS/LEADERS
$-Enrichment—R
WOMEN
$-Hello, Darling—R
$-Mother's Heart
Virtuous Woman

WRITERS
$-Fellowscript—R
$-Freelance Writer's
   Report—R

FILLERS: WORD PUZZLES
ADULT/GENERAL
American Chr. Voice—R
Believers Bay—R
$-CGA World
$-Christian Herald
Christian Journal—R
Christian Ranchman
$-Evangel—R
$-Faith & Friends—R
$-Gem, The—R
Joyful Living—R
$-Mature Years—R
Movieguide
$-Power for Living—R
$-War Cry—R

CHILDREN
$-Cadet Quest—R
Focus/Clubhouse
$-Guide—R
$-Nature Friend—R
$-Our Little Friend
$-Pockets—R
$-SHINE brightly—R
Skipping Stones—R

TEEN/YOUNG ADULT
$-Cadet Quest—R

WOMEN
Halo Magazine—R

FOOD/RECIPES
ADULT/GENERAL
$-Adoptee Search—R
Believers Bay—R
CBN.com—R
Christian Online
$-Homeschooling
    Today—R
$-Indian Life—R
Joyful Living—R
$-Mature Living
$-ParentLife
$-St. Anthony
    Messenger
$-World & I

CHILDREN
$-Animal Trails—R
Focus/Clubhouse
$-Focus/Clubhouse Jr.
$-Pockets—R
$-SHINE brightly—R
$-Sparkle—R

TEEN/YOUNG ADULT
Animal Trails—R

WOMEN
Dabbling Mum
Halo Magazine—R
$-Mother's Heart
Virtuous Woman

GRANDPARENTING
ADULT/GENERAL
American Chr. Voice—R
Believers Bay—R
Christian Journal—R
$-Christian
    Standard—R
$-Columbia
$-Good News, The –R
$-Indian Life—R
$-In Touch
Joyful Living—R
$-Mature Living
$-Prairie Messenger—R
$-Seek—R
$-War Cry—R

WOMEN
$-Brink Magazine—R
Halo Magazine—R
$-Mother's Heart

HEALING
ADULT/GENERAL
$-America
American Chr. Voice—R
$-Angels on Earth
Believers Bay—R
CBN.com—R
$-Celebrate Life
$-Christian Home &
    School
Christian Journal—R
Christian Online

Christian Ranchman
$-ChristianWeek
$-Gem, The—R
$-Guideposts—R
$-Home Times—R
$-Indian Life—R
Joyful Living—R
$-Light & Life
$-Mature Living
New Heart—R
$-Now What?—R
Our Sunday Visitor
Perspectives
$-St. Anthony
    Messenger
$-Seek—R
$-Testimony—R
$-United Church
    Observer
$-War Cry—R
$-World & I

CHILDREN
$-Animal Trails—R
Skipping Stones—R

DAILY DEVOTIONALS
Penned from the Heart

TEEN/YOUNG ADULT
$-Animal Trails—R
Single!—R

WOMEN
Halo Magazine—R
$-Mother's Heart
Share
Virtuous Woman

HEALTH
ADULT/GENERAL
$-Abilities
American Chr. Voice—R
$-Angels on Earth
Believers Bay—R
$-Brink Magazine—R
CBN.com—R
$-Celebrate Life
$-CGA World
$-Christian Courier—R

$-Christian Home &
   School
Christian Online
Christian Ranchman
$-ChristianWeek
$-Common Ground—R
$-Creative Nonfiction
$-Faith Today
Fit Christian—R
Genuine Motivation—R
$-Guideposts—R
Highway News—R
$-Home Times—R
$-Indian Life—R
Joyful Living—R
$-Light & Life
$-Lookout
$-Mature Living
$-Mature Years—R
$-Now What?—R
Our Sunday Visitor
$-ParentLife
Penned from the Heart
Pentecostal Evangel
$-Testimony—R
$-Vibrant Life—R
$-War Cry—R
$-World & I

CHILDREN
$-Guide—R
Skipping Stones—R
$-Sparkle—R

DAILY DEVOTIONALS
Penned from the Heart

PASTORS/LEADERS
$-Christian Century—R
$-InSite—R
$-L Magazine—R

TEEN/YOUNG ADULT
$-Devo'zine
Genuine Motivation—R
Single!—R

WOMEN
Dabbling Mum
$-Mother's Heart
Share

Treasure—R
Virtuous Woman

HISTORICAL
ADULT/GENERAL
American Chr. Voice—R
$-Angels on Earth
$-Arlington Catholic
Believers Bay—R
CBN.com—R
$-Celebrate Life
$-Christian Courier—R
$Christian History
Christian Journal—R
Christian Online
$-Columbia
$-Eureka Street
$-Faith Today
$-Indian Life—R
$-Homeschooling
   Today—R
$-Home Times—R
$-Indian Life—R
$-In Touch
$-Leben—R
$-Light & Life
$-Lutheran Digest—R
Our Sunday Visitor
Perspectives
$-Power for Living—R
Priscilla Papers
$-St. Anthony
   Messenger
Storyteller—R
$-War Cry—R
$-Wesleyan Life
$-World & I

CHILDREN
$-Focus/Clubhouse Jr.
$-Guide—R
$-Sparkle—R

PASTORS/LEADERS
$-Leadership—R
$-Ministry Today
$-Priest

HOLIDAY/SEASONAL
ADULT/GENERAL
$-Adoptee Search—R
$-Alive Now
American Chr. Voice—R
$-Angels on Earth
$-Arlington Catholic
Believers Bay—R
$-Brink Magazine—R
$-Catholic Digest
$-Catholic New York
CBN.com—R
$-CGA World
$-Chicken Soup Bks—R
$-Christian Courier—R
$-Christian Home &
   School
Christian Journal—R
Christian Online
$-Christian Retailing
$-ChristianWeek
$-City Light News
$-Columbia
$-Covenant
   Companion—R
Eternal Ink—R
$-Evangel—R
$-Family Smart—R
$-Gem, The—R
$-Gems of Truth
$-Good News, The –R
$-Good News, Etc.—R
Genuine Motivation—R
$-Guideposts—R
Highway News—R
$-Homeschooling
   Today—R
$-Home Times—R
$-Indian Life—R
$-In Touch
Joyful Living—R
$-Light & Life
$-Live—R
$-Living Light—R
$-Lookout
$-Mature Years—R
Our Sunday Visitor
$-ParentLife
Penned from the Heart
$-Point—R

$-Power for Living—R
$-Prairie Messenger—R
$-Psychology for
 Living—R
$-Purpose—R
$-St. Anthony
 Messenger
$-Seek—R
$-United Church
 Observer
$-U.S. Catholic
$-Vibrant Life—R
$-War Cry—R
$-Wesleyan Life
$-World & I

CHILDREN
$-Animal Trails—R
Focus/Clubhouse
$-Focus/Clubhouse Jr.
$-Guide—R
$-Juniorway
$-Nature Friend—R
$-Pockets—R
Skipping Stones—R
$-Sparkle—R

CHRISTIAN EDUCA-TION/LIBRARY
$-YouthWalk

DAILY DEVOTIONALS
$-Brink Magazine—R
Penned from the
 Heart—R

TEEN/YOUNG ADULT
$-Animal Trails—R
Genuine Motivation—R
Single!—R

WOMEN
Halo Magazine—R
$-Mother's Heart
Virtuous Woman

HOLY SPIRIT
ADULT/GENERAL
American Chr. Voice—R
Believers Bay—R
Christian Journal—R

$-Columbia
Eternal Ink—R
Genuine Motivation—R
Leaves—R
$-Live—R
$-Mature Living
$-War Cry—R

PASTORS/LEADERS
$-Brink Magazine—R

TEEN/YOUNG ADULT
Single!—R
$Young Salvationist—R

HOMESCHOOLING
ADULT/GENERAL
American Chr. Voice—R
Believers Bay—R
$-Columbia
$-Good News, The –R
$-Good News, Etc.—R
$-Homeschooling
 Today—R
$-Home Times—R
$-In Touch
Our Sunday Visitor
$-ParentLife

CHILDREN
$-Animal Trails—R
$-Guide—R
Skipping Stones—R

TEEN/YOUNG ADULT
$-Animal Trails—R
$-Insight

WOMEN
Halo Magazine—R
$-Mother's Heart
Virtuous Woman

HOMILETICS
ADULT/GENERAL
American Chr. Voice—R
Believers Bay—R
CBN.com—R
Christian Ranchman
$-Columbia
$-In Touch

Perspectives
Priscilla Papers
$-St. Anthony
 Messenger
$-Testimony—R
$-Wesleyan Life

PASTORS/LEADERS
$-Christian Century—R
$-Enrichment—R
$-L Magazine—R
$-Parish Liturgy
$-Preaching
$-Priest
Sharing the Practice—R

HOW-TO
ADULT/GENERAL
American Chr. Voice—R
Believers Bay—R
$-Brink Magazine—R
Canada Lutheran
$-CBA Retailers
CBN.com—R
$-Celebrate Life
Christian Journal—R
Christian Online
$-Christian Retailing
$-Faith Today
$-Family Smart—R
$-Good News, Etc.—R
$-Home Times—R
$-In Touch
$-Live—R
$-ParentLife
$-Presbyterians Today
$-St. Anthony
 Messenger
$-Testimony—R
$-Vibrant Life—R
$-World & I

CHRISTIAN EDUCA-TION/LIBRARY
$-Journal/Adventist
 Ed.—R
$-YouthWalk

PASTORS/LEADERS
$-Ministry Today
$-Net Results

$-Newsletter Newsletter
$-Outreach—R

WOMEN
Dabbling Mum
Virtuous Woman

WRITERS
$-Fellowscript—R
$-Freelance Writer's
Report—R
$-Poets & Writers
Writer's Digest

HOW-TO
ACTIVITIES (JUV.)
ADULT/GENERAL
Believers Bay—R
$-Christian Home &
School
Christian Online
$-Family Smart—R
Keys to Living—R
$-ParentLife
$-St. Anthony
Messenger
$-World & I

CHILDREN
$-Cadet Quest—R
Focus/Clubhouse
$-Focus/Clubhouse Jr.
$-Guide—R
$-Juniorway
$-Nature Friend—R
$-Pockets—R
$-SHINE brightly—R
$-Sparkle—R

TEEN/YOUNG ADULT
$-Cadet Quest—R

WOMEN
$-Mother's Heart
Virtuous Woman

HUMOR
ADULT/GENERAL
$-Abilities
American Chr. Voice—R
$-Angels on Earth

Believers Bay—R
$-Brink Magazine—R
$-Catholic Digest
CBN.com—R
$-Chicken Soup Bks—R
$-Christian Courier—R
$-Christian Home &
School
$-Christianity Today—R
Christian Journal—R
Christian Online
Christian Ranchman
$-Creative Nonfiction
$-City Light News
Eternal Ink—R
$-Family Smart—R
$-Gem, The—R
Genuine Motivation—R
$-Good News, The –R
$-Good News, Etc.—R
$-Homeschooling
Today—R
$-Home Times—R
$-Indian Life—R
$-In Touch
Joyful Living—R
$-Living Light—R
$-Lookout
$-Mature Living
Our Sunday Visitor
Penned from the
Heart—R
$-Psychology for
Living—R
$-Ruminate
$-St. Anthony
Messenger
$-Seek—R
Storyteller—R
$-Testimony—R
$-Thriving Family
$-U.S. Catholic
$-Weavings
$-Wildwood Reader—R
$-World & I

CHILDREN
$-Focus/Clubhouse Jr.
$-Guide—R
$-SHINE brightly—R

$-Sparkle—R

DAILY DEVOTIONALS
Penned from the
Heart—R

PASTORS/LEADERS
$-Enrichment—R
$-Leadership—R
$-L Magazine—R
$-Priest

TEEN/YOUNG ADULT
$-Direction
Genuine Motivation—R
Single!—R
$-TC Magazine
$Young Salvationist—R

WOMEN
Halo Magazine—R
$-Hello, Darling—R
$-Mother's Heart

WRITERS
$-Christian
Communicator—R
New Writer's Mag.
WritersWeekly.com—R

INNER LIFE
ADULT/GENERAL
American Chr. Voice—R
Believers Bay—R
Canada Lutheran
$-Catholic Digest
CBN.com—R
Christian Journal—R
Christian Ranchman
$-ChristianWeek
Genuine Motivation—R
$-In Touch
$-Light & Life
$-Mature Years—R
Our Sunday Visitor
Penned from the
Heart—R
$-Presbyterians Today
$-Seek—R
$-Testimony—R
$-Weavings

$-Wildwood Reader—R
$-World & I

TEEN/YOUNG ADULT
Single!—R
$-TC Magazine

WOMEN
$-FullFill
$-Mother's Heart

INSPIRATIONAL
ADULT/GENERAL
$-Alive Now
American Chr. Voice—R
$-Angels on Earth
$-Arlington Catholic
Believers Bay—R
$-Brink Magazine—R
CBN.com—R
$-Celebrate Life
$-Chicken Soup Bks—R
$-Christian Home &
    School
Christian Journal—R
Christian Online
Christian Ranchman
$-Columbia
$-Covenant
    Companion—R
$-Decision
$-Dreamseeker—R
Eternal Ink—R
$-Evangel—R
$-Gem, The—R
Genuine Motivation—R
$-Good News, The –R
$-Guideposts—R
Highway News—R
$-Homeschooling
    Today—R
$-Home Times—R
$-In Touch
Keys to Living—R
Leaves—R
$-Lookout
$-Lutheran Digest—R
$-Mature Living
New Heart—R
$-ParentLife

Penned from the
    Heart—R
$-Power for Living—R
$-Prairie Messenger—R
$-Presbyterians Today
$-Psychology for
    Living—R
$-Purpose—R
$-St. Anthony
    Messenger
$-Seek—R
Storyteller—R
SW Kansas Faith
$-Testimony—R
$-United Church
    Observer
$-War Cry—R
$-Wesleyan Life
$-Wildwood Reader—R
$-World & I

CHILDREN
$-Animal Trails—R
$-Cadet Quest—R

DAILY DEVOTIONALS
$-Brink Magazine—R
Penned from the
    Heart—R
$-Rejoice!

MISSIONS
$-Operation
    Reveille—R

PASTORS/LEADERS
$-L Magazine—R
$-Ministry Today
$-Priest

TEEN/YOUNG ADULT
$-Animal Trails—R
$-Cadet Quest—R
$-Devo'zine
$-Direction
Genuine Motivation—R
$-Insight
Single!—R
$Young Salvationist—R

WOMEN
$-FullFill
$-Hello, Darling—R
$-Mother's Heart
Right to the Heart—R
Share
Virtuous Woman

WRITERS
Writer's Digest

INTERVIEWS/
PROFILES
ADULT/GENERAL
$-Abilities
American Chr. Voice—R
$-Arlington Catholic
Believers Bay—R
$-Brink Magazine—R
$-Catholic New York
CBN.com—R
$-Celebrate Life
$-Charisma
$-Christianity Today—R
$-Christian Herald
Christian Journal—R
Christian News NW—R
Christian Online
Christian Ranchman
$-ChristianWeek
$-City Light News
$-Columbia
Encompass
Eternal Ink—R
$-Faith Today
$-Gem, The—R
$-Good News, The –R
$-Good News, Etc.—R
$-Guideposts—R
Highway News—R
$-Home Times—R
$-In Touch
$-Kindred Spirit—R
$-Light & Life
$-Living Light
    News—R
$-Lookout
New Heart—R
Our Sunday Visitor
$-ParentLife

$-Power for Living—R
$-Prism
$-St. Anthony
    Messenger
$-Testimony—R
$-United Church
    Observer
$-Vibrant Life—R
$-Weavings
$-World & I

CHILDREN
$-Cadet Quest—R
$-Pockets—R
$-SHINE brightly—R
Skipping Stones—R

MISSIONS
$-Operation
    Reveille—R

PASTORS/LEADERS
$-Christian Century—R
$-Enrichment—R
$-InSite—R
$-Ministry Today
$-Outreach—R
$-Priest

TEEN/YOUNG ADULT
$-Cadet Quest—R
$-Direction
Single!—R
$-TC Magazine
$Young Salvationist—R
$-YouthWalk

WOMEN
Halo Magazine—R
Virtuous Woman

WRITERS
$-Christian
Communicator—R
$-Fellowscript—R
New Writer's Mag.
$-Poets & Writers
$-Writer
Writer's Chronicle
Writer's Digest

LEADERSHIP
ADULT/GENERAL
American Chr. Voice—R
$-Angels on Earth
Believers Bay—R
CBN.com—R
$-Christian Courier—R
$-Christian Home &
    School
Christian Journal—R
$-Christian Retailing
$-Christian
    Standard—R
$-ChristianWeek
$-Columbia
$-EFCA Today
Encompass
$-Faith Today
$-Gem, The—R
$-Good News, Etc.—R
$-In Touch
$-Light & Life
$-Lookout
$-Mature Living
Men of the Cross
Our Sunday Visitor
$-Prairie Messenger—R
Priscilla Papers
$-St. Anthony
    Messenger
$-Testimony—R
$-United Church
    Observer
$-World & I

CHILDREN
$-SHINE brightly—R

**CHRISTIAN EDUCA-
TION/LIBRARIES**
$-Group Magazine
$-YouthWalk

PASTORS/LEADERS
$-Christian Century—R
$-Enrichment—R
$-Growth Points—R
$-InSite—R
$-Leadership—R
$-L Magazine—R

$-Ministry Today
$-Net Results
$-Outreach—R
Sharing the Practice—R
$-SmallGroups.com—R

TEEN/YOUNG ADULT
$-Boundless.org—R
$-Direction

WOMEN
Right to the Heart—R
Share
Women of the Cross

LIFESTYLE
ARTICLES
ADULT/GENERAL
American Chr. Voice—R
Believers Bay—R
$-Brink Magazine—R
byFaith
Canada Lutheran
CBN.com—R
Christian Journal—R
Christian Ranchman
$-ChristianWeek
$-City Light News
Eternal Ink—R
$-Faith Today
Fit Christian—R
Genuine Motivation—R
$-Good News, The –R
$-Good News, Etc.—R
$-Home Times—R
$-Indian Life—R
$-In Touch
$-Light & Life
$-Lookout
$-Mature Living
Our Sunday Visitor
$-ParentLife
$-Seek—R
Share
$-U.S. Catholic
$-Vibrant Life—R
$-War Cry—R

TEEN/YOUNG ADULT
$-Direction

Genuine Motivation—R
$-Insight
Single!—R
$-TC Magazine

WOMEN
$-FullFill
$-Mother's Heart
Virtuous Woman

LITURGICAL
ADULT/GENERAL
$-Alive Now
$-Arlington Catholic
Believers Bay—R
$-Columbia
$-Lutheran Journal—R
Our Sunday Visitor
Perspectives
$-Prairie Messenger—R
$-St. Anthony
    Messenger
$-Testimony—R
$-U.S. Catholic

PASTORS/LEADERS
$-Christian Century—R
$-L Magazine—R
$-Parish Liturgy
$-Reformed Worship
Sharing the Practice—R

MARRIAGE
ADULT/GENERAL
$-Adoptee Search—R
American Chr. Voice—R
$-Angels on Earth
$-Arlington Catholic
Believers Bay—R
$Bible Advocate—R
$-Brink Magazine—R
$-Catholic Digest
CBN.com—R
$-Celebrate Life
$-Christian Courier—R
$-Christian Examiner
$-Christian Home &
    School
Christian Journal—R
Christian Online

Christian Ranchman
$-Christian Research
$-Christian
    Standard—R
$-ChristianWeek
Church Herald &
    Holiness
$-Columbia
$-Decision
$-Evangel—R
$-Faith Today
$-Family Smart—R
$-Gem, The—R
$-Good News, The –R
$-Good News, Etc.—R
$-Guideposts—R
Highway News—R
$-Home Times—R
$-Indian Life—R
$-In Touch
Joyful Living—R
$-Light & Life
$-Living Light—R
$-Lookout
$-Mature Living
Men of the Cross
Our Sunday Visitor
$-ParentLife
Penned from the
    Heart—R
Perspectives
$-Point—R
$-Prairie Messenger—R
Priscilla Papers
$-Psychology for
    Living—R
$-Purpose—R
$-St. Anthony
    Messenger
$-Seek—R
$-Testimony—R
$-Thriving Family
$-U.S. Catholic
$-Vibrant Life—R
$-War Cry—R
$-Wesleyan Life
$-Wildwood Reader—R
$-World & I

DAILY DEVOTIONALS
Penned from the
    Heart—R

PASTORS/LEADERS
$-Christian Century—R
$-L Magazine—R
$-Ministry Today
$-SmallGroups.com—R

TEEN/YOUNG ADULT
$-Boundless.org—R
Genuine Motivation—R
$Young Salvationist—R

WOMEN
Dabbling Mum
Halo Magazine—R
$-Hello, Darling—R
$-Mother's Heart
Virtuous Woman
Women of the Cross

MEN'S ISSUES
ADULT/GENERAL
American Chr. Voice—R
$-Arlington Catholic
Believers Bay—R
$-Brink Magazine—R
CBN.com—R
$-Chicken Soup Bks—R
$-Christian Examiner
Christian Journal—R
Christian Online
Christian Ranchman
$-ChristianWeek
$-Columbia
$-Creative Nonfiction
$-EFCA Today
$-Evangel—R
$-Faith Today
$-Family Smart—R
$-Gem, The—R
Genuine Motivation—R
$-Good News, The –R
$-Good News, Etc.—R
$-Home Times—R
$-Indian Life—R
$-In Touch
Joyful Living—R

$-Light & Life
$-Live—R
$-Lookout
Men of the Cross
Our Sunday Visitor
Penned from the
    Heart—R
Perspectives
$-Point—R
Priscilla Papers
$-Psychology for
    Living—R
$-Purpose—R
$-St. Anthony
    Messenger
$-Testimony—R
$-United Church
    Observer
$-Vibrant Life—R
$-War Cry—R
$-Wesleyan Life
$-World & I

PASTORS/LEADERS
$-L Magazine—R
$-SmallGroups.com—R

TEEN/YOUNG ADULT
$-Boundless.org—R

WOMEN
Halo Magazine—R
$-Mother's Heart

MIRACLES
ADULT/GENERAL
American Chr. Voice—R
$-Angels on Earth
Believers Bay—R
CBN.com—R
$-Chicken Soup Bks—R
$-Christian Home &
    School
Christian Journal—R
$-Christianity Today—R
Christian Online
Christian Ranchman
$-Christian
    Standard—R
$-ChristianWeek

$-Columbia
$-Decision
$-Gem, The—R
Genuine Motivation—R
$-Guideposts—R
$-Home Times—R
$-Indian Life—R
$-In Touch
Joyful Living—R
Leaves—R
$-Light & Life
$-Lookout
$-Lutheran Journal—R
New Heart—R
Our Sunday Visitor
Penned from the
    Heart—R
Perspectives
$-Power for Living—R
Priscilla Papers
$-St. Anthony
    Messenger
$-Seek—R
$-Testimony—R

CHILDREN
$-Guide—R

DAILY DEVOTIONALS
Penned from the
    Heart—R

PASTORS/LEADERS
$-Ministry Today

TEEN/YOUNG ADULT
$-Devo'zine
Genuine Motivation—R
$-Insight
Single!—R

MISSIONS
ADULT/GENERAL
American Chr. Voice—R
Believers Bay—R
$-Brink Magazine—R
Canada Lutheran
$-Christian Home &
    School
Christian Ranchman

Church Herald &
    Holiness
$-City Light News
$-Columbia
$-EFCA Today
$-Faith Today
Genuine Motivation—R
$-Good News, The –R
$-Good News, Etc.—R
$-In Touch
$-Mature Living
Our Sunday Visitor
$-ParentLife

CHILDREN
$-Guide—R

**CHRISTIAN EDUCA-
TION/LIBRARIES**
$-Group Magazine

DAILY DEVOTIONALS
$-Brink Magazine—R

MISSIONS
$-Operation
    Reveille—R

PASTORS/LEADERS
$-Enrichment—R

TEEN/YOUNG ADULT
$-Direction
Genuine Motivation—R
Single!—R

WOMEN
Halo Magazine—R
$-Mother's Heart

MONEY
MANAGEMENT
ADULT/GENERAL
American Chr. Voice—R
Believers Bay—R
$-Brink Magazine—R
byFaith
$-CBA Retailers
CBN.com—R
Christian Journal—R
Christian Online

Christian Ranchman
$-ChristianWeek
$-Creative Nonfiction
$-Faith Today
$-Family Smart—R
$-Gem, The—R
Genuine Motivation—R
Highway News—R
$-Home Times—R
$-In Touch
Joyful Living—R
$-Lookout
$-Mature Years—R
Our Sunday Visitor
$-ParentLife
Penned from the
  Heart—R
$-St. Anthony
  Messenger
$-Testimony—R
$-War Cry—R
$-World & I

DAILY DEVOTIONALS
Penned from the
  Heart—R

PASTORS/LEADERS
$-Enrichment—R
$-SmallGroups.com—R

TEEN/YOUNG ADULT
$-Boundless.org—R
$-Direction
Genuine Motivation—R
Single!—R
$Young Salvationist—R

WOMEN
Halo Magazine—R
$-Mother's Heart
Treasure—R
Virtuous Woman

MOVIE REVIEWS
ADULT/GENERAL
$-Abilities
Believers Bay—R
byFaith
CBN.com—R
$-Christian Herald

Christian Journal—R
$-City Light News
$-Cresset, The
$-Eureka Street
$-Faith & Friends—R
Genuine Motivation—R
$-Good News, The –R
$-Home Times—R
$-Indian Life—R
Movieguide
Our Sunday Visitor
Perspectives
$-Prairie Messenger—R

TEEN/YOUNG ADULT
Genuine Motivation—R
Single!—R
$-TC Magazine

WOMEN
Virtuous Woman

MUSIC REVIEWS
ADULT/GENERAL
$-Arlington Catholic
Believers Bay—R
CBN.com—R
$-Charisma
$-Christian Herald
Christian Journal—R
$-Christian Retailing
$-City Light News
$-Cresset, The
$-Eureka Street
$-Faith & Friends—R
$-Faith Today
Genuine Motivation—R
$-Good News, The –R
$-Indian Life—R
Movieguide
Our Sunday Visitor
Perspectives
$-Presbyterians Today
$-Prism
$-Testimony—R
$-World & I

PASTORS/LEADERS
$-Christian Century—R
$-Ministry Today

Parish Liturgy
$-Reformed Worship

TEEN/YOUNG ADULT
$-Devo'zine
Genuine Motivation—R
Single!—R
$-TC Magazine
$Young Salvationist—R

WOMEN
Virtuous Woman

NATURE
ADULT/GENERAL
American Chr. Voice—R
Believers Bay—R
$-Brink Magazine—R
CBN.com—R
$-Christian Courier—R
Christian Journal—R
Creation
Creation Illust.
$-Creative Nonfiction
$-Gem, The—R
$-In Touch
Keys to Living—R
$-Lutheran Digest—R
Our Sunday Visitor
Penned from the
  Heart—R
$-Ruminate
$-St. Anthony
  Messenger
$-Seek—R
Storyteller—R
$-Testimony—R
$-Wildwood Reader—R
$-World & I

CHILDREN
$-Cadet Quest—R
$-Focus/Clubhouse Jr.
$-Guide—R
$-Nature Friend—R
Skipping Stones—R
$-Sparkle—R

TEEN/YOUNG ADULT
$-Cadet Quest—R

Genuine Motivation—R
Single!—R

WOMEN
Virtuous Woman

NEWS FEATURES
ADULT/GENERAL
Active Reliance
$-Catholic New York
$-Catholic Sentinel
CBN.com—R
$-Charisma
$-Christian Examiner
Christian News NW—R
Christian Ranchman
$-Christian Research
$-Christian Retailing
$-ChristianWeek
$-City Light News
$-Commonweal
$-Disaster News
Encompass
$-Eureka Street
$-Faith Today
Genuine Motivation—R
$-Good News, Etc.—R
$-Home Times—R
$-Indian Life—R
Movieguide
Our Sunday Visitor
$-St. Anthony
    Messenger
$-Testimony—R
$-War Cry—R
$-World & I

CHILDREN
$-Pockets—R

MISSIONS
$-Operation
    Reveille—R

PASTORS/LEADERS
$-Christian Century—R
$-Ministry Today

TEEN/YOUNG ADULT
Genuine Motivation—R

WRITERS
$-Poets & Writers

NEWSPAPERS/TABLOIDS
Active Reliance
$-Arlington Catholic
$-Catholic New York
$-Catholic Sentinel
Christian Chronicle
$-Christian Courier—R
$-Christian Examiner
$-Christian Herald
Christian Journal—R
Christian News NW—R
Christian Press
    Newspaper
Christian Ranchman
$-ChristianWeek
Church of England
    Newspaper
$-City Light News
$-Common Ground—R
Good News!
$-Good News, Etc.—R
Good News Rochester
$-Home Times—R
$-Indian Life—R
Kansas City Metro Voice
$-Living Light—R
Messianic Times
New Frontier
Our Sunday Visitor
$-Prairie Messenger—R
SW Kansas Faith

NOSTALGIA
ADULT/GENERAL
American Chr. Voice—R
Believers Bay—R
$-Good News, Etc.—R
$-Home Times—R
$-Indian Life—R
$-In Touch
$-Lutheran Digest—R
$-Seek—R
Storyteller—R
$-Testimony—R

PASTORS/LEADERS
$-Priest
News! Online
$-Homeschooling
    Today—R
$-Indian Life—R
$Kindred Spirit

ONLINE PUBLICATIONS
ADULT/GENERAL
$-America
American Chr. Voice—R
Answers Magazine
Believers Bay—R
$-Brink Magazine—R
$-Catholic Digest
CBN.com—R
$-Charisma
$-Christian Examiner
$-Christianity Today—R
Christian Journal—R
Christian Online
$-Christian Retailing
$-Christian
    Standard—R
$-Columbia
Converge Magazine
$-Decision
$-Disaster News
$-Drama Ministry—R
$-Dreamseeker—R
$-Eureka Street
Experience
$-Faith Today
$-Family Smart—R
$-Good News, The –R
Good News! Online
$-Homeschooling
    Today—R
$-Indian Life—R
$-Kindred Spirit
$-Leben—R
Light & Life Online
$-Lookout
Lutheran Witness
    Online
Men of the Cross
$-Now What?
Pentecostal Evangel

Perspectives
Priority Online
$-Reformed Worship
$-St. Anthony
  Messenger
$-Testimony—R
$Thriving Family
Urban Faith .com
$-U.S. Catholic
Wesleyan Life Online
$-World & I Online

CHILDREN
Compassion Explorer
  Online
Focus/Clubhouse
$-Focus/Clubhouse Jr.
Keys for Kids
Kids' Ark

DAILY DEVOTIONALS
$-Forward Day by Day
Mustard Seed Ministries

MISSIONS
$-Operation
  Reveille—R

PASTORS/LEADERS
$-Cook Partners
$-InSite—R
$-Leadership—R
L Magazine
$-Ministry Today
$-Net Results
$-Newsletter Newsletter
Plugged In Online
$-Preaching
$-Reformed Worship
$-SmallGroups.com—R
Worship Leader
$-YouthWorker

TEEN/YOUNG ADULT
$Young Salvationist—R

WOMEN
Christian Work at
  Home—R
Dabbling Mum

Empowering Everyday
  Women
$-FullFill
Right to the Heart—R
Virtuous Woman
Women's Ministry

WRITERS
$-Freelance Writer's
  Report—R
$-Reformed Worship
$-Testimony—R

OPINION PIECES
ADULT/GENERAL
American Chr. Voice—R
$-Arlington Catholic
Believers Bay—R
$-Brink Magazine—R
$-Catholic New York
CBN.com—R
$-Christian Courier—R
$-Christian Examiner
$-Christianity Today—R
Christian News NW—R
$-Christian Research
$-ChristianWeek
$-Eureka Street
$-Good News, The –R
$-Good News, Etc.—R
$-Home Times—R
$-Indian Life—R
$-In Touch
$-Lookout
Movieguide
Our Sunday Visitor
Perspectives
$-Prairie Messenger—R
$-St. Anthony
  Messenger
$-Testimony—R
$-United Church
  Observer
$-World & I

CHILDREN
Skipping Stones—R

MISSIONS
$-Operation
  Reveille—R

PASTORS/LEADERS
$-Ministry Today
$-Priest

WRITERS
New Writer's Mag.

PARENTING
ADULT/GENERAL
American Chr. Voice—R
$-Angels on Earth
$-Arlington Catholic
$-Bible Advocate—R
Canada Lutheran
$-Catholic Digest
CBN.com—R
$-Celebrate Life
$-Chicken Soup Bks—R
$-Christian Courier—R
$-Christian Home &
  School
Christian Journal—R
Christian Ranchman
$-Christian Research
$-ChristianWeek
$-Columbia
$-Family Smart—R
$-Gem, The—R
$-Good News, The –R
$-Good News, Etc.—R
$-Homeschooling
  Today—R
$-Home Times—R
$-Indian Life—R
$-In Touch
Joyful Living—R
$-Light & Life
$-Live—R
$-Living Light—R
$-Lookout
$-Lutheran Journal—R
Movieguide
Our Sunday Visitor
$-ParentLife
Penned from the
  Heart—R

Pentecostal Evangel
$-Point—R
$-Power for Living—R
$-Prairie Messenger—R
$-Psychology for
    Living—R
$-Purpose—R
$-St. Anthony
    Messenger
$-Seek—R
SW Kansas Faith
$-Testimony—R
$-Thriving Family
$-Vibrant Life—R
$-War Cry—R
$-Wesleyan Life
$-World & I

DAILY DEVOTIONALS
Penned from the Heart

WOMEN
$-FullFill
$-Hello, Darling—R
$-Mother's Heart
Right to the Heart—R
Share
Virtuous Woman

WRITERS
Dabbling Mum
$-Hello, Darling—R
$-Mother's Heart
Virtuous Woman

PASTORS' HELPS
PASTORS/LEADERS
Believers Bay—R
$-Christian Century—R
Christian Journal—R
$-Cook Partners
$-Enrichment—R
$-Growth Points—R
$-InSite—R
$-Leadership—R
$-L Magazine—R
$-Ministry Today
$-Net Results
$-Newsletter Newsletter
$-Outreach—R

$-Parish Liturgy
$-Preaching
$-Purpose—R
$-Reformed Worship
Sharing the Practice—R
$-SmallGroups.com—R

PEACE ISSUES
ADULT/GENERAL
American Chr. Voice—R
Believers Bay—R
CBN.com—R
$-ChristianWeek
$-Columbia
$-Eureka Street
Genuine Motivation—R
$-Indian Life—R
$-In Touch
$-Lookout
Our Sunday Visitor
Penned from the Heart
Perspectives
$-Prairie Messenger—R
$-Purpose—R
$-Seek—R
$-Testimony—R
$-U.S. Catholic

CHILDREN
$-Pockets—R
Skipping Stones—R

PASTORS/LEADERS
$-Christian Century—R
$-L Magazine—R

TEEN/YOUNG ADULT
Genuine Motivation—R
Single!—R

PERSONAL EXPERIENCE
ADULT/GENERAL
$-Adoptee Search—R
$-Alive Now
American Chr. Voice—R
$-Angels on Earth
Believers Bay—R
$Bible Advocate—R
$-Brink Magazine—R
$-Catholic Digest

$-Catholic New York
CBN.com—R
$-Celebrate Life
$-Chicken Soup Bks—R
$-Christian Courier—R
$-Christianity Today—R
Christian Journal—R
Christian Online
$-ChristianWeek
$-Columbia
$-Commonweal
$-Creative Nonfiction
$-Decision
Eternal Ink—R
$-Evangel—R
$-Gem, The—R
Genuine Motivation—R
$-Good News, Etc.—R
$-Guideposts—R
Highway News—R
$-Home Times—R
$-Indian Life—R
$-In Touch
Joyful Living—R
Keys to Living—R
Leaves—R
$-Light & Life
$-Lookout
$-Lutheran Journal—R
$-Mature Living
New Heart—R
$-Now What?—R
$-ParentLife
Penned from the
    Heart—R
$-Point—R
$-Power for Living—R
$-Prairie Messenger—R
$-Psychology for
    Living—R
$-Ruminate
$-St. Anthony
    Messenger
$-Seek—R
$-Testimony—R
$-U.S. Catholic
$-Vision—R
$-War Cry—R
$-Wesleyan Life
$-World & I

CHILDREN
$-Animal Trails—R
$-Guide—R
Skipping Stones—R
$-Sparkle—R

CHRISTIAN EDUCA-TION/LIBRARIES
$-Journal/Adventist
   Ed.—R

DAILY DEVOTIONALS
Penned from the Heart—R
   $-Rejoice!

PASTORS/LEADERS
$-Priest
$-YouthWorker

TEEN/YOUNG ADULT
$-Animal Trails—R
$-Boundless.org—R
$-Devo'zine
$-Direction
Genuine Motivation—R
$-Insight
Single!—R
$-TC Magazine
$Young Salvationist—R

WOMEN
$-Hello, Darling—R
$-Mother's Heart
Virtuous Woman

WRITERS
New Writer's Mag.
WritersWeekly.com—R

PERSONAL GROWTH
ADULT/GENERAL
$-Adoptee Search—R
$-Alive Now
American Chr. Voice—R
Believers Bay—R
$-Bible Advocate—R
$-Catholic Digest
CBN.com—R
$-Christian Courier—R
Christian Journal—R

Christian Online
Christian Ranchman
$-Columbia
$-Common Ground—R
$-Decision
$-Evangel—R
$-Faith & Friends—R
$-Gem, The—R
Genuine Motivation—R
$-Good News, The –R
$-Good News, Etc.—R
$-Home Times—R
$-Indian Life—R
$-In Touch
Keys to Living—R
$-Light & Life
$-Lookout
$-Lutheran Digest—R
$-Mature Years—R
New Heart—R
$-Now What?—R
$-ParentLife
Penned from the
   Heart—R
$-Psychology for
   Living—R
$-Purpose—R
$-St. Anthony
   Messenger
$-Seek—R
Share
$-Testimony—R
$-U.S. Catholic
$-War Cry—R
$-Wildwood Reader—R
$-World & I

CHILDREN
$-Animal Trails—R
$-Guide—R
Skipping Stones—R

CHRISTIAN EDUCA-TION/LIBRARY
$-Group Magazine

DAILY DEVOTIONALS
Penned from the
   Heart—R

PASTORS/LEADERS
$-L Magazine—R
$-Ministry Today

TEEN/YOUNG ADULT
$-Animal Trails—R
$-Boundless.org—R
$-Direction
Genuine Motivation—R
$-Insight
Single!—R
$Young Salvationist—R

WOMEN
Dabbling Mum
$-FullFill
Halo Magazine—R
$-Hello, Darling—R
$-Mother's Heart
Virtuous Woman

PHOTO ESSAYS
ADULT/GENERAL
Believers Bay—R
Genuine Motivation—R
$-Indian Life—R
Our Sunday Visitor
$-Prism
$-St. Anthony
   Messenger
$-U.S. Catholic
$-Wildwood Reader—R
$-World & I

CHILDREN
$-Animal Trails—R
Skipping Stones—R

CHRISTIAN EDUCA-TION/LIBRARY
$-Journal/Adventist
   Ed.—R

PASTORS/LEADERS
$-Outreach—R
$-Priest
$-YouthWorker

TEEN/YOUNG ADULT
$-Animal Trails—R
Genuine Motivation—R

PHOTOGRAPHS

Note: "Reprint" indicators (R) have been deleted from this section and "B" for black & white glossy prints or "C" for color inserted. An asterisk (*) before a listing indicates they buy photos with articles only.

ADULT/GENERAL

$-Adoptee Search—B/C
American Chr. Voice—B/C
*Animal Trails—B/C
$-Arlington Catholic—B
*Bible Advocate—C
Canada Lutheran—B
$-Catholic Digest—B/C
$-Catholic New York—B
$-Catholic Sentinel—B/C
$-CBA Retailers—C
$-Celebrate Life—C
*$-Charisma—C
*$-Christian Courier—B
*$-Christian Examiner—C
$-Christian Herald—C
$Christian History—B/C
$-Christian Home & School—C
*$-Christianity Today—C
*Christian Online
$-Christian Retailing—C
*$-Christian Standard—B/C
$-City Light News—B/C
$-Commonweal—B/C
$-Covenant Companion—B/C
$-Decision
$-Eureka Street—B/C
*$-Evangel—B
*$-Faith & Friends—C

*$-Faith Today
*$-Good News, The—C
*$-Homeschooling Today—B/C
*$-Home Times—B/C
$-Indian Life—B/C
*$-In Touch
*Joyful Living
*$-Kindred Spirit
*Leaves—B/C
*$-Leben—C
$-Light & Life—B/C
*$-Live—B/C
*$-Living Light—B/C
*$-Lookout—B/C
*$-Lutheran Journal—C
$-Lutheran Witness
**Mature Living—C
*Mature Years—C
*New Heart—R—C
*$Now What?—C
Our Sunday Visitor—B/C
Pentecostal Evangel—B/C
*Perspectives—B
*$-Point—C
$-Power for Living—B
$Prairie Messenger—B/C
*$-Presbyterians Today—B/C
*$-Prism—B/C
*$-Psychology for Living—C
*$-Purpose—B
*$-St. Anthony Messenger—B/C
*$-Seek—C
$-Sports Spectrum—C
*$-Testimony—B/C
*$-United Church Observer—B/C
*$-Vibrant Life—C
$-Vision—B/C
$-War Cry—C
*$-World & I—B/C

CHILDREN

$-Animal Trails—B/C

*Focus/Clubhouse—C
*$-Focus/Clubhouse Jr.—C
$-Nature Friend—B/C
*$-Pockets—C
$-SHINE brightly—C
Skipping Stones
$-Sparkle—C

CHRISTIAN EDUCATION/LIBRARIES

$-Journal/Adventist Ed.—B
$-YouthWalk—C

DAILY DEVOTIONALS

Secret Place—B
$-Upper Room

MISSIONS

$-Operation Reveille—B/C

PASTORS/LEADERS

$-Christian Century—B/C
*$-InSite—C
*$-Leadership—B
*$-Parish Liturgy
$-Priest
$-Reformed Worship
*$-YouthWorker

TEEN/YOUNG ADULT

$-Animal Trails—B/C
*$-Direction—B/C
Single!—B/C
$-Take Five Plus—B/C
*$-Young Salvationist—C

WOMEN

Halo Magazine—C
*$-Mother's Heart—C
Right to the Heart
*Virtuous Woman

WRITERS

$-Best New Writing—C
*New Writer's Mag.
*$-Poets & Writers

*Writer's Chronicle—B
*Writer's Digest—B

POETRY
ADULT/GENERAL
$-Alive Now
$-America
American Chr. Voice—R
Believers Bay—R
$-Bible Advocate—R
$-Christian Courier—R
Christian Journal—R
$-Christian Research
$-Commonweal
Creation Illust.
$-Cresset, The
Eternal Ink—R
$-Eureka Street
$-Evangel—R
$-Gem, The—R
$-Homeschooling
    Today—R
$-Home Times—R
$-Image
$-Indian Life—R
Keys to Living—R
Leaves—R
$-Light & Life
$-Live—R
$-Lutheran Digest—R
$-Lutheran Journal—R
$-Mature Years—R
New Heart—R
Penned from the Heart
Penwood Review
Perspectives
$-Prairie Messenger—R
$-Purpose—R
Relief Journal
$-Ruminate
$-St. Anthony
    Messenger
Storyteller—R
Studio—R
$-Testimony—R
Time of Singing—R
$-U.S. Catholic
$-Vision—R
$-War Cry—R
$-Weavings

$-World & I

CHILDREN
$-Animal Trails—R
$-Focus/Clubhouse Jr.
$-Pockets—R
$-SHINE brightly—R
Skipping Stones—R
$-Sparkle—R

CHRISTIAN EDUCATION/LIBRARIES
$-YouthWalk

DAILY DEVOTIONALS
Christian Devotions
God's Word for Today
Penned from the
    Heart—R
Secret Place

PASTORS/LEADERS
$-Christian Century—R

TEEN/YOUNG ADULT
$-Animal Trails—R
$-Devo'zine
$-Insight
$-Take Five Plus—R

WOMEN
Halo Magazine—R
$-Hello, Darling—R
Virtuous Woman

WRITERS
$-Best New Writing
$-Christian
    Communicator—R
New Writer's Mag.
Writer's Digest

POLITICS
ADULT/GENERAL
American Chr. Voice—R
$-Arlington Catholic
Believers Bay—R
$-Brink Magazine—R
CBN.com—R
$-Christian Courier—R
$-Christian Examiner

$-Christianity Today—R
Christian News NW—R
$-ChristianWeek
$-Commonweal
$-Creative Nonfiction
$-Cresset, The
$-Faith Today
$-Good News, The –R
$-Good News, Etc.—R
$-Home Times—R
$-Indian Life—R
$-In Touch
$-Light & Life
Movieguide
Our Sunday Visitor
Perspectives
$-St. Anthony
    Messenger
$-Testimony—R
$-U.S. Catholic
$-World & I

PASTORS/LEADERS
$-Christian Century—R

PRAISE
ADULT/GENERAL
American Chr. Voice—R
Believers Bay—R
Christian Journal—R
Eternal Ink—R
Genuine Motivation—R
Highway News—R
$-Mature Living
$-St. Anthony
    Messenger
TEEN/YOUNG ADULT
Single!—R

WOMEN
$-Brink Magazine—R
$-Mother's Heart

PRAYER
ADULT/GENERAL
$-Alive Now
American Chr. Voice—R
$-Angels on Earth
Believers Bay—R
$-Bible Advocate—R
$-Brink Magazine—R

$-Catholic Digest
CBN.com—R
$-Celebrate Life
$-Christian Home &
    School
$-Christianity Today—R
Christian Journal—R
Christian Online
Christian Ranchman
$-Christian Research
$-Christian
    Standard—R
$-ChristianWeek
$-Columbia
$-Covenant
    Companion—R
$-Decision
Eternal Ink—R
$-Evangel—R
$-Gem, The—R
Genuine Motivation—R
$-Good News, The –R
$-Good News, Etc.—R
Highway News—R
$-Home Times—R
$-Indian Life—R
$-In Touch
Leaves—R
$-Light & Life
$-Lookout
$-Lutheran Digest—R
$-Lutheran Journal—R
$-Lutheran Witness
$-Mature Living
$-Mature Years—R
Our Sunday Visitor
$-ParentLife
Penned from the Heart
Pentecostal Evangel
Perspectives
$-Point—R
$-Prairie Messenger—R
$-Presbyterians Today
$-St. Anthony
    Messenger
$-Seek—R
$-Testimony—R
$-U.S. Catholic
$-War Cry—R
$-Wesleyan Life

CHILDREN
$-Guide—R

DAILY DEVOTIONALS
$-Brink Magazine—R
Penned from the
    Heart—R

PASTORS/LEADERS
$-Leadership—R
$-L Magazine—R
$-Ministry Today
$-Parish Liturgy
$-Reformed Worship
$-SmallGroups.com—R

TEEN/YOUNG ADULT
$-Boundless.org—R
$-Devo'zine
$-Direction
$-Insight
Single!—R

WOMEN
Halo Magazine—R
$-Mother's Heart
Right to the Heart—R
Virtuous Woman

PROPHECY
ADULT/GENERAL
American Chr. Voice—R
Believers Bay—R
$-Bible Advocate—R
CBN.com—R
Christian Online
$-Christian Research
Eternal Ink—R
$-In Touch
$-Light & Life
Our Sunday Visitor
$-St. Anthony
    Messenger
$-Testimony—R
$-Vibrant Life—R
$-World & I

PASTORS/LEADERS
$-Ministry Today

WOMEN
Halo Magazine—R

PSYCHOLOGY
ADULT/GENERAL
American Chr. Voice—R
Believers Bay—R
CBN.com—R
$-Christian Courier—R
Christian Online
$-Creative Nonfiction
$-Gem, The—R
$-Light & Life
Our Sunday Visitor
$-Psychology for
    Living—R
$-St. Anthony
    Messenger
$-Testimony—R

PASTORS/LEADERS
Sharing the Practice—R

WOMEN
Halo Magazine—R
$-Mother's Heart

RACISM
ADULT/GENERAL
American Chr. Voice—R
Believers Bay—R
$-Brink Magazine—R
CBN.com—R
$-Christianity Today—R
$-Columbia
$-Creative Nonfiction
$-Eureka Street
$-Faith Today
Genuine Motivation—R
$-Indian Life—R
$-In Touch
$-Light & Life
$-Lookout
Our Sunday Visitor
Perspectives
$-Prairie Messenger—R
Priscilla Papers
$-Prism
$-St. Anthony
    Messenger

$-Testimony—R
$-U.S. Catholic
$-World & I

CHILDREN
$-Guide—R
$-Our Little Friend
$-Primary Treasure
Skipping Stones—R

PASTORS/LEADERS
$-L Magazine—R
$-Ministry Today

TEEN/YOUNG ADULT
$-Direction
Genuine Motivation—R
Single!—R

WOMEN
Halo Magazine—R

RECOVERY
ADULT/GENERAL
American Chr. Voice—R
Believers Bay—R
$-Bible Advocate—R
CBN.com—R
Christian Journal—R
$-Creative Nonfiction
$-Disaster News
$-Good News, The –R
$-Faith Today
$-Home Times—R
$-Indian Life—R
$-In Touch
$-Light & Life
$-Lookout
$-Now What?—R
Our Sunday Visitor
$-Prism
$-Ruminate
$-Seek—R
$-War Cry—R
$-Wildwood Reader—R

PASTORS/LEADERS
$-Ministry Today

TEEN/YOUNG ADULT
Single!—R

WOMEN
Right to the Heart—R

RELATIONSHIPS
ADULT/GENERAL
$-Adoptee Search—R
American Chr. Voice—R
$-Angels on Earth
Believers Bay—R
$Bible Advocate—R
$-Brink Magazine—R
Canada Lutheran
$-Catholic Digest
CBN.com—R
$-Celebrate Life
$-Chicken Soup Bks—R
$-Christian Home &
  School
Christian Journal—R
Christian Online
Christian Ranchman
$-ChristianWeek
$-Creative Nonfiction
$-Evangel—R
$-Family Smart—R
$-Gem, The—R
$-Gems of Truth
Genuine Motivation—R
$-Good News, The –R
$-Guideposts—R
$-Homeschooling
  Today—R
$-Home Times—R
$-Indian Life—R
$-In Touch
Joyful Living—R
Keys to Living—R
$-Light & Life
$-Live—R
$-Lookout
$-Mature Living
$-Mature Years—R
Men of the Cross
New Heart—R
$-Now What?—R
Our Sunday Visitor
$-ParentLife
Penned from the Heart
Pentecostal Evangel
Perspectives

$-Point—R
$-Prairie Messenger—R
Priscilla Papers
$-Seek—R
$-St. Anthony
  Messenger
$-Testimony—R
$-Vibrant Life—R
$-Vision—R
$-War Cry—R
$-Wesleyan Life
$-Wildwood Reader—R
$-World & I

CHILDREN
Skipping Stones—R

PASTORS/LEADERS
$-Leadership—R
$-L Magazine—R
$-SmallGroups.com—R

TEEN/YOUNG ADULT
$-Boundless.org—R
$-Direction
Genuine Motivation—R
$-Insight
Single!—R
$-TC Magazine
$Young Salvationist—R

WOMEN
Dabbling Mum
Halo Magazine—R
$-Hello, Darling—R
$-Mother's Heart
Virtuous Woman

RELIGIOUS
FREEDOM
ADULT/GENERAL
American Chr. Voice—R
$-Arlington Catholic
Believers Bay—R
$-Brink Magazine—R
CBN.com—R
$-Christian Examiner
$-Christian Home &
  School
$-Christianity Today—R
Christian News NW—R

Christian Online
Christian Ranchman
$-ChristianWeek
$-Columbia
$-Commonweal
$-Eureka Street
$-Faith Today
$-Gem, The—R
Genuine Motivation—R
$-Good News, The –R
$-Home Times—R
$-In Touch
$-Light & Life
$-Lookout
Our Sunday Visitor
Perspectives
$-Prairie Messenger—R
$-Prism
$-St. Anthony
    Messenger
$-Seek—R
$-Testimony—R
$-U.S. Catholic
$-War Cry—R
$-World & I

CHILDREN
$-Guide—R
Skipping Stones—R

MISSIONS
$-Operation
    Reveille—R

PASTORS/LEADERS
$-Christian Century—R

TEEN/YOUNG ADULT
$-Direction
Genuine Motivation—R
Single!—R

WOMEN
Virtuous Woman

**RELIGIOUS
TOLERANCE**
ADULT/GENERAL
American Chr. Voice—R
Believers Bay—R
$-Brink Magazine—R

CBN.com—R
$-Christian Examiner
$-Christian Home &
    School
$-Christianity Today—R
Christian Online
$-ChristianWeek
$-Columbia
$-Eureka Street
$-Faith Today
Genuine Motivation—R
$-Good News, Etc.—R
$-Indian Life—R
$-In Touch
$-Light & Life
$-Lookout
Our Sunday Visitor
Perspectives
$-Prairie Messenger—R
$-Seek—R
$-St. Anthony
    Messenger
$-Testimony—R
$-U.S. Catholic
$-War Cry—R
$-World & I

CHILDREN
$-Primary Treasure
Skipping Stones—R

MISSIONS
$-Operation
    Reveille—R
PASTORS/LEADERS
$-Christian Century—R

TEEN/YOUNG ADULT
$-Direction
Genuine Motivation—R
Single!—R

REVIVAL
ADULT/GENERAL
American Chr. Voice—R
Believers Bay—R
$-Bible Advocate—R
CBN.com—R
$-Christian Home &
    School
Christian Journal—R

Christian Ranchman
$-Columbia
$-Good News, Etc.—R
$-Home Times—R
$-In Touch
$-Light & Life
$-Lookout
$-Point—R
$-War Cry—R

PASTORS/LEADERS
$-Ministry Today

TEEN/YOUNG ADULT
$-Insight

WOMEN
Halo Magazine—R

**SALVATION
TESTIMONIES**
ADULT/GENERAL
American Chr. Voice—R
Believers Bay—R
CBN.com—R
$-Christian Home &
    School
Christian Journal—R
Christian Online
Christian Ranchman
$-Christian Research
$-Columbia
$-Decision
Eternal Ink—R
$-Evangel—R
$-Gem, The—R
$-Good News, Etc.—R
$-Guideposts—R
Highway News—R
$-Home Times—R
$-Indian Life—R
$-In Touch
$-Light & Life
$-Live—R
$-Mature Living
New Heart—R
$-Point—R
$-Power for Living—R
$-St. Anthony
    Messenger

$-Seek—R
$-Testimony—R
$-War Cry—R
$-Wesleyan Life

CHILDREN
$-Guide—R

TEEN/YOUNG ADULT
$-Direction
Single!—R

WOMEN
Halo Magazine—R

SCIENCE
ADULT/GENERAL
Answers Magazine
Believers Bay—R
CBN.com—R
$-Christian Courier—R
Creation
Creation Illust.
$-Creative Nonfiction
$-Eureka Street
$-Faith Today
$-Home Times—R
$-In Touch
$-Light & Life
Our Sunday Visitor
Perspectives
$-St. Anthony
    Messenger
$-Testimony—R
$-U.S. Catholic
$-World & I

CHILDREN
$-Animal Trails—R
$-Guide—R
$-Nature Friend—R
Skipping Stones—R

TEEN/YOUNG ADULT
$-Animal Trails—R

SELF-HELP
ADULT/GENERAL
American Chr. Voice—R
Believers Bay—R
$-Catholic Digest

CBN.com—R
Christian Journal—R
$-Family Smart—R
$-Home Times—R
$-In Touch
$-Light & Life
$-Lookout
Men of the Cross
$-St. Anthony
    Messenger
$-Seek—R
$-Testimony—R
$-Vibrant Life—R
$-World & I

CHILDREN
Skipping Stones—R

TEEN/YOUNG ADULT
Single!—R

WOMEN
$-FullFill
Virtuous Woman
Women of the Cross

SENIOR ADULT ISSUES
ADULT/GENERAL
American Chr. Voice—R
$-Angels on Earth
Believers Bay—R
byFaith
CBN.com—R
Christian Ranchman
$-Christian
    Standard—R
$-ChristianWeek
$-City Light News
$-Columbia
$-Evangel—R
$-Family Smart—R
$-Gem, The—R
$-Good News, The –R
$-Home Times—R
$-Indian Life—R
$-In Touch
Joyful Living—R
$-Light & Life
$-Live—R

$-Mature Years—R
Our Sunday Visitor
Penned from the Heart
$-Point—R
$-Power for Living—R
$-St. Anthony
    Messenger
$-Seek—R
$-Testimony—R
$-U.S. Catholic
$-War Cry—R
$-Wesleyan Life

DAILY DEVOTIONALS
Penned from the
    Heart—R

PASTORS/LEADERS
$-L Magazine—R

WOMEN
Halo Magazine—R

SERMONS
ADULT/GENERAL
$-Arlington Catholic
$-Lutheran Journal—R
$-St. Anthony
    Messenger
$-Testimony—R
$-Weavings

PASTORS/LEADERS
$-Ministry Today
$-Preaching
WOMEN
Halo Magazine—R

SHORT STORY: ADULT/GENERAL
Believers Bay—R
$-Best New Writing
CBN.com—R
Christian Journal—R
Halo Magazine—R
$-Indian Life—R
$-Lutheran Journal—R
New Writer's Mag.
Perspectives
$-Purpose—R
$-Ruminate

$-Seek—R
Storyteller—R
Studio—R
$-War Cry—R
$-Wildwood Reader—R

SHORT STORY: ADULT/RELIGIOUS

$-Alive Now
$-Angels on Earth
Believers Bay—R
CBN.com—R
$-Christian Century—R
$-Christian Courier—R
Christian Home1 &
     School
Christian Journal—R
Christian Online
Christian Ranchman
$-Christian Research
$-City Light News
$-Covenant
     Companion—R
$-Eureka Street
$-Evangel—R
$-Gem, The—R
$-Gems of Truth
Halo Magazine—R
$-Homeschooling
     Today—R
$-Home Times—R
$-Image
$-Indian Life—R
$-Live—R
$-Mature Living
Perspectives
$-Purpose—R
Relief Journal
$-Ruminate
$-Shades of Romance
$-St. Anthony
     Messenger
$-Seek—R
$-Testimony—R
$-U.S. Catholic
$-Vision—R
$-War Cry—R
$-Wesleyan Life

SHORT STORY: ADVENTURE

ADULT

$-Angels on Earth
Believers Bay—R
$-Best New Writing
CBN.com—R
Halo Magazine—R
$-Indian Life—R
Storyteller—R
$-Vision—R
$-Weavings

CHILDREN

$-Animal Trails—R
$-Cadet Quest—R
$-Focus/Clubhouse Jr.
Kids' Ark
Skipping Stones—R
$-Sparkle—R

TEEN/YOUNG ADULT

$-Animal Trails—R
$-Cadet Quest—R
$-Direction
Storyteller—R

SHORT STORY: ALLEGORY

ADULT

$-Alive Now
Believers Bay—R
CBN.com—R
Christian Journal—R
$-City Light News
$-Covenant
     Companion—R
$-Gem, The—R
$-Home Times—R
$-Indian Life—R
Men of the Cross
$-Vision—R
Women of the Cross

CHILDREN

$-Nature Friend—R

TEEN/YOUNG ADULT

$-Direction
$-Home Times—R

SHORT STORY: BIBLICAL

ADULT

$-Alive Now
Believers Bay—R
CBN.com—R
Christian Journal—R
Christian Online
Christian Ranchman
$-Evangel—R
$-Gem, The—R
$-Homeschooling
     Today—R
$-Lutheran Journal—R
$-Mature Living
$-Purpose—R
$-Seek—R
$-Wesleyan Life

CHILDREN

Christian Ranchman
Focus/Clubhouse
$-Nature Friend—R
$-Pockets—R
$-Sparkle—R

TEEN/YOUNG ADULT

Christian Ranchman
$-Direction
$-Home Times—R
$-SHINE brightly—R

SHORT STORY: CONTEMPORARY

ADULT

$-Alive Now
$-Angels on Earth
Believers Bay—R
CBN.com—R
$-Christian Century—R
$-Christian Courier—R
$-Christian Home &
     School
$-Covenant
     Companion—R
$-Eureka Street
$-Evangel—R
$-Gem, The—R
New Writer's Mag.
Perspectives

Relief Journal
$-Ruminate
$-Seek—R
$-Shades of Romance
Storyteller—R
$-U.S. Catholic
$-Vision—R
$-War Cry—R
$-Wildwood Reader—R

CHILDREN
$-Cadet Quest—R
Focus/Clubhouse
$-Focus/Clubhouse Jr.
Kids' Ark
$-Pockets—R
$-Sparkle—R

TEEN/YOUNG ADULT
$-Cadet Quest—R
$-Direction
$-Home Times—R
$-SHINE brightly—R
Storyteller—R

SHORT STORY: ETHNIC
ADULT
Believers Bay—R
$-Eureka Street
$-Gem, The—R
Relief Journal
$-Seek—R
$-U.S. Catholic

CHILDREN
Focus/Clubhouse
Kids' Ark
Skipping Stones—R
$-Sparkle—R

SHORT STORY: FANTASY
ADULT
Believers Bay—R
$-Eureka Street
$-Gem, The—R
Storyteller—R

CHILDREN
Focus/Clubhouse

TEEN/YOUNG ADULT
Storyteller—R

SHORT STORY: FRONTIER
ADULT
Believers Bay—R
$-Gem, The—R
$-Indian Life—R
Storyteller—R

CHILDREN
Kids' Ark

TEEN/YOUNG ADULT
$-Home Times—R
Storyteller—R

SHORT STORY: FRONTIER/ ROMANCE
ADULT
Believers Bay—R
$-Gem, The—R
$-Indian Life—R
$-Shades of Romance
Storyteller—R

SHORT STORY: HISTORICAL
ADULT
$-Alive Now
Believers Bay—R
CBN.com—R
$-City Light News
$-Gem, The—R
$-Homeschooling
    Today—R
$-Home Times—R
$-Indian Life—R
New Writer's Mag.
$-Purpose—R
$-Seek—R
Storyteller—R

CHILDREN
Christian Ranchman
Focus/Clubhouse
$-Focus/Clubhouse Jr.
$-Home Times—R
Kids' Ark

$-Nature Friend—R
$-Sparkle—R

TEEN/YOUNG ADULT
Christian Ranchman
$-Home Times—R
$-SHINE brightly—R
Storyteller—R

SHORT STORY: HISTORICAL / ROMANCE
ADULT
Believers Bay—R
CBN.com—R
$-Gem, The—R
$-Indian Life—R
$-Shades of Romance
Storyteller—R

SHORT STORY: HUMOROUS
ADULT
Believers Bay—R
CBN.com—R
$-Christian Courier—R
Christian Journal—R
$-City Light News
$-Covenant
    Companion—R
$-Eureka Street
$-Gem, The—R
Halo Magazine—R
$-Home Times—R
Joyful Living—R
$-Mature Years—R
Men of the Cross
New Writer's Mag.
$-Seek—R
Storyteller—R
$-U.S. Catholic

CHILDREN
$-Animal Trails—R
$-Cadet Quest—R
Christian Ranchman
Focus/Clubhouse
$-Home Times—R
Skipping Stones—R
$-Sparkle—R

TEEN/YOUNG ADULT
$-Animal Trails—R
$-Cadet Quest—R
Christian Ranchman
$-Direction
$-Home Times—R
$-SHINE brightly—R

**SHORT STORY:
JUVENILE**
$-Animal Trails—R
Believers Bay—R
$-Cadet Quest—R
CBN.com—R
Church Herald &
    Holiness
Focus/Clubhouse
$-Focus/Clubhouse Jr.
Halo Magazine—R
Keys for Kids
Kids' Ark
$-Pockets—R
$-Seek—R
$-SHINE brightly—R
Skipping Stones—R
$-Sparkle—R

**SHORT STORY:
LITERARY**
ADULT
Believers Bay—R
$-Christian Courier—R
$-Covenant
    Companion—R
$-Eureka Street
$-Gem, The—R
$-Indian Life—R
Perspectives
Relief Journal
$-Ruminate
$-Seek—R
Storyteller—R
Studio—R
$-U.S. Catholic
$-War Cry—R
$-Wildwood Reader—R

CHILDREN
$-Shine Brightly—R
Skipping Stones—R

TEEN/YOUNG ADULT
$-Home Times—R
$-SHINE brightly—R

**SHORT STORY:
MYSTERY/
ROMANCE**
Believers Bay—R
$-Direction
$-Gem, The—R
$-Shades of Romance
Storyteller—R

**SHORT STORY:
MYSTERY/SUSPENSE**
ADULT
Believers Bay—R
$-Best New Writing
CBN.com—R
$-Gem, The—R
Relief Journal
Storyteller—R

CHILDREN
$-Animal Trails—R
Kids' Ark
TEEN/YOUNG ADULT
$-Animal Trails—R
$-Direction
$-SHINE brightly—R

**SHORT STORY:
PARABLES**
ADULT
Believers Bay—R
$-Christian Courier—R
Christian Journal—R
$-Covenant
    Companion—R
$-Gem, The—R
$-Indian Life—R
$-Lutheran Journal—R
Perspectives
$-Seek—R
$-Testimony—R

CHILDREN
$-Focus/Clubhouse Jr.

TEEN/YOUNG ADULT
$-Home Times—R

$-Testimony—R

**SHORT STORY:
PLAYS**
$-Drama Ministry—R
$-SHINE brightly—R
Studio—R

**SHORT STORY:
ROMANCE**
Believers Bay—R
CBN.com—R
$-Gem, The—R
$-Shades of Romance
Storyteller—R
$-Wildwood Reader—R

**SHORT STORY:
SCIENCE FICTION**
ADULT
Believers Bay—R
$-Eureka Street
$-Gem, The—R
Storyteller—R
Studio—R
CHILDREN
Kids' Ark

TEEN/YOUNG ADULT
$-Direction
$-Home Times—R

**SHORT STORY:
SENIOR ADULT**
Believers Bay—R
$-Indian Life—R
$-Mature Years—R
$-St. Anthony
    Messenger
$-Seek—R
Storyteller—R
Studio—R

**SHORT STORY:
SKITS**
ADULT
$-Drama Ministry—R

CHILDREN
$-Drama Ministry—R

$-Focus/Clubhouse Jr.
$-SHINE brightly—R
$-Sparkle—R

TEEN/YOUNG ADULT
$-Drama Ministry—R
$-SHINE brightly—R

SHORT STORY: SPECULATIVE
ADULT
Believers Bay—R
$-Eureka Street
Relief Journal

TEEN/YOUNG ADULT
$-Home Times—R

SHORT STORY: TEEN/YOUNG ADULT
$-Animal Trails—R
Believers Bay—R
$-Cadet Quest—R
CBN.com—R
$-Direction
Halo Magazine—R
$-Indian Life—R
$-Seek—R
$-SHINE brightly—R
Skipping Stones—R
$-Sparkle—R
$-Testimony—R

SHORT STORY: WESTERNS
ADULT
Believers Bay—R
$-Indian Life—R
Storyteller—R

CHILDREN
Christian Ranchman
Kids' Ark

TEEN/YOUNG ADULT
Christian Ranchman

SINGLES' ISSUES
ADULT/GENERAL
American Chr. Voice—R

Believers Bay—R
$-Bible Advocate—R
$-Brink Magazine—R
CBN.com—R
$-Christian Examiner
Christian Journal—R
Christian Online
Christian Ranchman
$-ChristianWeek
$-Columbia
$-Evangel—R
$-Faith Today
$-Family Smart—R
$-Gem, The—R
Genuine Motivation—R
$-Good News, The –R
$-Home Times—R
$-In Touch
Joyful Living—R
$-Light & Life
$-Live—R
$-Lookout
$-Now What?—R
Our Sunday Visitor
Penned from the
    Heart—R
$-Point—R
$-Power for Living—R
Priscilla Papers
$-Psychology for
    Living—R
$-St. Anthony
    Messenger
$-Seek—R
$-Testimony—R
$-U.S. Catholic
$-Vibrant Life—R
$-Wesleyan Life
$-Wildwood Reader—R
$-World & I

DAILY DEVOTIONALS
$-Brink Magazine—R
Penned from the
    Heart—R

PASTORS/LEADERS
$-L Magazine—R
$-Ministry Today

TEEN/YOUNG ADULT
$-Boundless.org—R
Genuine Motivation—R
$-TC Magazine
$Young Salvationist—R

WOMEN
$-Mother's Heart
Virtuous Woman
Women of the Cross

SMALL-GROUP HELPS
ADULT/GENERAL
American Chr. Voice—R
Believers Bay—R
$-Ministry Today
$-SmallGroups.com—R

TEEN/YOUNG ADULT
$Young Salvationist—R

SOCIAL JUSTICE
ADULT/GENERAL
American Chr. Voice—R
$-Arlington Catholic
Believers Bay—R
$-Brink Magazine—R
Canada Lutheran
CBN.com—R
$-Christian Courier—R
$-Christianity Today—R
Christian Online
$-Christian
    Standard—R
$-ChristianWeek
$-Columbia
$-Commonweal
$-Covenant
    Companion—R
$-Creative Nonfiction
$-Cresset, The
$-Disaster News
$-Eureka Street
$-Faith Today
$-Gem, The—R
Genuine Motivation—R
$-Good News, The –R
$-Indian Life—R
$-In Touch

$-Light & Life
$-Lookout
Our Sunday Visitor
Penned from the
　　Heart—R
Perspectives
$-Prairie Messenger—R
Priscilla Papers
$-Prism
$-St. Anthony
　　Messenger
$-Seek—R
$-Testimony—R
$-United Church
　　Observer
$-War Cry—R
$-World & I

CHILDREN
$-Guide—R
$-Pockets—R
$-SHINE brightly—R
Skipping Stones—R
$-Sparkle—R

*CHRISTIAN EDUCA-
TION/LIBRARIES*
$-Group Magazine
$-Journal/Adventist
　　Ed.—R

PASTORS/LEADERS
$-Christian Century—R
$-L Magazine—R

TEEN/YOUNG ADULT
$-Devo'zine
Genuine Motivation—R
Single!—R
$-TC Magazine

SOCIOLOGY
ADULT/GENERAL
American Chr. Voice—R
Believers Bay—R
$-Christian Courier—R
Christian Online
$-ChristianWeek
$-Creative Nonfiction
$-Gem, The—R
$-In Touch

$-Light & Life
Our Sunday Visitor
Perspectives
Priscilla Papers
$-St. Anthony
　　Messenger
$-Testimony—R
$-World & I

CHILDREN
$-Primary Treasure

WOMEN
Women of the Cross

SPIRITUAL GIFTS
ADULT/GENERAL
American Chr. Voice—R
Believers Bay—R
$-Bible Advocate—R
$-Brink Magazine—R
CBN.com—R
$-Christian Home &
　　School
Christian Journal—R
$-Christianity Today—R
Christian Online
Christian Ranchman
$-Christian
　　Standard—R
$-ChristianWeek
$-Columbia
$-Covenant
　　Companion—R
$-Faith & Friends—R
$-Home Times—R
$-In Touch
Joyful Living—R
$-Light & Life
$-Live—R
$-Mature Living
$-Mature Years—R
Penned from the
　　Heart—R
Priscilla Papers
$-St. Anthony
　　Messenger
$-Seek—R
$-Testimony—R

CHILDREN
$-Guide—R
$-Our Little Friend
$-SHINE brightly—R
$-Sparkle—R

DAILY DEVOTIONALS
Penned from the
　　Heart—R

PASTORS/LEADERS
$-Ministry Today

TEEN/YOUNG ADULT
$-Direction
Single!—R
$-TC Magazine

WOMEN
Halo Magazine—R
Virtuous Woman

SPIRITUALITY
ADULT/GENERAL
$-Alive Now
American Chr. Voice—R
$-Angels on Earth
$-Arlington Catholic
Believers Bay—R
$-Bible Advocate—R
$-Brink Magazine—R
$-Catholic Digest
CBN.com—R
$-Christian Courier—R
$-Christianity Today—R
Christian Journal—R
Christian Online
$-ChristianWeek
$-Columbia
$-Common Ground—R
$-Covenant
　　Companion—R
Eternal Ink—R
$-Eureka Street
$-Faith & Friends—R
$-Faith Today
$-Gem, The—R
Genuine Motivation—R
$-Good News, The –R
$-Guideposts—R
$-Indian Life—R

$-In Touch
$-Light & Life
$-Lookout
$-Mature Years—R
New Heart—R
Our Sunday Visitor
Penned from the Heart
Penwood Review
$-Prairie Messenger—R
$-Presbyterians Today
Priscilla Papers
$-St. Anthony
    Messenger
$-Seek—R
$-Testimony—R
$-U.S. Catholic
$-Weavings
$-World & I

CHILDREN
Skipping Stones—R

CHRISTIAN EDUCA-TION/LIBRARIES
$-Group Magazine
DAILY DEVOTIONALS
Penned from the
    Heart—R

PASTORS/LEADERS
$-Christian Century—R
$-Leadership—R
$-L Magazine—R
$-Ministry Today
Sharing the Practice—R

TEEN/YOUNG ADULT
$-Direction
Genuine Motivation—R
Single!—R
$-TC Magazine
$Young Salvationist—R

WOMEN
Women of the Cross

SPIRITUAL LIFE
ADULT/GENERAL
American Chr. Voice—R
Believers Bay—R
$-Bible Advocate—R

$-Brink Magazine—R
$-Catholic Digest
CBN.com—R
$-Christian Examiner
$-Christian Home &
    School
Christian Journal—R
Christian Online
Christian Ranchman
$-Christian Research
$-ChristianWeek
$-Columbia
$-Covenant
    Companion—R
Eternal Ink—R
$-Faith & Friends—R
$-Good News, The –R
Highway News—R
$-Home Times—R
$-Indian Life—R
$-In Touch
Joyful Living—R
Leaves—R
$-Light & Life
$-Lookout
$-Lutheran Journal—R
$-Mature Living
New Heart—R
Our Sunday Visitor
$-ParentLife
Penned from the
    Heart—R
Perspectives
$-Prairie Messenger—R
$-Presbyterians Today
Priscilla Papers
$-Ruminate
$-St. Anthony
    Messenger
$-Seek—R
$-Testimony—R
$-War Cry—R
$-Weavings
$-Wildwood Reader—R

CHILDREN
$-Guide—R

CHRISTIAN EDUCA-TION/LIBRARIES
$-Group Magazine

DAILY DEVOTIONALS
$-Brink Magazine—R
Penned from the
    Heart—R

PASTORS/LEADERS
$-Leadership—R
L Magazine
$-Ministry Today
$-SmallGroups.com—R

TEEN/YOUNG ADULT
$-Boundless.org—R
$-Direction
Genuine Motivation—R
Single!—R
$-TC Magazine
$Young Salvationist—R

WOMEN
$-FullFill
$-Mother's Heart
Right to the Heart—R
Virtuous Woman

SPIRITUAL RENEWAL
ADULT/GENERAL
American Chr. Voice—R
Believers Bay—R
$-Bible Advocate—R
$-Brink Magazine—R
Canada Lutheran
CBN.com—R
$-Christian Home &
    School
Christian Journal—R
Christian Online
Christian Ranchman
$-ChristianWeek
$-Columbia
Eternal Ink—R
$-Evangel—R
Genuine Motivation—R
$-Good News, Etc.—R
$-Home Times—R
$-In Touch

$-Light & Life
$-Lookout
$-Mature Living
$-ParentLife
Pentecostal Evangel
$-Point—R
$-Seek—R
$-Testimony—R
$-War Cry—R
$-Wildwood Reader—R

*CHRISTIAN EDUCA-
TION/LIBRARIES*
$-Group Magazine

PASTORS/LEADERS
$-Christian Century—R
$-Leadership—R
L Magazine
$-Ministry Today

TEEN/YOUNG ADULT
$-Direction
Genuine Motivation—R
Single!—R
$-TC Magazine
$Young Salvationist—R
WOMEN
Halo Magazine—R
Right to the Heart—R
Virtuous Woman

SPIRITUAL
WARFARE
ADULT/GENERAL
American Chr. Voice—R
$-Angels on Earth
Believers Bay—R
$-Bible Advocate—R
$-Brink Magazine—R
CBN.com—R
$-Celebrate Life
$-Christian Home &
School
Christian Journal—R
$-Christianity Today—R
Christian Online
Christian Ranchman
$-Christian Research
$-ChristianWeek
$-Columbia

$-Faith & Friends—R
$-Gem, The—R
$-Good News, Etc.—R
$-Indian Life—R
Joyful Living—R
$-Light & Life
$-Lookout
$-Mature Living
New Heart—R
Penned from the Heart
$-St. Anthony
   Messenger
$-Seek—R
$-Testimony—R
$-War Cry—R

*CHRISTIAN EDUCA-
TION/LIBRARIES*
$-Group Magazine

DAILY DEVOTIONALS
Penned from the
   Heart—R

PASTORS/LEADERS
$-Growth Points—R
$-Ministry Today
$-Small Groups.
   com—R

TEEN/YOUNG ADULT
Single!—R
$Young Salvationist—R

WOMEN
Halo Magazine—R
$-Mother's Heart

SPORTS/
RECREATION
ADULT/GENERAL
$-Abilities
$-Angels on Earth
$-Arlington Catholic
Believers Bay—R
CBN.com—R
$-City Light News
$-Eureka Street
$-Family Smart—R
$-Gem, The—R
$-Good News, Etc.—R

$-Guideposts—R
$-Home Times—R
$-In Touch
$-Living Light—R
$-Lookout
Our Sunday Visitor
$-Sports Spectrum
$-St. Anthony
   Messenger
Storyteller—R
$-Testimony—R
$-U.S. Catholic
$-Vibrant Life—R
$-World & I

CHILDREN
$-Cadet Quest—R
$-Guide—R
$-SHINE brightly—R

TEEN/YOUNG ADULT
$-Cadet Quest—R
$-Direction
$-Insight
$-TC Magazine

STEWARDSHIP
ADULT/GENERAL
American Chr. Voice—R
$-Angels on Earth
Believers Bay—R
$Bible Advocate—R
Canada Lutheran
CBN.com—R
$-Celebrate Life
$-Christian Courier—R
Christian Journal—R
Christian Online
Christian Ranchman
$-Christian
   Standard—R
$-ChristianWeek
$-Columbia
$-Evangel—R
$-Faith Today
$-Gem, The—R
Genuine Motivation—R
$-Good News, The –R
$-Home Times—R
$-In Touch

$-Light & Life
$-Lookout
$-Lutheran Journal—R
$-Lutheran Witness
Our Sunday Visitor
Penned from the
    Heart—R
Perspectives
$-Power for Living—R
$-Prairie Messenger—R
$-Prism
$-Purpose—R
$-St. Anthony
    Messenger
$-Seek—R
$-Testimony—R
$-United Church
    Observer
$-U.S. Catholic
$-Wesleyan Life

CHILDREN
$-Guide—R
$-SHINE brightly—R
$-Sparkle—R

DAILY DEVOTIONALS
Penned from the
    Heart—R

PASTORS/LEADERS
$-InSite—R
$-L Magazine—R
$-Ministry Today
$-Net Results

TEEN/YOUNG ADULT
$-Boundless.org—R
$-Direction
Genuine Motivation—R
$-TC Magazine

WOMEN
Halo Magazine—R
$-Mother's Heart

**TAKE-HOME
PAPERS**
ADULT/GENERAL
$-Evangel—R
$-Gem, The—R

$-Gems of Truth
$-Power for Living—R
$-Purpose—R
$-Seek—R
$-Vision—R

CHILDREN
$-Guide—R
$-Juniorway
$-Our Little Friend
$-Primary Treasure

TEEN/YOUNG ADULT
$-Insight

THEOLOGICAL
ADULT/GENERAL
$-Alive Now
$-America
American Chr. Voice—R
$-Arlington Catholic
Believers Bay—R
$-Bible Advocate—R
$-Brink Magazine—R
byFaith
CBN.com—R
$-Christian Courier—R
$-Christianity Today—R
Christian Online
Christian Ranchman
$-Christian Research
$-Christian
    Standard—R
$-Cresset, The
$-Eureka Street
$-In Touch
$-Light & Life
$-Lookout
$-Mature Living
Movieguide
Our Sunday Visitor
Perspectives
$-Prairie Messenger—R
Priscilla Papers
$-St. Anthony
    Messenger
$-Testimony—R
$-United Church
    Observer
$-U.S. Catholic

**CHRISTIAN EDUCA-
TION/LIBRARIES**
$-Group Magazine

DAILY DEVOTIONALS
$-Brink Magazine—R
Penned from the
    Heart—R

PASTORS/LEADERS
$-Christian Century—R
$-Growth Points—R
$-L Magazine—R
$-Parish Liturgy
$-Reformed Worship
Sharing the Practice—R
$-SmallGroups.com—R

THINK PIECES
ADULT/GENERAL
$-Alive Now
American Chr. Voice—R
Believers Bay—R
$-Brink Magazine—R
$-Christian Courier—R
$-Christianity Today—R
Christian Online
$-ChristianWeek
$-City Light News
$-Eureka Street
$-Faith Today
$-Gem, The—R
Genuine Motivation—R
$-In Touch
$-Light & Life
$-Lookout
Men of the Cross
Our Sunday Visitor
Penned from the
    Heart—R
Penwood Review
$-St. Anthony
    Messenger
$-Seek—R
$-Testimony—R
$-World & I

CHILDREN
Skipping Stones—R

PASTORS/LEADERS
$-Enrichment—R
$-L Magazine—R
$-Ministry Today

TEEN/YOUNG ADULT
Genuine Motivation—R
Single!—R
$-TC Magazine

WOMEN
$-Hello, Darling—R
$-Mother's Heart
Women of the Cross

TIME
MANAGEMENT
ADULT/GENERAL
American Chr. Voice—R
Believers Bay—R
$-Brink Magazine—R
$-CBA Retailers
CBN.com—R
Christian Journal—R
Christian Online
$-ChristianWeek
$-Gem, The—R
Genuine Motivation—R
$-Home Times—R
$-In Touch
Joyful Living—R
$-Light & Life
$-Living Light—R
$-Lookout
Men of the Cross
$-ParentLife
Penned from the
    Heart—R
$-St. Anthony
    Messenger
$-Testimony—R
$-World & I

DAILY DEVOTIONALS
$-Brink Magazine—R
Penned from the
    Heart—R

PASTORS/LEADERS
$-Enrichment—R

TEEN/YOUNG ADULT
$-Boundless.org—R
$-Direction
Genuine Motivation—R

WOMEN
$-Mother's Heart
Single!—R
Virtuous Woman

WRITERS
$-Fellowscript—R
$-Writer

TRAVEL
ADULT/GENERAL
$-Abilities
American Chr. Voice—R
$-Arlington Catholic
$-Angels on Earth
Believers Bay—R
$-Brink Magazine—R
CBN.com—R
$-City Light News
$-Common Ground—R
$-Creative Nonfiction
$-Gem, The—R
Genuine Motivation—R
$-In Touch
$-Mature Years—R
Movieguide
$-ParentLife
$-Seek—R
Storyteller—R
$-Testimony—R
$-World & I

CHILDREN
$-Animal Trails—R
$-SHINE brightly—R
Skipping Stones—R
$-Sparkle—R

TEEN/YOUNG ADULT
$-Animal Trails—R
Genuine Motivation—R
Single!—R

TRUE STORIES
ADULT/GENERAL
$-Adoptee Search—R

American Chr. Voice—R
$-Angels on Earth
Believers Bay—R
$-Brink Magazine—R
byFaith
$-Catholic Digest
CBN.com—R
$-Celebrate Life
Christian Journal—R
Christian Online
Christian Ranchman
$-City Light News
$-Columbia
$-Creative Nonfiction
$-Disaster News
$-Gem, The—R
$-Gems of Truth
Genuine Motivation—R
$-Good News, The –R
$-Good News, Etc.—R
$-Guideposts—R
Highway News—R
$-Home Times—R
$-Indian Life—R
$-In Touch
Joyful Living—R
Leaves—R
$-Light & Life
$-Live—R
$-Lutheran Digest—R
$-Mature Living
Men of the Cross
New Heart—R
$-Now What?—R
$-ParentLife
Penned from the Heart
Pentecostal Evangel
$-Power for Living—R
$-St. Anthony
    Messenger
$-Seek—R
Storyteller—R
$-Testimony—R
$-Vision—R

CHILDREN
$-Animal Trails—R
$-Cadet Quest—R
$-Focus/Clubhouse Jr.
$-Guide—R

$-Our Little Friend
$-Pockets—R
$-Primary Treasure
$-SHINE brightly—R
Skipping Stones—R
$-Sparkle—R

MISSIONS
$-Operation
  Reveille—R

PASTORS/LEADERS
$-Leadership—R

TEEN/YOUNG ADULT
$-Animal Trails—R
$-Cadet Quest—R
$-Direction
Genuine Motivation—R
$-Insight
$-TC Magazine
$-YouthWalk

WOMEN
Halo Magazine—R
$-Hello, Darling—R
$-Mother's Heart

VIDEO REVIEWS
ADULT/GENERAL
$-Arlington Catholic
Believers Bay—R
CBN.com—R
$-Eureka Street
Genuine Motivation—R
$-Home Times—R
$-Indian Life—R
Movieguide
Our Sunday Visitor
Perspectives
$-Presbyterians Today
$-Testimony—R

PASTORS/LEADERS
$-Christian Century—R
$-Ministry Today

TEEN/YOUNG ADULT
$-Devo'zine
Genuine Motivation—R
Single!—R

$Young Salvationist—R

WOMEN
Dabbling Mum
$-Mother's Heart
Virtuous Woman

WEBSITE REVIEWS
ADULT/GENERAL
Believers Bay—R
CBN.com—R
$-Christianity Today—R
Christian Journal—R
Our Sunday Visitor
$-World & I

MISSIONS
$-Operation
  Reveille—R

TEEN/YOUNG ADULT
Single!—R

WOMEN'S ISSUES
ADULT/GENERAL
$-Abilities
$-Alive Now
American Chr. Voice—R
$-Arlington Catholic
Believers Bay—R
$-Brink Magazine—R
$-CBA Retailers
CBN.com—R
$-Celebrate Life
$-Chicken Soup Bks—R
$-Christian Courier—R
$-Christian Examiner
Christian Journal—R
Christian Online
Christian Ranchman
$-ChristianWeek
$-Columbia
$-Creative Nonfiction
$-EFCA Today
$-Evangel—R
$-Faith Today
$-Family Smart—R
$-Gem, The—R
$-Good News, The –R
$-Indian Life—R
Joyful Living—R

$-Light & Life
$-Live—R
$-Lookout
Our Sunday Visitor
$-ParentLife
Penned from the Heart
Perspectives
$-Point—R
Priscilla Papers
$-Psychology for
  Living—R
$-Purpose—R
$-St. Anthony
  Messenger
$-Seek—R
Share
$-Testimony—R
$-United Church
  Observer
$-U.S. Catholic
$-Vibrant Life—R
$-Wesleyan Life
$-World & I

CHILDREN
Skipping Stones—R

DAILY DEVOTIONALS
Penned from the
  Heart—R

PASTORS/LEADERS
$-L Magazine—R
$-SmallGroups.com—R

TEEN/YOUNG ADULT
$-Boundless.org—R
Single!—R

WOMEN
Dabbling Mum
$-FullFill
Halo Magazine—R
$-Hello, Darling—R
$-Mother's Heart
Right to the Heart—R
Share
Virtuous Woman
Women of the Cross

WORKPLACE ISSUES
ADULT/GENERAL
American Chr. Voice—R
Believers Bay—R
byFaith
CBN.com—R
$-Christian Examiner
Christian Journal—R
Christian News NW—R
Christian Online
Christian Ranchman
$-Christian Retailing
$-Eureka Street
$-Evangel—R
$-Faith & Friends—R
$-Faith Today
$-Good News, The –R
$-Good News, Etc.—R
$-In Touch
Joyful Living—R
$-Light & Life
$-Live—R
$-Lookout
New Heart—R
Our Sunday Visitor
$-ParentLife
Penned from the
    Heart—R
Perspectives
$-Point—R
$-Purpose—R
$-Seek—R
$-Testimony—R
$-World & I

MISSIONS
$-Operation
    Reveille—R

TEEN/YOUNG ADULT
$-Boundless.org—R
Single!—R

WOMEN
$-FullFill

WORLD ISSUES
ADULT/GENERAL
American Chr. Voice—R
$-Arlington Catholic

Believers Bay—R
$-Brink Magazine—R
CBN.com—R
$-Christian Examiner
Christian Online
$-ChristianWeek
$-Columbia
$-Creative Nonfiction
$-Eureka Street
$-Evangel—R
$-Gem, The—R
Genuine Motivation—R
$-Good News, Etc.—R
$-Home Times—R
$-Indian Life—R
$-In Touch
$-Light & Life
$-Lookout
Movieguide
Our Sunday Visitor
Penned from the
    Heart—R
Perspectives
$-Prism
$-Purpose—R
$-St. Anthony
    Messenger
$-Seek—R
$-Testimony—R
$-United Church
    Observer
$-World & I

CHILDREN
$-Guide—R
Skipping Stones—R

MISSIONS
$-Operation
    Reveille—R

PASTORS/LEADERS
$-Christian Century—R
L Magazine
$-Ministry Today

TEEN/YOUNG ADULT
Genuine Motivation—R
Single!—R
$-TC Magazine

WORSHIP
ADULT/GENERAL
American Chr. Voice—R
$-Angels on Earth
$-Arlington Catholic
Believers Bay—R
$-Bible Advocate—R
$-Brink Magazine—R
Canada Lutheran
CBN.com—R
$-Christian Examiner
$-Christianity Today—R
Christian Journal—R
Christian Online
Christian Ranchman
$-Christian
    Standard—R
$-ChristianWeek
$-Columbia
Eternal Ink—R
$-Evangel—R
Highway News—R
$-In Touch
$-Light & Life
$-Lookout
$-Lutheran Journal—R
Penned from the Heart
Perspectives
$-Point—R
$-Power for Living—R
$-Prairie Messenger—R
$-Presbyterians Today
Priscilla Papers
$-St. Anthony
    Messenger
$-Seek—R
$-Testimony—R
Time of Singing
$-United Church
    Observer
$-U.S. Catholic
$-Wesleyan Life
$-World & I

CHILDREN
Keys for Kids
$-Sparkle—R

CHRISTIAN EDUCATION/LIBRARIES
$-Group Magazine

DAILY DEVOTIONALS
$-Brink Magazine—R
Penned from the
    Heart—R

PASTORS/LEADERS
$-Enrichment—R
$-Growth Points—R
$-Leadership—R
$-L Magazine—R
$-Ministry Today
$-Parish Liturgy
$-Preaching
$-Reformed Worship

TEEN/YOUNG ADULT
$-Direction
$-Insight
Single!—R
$-TC Magazine
$Young Salvationist—R

WOMEN
Halo Magazine—R
$-Mother's Heart
Virtuous Woman

WRITING HOW-TO
ADULT/GENERAL
Believers Bay—R
Canada Lutheran
$-CBA Retailers
CBN.com—R
Christian Journal—R
Christian Online
$-Home Times—R
Penwood Review
$-St. Anthony
    Messenger
Storyteller—R
$-World & I

CHILDREN
$-SHINE brightly—R
Skipping Stones—R

PASTORS/LEADERS
$-Newsletter Newsletter

WOMEN
Dabbling Mum
$-Mother's Heart
Right to the Heart—R

WRITERS
$-Best New Writing
$-Christian
Communicator—R
$-Fellowscript—R
$-Freelance   Writer's
Report—R
New Writer's Mag.
$-Poets & Writers
$-Shades of Romance
$-Writer
Writer's Chronicle
Writer's Digest
WritersWeekly.com—R

YOUNG-WRITER MARKETS
Note: These publications
have indicated they will
accept submissions from
children or teens (C or T)
ADULT/GENERAL
$-Adoptee Search—(C
    or T)
American Chr. Voice (C
    or T)
CBN.com—R (T)
$-Celebrate Life (C or
    T)
$-Christian Herald
$-Christian Home &
    School (C or T)
Christian Journal (C
    or T)
Christian Online (C
    or T)
$-ChristianWeek (T)
Church Herald &
    Holiness (C or T)
$-City Light News (T)
$-Creative Nonfiction
    (T)

$-Drama Ministry (T)
$-Dreamseeker (C or T)
Eternal Ink (C or T)
$-Homeschooling Today
    (C or T)
$-Home Times (T)
Indian Life (C or T)
Joyful Living (C or T)
$-Leben (T)
$-Light & Life (C or T)
$-Lutheran Journal—R
    (C or T)
Men of the Cross (T)
Penned from the Heart
    (C or T)
$Prairie Messenger (T)
$-Priority! (C or T)
Storyteller (C or T

CHILDREN
$-Focus/Clubhouse (C)
Kids' Ark (C or T)
$-Pockets (C)

DAILY DEVOTIONALS
Penned from the Heart
    (C or T)

TEEN/YOUNG ADULT
$-Boundless.org (T)
$-Direction (T)
$-Insight (T)
$-SHINE brightly (T)
$-Take Five Plus (T)
$-TC Magazine (T)

WOMEN
Dabbling Mum (T)
$-Mother's Heart (T)
Women of the Cross (T)

WRITERS
$-Fellowscript—R (T)

YOUTH ISSUES
ADULT/GENERAL
American Chr. Voice—R
$-Arlington Catholic
Believers Bay—R
Canada Lutheran
CBN.com—R

$-Chicken Soup Bks—R
$-Christian Examiner
$-Christian Home &
    School
Christian Online
Christian Ranchman
$-ChristianWeek
$-Columbia
$-EFCA Today
$-Eureka Street
$-Family Smart—R
$-Good News, The –R
$-Homeschooling
    Today—R
$-Home Times—R
$-Indian Life—R
$-In Touch
Our Sunday Visitor
Penned from the Heart
$-Point—R
$-Prairie Messenger—R
$-St. Anthony
    Messenger
$-Seek—R
$-Testimony—R
$-U.S. Catholic
$-Wesleyan Life
$-World & I

$-Cadet Quest—R
$-Devo'zine
$-Direction
$-Insight
Sisterhood
$-Take Five Plus—R
$-TC Magazine
$Young Salvationist—R
$-YouthWalk

WOMEN
Halo Magazine—R
  $-Mother's Heart

CHILDREN
$-Animal Trails—R
$-Cadet Quest—R
$-Guide—R
Keys for Kids
$-SHINE brightly—R
Skipping Stones—R
$-Sparkle—R

CHRISTIAN EDUCA-TION/LIBRARIES
$-Group Magazine
$-Journal/Adventist
    Ed.—R

PASTORS/LEADERS
$-InSite—R
$-L Magazine—R
$-YouthWorker

TEEN/YOUNG ADULT
$-Animal Trails—R

BONUS SECTION

Writer's Helps

Popular Articles

Twelve Articles at a Glance

by Les Stobbe

1. Feature

A feature article may cover a topic, an event, a person, or a movement. An article in *The Boston Globe* on what churches in Massachusetts are doing to help the deaf worship carried the headline "Deaf 'at Home' at Grace Chapel." A feature article on how the Southern Baptists deal with racism was presented in World magazine under the headline "Rising from the Ashes of Racism." "Possessed or Obsessed?" in Christianity Today covered the issue of demon possession and American Christianity. Feature articles require in-depth and often broad research because so much information is needed to fully present the issue.

2. Inspirational

Inspirational articles present uplifting examples of kindness, sacrifice, and community spirit. The article "Help, Hard Work Create a 'Miracle'" is an excellent example, showing how two women made possible a huge improvement in the life of a single mother. Some inspirational articles, usually in first person, feature how a person or organization overcame huge odds to become successful.

3. Personality (or Profile)

Prominent speakers, authors, musicians, sports figures, artistic giants: all interest readers. People want to know as much as possible about their heroes. In smaller communities, a teacher who served 25 to 30 years may have influenced so many lives that a personality profile would interest a local newspaper.

4. Devotional

Designed to increase the reader's understanding of how spiritual truth applies to life, the devotional frequently uses brief illustrations of experiences with the Lord. Besides daily devotional publications, many other Christian periodicals are open to this kind of article.

5. How-To

How-to articles cover everything from how to pray more effectively to how to make your senior years count for eternity. Magazines covering such sports as golf, fishing, and hunting carry how-to articles. Magazines for gardeners and hobbyists of all kinds also use these pieces. You don't have to be the expert — just interview the expert. You enjoy the benefits of "borrowed credentials."

6. Seasonal

The Christian seasons, as well as school and community seasonal events, provide excellent opportunities. Specialized or denominational magazines, newspapers, and many other publications plan their seasonal articles well in advance — some periodicals by almost a year.

7. Expository

Christian magazines have a consistent diet of expository articles, in which the writer expounds on a Bible passage, often comparing Scripture with Scripture. The more interesting and life-changing ones provide application of biblical truth to life.

8. True Adventure

If you climb the highest mountain, get marooned at sea, are kidnapped by guerrillas in Colombia, or teach music to children of prisoners in Nepal, you have adventures that may well interest others. But it may also be kayaking down the Colorado River that gets you into an impossible situation from which you escape — with a story to tell.

And it may be something not nearly as dramatic. It's not the action itself, but what you experienced, that deepened your faith, love, and compassion (or gave you a new sense of the greatness of God) that makes such an article interesting and inspirational. These are all first-person articles with strong human interest. You can also write in the third person about someone else's adventure and what he or she learned from it, but you'll likely find that even their story is best told in the first-person.

9. Humorous

Humorous Christian writing, once rare, has become acceptable in recent decades. Many detail life experiences that, on reflection, were terribly funny. Other articles are by people to whom God has given a unique ability to see even tough experiences from a humorous perspective. Some articles poke fun at our foibles, helping us to laugh at ourselves.

10. Investigative

The investigative article has come into its own with Christianity Today and World magazines. These, however, require solid experience and special skills as a reporter, for there are many pitfalls for the writer in our litigious society. Usually this article type involves dealing with resistant sources.

11. Argumentative

Typically, the argumentative article is a reasoned presentation of apologetic truth designed to overcome the objections of unbelievers. It may, however, also cover an area of doctrine under dispute, such as raged in recent years over "open theism." Such an article may pit writers with opposing viewpoints against each other in a print version of TV's *Crossfire*.

12. Op-Ed

The Op-Ed article often appears in newspapers on the page opposite the editorial page. Also called a think piece or opinion piece, it presents a definite perspective on an issue that attempts to make people think differently about it. Religious issues, environmental issues, civil rights issues, war and peace, conflicts in another part of the world — all these and more can be discussed.

Used by permission of the Jerry Jenkins Writers Guild.

Five Essentials of Every Article
by Les Stobbe

REGARDLESS THE TOPIC OR APPROACH, every article needs these:

- A topic or subject that appeals to a large number of readers.

- A fresh approach to a topic or human relationship issue.

- Enough information to provide a factual basis for the discussion.

- Engaging writing that attracts readers.

- The stuff that life is made of: conflict, drama, pathos, and/or humor.

Ten Reasons to Use Story

by Les Stobbe

1. Stories provoke curiosity

You may have noticed how intensely curious your children or grandchildren are about your growing-up years. One story arouses curiosity about other aspects of your life. Kids want to hear the same story over and over (at least until they're teenagers). A writer starting an article with a story can evoke sustained curiosity throughout the whole piece.

2. Stories bind us to the universal human family

When I initiate conversation with a seatmate on an airplane, I usually bring up a story of how God has been at work in my life. The seatmate may be of any race or nationality, but a personal story ties us together while also serving as a vehicle of truth. Carefully selected stories in articles can bridge our differences. In his book *The Meaning of Shakespeare,* Harold Clarke Goddard writes, "The destiny of the world is determined less by the battles that are lost and won than by the stories it loves and believes in."

3. Stories help us remember

Stories about Jesus help us remember His gracious, loving way of dealing with people. Stories about the Holocaust help us remember the terror of sin run riot. Among the Bari in the jungles of Colombia, Bruce Olson discovered that their stories were told in song while lying in hammocks in their long house, so he joined them and sang the stories of the Bible. In time, almost every member of the tribe became a believer.

4. Stories let us communicate in a special language

Storyteller Robert Bela Wilhelm calls the declarative language of daylight hours our "daytime talk." At night, our minds are flooded with dreams, stories — the language of the subconscious with its marvelous images and fantasies. Wilhelm calls this "nighttime talk." Think of the special resonance created in the viewers of the movies *Chariots of Fire* (1981) and *Amistad* (1997), with their special languages of commitment to Christ.

5. Stories provide escape

Escaping isn't necessarily negative. It helps us get away from the tyranny of the urgent and gives us a chance to regroup, reform, and reenter life. All of us need to escape from hurts occasionally. We need the subliminal affirmations of a story. When families gather after the death of a loved one, funny, happy, touching stories about that person help them remember the good times and begin to heal.

6. Stories evoke tenderness and therefore wholeness

Because people have such different interests, experiences, temperaments, and dreams, we need to listen to each other's stories. Truly listening to their wives' stories evokes the tenderness God placed in men; they become whole persons, and marriages become better. When people hear the real stories of students, children, friends, coworkers, or spouses, they often replace annoyance with understanding. When you tell of deeds of kindness, of people reaching out to the hurting, your articles will also evoke tenderness.

7. Stories promote healing

A pastor's story of Mary Magdalene promoted healing in the congregation. David Seamands' books (for example, Healing for Damaged Emotions) contain wonderful stories that promote healing. For me, stories in In the Eye of the Storm, by Max Lucado, provided healing during a traumatic event in my life. Philip Yancey's excursions into the stories of Tolstoy and Dostoyevsky helped him heal spiritually.

8. Stories provide a basis for hope and morality

Peter asked Jesus, "How many times shall I forgive my brother when he sins against me? Up to seven times?" Jesus used hyperbole to make His point, then immediately launched into the story of the ungrateful forgiven debtor (Matthew 18:23-35). Anyone reading the story finds it a mirror, revealing both our unwillingness to forgive but also the way to release.

9. Stories are the basis for ministry

Need more Sunday school teachers in your church? Get a 20-year veteran to tell of the impact she had on a child — in fact, a whole family of children. Are you in the middle of a stewardship campaign? Have someone tell how God blessed bountiful giving. Write the stories and print them in your newsletter for double impact.

10. A story holds the reader accountable

This bears repeating: The memory hooks of a story give it longevity in the reader's mind and conscience. People will remember a powerful story in your article long beyond anything else you've written.

Used by permission of the Jerry Jenkins Writers Guild.

Six Ways to End an Article
by Les Stobbe

YOUR READER NEEDS TO FEEL that the end of the article ties up loose ends or projects ahead for a satisfying conclusion. These make effective endings:

- a wrap-up of the key idea

- a reference to a thought in the opening paragraph

- a concluding quote by a speaker or expert

- a surprise

- a stinger — an unexpected jab in the ribs

- a projection about what might happen

Be careful not to fall in love with one of these and overuse it. Variety will help you develop a reputation as a professional Christian writer. Try using several endings, then decide which is the most satisfying for each article.

Four Keys for Editing an Article

by Les Stobbe

1. Who ought to be interested?

As Christians, we assume that because truth is important, it will find a home in the hearts of the audience.

That's not how it works in articles or books. The dynamics of the marketplace dictate that you're irrelevant if you don't clearly define who ought to be interested in your writing.

This question will also determine both your article style and tone (such as warm and personal, third person and detached, or teaching). Professional nonfiction writers learn to match both style and the tone to each subject and intended audience. Writers eventually become known for their personal styles, but for beginners, experimenting with various styles and tones helps you develop.

Once you have your reader clearly in focus, determine if your style genuinely communicates to that type of person. This means you're asking more than "who?"; you're also asking "why?" That leads to the second general question.

2. What is the purpose for this article?

This is far more profound than it might seem. Your motives as a writer are on trial. You're asking, *Did I write this to please myself or to change lives? Did I write for the glory of God or to gain glory for myself?* And on a more mundane level, *What should this accomplish in the life of the reader?* Busy readers skim publications asking, "What's in this for me?" If they see no clear benefit, they'll move on.

You can lose sight of your purpose as you become emotionally involved in what you're writing.

These are tough things to ask after you've completed an article, but you can lose sight of your purpose as you become emotionally involved in what you're writing. Ideas come, anecdotes are added, more ideas come, more illustrations are added, and your article strays from your intended path. Knowing your goal allows you to identify, then trim material that's good, but not essential for readers.

As the apostle John wrote near the end of his Gospel, "Jesus did many other miraculous signs in the presence of his disciples, which are not recorded in this book. But these are written that you may believe that Jesus is the Christ, the Son of God, and that by believing you may have life in his name" (20:30–31).

The most effective way to force yourself to keep the purpose clearly before you is to write it in one short sentence. If you find yourself with a run-on sentence, your purpose is not sufficiently clear.

Having established the target reader and your purpose, you can move to the third step in self-editing.

3. How do I establish eye contact with my readers?

Once you've written your article, determine how well you're connecting with the reader.

Many writers think of their audience as a readership, a mass of people who need the truth the writer has discovered. But speakers know their audience is composed of individuals. Speakers make eye contact with one to three people and address them as though they were the only ones in the room. We writers need the same focus. Imagine one or two representative readers and address them individually. Don't refer to your reader as "Some of you," or "Many of you," but rather, "You ..."

When you read the Gospel according to Luke, do you feel Dr. Luke was writing it just for you? You have no reason to think otherwise. Yet Luke's mental eyes were clearly fixed on a new Christian — a Greek, Theophilus — and we just happen to be beneficiaries. In the same way, you will do your best work when you have a specific reader in your mind's eye.

How do speakers connect with the crowds? They may tell a story that illustrates a common dilemma, ask questions that identify a felt need, or cite statistics that include those in the room. A common device is to quote a recent mover and shaker in the field. You can make eye contact the same ways. Whether child, teen, or adult, we all respond to someone who identifies with our needs.

Beyond establishing eye contact, ask yourself if your manuscript is capable of achieving your purpose.

4. What have I included to help the reader initiate change?

You may be thinking, *But if I present truth, won't that initiate change?* Unfortunately, we prefer not to change. So truth that might call for change tends to be stored but not applied. Most Christians have truth granaries overflowing with tucked-away truth. Occasionally an event like September 11, 2001, shakes up that granary and some truth spills out, but maybe not enough to make a reader love Arab-American Muslims enough to befriend them, pray for them, and witness to them.

The Greek word for *truth* in John 8:32 can just as easily be translated "reality," and God's reality faced head-on calls for life change. Your job is to present truth as reality in a process that leads to change. That means you need to know something about the psychology of what persuades people to change. Ask yourself:

a. Do I have adequate information to initiate the process of change?
b. Do I have the imaginative content that touches people: word pictures, symbols, analogies, stories, poetry?
c. Have I built in motivational content: positive and negative role models, benefit statements, emotion-grabbing illustrations, how-to content?
d. Have I provided action opportunities that will lead to change?

Decision-making always involves process. We writers have to ask ourselves if we have built in the process that will lead the reader to make good decisions — decisions with eternal consequences.

Used by permission of the Jerry Jenkins Writers Guild.

Ten Ways to Analyze a Periodical

by Les Stobbe

MARKET ANALYSIS will help you:

- Discover the best place for your work.
- Become better acquainted with your target audience so you can more readily establish eye contact with them — and hold their attention.
- Establish writing priorities once you see what magazines carry today.

Solid market analysis is work. There's no easy way, no short cut. Grab a magazine for which you want to write, open a notebook or spreadsheet document, and get started.

1. Look at the cover.

Is it full color, two-color, or black and white? Is it well designed? How frequently is the magazine published? What do the article titles highlighted on the cover say about its target readers?

2. Open to the first two-page spread.

Are the advertisements about events sponsored by a pastor of a specific denomination? Turn page after page, looking at the ads, reading enough of the content to get a feel for the constituency. Does the publication appeal primarily to blue collar people or professional people, or does it try to reach both? Academic types or ministry types?

3. Look over the table of contents.

Solid market analysis is work.

3. How do I

The design alone will tell you if this is a professionally done magazine. Titles will give clues to its typical reader. The writers and their credentials will reveal your competition. Article descriptions reveal whether the magazine will be well written.

4. Examine the masthead.

That's the box listing the magazine staff, the mailing address, the website where you can get more information, and the email address. Request writers guidelines or download them from the website.

5. List the articles.

Note their approximate length, the names of the authors, the kinds of leads they used, their use of stories and quotes, and their theological orientation.

6. Determine the magazine's slant.

Is it positive and encouraging or negative and focused on controversy? Do articles major on one topic: the family, singleness, prayer, the future, prophecy?

7. Does it have editorials or opinion pieces?

Are they all staff written or are there guest editorials from freelancers?

8. Are the general articles primarily personal experience?

Or are they devotional? Inspirational? Investigative? Research oriented? Does it contain mostly first-person or third-person articles

9. Does it use poems?

If so, how long are they? Are the poems free or rhyming verse? Are they storytelling poems or reflective? (The market for poetry is so limited, market research is critical before trying to place one.)

10. Are fillers used?

How many?

Used by permission of the Jerry Jenkins Writers Guild.

Get Ready to Write Devotionals
by Les Stobbe

DEVOTIONAL MEDITATIONS, DONE RIGHT, can reach wide audiences and have staying power. How do you reach this vast readership?

- **Study devotional meditations** that speak to you, that encourage you. Analyze what elements they contain. Do they include a personal experience for every devotional, or do they use a wide variety of stories? How long are they?

- **Take time to deepen your own experience with God,** reading the Bible for how God speaks and acts, praying and listening to His voice.

- **Learn to pay attention to all your senses.** Experiencing God is not merely an intellectual exercise; it may involve all parts of your body. Notice how people talk: the tones of their voices, their dialects, how fast they speak. Notice the sounds around you. Observe how people sit, stand, and walk: posture, gestures, how they hold their heads, their gaits. Taste and smell are closely related, so if you monitor your taste, you'll also become more aware of aromas. Force yourself to be conscious of touch, and you'll be amazed at the richness of the experience.

- **Give your God-given imagination free rein.** Draw analogies between the earthly experiences gained through your senses and spiritual insights acquired during the practice of spiritual disciplines. Become aware of the heavenly meaning in earthly experiences. Write parables and poetry to sharpen your imagination.

- **Journal.** Write your experiences each day, enlisting your senses. Let the Holy Spirit remind you of when you were aware of God. Jot insights you gain as you read His Word and pray, listen to others, and wait quietly for His still, small voice.

- **Get started.** Begin writing devotional meditations for your church's website or your local newspaper. Soon you will have material with which to begin crafting devotionals and submitting them to various national publishers.

Used by permission of the Jerry Jenkins Writers Guild.

Five Traits of a Christian Inspirational Article

by Les Stobbe

INSPIRATIONAL ARTICLES ALSO APPEAR in non-Christian publications. They feature athletes who survive cancer and play on, successful people in all fields who face hardships and come back to become winners again, and officials who rise to the occasion during tragedy. You may write an inspirational article about an award-winning teacher. These do not, however, have the unique inspiration of the Christian article.

Special characteristics of a Christian inspirational article:

Human achievement is not the big feature.

While secular inspirational articles glorify the superhero, the Christian writer remembers that our strength and perseverance come from God — as does our reward. He alone deserves the glory.

They illustrate the power of choice.

The only power we really have is the power of choice. That power opens to us the resources of God through His Holy Spirit. Inspirational articles reveal how choices become the stepping-stones to victory over sin, disabling memories, physical disabilities, and failure.

They illustrate the source of power.

Jean Driscoll was a champion wheelchair racer as an unbeliever, but winning races was all she had. When she became a Christian, she not only raced better, but she also began to have an incredibly powerful witness. As a result, she retired from competition and became a public speaker, witnessing for her Savior. Any complete inspirational article featuring her would have to reveal the source of her power.

They reveal how hope fuels the Christian life.

The apostle Paul wrote that those without Christ are without hope, and he often presented the hope of the believer as eternal life both now and beyond the grave. Inspirational articles show how hope overcomes fear and provides an inner security that helps Christians surmount the most horrible difficulties.

They reveal the source of truth about life.

Inspirational articles point to Scripture as the source of strength, courage, and hope. What can be more inspiring than Paul's writing of Christ, "I can do everything through him who gives me strength" (Philippians 4:13)? Quotations from the Bible don't necessarily make an inspirational article Christian, but a Christian inspirational article will have at least one direct quote or specific reference from the Bible.

Used by permission of the Jerry Jenkins Writers Guild.

Elements of a Personality Profile
by Les Stobbe

WHILE USING MOST OF THE SAME TECHNIQUES as other article writers, personality profile writers have at their disposal five specialized approaches:

Narration
Personality profile writing calls for a well-developed narrative style. A personality profile is truly a story. Honing your storytelling skills will result in more acceptances than rejections. Above all, learn to show instead of tell about. Think and write visually. That's why you'll want to jot down everything you see, hear, smell, and feel about not only the person, but also the environment.

Interview
Much of the information you'll gather will be based on personal interviews not only with the subject, but also with his family, friends, and, at times, critics and even enemies. Don't short-circuit this important task, because that's where you pick up both information and direct quotes.

Flashback
More than any other article type, the personality piece thrives on the flashback technique. Grab the reader's interest, establish significance, then jump back to the beginning of the story you want to tell.

Always keep a notebook, smart phone, or audio recorder handy.

Direct Quotes
Always keep a notebook, smart phone, or audio recorder handy. The personality profile features many direct quotes, judiciously used to buttress the theme and illustrate the person's qualities and attitudes. Quotes from other authorities authenticate your insights.

Summary or Projection Ending
While many articles end with a reference to opening statements, another effective ending is a projection of plans and hopes, included in a quote from the subject or someone else integral to the story. The article is about someone else, so don't be pat, preachy, too personal, or chatty. Let the conclusion flow naturally. As textbook author Betsy Graham says, "Bear in mind the close relationship between the lead and the conclusion. If the relationship is complete, readers will have the satisfying feeling of completion. They will have come full circle, and they will remember what you have said."

Two Types of How-To Articles

by Les Stobbe

THERE'S AN ASTONISHING VARIETY of how-to subjects. Recently I faced a long layover because of a canceled flight, so I wandered into the magazine section of the news store. A third of the display was devoted to how-to magazines of all kinds.

How to Make and Do

Now that anyone can cook by sticking a package into the microwave and can create by learning how to use a computer software program, there's a real hunger for getting back to basics. People want to make what Grandma and Grandpa made back when they didn't have ready-made. Quilting has staged a comeback, as have knitting, needlepoint, crocheting, and macramé. How-to articles on cooking and baking seasonal foods fill entire magazines. Men want to build doghouses, a dollhouse, a workroom, or a boat.

For the best results in the how-to-make-and-do category, write about something you've done. Your research may include checking how others do it, but in reality your own skill makes the article come alive. We've all read how-to articles in our own fields of interest, and we can always tell if the writer is a fellow hobbyist or just reporting. Personal experience adds that ring of authenticity.

Things to keep in mind:

1. *Start at the beginning.* You may spark the interest of a first-timer, and they need to know all the materials they'll need and where they can get them.
2. *Be specific.* Nothing is more frustrating than generalized instructions.
3. *Include every step as simply as possible.* You know how to navigate the process, but don't make your reader guess what needs to be done.
4. *Document each step with illustrations or photos* if you want to make a sale in today's market. If you're not into photography, have a friend shoot for you. For a sale to a major magazine, you'll need a professional photographer skilled in specialized projects.
5. *Make it personal.* Communicate the joy and satisfaction you've experienced in making the item, maybe even telling some of where you found the needed parts.

How to Be

In the secular world, the emphasis is on self-help, being a better person, a better lover, a better parent, or a better leader by tapping into your inner resources.

The Christian writer knows that the inner man is flawed and that we must tap into the spiritual resources God has given us to become better Christians — establish priorities, develop spiritual gifts, be a soulwinner, become a better spouse or parent.

How-to-be articles require research, often documentation by experts. After you've written the how-to-be article, ask yourself:

1. Is my article rooted in truth and insights gained in Bible study and prayer?
2. Has my biblical documentation grown out of my reading — or have I simply looked for verses to support my ideas?
3. Do I have both biblical and life stories to illustrate the problem and the solution?
4. Have I adequately represented the power of the Holy Spirit to change lives?
5. Does my joy of living in a love relationship with Jesus Christ shine through?

How to Find Ideas for How-To Articles
by Les Stobbe

DETERMINE THE AREAS in which you have expertise, or at least enough know-how to develop a good article with a little research. Then analyze the opportunities at hand.

Around Your Home

- Do you have a recipe that's a family heirloom or that has a story attached to it? *Yankee* magazine regularly carries this kind of how-to article.

- Have you learned a craft and developed it enough to market items you make? A friend makes wreaths with another friend, and together they do house parties at which they take orders. A how-to article on making Christmas wreaths could at least get you into the local paper, if not a magazine.

- Maybe you've removed and replaced old wallpaper. Write a how-to article on the options you discovered as you began visiting wallpaper displays, tools you found helpful, how you overcame a problem, and how you finished difficult-to-get-at areas.

- You may have designed and built a patio that called for specialized construction and for which you used an unusual combination of wood, concrete, and brick. Or maybe you live in a condo and built your own soundproofing in the den so you could play your music as loud as you wished. Each experience could be the subject of a how-to article, complete with photos of every stage.

At Your Church

- A third-grade teacher has developed a new craft that uses household items. Your how-to article could focus on what she wants to achieve with the craft, what items she uses, what objects the children can make, and how the children are responding.

- A teacher seems to have a special way of dealing with troublesome kids. On the surface, it doesn't appear he or she is doing anything unusual, but when you probe, you discover a well-thought-out strategy. Develop a how-to article on steps to dealing with troublesome children.

- A teacher who has amazingly good relationships with her children and their parents. You discover it's a way of life for this teacher, but her action steps can be duplicated. Write a how-to article for a curriculum house to incorporate in a teacher's manual.

In Your Small Group

- Though there's lots of literature on small groups, you've got an extraordinarily creative group of couples who are forever coming up with new ideas. Do an article on harnessing the creative power of a small group.

- Someone in your group has special needs, so your group reaches out in love. That's the basis for a how-to article on caring for people with special needs.

In Your Spiritual Disciplines

- You find yourself continually distracted as you engage in prayer. Then you begin jotting down the distracting thoughts so you can continue in the spirit of prayer. You now have a how-to approach that, properly developed, can help others.

- You began meditating on the attributes of God after hearing Bill Bright or Anne Graham Lotz speak. Over time, you discovered clusters of attributes. Now you can develop a how-to article on studying the attributes of God.

- Your spouse has bouts of depression, but when you pray, his or her spirits are lifted. If this has happened in a variety of situations, you may be able write a how-to article on improving your marriage through prayer.

Used by permission of the Jerry Jenkins Writers Guild.

How to Begin a News Article
by Les Stobbe

THERE ARE TWO BASIC LEADS FOR NEWS STORIES: the direct and the delayed. Each has numerous variations. The inverted pyramid (which begins with the who, what, where, when, why, or how) always uses a direct lead.

Writers using a more creative style or writing a news feature often opt for the delayed lead. Either way, the writer must grab attention immediately or risk losing readers. Ways to start writing your news articles or features:

Direct Lead — summary of information or striking statement
This kind of lead offers summaries of key information, answering the five Ws & H.

> Five companies of fire fighters battled a stubborn fire last night at the Acme Company warehouse on Stenton Road, Centerville. The source of the fire is not immediately known.

Delayed — back into the story
A delayed lead backs into a story, grabbing the reader with an anecdote or colorful description, then transitioning into the body of the story.

Consider the following, about an urban legend concerning the attacks on 9/11:

> Two buildings tower above the others in the skyline, and one is in flames. On the ground far below are tiny figures, staring up in horror. In the thick black smoke, distinct features of a sinister face stare out at the city. It is, many who see this photograph believe, the face of Satan.

Although urban legends abounded following the terrorist attacks, the story above proved true. The Associated Press printed the photo, which reportedly had not been manipulated, and as reprinted in Time magazine, a creepy face is visible.

Question Lead — use sparingly
While the question lead is more often used for other types of articles, it can be used to stimulate interest in your story. Again, this should be used primarily for news features or human interest pieces.

> Interested in meeting other families and learning more about social, service, and instructional opportunities for families? Want to skip making lunch this Sunday? Then join the Baptist Family Club next Sunday, September 16, from 12:30-2:00 in Fellowship Hall for a free lunch and informational meeting.

Indirect Quote or Paraphrase — be accurate
The paraphrase or quote lead fits best with a news feature, a report on a conference or convention, or a special sermon by a pastor. For example, people are constantly asking why God lets evil men succeed in their nefarious plans. Consider these words by a senior pastor in California (adapted for this illustration):

> "God has given us a free will, the ability to make moral choices," said Pastor Rick Warren of Saddleback Community Church at yesterday's services, attended by a

record congregation of 15,000. "This one asset sets us apart from animals, but it is also the source of so much pain in our world. People, and that includes all of us, often make selfish, self-centered, and evil choices. Whenever that happens, people get hurt."

Now consider writing the lead as a paraphrase, leading into the direct quotes later:

Free will and evil choices cause events like the recent terrorism, said Pastor Rick Warren to a packed Saddleback Community Church yesterday.

"God has given us a free will, the ability to make moral choices," he told the record congregation of 15,000. "This one asset sets us apart from animals, but it is also the source of so much pain in our world."

Conclusions

While the conclusion to an article in the inverted pyramid style is simply the least essential bit of informational, many news stories have more creative endings. Some end with a summary of the event's impact or a projection of its future impact. A quote summing up the key idea of the speaker may also be used.

Some features or carefully crafted special articles might end with an unexpected or ironic twist. Just make sure the story ends smoothly and doesn't leave the reader confused. Think of the conclusion as tying the ribbon on a package — everything important is inside and the conclusion neatly wraps it up.

Used by permission of the Jerry Jenkins Writers Guild.

Opportunities for Seasonal Articles

by Les Stobbe

SOME ARE OBVIOUS, others more obscure. But written well, all hold potential for publication.

Christian Holidays and Seasons

Each year, magazines carry articles focusing on Easter and Christmas. Christian magazines carry seasonal articles for both, while secular magazines are loaded with seasonal articles at Christmas but feature little more than eggs and rabbits at Easter. Rather than doing another article decrying the world's emphasis on Santa, why not recall a Christmas memory from your childhood?

For Christian magazines, seasonal articles focus on the real meaning of the holiday — or some twist on that. An Easter meditation in *War Cry* turned on the question "Would the enemies of Jesus ever see the last of Him? No! They would not!"

> The enemies of Jesus did their worst. You have to give them full marks for thoroughness. They humiliated Him, they beat Him and they crowned Him with an excruciatingly painful diadem of thorns. They crucified Him with real nails, and for good measure thrust a spear into His side. They walled Him in a borrowed tomb, sealed it, and set guards so that no one could rob them of His very dead body. What else could they do to ensure that He could not bother them anymore?

What does the writer do to increase the impact of this meditation?

- He sets the tone with a short, striking-statement lead.
- He gives the enemies of Jesus grudging recognition, something I have never seen in another sermon or article in some 50 years of journalism.
- He describes their efforts using parallelism: humiliated, beat, crowned; walled, sealed, set guards. Note the active verbs!
- He uses a rhetorical question to, in effect, create a dialogue with the reader. This dignifies readers by treating them as thinkers.

In the same issue, a true story entitled "An Easter Awakening" tells of an Easter a single mother would never forget after a tornado destroyed her home. There is also an article focusing on the significance of the empty tomb. You could have written any or all of those three articles.

To make your seasonal article stand out, work on a new twist:

- How would a blind or deaf person celebrate Christmas, a holiday so rich in visual and auditory delights? Or how about a disabled father who can't get on the floor and assemble his son's train set?
- What is it like for a family with a father or mother in prison? Talk to someone doing Bible studies in prison for a contact on such a story.
- Visit a family that has adopted a child from another culture to observe the child's reaction to his or her first American Christmas. Take a camera along — and perhaps an audio recorder.
- Accompany a friend who often returns Christmas gifts and portray the experience through her eyes.

Historical and Regional Holidays

These opportunities require research and a new angle on an old story, but they can be enriched by an interview with someone who can provide historical perspective and possibly an unusual story.

- For President's Day, how about an article on one president's prayer life?
- For Patriot's Day in New England, get up early to see the re-creation of the battle on Lexington Green, and then do a "you are there" article.
- For Independence Day, compare the values of the signers of the Declaration of Independence with those of today's leaders.
- For Veteran's Day, interview a veteran of World War II, Korea, Vietnam, Iraq, or Afghanistan who has an unusual story.
- For Columbus Day, research what his faith meant to his journeys of discovery.

Annual Needs

Spring cleaning, preparing your taxes, caring for your lawn, planning your vacation, planning vacation Bible school, getting children ready for school, conducting your church's annual missions conference, winterizing your car.

The calendar is filled with opportunities to write articles tied to annual concerns and interests. Editors are always looking for a fresh approach that meets readers' seasonal needs.

Anniversaries

Almanacs of various kinds, as well as the internet, can provide lists of anniversaries that could spark article ideas. Personal experiences set against the backdrop of an anniversary can put a new perspective on it.

Used by permission of the Jerry Jenkins Writers Guild.

Timing Is Everything
by Les Stobbe

MOST WRITERS THINK of writing a Christmas article in September. But the editorial staff was looking for one months earlier in February. In July or August, editors are thinking about the coming Easter issue.

The more sophisticated the magazine, the further in advance it plans special issues. A Veteran's Day article should be submitted early in the year, unless it's for a local newspaper. Many magazines release an annual schedule so writers can submit articles in a timely fashion.

If you want to catch an editor's attention, December is a good month to send your query. Most writers are too busy to submit anything then, so there's less competition.

Work your way through the listing of magazines in publications like *The Christian Writer's Market Guide, LMP, Writer's Digest,* or *The Writer* in your local library for those that are especially interested in seasonal articles.

Adapted Used by permission of the Jerry Jenkins Writers Guild.

6

Alphabetical Listings of Periodicals

Visit a periodical's Website for a copy of their writer's guidelines and to learn more about what they publish. In addition to the guidelines, it is important that you send for a sample copy, or in some cases, simply study the samples on their website. Be sure to study the guidelines and the sample carefully before submitting.

For a detailed explanation of how to get the most out of these listings, as well as marketing tips, see "How to Use This Book" (see pages xv-xvii). Unfamiliar terms are explained in the Glossary (see pages 473-480).

(+) before a listing indicates it's a new market.
$ before a listing indicates it's a paying market.
(*) before a listing indicates unconfirmed information or no information update.

ADULT/GENERAL MARKETS

+$ **ABILITIES MAGAZINE,** (416) 923-1885, ext. 235. Jennifer@abilities.ca. Jennifer Rivkin, mng. ed. Canada's foremost cross-disability lifestyle magazine. Provides information about lifestyle topics, including travel, health, careers, education, relationships, parenting, new products, social policy and much more. Articles 500-2,000 wds. **Pays $50-$325.** No simultaneous submissions. Kill fee 50%. Guidelines at: http://abilities. ca/writers-guidelines.

+**ACTIVE RELIANCE,** PO Box 90711, Los Angeles CA 90009. (562) 895-2046. E-mail: cgreen@activereliance.com. Website: activereliance.com. Active Reliance Communication Group. A non-profit, Christian-based news, media, and publishing communications group whose focus is delivering reliable and useful information to its audience from a Christian world view. Clanford Green, ed. (Ads)

   Tip: "Our staff is dedicated to delivering breaking news from all around the world."

$ **ADOPTEE SEARCH,** E-mail: piecesoftymes@yahoo.com. This publication is devoted to finding biological families for adoptees. Writers are encouraged to share their stories of how Christ played a role in their own adoption reunions. Quarterly mag.; 40 pgs.; circ. 15,000; subscription $20. 85% unsolicited. Send complete ms. E-mail queries w/cover letter. **Pay $.02-.05,** on acceptance, for 1st rts. Articles 2,000-5,000 wds. (12/yr.). Responds in 8 wks. Seasonal 3 mos. ahead. Accepts simultaneous and reprints (tell when/where appeared). Regular sidebars. Accept submissions from children/teens. Prefers KJV. (No ads).

+$ **ALIVE NOW,** 1908 Grand Ave., PO Box 340004, Nashville TN 37203-0004. E-mail: alivenow@upperroom.org. Beth A. Richardson, ed. 48-page magazine. Publishes Scripture, prayers, meditations, stories, poetry, reflection aids, photos and art. For young adults through senior adults. Check Website for theme list. **Pays $35 and up,** on acceptance. Guidelines at: http://alivenow.upperroom.org/writers.

$ **AMERICA,** 106 W. 56th St., New York NY 10019-3893. (212) 581-4640. Fax (212)

399-3596. E-mail: articles@americamagazine.org. Website: www.americamagazine. org. Catholic. Submit to Editor-in-Chief. For thinking Catholics and those who want to know what Catholics are thinking. Weekly mag. and online version; 32+ pgs.; circ. 46,000. Subscription $56. 100% unsolicited freelance. Complete ms/cover letter; fax/e-query OK. **Pays $150-300** on acceptance. Articles 1,500-2,000 wds. Responds in 6 wks. Seasonal 3 mos. ahead. Does not use sidebars. Guidelines by mail/website: http://www. americamagazine.org/contact/submissions; copy for 9 x 12 SAE. Incomplete topical listings. (Ads)

Poetry: Buys avant-garde, free verse, light verse, traditional; 20-35 lines; $2-3/line.

AMERICAN CHRISTIAN VOICE, (formerly *The Ozarks Christian News*), 122 Lotus Ave., PO Box 336, Rockaway Beach MO 75740-0336. (417) 353-7598. E-mail: editor@AmericanChristianVoice.com. Website: www.AmericanChristianVoice.com. John G. Sacoulas, ed. Online version. Intelligent, inspirational and fun; serving the whole body of Christ. Monthly mag. (10X); 40 pgs.; circ. 20,000. Subscription $36. 50% unsolicited freelance. Query/clips; e-query OK. Trades promotion for articles; nonexclusive rts. Articles up to 500 wds. (100+/yr.); no fiction; reviews. Responds in 1 wk. Seasonal 3 mos. ahead. Accepts simultaneous submissions and reprints (tell when/where appeared). Requires e-mail submissions/attached file. Some sidebars. Accepts submissions from children/teens. Prefers NKJV. Guidelines by e-mail only. (Ads)

Fillers: All types. Up to 150 wds.

Columns/Departments: Query.

Poetry: Avant-garde, free verse, haiku, light verse, traditional. Submit max. 6 poems.

*$ ANGELS ON EARTH, 16 E. 34th St., New York NY 10016. (212) 251-8100. Fax (212) 684-1311. E-mail: submissions@angelsonearth.com. Website: www.angelsonearth. com. Guideposts. Colleen Hughes, ed-in-chief; Meg Belviso, depts. ed. for features and fillers. Presents true stories about God's angels and humans who have played angelic roles on earth. Bimonthly mag.; 75 pgs.; circ. 550,000. Subscription $19.95. 90% unsolicited freelance. Complete ms/cover letter; no phone/fax/e-query. **Pays $25-400** on publication for all rts. Articles 100-2,000 wds. (100/yr.); all stories must be true. Responds in 13 wks. Seasonal 6 mos. ahead. E-mail submissions from website form. Guidelines on website: http://www.guideposts.org/contact-us; copy for 7 x 10 SAE/4 stamps.

Fillers: Buys many. Anecdotal shorts of similar nature (angelic); 50-250 wds. $50-100.

Columns/Departments: Buys 50/yr. Messages (brief, mysterious happenings), $25. Earning Their Wings (good deeds), 150 wds. $50. Only Human? (human or angel?/mystery), 350 wds. $100. Complete ms.

Tips: "We are not limited to stories about heavenly angels. We also accept stories about human beings doing heavenly duties."

+$ ANGLICAN JOURNAL, 80 Hayden St., Toronto ON M4Y 3G2, Canada. 9416) 924-9199, ext. 307. Fax (416) 295-8811. E-mail: editor@national.anglican.ca. Anglican Church of Canada. Janet Thomas, ed. (jthomas@national.anglican.ca – submit to this e-mail). Monthly (10X) magazine. No unsolicited mss; send an e-query. **Pays .25/wd.** Guidelines at: http://www.anglicanjournal.com/about-us/guidelines.

$ ANIMAL TRAILS, E-mail: animaltrails@yahoo.com. Website: http://animaltrails-magazine.doodlekit.com. Tellstar Publishing. Shannon Bridget Murphy, ed. Teaching children and teens about animals and nature. Quarterly mag.; 40 pgs., circ. 15,000;

subscription $20.00. 85% unsolicited freelance. Complete ms/cover letter; e-query OK. **Pays .02-.05/wd.** on acceptance for 1st rts. Articles 2,000-5,000 wds. (12/yr.); fiction 2,000-5,000 wds. (12/yr.) Responds in 8 wks. Seasonal 3 mos. ahead. Accepts simultaneous submissions and reprints (tell when/where appeared). Prefers e-mail submissions (attached or copied into message). No kill fee. Regularly uses sidebars. Prefers KJV. Guidelines by e-mail. (No ads)

Poetry: Buys 10/yr. Avant-garde, free verse, haiku, light verse, traditional; any length. Pays variable rates. Submit max. 6 poems.

Fillers: Buys most types, to 1,000 wds. Accepts 10/yr.

Tips: "Most open to articles, stories, poetry, and fillers that explain the value of animals and their relationship with God. The value of animals is the mission of Animal Trails. Include a Scripture reference." Picture books are being accepted for publication.

$ ANSWERS MAGAZINE & ANSWERSMAGAZINE.COM, PO Box 510, Hebron KY 41048. (859) 727-2222. Fax (859) 727-4888. E-mail: nationaleditor@answersmagazine.com. Website: www.answersmagazine.com. Answers in Genesis. Bible-affirming, creation-based. Pam Sheppard, national ed. Submit a one paragraph article proposal; no unsolicited mss. Responds in 30 days. Quarterly mag. Subscription $24. Articles 300-600 wds. Responds in 30 days. **Pays $75-$400; $50-$225 for reprints.** Details on website: http://legacy-cdn-assets.answersingenesis.org/assets/pdf/about/writers-policy.pdf.
   **2010 EPA Award of Merit: General.

+$ ARLINGTON CATHOLIC HERALD, 200 N. Glebe Rd, St. 600, Arlington VA 22203. (703) 841-2590. Fax (703) 524-2782. E-mail: editorial@catholicherald.com. Michael F. Flach, ed. Guidelines at: http://www.catholicherald.com/contact_us.html.

BELIEVERS BAY, 1202 S. Pennsylvania St., Marion IN 46953. (765) 997-1736. E-mail: editor@BelieversBay.com. Website: www.BelieversBay.com. Online version. Tim Russ, ed. Nondenominational. To share the love of God with common sense. Daily to weekly online blog mag. 100% freelance; accepts as many as are submitted. One-time, electronic, nonexclusive rts. Seasonal 2 wks. ahead, or more. Accepts simultaneous submissions and reprints. No sidebars. No length restrictions. Open to almost all nonfiction topics and all fiction genres. **No payment** for 1st and electronic rts. (permanently archives pieces). Articles 500-1,000 wds. Guidelines at: www.believersbay.com/submissions.

Fillers: All types. To 500 wds.

Columns/Departments: Query. Columns 300-500 wds.

Poetry: All types. To 99 lines.

Special needs: Open to new columns; contact by e-mail.

Tips: "Easy to break in with quality writing; share something that shares the love of God with common sense, or share something that would be of value to the average person."

$ BIBLE ADVOCATE, PO Box 33677, Denver CO 80233. (303) 452-7973. Fax (303) 452-0657. E-mail: bibleadvocate@cog7.org. Website: http://baonline.org. Church of God (Seventh Day). Sherri Langton, assoc. ed. A denominational magazine that seeks to advocate the Bible and represent the Church of God (Seventh Day); one of the oldest religious publications still in print in the US. Bimonthly (6X) mag.; 32 pgs.; circ. 13,000. Subscription free. 20-25% unsolicited freelance. Complete ms/cover letter; accepts e-queries. **Pays $20-55** on publication for 1st, reprint, electronic, simultaneous rts. Articles 600-1,100 wds. (10/yr.). Responds in 4-10 wks. Seasonal 6 mos. ahead (no Christmas or Easter pieces). Accepts simultaneous submissions and reprints (tell when/

where appeared). Prefers requested ms by e-mail (attached or copied into message). Some kill fees. Some sidebars. Prefers NIV 1984, NKJV. Guidelines/theme list by mail/website: http://baonline.org/write-for-us; copy for 9 x 12 SAE/3 stamps. (No ads)

Poetry: Buys 5-10/yr. Free verse, traditional; 5-25 lines; $20. Submit max. 5 poems.

Special needs: Articles centering on upcoming themes (see Website).

Tips: "If you write well, all areas are open to freelance. Articles that run no more than 1,100 words are more likely to get in. Also, fresh writing with keen insight is most readily accepted."

+BREAKTHROUGH INTERCESSOR, PO Box 121, Lincoln VA 20160-0121. (540) 338-4131. E-mail: breakthrough@intercessor.org. Write about your personal experience with prayer; 1,000 wds. **Pays 5 copies.** Guidelines at: http://www.intercessors.org/writersguide.php.

$ THE BRINK MAGAZINE, 114 Bush Rd., Nashville TN 37217. Toll-free (800) 877-7030. (615) 361-1221. Fax (615) 367-0535. E-mail: thebrink@randallhouse.com or through the website: www.thebrinkonline.com. Randall House. David Jones, ed. Devotional magazine for young adults; focusing on Bible studies, life situations, discernment of culture, and relevant feature articles. Quarterly and online mag.; 64 pgs.; circ. 8,000. Subscription $6.99. Estab. 2008. 30% unsolicited freelance; 70% assigned. Query, query/clips; prefers e-query. Accepts full mss by e-mail. **Pays $50-150** on acceptance for all rts. Articles 500-2,000 wds. (10-15/yr.). Responds in 1-2 wks. Seasonal 6 mos. ahead. Accepts simultaneous submissions and reprints (tell when/where appeared). Requires accepted articles by e-mail (attached file). No kill fee. Regularly uses sidebars. Does not accept freelance devotions. Guidelines/theme list on website: http://www.thebrinkonline.com/magazine/write. (No ads)

Fillers: Buys 4/yr. Ideas, newsbreaks, book reviews, app reviews, quizzes; 50-100 wds. Pays $50-100.

Tips: "Pitch articles that are specific and relevant to young adults."
**2014 EPA Award of Excellence: Devotional

+BYFAITH (*byFaith*), 1700 N. Brown Rd., Ste. 105, Lawrenceville GA 30043. (678) 825-1005. E-mail: editor@byfaithonline.com. Presbyterian Church in America. Articles 500-3,000 wds. **No mention of payment.** Guidelines at: http://byfaithonline.com/about (scroll down).

+CAHABA RIVER LITERARY JOURNAL, 2413 Bethel Rd., Logansport LA 71049. (318) 564-6031. E-mail: https://www.facebook.com/groups/1505827313012865/Cahaba_River_Literary_Journal. Publishing Quality Fiction, Poetry, and Photography. Bimonthly journal. Debuts April 2015. Subscription $35. Fiction to 2,500 wds.; poetry to 25 lines (submit max. 3 poems); B & W photos (no more than 5 photos with a short story). No more than 150 words for a caption. **Pays in copies.** E-mail submissions only. Deadline for submissions is March 20, 2015.

Call for submissions: We work with new and seasoned writers. We need stories, poems, essays, color and B & W photos and artwork on all subjects in any form.

Tips: "Present me your best works: I want to laugh, cry, be sad, get angry at the story or poem, or just have fun sharing it with our readers. I want 'awe' when I see your photos."

$ CANADA LUTHERAN, 600—177 Lombard Ave., Winnipeg MB R3B 0W5, Canada. Toll-free (888) 786-6707, ext. 172. (204) 984-9171. Fax (204) 984-9185. E-mail: editor@elcic.ca. Website: www.elcic.ca/. Evangelical Lutheran Church in Canada. Provides information and inspiration to help our readers relate their faith to everyday life and foster a connection with their congregation, synods, and national office. Ken Ward, ed. Denominational. Monthly (8X) mag.; 32 pgs.; circ. 14,000. Subscription $22.60 Cdn.; $49.89 US. E-query or complete ms. **Pays $.10/wd. Cdn.** on publication for one-time rts. Articles 700-1,200 wds. Responds in 1-2 wks. Seasonal 6 mos. ahead. No simultaneous submissions; prefers first publication; very occasionally accepts reprints (tell when/where appeared). Prefers e-mail submission (attached file). Sometimes pays kill fee. Regularly uses sidebars. Prefers NRSV. Guidelines at: http://www.elcic.ca/clweb/writing.html; no copy. (Ads)

> **Columns/Departments:** Buys 8/yr. Practicing Our Faith (how-to piece to help readers deepen or live out their faith); 600 wds. Pays .20/wd.
>
> **Tips:** "Canadians/Lutherans receive priority; others considered but rarely used. Want material that is clear, concise, and fresh. Primarily looking for how-to articles."

THE CANADIAN LUTHERAN, 3074 Portage Ave., Winnipeg MB R3K 0Y2, Canada. Toll-free (800) 588-4226. (204) 895-3433. Fax (204) 897-4319. E-mail: info@ lutheranchurch.ca or through website: www.lutheranchurch.ca. Lutheran Church— Canada. Inspirational and educational articles. Matthew Block, ed. Bimonthly (6X) mag. Subscription $20. Open to unsolicited freelance. Guidelines at: http://www.lutheran-church.ca/canluth.php. Not in topical listings. (Ads)

+$ CANADIAN MENNONITE, 490 Dutton Dr., Unit C5, Waterloo ON N2L 6H7, Canada. (519) 884-3810. Fax (519) 884-3331. E-mail: submit@canadianmennonite. org. Dick Benner, ed/pub.; Ross W. Muir, mng. ed. Mennonite Church Canada. Open to theological reflections, sermons, opinion pieces, letters, reviews, and personal stories. Theme list on Website. Prefers e-mail submissions. **Pays .10/wd.** for solicited articles; no payment for unsolicited articles. Guidelines at: http://www.canadianmennonite.org/submissions.

+$ CATHOLIC DIGEST, 1 Montauk Ave., New London CT 06320. E-mail: queries@ catholicdigest.com. A lifestyle magazine that encourages and supports Catholics in a variety of life stage and circumstances. Published 9X/yr. Articles 1,500 wds. **Pays $200-300; $100 for reprints.** Seasonal 4-5 mos. ahead. No attachments. Guidelines at: http://www.catholicdigest.com/writers_guidelines.html.

$ CATHOLIC NEW YORK, 1011 First Ave., Ste. 1721, New York NY 10022. (212) 688-2399. Fax (212) 688-2642. E-mail: cny@cny.org. Website: www.cny.org. Catholic. John Woods, ed-in-chief (letters@cny.org). To inform New York Catholics. Biweekly newspaper; 40 pgs.; circ. 132,680. Subscription $26. 2% unsolicited freelance. Query or complete ms/cover letter. **Pays $15-100** on publication for onetime rts. Articles 500-800 wds. Responds in 5 wks. Guidelines on Website; copy $3.

> **Tips:** "Most open to columns about specific seasons of the Catholic Church, such as Advent, Christmas, Lent, and Easter."

+$ CATHOLIC SENTINEL, 5536 NE Hassalo, Portland OR 97213. (503) 281-1191. E-mail: sentinel@CatholicSentinel.org. Newspaper for the Archdiocese of Portland. Twice-monthly tabloid; 20 pgs. Articles 600-1,500 wds. Query first. Pays variable rates. Guidelines at: http://www.catholicsentinel.org/main.asp?SectionID=15&SubSectionID =60&ArticleID=11770.

$ CBA RETAILERS + RESOURCES, 9240 Explorer Dr., Colorado Springs CO 80920. Toll-free (800) 252-1950. (719) 272-3555. Fax (719) 272-3510. E-mail: info@cbaonline. org. Website: www.cbaonline.org. Christian Booksellers Assn. Submit queries to Cathy

Ellis, publications manager. To provide Christian retail store owners and managers with professional retail skills, product information, and industry news. Monthly trade journal (also in digital edition); 48-100 pgs.; circ. 5,000. Subscription $59.95 (for nonmembers). 10% unsolicited freelance; 80% assigned. Query/clips; fax/e-query OK. **Pays .30/wd.** on publication for all rts. Articles 800-2,000 wds. (30/yr. assigned); book/music/video reviews, 150 wds. ($35). Responds in 8 wks. Seasonal 4-5 mos. ahead. Prefers requested ms e-mailed in MS Word file. Regularly uses sidebars. Accepts any modern Bible version. Guidelines at: http://cbaonline.org/contact-us (Ads/Dunn & Dunn/856-582-0690)

> **Special needs:** Trends in retail, consumer buying habits, market profiles. By assignment only.
>
> **Tips:** "Looking for writers who have been owners/managers/buyers/sales staff in Christian retail stores. Most of our articles are by assignment and focus on producing and selling Christian products or conducting retail business. We also assign reviews of books, music, videos, giftware, kids products, and software to our regular reviewers."

$ CELEBRATE LIFE MAGAZINE, PO Box 1350, Stafford VA 22555. Phone (540) 659-4171; fax (540) 659-2586. E-mail: clmag@all.org. Website: www.clmagazine.org. Published by American Life League (www.all.org). Bonnie Seers, mng. ed. Quarterly full-color mag.; 32 pgs.; circ. 35,000; subscription $12.95. Covers all respect-for-life matters according to the Catholic Church's teaching. **Pays on publication,** according to quality of article, for 1st rights or work-for-hire assignments; rarely accepts reprints. No kill fee. Article length 600-1,800 wds. Seasonal 6 mos. ahead. Prefers Jerusalem Bible or New American Bible (Catholic) translations. Guidelines/theme list on Website. Prefers e-mail for queries and submissions; attached file. Accepts paid ads (see Website). Guidelines at: http://www.clmagazine.org/nav/index/heading/MjE/ (scroll down).

> **Ongoing needs:** Personal experience with abortion, post-abortion trauma/healing, adoption, pro-life activism/young people's involvement, disability, elder care, death/dying, euthanasia, eugenics, special-needs children, human personhood, chastity, large families, stem-cell science, and other respect-for-life topics.
>
> **Tips:** "We are pro-life, with no exceptions, in keeping with Catholic teaching. Looking for interviews with pro-life leaders and pro-life public figures, and nonfiction stories about pro-life activities and people who live according to pro-life ethics despite adversity. Photos are preferred for personal stories. No fiction, songs, art, or poetry. Break in by submitting work."

$ CGA WORLD, PO Box 249, Olyphant PA 18447. Toll-free (800) 836-5699. (855) 586-1091. Fax (570) 586-7721. E-mail: cgaemail@aol.com. Website: www.catholicgoldenage.org. Catholic Golden Age. Barbara Pegula, mng. ed. For Catholics 50+. Quarterly newsletter. Subscription/membership $12. Uses little freelance. Query. **Pays .10/wd.** on publication for 1st, onetime, or reprint rts. Articles 600-1,000 wds.; fiction 600-1,000 wds. Responds in 6 wks. Seasonal 6 mos. ahead. Accepts reprints (tell when/where appeared). Accepts requested ms on disk. Guidelines at: http://www.catholicgoldenage.org/About-CGA.html; copy for 9 x 12 SAE/3 stamps. (Ads).

$ CHARISMA, 600 Rinehart Rd., Lake Mary FL 32746. (407) 333-0600. Fax (407) 333-7100. E-mail: charisma@charismamedia.com. Website: www.charismamag.com. Primarily for the Pentecostal and Charismatic Christian community. Monthly and online mag.; 100+ pgs.; circ. 250,000. Subscription $14.97. 80% assigned freelance. Query only; accepts query letters or e-mails. **Pays up to $1,000** (for assigned) on publication for all rts. Articles 1,800-2,500 wds. (40/yr.); book/music reviews, 200 wds. ($20-35). Responds in 8-12 wks.

Seasonal 5 mos. ahead. Kill fee $50. Prefers accepted ms by e-mail. Regularly uses sidebars. Guidelines at: http://www.charismamag.com/about/write-for-us; copy $4. (Ads)

Tips: "Most open to news section, reviews, or features. Query (published clips help a lot)."

$ CHICKEN SOUP FOR THE SOUL BOOK SERIES, PO Box 700, Cos Cob CT 06807. Fax (203) 861-7194. E-mail: webmaster@chickensoupforthesoul.com. Website: www.chickensoup.com. Chicken Soup for the Soul Publishing, LLC. Submit questions/requests to Web master's e-mail. No submissions to Webmaster's e-mail. A world leader in self-improvement, helps real people share real stories of hope, courage, inspiration, and love that is open to all ages, races, etc. Quarterly trade paperback books; 385 pgs.; circ. 60 million. $14.95/book. 98% unsolicited freelance. Make submissions via website only. **Pays $200 (plus 10 free copies of the book, worth more than $110)** on publication for reprint, electronic, and nonexclusive rts. Articles 300-1,200 wds. Seasonal anytime. Accepts simultaneous submissions and sometimes reprints (tell when/where appeared). Submissions only through the website: Go to www.chickensoupforthesoul.com and click on "Submit Your Story" on the left toolbar. No kill fee. Accepts submissions from children and teens. Guidelines/themes on Website: http://www.chickensoup.com/story-submissions/story-guidelines; free sample. (No ads)

Special needs: See website for a list of upcoming titles.

Contest: See website for list of current contests.

Tips: "Visit our website and be familiar with our book series. Send in stories via our website, complete with contact information. Submit story typed, double-spaced, max. 1,200 words, in a Word document."

$ CHRISTIAN COURIER, 2 Aiken St., St. Catherines ON L2N 1V8, Canada. Toll-free (800) 969-4838. (905) 937-3314. Toll-free fax (800) 969-4838. (905) 682-8313. E-mail: editor@christiancourier.ca or through website: www.christiancourier.ca. Reformed Faith Witness. Angela Reitsma Bick, ed. (angela@christiancourier.ca); Cathy Smith, features ed. (cathy@christiancourier.ca). Mission: To present Canadian and international news, both religious and general, from a Reformed Christian perspective. Biweekly newspaper; 20-24 pgs.; circ. 2,500. Subscription $58 Cdn.; 20% unsolicited freelance; 80% assigned. Send queries to editor@christiancourier.ca. **Pays $40-$70, up to .10/wd. for assigned;** 30 days after publication for onetime, reprint, or simultaneous rts. Not copyrighted. Articles 700-1,200 wds. (40/yr.); fiction to 1,200-2,500 wds. (6/yr.); book reviews 750 wds. Responds in 1-2 wks. Seasonal 3 mos. ahead. Accepts simultaneous submissions and reprints (tell when/where appeared). Prefers accepted ms by e-mail (attached file). No kill fee. Uses some sidebars. Prefers NIV. Guidelines/deadlines on website: http://christiancourier.ca/writeForUs.php; no copy. (Ads)

Poetry: Buys 12/yr. Avant-garde, free verse, light verse, traditional; 10-30 lines; $20-30. Submit max. 5 poems.

Tips: "Suggest an aspect of the theme which you believe you could cover well, have insight into, could treat humorously, etc. Show that you think clearly, write clearly, and have something to say that we should want to read. Have a strong biblical worldview and avoid moralism and sentimentality." Responds only if material is accepted.

+CHRISTIAN BIBLE STUDIES.COM, Christianity Today, 465 Gundersen Dr., Carol Stream IL 60188. E-mail: CBSNewsletter@ChristianityToday.com. Draws men and women who represent a broad spectrum of denominations, backgrounds, education, experience, and expertise. Amy Jackson, mng. ed. No longer accepts unsolicited mss, but will consider including an excerpt from your published book in their Featured Article section. Guidelines at: http://www.christianitytoday.com/biblestudies/features/writers-guidelines.html.

+CHRISTIAN CHRONICLE, PO Box 11000, Oklahoma City OK 7313601100. (405) 425-5070. Fax (405) 425-5076. Erik Tryggestad, ed. International newspaper for Churches of Christ. Submit only through form on Website: http://www.christianchronicle.org/contact-us

$ CHRISTIAN EXAMINER, PO Box 2606, El Cajon CA 92021. (619) 668-5100. Fax (619) 668-1115. E-mail: info@christianexaminer.com. Website: www.christianexaminer.com. Selah Media Group. Lori Arnold and Scott Noble, eds. Reports on current events from an evangelical Christian perspective, inspirational articles, and church trends. Focus is on ministries in S. California and Minneapolis. Monthly and online newspaper; 24-36 pgs.; circ. 150,000. Subscription $19.95. 5% assigned. Query/clips. **Pays .10/wd.,** on publication for 1st and electronic rts. Articles 600-900 wds. Responds in 4-5 wks. Seasonal 2 mos. ahead. No simultaneous submissions or reprints. Prefers e-mail submissions (copied into message). No kill fee. Uses some sidebars. Guidelines at: http://www.christianexaminer.com/Pages/Aboutus.html. Not included in topical listings; copy $1.50/9x12 SAE. (Ads)

   Tips: "We prefer news stories."
   ** 2014 EPA Award of Merit: Newspaper & Newspaper-Portal (Digital); 2010 EPA Award of Merit: Online ; 2010, 2011 EPA Award of Excellence: Newspaper; 2012 EPA Award of Excellence: Online; 2012 EPA Award of Merit: Newspaper. Member of Association of Christian Newspapers (ACN).

+$ CHRISTIAN HERALD, PO Box 68526, Brampton ON L6R 0J8, Canada. (905) 874-1731. Fax (905) 874-1781. E-mail: info@christianherald.ca. Requires e-mail submissions; query first. **Pays $20-100 or .10/wd.** Not currently accepting poetry. Guidelines at: http://www.christianherald.ca/writersguideline.html.

+$ CHRISTIAN HISTORY.NET, 465 Gundersen Dr., Carol Stream IL 60188. (630) 260-0114. E-mail: cheditor@christianhistory.net. Jennifer Trafton, ed. Send a short query initially. "We give preference to scholars, graduate students, or experienced writers in the field of history. Articles 500-3,000 wds. Query only. **Pays .20-.25/wd.** Guidelines at: www.christianhistory.net.

$ CHRISTIAN HOME & SCHOOL, 3350 East Paris Ave. S.E., Grand Rapids MI 49512. Toll-free (800) 635-8288. (616) 957-1070, ext. 240. Fax (616) 957-5022. E-mail: rheyboer@csionline.org. Website: www.csionline.org/christian_home_and_school. Christian Schools Intl. Rachael Heyboer, mng. ed. For parents who send their children to Christian schools. Please note this is NOT a homeschooling magazine. Triannual mag.; 40 pgs.; circ. 66,000. Subscription $13.95. November and March issues focus on elementary and middle school; May issue on high school students. 25% unsolicited; 75% assigned. Complete ms or e-query. Accepts full mss by e-mail. **Pays $50-250** on publication for 1st rts. Articles 1,000-2,000 wds. (30/yr.); book reviews $25 (assigned). Responds in 4 wks. Seasonal 6 mos. ahead (no Christmas or summer). Accepts simultaneous queries. Regularly uses sidebars. Accepts submissions from children/teens. Prefers NIV. For guidelines/theme list/sample issues, check website: http://www.csionline.org/christian_home_and_school. (Ads)

   Tips: "Writers can break in by submitting articles based on the CH&S editorial calendar, geared from a Christian perspective and current with the times."

$ CHRISTIANITY TODAY, 465 Gundersen Dr., Carol Stream IL 60188-2498. (630) 260-6200. Fax (630) 260-9401. E-mail: cteditor@christianitytoday.com. Website: www.christianitytoday.com. Mark Galli, ed. For intentional Christians who seek to thoughtfully integrate their faith with responsible action in the church and world. 10X/year and online mag.; 65-120 pgs. Circ. 130,000. Subscription $24.95. Accepts a query or complete ms. Prefers e-query; no attachments. **Pays .25-.35/wd.** on publication for print 1st rts.; less for online. Articles 1,000-4,000 wds. (50/yr.); book reviews 800-1,200 wds. (pays per-page rate). Responds in 6 wks. Seasonal 6 mos. ahead. Accepts reprints (tell when/where appeared—payment 25% of regular rate). Kill fee 50%. Does not use sidebars. Prefers NIV. Guidelines on website: http://www.christianitytoday.com/ct/help/about-us/writers-guidelines.html; prefers online submissions. (Ads)

> **Tips:** "Read the magazine." Does not return unsolicited manuscripts.
> ** 2014 EPA Award of Merit: General. Various and sundry journalism awards through EPA and other professional associations.

THE CHRISTIAN JOURNAL, 1032 W. Main, Medford OR 97501. (541) 773-4004. Fax (541) 773-9917. E-mail: info@thechristianjournal.org. Website: www.TheChristianJournal.org. Chad McComas, ed. We write to those who are believers to encourage them. We write to those who are seeking Jesus to inspire them. We are a ministry of service from volunteers wanting to build the kingdom of God through our readers. Monthly and online newspaper; 12-20 pgs.; circ. 14,000. Subscription $20; most copies distributed free. Paper is sent to inmates across the country free. 50% unsolicited freelance; 50% assigned. Complete ms; e-query. **No payment** for onetime rts. Articles and fiction to 500 words (accepts 200-300/yr.); children's stories 500 wds (accepts 25/yr). Prefers articles by e-mail (attached file). Responds in 3 wks. Holiday/seasonal 2 mos. Ahead. Accepts simultaneous submissions and reprints. Sometimes uses sidebars. Also accepts submissions from children/teens. Accepts photos with articles only. Prefers modern translation. Guidelines/theme list on the Website: http://thechristianjournal.org/writers-information/guidelines-for-writers; copy online. (Ads)

> **Poetry:** Accepts very few/yr. Traditional; 3-20 lines. Submit max. 1 poem.
> **Reviews:** Book, music, video; 500 wds.
> **Fillers:** Accepts 25/yr. Anecdotes, cartoons, jokes, kid quotes, newsbreaks, prayers, quotes, short humor, or word puzzles; 50-300 wds.
> **Columns/Departments:** Accepts 6/yr. Youth; Seniors; Children's stories; all to 500 wds.
> **Tips:** "Send articles on themes; each issue has a theme. Theme articles get first choice. We are looking for real believers to share their journeys and what they are learning along the way."

+CHRISTIAN MOTORSPORTS ILLUSTRATED, PO Box 790, Quinlan TX 75474. (607) 742-3407. Designed to meet the spiritual needs of the motorsports community. Roland Osborne, pub. Articles 650-1,200 wds. **Pays in copies.** Guidelines at: http://www.christianmotorsports.com/index.php/from-the-publisher.

CHRISTIAN NEWS NORTHWEST, PO Box 974, Newberg OR 97132. Phone/fax (503) 537-9220. E-mail: cnnw@cnnw.com. Website: www.cnnw.com. John Fortmeyer, ed./pub. News of ministry in the evangelical Christian community in western and central Oregon and southwest Washington; distributed primarily through evangelical churches. Monthly newspaper; 20-24 pgs.; circ. 29,000 (free circulation); subscription by mail $22. 10% unsolicited freelance; 5% assigned. Complete ms; e-query and mail queries OK. **No payment.** Not copyrighted. Articles 700-1,000 wds. (few). Responds in 1-2 wks. Seasonal 3 mos. ahead. Accepts simultaneous submissions and reprints (tell when/where appeared). Accepts e-mail submissions (attached file or copied into message. Some sidebars. Prefers NIV. Guidelines at: http://cnnw.com/about-us; copy sent free. (Ads)

Columns: News or features primarily focused on churches or evangelical outreach here in the Northwest. Accepts few. Complete ms. No payment.
Tips: "Most open to ministry-oriented features. Our space is always tight, but stories on lesser-known, Northwest-based ministries are encouraged. Keep it very concise. Since we focus on the Pacific Northwest, it would probably be difficult for anyone outside the region to break into our publication."

CHRISTIAN ONLINE MAGAZINE, PO Box 262, Wolford VA 24658. E-mail: submissions@christianmagazine.org. Website: www.ChristianMagazine.org. Darlene Osborne, pub. (darlene@christianmagazine.org). Strictly founded on the Word of God, this magazine endeavors to bring you the best Christian information on the net. Monthly e-zine. Subscription free. 10% unsolicited freelance; 90% assigned. E-query. Articles 500-700 wds. Responds in 1 wk. Seasonal 2 mos. ahead. Prefers accepted ms by e-mail (attached file). **No payment.** Regularly uses sidebars. Also accepts submissions from children/teens. Prefers KJV. Guidelines at: http://www.christianonlinemagazine.com/submit_an_article_writer_guidelines. (Ads)
    Fillers: Accepts 50/yr. Prayers, prose, quizzes, short humor; 500 wds.
    Columns/Departments: Variety Column, 700-1,000 wds. Query.
    Tips: "Most open to solid Christian articles founded on the Word of God."

+CHRISTIAN PRESS NEWSPAPER, PO Box 145, Oxford MS 38655. (316) 644-6185. E-mail: russ@christianpress.com. Reports where news of the day and faith intersect; news, opinion, and features. Russ Jones, ed. Articles 500-750 wds. E-mail submissions. **No payment.** Guidelines at: http://www.christianpress.com/index.php/writers-guideline.

CHRISTIAN QUARTERLY (See *Joyful Living Magazine*)

THE CHRISTIAN RANCHMAN/COWBOYS FOR CHRIST, PO Box 7557, Fort Worth TX 76111. (817) 236-0023. Fax (817) 236-0024. E-mail: cwb4christ@cowboysforchrist. net, or CFCmail@cowboysforchrist.net, or through website: www.CowboysforChrist.net. Interdenominational. Dave Harvey, ed. Monthly tabloid; 16 pgs.; circ. 15,000. No subscription. 85% unsolicited freelance. Complete ms/cover letter. **No payment** for all rts. Articles 350-1,000 wds.; book/video reviews (length open). Does not use sidebars. Guidelines at: www.cowboysforchrist.net ("Contact Us"/ "Submit an Article"); sample copy.
    Poetry: Poetry: Accepts 40/yr. Free verse. Submit max. 3 poems.
    Fillers: Accepts all types.
    Tips: "We're most open to true-life Christian stories, Christian testimonies, and Christian or livestock news. Contact us with your ideas first."

*$ CHRISTIAN RESEARCH JOURNAL, PO Box 8500, Charlotte NC 28271-8500. (704) 887-8200. Fax (704) 887-8299. E-mail: submissions@equip.org. Website: www. equip.org. Christian Research Institute. Elliot Miller, ed-in-chief; Melanie Cogdill, ed. Probing today's religious movements, promoting doctrinal discernment and critical thinking, and providing reasons for Christian faith and ethics. Quarterly mag.; 64 pgs.; circ. 30,000. Subscription $39.50. 75% freelance. Query or complete ms/cover letter; fax query OK; e-query and submissions OK. **Pays .16/wd.** on publication for 1st rts. Articles to 4,200 wds. (25/yr.); book reviews 1,100-2,500 wds. Responds in 4 mos. Accepts simultaneous submissions. Kill fee to 50%. Guidelines by e-mail; copy $6. (Ads)
    Columns/Departments: Effective Evangelism, 1,700 wds. Viewpoint, 875 wds. News Watch, to 2,500 wds.
    Special needs: Viewpoint on Christian faith and ethics, 1,700 wds.; news pieces, 800-1,200 wds.
    Tips: "Be familiar with the *Journal* in order to know what we are looking for. We

accept freelance articles in all sections (features and departments). E-mail for writer's guidelines."

$ CHRISTIAN RETAILING, 600 Rinehart Rd., Lake Mary FL 32746. (407) 333-0600. Fax (407) 333-7133. E-mail: Retailing@charismamedia.com. Website: www.christianretailing.com. Charisma Media. Christine D. Johnson, mng. ed., print (chris.johnson@charismamedia.com). For Christian product industry manufacturers, distributors, retailers. Trade and online journal published 10X in 2015; circ. 5,600 (print), 40,000 (digital). Subscription $40 print/free digital/free print to authors and Christian retailers. 10% assigned. E-query with clips; no phone/fax query. **Pays varies depending on assignment.** No simultaneous submissions. Accepts requested mss by e-mail (attached file). Kill fee. Prefers MEV. Guidelines at: retailing@charismamedia.com (Ads)

> **Tips:** "Notify the editor, Christine D. Johnson (chris.johnson@charismamedia.com), of your expertise in the Christian products industry."

$ CHRISTIAN STANDARD, 8805 Governor's Hill Dr., Ste. 400, Cincinnati OH 45249. (800) 543-1301. Fax (513) 931-0950. E-mail: christianstandard@standardpub.com. Website: www.christianstandard.com. Standard Publishing/Christian Churches/Churches of Christ. Submit to: christianstandard@standardpub.com. Themed articles of special interest address challenges every Christian is facing and every congregation must consider. Practical insights for leaders and involved members of Christian Churches and Churches of Christ. Monthly and online mag.; 68 pgs.; circ. 19,200 (print). Subscription $37.99. 30% unsolicited freelance; 70% assigned. Query; e-query OK. **Pays $50-300** on acceptance, for nonexclusive, reprint and electronic rts. Articles 1,500-1,800 wds. (120-200/yr.). Responds in 6-8 wks. Seasonal 3-4 mos. ahead. Accepts simultaneous submissions and reprints (tell when/where appeared). Prefers e-mail submissions either attached or copied into message). Some kill fees. Regularly uses sidebars. Prefers NIV. Guidelines/copy on website: http://christianstandard.com/contact-us/submit-articles. (Ads)

> **Fillers:** Accepts 5-8 cartoons/yr.
>
> **Tips:** "We would like to hear ministers and elders tell about the efforts made in their churches. Has the church grown? Developed spiritually? Overcome adversity? Succeeded in missions?"

+$ CHRISTIANWEEK, Box 725, Winnipeg MB R3C 2K3, Canada. (204) 982-2060. Fax (204) 947-5632. Canada's only national interdenominational news publication. Articles 400-1,500 wds. E-query. **Pays .10/wd.** Website: www.christianweek.org.

CHURCH HERALD AND HOLINESS BANNER, 7407 Metcalf, Overland Park KS 66212. Fax (913) 722-0351. E-mail: editor@heraldandbanner.com. Website: www.heraldandbanner.com. Church of God (Holiness)/Herald and Banner Press. Dr. Gordon L. Snider, ed. Offers the conservative holiness movement a positive outlook on their church, doctrine, future ministry, and movement. Monthly mag.; 24 pgs.; circ. 500. Subscription $20.50. 5% unsolicited freelance; 50% assigned. Query; e-query OK. Accepts full mss by e-mail. **No payment** for onetime, reprint, or simultaneous rts. Not copyrighted. Articles 600-1,200 wds. (3-5/yr.). Responds in 9 wks. Seasonal 6 mos. ahead. Accepts simultaneous submissions and reprints (tell when/where appeared). Accepts requested ms on disk or by e-mail (attached file). Uses some sidebars. Prefers KJV. Also accepts submissions from children/teens. Guidelines at: http://www.heraldandbanner.com/banner; copy for 9 x 12 SAE/2 stamps. (No ads)

> **Fillers:** Anecdotes, quizzes; 150-400 wds.
>
> **Tips:** "Most open to short inspirational/devotional articles. Must be concise, well written, and get one main point across; 200-600 wds. Be well acquainted

with the Wesleyan/Holiness doctrine and tradition. Articles that are well written and express this conviction are very likely to be used."

+CHURCH OF ENGLAND NEWSPAPER. +44 20 7222 8700. E-mail: cen@church-newspaper.com. Looking for interesting stories about what's happening in your church or diocese. E-mail submissions/attached file. Guidelines at: http://www.churchnewspaper.com/services/add-your-story.

+CHURCH OF GOD EVANGEL, 1080 Montgomery Ave., Cleveland TN 37311. (423) 478-7592. E-mail: evangel@pathwaypress.org. Website: www.pathwaypress.org. Lance Colkmire, ed. Church of God (Cleveland TN). Official journal of the denomination. Open to freelance submissions; articles and reviews. Monthly print magazine; circ. 29,000; subscription $17.

+CITIZEN, 8605 Explorer Dr., Colorado springs CO 80920. (719) 531-3400. Karla.dial@fotf.org. Website: www.citizenlink.com/citizen-magazine. Focus on the Family. Karla Dial, ed. To inform, encourage, and inspire Christians of all denominations to engage the culture. Print mag. published 10X/yr.; circ. 50,000. Open to freelance submissions. (Ads)

+$ CITY LIGHT NEWS, Calgary AB, Canada. (403) 640-2011. Fax (886) 845-2019. E-mail: editor@Calgarychristian.com.Inter-denominational, for-profit Christian newspaper. Peter McManus, ed. Articles 550 wds.; fiction 300 wds.; reviews 300 wds. **Pays .10-.15/wd. Cdn.** Guidelines at: http://www.calgarychristian.com/adventures/guidelines.htm

$ COLUMBIA, 1 Columbus Plaza, New Haven CT 06510-3326. (203) 752-4398. Fax (203) 752-4109. E-mail: columbia@kofc.org. Website: www.kofc.org/columbia. Knights of Columbus. Alton Pelowski, ed.-in-chief. Geared to a general Catholic family audience; most stories must have a Knights of Columbus connection. Monthly and online mag.; 32 pgs.; circ. 1.5 million. Subscription $6; foreign $8. 25% unsolicited freelance; 75% assigned. Query; e-query OK. Accepts full mss by e-mail. **Pays $250-1,000** on acceptance for 1st and electronic rts. Articles 500-1,500 wds. (12/yr.). Responds in 4-6 wks. Seasonal 4 mos. ahead. Accepts e-mail submission (attachment preferred). Sometimes pays kill fee. Regularly uses sidebars. Prefers NAS. Guidelines at: http://www.kofc.org/un/en/columbia/guidelines.html; free copy. (No ads)

    Special needs: Essays on spirituality, personal conversion. Catholic preferred. Query first.

    Tips: "We welcome contributions from freelancers in all subject areas. An interesting or different approach to a topic will get the writer at least a second look from an editor. Most open to feature writers who can handle church issues, social issues from an orthodox Roman Catholic perspective. Must be aggressive, fact-centered writers for these features."

+COMMON CALL, The Baptist Standard Magazine, PO Box 259019, Plano TX 75025. (214) 630-4571. E-mail: marvknox@baptiststandard.com. Website: www.baptiststandard.com. Marv Knox, ed. Baptist Standard Publishing Co. To aid and support the denomination on such topics as missions, evangelism, family life, leadership, effective church ministry, and Texas Baptist history. Monthly denominational print magazine; circ. 18,500; subscription $24. Open to freelance submissions; articles and reviews. (Ads)

    ** 2014 EPA Award of Merit: Denominational (Digital)

+$ COMMON GROUND, 3152 W. 8th Ave., Vancouver BC V6K 2C3, Canada. (604) 733-2215. Fax: (604) 733-4415. E-mail: editor@commonground.ca. Prefer e-query; no attachments. Articles 600-1,500 wds. **Pays .10/wd.** Prefers Canadian authors. Guidelines at: http://commonground.ca/contribute.

+$ COMMONWEAL, 475 Riverside Dr., Rm. 405, New York NY 10115. (212) 662-4200. E-mail: editors@commonwealmagazine.org. Articles 750-3,000 wds. Query/attached file. **Pays $75-100** on publication for all rights. Guidelines at: https://www.commonwealmagazine.org/contact-us (scroll down).

CONVERGE MAGAZINE, 301-291 2nd Ave., Vancouver BC V5T 1B8, Canada. (604) 558-1982. E-mail: info@convergemagazine.com. Website: www.convergemagazine.com. Has print and online versions. Leanne Janzen print ed.; Kyle Stiemsma, web ed. Articles 300-1,000 wds. (to 800 wds. for online version). If no response in 4 wks., assume they are not interested. Guidelines at: http://convergemagazine.com/write.

+$ THE COVENANT COMPANION, 8303 W. Higgins Rd., Chicago IL 60631. (773) 907-3328. E-mail: communication@covchurch.org. Website: www.covchurch.org. The Evangelical Covenant Church. Edward Gilbreath, ed. Seeks to connect Covenanters to one another, and to challenge and inspire them in their faith. Monthly (10X) print magazine; circ. 8,000; subscription $19.95. Open to freelance submissions; articles and reviews. Articles 600-1,800 wds. **Pays $35-100** after publication for one-time or simultaneous rts. (Ads)

CREATION, PO Box 4545, Eight Mile Plains QLD 4113, Australia. 61-07 3340 9888. Fax 07 3340 9889. E-mail: mail@creation.info. Website: www.creation.com. Creation Ministries Intl. Carl Wieland, managing dir. A family, nature, science magazine focusing on creation/evolution issues. Quarterly mag.; 56 pgs.; circ. 46,000. Subscription $28. 10% unsolicited freelance. Query; phone/fax/e-query OK. **No payment** for all rts. Articles to 1,500 wds. (20/yr.). Responds in 2-3 wks. Prefers requested ms on disk or by e-mail (attached file). Regularly uses sidebars. For guidelines, see: http://creation.com/creation-magazine-writing-guidelines. (No ads)

> **Tips:** "Get to know the basic content/style of the magazine and emulate. Send us a copy of your article, or contact us by phone."

$ CREATION ILLUSTRATED, PO Box 7955, Auburn CA 95604. (530) 269-1424. Fax (888) 415-1989. E-mail: ci@creationillustrated.com. Website: www.creationillustrated.com. Tom Ish, ed./pub. An uplifting, Bible-based Christian nature magazine that glorifies God; for ages 9-99. Quarterly mag.; 68 pgs.; circ. 20,000. Subscription $19.95. 60% unsolicited freelance; 40% assigned. Query or query/clips; fax/e-query OK (put query submission in subject line). **Pays $75-125** within 30 days of publication for 1st rts. (holds North American Serial Rights, Archival Rights, and Internet Duplication of the Magazine in PDF Format). Articles 1,000-2,000 wds. (20/yr.). Response time varies. Seasonal 6 mos. ahead. Accepts simultaneous submissions and reprints (tell when/where appeared). Prefers e-mail submission (attached file or copied into message). Kill fee 25%. Uses some sidebars. Prefers NKJV. Guidelines/theme list on website: http://www.creationillustrated.com/article/8/writer-and-photographer-guidelines or by e-mail; copy $3/9 x 12 SAE/$3 postage. (Some ads)

> **Columns/Departments:** Creation Up Close feature, 1,500-2,000 wds. **$100;** Re-Creation and Restoration Through Outdoor Adventure, 1,500-2,000 wds. **$100;** Creatures Near and Dear to Us, 1,500-2,000 wds. **$100;** Children's Story, 500-1,000 wds. **$50-75;** My Walk with God, 1,000-1,500 wds. **$75;** Gardens from Eden Around the World, 1,000-1,500 wds., **$75;** Creation Day (a repeating series), 1,500-2,000 wds. **$100.**
>
> **Poetry:** Short, usually 4 verses. Needs to have both nature and spiritual thoughts. Pays about **$15.**
>
> **Tips:** "Most open to an experience with nature/creation that brought you closer

to God and will inspire the reader to do the same. Include spiritual lessons and supporting Scriptures—at least 3 or 4 of each."

+$ CREATIVE NONFICTION, 5501 Walnut St., Ste. 202, Pittsburgh PA 15232. (412) 688-0304. Fax (412) 688-0262. E-mail: information@creativenonfiction.org. Very open to unsolicited submissions; mailed or e-mailed. **Pays $50 flat fee, plus $10/printed page.** See Website for specific themes or needs under "Call for submissions." Guidelines at: http://www.creativenonfiction.org/submissions

+$ CRESSET, THE, The Editor, The Cresset, Mueller Hall, Valparaiso Univ., 1300 Chapel Dr., Valparaiso IN 46383. E-mail: cresset@valpo.edu. Journal address matters of import to those with some degree of theological interest and commitment. James Paul Old, ed.; Marci Rae Johnson, poetry ed. Prefers submissions through Website, but accepts e-mail submissions. Query. **Pays $100-500** on publication for all rts. Guidelines at: http://thecresset.org/submissions.html

+$ DECISION, 1 Billy Graham Pkwy., Charlotte NC 28201. (704) 401-2246. E-mail: decision@bgea.org. Website: www.billygraham.org/decision. Billy Graham Evangelistic Assn. Bob Paulson, ed. To set forth the Good News of salvation in Jesus Christ. Monthly (11X) print magazine; circ. 400,000; subscription $15. Open to freelance submissions. Articles 400-1,000 wds. Prefers queries. **Pays $200-500.**

+DESERT CHRISTIAN NEWS, PO Box 4196, Palm Desert CA 92261. (760) 772-2027. E-mail: smiller@desertchristiannews.org. To encourage communication and unity in the desert communities. Open to submissions. Susan Miller, pub. Articles to 500 wds. Prefers queries. Check this publisher at: www.desertchristiannews.org.

+$ DISASTER NEWS NETWORK, 10320 Little Patuxent Pkwy, Ste. 200, Columbia MD 21044. (443) 620-4230. Articles 1,000 wds. **Pays $100-150** on publication for all rts. E-query only. Guidelines at: www.disasternews.net.

+$ DRAMA MINISTRY, 2814 Azalea PL., Nashville TN 37204. Toll free: (866) 859-7622. E-mail: service@dramaministry.com. Open to unsolicited submissions. Send copies only; won't be returned. Articles 500-700 wds.; scripts 2-10 min. **Pays $100.** Guidelines at: http://www.dramaministry.com/faq (scroll down).

+$ DREAMSEEKER MAGAZINE, 126 Klingerman Rd., Telford PA 18969. (215) 723-9125. E-mail: DSM@CascadiaPublishingHouse.com. Michael A. King, ed. Quarterly mag. Articles 750-1,000 wds., or 1,500-2,000 wds. Submit by mail or e-mail. **Pays $5 or .01/wd.** Guidelines at: http://www.cascadiapublishinghouse.com/dsm/submit.htm.

+$ EFCA TODAY, PO Box 315, Charlottesville VA 22902. (434) 961-2500. E-mail: dianemc@journeygroup.com. Website: www.efcatoday.org. Diane McDougall, ed. Evangelical Free Church in America. Quarterly digital mag. Traffic 3,000. Articles 300-800 wds. Pays .23/wd., on acceptance, for 1st rights. Accepts reprints; payment varies. Guidelines at: http://www.efcatoday.org/site/writers-guidelines. (Ads)
     ** 2014 EPA Award of Excellence: Denominational (Digital)

+ENCOMPASS, 2296 Henderson Mills Rd. NE, Ste. 406, Atlanta GA 30345. (770) 414-1515. Email: rlundy@americananglican.org. Website: www.americananglican.org. Robert Lundy, ed. The American Anglican Council. To provide news, encouragement and information regarding the denomination; and to offer encouragement to the larger Christian community. Bimonthly print magazine; circ. 13,000. Open to freelance submissions. Articles 200-2,000 wds. Prefers queries. **No payment.**

ETERNAL INK, 4706 Fantasy Ln., Alton IL 62002. (618) 466-7860. E-mail:

eternallyours8@yahoo.com. EternallyYours8@groups.facebook.com. Interdenominational. Mary-Ellen Grisham, ed. (meginrose@gmail.com); Ivie Bozeman, features ed. (ivie@rose. net); Pat Earl, devotions ed. Personal sharing, witness, creativity, and outreach. Biweekly e-zine; 1 pg.; circ. 400. Subscription free. 50% unsolicited freelance. Complete ms/cover letter by e-mail only. **No payment** for onetime rts. Not copyrighted. Articles/devotions 300-500 wds. (25/yr.); reviews 300-500 wds. Responds in 2 wks. Seasonal 1 mo. ahead. Accepts simultaneous submissions and reprints (tell when/where appeared. Accepts e-mail submissions (copied into message). No kill fee or sidebars. Prefers NIV. Occasionally accepts submissions from children/teens. Guidelines/copy by e-mail (meginrose@charter. ney). (No ads)

> **Poetry:** Helen Down, poetry ed. (roybet@comcast.net). Accepts 24-30/yr. Free verse, light verse, traditional; 5-30 lines. Submit max. 3 poems.
>
> **Fillers:** Ivie Bozeman, features and fillers ed. (ivie@rose.net). Accepts 15/yr. Prayers, short humor; 25-100 wds.
>
> **Columns/Departments:** Ivie Bozeman, ed. Accepts 25-30/yr. See information in e-zine. Complete ms.
>
> **Special needs:** Devotions, meditations, and features.
>
> **Contest:** Annual Prose/Poetry Contest in November-December, with 1st, 2nd, and 3rd-place winners in each category. Book awards for first-place winners.
>
> **Tips:** "Please contact Mary-Ellen Grisham by e-mail with questions."

+$ EUREKA STREET.COM.AU, PO Box 553, Richmond VIC 3121, Australia. Phone: +61 3 9421 9666. E-mail: submissions@eurekastreet.com.au. Online publication of Australian Jesuits. Bimonthly. Articles 600-800 wds.; fiction 700-800 wds.; reviews 400 wds. (pays $100). Query for longer articles. Pays $200 for 1st rts. Guidelines at: http:// www.eurekastreet.com.au/article.aspx?aeid=33927#.UubCjJXTnIU..

> **Poetry:** Submit to: poetry@eurekastreet.com.au. Poets share $50 with other poets published that week.

$ EVANGEL, 770 N. High School Rd., Indianapolis IN 46214. (317) 244-3660. E-mail: evangeleditor@fmcusa.org. Free Methodist Church USA. Submit to: Julie Innes, ed. Printed quarterly for weekly distribution. Adult SS take home paper. 8 pgs. Circ. 6,000. Subscription rate $2.69. 100% freelance. Send complete mss with cover letter; e-mail or snail-mail queries OK. Prefers full mss by e-mail. **Pays $10-12** for articles or fiction, or **.06/wd.** Pay on publication, one-time rights. Copyrighted. Prefers NIV. Articles and fiction 300-1,200 wds. Responds in 4-10 wks. Seasonal 9-18 mos. in advance. Accepts simultaneous submissions and reprints. Occasional kill fee. Sometimes uses sidebars. Writer's guidelines by e-mail. Sample copy #10 env. and 2 first class stamps. Photos with articles only. Accepts teen submissions. (No ads

> **Nonfiction:** Send complete manuscript.
>
> **Fiction:** For adults.
>
> **Poetry:** Free verse, light verse, traditional; 7-15/yr. Max 5 at a time. **Pays $10 max.**
>
> **Fillers:** Cartoons, Crypto-Scriptures. **Pays $10-20.**

+THE EXPERIENCE, PO Box 12609, Oklahoma City OK 73157. (405) 792-7190. E-mail: trutland@iphc.org. Website: www.iphc.org/experience. LifeSprings Resources/ Intl. Pentecostal Holiness Church. Lee Grady, ed. To share what's happening in the denomination; reporting news from around the world; and providing articles and resources to assist in leadership development. Monthly online denominational magazine; traffic 10,000. Open to freelance submissions; articles and reviews.

+$ FAITH & FAMILY. (See *Catholic Digest*)

+$ **FAITH & FRIENDS,** The Salvation Army, 2 Overlea Blvd., Toronto ON M4H 1P4, Canada. (416) 422-6226. Fax: (416) 422-6120. E-mail: faithandfriends@can.salvationarmy.org. Publishes testimonials and personal stories. Circ. 50,000. Prefers e-mail submissions. Articles 500-1,000 wds. Accepts reprints. **Pays up to $200 Cdn.** Guidelines at: http://salvationist.ca/editorial/writers-guidelines.

$ **FAITH TODAY:** To Connect, Equip and Inform Evangelical Christians in Canada, PO Box 5885, West Beaver Creek, Richmond Hill, ON L4B 0B8, Canada. (905) 479-5885. Fax (905) 479-4742. E-mail: editor@faithtoday.ca. Website: www.faithtoday. ca. Company blog: blog.faithtoday.ca; free digital editions at www.faithtoday.ca/digital. Evangelical Fellowship of Canada. Bill Fledderus, sr. ed.; Karen Stiller, assoc. ed. Connects, equips, and informs Canada's four million Evangelicals with 6 printed issues per year, plus more online. Bimonthly mag. and e-zine; 56-80 pgs.; circ. 20,000. US print subscription $35.99, online free. 20% unsolicited freelance; 60% assigned. Query/clips; e-query preferred. Prefers a cover letter. **Pays $60-750 (.15-.25 Cdn./wd.)** on acceptance for 1st, one-time or electronic rts.; reprints .15/wd. Features 800-1,700 words; cover stories 2,000 wds.; essays 650-1,200 wds.; profiles 900 words; articles 300-2,000 wds. (50/yr.); book/music/video reviews 300 wds. (75-100/yr.); pays $50. Responds in 2 wks. Seasonal 6 mos. ahead. Accepts simultaneous submissions; no reprints. Requires e-mail submissions, attached or copied into message. Kill fee 30%. Regularly uses sidebars. Prefers NIV. Guidelines at: www.faithtoday.ca/writers; copy at www.faithtoday.ca/digital. (Ads)
>   **Columns/Departments:** Query. Buys 20/yr. Pays $50 for 300 wd. Reviews; $100 or more for 700 wd. column.
>   **Special needs:** Images of work by Canadian Christian visual artists. Anything with an explicit Canadian-Christian connection/angle.
>   **Tips:** "Most open to short, colorful items, statistics, stories, profiles (400 wds.) for Kingdom Matters department. Content (not author) must have a Canadian connection." Unsolicited manuscripts will not be returned.

+$ **FAMILY SMART E-TIPS,** PO Box 1125, Muriette CA 9256 325 University Drive, Hershey, PA 17033; February 5-7, 2016. (727) 596-7625. Fax: 4-1125. (858) 513-7150. E-mail: plewis@smartfamilies.com. A pro-family, pro-child, and pro-marriage message. Paul Lewis, ed./pub. Bimonthly E-newsletter. Articles 200-1,000 wds. Prefers complete ms. Pays $50-250. Guidelines at: http://www.smartfamilies.com/fslinks/fsEditorial_Privacy.html

THE FIT CHRISTIAN MAGAZINE, PO Box 2824, Key West FL 33045. (206) 305-407-0555. E-mail: editor@fitchristian.com. Website: www.fitchristian.com. His Work Christian Publishing. Rev. Angela J. Willard Perez, ed. A Christian rendering health and fitness. Seasonal mag. Subscription free. Open to unsolicited freelance. Reprints encouraged. Guidelines online at: http://www.fitchristian.com/articles/article_submissions. html#axzz2rkAu9CED, or www.fitchristian.com/jobs.html. Features and articles in the magazine and online. Topics on health, fitness, diet, nutrition, family, faith.

+**FOUNDERS JOURNAL,** Founders Press, PO Box 150931, Cape coral FL 33915. (239) 772-1400. Fax: (239) 772-1140. Kenneth Puls, ed. Southern Baptist. Quarterly theological publication. Articles and book reviews. Guidelines at: http://www.founders. org/journal/fjguide.pdf

+**FRIENDS JOURNAL,** 1216 Arch St., Ste. 2A, Philadelphia PA 19107. (215) 563-8629. E-mail: martink@friendsjournal.org. An independent magazine serving the entire Religious Society of Friends. Martin Kelly, sr. ed. Theme list on Website. Articles to 2,500 wds. No payment. Guidelines at: http://www.friendsjournal.org/submissions/.

*$ GEM, 700 E. Melrose Ave., Box 926, Findlay OH 45839-0926. (419) 424-1961. Fax (419) 424-3433. E-mail: communications@cggc.org, or through website: www.cggc.org. Churches of God, General Conference. Rachel L. Foreman, ed. To encourage and motivate people in their Christian walk. Monthly (13X) take-home paper for adults; 8 pgs.; circ. 6,000. Subscription $14. 95% unsolicited freelance; 5% assigned. Complete ms/cover letter; phone/fax/e-query OK. **Pays $5-15** after publication for onetime rts. Articles 300-1,200 wds. (125/yr.); fiction 1,200 wds. (125/yr.). Responds in 12 wks. Seasonal 3 mos. ahead. Accepts simultaneous submissions and reprints (tell when/where appeared). Prefers submissions by e-mail. Uses some sidebars. Prefers NIV. Copy for #10 SAE/2 stamps. (No ads)

> **Poetry:** Buys 100/yr. Any type, 3-40 lines; $5-15. Submit max. 3 poems.
> **Fillers:** Buys 25/yr. All types except party ideas; 25-100 words; $5-10.
> **Special needs:** Missions and true stories. Be sure that fiction has a clearly religious/ Christian theme.
> **Tips:** "Most open to real-life experiences where you have clearly been led by God. Make the story interesting and Christian."

$ GEMS OF TRUTH, PO Box 4060, 7407-7415 Metcalf Ave., Overland Park KS 66204. (913) 432-0331. Fax (913) 722-0351. Website: www.heraldandbanner.com. Church of God (Holiness)/Herald & Banner Press. Arlene McGehee, Sunday school ed. Denominational. Weekly adult take-home paper; 8 pgs.; circ. 14,000. Subscription $2.45. Complete ms/cover letter; phone/fax/e-query OK (prefers mail or e-mail). **Pays .005/wd.** on publication for 1st rts. Fiction 1,000-2,000 wds. Seasonal 6-8 mos. ahead. Accepts simultaneous submissions and reprints (tell when/where appeared). Prefers KJV. Guidelines at: http://www.heraldandbanner.com/hb/gems-of-truth; theme list/copy by mail. Not in topical listings. (No ads)

*GENUINE MOTIVATION: YOUNG CHRISTIAN MAN, PO Box 573, Clarksville AR 72830. (479) 439-4891. E-mail: thebeami@juno.com; Website: www.onmyownnow.com; On My Own Ministries, Inc. Rob Beames, ed. Christian alternative to the men's magazine. For young, single men ages 17-23 who are sincerely seeking to be disciples of Christ. Monthly e-zine; 18 pgs; circ. 1,000. Free subscription. Estab. 2009; 40% unsolicited. 60% assigned. Complete manuscript by e-mail. E-mail query OK. **No payment,** nonexclusive rights. Prefer NIV. 800-1200 wds. Accepts 24 nonfiction mss/yr. Responds in 2 weeks. Seasonal 2 mo ahead. Accepts simultaneous and reprints. (Tell when/where appeared). Require articles by e-mail. No kill fee. Always inc. bio on feature article. Guidelines on website. Book, Music, Video review 800 wds. Accept submissions from teens. Column: Tool Box (resources for young adult men) 450-550 wds; Faith and Finance (good and godly stewardship) 700-1000 wds; The Recap (review of books, movies, music, etc) 600-1000 wds; Election Year (where faith and politics intersect) 800-1200 wds. Accepts 18 mss/yr. Query, send complete manuscript. Guidelines at: www.onmyownnow.com.

> **Tips:** "Looking for guest columnists for Faith and Finance, Tool Box, and The Recap. Also seek new writers for feature articles." (No ads)

+$ GOOD NEWS, PO Box 132076, The Woodlands TX 77393-2076. (832) 813-8327. Fax: (832) 813-5327. Leading United Methodists to a faithful future. Steve Beard, ed. Articles 1,500-1,850 wds. **Pays $100-150** on publication for one-time rts. Subscription $25. Guidelines at: www.goodnewsmag.org.

+GOOD NEWS!, 440 W. Nyack Rd., West Nyack NY 10994, (845) 629-7438, E-mail: warren.maye@use.salvationarmy.org. Website: www.sagoodnews.com. The Salvation

Army – Eastern Territory. Warren L. Maye, ed. To inform, inspire, and equip Salvationists to grow in holiness, to serve together in supportive, healing communities, and to reach others for Jesus Christ. Monthly newspaper; circ. 35,000. Open to freelance submissions by e-mail/attached or embedded; articles and reviews. Guidelines at: http://www.sagoodnews.org/submission.php. (Ads)

+ **GOOD NEWS! ONLINE.** (See *Good News!*) Traffic: 1,166.

+$ **GOOD NEWS, THE (FL),** 5601 Powerline Rd., Fort Lauderdale FL 33309. (954) 564-5378. Shelly Pond, ed. Articles 500-800 wds. Query/clips. **Pays .10/wd.** Guidelines at: www.goodnewsfl.org.

+$ **GOOD NEWS, ETC,** PO Box 2660, Vista CA 92085. (760) 724-3075. E-mail: goodnewseditor@cox.net. Website: www.goodnewsetc.com. Abiding Media Group, Inc. Rick Monroe, ed. To provide local Christian news and features to believers and seekers in San Diego County. Monthly print newspaper; circ. 36,000; subscription $30. Open to freelance submissions; articles and reviews. E-query. Articles 500-900 wds. **Pays $40-150.** (Ads)

+**GOOD NEWS JOURNAL,** PO Box 170069, Austin TX 78717-0069. (512) 461-2964. E-mail: goodnewsjournal10@gmail.com. Articles 350 wds. Prefers e-query. **No payment.** Check this publication at: www.thegoodnewsjournal.net

+**GOOD NEWS ROCHESTER,** PO Box 18204, Rochester NY 14618. (585) 271-4464. E-mail: thegoodnewsrochester@frontiernet.net. Website: www.thegoodnewswny.com. Good News Rochester. Alexandre V. Boutakov. Bimonthly print newspaper; subscription $20. A nondenominational, biblically based Christian newspaper. Open to freelance submissions; articles and reviews. (Ads).

+**GRACECONNECT,** PO Box 544, Winona Lake IN 46590. (574) 268-1122. E-mail: lcgates@bmhbooks.com. Website: www.graceconnect.us. Brethren Missionary Herald Co. Liz Cutler Gates, ed. Connecting people and churches of the Fellowship of Grace Brethren Churches. Quarterly denominational print magazine; circ. 16,000. Open to freelance submissions. (Ads)

$ **GUIDEPOSTS,** (212) 251-8100. E-mail: submissions@guideposts.org. Website: www.guideposts.org. Interfaith. Submit to Articles Editor. Personal faith stories showing how faith in God helps each person cope with life in some particular way. Monthly mag.; 68 pgs.; circ. 2 million. Subscription $16.97. 40% unsolicited freelance; 20% assigned. Complete ms/cover letter by e-mail (attached or copy into message). **Pays $100-500** on publication for all rts. Articles 750-1,500 wds. (40-60/yr.), shorter pieces 250-750 words (**$100-250**). Responds only to mss accepted for publication in 2 mos. Seasonal 3 mos. ahead. Accepts simultaneous submissions and reprints. Kill fee 20%. Uses some sidebars. Free guidelines on website: www.guideposts.org/tellusyourstory; copy. (Ads)

> **Columns/Departments:** Mysterious Ways (divine intervention), 250 wds. What Prayer Can Do, 250 wds. Divine Touch (tangible evidence of God's help), 400 wds.
> **Contest:** Writers Workshop Contest held on even years with a late June deadline. Winners attend a week-long seminar (all expenses paid) on how to write for *Guideposts*.
> **Tips:** "Be able to tell a good story, with drama, suspense, description, and dialog. The point of the story should be some practical spiritual help that the subject learns through his or her experience. Use unique spiritual insights, strong and unusual dramatic details. We rarely present stories about deceased or professional religious people." First person only.

+$ **HAVOK,** Splickety Publishing Group. E-mail: submissions@splicketypubgroup.com. Avily Jerome, ed. Publishes concise, poignant fiction under 1,000 wds.; stories that hit fast and stick hard—stories that, no matter the genre, can cut through the day's troubles and grip readers with short attention spans. Short stories 300-1,000 wds.; prefers 700 wds. or less. Open to submissions for nano-fiction stories in 100 wds. or less; need to fit the theme. Theme list with deadlines on the Website. Send e-mail submissions/attachment only. **Pays .02/wd.** Guidelines on Website.

Artwork: Also accepts submissions from artists, graphic designers, and photographers.

+**HEARTBEAT,** PO Box 9, Hatfield AR 71945. (870) 389-6196. E-mail: heartbeat@ cmausa.org. Website: www.cmausa.org. Christian Motorcyclists Assn. Misty Bradley, ed. To inspire our leaders and members to be the most organized, advanced, equipped, financially stable organization, full of integrity in the motorcycling industry and the kingdom of God. Monthly print magazine; circ. 18,000; subscription $20. Open to freelance submissions. (Ads)

HIGHWAY NEWS AND GOOD NEWS, 1525 River Rd., PO Box 117, Marietta PA 17547-0117. (717) 426-9977. E-mail: editor@transportforchrist.org. Website: www. transportforchrist.org. Transport for Christ, Intl. Inge Koenig, ed. For truck drivers and their families; evangelistic, with articles for Christian growth. Monthly mag. and e-zine; 16 pgs.; circ. 20,000. Subscription free. 5-10% unsolicited freelance. E-query preferred. **Pays in copies** for rights offered. Articles 600 to 800 wds. Seasonal 4 mos. ahead. Accepts simultaneous submissions and reprints (tell when/where appeared). Prefers requested ms by e-mail (attached or copied into message). Uses some sidebars. Prefers NIV 1984 or ESV. Guidelines/idea list at: http://www.transportforchrist.org/highway/about.cfm; free copy mailed upon request. (No ads)

Poetry: Accepts 2/yr. 3-20 lines. Submit max. 1 poem. Rarely uses poetry; should be related to the trucking life, with a Christian focus.

Tips: "As a magazine with truckers as its primary audience, we especially look for articles dealing with issues of interest to truckers (not necessarily Christian— for example, we may publish an article addressing new DOT rulings); also experiences and testimonies that address or are related to the trucking life, its challenges, problems, rewards, etc."

+$ **HOLINESS TODAY,** 17001 Prairie Star, Lenexa KS 66220. (913) 577-0500x2565. E-mail: holinesstoday@nazarene.org. Website: www.holinesstoday.org. General Board, Church of the Nazarene. Carmen Ringhiser, ed. To keep readers connected with the Nazarene experience and provide tools for everyday faith. Bimonthly denominational print magazine; circ. 20,000; subscription $12. Open to freelance submissions. Query first. **Pays.**

+$ **HOMESCHOOLING TODAY.** E-mail: editor@homeschoolongtoday.com. To encourage the hearts of homeschoolers and give them tools to install a love of learning in their children. Published 4X/yr. Does not accept queries; send full ms. as an attachment. Articles 900-1,200 wds. No reprints. **Pays .10/published word.** Accepts simultaneous submissions (tell them). Guidelines at: http://homeschoolingtoday.com/write-for-us/ .

$ **HOME TIMES FAMILY NEWSPAPER,** 4078 Colle Dr., Lake Worth FL 33461. (888) 439-3509. E-mail: hometimes2@aol.com. Website: www.hometimes.org. Neighbor News, Inc. Dennis Lombard, ed./pub. Conservative, pro-Christian community newspaper. Quarterly broadsheet 8 pgs.; circ. 2,000. Subscription $15/yr. 15% unsolicited freelance; 15% assigned. Complete ms only/cover letter; no phone/fax/e-query. **Pays $5-25** on acceptance for onetime rts. Articles 100-1,200 wds. (15/yr.); fiction 300-1,500 wds. (1-2/yr.). Responds in 2 wks. Seasonal 2 mos. ahead. Accepts simultaneous submissions and reprints (tell when/where appeared). No kill fee. Regularly uses sidebars. Also accepts submissions from teens. Any Bible version. Guidelines on Website; sample issue $3. (Ads)

Poetry: Buys almost none. Free verse, traditional; 2-16 lines; **$5.** Submit max. 3 poems.

Fillers: Uses a few/yr. Anecdotes, cartoons, facts, ideas, jokes, kid quotes, newsbreaks, prayers, quotes, short humor, tips; to 100 wds. **Pays 2 copies,** if requested.

Columns/Departments: Buys 30/yr. See guidelines for departments, to 800 wds. **$5-15.**

Special needs: Good short stories (creative nonfiction or fiction). Home and family, parenting, education, etc. More faith, miracles, personal experiences, local people stories, some on assignment.

Tips: "Most open to personal stories or home/family pieces. Very open to new writers, but study guidelines and sample first; we are different. Published by Christians, but not 'religious.' Looking for more positive articles and stories. Occasionally seeks stringers to write local people features with photos. Journalism experience is preferred. E-mail query for more info with your name, background, and address to hometimes2@aol.com. We strongly suggest you read *Home Times.* Also consider our manual for writers: *101 Reasons Why I Reject Your Manuscript* (reduced to $12, reg. $19)."

+HOPEKEEPERS MAGAZINE, PO Box 502928, San Diego CA 92150. E-mail: rest@restministries.org. Rest Ministries, Inc. Serves people who live with chronic pain. Currently digital only. Quarterly. Prefers e-queries. Articles 375-1,500 wds.; book reviews 300 wds. **Pays in copies.** Guidelines at: http://www.restministries.org/hk_mag/writers-guidelines.htm. Copy for $3/6x9 SAE.

+$ IMAGE, 3307 Third Ave. W., Seattle WA 98119. E-mail: mkenagy@imagejournal. org. Mary Kenagy Mitchell, mng. ed. Open to unsolicited submissions. Accepts e-mail queries, but not submissions; mailed submissions only. 6,000 wds. Max. Responds in 5 mos. Buys 1st serial rts. **Pays $10/pg. ($200 max.)** Guidelines at: http://imagejournal.org/ page/about/submission-guidelines.

$ INDIAN LIFE, 188 Henderson Hwy., Winnipeg MB R2L 1L6, Canada. (204) 661-9333. Fax (204) 661-3982. E-mail: ilm.editor@indianlife.org or through website: www. indianlife.org. Intertribal Christian Communications. Online site: www.newspaper@indi-anlife.org. Jim Uttley, ed. Primary audience is North America's First Peoples (Indigenous); includes Native Americans and Native Canadians; only evangelical publication produces for this audience. Bimonthly tabloid newspaper; 20 pgs.; circ. 14,500. Subscription $18. 30% unsolicited freelance; 40% assigned; 30% in-house. Query (query or complete ms for fiction); snail mail and e-query OK. Pays **.15-.25/wd ($50-$200)** on publication for 1st and reprint rts. Articles 150-2,500 wds. (20/yr.); fiction 1,000-2,500 wds. (15/yr.); book and music reviews, 500-800 wds.; video reviews 500-1,500 wds **(pays .25/wd.).** Responds in 6 wks. Seasonal 6 mos. ahead. Accepts simultaneous submissions and reprints (tell when/where appeared). Accepts requested ms by e-mail (copied into message preferred). Some kill fees 50%. Some sidebars. Accepts submissions from children/teens. Prefers New Life Version, The Message. Guidelines by e-mail/website: http://www.indianlife. org/index.php; copy for 9 x 12 SAE/$2 postage (check or money order). (Ads)

Poetry: Buys 10-12 poems/yr.; free verse, light verse, traditional, 10-100 wds. Or 5-25 lines; **pays $40.** Submit max. 3 poems.

Fillers: Buys 12 or less. Anecdotes, cartoons, facts, jokes, prose, quotes; 25-100 wds.; **$15.**

Columns: Query for columns. Pays **$40-$80.**

Special needs: Articles on suicide, environment, and sexual issues as related to indigenous communities. We don't accept freelance materials for columns except for articles on Native legends and how they relate to the Christian life.

Tips: "Most open to testimonies from Native Americans/Canadians—either first person or third person—news features, or historical fiction with strong and accurate portrayal of Native American life from the Indian perspective. A writer should have understanding of some Native American history and culture. We suggest reading some Native American authors. Native authors preferred, but some others are published. Aim at a 10th-grade reading level; short paragraphs; avoid multisyllable words and long sentences."

**2010 EPA Award of Merit: Newspaper.

+IN PART, 431 Grantham Rd., Mechanicsburg PA 17055. (717) 697-2634. E-mail: inpart@bic-church.org. Website: www.inpart.org. Brethren in Christ Church in the U.S. Kristine N. Frey, ed. To communicate the life, teachings, and mission of the denomination. Quarterly denominational print magazine; circ. 19,000. Accepts freelance submissions; articles and reviews.

**2014 EPA Award of Merit: Denominational

+$ IN TOUCH, 3836 DeKalb Technology Pkwy, Atlamta GA 30340. E-mail: cameron.lawrence@intouch.org. Website: www.intouch.org. In Touch Ministries. Cameron Lawrence, ed. To inspire, encourage, educate and change lives by communicating God's truth and connect people to God's work through In Touch Ministries. Monthly devotional print magazine; circ. 1,500,000. Open to freelance submissions. Articles 800-2,000 wds. **Pays varying rates.**

** 2014 EPA Award of Merit: Most Improved.

JOBTOJOY.US, 5042 E. Cherry Hills Blvd., Springfield MO 65809. (417) 832-8409. Fax (508) 632-8409. E-mail: editor@JobToJoy.us, e-mail submissions only (attachment formats are fine in Word, WordPerfect, Works, or the free OpenOffice word processor; not PDF files). Also attach a brief author's bio, and digital photo if available. E-query OK. Open to 80% unsolicited freelance! Reprints fine, electronic rights. Future selection for inclusion in a book is a possibility. Get in on the ground floor. We are a start-up with a small staff; if your writing requires edits, it will delay posting it online. J. R. Chrystie, managing director. All submissions should have a positive focus. **No payment.** In lieu of payment, accepted authors will be featured on Our Authors page with their bio, photo, and link to their website or blog. Devotions 300-500 words; include Scripture and ending prayer. Book reviews (query first) 400-800 words; books about careers, change, moving, retirement, job-related issues. Inspiring testimonials (successful job change, career change, new retirement years' career transition into ministry or volunteerism) 600-1000 words. Keep it positive. Some poetry, any form.

Fillers: Inspiring quotations 20-75 words; humorous short stories about a job change 70-150 words; positive job change how-to tips 50-150 words; review of a helpful job-related website 30-50 words; a Bible verse and how it helped you through a job change 20-50 words; cartoons should be attached as a .jpg file (remember this is a Christian site).

Special Needs: Feature articles (query first) such as how to know when God wants you elsewhere, what is the difference between a job and a ministry, and relevant interviews. Read our online mission statement and be creative.

+JOYFUL LIVING MAGAZINE, (formerly Christian Quarterly), PO Box 311, Palo Cedro CA 97073. Phone/fax (530) 247-7500. E-mail: Cathy@joyfullivingmagazine.com. Nondenominational. Cathy Jansen, pub. E-mail: cathy@christianquarterly.org. Christian-based magazine in Northern CA; also distributes in Southern OR. Quarterly magazine; circ. 15,000. Subscription $35. 100% unsolicited freelance. Complete ms; e-queries OK. **No payment.** Not copyrighted. All rights. Articles and fiction under 700 wds. Responds in 2 wks. Seasonal 6 mos. ahead. Accepts simultaneous submissions and reprints (tell when/where appeared). Requires e-mail submissions (attached or copied into message). Some sidebars. Also accepts submissions from children/teens. Modern English Version. Guidelines on Website; copy for 10 x 12 SAE/$3 postage. (Ads).

> **Poetry:** Accepts 6-10/yr. Free verse, traditional.
> **Fillers:** 200-250 wds. Accepts cartoons, games, jokes, short humor, tips, and word puzzles.
> **Columns/Departments:** Uses many. Marriage and family; Health; Financial; Testimonies.
> **Special needs:** "Looking for articles that inspire and encourage, not too preachy or not coming off like a Bible study. Content that stimulates readers to ponder on the good things of God."

+KANSAS CITY METRO VOICE, 1114, Lee's summit MO 64063. (816) 524-4522. E-mail: dwight@metrovoicenews.com. Website: www.metrovoicenews.com. Widamon Communications, Inc. Dwight Widamon, ed. Through two zoned editions, to inform and encourage the evangelical community in the Kansas City metropolitan area and Topeka/ Northeast Kansas, on issues of the day so that they might pray more effectively. Monthly print newspaper; circ. 42,500; subscription $24. Open to freelance submissions; articles and reviews. (Ads).

KEYS TO LIVING, 105 Steffens Rd., Danville PA 17821. (570) 437-2891. E-mail: owcam@verizon.net. Website: http://keystoliving.homestead.com. Connie Mertz, ed./ pub. Educates, encourages, and challenges readers through devotional and inspirational writings; also nature articles, focusing primarily on wildlife in eastern US. Quarterly news-letter; 16 pgs. Subscription $10. 30% unsolicited freelance (needs freelance). Complete ms/cover letter; prefers e-mail submissions; no phone query. **Pays 2 copies** for onetime or reprint rts. Articles 350-500 wds. Responds in 4 wks. Accepts reprints. No disk; e-mail submission OK (copied into message). Prefers NIV. Guidelines/theme list at: http://key-stoliving.homestead.com/GuidelinesSubscription.htm; copy for 7 x 10 SAE/2 stamps. (No ads)

> **Poetry:** Accepts if geared to family, nature, personal living, or current theme. Traditional with an obvious message.
> **Special needs:** More freelance submissions on themes only.
> **Tips:** "We are a Christ-centered family publication. Seldom is freelance material used unless it pertains to a current theme. No holiday material accepted. Stay within word count."

$ KINDRED SPIRIT, 3909 Swiss Ave., Dallas TX 75204. Fax (972) 222-1544. E-mail: sglahn@dts.edu. Website: www.dts.edu/ks. Dr. Sandra Glahn, ed-in-chief. Publication of Dallas Theological Seminary. We use freelancers for profiles of our graduates only. Triannual and online mag.; 16-20 pgs.; circ. 30,000. Subscription free. 30% unsolicited freelance; 50% assigned. Query/clips; mail and e-query OK. **Pays $300-350** on publication for 1st and electronic rts.; also First North American rts. Articles 1,000 wds. (or 1,100 including sidebar); accepts 6/yr. Responds in 6 wks. No seasonal. Accepts simulta-neous submissions and reprints (**pays $150**). Requires accepted mss by e-mail (attached or copied into message). Kill fee 75%. Regularly uses sidebars. Prefers NIV. Guidelines at: http://www.dts.edu/publications/kindredspirit/submissions; copy online. (No ads)

Special needs: Profiles/interviews of DTS grads and faculty are open to anyone.

Tips: "Any news or profiles or expositions of Scripture with a link to DTS will receive top consideration; all topics other than interviews need to come from DTS graduates."

** 2010 EPA Award of Merit: Cause of the Year.

LEAVES, PO Box 87, Dearborn MI 48121-0087. (313) 561-2330. Fax (313) 561-9486. E-mail: leaves-mag@juno.com. Website: www.mariannhill.us. Catholic/Mariannhill Fathers of Michigan. Rev. Thomas Heier, CMM, ed-in-chief. For all Catholics; promotes devotion to God and his saints and publishes readers' spiritual experiences, petitions, and thanksgivings. Bimonthly mag.; 24 pgs.; circ. 19,000. Subscription free. 25% unsolicited freelance. Complete ms/cover letter; mail/e-query OK. **No payment** for one-time rts. Not copyrighted. Articles 500 wds. (4/yr.). Responds in 2 wks. Seasonal 4 mos. ahead. Accepts simultaneous submissions and reprints (tell when/where appeared). Prefers e-mail submissions (attached file). No sidebars. Prefers NAB. Guidelines at: http://www. mariannhill.us/leaves.html; no copy. (No ads)

Poetry: Accepts 6/yr. Light verse, traditional; 8-16 lines. Submit max. 3 poems.

Tips: "Besides being interestingly and attractively written, an article should be confidently and reverently grounded in traditional Catholic doctrine and spirituality. The purpose of our magazine is to edify our readers. Read some of our articles."

$ LEBEN, 2150 River Plaza Dr., Ste. 150, Sacramento CA 95833. (916) 473-8866, ext. 4. E-mail: editor@leben.us or through website: www.leben.us. City Seminary Press. Wayne Johnson, ed. Tells stories of the Protestant Reformers and those who have followed in their footsteps through the ages. Quarterly and online mag.; 24 pgs.; circ. 5,000. Subscription $19.95. 20% unsolicited freelance; 80% assigned. Complete ms; e-query OK. Accepts full mss by e-mail. **Pays .05/wd.** (copies and subscription) on acceptance for 1st and electronic rts. Articles 500-2,500 wds. (4/yr.). Responds in 2 wks. Accepts simultaneous submissions and reprints (tell when/where appeared). Prefers e-mail submissions (attached file). Uses some sidebars. Also accepts submissions from teens. Prefers KJV. Guidelines at: http:// www.leben.us/writers; copy for 9 x 12 SAE/$2 postage. (Ads)

Fillers: Buys 4-6/yr. Short humor. **Pays $5-10.**

Special needs: Reprints from old publications; historical, humor, etc.

Tips: "We feature stories that are biographical, historically accurate, and interesting—about Protestant martyrs, patriots, missionaries, etc., with a 'Reformed' slant."

$ LIGHT & LIFE MAGAZINE, Box 535002, Indianapolis IN 46253-5002. (317) 244-3660. Fax (317) 244-1247. E-mail: jeff.finley@fmcusa.org. Website: http://llcomm. org/writersguidelines. Free Methodist Church - USA. Jeff Finley, mng. ed. Interactive magazine for maturing Christians; contemporary-issues oriented, thought-provoking; emphasizes spiritual growth, discipline, holiness as a lifestyle. Monthly mag.; 32 pgs. (plus pullouts); circ. 45,000. Subscription $12. 95% unsolicited freelance. Query first; e-query OK. **Pays .15/wd.** on acceptance for 1st rts. Articles 800-1,500 wds. (24/yr.). Responds in 8-12 wks. Seasonal 12 mos. ahead. No simultaneous submissions. Prefers e-mail submission (attached file) after acceptance. No kill fee. Uses some sidebars. Prefers NIV. Also accepts submissions from children/teens. Guidelines at: http://llcomm.org/ writersguidelines; copy $4. (Ads).

Tips: "Best to write a query letter. We are emphasizing contemporary issues articles, well researched. Ask the question, 'What topics are not receiving adequate coverage in the church and Christian periodicals?' Seeking unique angles on everyday topics."

+LIGHT AND LIFE MAGAZINE ONLINE, 3 (See *Light & Life Magazine*). E-mail: llmeditor@fmcna.org. Website: www.llcomm.org. Jay Cordova, ed.

+$LIGUORIAN, Attn: Managing Editor, One Liguori Dr., Liguori MO 63057. E-mail: liguorianeditor@liguori.org. Requires e-mail submission/attached file. Articles to 2,200 wds,; fiction 2,000 wds. **Pays .12-.15/wd.** No simultaneous submissions or reprints. Seasonal 8 mos. ahead. Responds in 8-10 wks. Guidelines at: http://www.liguorian.org/index.php?option=com_content&view=article&id=212&Itemid=78.

$LIVE, 1445 N. Boonville Ave., Springfield MO 65802-1894. (417) 862-2781. E-mail: rl-live@gph.org. Website: www.gospelpublishing.com. Assemblies of God/Gospel Publishing House. Wade Quick, ed. For Christian adults. Accepts true stories, stories based on true stories, personal experience, and fiction; must show God working in individual lives. Weekly take-home paper; 8 pgs./week; 112/quarter; circ. 20,000. Subscription $3.99/quarter. 100% unsolicited freelance. Complete ms.; accepts full ms by e-mail. **Pays .07-.10/wd.** (.07/wd. for reprints) on acceptance for 1st or reprint rts. Articles 450-1,200 wds. (96/yr.); fiction 450-1,200 wds. (8/yr.). Responds in 8 wks. Seasonal 8-12 mos. ahead. Accepts simultaneous submissions and reprints (tell when/where appeared). Prefers e-mail submissions (attached file). Some sidebars. Prefers 2011 NIV. Guidelines at: www.gospelpublishing.com ("Writer's Guides"); copy for #10 SAE/2 stamps. (No ads)

> **Poetry:** Paul Smith, ed. Buys 12/yr. Traditional; 6-15 lines; $60 (payment for reprints varies) when scheduled. Submit max. 4 poems.
>
> **Tips:** "We are often in need of good shorter stories (400-600 wds.), especially true stories or based on true stories. Often need holiday stories that are not 'how-to' stories, particularly for patriotic or nonreligious holidays. All areas open to freelance—human interest, inspirational, and difficulties overcome with God's help. Fiction must be in first person, and must have a spiritual point for Christians. Follow our guidelines. Most open to well-written personal experience with biblical application.

+THE LIVING CHURCH, 816 E. Juneau Ave., Milwaukee WI 53202. (414) 276-5420. E-mail: dleblanc@livingchurch.org. Website: www.livingchurh.org. The Living Church Foundation. Christopher Wells, ed. To seek and serve the Catholic and evangelical faith of the one Church, to the end of visible Christian unity throughout the world. Denominational print magazine published 26X/yr; circ. 5,000; subscription $39. Open to freelance submissions; articles and reviews. (Ads)

$ LIVING LIGHT NEWS, #200, 5306—89th St., Edmonton AB T6E 5P9, Canada. (780) 468-6397. Fax (780) 468-6872. E-mail: shine@livinglightnews.com. Website: www.livinglightnews.com. Living Light Ministries. Jeff Caporale, ed. To inspire and encourage Christians; witnessing tool to the lost. Bimonthly tabloid; 20 pgs.; circ. 60,000. Subscription $24.95 US. 20% unsolicited freelance; 70% assigned. Query; e-query OK. **Pays $20-125** (.10/wd. Cdn. or .10/wd. US) on publication for all, 1st, onetime, simultaneous, or reprint rts. Articles 600-700 wds. (75/yr.). Responds in 4 wks. Accepts simultaneous submissions and reprints (tell when/where appeared). Guidelines by e-mail/website: http://www.livinglightnews.org/writing.htm; copy for 9 x 12 SAE/$4.50 Cdn. postage or IRCs (no US postage). (Ads)

> **Special needs:** Celebrity interviews/testimonials of well-known personalities and inspiring stories of Christians serving the Lord.

Tips: "Most open to a timely article about someone who is well known in North America, in sports or entertainment, and has a strong Christian walk."

$ THE LOOKOUT, 8805 Governor's Hill Dr., Ste. 400, Cincinnati OH 45249. (513) 931-4050. Fax (513) 931-0950. E-mail: lookout@standardpub.com. Website: www.lookoutmag.com. Standard Publishing. Kelly Carr, ed. For adults who are interested in learning more about applying the gospel to their lives. Weekly and online mag.; 16 pgs.; circ. 52,000. Subscription $45, or $10 for online only. Only purchases manuscripts submitted for theme list. E-query only; no mailed submissions. **Pays $145-200** on acceptance (after contract is signed), for 1st rts. Articles 1,000-1,400 wds. Responds in 12 wks. Prefers NIV. Guidelines/theme list and digital sample onWebsite: www.lookoutmag.com/about-us/write-for-us. (Ads)

Tips: "Open to feature articles according to our theme list. Get a copy of our theme list and query about a theme-related article at least six months in advance. Request sample copies of our magazine to familiarize yourself with our publishing needs (also available online)."

$ THE LUTHERAN DIGEST, 6160 Carmen Ave. E., Inver Grove MN 55076. (651) 451-9945. E-mail: editor@lutherandigest.com. Website: www.lutherandigest.com. Lori Rosenkvist, ed. Blend of general and light theological material used to win nonbelievers to the Lutheran faith. Quarterly literary mag.; 64 pgs.; circ. 60,000. Subscription $16. 100% unsolicited freelance. Complete ms/cover letter; e-query preferred. **Pays $35 ($25 for reprints)** on publication for onetime and reprint rts. Articles 300 to 1,000 wds. Prefers full mss by e-mail. Responds in 4-9 wks. Seasonal 6-9 mos. ahead. Accepts simultaneous submissions and reprints (tell when/where appeared). No kill fee. Uses some sidebars. Rarely accepts submissions from children/teens. Guidelines at: http://lutherandigest.com/write-for-us; copy $3.50/6 x 9 SAE. (Ads)

Poetry: Accepts 20+/yr. Light verse, traditional; short/varies; no payment. Submit max. 3 poems/quarter.

Fillers: Anecdotes, facts, short humor, tips; length varies; no payment.

Tips: "We want our readers to feel uplifted after reading our magazine. Short, hopeful pieces are encouraged. We need well-written short articles that would be of interest to middle-aged and senior readers—Christian and non-Christian. We prefer real-life stories over theoretical essays. Personal tributes and testimony articles are discouraged. Please read sample articles and follow our writers' guidelines prior to submission to make your submissions relevant."

$ THE LUTHERAN JOURNAL, PO Box 28158, Oakdale MN 55128. (651) 702-0086. Fax (651) 702-0074. E-mail: christianad2@msn.com. Vance Lichty, pub.; Roger S. Jensen, ed.; submit to Editorial Assistant. Family magazine for, by, and about Lutherans, and God at work in the Lutheran world. Annual mag.; 48 pgs.; circ. 200,000. Subscription $6. 60% unsolicited freelance; 40% assigned. Complete ms/cover letter; fax query OK. **Pays .01-.04/wd.** on publication for all or 1st rts. Articles 750-1,500 wds. (25-30/yr.); fiction 1,000-1,500 wds. Response time varies. Seasonal 4-5 mos. ahead. Accepts reprints. Uses some sidebars. Prefers NIV, NAS, KJV. Accepts requested ms on disk. Also accepts submissions from children/teens. Guidelines by mail; copy for 9 x 12 SAE/2 stamps. (Ads)

Poetry: Buys 4-6/yr. Light verse, traditional; 50-150 wds. **$10-30.** Submit max. 3 poems.

Fillers: Buys 5-10/yr. Anecdotes, facts, prayers, quotes; 50-300 wds. **$5-30.**

Columns/Departments: Buys 1st time rights only.

Tips: "Most open to Lutheran lifestyles or Lutherans in action." Does not return rejected manuscripts.

+$ **LUTHERAN WITNESS,** 1333 S. Kirkwood Rd., St. Louis MO 63122-7226. E-mail: adriane.door@lcms.org. The Lutheran Church—Missouri Synod. Adriane Heins, ed. Denominational print magazine published 11X/yr.; circ. 160,000; subscription $22. Prefers complete ms. Articles 500, 1,000, or 1,500 wds. Buys 1st NASR. Subscription $24; circ. 185,000. **Pays $150-500.** Guidelines at: http://blogs.lcms.org/the-lutheran-witness/writers-guidelines-for-the-lutheran-witness. (Ads)

   **2014 EPA Award of Merit: Denominational.

+**LUTHERAN WITNESS ONLINE** (See *Lutheran Witness*).

$ **MATURE LIVING,** One Lifeway Plaza, MSN 136, Nashville TN 37234-0175. (615) 251-2000. E-mail: matureliving@lifeway.com. Website: www.lifeway.com. LifeWay Christian Resources/Southern Baptist. Debbie Dickerson, content ed. Primary audience is adults 50 and older who desire to live a Christian legacy. Monthly mag.; 60 pgs.; circ. 222,670. Query; accepts e-queries or mail queries. Accepts full mss by e-mail (attached or copied into message). **Pays $100-350** on acceptance for all rts. Articles 300-1,200 wds.; senior adult fiction 1,000-1,200 wds. Responds in 6-8 wks. Seasonal 6-8 mos. ahead. No simultaneous submissions or reprints. Prefers e-mail submissions/attached file. Some sidebars. Prefers HCSB. Guidelines by mail/e-mail (rene.holt@lifeway.com), or at: http://www.lifeway.com/n/Product-Family/Mature-Living-Magazine. To see sample, www.lifeway.com/matureliving.

   Fillers: Word puzzles. Grandchildren stories, 50-100 wds. No payment.

   Tips: "Almost all areas open to freelancers except medical and financial matters. Study the magazine for its style. Write for our readers' pleasure and inspiration. Fiction for 55+ adults needs to underscore a biblical truth."

$ **MATURE YEARS,** (Christian Living in the Mature Years), PO Box 801, Nashville TN 37202. (801) 672-1789. Fax (615) 749-6512. E-mail: matureyears@umpublishing.org. Website: www.cokesbury.com. United Methodist Publishing House. Pamela Dilmore, lead ed. To help persons in and nearing retirement years understand and appropriate the resources of the Christian faith in dealing with specific problems and opportunities related to aging. Quarterly mag.; 96 pgs.; circ. 35,000. $8.99/issue. 50% unsolicited freelance. Complete ms/cover letter; e-query OK. **Pays .07-.10/wd.** on acceptance for onetime or reprint rts. Articles 600-1,400 wds. (40/yr.). Responds in 24-28 wks. Seasonal 12 mos. ahead. Accepts reprints. Prefers accepted ms by e-mail (attached file). Some sidebars. Prefers CEB. Guidelines by e-mail; copy $5. (No ads)

   Poetry: Buys 12-16/yr. Avant-garde, free verse, haiku, light verse, traditional; 4-16 lines; **.50-1.00/line.** Submit max. 4 poems.

   Fillers: Anecdotes (to 300 wds.), cartoons, jokes, short humor, word puzzles (religious only); to 30 wds. **$5-25.** Must be uplifting, not scathing or sarcastic.

MEN OF THE CROSS, 920 Sweetgum Creek, Plano TX 75023. (972) 517-8553. E-mail: info@menofthecross.com. Website: www.menofthecross.com. Greg Paskal, content mngr. (greg@gregpaskal.com). Encouraging men in their walk with the Lord; strong emphasis on discipleship and relationship. Online community. 50% unsolicited freelance. Query by e-mail. No payment. Not copyrighted. Articles 500-1,500 wds. (10/yr.). Responds in 2-4 wks. Seasonal 3 mos. ahead. Accepts simultaneous submissions; no reprints. Prefers e-mail submissions (attached or copied into message). Uses some sidebars. Prefers NIV, NKJV, NAS. Also accepts submissions from teens. Guidelines at: www.menofthecross.com; copy online. (No ads)

   Special needs: Christian living in the workplace.

   Tips: "Appropriate topic could be a real, firsthand account of how God worked in the author's life. We are looking for humble honesty in hopes it will minister to those in similar circumstances. View online forums for specific topics."

+**MESSAGE OF THE OPEN BIBLE,** 32020 Bell Ave., Des Moines IA 50315. (515) 288-6761. E-mail: message@openbible.org. Website: www.openbible.org. Open Bible Standard Churches. Andrea Johnson, ed. Bimonthly denominational print magazine; circ. 2,000; subscription $9.95. Open to freelance submissions; articles 750 wds. and reviews. **Pays 5 copies.**

+**MESSAGE OF THE OPEN BIBLE.ORG** (See *Message of the Open Bible*)

$ THE MESSENGER, 440 Main St., Steinbach MB R5G 1Z5, Canada. (204) 326-6401. Fax (204) 326-1613. E-mail: messenger@emconf.ca or through website: www.emconf.ca/Messenger. Evangelical Mennonite Conference. Terry M. Smith, ed. Serves Evangelical Mennonite Conference members and general readers. Monthly mag.; 36 pgs. Subscription $24. Uses little freelance, but open. Query preferred; phone/fax/e-query OK. Accepts full mss by e-mail. Articles to 1,200 wds. **Pays $50-135** on publication for 1st rts. only. Articles. Brief guidelines on website: http://www.emconference.ca/the-messenger/submission-guidelines. Not included in topical listings.

THE MESSIANIC TIMES, PO Box 2096, Niagara Falls NY 14302. (780) 329-5399. Fax (951) 677-7353. E-mail: editor.messianictimes@gmail.com or through website: www.messianictimes.com. Times of the Messiah Ministries. Eric Tokajer, publisher; Karen S. Meissner, managing editor. To unify the International Messianic Jewish community to serve as an evangelistic tool to the Jewish community, and to educate Christians about the Jewish roots of their faith. Bimonthly newspaper; circ. 35,000. Subscription $29.99. Accepts freelance. Query preferred. Submit with online form. Articles and reviews. Not in topical listings. Guidelines at: http://www.messianictimes.com/about (Ads)

+**METHODIST HISTORY,** 36 Madison Ave., Madison NJ 07940. (973) 408-3189. E-mail: atday@gcah.org. United Methodist Church. Prefers e-mail submissions/attached file. Articles 20 pages or 5,000 wds. max. E-query. **Pays 3 copies.** Guidelines at: http://www.gcah.org/resources/guidelines-for-publication

*****MOVIEGUIDE,** 1151 Avenida Acaso, Camarillo CA 93012. Toll-free (800) 577-6684. (770) 825-0084. Fax (805) 383-4089. E-mail: info@movieguide.org. Website: www.movieguide.org. Good News Communications/Christian Film & Television Commission. Dr. Theodore Baehr, pub. Family guide to media entertainment from a biblical perspective. 10% unsolicited freelance. Query/clips. **Pays in copies** for all rts. Articles 1,000 wds. (100/yr.); book/music/video/movie reviews, 750-1,000 wds. Responds in 6 wks. Seasonal 6 mos. ahead. Accepts requested ms on disk. Regularly uses sidebars. Guidelines/theme list; copy for SAE/4 stamps. (Ads)

> **Fillers:** Accepts 1,000/yr.; all types; 20-150 wds.
> **Columns/Departments:** Movieguide; Travelguide; Videoguide; CDguide, etc.; 1,000 wds.
> **Contest:** Scriptwriting contest for movies with positive Christian content. Go to www.kairosprize.com.
> **Tips:** "Most open to articles on movies and entertainment, especially trends, media literacy, historical, and hot topics."

+**MUTUALITY,** 122 W. Franklin Ave., Ste. 218, Minneapolis MN 55404. (612) 872-6898. Fax: (612) 872-6891. Christians for Biblical Equality. Submit articles as attachments through contact form on Website. Theme list on Website. Articles 800-1,800 wds.; reviews

500-800 wds. Responds in 4 wks or more. **Pays a gift certificate to their bookstore.** Guidelines at: http://www.cbeinternational.org/content/mutuality-writers-guidelines.

NEW FRONTIER CHRONICLE, 180 E. Ocean Blvd., 4th Fl., Long Beach CA 90802. (562) 491-8723. Fax (562) 491-8791. Email: new.frontier@usw.salvationarmy.org. www.newfrontierpublications.org. The Salvation Army Western Territory. Robert L. Docter, ed. News of The Salvation Army in the Western United States and from 126 countries where the Army is at work. Biweekly newspaper; circ. 25,000. Subscription $15. Open to freelance. Prefers query. **No payment.** Articles and reviews; no fiction. Not in topical listings. More about this publication at: http://www.newfrontierchronicle.org. (Ads)

A NEW HEART, PO Box 4004, San Clemente CA 92674-4004. (949) 496-7655. Fax (949) 496-8465. E-mail: HCFUSA@gmail.com. Website: www.HCFUSA.com. Aubrey Beauchamp, ed. For Christian healthcare givers; information regarding medical/Christian issues. Quarterly mag.; 16 pgs.; circ. 5,000. Subscription $25. 20% unsolicited freelance; 10% assigned. Complete ms/cover letter; phone/fax/e-query OK. **Pays 2 copies** for one-time rts. Not copyrighted. Articles 600-1,800 wds. (20-25/yr.). Responds in 2-3 wks. Accepts simultaneous submissions and reprints. Accepts e-mail submission. Does not use sidebars. Guidelines at: http://www.hcfusa.com/LinkClick.aspx?fileticket=MMyGCr6sh 80%3d&tabid=65; copy for 9 x 12 SAE/3 stamps. (Ads)

   Poetry: Accepts 1-2/yr. Submit max. 1-3 poems.

   Fillers: Accepts 3-4/yr. Anecdotes, cartoons, facts, jokes, short humor; 100-120 wds.

   Columns/Departments: Accepts 20-25/yr. Chaplain's Corner, 200-250 wds. Physician's Corner, 200-250 wds.

   Tips: "Most open to real-life situations which may benefit and encourage healthcare givers and patients. True stories with medical and evangelical emphasis."

+NEW IDENTITY MAGAZINE, PO Box 375, Torrance CA 90508. (310) 947-8707. E-mail: submissions@newidentitymagazine.com. Provides diverse, Bible-centered content to help lead new believers and seekers to a fuller understanding of the Christian faith. Cailin Briody Henson, ed.-in-chief. Quarterly magazine. Articles 1,000-4,000 wds. Prefers e-submissions, imbedded or attached. Responds in 6-8 wks. **No payment.** Guidelines at: http://www.newidentitymagazine.com/WritersGuidelines.pdf .

+NOSTALGIA, PO Box 8466, Spokane WA 99203. E-mail: editor@nostalgismagazin.net. Gathers photos, personal remembrance stories, diaries, and researched stories of people, places, and events. Prefers e-mail submissions. Articles 400-1,500 wds. **No payment.** Guidelines at: http://www.nostalgiamagazine.net/submit.html

   Tips: "Especially interested in photo essays."

$ NOW WHAT?, PO Box 33677, Denver CO 80233. (303) 452-7973. Fax (303) 452-0657. E-mail: nowwhat@cog7.org. Website: http://nowwhat.cog7.org. Church of God (Seventh Day). Sherri Langton, assoc. ed. Articles on salvation, Jesus, social issues, life problems, that are seeker sensitive. Monthly online mag.; available only online. 100% unsolicited freelance. Complete ms/cover letter; no query. **Pays $25-55** on publication for first, electronic, simultaneous, or reprint rts. Articles 1,000-1,500 wds. (10/yr.). Responds in 4-10 wks. Accepts simultaneous submissions and reprints (tell when/where appeared). Accepts requested ms by e-mail. E-mail preferred. Regularly uses sidebars. Prefers NIV 1984. Guidelines by mail/website: http://nowwhat.cog7.org/InfoPage/Send_Us_Your_Story.html.

   Special needs: "Personal experiences must show a person's struggle that either brought him/her to Christ or deepened faith in God. The entire *Now What?* site is built around a personal experience each month."

Tips: "The whole e-zine is open to freelance. Think how you can explain your faith, or how you overcame a problem, to a non-Christian. It's a real plus for writers submitting a personal experience to also submit an objective article related to their story. Or they can contact Sherri Langton for upcoming personal experiences that need related articles. No Christmas or Easter pieces."

$ OUR SUNDAY VISITOR NEWSWEEKLY, 200 Noll Plaza, Huntington IN 46750. Toll-free (800) 348-2440. (260) 356-8400. Fax (260) 356-8472. E-mail: oursunvis@ osv.com. Website: www.osv.com. Catholic. John Norton, ed.; Sarah Hayes, article ed. Vital news analysis, perspective, spirituality for today's Catholic. Weekly newspaper; 24 pgs.; circ. 68,000. 10% unsolicited freelance; 90% assigned. Query or complete ms; fax/e-query OK. **Pays $100-800** within 4 wks. of acceptance for 1st and electronic rts. Articles 500-3,500 wds. (25/yr.). Responds in 4-6 wks. Seasonal 2 mos. ahead. No simultaneous submissions; rarely accepts reprints (tell when/where appeared). Kill fee. Regularly uses sidebars. Prefers RSV. Guidelines by mail/e-mail/website (click on "About Us"/"Writers' Guidelines" in left column); copy for $2/10 x 13 SAE/$1 postage. (Ads)

Columns/Departments: Faith; Family; Trends; Profile; Heritage; Media; Q & A. See guidelines for details.

Tips: "Our mission is to examine the news, culture, and trends of the day from a faithful and sound Catholic perspective—to see the world through the eyes of faith. Especially interested in writers able to do news analysis (with a minimum of 3 sources) or news features." Guidelines at: https://www.osv.com/ OSVNewsweekly/More/WritersGuidelines.aspx.

+$ PARENTLIFE, One Lifeway Plaza, Nashville TN 37234-0172. (615) 251-2196. E-mail: parentlife@lifeway.com. To support the family, strengthen marriage, and encourage parents. Articles 500-1,500 wds. E-query. Pays $150-500 on acceptance for nonexclusive rts. Guidelines at: https://support.lifeway.com/app/answers/detail/a_id/321/session/ L3RpBWUvMTM5MDg2Mjk1NC9zaWQvOE55cnpzTGw%3D

$ PENTECOSTAL EVANGEL, 1445 N. Boonville, Springfield MO 65802-1894. (417) 862-2781. Fax (417) 862-0416. E-mail: pe@ag.org. Website: www.pe.ag.org. Assemblies of God. Ken Horn, ed.; submit to Scott Harrup, sr. assoc. ed. Assemblies of God. Weekly and online mag.; 32 pgs.; circ. 170,000. Subscription $28.99. 5% unsolicited freelance; 95% assigned. Complete ms/cover letter; or e-submission/attached file. Accepts full mss by e-mail. **Pays .06/wd. (.04/wd.** for reprints) on acceptance for 1st or reprint and electronic rts. Articles 500-1,200 wds. (10-15/yr.); testimonies 200-300 wds. Responds in 6-8 wks. Seasonal 6-8 mos. ahead. No simultaneous submissions; accepts reprints (tell when/where appeared). Kill fee 100%. Prefers e-mail submissions (attached file). Uses some sidebars. Prefers NIV, KJV. Guidelines at: http://www.pe.ag.org/about_us/writers_guidelines.cfm ; copy for 9 x 12 SAE/$1.39 postage. (Ads)

Fillers: Anecdotes, facts, personal experience, testimonies; 250-500 wds. Practical, how-to pieces on family life, devotions, evangelism, seasonal, current issues, Christian living; 250 wds. Pays about $25.

Special needs: "The *Pentecostal Evangel* offers a free e-mail/online devotional, *Daily Boost.* Contributors are not paid, but a number of these writers have been published in the magazine."

Tips: "True, first-person inspirational material is the best bet for a first-time contributor. We reserve any controversial subjects for writers we're familiar with.

Positive family-life articles work well near Father's Day, Mother's Day, and holidays."

Note: This publication is not currently accepting freelance submissions. Check Website for update.

**2010 EPA Award of Excellence: Denominational.

+PENTECOSTAL MESSENGER, PO Box 211866, Bedford TX 76095. (817) 554-5900. E-mail: randy@pcg.org. Website: www.pcg.org. Pentecostal Church of God. Randy Lawrence, Jr., ed. Denominational publication. Quarterly denominational print magazine; circ. 5,000; subscription $12. Open to freelance submissions. Prefers e-mail submissions. (Ads).

**2014 EPA Award of Excellence: Denominational; 2014 EPA Award of Merit: Most Improved

THE PENWOOD REVIEW, PO Box 862, Los Alamitos CA 90720-0862. E-mail: submissions@penwoodreview.com. Website: www.penwoodreview.com. Lori Cameron, ed. Poetry, plus thought-provoking essays on poetry, literature, and the role of spirituality and religion in the literary arts. Biannual jour.; 40+ pgs.; circ. 80-100. Subscription $12. 100% unsolicited freelance. **No payment** ($2 off subscription and 1 free copy), for one time and electronic rts. Articles 1 pg. (single spaced). Responds in 9-12 wks. Accepts requested ms by e-mail/attached file. Guidelines at: http://www.penwoodreview.com/?page_id=11; copy $6.

Poetry: Accepts 120-160/yr. Any type, including formalist; to 2 pgs. Submit max. 5 poems.

Special Needs: Faith and the literary arts; religion and literature. Needs essays (up to 2 pgs., single spaced).

Tips: We publish poetry almost exclusively and are looking for well-crafted, disciplined poetry, not doggerel or greeting-card-style poetry. Poets and writers should study poetry, read it extensively, and send us their best, most original work. Visit our website or buy a copy for an idea of what we publish.

PERSPECTIVES: A Journal of Reformed Thought, 4500—60th Ave. S.E., Grand Rapids MI 49512-0670. (616) 698-7071. Fax (616) 698-6606. E-mail: submissions@perspectivesjournal.org. Website: www.perspectivesjournal.org. Online version. Independent. Malcolm McBryde, mng. ed.; Dawn Boelkins, nonfiction ed. Our purpose is to publish Christian writing that delights readers and engages the world in a Reformed way; primary audience is educated people in the Reformed and Presbyterian tradition. Bimonthly online mag.; 24 pgs.; circ. 2,200. Subscription $20. 100% unsolicited freelance. Complete ms, e-query OK. **No payment** for 1st rts. Articles 600-3,000 wds. (12/yr.) and fiction (8/yr.), 2,500-3,000 wds.; book/music/video reviews 800 wds. Responds in 4 wks. Seasonal 6 mos. ahead. No simultaneous submissions or reprints. Requires submissions by e-mail/attached file. Regularly uses sidebars. Prefers NIV. Guidelines at: http://www.perspectivesjournal.org/submissions; copy for 9x12 envelope. (Ads)

Poetry: Accepts 15/yr. All types. Submit max. 3 poems.

Tips: "Most open to feature-length articles. Must be theologically informed, whatever the topic. Avoid party-line thinking and culture-war approaches. A reading of past issues and a desire to join in a contemporary conversation on the Christian faith would help you break in here."

+PERSPECTIVES ON SCIENCE & CHRISTIAN FAITH, Roanoke College, 221 College Lane, Salem VA 24153. E-mail: jpeterson@roanoke.edu. James C. Peterson, ed. Requires e-mail submission/attached file. Articles 2,000-3,000 wds. Responds within 10

days. An abstract of 50-1250 words is required. No reprints. **No payment.** Guidelines at: http://network.asa3.org/?PSCFsubmissions. (Ads)

+THE PLAIN TRUTH, 1710 Evergreen St., Duarte CA 91010. (626) 298-8011. E-mail: managing.editor@ptm.org. Website: www.ptm.org. Plain Truth Ministries. Greg Albrecht, ed. Combats the deadly virus of legalism and gives hope, inspiration and encouragement to those burned out by religion. Quarterly print magazine; circ. 15,000. Open to freelance submissions.

+$ POINT, 11002 Lake Hart Dr., Orlando FL 32832. (407) 563-6083. E-mail: point@convergeww.org. Website: www.convergeworldwide.org. Converge Worldwide/Baptist General Conference. Bob Putman, ed. To increase movement awareness, ownership and involvement by publishing captivating God-stories of Converge people and regional ministries. Denominational print magazine published 5X/yr.; circ. 43,000. Open to freelance submissions. E-query/clips. Articles 300-1,400 wds. **Pays $60-280** on publication for 1st, reprint and electronic rts. (Ads)

$ POWER FOR LIVING, #104—Manuscript Submission, 4050 Lee Vance View, Colorado Springs CO 80918. Toll-free (800) 708-5550. (719) 536-0100. Fax (719) 535-2928. Website: www.cookministries.org. Cook Communications/Scripture Press Publications. Not currently accepting freelance submissions.

$ PRAIRIE MESSENGER: Catholic Journal, PO Box 190, Muenster SK S0K 2Y0, Canada. (306) 682-1772. Fax (306) 682-5285. E-mail: pm.canadian@stpeterspress.ca. Website: www.prairiemessenger.ca. Catholic/Benedictine Monks of St. Peter's Abbey. Maureen Weber, assoc. ed. Our audience is primarily prairie Catholics, but our publication emphasizes ecumenical and interfaith relations with a decidedly liberal slant, yet still faithful to the Roman Catholic Church. Weekly tabloid newspaper (46X); 16-20 pgs.; circ. 4,900. Subscription $37 Cdn. 10% unsolicited freelance; 90% assigned. Query; e-query OK. **Pays $60 Cdn. ($2.75/column inch for news items)** on publication for 1st rts. Not copyrighted. Articles 1,000 wds. (5/yr.); book reviews 550 wds. ($27.50). Responds in 6 wks. Seasonal 3 mos. ahead. Accepts simultaneous submissions and reprints (tell when/where appeared). Prefers e-mail submission (attached file or copied into message). Some sidebars. Accepts submissions from teens. Prefers NRSV. Guidelines by e-mail/website: http://www.prairiemessenger.ca/Submit.html; copy for 9 x 12 SAE/$1 Cdn./$1.50 US postage. (Ads)

> **Poetry:** Accepts 20/yr. Avant-garde, free verse, haiku, light verse; 3-30 lines. **Pays $25 Cdn.** Send max. 8 poems.
> **Columns/Departments:** Complete ms. Accepts 5/yr. **Pays $60 Cdn.**
> **Special needs:** Ecumenism; social justice; native concerns.
> **Tips:** "Comment/feature section is most open; send good reflection column of about 800 words; topic of concern or interest to Prairie readership. It's difficult to break into our publication. Piety not welcome." This publication is limited to Canadian writers only.

$ PRESBYTERIANS TODAY, 100 Witherspoon St., Louisville KY 40202-1396. Toll-free (800) 728-7228x5627. E-mail: today@pcusa.org. Website: www.pcusa.org/today. Presbyterian Church (USA). Patrick Heery, ed. Denominational. Primary focus on mission and ministry of the Presbyterian Church (USA)'s Presbyterian Mission Council Agency. Monthly (11X) mag.; 52 pgs.; circ. 30,000. Subscription $24.95. 25% freelance. Query or complete ms/cover letter; phone/fax/e-query OK to editor@pcusa.org. (502) 569-5635. **Pays $100-300** on acceptance for 1st rts. Articles 800-2,000 wds. (prefers 1,000-1,500); (20/yr.). Also uses short features 250-600 wds. Responds in 2-5 wks. Seasonal 3 mos. ahead. Few reprints. Accepts requested ms by e-mail. Kill fee 50%. Prefers NRSV. Guidelines on website: www.presbyterianmission.org/ministries/today/ writers-guidelines.

> **Tips:** "Most open to feature articles about Presbyterians—individuals, churches with special outreach, creative programs, or mission work. Do not often use inspirational or testimony-type articles."
> **Note:** Will become bimonthly beginning July 2015.
> ** This periodical won a "Best in Class" award from the Associated Church Press (2012) and from the Religion Communicators Council (2013).

+$ PRIORITY, 440 W. Nyack Rd., West Nyack NY 10994. (845) 620-7450. E-mail: cheryl.maynor@use.salvationarmy.org. Website: www.prioritypeople.org. The Salvation Army – Eastern Territory. Linda D. Johnson, ed. Promotes holiness, prayer, and evangelism through the life stories of God's people. Quarterly print mag.; circ. 26,000; subscription $8.95. Open to freelance submissions. Query/clips. Articles 400-1,700 wds. **Pays $200-800** on acceptance for 1st rts. (Ads accepted from non-profits only)

+PRIORITY! ONLINE (See *Priority!*)

PRISCILLA PAPERS, 122 W. Franklin Ave., Ste. 218, Minneapolis MN 55404-2451. (612) 872-6898. E-mail: priscillapaperseditor@gmail.com.. Website: www.cbeinternational.org. Christians for Biblical Equality. Jeff Miller, ed. Addresses biblical interpretation and its relationship to women and men sharing authority and ministering together equally, not according to gender, ethnicity, or class but according to God's gifting. Quarterly jour.; 32 pgs.; circ. 2,500. Subscription $40 (print only). 85% unsolicited freelance; 15% assigned. Query preferred; e-query OK. **Pays 3 copies** for 1st and electronic rts. Articles 600-5,000 wds. (1/yr.); no fiction; book reviews 600 wds. (free book). Slow and careful response. No reprints. Seasonal 12 mos. ahead. Prefers proposed ms on disk or by e-mail (attached file) with hard copy. No kill fee. Uses some sidebars. Guidelines at: http://www.cbeinternational.org/content/write-priscilla-papers; copy for 9 x 12 SAE/$2.07 postage. (Ads)

> **Tips:** "Priscilla Papers is the academic voice of CBE. Our target is the informed lay reader. All sections are open to freelancers. Any well-written, single-theme article (no potpourri) presenting a solid exegetical and hermeneutical approach to biblical equality from a high view of Scripture will be considered for publication." Seeks original cover artwork. Use *Chicago Manual of Style.*

+$ PRISM MAGAZINE, PO Box 367, Wayne PA 19087. (267) 257-4968. E-mail: kkomarni@eastern.edu. Website: www.evangelicalsforsocialaction.org/prism. Evangelicals for Social Action. Kristyn Komarnicki, ed. To challenge Christians to live out their faith holistically, in word and deed, to invite them to a whole-life discipleship. Bimonthly print magazine; circ. 3,000; subscription $30. Open to freelance submissions. Complete ms/ cover letter; or e-query. Articles 1,500-3,000 wds. **Pays $75-450.** (Ads)

+$ PSYCHOLOGY FOR LIVING, 250 W. Colorado Blvd., Ste. 200, Arcadia CA 91007. E-mail: editor@ncfliving.org. Robert and Melanie Whitcomb, co-eds. Narramore Christian Foundation. Applied Christian psychology. One full issue and 3 limited editions/yr. Circ. 7,000. Query not necessary. **Pays $200** for articles 1,200-1,700 wds.; $125 or less than 1,200 wds.; reprints $75. Guidelines at: http://www.ncfliving.org/guidelines.php.

$ PURPOSE, 718 N. Main St., Newton KS 67114. (316) 281-4412. Fax (316) 283-0454. E-mail: info@mennomedia.org. Website: www.mpn.net. Mennonite Publishing Network/ Agency of Mennonite Church USA and Canada. Carol Duerksen, ed. Denominational, for older youth and adults. Monthly take-home paper; 32 pgs.; circ. 8,900. Subscription $22.65; $23.78 Cdn. 80% unsolicited freelance; 20% assigned. Complete ms (only)/cover letter; e-mail submissions preferred. **Pays $10-42 or .06-.07/wd.** on acceptance (or when editor chooses) for onetime rts. Articles and fiction, 400-600 wds. (95/yr.). Responds in 6 mos. Seasonal 1 yr. ahead. Accepts simultaneous submissions and reprints (tell when/ where appeared). Regularly uses sidebars. Guidelines at: http://store.mennomedia.org/ Purpose-C1273.aspx; copy $2/6 x 9 SAE/2 stamps. (No ads)

Poetry: Buys 120/yr. Free verse, haiku, traditional; 3-12 lines; **up to $2/line ($7.50-20).** Submit max. 5 poems.

Fillers: Buys 25/yr. Anecdotes, prose; up to 300 wds., **up to .06/wd.**

Tips: "Read our guidelines. All areas are open. Articles must carry a strong story line. First person is preferred. Don't exceed maximum word length, send no more than 3 works at a time."

+QUAKER LIFE, 101 Quaker Hill Dr., Richmond IN 47374. (765) 962-7573. E-mail: quakerlife@fum.org. Inspirational essays, 500-750 wds.; articles 750-1,300 wds. Theme list on Website. Prefers e-mail submissions/attached file. **Pays 3 copies.** Guidelines at: http://fum.org/quaker-life-a-call-for-writers/

+REFRESHED, PO Box 2606, El Cajon CA 92021. (619) 668-5100. E-mail: info@ refreshedmag.com. Website: www.refreshedmag.com. Selah Media Group. Lori Arnold and Scott Noble, eds. An inspirational lifestyle magazine serving San Diego and Minneapolis; seeking to generate vibrant cultural dialogue within the framework of faith and to present engaging, real stories and feature that offer our readers practical solutions to the challenges and complexities of life. Monthly print mag.; circ. 60,000; subscription $24.95. Open to freelance submissions; articles and reviews.

+REGENT GLOBAL BUSINESS REVIEW, 1333 Regent Univ. Dr., Virginia Beach VA 23464. E-mail: rgbr@regent.edu. Dr. Bruce Winston, interim exec. ed. bwinston@regent. edu; (757) 352-4306]. Includes biblical or values-based perspectives on the advancement of global business. Feature articles, 1,200-2,500 wds.; case studies, 2,500-4,000 wds.; Toolkit/Executive Summaries, 250-500 wds. Submit through Website. Requires an abstract of 150 wds. or less. **No payment.** Guidelines at: http://www.regent.edu/acad/global/publications/rgbr/submissions.shtml

+$ RELEVANT & RELEVANTMAGAZINE.COM. E-mail: submissions@relevant-mediagroup.com. Covers faith, culture, and intentional living. Monthly magazine and iPad edition; bimonthly. Most articles 750-1,000 wds. See Website for description of various types of articles needed. Submit through Website or e-mail; prefers e-mail submissions/attached file. **Pays $100-400.** Guidelines at: http://www.relevantmagazine.com/how-write-relevant

RELIEF JOURNAL: A Christian Literary Expression, 8933 Forestview, Evanston IL 60203. E-mail: editor@reliefjournal.com. Website: www.reliefjournal.com. Looking for unpublished poetry and stories that reflect reality. Brad Fruhauff, ed-in-chief; Brady Clark, nonfiction ed.; Joshua Hren, fiction ed.; Tania Runyan, poetry ed. Semiannual mag.; 140 pgs.; circ. 300. Subscription $23. 90% unsolicited freelance; 10% assigned. Online submission: e-mail submissions. Complete ms. **Pays in copies** for 1st rts. Writer pays $2 for each submission. Creative nonfiction to 5,000 wds (10/yr); fiction to 8,000 wds. (12/yr.). Poetry to 5 poems (50/yr); images to 5 pieces (8/yr). Responds in 16 wks. Two reading periods: January 1 – March 1; July 1 – September 1. Accepts simultaneous submissions and reprints (only when solicited). Any Bible version. Guidelines at: http://www.reliefjournal.com/submit-your-work. Incomplete topical listings. (Ads)

Poetry: Tania Runyan, poetry ed. Accepts 50-60/yr. Poetry that is well-written, concrete, and grounded and makes sense; to 1,000 wds. Submit max. 5 poems.

CNF: Brady Clark, CNF ed. Accepts 6-10/yr. Personal essays, nonfiction with a narrative and/or emotional arc; to 5,000 wds.

Fiction: Joshua Hren, fiction ed. Accepts 9-12/yr. Fiction unafraid of the tough questions and willing to live in the ambiguity that requires faith; to 8,000 wds.

Images: Brad Fruhauff, image ed. Accepts 6-10/yr. B/W photos, drawings, or paintings that strike the eye and engage the imagination; to 5 images.

+$ RUMINATE, 1041 N. Taft Hill Rd., Fort Collins CO 80521. Brianna VanDyke, ed.-in-chief; Amy Lowe, sr. ed. No reprints or simultaneous submissions. Buys 1st serial rts. Submissions only through online form. See Website for established reading periods for different genres—fiction and nonfiction. Short reviews, 500 wds.; longer reviews 800-2,500 wds; **pays $15/400 wds.** Guidelines at: http://www.ruminatemagazine.com/submit/.

Poetry: Kristin George Bagdanov, poetry ed. Submit max. 5 poems (prefers 3-5).

Contests: Sponsors 4 contests/yr.

+SAMARITAN MINISTRIES' CHRISTIAN HEALTHCARE NEWSLETTER, PO Box 3618, Peoria IL 61612. (309) 689-0442. E-mail: ray.king@samaritanministries. org. Website: www.samaritanministries.org. Samaritan Ministries Intl. Ray King, ed. Information related to the Christian life, health care, and the direct sharing of health care needs. Monthly print newsletter; circ. 23,300; subscription $180. Open to freelance submissions; articles and reviews.

+SCP JOURNAL, PO Box 4308, Berkeley CA 94704. E-mail: scp@scp-inc.org. Confronts the occult, the cults, and the New Age movement, and explains why they are making an impact on our society. Tal Brooke, ed. Quarterly journal; circ. 15,000. Query only. Check this publication at: http://www.scp-inc.org.

$ SEEK, 8805 Governor's Hill Dr., Ste. 400, Cincinnati OH 45249. E-mail: seek@standardpub.com. Website: www.Standardpub.com. Standard Publishing. Submit to Editor. Light, inspirational, take-home reading for young and middle-aged adults. Weekly take-home paper; 8 pgs.; circ. 29,000. Subscriptions $18.49 (sold only in sets of 5). 75% unsolicited freelance; 25% assigned. Complete ms; no phone/fax/e-query. **Pays .07/wd.** on acceptance for 1st rts., **.05/wd. for reprints.** Articles 750-1,000 wds. (150-200/yr.); fiction 500-1,200 wds. Responds in 18 wks. Seasonal 1 yr. ahead. Accepts reprints (tell when/where appeared). Prefers submissions by e-mail (attached file). Uses some sidebars. Guidelines/theme list by mail/website: http://www.standardpub.com/view/seek-guidelines.aspx; copy for 6x9 SAE/2 stamps. (No ads)

Fillers: Buys 50/yr. Ideas, short humor per word count.

Tips: "We now work with a theme list. Only articles tied to these themes will be considered for publication. Check website for theme list and revised guidelines."

+SHARING, PO Box 780909, San Antonio TX 78278-0909. (210) 348-8315. Toll free: (877) 992-5222. E-mail: sharing@orderofstluke.org. Website: www.orderofstluke. org. International Order of St. Luke the Physician. Interdenominational magazine of Christian healing, dedicated to the healing of body, soul, and spirit. Published 6X/yr. For information on upcoming themes, e-mail or call the editor. Articles 200-1,500 wds. Prefers e-submissions/attached files, but will accept mailed submissions. **No payment.** Guidelines at: http://www.orderofstluke.org/images/documents/Submission-Guidelines.pdf.

Poetry/Prayers: Poetry 30-50 wds. (longer will be considered).

+SHATTERED MAGAZINE, 101 Stone River Rd., Huntsville AL 35811. (256) 783-8350. E-mail: rachael@shatteredmagazine.net. Website: http://shatteredmagazin.net. Emily Rogers, ed. We want people to have a perspective on life that is hard to come by—where we realize our greater purpose and how that purpose should free us to live full and meaningful lives, celebrating our own unique, God-given stories for His Glory. Quarterly print mag.; circ. 8,000; subscription $19.99. Accepts freelance submissions; articles and reviews. (Ads)

** 2014 EPA Award of Merit: General.

+SINGLE AGAIN MAGAZINE, 7405 Greenback Ln., #129, Citrus Heights CA 95610-5603. (916) 773-1111. Fax (916) 773-2999. E-mail: publisher@singleagain.com. Paul V. Scholl, pub. Articles 500 wds. and up. Responds in 6 wks. **No payment.** Check out this publication at: www.singleagain.com..

+SOJOURNERS, 3333 – 14th St. NW, Ste. 200, Washington DC 20010. (202) 328-8842. E-mail: sojourners@sojo.net. Website: www.sojo.net. Jim Rice, ed. Offer discernment of social issues, reflections on spirituality, and commentary on popular culture from a biblical perspective. Monthly (11X) mag; circ. 30,600; subscription $39.95. Open to freelance submissions; articles and reviews. (Ads)

SOUTHWEST KANSAS FAITH AND FAMILY, PO Box 1454, Dodge City KS 67801. (620) 225-4677. Fax (620) 225-4625. E-mail: stan@swkfaithandfamily.org. Website: www. swkfaithandfamily.org. Independent. Stan Wilson, pub. Dedicated to sharing the Word of God and news and information that honors Christian beliefs, family traditions, and values that are the cornerstone of our nation. Monthly newspaper; circ. 9,000. Subscription $25. Accepts freelance. Prefers e-query; complete ms OK. Articles; no reviews. Guidelines at: http://www.swkfaithandfamily.org/submitarticle.html. Incomplete topical listings. (Ads)

+$ SPLICKETY LOVE, Splickety Publishing Group. E-mail: submissions@splickety-pubgroup.com. Bonita Jewel, ed. Publishes concise, poignant fiction under 1,000 wds.; stories that hit fast and stick hard—stories that, no matter the genre, can cut through the day's troubles and grip readers with short attention spans. Short stories 300-1,000 wds.; prefers 700 wds. or less. Open to submissions for nano-fiction stories in 100 wds. or less; need to fit the theme. Theme list with deadlines on the Website. Send e-mail submissions/attachment only. **Pays .02/wd.** Guidelines on Website.

   Artwork: Also accepts submissions from artists, graphic designers, and photographers.

+$ SPLICKETY PRIME, Splickety Publishing Group. E-mail: submissions@splickety-pubgroup.com. Sarah Grimm, ed. Publishes concise, poignant fiction under 1,000 wds.; stories that hit fast and stick hard—stories that, no matter the genre, can cut through the day's troubles and grip readers with short attention spans. Short stories 300-1,000 wds.; prefers 700 wds. or less. Open to submissions for nano-fiction stories in 100 wds. or less; need to fit the theme. Theme list with deadlines on the Website. Send e-mail submissions/attachment only. **Pays .02/wd.** Guidelines on Website.

   Artwork: Also accepts submissions from artists, graphic designers, and photographers.

+$ SPORTS SPECTRUM, PO Box 2037, Indian Trail NC 28979. E-mail: editor@ sportsspectrum.com. Reaching non-Christians through sports; featuring testimonies of strong Christian sport figures. Audience is sports fans, usually between 20 and 55. No unsolicited submissions. Send e-queries and they give assignments, if interested. Articles 1,500-2,000 wds, plus 1 or 2 sidebars (about 150 wds). **Pays .21/wd. and up,** on acceptance, for all rts. Accepts reprints. Prefers NIV. Guidelines at: http://www.sportsspectrum. com/about/writers-guide.php

$ ST. ANTHONY MESSENGER, 28 W. Liberty St., Cincinnati OH 45202-6498.

(513) 241-5615. Fax (513) 241-0399. E-mail: MagazineEditors@Franciscanmedia.org. Website: www.FranciscanMedia.org. John Feister, ed.-in chief. For Catholic adults and families. Monthly and online mag.; 64 pgs.; circ. 100,000. Subscription $39. 55% unsolicited freelance. Query first; all correspondence by e-query. **Pays .20/wd.** on acceptance for 1st publication and shared rights thereafter. Articles 1,500-2,300 wds., (35-50/yr.); fiction 1,500-2,500 wds. (12/yr.); book reviews by assignment only. Responds in 3-9 wks. Seasonal 8-12 mos. ahead. Uses sidebars. Prefers NAB. Guidelines at: http://www.stanthonymessenger.org/ContactUs.aspx; copy for 9 x 12 SAE/4 stamps. (Ads).

Poetry: Christopher Heffron, poetry ed. Buys 20/yr. Free verse, haiku, traditional; 3-15 lines; $2/line ($20 min.). Submit max. 2 poems.

Tips: "Study writer's guidelines. Read some sample articles there. Query first. Writing must be professional; written with a Catholic audience in mind. Writing must be faithful to Catholic belief and teaching, life, and experience."

THE STORYTELLER, 2441 Washington Rd., Maynard AR 72444. (870) 647-2137. E-mail: storytellermag1@yahoo.com. Website: www.thestorytellermagazine.com. Fossil Creek Publishing. Regina Cook Williams, ed./pub. Adult audience (although we have children who write for us); unique in that we are one of the last magazines to accept a wide range of genres. Quarterly literary magazine; 72 pgs.; circ. 2,000. Subscription $24. 95.5% unsolicited freelance. Complete ms/cover letter; phone/e-query OK. No payment. 1st rts. Articles 2,500 wds. (75/yr.); fiction 2,500 wds. (125/yr.). Responds in 1-3 wks. Seasonal 4 mos. ahead. Accepts simultaneous submissions and reprints (tell when/where appeared). Responds in 1-2 wks. Accepts e-mail submissions (attached file); no sidebars. Also accepts submissions from children/teens (not children's stories). Prefers KJV. Guidelines by e-mail/website: www.thestorytellermagazine.com (scroll down); copy $8/9 x 12 SAE/5 stamps. (Ads)

Poetry: Jamie Johnson, poetry ed. Accepts 175+/yr. Avant-garde, free verse, haiku, light verse, traditional; 4-40 lines. Submit max. 3 poems.

Fillers: Accepts 10-20/yr. Cartoons, quotes, tips; 25-50 wds. Writing-related only.

Special needs: Original artwork. Funny or serious stories about growing up as a pastor's child or being a pastor's wife. Also westerns and mysteries.

Contest: Offers 1 or 2 paying contests per year, along with People's Choice Awards, and Pushcart Prize nominations. Go to www.thestorytellermagazine.com for announcements of all forthcoming contests for the year.

Tips: "We look for stories that are written well, flow well, have believable dialogue, and good endings. So many writers write a good story but fizzle at the ending. All sections of the magazine are open except how-to articles. Study the craft of writing. Learn all you can before you send anything out. Pay attention to detail, make sure manuscripts are as free of mistakes as possible. Follow the guidelines—they aren't hard." Always looking for B & W photos for front cover.

STUDIO, 727 Peel St., Albury NSW 2640, Australia. E-mail: studio00@bigpond.net.au. Paul Grover, ed. Offers a venue for previously published, new, or aspiring writers, and seeks to create a sense of community among Christians writing. Quarterly mag.; 36 pgs.; circ. 250. Subscription $60 AUD. 90% unsolicited freelance; 10% assigned. Complete ms. Mail or e-mail queries OK; prefers a cover letter. **Pays a free copy of magazine and reduced rates;** for nonexclusive rts. Articles 2,000 wds. (15/yr.); fiction 2,000 wds. (50/yr.); book reviews 300 wds. Responds in 3 wks. Accepts simultaneous submissions and reprints (tell when/where appeared). E-mail submissions OK. No sidebars. Accepts submissions from teens. Guidelines by e-mail; no copy overseas. (Ads)

Poetry: Accepts 50/yr. Avant-garde, free verse, haiku, light verse, traditional; 4-100 lines. Submit max. 3 poems.

Tips: "We accept all types of fiction and literary article themes."

SUCCESS/VICTORY NEWS, Franklin Publishing Company, 2723 Steamboat Circle, Arlington TX 76006. (817) 548-1124. E-mail: ludwigotto@sbcglobal.net. Website: www. franklinpublishing.net. Submit to Dr. Ludwig Otto, publisher. Bimonthly journal. 170 pgs; circ. 8,000. Subscription $80. **No payment.** 100% unsolicited. Responds in 3 wks. E-mail queries. Send submissions by e-mail attachment. Book reviews 3 pgs. Audience general public with a Christian message. Guidelines at: http://www.franklinpublishing. net/submission.html

$ TESTIMONY, 2450 Milltower Ct., Mississauga ON L5N 5Z6, Canada. (905) 542-7400. Fax (905) 542-7313. E-mail: testimony@paoc.org. Website: www.testimony-mag.ca. The Pentecostal Assemblies of Canada. Stephen Kennedy, ed. To encourage a Christian response to a wide range of issues and topics, including those that are peculiar to Pentecostals. Monthly and online mag.; 24 pgs.; circ. 8,000. Subscription $30 US/$24 Cdn. (includes GST). 10% unsolicited freelance; 90% assigned. Query; fax/e-query OK. Unsolicited mss not accepted or returned. **Pays $100** on publication for 1st rts. (no pay for reprint rts.). Articles 800-1,000 wds. responds in 6-8 wks. seasonal 4 mos. ahead. accepts reprints (tell when/where appeared). prefers e-mail submission (copied into message). regularly uses sidebars. prefers niv. guidelines/theme list by mail/e-mail/website: http://www.testimonymag.ca/index.php?option=com_content&view=article&id=50&itemid=34; $3 us or $2.50 cdn./copy 9 x 12 sae. (ads)

Tips: "View theme list on our website and query us about a potential article regarding one of our themes. Our readership is 98% Canadian. We prefer Canadian writers or at least writers who understand that Canadians are not Americans in long underwear. We also give preference to members of this denomination, since this is related to issues concerning our fellowship."

+TESTIMONY ONLINE (See *Testimony).* Traffic: 500

+$ THIS I BELIEVE ESSAYS, 323 W. Broadway, Ste. 503, Louisville KY 40202. (502) 259-9889. Write and submit your own statement of personal belief; 500-600 wds. **Pays $200.** Guidelines at: www.npr.org/thisibelieve/guide.html

$ THRIVING FAMILY, 8605 Explorer Dr., Colorado Springs CO 80920. E-mail: thrivingfamily.submissions@family.org. Website: www.thrivingfamily.com. Focus on the Family. Submit to Submissions Editor. Focuses on marriage and parenting from a biblical perspective; mostly for families with 4- to 12-year-old children. Monthly and online mag. Open to unsolicited freelance. Complete ms or query; e-query OK (no attachments). **Pays .25/wd.** Feature articles 1,200.; online articles 800-1,200 wds. Guidelines/theme list: http://www.thrivingfamily.com/www.thrivingfamily.com/~/media/thriving/1-articles/pdfs/tf-writers-guidelines.pdf; copy online. incomplete topical listings.

Columns/departments: family stages (practical tips), 50-200 wds. (Pays $50); For him (male perspective), 450 wds. For her (female perspective), 450 wds. Blended family (concerns of blended families), 450 wds. Single parents (issues related to single parenting), 450 wds.; adoption/special needs 450 wds.
** 2014 EPA Award of Excellence: General. 2014 EPA Award of Excellence: General (Digital

+TIFERET, E-mail: editors@tiferetjournal.com. To help raise individual and global consciousness, we publish writing from a variety of religious and spiritual traditions. Published 4X/yr; subscription $24.95. Online submissions only; no mailed submissions.

1st NA Serial rts. **Pays 1 copy.** Fiction and nonfiction. Guidelines at: http://tiferetjournal. com/submit.

Poetry: Submit max. 6 poems; each on a separate page.

Photos/Artwork: Open to submissions of photos and artwork.

TIME OF SINGING: A Magazine of Christian Poetry, 3PO Box 5276, Conneaut Lake PA 16316. E-mail: timesing@zoominternet.net. Website: www.timeofsinging.com. Wind & Water Press. Lora Homan Zill, ed. *TOS* is a literary Christian poetry magazine, so I prefer poems without religious jargon, that "show" and don't "tell," and that take creative chances with faith and our walk with God. Quarterly journal; 44 pgs.; circ. 200. Subscription $17. 95% unsolicited freelance; 5% assigned. Complete ms; e-query and mail query OK. **Pays in copies** for 1st, onetime, or reprint rts. Poetry only (some book reviews by assignment). Responds in 12 wks. Seasonal 6 mos. ahead. Accepts simultaneous submissions and reprints (tell when/where appeared). Accepts e-mail submission (attached file). Any Bible version. Responds in 12-16 wks. Seasonal 6 mos. ahead. Accepts submissions from teens. Accepts simultaneous submissions and reprints (tell when/where appeared). Guidelines by e-mail/website: http://www.timeofsinging.com/ guidelines.html; copy $4 ea. or 2/$7 (Checks, money orders payable to Wind & Water Press.) (No ads)

Poetry: Accepts 150/yr. Avant-garde, free verse, haiku, light verse, traditional; 3-40 lines. Submit max. 5 poems. Always need form poems (sonnets, villanelles, triolets, etc.) with Christian themes. Fresh rhyme. "Cover letter not needed; your work speaks for itself."

Tips: "Study poetry, read widely—both Christian and non-Christian. Work at the craft. Be open to suggestions and critique. If I have taken time to comment on your work, it is close to publication. If you don't agree, submit elsewhere. I appreciate poets who take chances and a fresh look at abstract, but substantive, Christian concepts like grace, faith, etc. *Time of Singing* is a literary poetry magazine, so I'm not looking for greeting card verse or sermons that rhyme."

+$ TODAY'S CHRISTIAN LIVING, PO Box 5000, Iola WI 54945. Toll free(800) 223-3161, (715) 445-5000. Fax: (715) 445-4053. E-mail: editor@todayschristianliving. org. Website: www.todayschristianliving.org. Diana Jones, pub. (dianaj@jonespublish-ing.com). Submit to: Dan Brownell (danb@jonespublishing.com). Encourages, equips, and engages Christians of all ages. Bimonthly. Prefers complete ms; discourages queries. Personality Profiles, 1,400-1,600 wds + sidebar 150-250 wds. Ministry Profile 1,400-1,600 wds.+ sidebar 150-250 wds. Personal Story/Anecdote 700-1,500 wds. Grace Notes 650-700 wds. Hospitality 700-1,500 wds. Humor 50-200 wds. **Pays $25-150.** Guidelines at: http://todayschristianliving.org/writers-guidelines.

Photos: Color, digital.

Contest: Annual writing contest. Top 3 winners published in the November issue.

+$ UNITED CHURCH OBSERVER, 478 Huron St., Toronto ON M5R 2R3, Canada. E-mail: dnwilson@ucobserver.org. Website: www.ucobserver.org. Observer Publications, Inc. United Church of Canada. David Wilson, ed. Published 11X/yr. Prefers e-mail submissions. Responds in 1-2 wks. Articles to 1,200 wds. **Payment negotiable.** Seasonal 6 mos. ahead. Guidelines at: http://www.ucobserver.org/2011/11/submission%20guide-lines.pdf.

+URBAN FAITH.COM, 1551 Regency Ct., Calumet City IL 60409. (708) 832-3309. E-mail: jrichards@urbanministries.com. Website: www.urbanfaith.com. Urban Ministries

Inc. John Richards, ed. Features news and Christian commentary on faith and culture from a uniquely urban and multiethnic perspective. Online magazine. Open to freelance submissions; articles and reviews. (Ads)

+$ **U.S. CATHOLIC,** 205 W. Monroe St., Chicago IL 60606. (312) 236-7782. Fax (312) 236-8207. E-mail: submissions@uscatholic.org. Website: www.uscatholic.org. Rev. John Molyneux C.M.F., ed. Catherine O'Connell-Cahill, sr. ed. Responds in 6-8 wks. No reprints or simultaneous submissions. Print and online editions (separate guidelines for online). Feature articles, 2,500-3,200 wds, **$500;** Stand-alone essays, 700-1,400 wds, **$150;** Practicing Catholic, 800 wds. + 150 wd. sidebar, **$200;** Sounding Board, 1,400 wds., **$200;** In Person, 800 wds., **$200;** Wise Guide essay, 975 wds. + 2-4 quotes from subject, **$200;** reviews, 350 wds., **$75 and up**. Samples of each type of article on Website. Subscription $29. Guidelines at: http://www.uscatholic.org/writers-guide.

> **Fiction:** 1,500 wds. **Pays $300.** Submit to literaryeditor@uscatholic.org.
>
> **Poetry:** Submit max. 3-5 poems to literaryeditor@uscatholic.org. **Pays $75.**

+$ **VIBRANT LIFE,** PO Box 5353, Nampa ID 83653-5353. (208) 465-2584. Fax: (208) 465-2531. E-mail: vibrantlife@pacificpress.com. Heather Quintana, ed. Promotes physical health, mental clarity, and spiritual balance from a practical Christian perspective. Bimonthly mag. Short articles 450-650 wds.; feature articles to 1,000 wds. (+ 1 sidebar if informational). **Pays $100-300,** on acceptance, for 1st and reprint rts. Complete ms by snail mail. Guidelines at: http://www.vibrantlife.com/?page_id=1369.

> **Photos:** To illustrate article only.

$ **WAR CRY,** 615 Slaters Ln., Alexandria VA 22314. (703) 684-5500. Fax (703) 684-5539. E-mail: war_cry@usn.salvationarmy.org. Website: www.thewarcry.org. The Salvation Army. Lt. Colonel Allen Satterlee, ed-in-chief; Jeff McDonald, mng. ed. Represents the Army's mission through news, profiles, commentaries and stories. It looks to bring people to Christ, help believers grow in faith and character, and promotes redemptive cultural practices from the perspective of Salvation Army programs, ministries, and doctrines. Monthly mag. and e-zine, plus special Easter and Christmas issues, and a Heritage edition. 44 pgs., circ. 180,000. 30% freelance. Complete ms, no cover letter. Prefers full mss by e-mail (attached or copied into message); e-query OK. **Pays .25/wd.** upon publication, and **.15/wd.** for reprints; for 1st, one-time, simultaneous, electronic, or reprint rights. Articles 600-1,200 wds. (80/yr.); fiction 800-1,500 wds. (5/yr); book reviews 350-500 wds. Responds in 8 wks. Seasonal 6 mos. ahead. Accepts simultaneous submissions and reprints (tell when/where appeared). Prefers e-mail submissions (attached file). Some sidebars. Prefers NLT. Guidelines by e-mail or Website: http://publications.salvationarmyusa.org/writers-submissions; copy for 9 x 12 SASE/3 stamps; copies online. (Ads)

> **Poetry:** Free verse, traditional. Accepts 7/yr. Submit max. 5. Length: 20-25 lines.
>
> **Fillers:** Accepts 20/yr.; 200-400 wds. Anecdotes, cartoons, facts, newsbreaks, prayers, prose, tips, word puzzles.
>
> **Tips:** Most open to holiday material, theme-related features, and articles for the unchurched.

$ **WEAVINGS,** 908 Grand Ave., PO Box 340004, Nashville TN 37203-0004. (615) 340-7254. E-mail: weavings@upperroom.org. Website: www.weavings.org. Publisher: The Upper Room. Submit to The Editor. For clergy, lay leaders, and all thoughtful seekers who want to deepen their understanding of, and response to, how God's life and human lives are being woven together. Quarterly mag. Subscription $29.95. Open to freelance that relates to a specific upcoming theme. Complete ms. **Pays .12/wd. and up.** Articles, sermons, meditations, stories 2,000 wds. maximum; poetry. Responds within 13 wks. Considers submissions sent by e-mail. Guidelines/theme list on website: http://www.upperroom.org/about/writer-guidelines/weavings; sample copy for 6.5 x 9.5 SAE/5 stamps.

+$ WESLEYAN LIFE ONLINE, PO Box 50434, Indianapolis IN 46250. (317) 774-7900. Wesleyan Church. Wayne MacBeth, exec. ed. (macbethw@wesleyan.org; Kerry Kind, ed., kindk@wesleyan.org. Digital magazine. Articles 400-500 wds. E-submissions only. **Pays $50-80.** Guidelines at: http://www.wesleyan.org/700/wesleyan-life-magazine..
**2014 EPA Award of Merit: Denominational; 2014 Award of Merit: Denominational (Digital); 2014 EPA Award of Excellence: Most Improved.

+$THE WILDWOOD READER, PO Box 1154, Rockville MD 20850. (904) 705-6806. E-mail: publisher@wildwoodreader.com. Website: www.wildwoodreader.com. Timson Edwards Co. Alex Gonzalez, pub. Focus is on adult, literary short fiction that is uplifting and motivational for living life in wellness and spirit. Quarterly jour.; 16 to 32 pgs.; circ. 1,000. Subscription $24. 100% unsolicited freelance. Query in writing. **Pays $10-75,** 60 days after publication for onetime rts. Fiction 800-2,400 wds. (18/yr.). Responds in 8 wks. Seasonal 4 mos. ahead. Accepts simultaneous submissions and reprints (tell when/where appeared). Requires CD by mail. Guidelines on Website; no copy. (Ads)

   Contest: Sponsors regular contests with winners being published. Readers pick the best of the year for an annual award.

   Tips: "Most open to good, solid, ready-to-print short stories that follow the indications above. I prefer new and emerging writers; we are not a high end publication yet, but working our way there. Your work must be edited and ready to publish."

WORD & WAY, 3236 Emerald Ln., Ste. 400, Jefferson City MO 65109-3700. (573) 635-5939, ext. 205. Fax (573) 635-1774. E-mail: wordandway@wordandway.org. Website: www.wordandway.org. Baptist. Bill Webb, ed. (bwebb@wordandway.org). Contact: Vicki Brown, Assoc. ed. (vbrown@wordandway.org). Biweekly. Subscription $17.50. To share the stories of God at work through Baptists in Missouri and surrounding areas. Guidelines at: http://www.wordandway.org/content/view/825/199.

+$ WORLD & I ONLINE, 3600 New York Ave. NE, Washington DC 20002. (202) 636-3334. Fax (202) 636-3323. E-mail: education@worldandi.com. Charles Kim, pub.; Steve Osmond, ed. Monthly online publication. E-query only. Articles 1,000-2,000 wds. **Pays $25.** Guidelines at: http://www.worldandi.com/about.asp.

+XAVIER REVIEW, Xavier University, 1 Drexel Dr., Box 89, New Orleans LA 70125. E-mail: radamo@xula.edu. Ralph Adamo, ed. A literary journal based at a historically Black university. Articles 250-5,000 wds.; fiction 250-5,000 wds.; book reviews 250-750 wds. **Pays in copies.** Check this publication at: http://www.xula.edu/review/ (scroll down).

CHILDREN'S MARKETS

$ CADET QUEST, 1333 Algers St. SE, Grand Rapids MI 49507. (616) 241-5616. Fax (616) 241-5558. E-mail: submissions@CalvinistCadets.org. Website: www.CalvinistCadets.org. Calvinist Cadet Corps. G. Richard Broene, ed. To show boys ages 9-14 how God is at work in their lives and in the world around them; helping boys to grow more Christ-like in all areas of life. Mag. published 7X/yr.; 24 pgs.; circ. 7,000. Subscription $16.45. 50% unsolicited freelance. Complete ms/cover letter. **Pays 04-.05/wd.,** on acceptance, for 1st, one-time, or reprint rts. Articles 700-1,100 wds. (7-10/yr.); fiction 1,000-1,300 wds. (14-15/yr.). Responds in 8-10 wks. Accepts simultaneous submissions and reprints (tell when/where appeared). Accepts ms by e-mail (copied into message). No kill fees. Some sidebars. Prefers NIV. Guidelines/theme list by mail/

website: www.calvinistcadets.org ("Submissions/Help"/"Cadet Quest Author's Info"); copy for 9 x 12 SAE/3 stamps. (Ads)

Fillers: Buys 14/yr. Games, word puzzles; 20-200 wds. **$5 and up**.

Tips: "Most open to fiction or fillers tied to themes; request new theme list in January of each year (best to submit between February and April each year). Also looking for simple projects/crafts, and puzzles (word, logic)."

+COMPASSION EXPLORER MAGAZINE & ONLINE, 12290 Voyager Pkwy, Colorado Springs CO 80921. (719) 487-7000. E-mail: compassionmagazine@us.ci. org. Website: http://compassion.com/exploreremagazine. Leanna Summers, ed. Compassion Intl. To broaden American children's perspective as they learn about children from the developing world in a fun, engaging way, creating a desire to help those in need. Triannual print and online magazine; circ./traffic 28,000. Open to freelance submissions.

** 2014 EPA Award of Merit: Organizational & Organizational (Digital).

+$ CRICKET, Carus Publishing, 700 E. Lake St., Ste. 800, Chicago IL 60601. Publishes highest quality fiction, poetry, and literary nonfiction for middle-grade readers. General publication; nothing overtly Christian. Open to unsolicited submissions; complete ms only; no e-mail submissions. Responds in 3-6 mos. No theme list. Accepts reprints. Nonfiction and fiction 1,200-1,800 wds.; fiction serials to 6,000 wds. **Pays .25/wd.;** activities and recipes $75 flat fee. Guidelines at: https://cricketmag.submittable.com/submit.

Fiction: Folk tales, myths and legends; sci-fi and fantasy; historical; contemporary. Some shorter pieces, 600-900 wds.

Poetry: Serious and humorous. Most 8-15 lines, but accepts 3-35 lines. Submit max. 6 poems. Pays up to $3/line, $25 min.

Art: Submission guidelines on Website.

$ FOCUS ON THE FAMILY CLUBHOUSE, 8605 Explorer Dr., Colorado Springs CO 80920. (719) 531-3400. Website: www.clubhousemagazine.com. Focus on the Family. Jesse Florea, ed.; submit to Stephen O'Rear, asst. ed. For children 8-12 years who desire to know more about God and the Bible. Monthly and online mag.; 32 pgs.; circ. 46,000. Subscription $19.99. 25% unsolicited freelance; 40% assigned. Complete ms/cover letter by mail only; no phone/fax/e-query. **Pays .15-.25/wd. for articles, up to $300 for fiction** on acceptance for nonexclusive license. Nonfiction 400-500 or 800-1,000 wds. (5/yr.); fiction 500-1,800 wds. (30/yr.). Responds within 8 wks. Seasonal 8 mos. ahead. Accepts simultaneous submissions; no reprints. No disk or e-mail submissions. Kill fee. Uses some sidebars. Prefers HCSB. Guidelines at: http://www.clubhousemagazine.com/en/submission-guidelines.aspx; copy (call 800-232-6459). (Minimal ads accepted)

Fillers: Buys 6-8/yr. Quizzes, crafts, word puzzles, recipes; 200-800 wds., **.15-.25/wd.**

Tips: "Most open to fiction, personality stories, quizzes, and how-to pieces with a theme. Avoid stories dealing with boy-girl relationships, poetry, and contemporary, middle-class family settings. We look for fiction in exciting settings with ethnic characters. True stories of ordinary kids doing extraordinary things and historical fiction are good ways to break in. Send manuscripts with list of credentials. Read past issues."

** 2014, 2012, 2011, 2010 EPA Award of Merit: Youth.

$ FOCUS ON THE FAMILY CLUBHOUSE JR., 8605 Explorer Dr., Colorado Springs CO 80920. (719) 531-3400. Fax (719) 531-3499. E-mail: jesse.florea@fotf.org. Website:

www.clubhousejr.com. Focus on the Family. Jesse Florea, ed. Submit to Joanna Echols, sr. assoc. ed. For 3- to 7-year-olds. Monthly and online mag.; 32 pgs.; circ. 60,000. Subscription $19.99. 30% unsolicited freelance; 30% assigned. Complete ms/cover letter; no phone/fax/e-query. **Pays $30-200 ($50-200 for fiction)** on acceptance for nonexclusive rts. Articles 100-600 wds. (1-2/yr.); fiction 250-500 wds. (10/yr.); Bible stories 250-600 wds.; one-page rebus stories to 350 wds. Responds within 8 wks. Seasonal 9 mos. ahead. Kill fee. Prefers NIRV. Uses some sidebars. Guidelines at: http://www.clubhousejr.com/en/submission-guidelines.aspx; copy (call 800-232-6459). (No ads)

Poetry: Buys 4-8/yr. Traditional; 10-25 lines (to 250 wds.); **$50-100.**

Fillers: Buys 4-8/yr. Recipes/crafts; 100-500 wds. **$30-100.**

Special needs: Bible stories, rebus, fiction, and crafts.

Tips: "Most open to short, non-preachy fiction, beginning reader stories, and read-to-me. Looking for true stories of ordinary kids doing extraordinary things. Be knowledgeable of our style and try it out on kids first. Looking for stories set in exotic places; nonwhite, middle-class characters; historical pieces; humorous quizzes; and craft and recipe features are most readily accepted."

** 2010 EPA Award of Excellence: Youth; 2012, 2011 EPA Award of Merit: Youth.

+GEMS GIRLS' CLUBS, 1333 Alger St. SE, Grand Rapids MI 49507. (616) 241-5616. E-mail: webmaster@gemsgc.org. Website: www.gemsgc.org. Dynamic Youth Ministries. Kelli Gilmore, ed. To help bring girls into a dynamic relationship with Jesus Christ, a relationship that empowers them to see how God can work through their individual personalities, situations, and talents. Digital magazine. Open to freelance submissions.

$ GUIDE, PO Box 5353, Nampa ID 83653-5353. E-mail: Guide@pacificpress.com. Website: www.guidemagazine.org. Seventh-day Adventist/Pacific Press. Randy Fishell, ed. A Christian journal for 10- to 14-yr.-olds, presenting true stories relevant to their needs. Weekly mag.; 32 pgs.; circ. 26,000. 75% unsolicited freelance; 20% assigned. Prefers complete ms/cover letter, rather than queries. **Pays .07-.10/wd. ($25-140)** on acceptance for 1st, reprint, simultaneous, and electronic rts. Feature articles 1,000-1,200 wds. (some shorter pieces 450 wds. and up); adventure, personal growth, humor, inspirational, biography, series (serials 2-12 parts), nature, games and puzzles. Sometimes accepts quizzes and other unique non-story formats; must include a clear spiritual element. Responds in 4-6 wks. Seasonal 8 mos. ahead. Accepts simultaneous submissions and reprints (tell when/where appeared; pays 50% of standard rate). Prefers requested ms by e-mail (attached). Kill fee 20-50%. Regularly uses sidebars. Accepts submissions from teens (14 or older). Prefers NIV. Guidelines at: http://www.guidemagazine.org/writers-guidelines or by mail; copy for 6 x 9 SAE/2 stamps. (Ads)

Fillers: Buys 40-50/yr. Cartoons, games, quizzes, word puzzles on a spiritual theme; 20-50 wds. **$20-40.** Accepting very few games, only the most unusual concepts.

Columns/Departments: All are assigned.

Special needs: "Most open to true action/adventure, Christian humor, and true stories showing God at work in a 10- to 14-year-old's life. Stories must have energy and a high level of intrinsic interest to kids. Put it together with dialog and a spiritual slant, and you're on the 'write' track for our readers. School life."

Tips: "We are very open to freelancers. Use your best short-story techniques (dialogue, scenes, a sense of 'plot') to tell a true story starring a kid ages 10-14. Bring out a clear spiritual/biblical message. We publish multipart true stories regularly; 3-12 chapters, 1,200 words each. We can no longer accept nature or historical stories without documentation. All topics indicated need to be addressed within the context of a true story."

*\$ JUNIORWAY, PO Box 436987, Chicago IL 60643. Fax (708) 868-6759. Website: www.urbanministries.com. Urban Ministries, Inc. K. Steward, ed. Sunday school magazine with accompanying teacher's guide and activity booklet for 4th-6th graders. Open to freelance queries; 100% assigned. Query and/or e-query with writing sample and/or clips; no phone queries. **Pays \$150** for curriculum, 120 days after acceptance for all rts. Articles 1,200 wds. (4/yr.), **pays \$80.** Responds in 4 wks. No simultaneous submissions. Requires requested material by e-mail (attached file). Guidelines by e-mail. Incomplete topical listings. (No ads).

Poetry: Buys 8/yr.; 200-400 wds. Pays \$40.

Tips: Juniorway principally serves an African American audience; editorial content addresses broad Christian issues. Looking for those with educational or Sunday school teaching experience who can actually explain Scriptures in an insightful and engaging way and apply those Scriptures to the lives of children 9-11 years old."

\$ KEYS FOR KIDS, PO Box 1001, Grand Rapids MI 49501-1001. (616) 647-4500. E-mail: editorial@keysforkids.org. Website: keysforkids.org. Keys for Kids Publishing. A daily devotional book for children (6-12) or for family devotions. Quarterly booklet and online version; 112 pgs.; circ. 50,000 (print). Subscription free. 100% unsolicited freelance. Complete ms; e-query OK. Accepts full mss by e-mail. **Pays \$25** on acceptance for worldwide rights. Devotionals (includes short fiction story) 350 wds. (30-40/yr.). Responds in 4-8 wks. Seasonal 4-5 mos. ahead. Accepts simultaneous submissions (please advise in cover letter). Prefers NKJV. Guidelines at: keysforkids.org; copy for \$1.50 postage/handling. Send stories to the attention of Editorial Submissions. (No ads)

Tips: "We want children's devotions. If your story is rejected, refer to the writer's guidelines. Sometimes we reject stories that use common or overly used themes/ illustrations."

\$ THE KIDS' ARK CHILDREN'S CHRISTIAN MAGAZINE, PO Box 3160, Victoria TX 77903. Toll-free (800) 455-1770. (361) 485-1770. E-mail for queries: editor@thekidsark.com. Website: http://thekidsark.com. Interdenominational. Submit to: Joy Mygrants, sr. ed., at thekidsarksubmissions@yahoo.com. To give kids, 6-12, a biblical foundation on which to base their choices in life. Quarterly and online mag.; 36 pgs.; circ. 8,000. 100% unsolicited freelance. Complete ms; e-query OK. Accepts full ms by e-mail. **Pays \$100 max.** on publication for 1st, reprint (\$25), electronic, worldwide rts. Fiction 600 wds. (Buys 4 stories/issue—16/yr., must match issue's theme); no articles. Responds in 3-4 wks. No reprints. Prefers accepted submissions by e-mail (attached file). Kill fee 15%. Uses some sidebars. Also accepts submissions from children/teens. Prefers NIV. Guidelines/theme list at: http://thekidsark.com/guidelines.htm; paper copy for \$1postage. Sample magazine on website. (Ads—limited)

Tips: "Open to fiction only (any time period). Think outside the box! Must catch children's attention and hold it; be biblically based and related to theme. We want to teach God's principles in an exciting format. Every issue contains the Ten Commandments and the plan of salvation."

\$ NATURE FRIEND: Helping Families Explore the Wonders of God's Creation, 4253 Woodcock Ln., Dayton VA 22821. (540) 867-0764. Fax (540) 867-9516. E-mail: editor@naturefriendmagazine.com. Website: www.naturefriendmagazine.com. Dogwood

Ridge Outdoors. Kevin Shank, ed. For ages 6-16. Monthly mag.; 28 pgs; circ. 10,000. Subscription $38. 50-80% freelance written. Complete ms/cover letter; no phone/fax/e-query. **Pays .05/wd.** on publication for 1st rts. Articles 250-900 wds. (50/yr.); or fiction 500-750 wds. (40/yr.). Seasonal 4 mos. ahead. Accepts simultaneous submissions and reprints. Submit accepted articles on disk (Word format) or by e-mail. Uses some sidebars. KJV only. Guidelines $5 (www.naturefriendmagazine.com/index. pl?linkid=12;class=gen); copy $5/SAE/$2 postage. (No ads)

Fillers: Buys 12/yr. Quizzes, word puzzles; 100-500 wds. **$10-15.**

Columns/Departments: "While we need both stories and articles, what we need most are good stories. Children/families out doing things in nature. We regularly need materials on: Wild birds and animals, Camp & Cabin Cookin', nature-friendly gardening, activity-oriented material for our "Learning by Doing" feature, nature photography lessons, survival/wilderness first-aid, weather, astronomy, flowers, and marine life. Tell us about the activities you enjoy in nature."

Tips: "We want to bring joy and knowledge to children by opening the world of God's creation to them. We endeavor to create a sense of awe about nature's Creator and a respect for His creation. I'd like to see more submissions of hands-on things to do with a nature theme. The best way to learn about the content we use is to be a current, active subscriber."

+$ OUR LITTLE FRIEND, PO Box 5353, Nampa ID 83653. E-mail: ailsox@pacific-press.com. For ages 1-5 (through kindergarten). Seventh Day Adventist/Pacific Press. Aileen Andres Sox, ed. Prefers e-mail submissions/attached file. Send complete ms; no queries except for series. **Pays $25-50,** on acceptance, for one-time print and electronic rts. One to two page ms. No talking animals or fantasy stories, poetry, games, puzzles, or photos. Seasonal 7 mos. ahead. Accepts reprints. Guidelines at: http://www.primarytreasure.com/?page=authors.

$ POCKETS, PO Box 340004, Nashville TN 37203-0004. (615) 340-7333. Fax (615) 340-7267. E-mail: pockets@upperroom.org. Website: pockets.upperroom.org. United Methodist/The Upper Room. Submit to Attn: Editor. Devotional magazine for children (6-12 yrs.). Monthly (11X) mag.; 48 pgs.; circ. 67,000. Subscription $21.95. 75% unsolicited freelance. Complete ms/brief cover letter; no phone/fax/e-query. **Pays .14/wd.** on acceptance for onetime rts. Articles 600-1,000 wds. (10/yr.) and fiction 600-1,400 wds. (40/yr.). Responds in 8 wks. Seasonal 1 yr. ahead. Accepts simultaneous submissions and reprints (tell when/where appeared). No mss by e-mail. Uses some sidebars. Prefers NRSV. Also accepts submissions from children through age 12. Theme list available by mail/SASE. Guidelines at: http://pockets.upperroom.org/write-for-us/writers-guidelines; copy for 9 x 12 SAE/4 stamps. (No ads)

Poetry: Buys 25/yr. Free verse, haiku, light verse, traditional; to 20 lines; **$25-48.** Submit max. 7 poems. Seasonal and theme related.

Fillers: Buys 50/yr. Games, word puzzles; **$25-50.**

Columns/Departments: Buys 20/yr. Complete ms. Kids Cook; Pocketsful of Love (ways to show love in your family), 200-300 wds. Peacemakers at Work (children involved in environmental, community, and peace/justice issues; include action photos and name of photographer), to 600 wds. Pocketsful of Prayer, 400-600 wds. Someone You'd Like to Know (preferably a child whose lifestyle demonstrates a strong faith perspective), 600 wds. **Pays .14/wd.**

Special needs: Two-page stories for ages 5-7, 600 words max. Need role model stories, retold biblical stories, Someone You'd Like to Know, and Peacemakers at Work.

Contest: Fiction-writing contest; submit between March 1 and August 15 every year. Prize $1,000 and publication in Pockets. Length 1,000-1,600 wds. Must be unpublished and not historical fiction. Previous winners not eligible. Send to Pockets Fiction Contest at above address, and include an SASE for return of manuscript and response. Write "Fiction Contest" on envelope and on title/first page of manuscript.

Tips: "Well-written fiction that fits our themes is always needed. Make stories relevant to the lives of today's children and show faith as a natural part of everyday life. All areas open to freelance. Nonfiction probably easiest to sell for columns (we get fewer submissions for those). Read, read, read, and study. Be attentive to guidelines, themes, and study past issues."

+$ PRIMARY TREASURE, PO Box 5353, Nampa ID 83653. E-mail: ailsox@pacificpress.com. For ages 7-9 (grades 1-4). Seventh Day Adventist/Pacific Press. Aileen Andres Sox, ed. Prefers e-mail submissions/attached file. Send complete ms; no queries except for series. Ms up to 5 pages. **Pays $25-50,** on acceptance, for one-time print and electronic rts. No talking animals or fantasy stories, poetry, games, puzzles, or photos. Seasonal 7 mos. ahead. Accepts reprints. Guidelines at: http://www.primarytreasure. com/?page=authors.

$ SHINE BRIGHTLY, 1333 Alger St. SE, Grand Rapids MI 49507. (616) 241-5616, ext. 3035. E-mail: kelli@gemsgc.org. Website: www.gemsgc.org. GEMS Girls Clubs. Kelli Gilmore, mng. ed. For girls ages 9-14, to equip, motivate, and inspire girls to become activists for Christ. Monthly mag.; 24 pgs.; circ. 14,500. Subscription $13.95. 25% unsolicited freelance. Complete ms; e-mail queries. **Pays $35; or .03-.05/wd.** on publication for 1st, reprint, or simultaneous rts. Articles 200-800 wds. (5/yr.); fiction 700-900 wds. (8/yr.). Responds in 6-8 wks. Seasonal 5 mos. ahead. Accepts simultaneous submissions and reprints (tell when/where appeared). Require submissions by e-mail (copied into message). Pays some kill fees. Regularly uses sidebars. Prefers NIV. Guidelines/theme list on website www.gemsgc.org/main/shine_guidelines.html. Copy $1/9 x 12 SAE/3 stamps. (No ads)

> **Fillers:** Buys 10/yr. Facts, games, ideas, jokes, party ideas, prayers, quizzes, short humor, word puzzles; 50-200 wds. **$5-10.**
>
> **Poetry:** Haiku, light verse, traditional. Accepts 2-3/yr.
>
> **Special needs:** Craft ideas that can be used to help others. Articles on how words can help build others up or tear people down.
>
> **Tips:** "Be realistic—we get a lot of fluffy stories with Pollyanna endings. We are looking for real-life-type stories that girls relate to. We mostly publish short stories but are open to short reflective articles. Know what girls face today and how they cope in their daily lives. We need angles from home life and friendships, peer pressure, and the normal growing-up challenges girls deal with."

SKIPPING STONES: A Multicultural Literary Magazine, PO Box 3939, Eugene OR 97403. (541) 342-4956. E-mail: editor@skippingstones.org. Website: www.skippingstones.org. Interfaith/multicultural. Arun N. Toké, exec. ed. A multicultural awareness and nature appreciation magazine for young people 7-17, worldwide. In 27th year. Quarterly mag.; 36 pgs.; circ. 2,000. Subscription $25. 85% unsolicited freelance; 15% assigned. Query or complete ms/cover letter; no phone query; e-query/submissions OK. **Pays in copies** (2-8) (40% discount on extra issues) for 1st, electronic, and nonexclusive reprint rts. Articles (15-25/yr.) 750-1,000 wds.; fiction for teens, 750-1,000 wds.

Responds in 9-13 wks. Seasonal 2-4 mos. ahead. Accepts simultaneous submissions. Accepts ms on disk or by e-mail. Regularly uses sidebars. Guidelines/theme list by mail/e-mail/website: http://www.skippingstones.org/submissions.htm#adult; copy $7. (No ads) Winner of many awards.

Poetry: Only from kids under 18. Accepts 100/yr. Any type; 3-30 lines. Submit max. 4-5 poems.

Fillers: Accepts 10-20/yr. Anecdotes, cartoons, games, quizzes, short humor, word puzzles; to 250 wds.

Columns/Departments: Accepts 10/yr. Noteworthy News (multicultural/nature/international/social, appropriate for youth), 200 wds.

Special needs: Stories and articles on your community, culture and country, peace, nonviolent communication, compassion, kindness, spirituality, tolerance, understanding of nature, and giving.

Contest: Annual Book Awards for published books and authors (deadline February 1); Annual Youth Honor Awards for students 7-17 (deadline June 20). Send SASE for guidelines, or check the website.

Tips: "Most of the magazine is open to freelance. We're seeking submissions by minority, multicultural, international, and/or youth writers. Do not be judgmental or preachy; be open or receptive to diverse opinions."

$ SPARKLE, 1333 Alger St. SE, Grand Rapids MI 49507. (616) 241-5616. E-mail: kelli@gemsgc.org; elli@gemsgc.org; servicecenter@gemsgc.org;+ sparkle@gemsgc.org. Website: www.gemsgc.org/main/magazine.html. GEMS Girls' Clubs (nondenominational). Kelli Gilmore, articles and fiction ed. To prepare girls, grades 1-3, to discover who God is and how He works in His world and their lives; to help girls sparkle Jesus' light into the world. Published monthly (October-March); 16 pgs. Subscription $10.70. 20% unsolicited freelance; 20% assigned. Circ. 9,000. Complete ms; no e-query. **Pays .03/wd.** on publication for 1st, reprint, or simultaneous rts. Articles 100-400 wds. (2-3/yr.); fiction 100-400 words (3-5/yr.). Responds in 6-8 wks. Seasonal 5 mos. ahead. Accepts simultaneous submissions and reprints (indicate where sold). Requires full ms by e-mail (copied into message). Sometimes pays kill for assigned articles. Regularly uses sidebars. Never includes byline. Prefers NIV. Accepts color photos. Sends 2 contributor's copies. Accepts submissions from teens. Guidelines/theme list at: www. gemsgc.org/main/sparkle_guidelines.html. copy $1/9x12 SAE/1.19 postage. (No ads).

Fillers: Fillers: Buys 10/yr. Games, party ideas, prayers, quizzes, short humor; 50-200 wds. **$5-15**.

Poetry: Kelli Gilmore, poetry ed. Uses haiku, light verse, traditional; 2-3/yr. **Pays $15.**

Tips: "Send in pieces that teach girls how to be world changers for Christ, or that fit our annual theme. We also are always looking for games, crafts, and recipes. Keep the writing simple. Keep activities short. Engage a 3rd grader, while being easy enough for a 1st grader to understand."

CHRISTIAN EDUCATION/LIBRARY MARKETS

+$ CATECHIST, 1 Montauk Ave., Ste. 2, New London CT 06320. E-mail: robyn.lee@ bayard-inc.com. National Society of Volunteer Catechists. Robyn Lee, ed. For catechists in parish religious education programs and religion teachers in Catholic schools. Needs age-specific articles (about teaching specific age groups). Articles up to 1,200 wds. Submit hard copy by mail, or by e-mail/attachments. **Negotiable payment** on publication. No reprints or simultaneous submissions. Present your credentials in cover letter. Guidelines at: http://www.catechist.com/guidelines.php

+**CHRISTIAN LIBRARIAN,** 7318 N. Pittsburg St., Spokane WA 99217. E-mail: trobinson@whitworth.edu. Assn. Of Christian Librarians. Tami Robinson, mng. ed. Scholarly articles to 5,000 wds.; some longer. Shorter papers, 1,000-3,000 wds., are generally preferable for practical and non-research papers. Include a 100 wd. abstract. **No payment** for one-time rts. No reprints or simultaneous submissions. Mail or e-mail submissions. Guidelines at: http://www.acl.org/index.cfm/publications/the-christian-librarian/guidelines-for-authors/

$ **GROUP MAGAZINE,** 1515 Cascade Ave, Loveland CO 80538. (970) 669-3836. Fax (970) 292-4374. E-mail: puorgbus@group.com. Website: http://group.com/customer-support/submissions. Submit to Proposal Review Team. We equip churches to help children, youth, and adults grow in their relationship with Jesus. Quarterly mag/ezine. 90pg. Circ. 15,000. Sub $24.95. 60% unsolicited freelance; 20% assigned. Send complete ms. Accepts e-mail submissions. Cover letter. Accepts full mss by e-mail. **Pays $50-350,** on acceptance, for all rts. Preferred Bible version: NLT. Articles up to 2,000 wds. Accept 300 nonfiction mss/yr. from freelancers. Responds 1-12 wks. Seasonal 9-10 mos. ahead. Accepts simultaneous submissions. Accepts articles on disk or e-mail (attached file). No kill fee. Regular sidebars. Sometimes inc. bio notes on writer of feature articles. Guidelines at: http://www.group.com/customer-support/submissions. No photos. Sends contributor copies upon request. (ads to breynolds@group.com/970-292-4675)

> **Fillers:** Games, ideas, tips. (6/yr) 150-200 wds. **Pays $25-50.**
> **Tips:** Try this one!

$ **THE JOURNAL OF ADVENTIST EDUCATION,** 12501 Old Columbia Pike, Silver Spring MD 20904-6600. (301) 680-5069. Fax (301) 622-9627. Email: goffc@gc.adventist.org. Website: http://jae.adventist.org. General Conference of Seventh-day Adventists. Faith Ann McGarrell, ed. For Seventh-day teachers teaching in the church's school system, kindergarten to university and educational administrators. Bimonthly (5X) jour.; peer reviewed; 48 pgs.; circ. 13,500. Selected articles are translated into French, Spanish, and Portuguese for a twice-yearly international edition. Subscription $18.25 (add $3 outside US). Percentage of freelance varies. Query or complete ms; phone/fax/e-query OK. **Pays $25-300** on publication for 1st North American and translation rts., and permission to post on website. Articles 1,000-2,000 wds. (2-20/yr.). Responds in 6-17 wks. Seasonal 6 mos. ahead. Accepts reprints (tell when/where appeared). Accepts requested ms on disk. All manuscripts must be submitted in electronic form. Regularly uses sidebars. Guidelines at: http://jae.adventist.org/authors.htm; copy for 10 x 12 SAE/5 stamps.

> **Fillers:** Cartoons only, no payment.
> **Special needs:** "All articles in the context of parochial schools (not Sunday school tips); professional enrichment and teaching tips for Christian teachers. Need feature articles and articles on the integration of faith and learning."

+**JOURNAL OF CHRISTIAN EDUCATION,** PO Box 602, Epping NSW 1710, Australia. Phone/fax: (+612) 9868 6640. E-mail: editorjce@acfe.org.au. Faith shaping leadership, teaching and learning. Grant Maple, ed. Prefers e-mail submissions/attached file. Articles 3,000-6,000 wds.; book reviews 400-600 wds. **No payment.** Guidelines at: http://www.jce.org.au/about-guidelines-for-authors.php

+**JOURNAL OF CHRISTIANITY AND FOREIGN LANGUAGES,** Spanish Dept., Calvin College, Grand Rapids MI 49546. (616) 526-6426. E-mail: cslagter@calvin.edu. Website: www,nacfla.net. A forum for educators who wish to publish research undertaken from a Christian perspective. Dr. Cynthia Slagter, ed. Yearly publication. Prefers mss in English, but does accept some in foreign languages. No reprints or simultaneous submissions. Prefers e-mail submissions. Articles 2,500-4,000 wds.; Forum contributions 1,000-1,500 wds.; reviews 750-1,000 wds. Include an abstract of 50-80 wds. **Pays in copies or off-prints.** Guidelines at: http://www.nacfla.net/pJournals.aspx

+JOURNAL OF RESEARCH ON CHRISTIAN EDUCATION, Information Services Bldg. Ste 101, Andrews University, Berrien springs MI 49104-1800. (269) 471-6080. Fax: (269) 471-6224. E-mail: jrce@andrews.edu. School of Education at Andrews University. Larry D. Burton, ed. Semi-annual. Prefers e-mail submissions/attached file. No simultaneous submissions. Articles 10-30 double-spaced pages. Include a 100 word abstract with feature articles. **No payment.** Submit tables and figures as camera-ready copy. Guidelines at: http://www.andrews.edu/jrce/guidelines.html

+$ KIDS' MINISTRY IDEAS, PO Box 5353, Nampa ID 83653-5353. (208) 465-2584. Fax (208) 465-2531. E-mail: kidsmin@pacificpress.com. Seventh-day Adventist/ Pacific Press. For those leading children to Jesus. Quarterly. Two-page articles 800 wds.; 1-page 300 wds. Seasonal 6-12 mos. ahead. Queries welcome. **Pays $20-100** for 1st NASR. Guidelines at: http://www.kidsministryideas.org/content/writers_guidelines

+$ TEACHERS OF VISION, 227 N Magnolia Ave, Ste. 2, Anaheim CA 92801. (714) 761-1476. E-mail: jturpen@ceai.org. Website: www.ceai.org. Christian Educators Assn. Intl. Judy Turpen, ed. To encourage, equip, and empower Christian serving in public and private schools and to demonstrate God's love to the educational community. Quarterly print mag; circ. 6,500; subscription $29. Open to freelance submissions; articles 600-2,500 wds. and reviews. **Pays $20-50 ($30 for reprints).** (Ads)

+$ TODAY'S CATHOLIC TEACHER, 92651 Dryden Rd., Ste. 300, Dayton OH 45439. Toll free: (800) 523-4625 x 1139. E-mail: bshepard@peterli.com. Peter Li Education Group. For K-8 educators concerned with private education in general and Catholic education in particular. Prefers material for teachers of grades 4-8. Articles 600-800 wds.; 1,000-1,200 wds., and 1,200-1,500 wds. **Pays $100-250.** Guidelines at: http://www.catholicteacher.com/contacttodayscatholicteacher.html; copy $3.
   Photos: Send electronically.

DAILY DEVOTIONAL MARKETS

Due to the nature of the daily devotional market, the following market listings give a limited amount of information. Because most of these markets assign all material, they do not wish to be listed in the usual way.

If you are interested in writing daily devotionals, send to the following markets for guidelines and sample copies, write up sample devotionals to fit each one's particular format, and send to the editor with a request for an assignment. *Do not* submit any other type of material to these markets unless indicated.

CHRISTIAN DEVOTIONS.US, PO Box 6494, Kingsport TN 37663. E-mail: cindyksproles@gmail.com. Website: www.christiandevotions.us. Cindy Sproles and Eddie Jones, exec. eds. Prefers completed devotions; 400 wds. **No payment or $10/devotion.** Accepts poetry. Accepts reprints and e-mail submissions. Guidelines at: http://www.christiandevotions.us/pdfs/CDWritingGuidelinesAugust2012.pdf

DAILY DEVOTIONS FOR THE DEAF, c/o Deaf Missions, 21199 Greenview Rd., Council Bluffs IA 51503-4190. (712) 322-5493. Fax (712) 322-7792. E-mail:

JoKrueger@deafmissions.com. Website: www.deaf missions.com. Jo Krueger, ed. Published 3 times/yr. Circ. 26,000. Prefers to see completed devotionals; 200-225 wds. **No payment.** E-mail submissions OK. Accepts reprints. Guidelines at: http://www. deafmissions.com/?PageID=54

+$ EVERY DAY WITH THE WORD (formerly *My Daily Visitor*), Our Sunday Visitor, 200 Noll Plaza, Huntington IN 46750. toll free: (800) 348-2440. (260) 356-8400. Fax (260) 356-8472. Web exclusive version. **Pays $500 for a month's devotions.** Check this publication at: https://www.osv.com/EverydayWithTheWord/TabId/2143/ArtMID/18793/ArticleID/16741/January-22-2015-%e2%80%93-Day-of-Prayer-for-the-Legal-Protection-of-Unborn-Children.aspx.

$ FORWARD DAY BY DAY, 412 Sycamore St. #2, Cincinnati OH 45202-4110. Toll-free (800) 543-1813. (513) 721-6659. Fax (513) 721-0729. E-mail: dailydevo@ forwardmovement.org, or editorial@forwardmovement.org. Website: www.forward-movement.org. The Episcopal Church. Kelly Harris, ed. A daily devotional that offers meditation and scripture. Also online version. Send three sample devotions according to guidelines posted on website. Likes author to complete an entire month's worth of devotions. Subscription $13. Accepts e-mail submissions. Responds in 4-6 wks. Length: 210 wds., including scripture. **Pays $300 for a month of devotions.** No reprints. (No ads.) Guidelines at: http://www.forwardmovement.org/Pages/About/Writers_Guidelines.aspx

+FRUIT OF THE VINE, 211 N. Meridian St. #101, Newberg OR 97132. (503) 538-9775. E-mail: fv@barclaypress.com. Website: www.barclaypress.com. Barclay Press/ Friends. Devotional quarterly. Submit devotional readings for 7 day, starting with Sunday. Choose your own theme and Bible readings. Devotion + prayer 250 wds., not more than 290 wds. Prefers e-mail submission. **Pays a 1-year subscription and 6 copies.** Prefers NIV. Guidelines at: https://www15.corecommerce.com/~barclaypress/files/Fruit%20of%20the%20Vine%20writer%20guidelines.pdf

$ GOD'S WORD FOR TODAY, 1445 N. Boonville Ave., Springfield MO 65802. (417) 862-2781. Fax: (417) 862-0416. E-mail: rl-gwft@gph.org. Website: www. GospelPublishing.com. Assemblies of God. Wade Quick, team leader for dated curriculum projects. Writing is by assignments only; inquiry required. New writers will need to write two assigned sample devotions. Prefers 210 wds. **Pays $25.** Accepts poetry and e-mail submissions. No reprints. Guidelines at: http://gospelpublishing.com/store/startitem.cfm?item=693101&cat=GPINDEX&mastercat=&path=GPINDEX

$ LIGHT FROM THE WORD, PO Box 50434, Indianapolis IN 46250-0434. (317) 774-7900. E-mail: submissions@wesleyan.org. Website: www.wesleyan.org/wg. Wesleyan. Craig A. Bubeck, ed. dir. Devotions 200-250 wds. Pays $100 for seven devotions. Electronic submissions only. Send a couple of sample devotions to fit their format and request an assignment. Accepts e-mail submissions. No reprints. Guidelines at: www.wesleyan.org/wg

MUSTARD SEED MINISTRIES DEVOTIONAL, 1225 Summit Ave., Bluffton IN 46714. E-mail: devotionals@mustardseedministries.org. Website: www.mustard-seedministries.org. Online devotional mag. 100% unsolicited freelance. Complete ms; e-mail submissions preferred. Devotions 225-275 wds. Indicate Bible version used. **No payment** for non-exclusive rts. Example devotional in guidelines. Guidelines at: http://www.mustardseedministries.org/guidelines/

> **Tips:** "We do not return any submissions and prefer that they are e-mailed to us. We are looking for submissions that are biblically based. Sincerity is as important as your writing skills. Most of us have a story to tell about how Christ

touched our life in some situation that others in this world would benefit from; please send this to us."

PENNED FROM THE HEART, 143 Greenfield Rd., New Wilmington PA 16142. (724) 946-9057. E-mail: nutter4penned@gmail.com. Annual daily devotional book; about 240 pgs. Prefers to see completed devotions. 100% unsolicited freelance. Complete ms/cover letter; phone/e-query OK. Prefers 225 wds. **Pays one copy of the book**; opportunity to purchase books at a discount. Accepts poetry and reprints. Guidelines at: http://www.marilynnutter.com/writers-guidelines.html

$ THE QUIET HOUR, David C Cook, 4050 Lee Vance View, Colorado Springs CO 80918. Scott Stewart, ed. Quarterly subscription. **To be considered for paid assignment** on seven preselected passages, send short bio and a sample devotional encouraging a life of faith from a truth in a Scripture passage of your choice. Limit 210 wds. Use anecdotal launch, bring biblical insight as a companion in faith.

$ REFLECTING GOD: Devotions for Holy Living, 2923 Troost Ave., Kansas City MO 64109. (816) 931-1900. Fax: (816) 412-8306. E-mail: dcbrush@wordaction.com. Website: www.WordAction.com. Duane Brush, ed. Send a couple sample devotions to fit format and request an assignment. Prefers 180-200 wds. **Pays $115.00 for a week's devotions** (7). Guidelines at: http://reflectinggod.com/about. E-mail for application. Daily devotional guide published quarterly.

*$ REJOICE!, 35094 Laburnum Ave., Abbotsford BC V2S 8K3, Canada. (778) 549-8544. E-mail: RejoiceEditor@MennoMedia.org. Website: www.faithandliferesources. org/periodicals/rejoice. Faith & Life Resources/MennoMedia. Jonathan Janzen, ed. Daily devotional magazine grounded in Anabaptist theology. Quarterly mag.; 112 pgs.; circ. 12,000. Subscription $29.40. 5% unsolicited freelance; 95% assigned. **Pays $100-125 for 7-day assigned meditations,** 250-300 wds. each; on publication for 1st rts. Also accepts testimonies 500-600 wds. (8/yr.). Prefers that you send a couple of sample devotions and inquire about assignment procedures; fax/e-query OK. Accepts assigned mss by e-mail (attached). Responds in 4 wks. Seasonal 8 mos. ahead. No simultaneous submissions or reprints. Some kill fees 50%. No sidebars. Prefers NRSV. Guidelines by e-mail/website: http://www.faithandliferesources.org/Authors.

Poetry: Buys 8/yr. Free verse, light verse; 60 characters. **Pays $25.** Submit max. 3 poems.

Tips: "Don't apply for assignment unless you are familiar with the publication and Anabaptist theology."

$ THE SECRET PLACE, PO Box 851, Valley Forge PA 19482-0851. (610) 768-2434. Fax (610) 769-2441. E-mail: thesecretplace@abc-usa.org. Website: www.judsonpress.com. Ingrid and Dave Dvirnak, eds. Send only completed devotionals, 200 wds. (use unfamiliar Scripture passages). 64 pgs. Circ. 250,000. 100% freelance. **Pays $20** for 1st rts. Accepts poetry. Prefers e-mail submissions. No reprints. Guidelines by mail, e-mail, or Website: http://www.judsonpress.com/catalog_sp_guidelines.cfm.

$ THESE DAYS, 100 Witherspoon St., Louisville KY 40202-1396. (502) 596-5060. Fax (502) 569-5113. E-mail: lcheifetz@presbypub.com. Website: www.ppcbooks. com. Presbyterian Publishing Corp. Laura M. Cheifetz, ed. Quarterly booklet; circ. 100,000. Subscription $7.95. Query/samples. 95% unsolicited freelance. Open to submissions from members of The Cumberland Presbyterian Church, the Presbyterian Church (USA), the United Church of Canada, or The United Church of Christ. **Pays $14.25/devotion** on acceptance for 1st and nonexclusive reprint rts. (makes work-for-hire assignments); 200 wds. (including key verse and short prayer). Wants short, contemporary poetry ($15) on church holidays and seasons of the year—overtly religious (15 lines, 33-character/line maximum). Query for their two feature segments (short articles): "These Moments" and "These Times." Guidelines at: http://www.ppc-books.com/thesedays.asp; copy for 6 x 9 SAE/3 stamps.

Poetry: Accepts poetry.

Photos: Buys digital photos for the cover.

$THE UPPER ROOM, PO Box 340004, Nashville TN 37203-0004. (615) 340-7252. Fax (615) 340-7267. E-mail: TheUpperRoomMagazine@upperroom.org. Website: www.upperroom.org. Mary Lou Redding, ed. dir. 95% unsolicited freelance. **Pays $30/ devotional** on publication. 72 pgs. This publication wants freelance submissions and does not make assignments. Phone/fax/e-query OK. Send devotionals up to 250 wds. Seasonal 15 mos. ahead. Buys explicitly religious art, in various media, for use on covers only (transparencies/slides requested); buys onetime, worldwide publishing rts. Accepts e-mail submissions (copied into message). Guidelines at: http://www.upperroom.org/about/writer-guidelines/upper-room; copy for 5x7 SAE/2 stamps. (No ads)

Tips: "We do not return submissions. Accepted submissions will be notified in 6-9 wks. Follow guidelines. Need meditations from men." Always include postal address with e-mail submissions.

$THE WORD IN SEASON, 100 S. 5th St., Ste. 600, Minneapolis MN 55402. Fax (612) 330-3215. E-mail: rochelle@writenowcoach.com. Website: www.augsburgfortress. org. Augsburg Fortress. Rev. Rochelle Y. Melander, ed./mngr. 96 pgs. Devotions to 200 wds. **Pays $20/devotion; $75 for prayers.** Accepts e-mail submissions (copied into message) after reading guidelines. Guidelines at: http://www.augsburgfortress.org/company/submit.jsp.

Tips: "We prefer that you write for guidelines. We will send instructions for preparing sample devotions. We accept new writers based on the sample devotions we request and make assignments after acceptance."

$ WORSHIPMINISTRYDEVOTIONS.COM, 65 Shepherds Way, Hillsboro MO 63050-2605. (636) 789-4522. E-mail: staff@training-resources.org. Website: www.worshipministrydevotions.com. Tom Kraeuter, ed. Prefer to see completed devotions, 500-750 wds. Pays $50 and up. Accepts submissions by e-mail. Guidelines at: http://www.worshipministrydevotions.com/writeforus.html

Tips: "Please check the website and follow guidelines. We won't consider any submission that does not follow our guidelines."

MISSIONS MARKETS

+ACTION MAGAZINE, 941 Fry Rd., Greenwood IN 46142. (317) 881-6752. E-mail: mfmi@onemissionsociety.org. Website: www.mfmi.org. One Mission Society. Editor: Gene Bertolet. Published 3X/yr. Circ. 15,500. Articles 500-600 wds. To inform the public of ministry opportunities and report on ministry of various mission teams. Incomplete topical listings.

+$ EVANGELICAL MISSIONS QUARTERLY, PO Box 794, Wheaton IL 60187. (630) 752-7158. E-mail: emq@wheaton.edu. A professional journal serving the worldwide mission community. A. Scott Moreau, ed. Articles 3,000 wds.; book reviews 400 wds. No reprints. Prefers e-submissions. **Pays $100** on publication. Guidelines at: http://www.emqonline.com/submit-an-article.

Photos: B & W or color. E-mail or mail photos. Details in guidelines.

+**INTERNATIONAL JOURNAL OF FRONTIER MISSIOLOGY**, 1539 E. Howard St., Pasadena CA 91104. (626) 398-2108. Fax (626) 398-2185. E-mail: ijfm@wciu.edu. International Student Leaders Coalition for Frontier Missions. Rory Clark, ed. E-query first. Articles 2,000-6,000 wds. **No payment.** Seasonal 3 mos. ahead. Guidelines at: http://www.ijfm.org/author_info.htm

+**LAUSANNE WORLD PULSE**, PO Box 794, Wheaton IL 60189. (630) 752-7158. Fax: (630) 752-7155. E-mail: submissions@lausanneworldpulse.com, or editor@lausanneworldpulse.com. Accepts articles on current world missions and evangelism topics. Submit to The Editor. Articles 800-2,000 wds. Requires electronic submissions. **No payment.** Editorial calendar on Website. Guidelines at: http://www.lausanneworldpulse.com/submit.php

+**ON MISSION**, 4200 North Point Pkwy, Alpharetta GA 30022. (770) 410-6497. E-mail: jconway@namb.net. Website: www.onmission.com. Joe Conway, ed. Highlights the work of missionaries and on mission Christians throughout North America who are impacting their world for Christ. Quarterly print magazine; circ. 177,000. Open to freelance submissions; articles and reviews.
    ** 2014 EPA Award of Excellence: Missionary

$ **OPERATION REVEILLE E-JOURNAL**, PO Box 3488, Monument CO 80132-3488. (800) 334-0359. Fax (775) 248-8147. Website: www.oprev.org. Mission To Unreached Peoples. Bruce T. Sidebotham, dir. Provides information to equip US military Christians for cross-cultural ministry. Bimonthly e-zine. Subscription free. 20% unsolicited freelance; 80% assigned. Query; e-query OK. Accepts full mss by e-mail. **Pays in copies or up to $99** for electronic, reprint, or nonexclusive rights (negotiable). Articles 500-2,500 wds. (2/yr.); book reviews 700 wds. Responds in 2 wks. Accepts simultaneous submissions and reprints (tell when/where appeared). Accepts requested ms by e-mail (attached file). Uses some sidebars. Prefers NIV. Guidelines at: http://www.oprev.org/about; copy online. (Ads)
    Fillers: Accepts 4/yr. Facts; newsbreaks; commentary, to 150 wds.
    Columns/Departments: Accepts 4/yr. Agency Profile (describes a mission agency's history and work), 200-300 wds. Area Profile (describes spiritual landscape of a military theater of operations), 300-750 wds. Resource Review (describes a cross-cultural ministry tool), 100-200 wds. Query.
    Special needs: Commentary on service personnel in cross-cultural ministry situations and relationships.
    Tips: "We need insights for military personnel on understanding and relating the gospel to Muslims."

+**THRIVE**, PO Box 151297, Lakewood CO 80215. (303) 985-2148. Fax (303) 988-2996. E-mail: Through Customer Service Portal on Website. Submit to The Editor. Seeks to empower and encourage women in cross-cultural work. Articles and recipes. Feature articles 500-1,000 wds. **No payment.** Guidelines at: http://thriveconnection.com/write-for-us.

+**WOMEN OF THE HARVEST** (see *Thrive*)

PASTOR/LEADERSHIP MARKETS

$ **THE CHRISTIAN CENTURY,** 104 S. Michigan Ave., Ste. 1100, Chicago IL 60603. (312) 263-7510 (no phone calls). Fax: (312) 263-7540. Website: http://christiancentury.org. Christian Century Foundation. Senior Editors: Debra Bendis and Richard A. Kaufman. Submit queries by e-mail to: submissions@christiancentury.org. For ministers, educators, and church leaders interested in events and theological issues of concern to the ecumenical church. Biweekly mag.; 48 pgs.; circ. 30,000. Subscription $59. 10% unsolicited freelance; 90% assigned. **Pays $150** on publication for all or one-time rts. Articles 1,500-3,000 wds. (150/yr.); book reviews, 800-1,500 wds. (Attn: Book Reviews); music or film reviews 1,000 wds.; pays $0-75. No fiction submissions. Responds in 4-6 wks. Seasonal 4 mos. ahead. No simultaneous submissions. Accepts reprints (tell when/where appeared). No kill fee. Regularly uses sidebars. Prefers NRSV. Guidelines/theme list by e-mail/website: http://www.christiancentury.org/submission-guidelines; copy $10. (Ads)

> **Poetry:** Poetry Editor – Jill Pelaez Baumgaertner (poetry@christiancentury.org). Buys 50/yr. Any type (religious but not sentimental); to 20 lines; **$50.** Submit max. 10 poems.
> **Special needs:** Film, popular-culture commentary; news topics and analysis.
> **Tips:** "Keep in mind our audience of sophisticated readers, eager for analysis and critical perspective that goes beyond the obvious. We are open to all topics if written with appropriate style for our readers."

CHRISTIAN EDUCATION JOURNAL, 13800 Biola Ave., La Mirada CA 90639. (562) 903-6000, ext. 5528. Fax (562) 906-4502. E-mail: editor.cej@biola.edu. Website: www.biola.edu/cej. Talbot School of Theology, Biola University. Kevin E. Lawson, ed. Academic journal on the practice of Christian education; for students, professors, and thoughtful ministry leaders in Christian education. Semiannual jour.; 200-250 pgs.; circ. 750. Subscription $32. Open to freelance. Query; e-query OK. Accepts full mss by e-mail. **No payment** for 1st rts. Articles 3,000-6,000 wds. (20/yr.); book reviews 2-5 pgs. Responds in 4-6 wks. No seasonal. Might accept simultaneous submissions and reprints (tell when/where appeared). Requires e-mail submissions (attached file in Word format). Does not use sidebars. Any Bible version. Guidelines at: http://journals.biola.edu/cej/assets/19/cejwritingguidelines.pdf; no copy. (Ads)

> **Tips:** "Focus on foundations and/or research with implications for the conception and practice of Christian education." Book reviews must be preassigned and approved by the editor; guidelines on website.

+CHURCH LAW AND TAX.COM, 465 Gundersen Dr., Carol Stream IL 60188. (630) 260-6200. E-mail: mbranaugh@christianitytoday.com. Website: www.churchlawandtax.com. Matthew Branaugh, ed. Christianity Today Intl. Provides local church leaders with the most comprehensive and trustworthy law, tax, finance, and risk management content available anywhere to help those leaders keep their churches safe, legal, and financially sound. Digital publication; traffic 16,000; subscription $119.95. Open to freelance submissions. (Ads)

> ** 2014 EPA Award of Excellence: Christian Ministry and Award of Merit: Christian Ministry (Digital)

*$ COOK PARTNERS, 4050 Lee Vance View, Colorado Springs CO 80918. (719) 536-0100. Fax (719) 536-3266. Website: www.cookinternational.org. Cook International. Submit to Marie Chavez. Seeks to encourage self-sufficient, effective indigenous Christian publishing worldwide to spread the life-giving message of the gospel. Bimonthly online publication; circ. 2,000. Subscription free. Open to unsolicited freelance. Query or complete ms. Articles and reviews 400-1,500 wds. Responds in 1-4 wks. Most writers donate their work, but **will negotiate for payment if asked.** Wants all rts. Incomplete topical listings. (No ads)

+CROSSCURRENTS, 475 Riverside Dr., Ste. 1945, New York, NY 10115. (212)

870-2544. cph@crosscurrents.org. Charles Henderson, ed. For thoughtful activists for social justice and church reform. Articles 3,000-5,000 wds. Accepts e-mailed and mailed submissions. Responds in 4-8 wks. **Pays in copies.** No unsolicited book reviews, reprints, or simultaneous submissions. Guidelines at: http://www.aril.org/submissions.htm

$ ENRICHMENT: A Journal for Pentecostal Ministry, 1445 N. Boonville Ave., Springfield MO 65802. (417) 862-2781, ext. 4095. Fax (417) 862-0416. E-mail: hhartman@ag.org, or enrichmentjournal@ag.org. Website: www.enrichmentjournal.ag.org. Assemblies of God. George P. Wood, ed; Rick Knoth, mng. ed. For Assembly of God ministers and other Pentecostal/charismatic leaders. Quarterly jour.; 128-144 pgs.; circ. 33,000. Subscription $24; foreign add $30. 15% unsolicited freelance. Complete ms/ cover letter. **Pays .10/wd.** on publication for 1st rts. Articles 1,000-2,800 wds. (25/yr.); book reviews, 250 wds. **($25).** Responds in 8-12 wks. Seasonal 1 yr. ahead. Accepts simultaneous submissions and reprints (tell when/where appeared). Requires requested ms by e-mail (copied into message or attached). Kill fee up to 50%. Regularly uses sidebars. Prefers NIV. Guidelines at: http://www.enrichmentjournal.ag.org/extra/EJ_ Writer_Guidelines.pdf; copy for $7/10 x 13 SAE. (Ads)

> **Fillers:** Buys over 100/yr. Anecdotes, cartoons, facts, short humor, tips; **$25-40,** or .10-.20/wd.
>
> **Columns/Departments:** Buys 40/yr. for Women in Ministry (leadership ideas), Associate Ministers (related issues), Managing Your Ministry (how-to), Financial Concepts (church stewardship issues), Family Life (minister's family), When Pews Are Few (ministry in smaller congregation), Worship in the Church, Leader's Edge, $ Preaching That Connects, Ministry & Medical Ethics; all 1,200-2,500 wds. **$75-275.** Query or complete ms.
>
> **Tips:** "Most open to EShorts: short, 150-250 word, think pieces covering a wide range of topics related to ministry and church life, such as culture, worship, generational issues, church/community, trends, evangelism, surveys, time management, and humor."
> ** 2010 and 2014 Award of Merit: Christian Ministry.

+FACTS & TRENDS, 1 Lifeway Plaza, Nashville TN 37234. (615) 251-2000. E-mail: carol.pipes@lifeway.com. Website: www.factsandtrends.net. LifeWayChristian Resources. Carol Pipes, ed. To help pastors, church staff, and denominational leaders navigate the issues and trends impacting the church by providing information, insight, and resources for effective ministry. Quarterly print mag.; circ. 65,000. Open to freelance submissions; articles and reviews. (Ads)

+GREAT COMMISSION RESEARCH JOURNAL, Cook School of Intercultural Studies, 13800 Biola Ave., LaMirada CA 90639-0001. (562) 903-4844. Dr. Alan McMahan, ed. Deals with all aspects of church growth, effective evangelism, and successful Great Commission strategies. Biannual journal. Articles 12-15 pages, double-spaced; plus a 100-word abstract. Complete ms/cover letter, or e-submission. Pays in copies for one-time rts. Guidelines at: http://journals.biola.edu/gcr/submission-guidelines/

$ GROWTH POINTS, PO Box 892589, Temecula CA 92589-2589. Phone/fax (951) 506-3086. E-mail: cgnet@earthlink.net. Website: www.churchgrowthnetwork.com. Dr. Gary L. McIntosh, ed. For pastors and church leaders interested in church growth. Monthly newsletter; 2 pgs.; circ. 8,000. Subscription $19. 10% unsolicited freelance; 90% assigned. Query; fax/e-query OK. **Pays $25** for onetime rts. Not copyrighted. Articles 1,000-2,000 wds. (2/yr.). Responds in 4 wks. Accepts simultaneous submissions and reprints. Accepts requested ms on disk. Does not use sidebars. Guidelines at:

http://churchgrowthnetwork.com/resources/newsletters/2010/01/01/growth-points-executive-subscription; copy for #10 SAE/1 stamp. (No ads)

Tips: "Write articles that are short (1,200 words), crisp, clear, with very practical ideas that church leaders can put to use immediately. All articles must have a pro-church-growth slant, be very practical, have how-to material, and be very tightly written with bullets, etc."

$ INSITE & THURSDAY MAIL E-NEWSLETTER, PO Box 62189, Colorado Springs CO 80962-2189. (719) 260-9400. Fax (719) 260-6398. E-mail: editor@ccca.org, or info@ccca.org. Website: www.ccca.org. Christian Camp and Conference Assn. Kris Hardy, ed. These publications reach 850 professional camp members with columns and features that provide education, encouragement, new ideas, business sense, youth and culture trends, graphics and devotionals to help our members maximize their ministries by learning and staying inspired while serving God's people. InSite bimonthly mag., *Thursday Mail* biweekly; 60 pgs. Query; mail and e-mail queries OK. 15% unsolicited freelance; 85% assigned. Query; e-query OK. **Pays .20/wd.** on publication for 1st and electronic rts. Cover articles 1,500-2,000 wds. (12/yr.); features 1,200-1,500 wds. (30/yr.); sidebars 250-500 wds. (15-20/yr.). Responds in 4 wks. Seasonal 6 mos. ahead. Accepts simultaneous submissions and reprints (tell when/where appeared). Prefers e-mail submission (attached file). Kill fee. Regularly uses sidebars. Prefers NIV. Guidelines at: http://www.ccca.org/documents/insite/isguidelines.pdf; copy $4.99/9 x 12 SAE/$1.73 postage. (Ads)

Special needs: Outdoor setting; purpose and objectives; administration and organization; leadership; personnel development; camper/guest needs; programming; health and safety; food service; site/facilities maintenance; business/operations; marketing and PR; relevant spiritual issues; and fund-raising.

Tips: "Most open to how-to pieces; get guidelines, then query first. Don't send general camping-related articles. We print stories specifically related to Christian camp and conference facilities; innovative programs or policies; how a Christian camp or conference experience affected a present-day leader; spiritual renewal and leadership articles. Review several issues so you know what we're looking for."
** 2010 EPA Award of Merit: Christian Ministries'

+JOURNAL OF PASTORAL CARE & COUNSELING, 26 E. 60th St., Savannah GA 51405. Rabbi Terry R. Bard D.D., ed.-in-chief; Brian Childs, Ph.D., book review ed. Quarterly. Articles related to pastoral/spiritual care, counseling, and education. Register before submitting (see guidelines), followed by your e-mail query on Website. Articles to 14 pages, plus a 75-word abstract. Maintains a 10-18 month backlog of mss. No reprints. **Pays 10 copies.** Guidelines at: http://www.jpcp.org/guidelines_jpcc.htm.

Poetry: Dale M. Kushner, poetry ed

$ LEADERSHIP JOURNAL, 465 Gundersen Dr., Carol Stream IL 60188. (630) 260-6200. Fax (630) 260-0451. E-mail: LJEditor@LeadershipJournal.net. Website: www.leadershipjournal.net. Christianity Today Intl. Marshall Shelley, ed-in-chief. Practical help for pastors/church leaders, covering the spectrum of subjects from personal needs to professional skills. Quarterly and online jour.; 104 pgs.; circ. 45,000. Subscription $24.95. 20% unsolicited freelance; 80% assigned. Prefers electronic submissions; query through guidelines. Accepts full mss by e-mail. **Pays .15-.20/wd.** on acceptance for 1st and electronic rts. Articles 500-3,000 wds. (10/yr.); book reviews 100 wds. (**pays $25-50**). Responds in 6 wks. Seasonal 6 mos. ahead. Accepts reprints (tell when/where appeared). Accepts requested ms by e-mail (copied into message or attached Word doc).

Kill fee 30%. Regularly uses sidebars. Prefers NLT. Guidelines on website: http://www.christianitytoday.com/le/help/writersguidelines; copy for 9 x 12 SAE/$2 postage. (Ads)

Fillers: Buys 80/yr. Cartoons, short humor; to 150 wds. **$25-50.**

Columns/Departments: Skye Jethani, mng. ed. Buys 12/yr. Tool Kit (practical stories or resources for $ Preaching, worship, outreach, pastoral care, spiritual formation, and administration); 100-700 wds. Complete ms. **Pays $50-250.**

Tips: "*Leadership* is a practical journal for pastors. Tell real-life stories of church life—defining moments—dramatic events. What was learned the hard way—by experience. We look for articles that provide practical help for problems church leaders face, not essays expounding on a topic, editorials arguing a position, or homilies explaining biblical principles. We want 'how-to' articles based on first-person accounts of real-life experiences in ministry in the local church."
** 2010 EPA Award of Excellence: Christian Ministry; 2014 EPA Award of Merit: Christian Ministry.

+LEADERSHIP JOURNAL.NET, (See *Leadership Journal*). Traffic 85,000.
**2014 EPA Award of Excellence: Christian Ministry (Digital)

$ L MAGAZINE, 9764 Gares Ave., Cleveland OH 44105-6055. (888) 317-7270. Fax (888) 317-0342. E-mail: info@myliterarycoach.com. Website: www.LMagazine.net. Online version of a 4-color print edition. Empowering ELCA (Evangelical Lutheran Church in America) leaders. Timothy Staveteig, exec. ed. Aimed at ordained and lay ministers in the Evangelical Lutheran Church in America (ELCA). Bimonthly magazine; 36 pgs. Circulation 16,000. Free. 80% unsolicited, 20% assigned. Writers should query. Prefer cover letter, full mss by e-mail up to 1,500 wds. **Pay up to $100** on publication for one-time and electronic rights. Not copyrighted. Prefer NRSV. Articles 750, lead articles 1,500 wds. (30/yr.); book reviews 750 wds. **($50).** Responds in 1 wk. Holiday/seasonal 4 mos. ahead. Accepts simultaneous and reprints (tell when and where). Accepts ms by e-mail in attached file. Never uses sidebars. Some kill fees. Accepts submissions from teens. Guidelines at: http://www.logosproductions.com/content/l-magazine-advertising-rates-and-guidelines-0 (Ads).

Columns/Departments: Accepts 24 mss/yr. Complete ms. Pays $50.

+LUTHERAN FORUM, PO Box 327, Delhi NY 13753-0327. (607) 746-7511. E-mail: editor@lutheranforum.org, Sarah Hinlicky Wilson, ed. American Lutheran Publicity Bureau. Articles 2,000-3,000 wds. Requires e-mail queries or complete mss. Preface the piece with a 50-word synopsis. Responds in 3 mos. No reprints or simultaneous submissions. **Pays in copies.** Guidelines at: http://www.lutheranforum.org/folder.2007-08-22.9250967752/submissions.

Art: B & W for covers or inside. Submit to: editor@lutheranforum.org. Art guidelines on Website.

Hymns: Submit to messner@lutheranforum.org. Hymn guidelines on Website.

+MANAGING YOUR CHURCH.COM, 465 Gundersen Dr., Carol Stream IL 60188. (630) 260-6200. E-mail: mdowell@christianitytoday.com. Website: www.blog.managingyourchurch.com. Christianity Today, Intl. Matthew Branaugh, ed. Serves church leaders by providing accurate, authoritative, and timely law, tax, finance and risk management articles and resources that help them keep their congregations safe, legal, and financially sound. Digital magazine; traffic 9,000. Open to freelance submissions; articles and reviews. (Ads)
**2014 EPA Award of Merit: Christian Ministry (Digital); 2014 EPA Award of Excellence: Newsletter Email (Digital)

+$ MINISTRY MAGAZINE, International Journal for Pastors, 112501 Old Columbia Pike, Silver Spring MD 20904. (301) 680-6518. Fax: (301) 680-6502. E-mail: trobinson@whitworth.edu. Derek K. Morris, ed. Seventh-day Adventist. Articles to 2,500 wds.; book reviews and resources to 500 wds. For all submissions, complete their biographical information form (in guidelines). **Pays $50-300** on acceptance for all rts. E-mail submissions. Prefers no simultaneous submissions. Guidelines at: https://www.ministrymagazine.org/article-submissions.

$ MINISTRY TODAY, 600 Rinehart Rd., Lake Mary FL 32746. (407) 333-0600. Fax (407) 333-7100. E-mail: ministrytoday@charismamedia.com. Website: www.ministrytodaymag.com. Charisma Media. Submit to The Editor. Helps for pastors and church leaders, primarily in Pentecostal/Charismatic churches. Quarterly and online mag.; 112 pgs.; circ. 30,000. Subscription $14.97. 60-80% freelance. Query; e-query required. **Pays $50 or $500-800** on publication for all rts. Articles 1,800-2,500 wds. (25/yr.); Department articles, to 700 wds.; book/music/video reviews, 300 wds. **$25.** If no response is 2 wks., assume they're not interested, . Prefers accepted ms by e-mail. Kill fee. Regularly uses sidebars. Prefers NIV. Guidelines at: http://ministrytodaymag.com/index.php/write-for-us; copy $6/9 x 12 SAE. For free subscription to online version go to: ministrytodaymag.com/index.php/ministry-today-digital. (Ads)

Tips: "Most open to Departments. Study guidelines and the magazine."

+$ NET RESULTS, 308 West Blvd. N., Columbia MO 65203. (888) 470-2456. E-mail: submissions@netresults.org. Shares great ideas for vital ministry among Christian leaders. Bimonthly print and digital magazine. Requires e-mail submissions/attached file. Responds in 4-6 wks. Articles 1,000-2,000 wds. **Pays on publication** for one-time rts. **Cartoons $25.** Guidelines at: http://netresults.org/writers/writers-guidelines

*$ THE NEWSLETTER NEWSLETTER, PO Box 36269, Canton OH 44735. Toll-free (800) 992-2144. E-mail: service@newsletternewsletter.com or through website: www.newsletternewsletter.com. Communication Resources. Stephanie Martin, ed. To help church secretaries and church newsletter editors prepare high-quality publications. Monthly and online newsletter; 14 pgs. Subscription $71.80. 100% assigned. Complete ms; e-query OK. **Pays $50-150** on acceptance for all rts. Articles 800-1,000 wds. (12/yr.). Responds in 4 wks. Seasonal 4 mos. ahead. Requires requested ms by e-mail. Guidelines at: http://www.newsletternewsletter.com.

Tips: "Most open to how-to articles on various aspects of producing newsletters and e-newsletters — writing, layout and design, distribution, etc."

+$ OUTREACH MAGAZINE, Story Ideas, 5550 Tech Center, Colorado Springs CO 80919. E-mail: tellus@outreachmagazine.com. The gathering place of ideas, insights, and stories for Christian churches focused on reaching out to their community—locally and globally—with the love of Christ. Articles 1,200-2,500 wds.; features 1,500-2,500 wds.; Pulse 200-300 wds.; Ideas 300 wds.; and Soulfires 600 wds. **Feature articles $700-1,000.** Seasonal 6 mos. ahead. Responds in 8 wks. Send published clips with submissions. Accepts reprints (tell when/where). Subscription $29.95. Guidelines at: http://www.outreachmagazine.com/magazine/3160-writers-guidelines.html

$ PARISH LITURGY, 16565 S. State St., South Holland IL 60473. (708) 331-5485. Fax (708) 331-5484. E-mail: acp@acpress.org. Website: www.americancatholicpress. org, or acpress.org. American Catholic Press. Rev. Michael Gilligan Ph.D, exec. dir. Serves parish priests, musicians, and others who plan the liturgy; features resources for Sunday Mass, e.g., articles, sermons, petitions, and music suggestions. Quarterly mag.; 48 pgs.; circ. 950. Subscription $26. 10% unsolicited freelance. Query; mail queries

OK. **Pays $50,** on publication, for all (exclusive) rts. Articles 400 wds.(2/yr.) Responds in 8 wks. No simultaneous submissions or reprints. Accepts articles by e-mail (copied into message). No kill fees. Some sidebars. Prefers NAB. Guidelines at: http://www. americancatholicpress.org; copy available. (No ads)

Tips: "We only use articles on the liturgy—period. Send us well-informed articles on the liturgy."

PLUGGED IN ONLINE, 8605 Explorer Dr., Colorado Springs CO 80920. Website: www.pluggedin.com. Focus on the Family. Not currently accepting outside submissions. **2010 EPA Award of Excellence: Online, 2013 NRB Award for Best Website.

$ PREACHING, PREACHING ONLINE & PREACHING NOW, 402 BNA Dr., Ste. 400, Nashville TN 37217. (615) 386-3011. Fax (615) 312-4277. E-mail: Alee@ SalemPublishing.com. Salem Communications. Dr. Michael Duduit, ed. Bimonthly; circ. 9,000. Subscription $24.95/2 yrs. 50% unsolicited freelance; 50% assigned. Query; fax/e-query OK. Pays a subscription for onetime and electronic rts. Responds in 1-2 days. Seasonal 10-12 mos. ahead. Reprints from books only. Prefers requested ms by e-mail (attached file). Uses some sidebars. Guidelines on website; copy online. (ads). Preaching Online is a professional resource for pastors that supplements Preaching magazine. Includes all content from magazine, plus additional articles and sermons. Feature articles, 2,000-2,500, **$50.** Sermons 1,500-2,000 wds. **$35.** Preaching Now is a weekly e-mail/e-zine; circ. 43,500. Subscription $39.95. Accepts books for review. Guidelines on website (scroll down to bottom of home page and click on "Site Map"/ scroll down to "Help"/ "Writing for Us"); Copy $8. (Ads)

*$ THE PRIEST, 200 Noll Plaza, Huntington IN 46750-4304. Toll-free (800) 348-2440. (260) 356-8400. Fax (260) 359-9117. E-mail: tpriest@osv.com. Website: www. osv.com. Catholic/Our Sunday Visitor Inc. Msgr. Owen F. Campion, ed.; submit to Murray Hubley, assoc. ed. For Catholic priests, deacons, and seminarians; to help in all aspects of ministry. Monthly jour.; 56 pgs.; circ. 6,500. Subscription $43.95. 40% unsolicited freelance. Query (preferred) or complete ms/cover letter; phone/fax/e-query OK. **Pays $50-250** on acceptance for 1st rts. Not copyrighted. Articles to 1,500 wds. (96/ yr.); some 2-parts. Responds in 5-13 wks. Seasonal 3 mos. ahead. Uses some sidebars. Prefers disk or e-mail submissions (attached file). Prefers NAB. Guidelines at: https:// www.osv.com/Magazines/ThePriest.aspx; free copy. (Ads)

Fillers: Murray Hubley, fillers ed. Cartoons; **$35.**

Columns/Departments: Buys 36/yr. Viewpoint, to 1,000 wds. **$75.**

Tips: "Write to the point, with interest. Most open to nuts-and-bolts issues for priests, or features. Keep the audience in mind; need articles or topics important to priests and parish life. Include Social Security number."

Special needs: Anglican and Episcopal theology, religion, history, doctrine, ethics, homiletics, liturgies, hermeneutics, biography, prayer, practice.

+$ REFORMED WORSHIP, 1700 - 28th St. SE, Grand Rapids MI 49508-1407. Toll free (800) 777-7270. E-mail: info@reformedworship.org. Christian Reformed Church. Quarterly and online magazine. Resources for planning and leading worship. Short articles to 800 wds.; longer 1,600-2,400 wds. E-query. **Pays .05/wd.** on publication for 1st and electronic rts. Subscription $29.99. Guidelines at: http://www.reformedworship.org/content/writers-guidelines

SHARING THE PRACTICE, 4705 Alton Dr., Troy MI 48085-5001. (248) 644-0512. Website: www.apclergy.org. Academy of Parish Clergy/Ecumenical/Interfaith. Rev. Dr. Robert Cornwall, ed-in-chief (drbobcornwall@msn.com). Website: http://

apclergy.org. Articles written for clergy by practicing clergy. Quarterly international jour.; 24 pgs.; circ. 215. Membership $75; subscription $30/yr. (send to APC, 2249 Florinda St., Sarasota FL 34231-1414). 70% unsolicited freelance. Query; e-query OK; query/clips for fiction. **No payment** for 1st rts. Articles 1,500-2,500 wds. (8-12/yr.); book reviews 500-1,000 wds.; music and video reviews 500 wds. (40/yr.) Responds in 3-4 wks. Occasionally accepts simultaneous submissions and reprints (tell when/where appeared). Requires e-mail submissions (attached file). No sidebars. Prefers NRSV. Guidelines/theme list by e-mail/Website; will send PDF for sample. (Ads)

Poetry: Occasionally accepts ministry-related poetry. Any type; 25-35 lines. Submit max. 2 poems.

Tips: "We desire articles by practicing clergy of all kinds who wish to share their practice of ministry. Join the Academy."

$ SMALLGROUPS.COM, 65 Gundersen Dr., Carol Stream IL 60188. (630) 260-6200. Fax (630) 260-8428. E-mail: smallgroups@christianitytoday.com. Website: www.smallgroups.com. Christianity Today. Amy Jackson, mng. ed. Serves small-group leaders and churches and provides training and Bible studies that are easy to use. Weekly e-newsletter; circ. 50,000. Subscription $99. 10% unsolicited freelance; 50% assigned. Complete ms/cover letter; e-query OK. Accepts full mss by e-mail. **Pays $75-150 for articles; $350-750 for curriculum;** on acceptance for electronic and nonexclusive rts. Articles 1,200-1,800 wds. Responds in 2 wks. Seasonal 2 mos. ahead. Accepts simultaneous submissions and reprints (tell when/where appeared). Prefers requested ms by e-mail (attached file). Some kill fees 50%. No sidebars. Accepts reprints. Prefers NIV. Guidelines at: Small Groups – http://www.smallgroups.com/help/downloadablecontent/howcanisharematerial.html. (Ads)

Fillers: Icebreakers and other small-group learning activities.

Special needs: Journalistic pieces on the small-group movement; creative, practical ideas for small-group ministry, esp. from experience.

Tips: "We prefer writers who are currently involved in small-group ministry."
**2010 EPA Award of Merit: Online; 2012 EPA Award of Excellence: Online Newsletter.

+TECHNOLOGIES FOR WORSHIP, 103 Niska Dr., Waterdown ON L0R 2H3 Canada. (705) 734-7696 or (705) 500-4978. E-mail: mm@tfwm.com. Michelle Makariak, ed. Leading educational resource publication for houses of worship. Print published 10X/yr.; 12X/yr. digitally. Free in North America. Articles 700-1,200 wds. Responds in 2 wks. Seasonal 2 mos. ahead. **No payment.** Check out this publication at: www.tfwm.com

+WORSHIP LEADER, 29222 Rancho Viejo, Ste. 215, San Juan Capistrano 92675. (949) 240-9339. Fax: (949) 240-0038. E-mail: submit through form on Website. Open to unsolicited submissions for the Web. Bimonthly and online magazine. Articles 700-900 wds. Query/clips or complete ms. Subscription $24.99. **No payment.** Guidelines at: http://worshipleader.com/submit-an-article.

$ YOUTHWORKER JOURNAL, c/o Salem Publishing, 402 BNA Drive, Suite 400, Nashville TN 37217-2509. (615) 386-3011. Fax (615) 386-3380. E-mail: proposals@youthworker.com. Website: www.Youthworker.com. Salem Communications. Tim Baker, ed. For youth workers/church and parachurch. Bimonthly and online jour.; 72 pgs.; circ. 15,000. Subscription $39.95. 100% unsolicited freelance. Query or complete ms (only if already written); e-query preferred. **Pays $50-300** on publication for 1st/perpetual rts. Articles 250-3,000 wds. (30/yr.); length may vary. Responds in 1-2 days.

Seasonal 6 mos. ahead. No reprints. Kill fee $50. Guidelines/theme list on website: http://www.youthworker.com/help, or www.youthworker.com/editorial_guidelines. php. (Ads)

Columns/Departments: Buys 10/yr. International Youth Ministry, and Technology in Youth Ministry.

Tips: "Read *YouthWorker;* imbibe its tone (professional, though not academic; conversational, though not chatty). Query me with specific, focused ideas that conform to our editorial style. It helps if the writer is a youth minister, but it's not required. Check website for additional info, upcoming themes, etc. WorldView column on mission activities and trips is about the only one open to outsiders."

TEEN/YOUNG-ADULT MARKETS

BOUNDLESS, Focus on the Family, Colorado Springs CO 80995 (no street address needed). (719) 531-3419. E-mail: editor@boundless.org. Website: www.boundless. org. Martha Krienke, ed., producer. For Christian young adults who want to grow up, own their faith, date with purpose, and prepare for marriage and family. Weekly e-zine; 300,000 visitors/mo.; 130 page views/mo. on blog. Free online. 10% unsolicited freelance; 90% assigned. Query/clips; e-query OK. Accepts full ms by e-mail. **Pays $300-$500** on acceptance for nonexclusive rts. Articles 1,200-1,600 wds. (52/yr.). Responds in 4 wks. Seasonal 4 mos. ahead. Accepts simultaneous submissions and reprints (tell when/where appeared). Requires e-mail submission (attached). May pay kill fee. No sidebars. Prefers ESV. Guidelines on website (click on "About Us"/scroll down to "Write for Us"/"Writers' Guidelines") or http://www.boundless.org/about/write-for-us; copy online. (Ads)

Tips: "See author guidelines on our website. Most open to conversational, winsome, descriptive, and biblical."

** 2014 EPA Award of Excellence: Youth (Digital)

+$ DEVO'ZINE, 1908 Grand Ave., PO Box 340004, Nashville TN 37203-0004. E-mail: devozine@gbod.org. (smiller@gbod.org for queries). Sandy Miller, ed. For teens (ages 14-19), written by teens and adults who love them. Daily meditations and weekend articles. Bimonthly, 64-page magazine. Theme list in guidelines. Meditations 150-250 wds., pays $25 ($10-15 if part of a group). Weekend feature articles 500-600 wds.; **pays $100;** query for an assignment. Guidelines at: http://www.devozine.org (click on "write for Us").

Poetry: Up to 20 lines.

$ DIRECTION MAGAZINE, 114 Bush Rd., PO Box 17306, Nashville TN 37217. (615) 361-1221. Fax (615) 367-0535. E-mail: direction@d6family.com. Website: www. randallhouse.com. Randall House Publications. David Jones, ed.; submit to Derek Lewis, ed. asst. Bringing junior high students to a closer relationship with Christ through devotionals, relevant articles, and pertinent topics. Quarterly print mag.; 56 pgs.; circ. 4,500. Open to freelance. Complete ms/cover letter; query for fiction. Accepts full mss by e-mail. **Pays $35-150 for nonfiction; $35-150 for fiction;** on publication for 1st rts. Articles 600-1,500 wds. (35/yr.); book reviews 500-600 wds. **($35).** Responds in 6 wks. Seasonal 6 mos. ahead. Accepts simultaneous submissions; no reprints. Prefers e-mail submissions (attached file). No kill fee. Regularly uses sidebars. Also accepts submissions from teens. Guidelines by e-mail/website; copy for 9 x 12 SAE. (No ads)

Columns/Departments: Buys 10/yr. Changing Lanes (describe how God is changing you; teens only), 500-1000 wds. Between the Lines (review of book approved by Randall House), 500-600 wds. **$35-50.** Missions (describe a personal opportunity to serve others), 500-1000 wds.

Tips: "We are open to freelancers by way of articles and submissions to 'Changing Lanes,' 'Between the Lines,' 'Missions,' and feature articles/interviews. All articles should be about an aspect of the Christian life or contain a spiritual element, as the purpose of this magazine is to bring junior high students closer to Christ. We are happy to accept personal testimonies or knowledgeable articles on current hot topics and how they compare to biblical standards."

+FCA MAGAZINE, Fellowship of Christian Athletes, 8701 Leeds Rd., Kansas City MO 64129. (816) 921- 0909, Fax: (816) 921-8755. Toll free: (800) 289-0909. E-mail: mag@fca.org. Website: www.fca.org/magazine. Check out this publication at: http://www.fca.org/about-fellowship-of-christian-athletes/contactus/

+$ INSIGHT, PO Box 5353, Nampa ID 83653-5353. (208) 465-2579. E-mail: insight@pacificpress.com. Seventh-Day Adventist/Pacific Press. Magazine for teens 13-19. Articles 1,200-1,700 wds. E-mail submissions. **Pays $50-85** on publication for 1st rts. Seasonal 6 mos. ahead. Guidelines at: http://www.insightmagazine.org/guidelines/index.asp

***SISTERHOOD: Magazine for Teen Girls,** (888) 817-8743. E-mail: susieshell@comcast.net. Susie Shellenberger, editor. A publication appealing and relevant for today's teen girl. Estab. 2009. Bimonthly mag. Open to unsolicited freelance. E-mail complete manuscripts labeled "Free Freelance." No payment. Nonfiction and fiction. Not included in topical listings.

$ TAKE FIVE PLUS YOUTH DEVOTIONAL GUIDE, 1445 N. Boonville Ave., Springfield MO 65802-1894. (417) 862-2781. Fax (417) 862-0416. E-mail: rl-take5plus@gph.org. Assemblies of God. Wade Quick, ed. Devotional book for teens. Quarterly mag; 104 pgs.; circ. 6,000; subscription $3.99/quarter. 100% freelance. Query. Accepts full ms by e-mail. **Pays $25/devotion,** on acceptance, for all rts. Devotions may range from 210 to 235 wds. (max.). Accepts submissions from teens. Prefers 2011 NIV. Guidelines on request.

Poetry: Accepts poetry from teens; no more than 25 lines.

Tips: "The sample devotions need to be based on a Scripture reference available by query. You will not be paid for the sample devotions." Also accepts digital photos, and artwork from teens.

+$ TC MAGAZINE, HU Box 10750, Searcy AR 72149. (501) 279-4530. E-mail: season@harding.edu. Mitchell Center for Leadership & Ministry. Mostly staff written, but open to unique queries. Articles 500-1,200 wds.; no fiction. Prefers true stories. **Pays variable rates** on publication for all rts. Guidelines at: http://www.tcmagazine.org/pages/page.asp?page_id=220597

$ YOUNG SALVATIONIST, PO Box 269, Alexandria VA 22313-0269. (703) 684-5500. Fax (703) 684-5539. E-mail: ys@usn.salvationarmy.org. Website: www.youngsalvationist.org. The Salvation Army. Captain Pamela Maynor, ed. For teens and young adults in the Salvation Army. Monthly (10X) and online mag.; 28 pgs.; circ. 40,000. Subscription $5.00. 20% unsolicited freelance; 80% assigned. Complete ms preferred; e-query OK. **Pays .15-.25/wd.;** on publication for 1st, onetime, simultaneous, electronic, or reprint rts. Articles 350-1,000 wds. (30/yr.); short evangelistic pieces, 350-600 wds.; book, music, video reviews (.25/wd.). No fiction. Responds in 3-4 wks. Seasonal 3 mos. ahead. Accepts simultaneous submissions and reprints (tell when/where appeared). Prefers e-mail submissions (prefers attached file). Some sidebars. Prefers NLT. Guidelines at: http://www.youngsalvationist.org; copy for 9 x 12 SAE/3 stamps. (Ads)

Tips: "Submit interviews/profiles of Christian in the spotlight; also mss related to growing up in faith.
Contest: Creativity Contest: Annual contest that runs from January-March. Categories include original art, poetry, fiction, nonfiction, etc. Details advertised in the YS magazine in the months preceding the contest.
** 2014 EPA Award of Merit: Most Improved.

+$ **YOUTHWALK,** 4201 N. Peachtree Rd., Atlanta GA 30341. (770) 451-9300. Fax (770) 454-9313. E-mail: yw@ywspace.org. Website www.ywspace.org. Walk Thru the Bible Ministries. Lauren Makohon, ed. Real life stories that give us a glimpse at what God is doing in student's lives. Complete ms. Articles 600-1,500 wds. **Pays $50-250.** Guidelines at: http://www.walk-thru.org/yw-contact

WOMEN'S MARKETS

+**BEYOND THE BEND,** 22 Williams St., Batavia NY 14020. (585) 343-2810. (585) 813-8304. E-mail: submissions@beyondthebend.com, or info@beyondthebend.com. Division of PC Publications. Provides encouragement and hope for women who are approaching or are already in the second half of life. Articles 500-1,000 wds. **Prefers e-mail submissions.** Pays free books. Guidelines at: http://beyondthebend.com/writersguidelines.htm

+**CHRISTIAN WOMAN'S PAGE,** E-mail: writer@christianwomanspage.org. Janel Messenger, ed. Send complete ms. Articles 1,100-1,500 wds., not more than 1,700. Requires e-mail submissions/attached file; no queries or mailed submissions. Responds in 2-4 wks. Theme list at end of guidelines. **No payment.** Guidelines at: http://www.christianwomanspage.org/cwpwrite4us.aspx

CHRISTIAN WORK AT HOME MINISTRIES, PO Box 974, Bellevue NE 68005. E-mail: jill@cwahm.com. Website: www.cwahm.com. Christian Work at Home Inc. Jill Hart, pres. Primary audience is moms looking for information and advice about working from home. Weekly online mag.; 2,000 pgs. Sitewide; circ. 30,000-35,000 unique visitors/mo. Subscription free online. 50% unsolicited freelance; 50% assigned. Query or complete ms; e-query ok. Accepts full mss by e-mail. **No payment** for nonexclusive rts. Articles 600 wds. and up (50-75/yr.); reviews 300 wds. Responds in 2 wks. Seasonal 2 mos. ahead. Accepts reprints. Requires accepted mss by e-mail (copied into message). Uses some sidebars. Guidelines at: www.cwahm.com. (Ads).
    Special needs: Turning writing into a career from home. Advice on treating writing like a business.
    Tips: "We are always looking for how-to articles related to running a home business, and profiles of successful work-at-home people."

*$ **THE DABBLING MUM,** 508 W. Main St., Beresford SD 57004. (866) 548-9327. E-mail: dm@thedabblingmum.com. Website: www.thedabblingmum.com. Alyice Edrich, ed. The Dabbling Mum is an inspirational e-Magazine featuring how-to articles, step-by-step craft tutorials, creative writing tips, and business coaching articles for busy, creative entrepreneurs who work out of their home offices. Weekly blog; monthly e-zine; circ. 30,000-40,000. Subscription free online. 90% unsolicited freelance; 10% assigned. Complete ms submitted online; e-query OK. Accepts full mss by e-mail. **Pays $20 to $40** on acceptance for 1st rts., and exclusive indefinite archival rts. **$10 for reprint** rts. Accepts guest posts (donated material). Articles 500-1,500 wds. (48-96/yr.); book and video reviews 500 wds. (no payment). Responds in 4-12 wks. Seasonal 1

mo. ahead. No simultaneous submissions; accepts reprints (tell when/where appeared). Accepts e-mail submissions (copied into message). No kill fee or sidebars. Also accepts submissions from teens. Prefers KJV or NAS. Guidelines/editorial calendar/copy on website ("E-Magazine"/ "Women"). (Ads)

> **Special needs:** Small-business ideas; grammar and style tips; do-it-yourself tutorials and arts and crafts projects
> **Tips:** "Please use e-mail and submissions forms when contacting us. We're looking for material that is not readily available on the Internet. When adding a personal twist to your how-to piece, make sure you write in a way that is universal. In other words, it's not enough to say how you did it; we want you to teach others how to do it too. Write in a conversational tone so that readers feel as though you're speaking to them over the kitchen table, but keep it professional."

+EMPOWERING EVERYDAY WOMEN. E-mail: submissions@eewmagazine.com, or testify@empoweringeverydaywomen.com. Diana Hobbs, ed-in-chief. The nation's leading web publication for women of color. Online magazine. Complete ms or query by e-mail only. Articles/testimonies 800-1,500 wds. **No payment.** Check out this publication at: http://www.empoweringeverydaywomen.com/share-your-story.html

+FOR EVERY WOMAN, 1445 Springfield MO 65802. (417) 862-2781. E-mail: dknoth@ag.org. Website: www.women.ag.org. Assemblies of God National Women's Dept. Darla Knoth, ed. To provide encouragement, inspiration, and information from a Christian perspective to support women of all ages and interests in their walk with God, daily life, and personal ministry. Digital devotional publication. Accepts freelance submissions; articles 500-800 wds. and reviews. No payment. (Ads)

+$ FULLFILL, PO Box 461546, Aurora CO 80046. (303) 690-2083. E-mail: emorgan@fullfill.org. Website: http://fullfill.org. Mission: Momentum. Mary Byers, ed. To mobilize women to live out their influence; leadership development, spiritual formation, and personal development. Biannual digital magazine and weekly blog; traffic 9,999. Articles 1,000-1,500 wds. Open to freelance submissions. **Pays varying amounts.** (Ads)

HALO MAGAZINE, 148 Banks Dr., Winchester VA 22602. (540) 877-3568. E-mail: halomag@aol.com. Website: halomag.com. Marian Newman Braxton, sr. ed. Our primary audience is women, and most of our articles are written by women. Quarterly mag.; 35 pgs., subscription $20. 100% freelance. Complete ms; e-queries OK. **No payment** for one-time or reprint rts. Articles 1,000 wds. (4/yr); fiction 2,000 wds.; book reviews 250 wds. (25/yr.) Responds in 2 wks. Seasonal 2 mos. ahead. Accepts simultaneous submissions and reprints. Requires e-mail submissions (prefers attached file). Some sidebars. Accepts submissions from teens. Prefers NIV, NASV, KJV. Guidelines by e-mail/Website; copy for large envelope/$3 postage. (Ads)

> **Fiction:** Delbert Teachout, ed. For adults. Complete ms.
> **Poetry:** Delbert Teachout, ed. Accepts 8/yr. Free verse, traditional. Submit max. 2 poems. 4-12 lines.
> **Fillers:** Delbert Teachout, ed. Anecdotes, facts, kid quotes, prayers, quotes, word puzzles (using scripture). Accepts 12/yr. 25-100 wds.
> **Columns/Departments:** Delbert Teachout, ed. Men, prayer, poetry; evangelical slant. Accepts 12/yr. Complete ms.
> **Special needs:** True salvation experiences.
> **Tips:** Submit an article about spiritual growth, prison ministry, women's issues.

+$ **HELLO, DARLING** (formerly *MomSense*), 2370 S. Trenton Way, Denver CO 80231-3822. (303) 733-5353. Fax (303) 733-5770. E-mail: magazines@mops.org, or info@MOPS.org. Website: www.MOPS.org/blog. MOPS Intl. Inc. (Mothers of Preschoolers). Jackie Alvarez, ed. Nurtures mothers of preschoolers and school-age kids from a Christian perspective with articles that both inform and inspire on issues relating to womanhood and motherhood. Bimonthly mag.; 32 pgs.; circ. 100,000. Subscription $24.95. 25% unsolicited freelance; 75% assigned. Complete ms/bio. Accepts full mss by e-mail. **Pay .15/wd** on publication for 1st and reprint rts. Articles 450-650 wds. (15-20/yr.). Responds in 12 wks. Seasonal 6 mos. ahead. Accepts simultaneous submissions and reprints (tell when/where appeared). Prefers requested mss by e-mail (attached file or copied into message). Some kill fees 10%. Uses some sidebars. Prefers NIV. Guidelines at: http://www.mops.org/writers-guidelines (scroll down); copy for 9x12 SAE/$1.39 postage. (Ads)

> **Special needs:** "We always need practical articles to the woman as a woman, and to the woman as a mom."
>
> **Contests:** Sponsors several contests per year for writing and photography. Check Website for details on current contests.
>
> **Tips:** "Most open to theme-specific features."

+**HISTORY'S WOMEN,** 22 Williams St., Batavia NY 14020, (585) 297-3009. E-mail: submissions@historyswomen.com. Looks at history from a Christian worldview. Patti Chadwick, ed. Monthly e-zine. Requires e-mail submissions/no attachments. Subscriptions 21,000. Articles 400-1,200 wds. E-query/e-submissions only. **No payment.** Guidelines at: http://www.historyswomen.com/articlesubmissions.html.

+**JUST BETWEEN US,** 777 S. Barker Rd., Brookfield WI 53045. (800) 260-3342. E-mail: jbu@justbetweenus.org. Website: www.justbetweenus.org. Elmbrook Church Inc. Shelly Esser, ed. To encourage and equip women for a life of faith and service. Quarterly print mag.; circ. 8,000; subscription $19.95. Open to freelance submissions; articles and reviews. Articles 1,200-1,500 wds. or less. E-query. **No payment.** (Ads)

MOMSENSE PO (See *Hello, Darling*)

+$ **MOTHER'S HEART MAGAZINE, THE,** PO Box 231, Oxford MI 48370. E-mail: edior@TMHMag.com, or Kym@kymwright.com. Website: www.the-mothers-heart.com. Kym Wright, ed. Interested in heart and informational articles on all facets of motherhood. Short articles: 750-1,000 wds.; feature articles 1,250-1,750 wds. Prefers e-mail submissions/attached file, but will accept embedded in e-mail. **Pays $10-75.** Guidelines at: http://www.the-mothers-heart.com/Writers%20Guidelines%202010-12.pdf

+**PRECIOUS TIMES,** 3857 Birch St., Ste. 215, Newport Beach CA 92660. (949) 427-0688. E-mail: precioustimesmag@gmail.com. The magazine for today's Black Christian woman. Articles 1,800-2,400 wds.; fiction 2,400-3,200 wds. **Pays 5 copies.** Check this publication at: www.precioustimesmag.com

*****RIGHT TO THE HEART OF WOMEN E-ZINE,** PO Box 6421, Longmont CO 80501. (303) 772-2035. Fax (303) 678-0260. E-mail: righttotheheart@aol.com. Website: www.righttotheheartofwomen.com. Linda Shepherd, ed. Encouragement and helps for women in ministry. Weekly online e-zine; 5 pgs.; circ. 20,000. Subscription free. 10% unsolicited freelance; 90% assigned. Query; e-query OK. **No payment** for nonexclusive rts. Articles 100-800 wds. (20/yr.). Responds in 2 wks. Seasonal 2 mos. ahead. Accepts simultaneous submissions and reprints (tell when/where appeared). Requires accepted mss by e-mail (copied into message). Does not use sidebars. Guidelines at: www.righttotheheartofwomen.com; copy on website. (Ads)

> **Columns/Departments:** Accepts 10/yr. Women Bible Teachers; Profiles of

Women in Ministry; Women's Ministry Tips; Author's and Speaker's Tips; 100 wds. Query.

Special needs: Book reviews must be in first person, by the author. Looking for women's ministry event ideas. Topics related to women and women's ministries. **New department:** Articles needed for helps for hurting or suicidal. 500 wds. **$10** on acceptance. See www.thinkingaboutsuicide.com to see existing article format and topics.

Tips: "For free subscription, subscribe at website above; also view e-zine. We want to hear from those involved in women's ministry or leadership. Also accepts manuscripts from AWSAs (see www.awsawomen.com). Query with your ideas."

SHARE, 10 W. 71st St., New York NY 10023-4201. (212) 877-3041. Fax (212) 724-5923. E-mail: cdashare@aol.com. Website: www.catholicdaughters.org. Catholic Daughters of the Americas. Submit to Tom Panas, ed. For Catholic women. Quarterly mag.; circ. 85,000. Stories 50-125 wds. Free with membership. Most articles come from membership, but is open. **No payment.** Buys color photos and covers. Guidelines at: http://www.catholicdaughters.org/documents/Procedure_to_Submit_Stories_for_SHARE_Magazine.pdf/copy by mail. (Ads)

Tips: "We use very little freelance material unless it is written by Catholic Daughters."

SINGLE! YOUNG CHRISTIAN WOMAN, 1000 N. Dove Dr., Rogers AR 72756. E-mail: donna@onmyownnow.com. Website: www.onmyownnow.com. On My Own Now Ministries, Inc. Donna Lee Schillinger, pub. Christian alternative to the fashion magazine. For young, single women ages 17-23, promoting wise life choices and Christ-likeness in all aspects of daily life. Quarterly e-zine; 22 pgs.; circ. 1,500. Free subscription. 50% unsolicited, 50% assigned. Query; e-queries accepted. **No payment.** Simultaneous, electronic, nonexclusive rts. Prefers NIV. Articles 800-1,800 wds.; book, music, video reviews 800 wds. Accepts 24 nonfiction mss/yr. Responds in 4 wks. Holiday/seasonal 2 mos. ahead. Accepts simultaneous submissions and reprints (tell when/where published). Require articles on e-mail (attached preferred). No kill fee. Some sidebars. Accept submissions from teens. Sample copy online; guidelines by e-mail or Website: http://singleycw.wordpress.com/about. (No ads)

Columns/Departments: Just What You Need (resources for young adult women), 450-550 wds; Fashion DIVinA (how to look good and remain godly), 700-1000 wds.; The Recap (reviews of books, movies, music, etc.), 600-1,000; Accepts 18 mss/yr. Query.

+$ TODAY'S CHRISTIAN WOMAN, 465 Gundersen Dr., Carol Stream IL 60188. (630) 260-6200, E-mail: tcw@christianitytoday.com. Website: www.todayschristianwoman.com. Christianity Today Intl. Marian Liautaud, ed. To strengthen and encourage Christian women as they live out their faith in the grit of everyday life. Digital magazine; 52 issues/yr; traffic 236,000; subscription $14.95. Open to freelance submissions; articles and reviews. **Pays.** (Ads)

**2014 EPA Award of Merit: General (Digital)

TREASURE, PO Box 5002, Antioch TN 37011. Toll-free (877) 767-7662. (615) 731-6812. Fax (615) 727-1157. E-mail: treasure@wnac.org. Website: www.wnac.org. Women Nationally Active for Christ of National Assn. of Free Will Baptists. Phyllis York, mng. ed. A women's Bible study guide with emphasis on missions and mentoring. Quarterly publication; 48 pgs.; circ. 3,700. Subscription $12. Estab. 2011. 25% unsolicited freelance; 75% assigned. Complete ms/cover letter. Accepts full ms by e-mail. **Pays**

in copies for 1st rts. Articles 750-1,200 wds. (10/yr.). Responds in 8 wks. Seasonal 12 mos. ahead. No simultaneous submissions; accepts reprints (tell when/where appeared). Prefers e-mail submissions (attached file). Regularly uses sidebars. Also accepts submissions from teens. Prefers KJV. Guidelines/theme list at: www.wnac.org treasure@wnac.org; copy for 5.35 x 8.5 SAE/$1. (No ads)

   Columns/Departments: What Works (practical tips/lists about women's health, homes, fitness, fashion, or finances).

   Special needs: Spiritual formation, family issues, life coaching/mentoring, church life, community outreach and global evangelism.

   Tips: "Most open to articles. Bulk of material comes from Women Active for Christ or Free Will Baptist writers."

A VIRTUOUS WOMAN, 594 Ivy Hill, Harlan KY 40831. (606) 573-6506. E-mail: melissaringstaff@avirtuouswoman.org. Website: www.avirtuouswoman.org. Independent Seventh-day Adventist ministry. Melissa Ringstaff, dir./ed. Strives to provide practical articles for women ages 20-55 years; focusing on the 10 virtues of the Proverbs 31 woman under the categories of Abundant Living, At Home, and Family Life and offers women practical ideas and encouragement for living God's will for their lives. Weekly e-zine; circ. 200,000 page views. Query; e-query OK. Accepts full mss by e-mail. No payment for reprint, electronic, nonexclusive rts. Articles 300-1,000 wds. (150+/yr.); book, music, video reviews 500 wds. Responds in 4 wks. Seasonal 2 mos. ahead. No simultaneous submissions; accepts reprints (tell when/where appeared). Requires e-mail submissions/attached file. Some sidebars. Prefers KJV, NIV, NLT. Guidelines/theme list on website: http://avirtuouswoman.org/writers-guidelines. (No ads)

   Poetry: Accepts 5/yr. Free verse, traditional. Submit max. 2 poems.

   Fillers: Accepts 12/yr. Anecdotes, facts, ideas, jokes, party ideas, prayers, quizzes, and tips; to 200 wds.

   Tips: "Write practical articles that appeal to the average woman—articles that women can identify with. Do not preach. Read our writer's helps for ideas."

*WOMEN OF THE CROSS, 920 Sweetgum Creek, Plano TX 75023. (972) 517-8553. Website: www.womenofthecross.com. Greg Paskal, content mngr. (greg@gregpaskal.com). Encouraging women in their walk with the Lord; strong emphasis on discipleship and relationship. Online community. 50% unsolicited freelance. Complete ms by e-mail; e-query OK. No payment. Articles 500-1,500 wds. (10/yr.). Responds in 2-4 wks. Seasonal 3 mos. ahead. Accepts simultaneous submissions; no reprints. Prefers e-mail submissions (attached or copied into message). Uses some sidebars. Prefers NIV, NKJV, NAS. Also accepts submissions from teens. Guidelines at: www.womenofthecross.com greg@gregpaskal.com. (No ads)

   Poetry: Accepts 2/yr. Avant-garde, free verse, haiku, or light verse; 50-250 lines. Submit max. 1 poem.

   Columns/Departments: Accepts 10/yr. Features (Christian living, encouragement); article (to other women); all 500-1,500 wds.

   Special needs: Personal stories of growing in the Lord; faith-stretching stories about international adoption.

   Tips: "Appropriate topics could be firsthand accounts of how God worked in the author's life through a personal or family experience. View online forum for specific topics."

+WOMEN'S MINISTRY MAGAZINE, 4319 S. National Ave., Ste. 303, Springfield MO 65810-2607. (417) 888-2067, Fax (866) 360-2611. E-mail: publisher@womensministry.net. Jennifer Rothschild, ed. Where women's ministry leaders find news, events, and tips for women's ministry in the local church. Online newsletter. Open to submissions. Check this publication at: http://www.womensministry.net/public/department53.cfm

WRITERS' MARKETS

+AUTHOR-ME.COM, 1407 Getzelman Dr., Elgin IL 60123. E-mail: cook comm@ gmail.com. Dr. Bruce Cook, ed. To encourage and nurture emerging writers in their craft. E-mail submissions/attached or embedded. Submissions only from ages 14 and older. **No payment.** Guidelines at: http://author-me.com/guidelines.htm

$ BEST NEW WRITING, PO Box 11, Titusville NJ 08560. E-mail: bfonte@bestnewwriting.com. Website: www.bestnewwriting.com. Brittany Fonte, mng. ed. This annual anthology carries the results of the Eric Hoffer Award for Books and Prose and the Gover Prize for short-short writing. Submit books via mail; no queries. Submit prose online. The prose category is for creative fiction and nonfiction less than 10,000 wds. (Hoffer Award) and less than 500 wds (Gover Prize). Annual award for books features 18 categories, including self-help and spiritual. **Pays $250 for winning prose; $2,000 for winning book; $250 for short-short prose; $75 for cover art.** Guidelines at: http://www.hofferaward.com/HofferBookForm.html

$ CHRISTIAN COMMUNICATOR, 9118 W. Elmwood Dr., Ste. 1G, Niles IL 60714-5820. (847) 296-3964. Fax (847) 296-0754. E-mail: ljohnson@wordprocommunications.com. Website: www.ACWriters.com. American Christian Writers/Reg Forder, P.O. Box 110390, Nashville TN 37222. E-mail: ACWriters@aol.com (for samples, advertising, or subscriptions). Lin Johnson, mng. ed. For Christian writers/ speakers who want to improve their writing craft and speaking ability, stay informed about writing markets, and be encouraged in their ministries. Monthly (11X) mag.; 20 pgs.; circ. 3,000. Subscription $29.95. 50% unsolicited freelance. Queries by e-mail, or complete ms. **Pays $5-10** on publication for 1st or reprint rts. Articles 650-1,000 wds. (60/yr.); reviews 250-350 wds. (**pays $5**). Responds in 6-8 wks. Seasonal 6 mos. ahead. No simultaneous submissions. Accepts reprints (tell when/where appeared). Requires e-mail submission Prefers attached file). Some sidebars. Prefers NIV. Guidelines by e-mail or Website: *Christian Communicator - ljohnson@wordprocommunications. com; copy for 9 x 12 SAE/3 stamps to Nashville address. (Ads)

> **Poetry:** Buys 25/yr. Free verse, haiku, light verse, traditional; to 20 lines. Poems on writing or speaking only; **$5-$20.** Send to Sally Miller: sallymiller@ ameritech.net. Send max. 3 poems.
>
> **Columns/Departments:** Buys 22/yr. A Funny Thing Happened on the Way to Becoming a Communicator (humor), 75-300 wds. Interviews (well-published authors with unique angle or editors), 650-1,000 wds. Speaking (techniques for speakers), 650-1,000 wds.
>
> **Tips:** "I need anecdotes for the 'Funny Thing Happened' column and articles on research, creativity, and writing nonfiction."

$ FELLOWSCRIPT, Canada. E-mail: fellowscripteditor@gmail.com. Website: www. inscribe.org/fellowscript. Submit to: FellowScript Editor. Writer's quarterly newsletter for, by, and about writers/writing. 30 pgs.; circ. 150-200. Subscription with InScribe membership. Submit complete ms. by e-mail. **Pays 2.5 cents per word** (Canadian funds) for onetime rights, or **1.5 cents per word for reprint rights,** paid by PayPal on publication; an extra half cent paid for publication (with author's permission) on our website for a period of no more than three months. Feature articles 750-1,000 wds.;

columns 500-750 wds.; reviews 150-300 wds.; fillers/tips 25-500 wds.; general articles 700 wds. Responds in 4 weeks. Submissions deadlines are January 1, April 1, July 1, and October 1. Plans 6 months ahead. Guidelines at: http://inscribe.org/fellowscript/ submission-guidelines. (Ads)

> **Tips:** "We always prefer material specifically slanted toward the needs and interests of Canadian Christian writers. We do not publish poetry except as part of an instructional article, nor do we publish testimonials. We give preference to members and to Canadian writers."

+FICTION FIX NEWSLETTER. E-mail through Website. Carol Lindsay, ed. For aspiring novelists and short story writers; offers how-to advice. Does not publish fiction. Monthly; circ. 5,000. E-queries only/no attachments. Articles 1,500 wds. max. **No payment** for one-time rts. Deadline the 10th of the previous month. Guidelines at: http://www.coffeehouseforwriters.com/fictionfix/writeguide.html

$ FREELANCE WRITER'S REPORT, 45 Main St., PO Box A, North Stratford NH 03590-0167. (603) 922-8338. E-mail: editor@writers-editors.com. Website: www.writers-editors.com. General/CNW Publishing Inc. Dana K. Cassell, ed. Covers marketing and running a freelance writing business. Monthly newsletter; 8 pgs. 25% freelance. Complete ms via e-mail (attached or copied into message). **Pays .10/wd.** on publication for onetime rts. Articles to 900 wds. (50/yr.). Responds within 1 wk. Seasonal 2 mos. ahead. Accepts simultaneous submissions and reprints (tell when/where appeared). Does not use sidebars. Guidelines on website; copy for 6 x 9 SAE/2 stamps (for back copy); $4 for current copy; or download PDF copy at http://danasuggests.info/FWR.

> **Fillers:** Prose fillers to 400 wds.
>
> **Contest:** Open to all writers. Deadline March 15, 2015 (annual). Nonfiction, fiction, children's, poetry. Prizes: $100, $75, $50. Details on website.
>
> **Tips:** "No articles on the basics of freelancing; our readers are established freelancers. Looking for marketing and business building for freelance writers/ editors/book authors."

*$ NEW WRITER'S MAGAZINE, PO Box 5976, Sarasota FL 34277-5976. (941) 953-7903. E-mail: newriters@aol.com. General/Sarasota Bay Publishing. George S. Haborak, ed. Bimonthly mag.; circ. 5,000. 95% freelance. Query or complete ms by mail. **Pays $10-50 ($20-40 for fiction)** on publication for 1st rts. Articles 700-1,000 wds. (50/yr.); fiction 700-800 wds. (2-6/yr.). Responds in 5 wks. Guidelines by mail; copy $3.

> **Poetry:** Buys 10-20/yr. Free verse, light verse; 8-20 lines. **Pays $5** min. Submit max. 3 poems.
>
> **Fillers:** Buys 25-45/yr. Writing-related cartoons; buys 20-30/yr.; pays $10 max. Anecdotes, facts, newsbreaks, short humor; 20-100 wds. Buys 5-15/yr. **Pays $5** max.
>
> **Tips:** "We like interview articles with successful writers."

OCACW NEWSLETTER, 5042 E. Cherry Hills Blvd., Springfield MO 65809. (417) 832-8409. Fax (508) 632-8409. E-mail: OzarksACW@yahoo.com. Jeanetta Chrystie, pres. (DrChrystie@mchsi.com); James Cole-Rous, newsletter ed. Writing how-to and Christian encouragement aimed at beginning writers. Ozarks Chapter of American Christian Writers. Bimonthly newsletter; 8 pgs.; circ. 60; subscription $10. 95% freelance; 5% assigned. Query/published clips; e-queries OK. **No payment** (copies and publicity) for one-time and reprint rights. Also attach a brief author's bio and digital photo. E-query OK. Open to 90% unsolicited freelance! Reprints welcome, electronic rights requested. Articles 200-1,000 wds. (60/yr.); writing book reviews 450 wds. Responds in 3 wks. Seasonal 2 mos. ahead. Accepts simultaneous submissions and reprints (tell when/where appeared). Requires e-mail submissions/attached file. Uses some sidebars. Any Bible version. Copy for 2 first-class stamps; guidelines on website: www.ozarksacw.org/columns.php, or http://www.ozarksacw.org/guidelines.php. (Ads)

Fillers: Anecdotes, facts, ideas, jokes, newsbreaks, prayers, quotes, sermon illustrations, tips—all related to writing. Accepts 12/yr.; 25-100 wds.

Poetry: Avant-garde, free verse, haiku, light verse, traditional; 3-40 lines. Accepts 10/yr.; submit max. 5 poems.

Columns/Departments: Accepts 12/yr. Query. All submissions should relate to writing: how-to, personal experience, book reviews, encouragement, marketing ideas, Christian growth of writer, grammar tips, self-editing tips, related poetry.

Special needs: Looking for new columnists to provide 3-5 articles/yr.

Contest: Each spring sponsors an open writing contest; details change annually and are posted on our Website.

Tips: "We want content that speaks to Christian writers by teaching and encouraging them. E-mail us a well-written query that presents your idea. We welcome new writers, and advertise you on our Website as part of your payment."

$ POETS & WRITERS MAGAZINE, 90 Broad St., Ste. 2100, New York NY 10004-2272. (212) 226-3586. Fax (212) 226-3963. E-mail: editor@pw.org. Website: www. pw.org. General. Submit to The Editors. Professional trade journal for poetry, fiction, and nonfiction writers. Subscription $19.95. Bimonthly mag.; circ. 100,000. E-query/clips, or by mail. **Pays $150-500** on acceptance for 1st and nonexclusive rts. News & Trends 500-1,200 wds.; The Literary Life 1,500-2,500 wds.; The Practical Writer 1,500-2,500 wds.; features (profiles and interviews) 2,000-3,000 wds. (35/yr.). Responds in 4-6 wks. Seasonal 4 mos. ahead. Some kill fees 25%. Guidelines at: https://www. pw.org/about-us/about_poets_%2526amp%3B_writers_magazine; copy $5.95. (Ads)

Tips: "Most open to News & Trends, The Literary Life, and The Practical Writer (columns)."

+$ SHADES OF ROMANCE MAGAZINE, 7127 Minnesota Ave., St. Louis MO 63111. E-mail: sormag@yahoo.com. Caters to readers and writers of multi-cultural literature. LaShaundra Hoffman, ed. Devotionals 200-500 wds.; fillers 200-500 wds.; **$15;** short stories (romance) 500-1,500 wds., **$25.** Payment on publication. Query first. Responds in 2-4 wks. Themes on Website. Guidelines at: http://www.sormag. com/guidelines.htm

$ THE WRITER, 21027 Crossroads Cir., Waukesha WI 53187. (262) 796-8776. Fax (262) 798-6468. E-mail: queries@writermag.com. Website: www.writermag.com. General. Alicia Anstead, ed.-in-chief (aanstead@writermag.com); Aubrey Everett, mng. ed. (aeverett@madavor.com). How-to for writers; lists religious markets on web-site. Monthly mag.; 60-68 pgs.; circ. 30,000. Subscription $32.95. 80% unsolicited freelance. Articles 300-3,000 wds. Query (prefers hard copy or e-query). Send hard copies to: Attn: Editorial, Madavor Media, 25 Braintree Hill Office Park, Ste. 404, Briantree M 02184. **Pays $250-400 for feature articles; book reviews ($40-80, varies);** on acceptance for 1st rts. Features 600-3,500 wds. (60/yr.). If no response in two weeks, they probably aren't interested; move on. Uses some sidebars. Guidelines at: http:// www.writermag.com/the-magazine/submission-guidelines. (Ads)

Fillers: Prose; writer-related cartoons $50. Send cartoons to slange@writermag.com.

Columns/Departments: Buys 24+/yr. Freelance Success (shorter pieces on the business of writing), 1,000 wds.; Off the Cuff (personal essays about writing; Breakthrough 700 wds.; Writing Essentials 800 wds.; How to Write 600 wds.;

Literary Spotlight 500 wds.; Market Focus 1,000 wds.; Poet to Poet 500-750 wds.; Writers at Work 750-1,500 wds.; Write Stuff 500-750 wds. Pays $100-300 for columns; $25-75 for Take Note, 200-500 wds. Query 4 months ahead.

Special needs: How-to on the craft of writing only.

Contests: Currently running two to three contests a year, generally in personal-essay or short-story categories.

Tips: "Get familiar first with our general mission, approach, tone, and the types of articles we do and don't do. Then, if you feel you have an article that is fresh and well suited to our mission, send us a query. Personal essays must provide takeaway advice and benefits for writers; we shun the 'navel-gazing' type of essay. Include plenty of how-to, advice, and tips on techniques. Be specific. Query for features six months ahead. All topics indicated must relate to writing."

$ THE WRITER'S CHRONICLE: The Magazine for Serious Writers, The Association of Writers & Writing Programs, George Mason University, MSN 1E3, 4400 University Dr., Fairfax VA 22030-4444. (703) 993-4301. Fax (703) 993-4302. E-mail: awp@awp-writer.org. Website: www.awpwriter.org. Supriya Bhatnagar, ed. Magazine for serious writers; articles used as teaching tools. Mag. published 6X during academic yr.; 96 pgs.; circ. 35,000. Subscription $20/yr.; $34.2/yr. 90% unsolicited freelance; 10% assigned. Paper submissions only. Accepts submissions February 1 through August 31st. No full mss by e-mail. **Pays $14/100 wds.** on publication for 1st serial rts. and electronic rts. Articles 3,000-6,000 wds.; Interviews 4,000-7,000 wds.; Essays on Craft of Writing or Literary Trends 2,000 to 6,000 wds.; Appreciations 2,000-5,000 wds.; News/Features 3,000 wds. Responds in 12 wks. No simultaneous submissions. No reprints. No articles on disk or by e-mail. No kill fee. Uses some sidebars. Guidelines/theme list at: https://www.awpwriter.org/magazine_media/writers_chronicle_submission_guidelines; copy for 10 x 13 SAE/first-class postage. (Ads)

Special needs: Articles on the craft of writing and interviews with established writers from all over the world. Essays, trends, and literary controversies. No poetry or fiction.

Contests: Grace Paley Prize for Short Fiction, $6,000 and publication; AWP Prize for Creative Nonfiction, $3,000 and publication; Donald Hall Prize for Poetry, $6,000 and publication; AWP Prize for the Novel, $3,000 and publication. Website: www.awpwriter.org.

$ WRITER'S DIGEST, 10151 Carver Rd., Suite 200, Cincinnati OH 45242. (513) 531-2690, ext. 11483. Fax (513) 891-7153. E-mail: writersdigest@fwmedia.com. Website: www.writersdigest.com. General/F+W. Submit to Acquisitions Editor. To inform, instruct, or inspire the freelancer and author. Media (8X) mag.; 76 pgs.; circ. 110,000. Subscription $24.96. 20% unsolicited; 60% assigned. E-mail submissions only. Responds within 4 mos. **Pays .30-.50/wd.** on acceptance for 1st and electronic rts. Articles 800-1,200 wds. (75/yr.). Seasonal 8 mos. ahead. Requires requested ms by e-mail (copied into message). Kill fee 25%. Regularly uses sidebars. Guidelines/editorial calendar on website: www.writersdigest.com; no copy. (Ads)

Contests: Sponsors annual contest for articles, short stories, poetry, and scripts. Also annual Self-Published Book Awards. Check website for rules.

Tips: "We're looking for technique pieces by published authors. The Inkwell section is the best place to break in."

THE WRITER'S MONTHLY REVIEW, 106 Fletcher Dr., Logansport LA 71049. (318) 469-5481. Marcella Simmons, pub./ed. E-mail: writersmonthlyreview@gmail.com or marcies04@yahoo.com. Website: http://writersmonthlyreview.com. Debuted in

January 2015. Monthly mag. where creative writers of every genre can come together and learn, hone their crafts, and interact with others who share their passion of writing. US sub. $25/Foreign $35. Features 550-1,000 wds./essay 550-1,000/humor 50-500. All accepted submissions will receive **one copy of magazine.** Subscribers get a free manuscript critique.

Poetry: Well-crafted in any style and on the subject of writing. Max. 20 lines.

+$ WRITERSWEEKLY.COM, 15726 Cortez Rd. W., #349, Bradenton FL 34210. (305) 768-0261. E-mail: angela@booklocker.com. Website and blog: www.writersweekly.com. Angela Hoy, pub. General publication, but how-to articles can include the religious market. Distributed to freelancers every Wednesday. 20% freelance. Articles up to 600 wds. **Pays $60** for non-exclusive e-rights or reprint rts. only. Submit query with credits by e-mail to: Angela@writersweekly.com. Guidelines at: http://writersweekly.com/misc/guidelines.php. Incomplete topical listings.

+WRITING CORNER, (410) 536-4610. E-mail: editor@writingcorner.com. Open to how-to articles on fiction, nonfiction, writing life, tips, and tricks; basic and advance writing techniques. Requires e-mail submissions. Accepts reprints. **No payment** for non-exclusive rts.; regular contributors get free sidebar ads on their site. Responds in 2 wks. Guidelines at: http://www.writingcorner.com/main-pages/submission-guidelines/.

BONUS SECTION

Writer's Helps

Nonfiction Books

What Do Readers Want?

by Dennis E. Hensley

WHEN SOLOMON WROTE THERE WAS NOTHING NEW under the sun, he could have been referring to nonfiction book topics. Although styles vary, formats change, and media delivery modes alter, this core list of topics that fascinate readers holds steady from generation to generation.

Money

Jesus spoke so much about money matters because money matters. People want to know how to spend, save, collect, invest, conserve, earn, share, and understand it. The popularity of money management books by Ron Blue, Larry Burkett, and Dave Ramsey show that people want to know how to plan for retirement, set aside cash for their children's education, invest wisely, support Christian ministries, and become good stewards. Solid information related to finances, explained on a layperson's level, will always find a market.

Improved Physical Health

People want to feel, look, and perform better. They are always looking for new diets, more effective exercise regimens, the latest medical advice on total body wellness. You don't have to be an expert on these topics to write about them; you merely have to gain access to the experts. Consider also ways to write about controversial topics, such as whether Christians should have plastic surgery, what the church's stance will be regarding stem cell research, or how to decide whether a computer chip should be implanted under your baby's skin so you'll always be able to track him or her.

Personal Advancement

Traditional how-to books become standards because they continue to gain new generations of readers seeking to get ahead. Articles that teach "Seven Ways to Write a Dazzling Resume" or books on *Home Repairs Made Easy* will always find an audience. If your book can improve the life of your reader, you will be certain to find a market for it.

Activities

Because technology has led to isolation, many today have forgotten how to have fun together. Years ago people would sit around a Monopoly board laughing together. Today people turn on their computers, and play video games alone. Backyard parties are rare; people tend to stay inside and do virtual bowling on Wii.

People need help knowing what to do when groups get together. A young mom has Brownies coming to her home; after they have a snack, what projects can she engage them in? Grandparents pick up their young grandsons for a 300-mile car trip; how do they keep them entertained for six hours without having to resort to a Game Boy or an iPod? Come up with mentally or physically engaging activities — whether as icebreakers for a company retreat or group events — and you'll find eager readers.

Profiles

People never tire of reading about other people. Magazine racks carry a sea of publications like People and Us. For decades the most popular TV shows have had titles such as *Lifestyles of the Rich and Famous, Entertainment Tonight,* and *The Apprentice.* The common denominator is their focus on people, whether famous like Donald Trump or someone who fascinates because he became the first blind man to scale Mount McKinley.

The largest advances for nonfiction books in the past 20 years have been paid for biographies and autobiographies (Colin Powell, Hillary Clinton, Barak Obama, Michael Phelps, Britney Spears, Stephen King). Keep in mind that the person you write about does not have to be a senator, a televangelist, or a Nobel laureate. The person just has to be distinctive and interesting enough to hold your readers.

Schooling and Educational Innovations

Although modern public schools train thousands of students via satellite feeds for in-class news and specialized programs, thousands of other students are being educated at home, a concept that dates to the colonial era. If you ask parents why they prefer public schools, they will talk about modern science labs, diverse sports programs, a broad range of teachers and counselors and administrators, and the opportunity for students to gain social skills. Parents who homeschool talk about personalized attention, a more conservative curriculum, protection from gangs and drugs, no restrictions on prayer, and more field trips.

Your job as a writer is to investigate, analyze, and report on all aspects of education. Why have online courses become so popular? What causes school violence? Does playing music by Mozart really help students remember? The range of topics is limitless because the interest for readers is equally limitless. Share what you've learned about learning.

This list is not exhaustive, but it will give you a foundation of topics that never fail to find a market if they are given new insights and written in a lively, clear manner.

Used by permission of the Jerry Jenkins Writers Guild.

The Seven Cs of Writing
by Dennis E. Hensley

NO MATTER WHAT METHOD you choose, think about certain structural foundations before you write.

1. Certainty

Accuracy is essential. No careless handling of the truth and no trifling with facts.

2. Concern

Have a concerned heart, but not a bleeding heart. Be sensitive to a reader's desire for more knowledge, hope, recognition, and understanding. Deliver information in gracious but pragmatic ways.

3. Creativity

The writer needs imagination, freshness, new information, new insights, and a desire to say old things in new, clever ways.

4. Character

Identify the strengths in your writing, then develop and improve those strengths. Copying other writers is a waste of time. Be original and give your writing its own character.

5. Completeness

Mention only necessary facts, but don't omit important details. Tell the full story. If you have too much information, narrow the scope and use the rest in a second article. Both articles can then become sections of a chapter in your next book.

6. Clarity

Make your writing simple, direct, readable, and precise. Rewrite as many times as necessary to eliminate what's dull or fuzzy. Paint clear word pictures. Don't try to impress editors or readers with your vocabulary; just give them the facts.

7. Conciseness

Weed out anything that doesn't advance the action or provide necessary explanations. Make your words count. Keep your writing crisp, tight, and on-topic. The best writers say the most in the fewest words.

Why a Book?

by Les Stobbe

WHY WRITE A BOOK AND NOT AN ARTICLE? When my wife and I drove from Massachusetts to Arkansas, we filled our gas tank at the start of the journey. We knew it would get us only about 350 miles down the road, and it would need several refillings to get us to our destination. An article might be compared to that gas tank; it will get us started, but it can't hold enough fuel for a long journey.

That's the role of a book, which can remotivate us and further equip us, chapter after chapter, to keep on in our journey of faith and life — to let the Holy Spirit make the adjustments to behavior so we please our Master and encourage others to make the journey with us.

To accomplish that, we must think of the book as a movement. Through our words, we ask our readers to join us in our quest for a life that pleases God. We summon them to participate in a process that brings pleasure in the beauty of God's creation, joy even in suffering, and an unshakable hold on our hope in Christ. That means, of course, a life that lives out the Great Commandment of Christ and seeks to fulfill His Great Commission.

Through our words we ask our readers to join us in our quest for a life that pleases God.

That mindset is foreign even to many writers who consider themselves Christians. Our age has so imbued us with self-importance, we tend to believe that what we have to offer is so fabulous that we need to share it.

Yet even when we're providing information, we ought to be writing to change lives rather than for mere self-expression. Luke, John, Paul, and other biblical writers focused on their readers and what their needs were, and that outward focus was part of the divine inspiration God gave them.

Books Come in Different Shapes

by Les Stobbe

Like articles, books come in a variety of genres, of which these are the most common:

Autobiographical

You will either have to be famous or have an incredible life or experience — such as being a missionary held hostage — to get readers interested in an autobiographical book. That doesn't mean your story is unimportant. But it does mean that instead of telling your story chronologically, you'll need to incorporate your experiences as illustrations in a book with a theme that speaks to many people. *First We Have Coffee* by Margaret Jensen did that — and its success resulted in an annual compilation of stories under a central theme.

Biographical

This is another category not in favor with Christian publishers. A biography of a prominent university president will typically draw a yawn from an editor — and most alumni. If you can do biographies of historical figures, they may find a market in education or home-schooling circles. An excellent example is *A Passion for the Impossible*, the biography of missionary Lilias Trotter by Miriam Huffman Rockness. In the secular market, *John Adams* by David McCullough achieved best-seller status.

How-To

This category has lots of potential — and many competitors. Because topics can be covered in so many different ways, how-to books will constantly find an audience. Look at the spate of books on praying for your spouse and your family. With creativity, you can find areas of Christian living about which no one has recently written. That was true with Jim Talley's manuscript for *Reconcilable Differences;* no one else was writing about how divorced and separated people could be reconciled. The same was true of a book based on interviews with successful single moms. So check what's on the market — and then develop your own angle.

Motivational

This is a major category in general market publishing, with the best-selling *Seven Habits of Highly Effective People* by Steven Covey a striking example. In the Christian field, books by John Maxwell and the late Zig Ziglar have even crossed over into the general market. Bruce Wilkinson's *The Prayer of Jabez* tapped a deeply felt need among Christians for a positive, can-do book.

Christian Living

This catchall category encompasses many types of books. All are designed to help people "walk the walk" more successfully; many are motivational. One of the best is *Stretching the Soul* by Ronald E. Wilson. Another valuable work is Janet Chester Bly's *Hope Lives Here*. In the past several years, Rick Warren's *The Purpose-Driven Life* has prompted multiple follow-up books.

Inspirational

These are books with stories of people who've overcome a debilitating disease, injury, or some other obstacle. An outstanding example is the book *Joni* by Joni Eareckson

Tada with Joe Musser. There are many more stories like Joni's, but few will have the inspirational value. Commercial editors have seen so many stories of overcoming grief, they usually turn them down automatically. But every so often one breaks through.

Exposition

This category tends to be dominated by preachers and professors, as they regularly do exposition of Scripture. But a topical, popular-level approach by a lay Bible teacher with a sufficient promotional platform may also break through and catch readers' attention.

Apologetic/Evangelistic

Each year brings a new crop of books in this category. You have to become a specialist — and most likely be affiliated with a ministry doing evangelism. Rebecca Manley Pippert's *Out of the Salt Shaker and Into the World* has become a classic.

Issues and Problems

Issues such as racial reconciliation, taking care of aging parents, recovery from addictions, and theological disagreements fall into this category. One of the better examples is *Enjoying Your Best Years* by J. Oswald Sanders, which focuses on staying younger while growing older. Another example is *Winning the Race to Unity: Is Racial Reconciliation Really Working?* by Clarence Shuler.

Curriculum

With the emergence of adult small groups, books that were once designed for use only in adult Bible classes took on a new format, and regular nonfiction books had study guides added. In addition, writers emerged who specialized in interactive study in the small-group setting. This promises to be a continuing market.

Used by permission of the Jerry Jenkins Writers Guild.

Nonfiction Dialogue Tips
by Les Stobbe

1. **Don't let dialogue become preachy.**
   Consider three sentences at a time the maximum length.

2. **Dialogue should rarely be expositional.**
   That slows the exchange too much.

3. **Dialogue should be as natural as conversation.**
   The writer needs imagination, freshness, new information, new insights, and a desire to say old things in new, clever ways.

4. **Accents or dialects do not work well in written dialogue.**
   Unless there is a compelling reason to have one person use dialect briefly, don't. Just one or two phonetically spelled or carefully chosen words can accomplish what you want.

5. **If your story is moving well, dialogue will come.**
   Let the characters interact naturally and don't force dialogue into a situation where it would be awkward.

Before You Start to Write Your Book

by Les Stobbe

FIRST YOU NEED A CLEAR PURPOSE — what you want to achieve in the lives of your readers. If you can condense that to one sentence, it can become a laser beam to keep you on course throughout writing and revision. When good ideas pop into your head, you can check them against that purpose. If they don't further the purpose, you can cast them aside. They may be okay for a later book, but not the one you're writing now.

A Rough Outline

So what's your book idea? What concept — what biblical truth, argument, behavior, or experience — has the strength to sustain a full-length book?

Bruce Wilkinson's preaching and teaching on the prayer of Jabez in 1 Chronicles 4:9-10 convinced him he needed to write a book. He developed an outline and began writing. The result was a 280-page masterpiece — from his perspective. Unfortunately, no publisher agreed. Years later, he was challenged to try again.

This time writer/editor David Kopp was enlisted to help distill Bruce's concepts. The result? A 92-page book — one-third the length of the original — saw daylight as *The Prayer of Jabez*. The market responded with unbridled enthusiasm, propelling it into publishing history as the best-selling nonfiction book ever in first-year sales.

The lesson? No matter how good your idea, no matter how great your outline and content, it still has to be published in a format that will appeal to a large number of readers. Keeping that in mind can save you many hours of effort.

Initially, all outlines are tentative. You're moving from concept to process. What steps will change a static idea into a life-changing experience? What can you include that will motivate acceptance of new ideas and behaviors?

Research can lead you to make dramatic changes. Those revisions will be based on conclusions developed through study and interviews — not on your initial, less-informed ideas of where you want to go. Yet those ideas give you a starting place.

As you develop the outline, remember you're mapping a journey for your reader designed to lead to life change. When we're cooperating with the Holy Spirit through prayer, drawing on His Word, and moving a reader step by step, chapter by chapter, we can be used by the Lord to effect a shift in mind, in attitude, and ultimately in behavior. The outline makes that possible.

Whenever you have a nonfiction book idea, try this: Write the key ideas in outline form. Then put the chapter headings on separate pages. For each chapter, write insights and information you already have. Add imaginative devices you may want to use: story (illustrations), word pictures, extended metaphors. List the motivational tools you want to use: benefits, role models, emotional grabbers, how-to. Now put down the action you hope readers will take.

This can take more time than you think it deserves. But unless you're an experienced writer for whom these elements just flow, this step can save you considerable time in the actual writing.

Research

No matter how well you've thought through a topic, you'll need to engage in thorough research. Not only will it uncover additional information, stories, and insights, but it also may challenge your firmly held positions and force you to think differently about your topic. It's like assembling a group and tossing your concept on the table for their reaction.

Online research adds dramatically to what is available through traditional means. Insert the word *righteousness* in a search dialogue box, and the first screen displays 10 potential sources of information — followed by listings from every possible viewpoint and degree of credibility. As I wrote this, I inserted "heaven + Billy Graham" in the Google.com search box, and in less than a second I had access to the first page of thousands of references. The second page included a link to an article in *USA Today* on Anne Graham Lotz's book on heaven, complete with a salvation message excerpted from it.

At this stage of your research, the landscape of your book should be taking shape. You'll still need to do more hours of research, but having the big picture means you have a working knowledge of your best sources for corroborating information and quotes.

Each book requires a somewhat different approach to research. Especially if you are writing on a biblical theme, you'll be digging into Scripture — finding key verses on a specific topic and digging into manners and customs books to understand the culture of Bible times. Then you can use a site such as BibleGateway.com to cut and paste Scripture verses into the text to present God's perspective on your topic. By taking such an approach, you can be careful to avoid proof-texting: just pulling in verses to support an argument you develop.

For a book on why so many teens leave the church, you'll need to meet with parents, youth pastors, teens dropping out of church, and disaffected young adults. A book on prayer may require a tour through books on prayer that go back to medieval times, but you could also elicit stories of answered prayer through an internet or email site for Christian writers.

Used by permission of the Jerry Jenkins Writers Guild.

A Sample Structure for Nonfiction Books
by Les Stobbe

AFTER ANALYZING many nonfiction books — and writing a few myself — I've reached the conclusion that except for biography, this pattern works well:

- **Chapter 1** grabs the reader and introduces the topic, writer, and benefits.
- **Chapter 2** establishes the significance of the topic, providing some background.
- **Chapters 3 and following** each develop a key point to be made, richly illustrated from Scripture and life.
- **The closing chapter** wraps up the discussion, with a clear indication of the life change expected.

Each chapter needs to grab the reader anew, so the initial paragraphs require the same power to engage the reader as the lead in chapter 1. Each chapter needs to include motivation for life change — and end with a promise of the benefit of reading the next chapter. Internally, each chapter has the characteristics of a magazine article.

Even exposition can follow this pattern, for today's readers want biblical truth in life settings, not merely for information's sake. In his books, Chuck Swindoll consistently follows a biblical example with a story that illustrates the same point from modern life — often from his own life. As a result, readers are less likely to dismiss the biblical story as irrelevant.

Does Your Book Need These Sections?
by Les Stobbe

AS YOU PLAN YOUR BOOK you'll need to decide whether to include some parts that have traditionally been common. We've all read books with a foreword (be sure you spell that word correctly), a preface, and an introduction. Let's examine them.

The Foreword
In most cases, the foreword is the last piece added to your manuscript. Marketers don't recommend a foreword written by your best friend or pastor, but one from the most widely known personality available — or someone with credentials who is well known in this field.

Usually the person who writes the foreword will want to see the whole manuscript. Once when I was an editor at a book publisher, I enlisted a pastor/writer to provide a foreword for a book on fathering a son. He agreed to do it only if the authors made some specific changes. The authors consented, and the book sold so well, the publisher kept it in print for 10 years.

In another case I enlisted Dr. C. Everett Koop, then head of pediatric surgery at a Philadelphia hospital, to write the foreword for a book on living with cancer. He delivered a six-page piece that undoubtedly contributed to the extraordinary sales of the book. Not all forewords make that kind of impact!

The Preface
Once extremely popular, prefaces have largely disappeared from today's books. They are often an attempt to attract another well-known personality to endorse the book. The preface may focus on the book's content or the qualities of the writer. Sometimes in a second or third edition, an author will add a preface to tackle issues raised by readers.

In reality, few readers even glance at a preface. They want to get to chapter 1. So unless you have a very good reason, don't bother with it.

The Introduction
Should you write an introduction? Most authors who write one see it as an opportunity to explain who they are and why they've written the book. Such introductions can fill several pages.

Cheri Fuller, in When Couples Pray, has a six-page introduction. Subtitled "How to Get the Most from This Book," it opens with:

> Last weekend, we attended yet another wedding. In a gorgeous silk and brocade dress, the glowing bride floated down the aisle to the sound of trumpets and organ music to meet her groom at the altar. Candles flickered as the couple gazed into each other's eyes and promised to love forever.

Doesn't that feel like the opening of a chapter? By the time I'd scanned the introduction, I knew it had all the earmarks of a first chapter. But its good content will be lost to all those readers who skip the introduction. Why not let the first chapter do the work of both the preface and the introduction? You'll get to the reader much faster!

Used by permission of the Jerry Jenkins Writers Guild.

Make the Most of Chapter 1

by Les Stobbe

EVER WATCH PEOPLE IN A STORE picking up nonfiction books? Most likely they will scan the cover, quickly noticing the title, author's name, and additional information. Next they will scan the back cover. Then they'll open to the contents page and glance at the chapter titles. If they're still intrigued, they'll open to the first chapter.

That's why you want the first paragraph of chapter 1 to be a real grabber — with the rest of the chapter so strong, it holds a reader's attention.

In *Learning to Hear the Whispers of God,* Donna Fitzpatrick opens with:

> Kevin shifted from one foot to the other in the doorway of my room while his gaze roamed the walls in search of words. The book in my lap fell aside; my easygoing teen had seized my full attention. Sitting up straighter, I watched and waited until at last his eyes met mine, and he softly asked, "Mom ... how do you know when God is talking to you?"

Her opening anecdote ties in directly with her book's title. And because it's her son, we know she'll be transparent.

Far too many writers charge in with their big idea in the first chapter —then try to figure how to stretch it to fill a book. In road-building terminology, they "dump the whole load" of gravel, then try to spread it for half a mile. It gets mighty thin.

Hook and Intrigue

Instead, use the first chapter to hook readers, intrigue them, and let them sense this book will provide excellent content by a qualified author — that the benefits will be worth the investment of time.

What should be your goals in the first chapter? Here are five objectives:

- warm readers to your topic
- establish your credentials as a writer/expert
- acquaint readers with your style of writing
- establish the boundaries of the discussion
- point to the benefits of reading the rest of the book

Warm Readers to Your Topic

Here's where we take a page from article writers. What are the key ways to hook readers in the lead? In a book you have more space to set up the opening story, to do justice to it or give more of a catchy quote. With that, you want to establish eye contact with readers at a point of felt need. You want them to feel you know what's important to them, that you're going with them on a journey of discovery.

In *Will God Heal Me?* Ron Dunn opens the first chapter with:

> "Does God heal today?" That question is as relevant as your next headache. Even more relevant is, "Will God heal me?"
>
> It's easy to philosophize about suffering when you're not doing any. But when the beast crouches at your own door, it's another ball game — the answers don't come as easily then, and the explanations often don't satisfy.

What has the author done to establish connection with his readers? How has he helped them picture suffering?

I call this building a bridge across felt need to the readers' real need. These real need may be forgiveness, a deepened relationship with Jesus Christ, a better understanding of the life of holiness, or a confronting of their own weakness in the light of God's strength. But if you don't cross the bridge of felt need, readers may stop reading before they get help. Or they may never see their need to take the step of personal application.

Establish Your Credentials

A formal description of your job credentials may appear on the back cover. But it doesn't provide a warm enough context to portray you as a writer communicating a message from the Lord.

So how do you get across your spiritual or experiential credentials? Through a personal experience or two that you relate in the first chapter. People want to know you're a regular person and have faced the issues you'll be writing about. No affectation, no boasting — just letting readers look enough into your life to gain confidence that you understand them and have been where they are.

In *When Couples Pray,* Cheri Fuller establishes her credentials by telling how her silent-about-his-faith husband eventually became her prayer partner. Instead of withdrawing to his room when he felt threatened, he began joining her in prayer.

Acquaint Readers with Your Style

While the first chapter may be significantly shorter than the rest, it provides a window into the book that lets readers see if you're information-oriented or story-based, informal or formal, real or artificial. An easy-reading, anecdote-based opening chapter may capture your reader — but only temporarily if the following chapters are more formal or academic.

Readers will quickly sense if you're dumping information or engaging in a dialogue, providing authoritarian answers or embarking on a shared journey of discovery. The vocabulary level, number of anecdotes, frequency of allusions to real life, use of word pictures, and references to Scripture — all give readers a feel for the kind of communication they'll receive.

Establish the Discussion

After reading the first chapter, readers should have a good idea how wide-ranging the book's discussion will be. They want to know what they're getting themselves into. If the discussion is not sufficiently in-depth, they want to move on. You want readers to feel they're getting what the title and cover promise.

Point to the Benefits of Reading

There's a lot at stake when readers open your book and start into chapter 1. To hook them, the skillful writer includes references to the benefits to be gained by reading the whole book. These may be stated in only one sentence, if presented in a way the reader can't miss. They may even be in the form of a promise, as at the end of chapter 1 in *The Prayer of Jabez:*

> God really does have unclaimed blessings waiting for you, my friend. I know it sounds impossible — even embarrassingly suspicious in our self-serving day. ... At that moment, you will begin to let the loving currents of God's grace and power carry you along. God's great plan for you will surround you and sweep you forward into the profoundly important and satisfying life He has waiting. If that is what you want, keep reading.

Used by permission of the Jerry Jenkins Writers Guild.

Think Hollywood

by Virelle Kidder

As you write a personal nonfiction account, think of yourself as a film director. Imagine sounds, camera angles, color, tension, emotion, pacing, and urgency.

Because you're engaging the theater of your reader's mind, you have more tools than a film director. You have all the five senses. Show readers how it looked and felt to dangle from the bridge while fishing. Let him feel the thrill of catching that trout — and seeing your mom's face when you brought it home. Let readers feel the snow alighting on your eyelashes during a blizzard, the tenderness of your first kiss, the pain of failure.

Let readers feel the snow alighting on your eyelashes, the tenderness of your first kiss, the pain of failure.

You are your reader's eyes and ears. When writing about a friend or grandparent, describe how he dresses and walks. Does he have pet expressions or annoying quirks? How loud is his voice? What do his words reveal? Put us in a scene with this person and let us watch you relate to him, smell the coffee you share over a campfire, watch him perform simple tasks, feel his hands, and look in his eyes.

You need the skills of a fiction writer, not because the account isn't true, but because you want to evoke the senses of your reader. While you are limited to only your words, words are powerful enough to bring long dead relatives and friends back to life for your reader. Tips for creating memorable scenes:

- **Use dialogue.**
  Let readers hear the voices and see the people speaking. Don't just summarize what someone said.

- **Show the setting with subtle details.**
  What rivets this scene in your memory? A broken plate after an angry exchange? Finding an empty dog bed?

- **Reveal emotion through action.**
  Describe your mother's hug. How about your fear when your father rose quickly from his chair? Share the deep disappointment of losing a job. Don't just say it; show it.

Four Tracks for Life-Changing Communication

by Les Stobbe

Communication designed to move the reader from point A to point Z travels best on four tracks:

1. Information

Information provides the building blocks of sound thinking. Ideas not only excite us, but also help us to make sense of what's going on. We live by information every day. But to effect life change, such information must include the knowledge of what God has said and does, for the Word of God is quick and active and sharper than any two-edged sword (see Hebrews 4:12).

2. Imagination

Undoubtedly, imagination is our most-effective tool in communicating transcendent ideas in humanly receivable form. Without the help of story, symbol, and metaphor, our finite minds cannot receive the rich fullness of who God is and how He works. As we have seen, the metaphor that God seems to especially delight in using is story.

3. Motivation

All through Scripture, God offers motivation to move people. If we want to get beyond tickling the intellect, we also need to build into our books motivation for change. Four keys to motivating people:

- **Benefits:** God knows benefits are important to us. Even Abraham, that great man of faith, had to be reminded again and again of what his benefits would be if he followed God wholeheartedly. We can't promise descendants as numerous as the stars in the sky, but we can project the benefits of reading and applying biblical truth.

- **Role models:** Throughout Scripture, God kept reminding His people of the positive role models He had given them: Moses, Abraham, Isaac, and Jacob. The apostle Paul also referred to role models in his letters. But even these were presented realistically — acknowledging failures such as when Abraham denied that Sarah was his wife, when Moses disobeyed God and struck the rock, and when David committed adultery with Bathsheba, then arranged to have her husband killed.

- **Emotion-involving content:** People in show business know they need to make their audience laugh and cry. Some years ago, John Stott wrote that we in the West need more emotional content in our communications. Such writers as Margaret Jensen, Max Lucado, Patsy Clairmont, and Liz Curtis Higgs effectively communicate with emotion-laden content.

- **How-to:** Benefits get the reader's interest. Role models portray the values you're trying to communicate. Emotional content grabs the heart and helps the story stick in the memory so it can go off like a time bomb when life experiences parallel it. Finally, how-to content releases the reader for action.

Motivation alone may produce only guilt; how-to shows the reader a way to get past guilt and initiate life change.

4. Action Application

Information provides the building blocks of sound thinking. Ideas not only excite us, but also help us to make sense of what's going on. We live by information every day. But to effect life change, such information must include the knowledge of what God has said and does, for the Word of God is quick and active and sharper than any two-edged sword (see Hebrews 4:12).

Used by permission of the Jerry Jenkins Writers Guild.

PART 3

Specialty
Markets

7

Greeting Card/Gift/Specialty Markets

This list contains both Christian/religious card publishers and general publishers that have religious lines or produce some religious or inspirational cards. General companies may produce other lines of cards that are not consistent with your beliefs, and for a general company, inspirational cards usually do not include religious imagery. Support groups for greeting card writers can be found at http://groups.yahoo.com/group/GreetingCardWriters.

CARD PUBLISHERS

BLUE MOUNTAIN ARTS INC., Editorial Dept., PO Box 1007, Boulder CO 80306. (303) 449-0536. Fax (303) 447-0939. E-mail (submit to): editorial@sps.com (no attachments). Website: www.sps.com. Submit to Editorial Department. General card publisher that does a few inspirational cards. Open to freelance; buys 50-100 ideas/yr. Prefers outright submissions. Pays $300 for all rts. for use on a greeting card, or $50 for onetime use in a book, on publication. No royalties. Responds in 12-16 wks. Uses unrhymed or traditional poetry; short or long, but no one-liners. Produces inspirational and sensitivity. Needs anniversary, birthday, Christmas, congratulations, Easter, Father's Day, friendship, get well, graduation, keep in touch, love, miss you, Mother's Day, new baby, reaching for dreams, relatives, sympathy, thank you, valentines, wedding. Holiday/seasonal 6 mos. ahead. Open to ideas for new card lines. Send any number of ideas (1 per pg.). Open to ideas for gift books. Guidelines at: http://www.sps.com/help/greetingcardwritings.html; no catalog. To request a copy of full guidelines, send a blank e-mail to writings@sps.com with "Send Me Guidelines" in the subject line.

   Contest: Sponsors a poetry card contest online. Details on Website.

   Tips: "We are interested in reviewing poetry and writings for greeting cards, and expanding our field of freelance poetry writers."

DAYSPRING CARDS INC., Editorial Department, PO Box 1010, 21154 Hwy. 16 East, Siloam Springs AR 72761. Fax (479) 524-9477. E-mail: info@dayspring.com (type "write" in message or subject line). Website: www.dayspring.com. Attn: Freelance Editor. Christian/religious card publisher. Please read guidelines before submitting. Prefers outright submission. Pays $60/idea on acceptance for all rights. No royalty. Responds in 4–8 wks. Uses unrhymed, traditional, light verse, conversational, contemporary; various lengths. Looking for inspirational cards for all occasions, including anniversary, birthday, relative birthday, congratulations, encouragement, friendship, get well, new baby, sympathy, thank-you, wedding. Also needs seasonal cards for friends and family members for Christmas, Valentine's Day, Easter, Mother's Day, Father's Day, Thanksgiving, graduation, and Clergy Appreciation Day. Include Scripture verse with each submission. Send 10 ideas or fewer. Guidelines at: http://about.dayspring.com/corporate/contact/editorial.asp; no catalog.

   Tips: "Currently we are accepting submissions only from writers who have previously had work published."

+DESIGN DESIGN INC., 19 LaGrave Ave., SE, Grand Rapids MI 49503-4205.

(616) 774-2448. Fax (616) 744-4020. Website: www.designdesign.us. Greeting card designs. Send copies, not originals to: Susan Birnbaum, creative dir. (greeting cards), (616) 771-8359, susan.birnbaum@designdesign.us. Submit by mail or e-mail. Guidelines at: http://designdesign.us/media/materials/2012_DDi_Artist_Guidelines.pdf.

+INSPIRATIONART & SCRIPTURE INC., PO Box 5550, Cedar Rapids IA 52406. "World's Largest Christian Poster Publisher." Art submissions welcome to: customerservice@inspirationart.com, with "Art Submission" in subject line. Responds in 3–4 months. Art purchased two times a year. Guidelines at: http://www.inspirationart.com/art-guidelines.html.

+P.S. GREETINGS/FANTUS PAPER PRODUCTS, 5730 N. Tripp Ave., Chicago IL 60646. No phone calls. Submit to Design Director. Open to greeting card verses or poems. Submit as photocopies with black ink on white paper. No royalties; pays flat fee. Responds in 30 days. Guidelines at: http://www.psg-fpp.com/creative_guidelines.htm.

WARNER PRESS INC., 1201 E. 5th St., PO Box 2499, Anderson IN 46018-9988. (800) 741-7721. Fax (765) 640-8005. E-mail: rfogle@warnerpress.org or krhodes@warnerpress.org. Website: www.warnerpress.org. Karen Rhodes, sr. ed.; Robin Fogle, product ed. Produces church bulletins (submission deadline September 30; pays $35 on acceptance); children's coloring & activity books (submissions deadlines January 31 & July 31; payment varies); greeting cards (submission deadline July 31; pays $35 on acceptance); children's picture books (not accepting at this time). Also produces ministry resource books and teaching resource books. No royalties. Prefers e-mail submissions. Responds in 6–8 wks. Uses unrhymed, traditional verse, and devotionals for bulletins; 16–24 lines. Accepts 10 ideas/submission. Guidelines at: http://www.warnerpress.org/custom.aspx?id=3; no catalog.

> **Photos/Artwork:** Accepts freelance photos and queries from freelance artists. E-mail curtis@warnerpress.org, Curtis Corzine, creative director.

GIFT/SPECIALTY-ITEM MARKETS

+ARTBEATS, New York Graphic Society, Art Submissions, 129 Glover Ave., Norwalk CT 06850. (800) 677-6947. Send art submissions by mail, express mail, or by e-mail to: donna@nygs.com. Send high quality color copies and/or digital files in JPG format only, not originals. If no response in a few weeks, assume they are not interested (do not call). Guidelines at: http://www.nygs.com/submit/index.html.

LORENZ CORP., Editorial Dept., 501 E. Third St., Dayton OH 45402. Toll-free (800) 444-1144, ext. 1. (937) 228-6118. Fax (937) 223-2042. E-mail: submit@lorenz.com or through website: www.lorenz.com. Open to submissions of sacred music, sacred organ, sacred choral, educational choral, handbells, and sacred instrumental. Electronic submissions only as a PDF of your work. If no response within 60 days, you are free to submit elsewhere. Guidelines online for music submissions: http://www.lorenz.com/Submissions.aspx

> **Tips:** "Also open to lessons, worksheets, or other teaching materials for our music classroom magazine, Activate!"

BONUS SECTION

Writer's Helps

Books Plus

Interviews: The Art of Listening

by Les Stobbe

TO BE AN EFFECTIVE INTERVIEWER, learn to master the art of careful listening. As you practice basic listening techniques, you'll discover that people are willing to tell you what they know. Five steps to apply:

1. Maintain eye contact.

People appreciate undivided attention. If you are checking your watch or following a fly buzz around the room, your mind is not on the topic. Be careful not to simply stare without blinking. Instead, give the person your full attention for 20 to 30 seconds, then briefly break eye contact to nod or make an expression that indicates you are weighing what's been said. Then come back to direct eye contact.

2. Use good body language.

Your job as an interviewer is to instill confidence, not to intimidate. Sit near enough to engender trust. Lean forward, indicating you are hanging on every word. By not interrupting the speaker, he or she will continue to talk. Your smile or nod will show you understand. Let your body talk, but mostly keep quiet.

3. Keep your mind on the topic.

People talk at about 125 words per minute but listen at 600 words per minute. So it takes discipline to stay focused on what someone is saying. Try not to anticipate what the speaker will say so you can come up with a clever response. Your job is to listen, not to talk except to keep the interview on track. Don't be afraid to let the other person take control for awhile. It may lead into new, valuable topics.

4. Use short lulls.

Inexperienced interviewers can become terrified of dead air, thinking it makes them look unprepared. They rush into a new question and miss the benefit of a completed answer for the previous one. Take your time. Study your interviewee. If he or she is pondering a question or probing a memory to answer more carefully, be courteous enough to provide silence. If the person says, "I'm not sure how to answer," don't abandon the question. Phrase it another way, offer an example, or paraphrase what has been stated and ask for clarification. Sometimes silence truly is golden.

5. Observe common courtesy.

Don't put words in people's mouths. Don't finish sentences for them. Don't interrupt with your own observations unless it helps bond you to the interviewee. And in that case, set down your pencil or even pause your recorder and say, "I know what you mean. A similar thing happened to me … ." That shows you want to connect, but that you aren't implying your own experience is part of the research. And don't make critical comments. If you must take issue, begin with a positive statement, such as, "You hit on a real problem there, but I wonder why a lot of people don't hold your opinion on that?" An excellent way to prove to the interviewee that you have been listening is to read back your notes and say, "So, if I have this correct, you are saying…" The other person can then confirm, modify, or retract it. This will show you have been paying close attention.

Used by permission of the Jerry Jenkins Writers Guild.

Prepare for a Successful Interview
by Les Stobbe

ONCE YOU HAVE CALLED to set up an interview, follow these steps:

Tell the interviewee specifically what you want to talk about.
This will allow him or her to prepare and will put the person at ease.

Read all you can about that person and his or her field.
Check websites, other publications, and even company public relations offices. This will enable you to save time by not asking for information that can be found elsewhere. You might ask, "Are all the details in your media sheet up to date or is there something else I should know?"

Prepare a list of questions in logical order.
But save your harder questions for later. This will allow you time to establish rapport before you get to sensitive topics.

Write a lot of open-ended questions.
Seek the person's opinions, ideas, thoughts, feelings, and experiences rather than statistics, facts, and other data. Say things such as, "How did you respond to the news about your son?" or "What do you think will happen if that legislation is passed?"

Conduct the interview on the subject's home turf.
Go to his house or office. This not only makes the person feel more relaxed, but it also provides access to photo albums, files, trophies, and other supplemental information. Avoid interviews in public places. They are noisy, and there is the chance a stranger will come up and interrupt.

Bring an audio recorder to record everything that's said.
If the subject feels nervous, say, "This is just to make sure I quote you accurately. It isn't for broadcast. If you wish to tell me something off the

---

Interview Icebreakers
by Les Stobbe

IF YOU FEEL NERVOUS about conducting your interview, be assured that many of the people you talk to will also be nervous. If time allows, begin with generic questions that create an easy flow of conversation. Some sample ice-breaker questions:

• What in the past year has given you the most pleasure, personally or in your career?

• Who are your heroes?

• Which have you enjoyed more, getting to the top or being at the top? Why?

• For what act or achievement would you most like to be remembered?

• Is there anything you have not accomplished yet that you would still like to achieve?

• What do you like to read, and what are some of your favorite books?

• If you could go back and talk to yourself at age 18, what would you say?

• If you were not in your current career, what other field would you enjoy?

• Where do you envision yourself ten years from now?

record, I'll be glad to stop the recorder for a moment." Once the person feels he or she has control over the recorder, it will no longer be an issue. Use clip-on microphones for both of you, connected to the recorder with a Y-adapter. And don't depend on the recorder's batteries; plug the unit into a wall outlet.

Take a notepad.

It may seem redundant, but there is a psychological value in taking notes. First, it gives you something to do with your hands. Second, it enables to you write the things beyond what is said, such as the room décor, how the person was dressed, his or her body language and any idiosyncrasies (gestures, biting the lower lip, twirling a strand of hair). And if your recorder fails, good notes can salvage the interview.

Ask one question at a time, no multi-parters.

Allow time for the person to think and give you a thorough answer. Pace yourself so you are neither slow nor racing through and getting only surface responses. Base a lot of your questions on your interviewee's responses; be careful not to stick to your list if the conversation leads profitably elsewhere.

Try not to allow others to be present.

Public relations executives will try to steer your interview in a certain direction. Spouses may try to tell a different version of a story or memory. Children will be distracting.

Don't wait to prepare the first draft of your interview.

Many of your immediate impressions will fade unless captured as soon as possible. Transcribe your recordings and block out an initial version of the interview. You can polish it later.

Don't agree to let the subject proofread your interview before it goes to press.

If you agree to this, it will no longer be your interview. The other person will insert long paragraphs about his golf game or her pet poodle. He or she will delete any references to grey hair or wrinkles. In short, your interview will become a fluff piece. You cannot allow that.

Used by permission of the Jerry Jenkins Writers Guild.

Attracting Your Reader

by Les Stobbe

HAVE YOU EVER WANDERED THROUGH A BOOKSTORE and watched the customers? Some know what they want, head to a specific section, take a book off the shelf, then head for the checkout counter.

Others stand before a section, scan the shelves, and begin to examine a book. There's a glance at the title and author's name, then they turn to the back cover. At that point they either put the book back on the shelf or make a truly fateful move — they open the book near the front.

If it's a book you've written, you hold your breath. They may scan the contents page. If that seems to satisfy them, they turn to the next page. What — besides introducing yourself as the author — do you think will catch the reader and ensure a sale? You've piqued their interest with the title and list of chapters, so how do you sink the hook deep enough for them to pull out their wallet?

A Test Run

To find out what authors do to grab the reader, I pulled book after book off my own shelves to see what authors had done to grab and hold my attention.

An autobiography of a well-known athlete follows the contents page with a "Chronology of Events." Next comes a foreword by a well-known pastor — useful if either the subject or the author are not well enough known to be trusted to make a significant contribution to the reader's life. Then come two pages of acknowledgments and a prologue. On page 21 we finally start getting the experiences of the athlete. Can you see the browser paging and paging as he tries to find out if he'll like the book enough to buy it? Would you have kept going through all those introductory pages?

The next book is a title on the interior life by a well-known writer. Uh-oh, the same pastor wrote the foreword as for the previous book. (Don't you wonder if these endorsers really have time to read every book they recommend?) That's followed by a five-page preface by the author — well written but aimed at only one segment of his readers. At least we've made some progress in page-count; we need to get only to page 13 to find the first chapter.

The next book is on marriage, though not by a counselor or psychologist. The writer is well-known and highly creative. No foreword, preface, or introduction — immediately after the contents page we are at the first chapter. And what a first chapter!

Now let's look at a true best seller, The Prayer of Jabez, by Bruce Wilkinson. Look at the preface. Did you read it when you read the book? My research indicates only 20 percent of readers ever read a preface or introduction. In this case, look at the first paragraph of chapter 1 — doesn't it do what Bruce Wilkinson tries to accomplish in the preface? Let's assume you did open this little book directly to the first chapter. How does this opening statement grab you?

> The little book you're holding is about what happens when ordinary Christians decide to reach for an extraordinary life — which, as it turns out, is exactly the kind God promises.

A wonderful statement. Because it leads into Wilkinson's own experience with the prayer of Jabez, it's a most appropriate opening sentence.

So what will most effectively catch your readers and get them to read your book?

Techniques to Engage Your Reader

by Les Stobbe

THE MOST FREQUENT REASON PEOPLE REJECT A BOOK is that it did not grab or hold their attention.

You need to do more than provide quick access to chapter 1 and content that speaks clearly to the reader's felt need, that holds promise of being a satisfying read.

Each subsequent chapter must present engaging material that leaves the reader feeling in touch with a real person who knows how God is at work in our world.

To engage your reader, you must know who he is. It's astonishing how few authors seriously consider this. As far as they're concerned, having a great idea or having received a message from the Lord is enough. When their book doesn't sell, they blame everyone but themselves.

Once you engage your target reader, you need to provide stimulating content.

Active, Colorful Writing

To a large extent, our personality determines our writing style. The laid-back person more easily adopts a reflective style, while the energetic person tends toward more active writing. But just as I need to overcome my desire to sleep too late, avoid the gym, and linger over the newspaper, I must consciously adopt a more active, vivid writing style.

As you've worked on your book, have you remembered to use active verbs, a variety of sentence lengths, and vivid imagery? If you're struggling to do that, read contemporary authors who write vividly until it becomes a part of your psyche. Then read and edit, read and edit, until your paragraphs spring to life.

Interactive Writing

At its most elemental level, interactive writing reflects an attitude — the attitude the apostle Paul emphasizes in his letters. Paul's reflections in the opening verses of Philippians 2 are but one example. Verse 3 becomes the springboard for his vivid depiction in verses 5-11 of the Incarnation:

> Do nothing out of selfish ambition or vain conceit, but in humility consider others better than yourselves.

Paul's writing reveals a basic humility that gives the reader credit for being intelligent and open to the Holy Spirit's leading. He writes things like, "Therefore, my dear friends, as you have always obeyed," and "All of us who are mature should take such a view of things." Even when he recounts his sufferings, it's done reluctantly and only because people questioned his credentials as God's messenger.

Let Stories Do the Talking

When Luke wanted to demonstrate that Jesus, despite His humanity, had authority on earth, he could have made that plain by the use of argument. Instead, starting with chapter 4 we read a series of accounts that illustrate this theme.

- Jesus goes to Capernaum, where there is a demon-possessed man, and Jesus orders the evil spirit, "Be quiet! Come out of him!" (4:35).

- He visits Simon's home, where Simon's mother-in-law is ill with a fever. Jesus demonstrates authority over disease by healing her.
- Jesus tells the disciples to let their net down on the other side of the boat, and they catch so many fish their nets start breaking — demonstrating His power over the fish in the lake.
- In a crowded room where Jesus is speaking, a paralytic suddenly comes through the roof — and has his sins forgiven, demonstrating Jesus' God-given authority over sin.
- Jesus then calls Matthew, a tax collector, to follow Him — demonstrating His authority to break cultural conventions.

No lecture or exposition of Jesus' authority would have the impact of this series of stories.

If I were writing a chapter, what story could I use to parallel these biblical ones? Powerful stories may be hard to find, but if you want readers to become emotionally engaged, you must find them.

Touch the Heart

Luke chapter 3 tells the story as if he were there. There's John in the wilderness along the Jordan, "preaching a baptism of repentance for the forgiveness of sins" (v. 3). Luke gives us the scene: "John said to the crowds coming out to be baptized by him …" (v. 7). He reports the crowd asking, "What should we do then?" (v. 10). John has answers for the crowd, for the tax collectors, for the soldiers. I imagine that after every answer, the crowd must have roared approval, for who wouldn't cheer when John said to the soldiers, "Don't extort money and don't accuse people falsely — be content with your pay" (v. 14). Then Luke reports, "The people were waiting expectantly and were all wondering in their hearts if John might possibly be the Christ" (v. 15).

Why is Joni Eareckson Tada's writing so widely accepted? Her stories touch the heart. Why was *Comeback* by Dave Dravecky so popular? Because the story, of a highly successful baseball pitcher losing his arm to cancer, touches the heart.

I've found that stories about abuse and injustice touch the heart, as do stories involving children and pets. Who isn't moved when reading Marjorie Williams' *The Velveteen Rabbit?* From that book Charles Swindoll adds the story of the skin horse at the end of chapter 1 of *Improving Your Serve,* because he knew it would touch the heart.

As writers, we face enormous odds in getting our material read. We can reduce those odds by so engaging our readers, they feel part of the story.

Used by permission of the Jerry Jenkins Writers Guild.

Using Others' Stories

by Les Stobbe

PEOPLE LOVE TELLING THEIR STORIES, and as writers it's up to us to use them well. Record the facts and sequence of events immediately so you're sure you have it right.

Before we get into how to best use other people's stories, let's discuss when using another person's story may cause problems.

Legal Precautions

Be careful not to tell stories, even old ones, that put a living person in a negative light. Even true stories, if they harm someone's reputation, can result in lawsuits.

Suppose you come from a colorful family where unchristian behavior is the norm. In portraying such behavior in an article or book, you will need to eliminate any identifying references, or an irate family member may sue you. Even if all but one physical or behavioral identification of the person are changed, you can still face legal action.

How do you avoid problems if you're using stories by other people or about them? Use a permissions release form with everyone whose story you have told. Some traditional publishers will not release any of the advance against royalty until all permissions are in. Use your favorite search engine to find a release form compatible with your purpose, or ask the publisher for theirs (not all publishers offer a form).

Shaping Stories

Stories are like rough diamonds — of little use until shaped to fit an article or chapter and its theme. Some areas to work on:

Focus on the central character. Most stories have interaction between several characters. We may want to tell about every participant, but as in fiction, readers want to identify with a central character. We also want to make sure readers understand the

---

Acquiring Stories
by Les Stobbe

HOW CLOSE ARE YOU to someone else's story?

- On a flight from Chicago to Orlando, I discovered the person next to me was a small-town librarian acquiring Christian books. I asked if she had acquired a book I had written with Dale Evans Rogers, and she came alive as she told me of her infatuation as a child with Dale Evans.
- I ride a Lifecycle in a local gym. My frequent companion on the adjoining bike is a retired AT&T technician who leads a small group of seniors who sing in nursing homes. He also does volunteer work with other former AT&T technicians, runs a train at a train museum, and performs as Santa Claus at private parties before Christmas. Guess how many stories he can tell.
- Our church prints the conversion stories of some of the people applying for membership. There are extraordinary stories of God keeping after people until they finally bow the knee, and of others invited by friends to special evangelistic outreaches.
- Your local newspaper's human interest stories: the inventor of a widely used device; the painter of celebrities; the airline pilot who turned over some of his acreage to Cambodian families to raise vegetables to sell in their markets; the family whose elementary school children helped develop an amazingly effective Thanksgiving food distribution effort. Clip and file by topic.
- The missionary newsletters that arrive via e-mail have astonishing stories of heroism and persistence in the face of opposition.

story's circumstances, so we may just spill out the material. Keep the focus on the key person as she interacts with others and the circumstances.

Use dialogue when possible. One great weaknesses of nonfiction writers is their seeming lack of interest in dialogue. It's so much easier to report the events, rather than introduce readers to the interaction between people. I'm struck by how the Gospel writer Luke often went beyond the facts to show the human interaction.

The first prerequisite of dialogue is to capture it when you encounter the story. As we read of the apostle Paul coming out of his prison cell in Caesarea to present his case before King Agrippa (Acts 26), it's clear that Luke is a participant who recorded what he heard.

Write it tight and write it right. The very nature of story makes it susceptible to embellishment. But when using a story in an article or chapter, include only what will advance the story. That does not mean omitting essential description, but making sure you include only what's essential.

The challenge to Christian communicators is to escape the Greek philosophical approach — where factual presentation is paramount — and accept the Hebraic tradition of our Bible: the story as the truth-bearer. That means taking great care with stories and using dialogue to enhance the impact of the truth being absorbed through the story.

Used by permission of the Jerry Jenkins Writers Guild.

Converting Chapters to Articles
by Les Stobbe

THROUGH EXCERPTED ARTICLES, an author can influence tens of thousands more readers than will most books. Use the same tactics as for writing articles when you write your book, and you will have chapters that can do double duty.

Edit for length. It's rare that a chapter will be too short. Some cautions as you edit a chapter to article length:

Don't eliminate the reader-grabbing introduction. There's a tendency to look at a chapter introduction and say, "I can get into this topic faster by eliminating my anecdote." Bad idea. Book readers tend to settle in for the rest of the book once past the first chapter. But you have a much shorter time to grab readers paging through a magazine. Keep the material that helps you quickly establish reader eye contact.

Don't eliminate the stories. Another temptation is to eliminate one or more of the stories. Nonfiction writers may think their explanations and arguments are the important part. But carefully selected, properly told stories are the diamonds.

If you have two or more stories illustrating one point, you may be able to sacrifice all but one. Decide which most effectively embodies the truth you wish to communicate.

Edit for repetition. I recently was asked to evaluate a book manuscript for a pastor. After reading about halfway through, I urged him to edit out his plethora of repetitions. He accepted the challenge and reduced the length by one-third. Then he asked me to edit it, and I cut even more.

You may say, "There's no way I can cut my material any further." If you want to be a selling writer, you need to develop a hard-nosed approach to your own writing. Often self-editing is more important than actually writing a chapter; it can dramatically enhance the readability.

Edit for a more active voice. You've heard this so many times. Yet even those of us who teach writing find ourselves overusing is and was. We also use words that slow the reader instead of enhancing his understanding."

Traditional Marketing Methods That Still Work

by Dennis E Hensley

While most royalty publishers have advertising and public relations people, new authors are often stunned to discover how little is budgeted to promote their book. If you're taking the self-publishing route, it will be up to you to decide how much you want to invest in professional services to help with your book's publicity. There's no getting around it, you must work to make your book known.

Today many writers think first about online promotion and concentrate on using social media. But let's review some more traditional — and still effective — measures you can take to promote sales.

At Your Church

Check with your church's media center about setting up a display. If your church is large enough, you may be allowed an autograph party after a weekend service. Even if you sell only 20 books, this will make many people aware of it, and word-of-mouth is the most effective way to promote a book.

Action item: Call your church office and request an autograph party and book display.

Community Organizations

Contact organizations whose members would enjoy having you speak about the subject of your book. Groups such as the Rotary Club and the Lions Club always need luncheon and dinner speakers. Call their local presidents, name a topic you could address for 30 to 45 minutes, then send a follow-up letter with your photo and contact information. Although your only pay will likely be a free meal, you can ask to set up a book table where you can sell and autograph copies after your speech. Depending on your topic, consider military groups, such as the VFW or American Legion, PTA organizations, the Girl or Boy Scouts, women's auxiliary groups, couples retreats, unions, and professional associations.

Action item: Get your Yellow Pages and list organizations to contact about speaking engagements.

Alumni Offices

Contact the alumni office of any school you've graduated from. If you send a photo, along with a one-page press release, colleges and universities will usually run this information in their alumni newsletters and bulletins, as well as post it on alumni websites.

Action item: Go online to track down addresses of the schools from which you've graduated. Send each a press release about your book, along with a recent photo.

Personal Contacts

Encourage everyone you know to go online or to a bookstore to buy your book. Early sales create momentum, so send emails, postcards, and letters to relatives, friends, neighbors, and co-workers, encouraging them to buy your book as soon as it's available. Provide the title, ISBN, and publisher so it can be ordered if necessary.

Action item: Prepare a list of names and addresses of people to notify right before your book is published.

Press Releases

Gain as much free publicity as possible. Prepare a succinct press release, usually one double-spaced page, and send it to the bulletin and newsletter editors of the church, neighborhood association, literary societies, book clubs, and social organizations you are active in. Attach a handwritten note to the effect of, "I'd appreciate it if you could run this notice in your next newsletter." Customize each release so it mentions how you are affiliated with that organization. Again, mention the book's publisher and ISBN so people will have no problem ordering it.

Action item: List every organization you belong to that issues a mailed or online publication. Send each a customized press release about your new book.

Endorsements

Obtain endorsement quotes. If you know experts who will endorse your book, get those in writing. Use the quotes on your own website, in your press releases, and in your mailings. Keep the endorsements short, appropriate, and diverse. Don't have three medical doctors all say, "This book helps you lose weight." Have one say it has break-through medical information, another say it is easy to understand, and a third say your research is solid and that you are a great communicator. After each endorser's name, put something to draw attention to this endorsement, such as an academic title (M.D., Ph.D., MBA), a tagline like "author of *Healthy Foods for Your Baby*," or a publicity iden-tifier such as "Host of WDEK radio's *Financial Freedom*." Endorsers do not have to be famous (although that is nice), so long as they have credentials pertinent to your topic.

Action item: Contact people who will endorse you book in writing, and as soon as you receive their endorsements, send them to your publisher for use on the back cover.

Promotional Items

Create gimmicks to promote your book. You needn't spend thousands to hire media specialists to develop video trailers. You can invest much less and get surprisingly good results. Bookmarks featuring your book's cover, your photo, and short blurbs about the book can be produced and distributed inexpensively. Pens or notepads with slogans will also keep your book's name before the public. One author who wrote on stock and bond trading had the title stamped on wooden nickels he gave to his investment clients and friends. Use your imagination.

Action item: Collect catalogues from advertising businesses and brainstorm how you can use specific products to promote your book.

Libraries

Introduce yourself to librarians. Visit librarians at public libraries, high schools and colleges, churches and private schools, and military bases. These people have budgets to purchase new books. Make them aware of yours and give them your publicity materials. You will gain not only a possible sale to their library, but you will also get your book in front of the reading public. One author visited her city's head librarian and gave him information on her new book. That librarian was so impressed, he ordered 25 copies so the main library and all the branches would have it.

Action item: Develop a list of area libraries you can visit as soon as your book is released.

Publicity Photos

Have professional photos made of yourself and your book. Image is important, so don't use your graduation picture or a cropped head shot from your vacation as your official author photo. Make an appointment with a professional photographer and get a series of shots, including some of you holding your book and some of just the book. These can be used for posters promoting your speaking engagements. Looking professional will attract people to hear you speak and buy your book.

Action item: Set up an appointment with a professional photographer and get a series of photos to use in promotions.

Review Copies

Get your book into the hands of reviewers. Most book contracts provide the author ten free copies, but you'll need more. Buy several dozen. Take a copy to each of your local newspapers and put it in the hands of the arts page editor, asking it be sent to the book reviewer. If the denomination you belong to has a magazine that prints book reviews, send an autographed copy along with a cover letter explaining you are a member of such and such church and that you'd appreciate a review. Many traditional publishers send review copies to major publications, such as *Publisher's Weekly* and *Christian Book Previews.* But it will be up to you to see that reviewers at your local papers and specialty periodicals get copies.

Action item: Make a detailed list of all the publications you will want to review your book. Find out the reviewers for those publications, and learn how you can get your book into their hands.

Teach on Your Topic

Consider leading a class or seminar. One of the best ways to sell 50 copies of your book in one day is to lead a seminar in which participants need to buy your book. (You might build the book's cost into the price of the seminar.) If you are a nurse who has written a book on prenatal care, you could offer a seminar and use your book for the class. Authors such as Gary Chapman with his *Five Love Languages* and John Gray with his *Men Are from Mars, Women Are from Venus* hold retreats and seminars that are attended by hundreds of couples, who all buy their books.

Action item: Create a workshop or seminar based on your book. Practice the presentation so as soon as your book comes out, you will be ready to contact schools, hospitals, churches, and conventions, notifying them of your availability to teach.

On the Road

Capitalize on your vacation travels. Whether flying across the country to attend a class reunion or driving to a nearby state to visit your in-laws, take advantage of opportunities to promote your book in new locations. While you are in town, visit libraries and bookstores to speak with managers about your book. Notify your publicist in advance of your travels and see if she can arrange for you to be interviewed on local radio or TV talk shows. Maybe you can set up an interview with local newspapers or even arrange to speak at a service club luncheon. The more visibility you gain for yourself and your book, the better the book's sales.

Action item: Look ahead to travel plans for holidays, business trips, and vacations. Advise your publicist of your pending travels and try to coordinate some publicity events in those locales.

Magazine Excerpts

Maximize the use of serializations. Your book is already divided into chapters, and those contain sidebars, sections, and subhead units. So it shouldn't be hard to convert material into articles for print or online magazines. By creating a three-part series on

"Preparing for Retirement" or a yearlong column on "Maximizing Your Time," you can cannibalize your book and give it continuous visibility. At the end of each installment, add a tagline that says something like, "Adapted from *The Power of Positive Productivity* by Dennis E. Hensley (Possibility Press)." These excerpts will earn you byline visibility and cash, while also promoting your book. It's a win-win-win situation.

Action item: Determine which sections or chapters of your manuscript could be subdivided into independent articles. Block out a series of related articles. Look for publications that would consider running such a series and contact them to pitch the idea.

Broadcast Interviews

Make things easy for talk show hosts. You can be a guest, live or recorded, on dozens of radio talk shows by phone without ever leaving your home. Because you're a new author, the interviewer won't be familiar with you or your book, so provide the information to conduct a fantastic interview. Give your publicist a single page that features your photo, a tightly written synopsis, a one-paragraph summary of your credentials, and several interview questions. This will enable the interviewer to sound knowledgeable about your book, and you'll be answering questions you've prepared. You'll both sound like experts. Talk show hosts don't have time to read a new book every day, yet they usually need to interview a new author daily. They appreciate prepared questions. You or your publicist can send interview set-up sheets to talk show hosts and use them to schedule interviews.

Action item: Record an interview with yourself. Play it back and pull from that a list of the best questions related to your book.

Publicity Material

Enhance your press kit. If you have a publicist create a press kit, do all you can to keep it up-to-date. Each time you're interviewed by a print publication, send a hard copy to the publicist so it can be added to your press kit. After you've made a series of radio interviews (a copy of which will always be given to you on request), consider assembling some prime audio excerpts into a CD to include in your press kit. The best way to gain coverage in large-circulation periodicals and large broadcast markets is by first getting massive amounts of press coverage in small to medium ones. Build momentum. Make yourself someone who can't be ignored by the larger media.

Action item: Create a file to keep copies of all published stories about you and your book.

Summary

Some writers resist getting involved in publicity. If you have written a quality book with the potential to help thousands, you are obligated to make that book known. What good did it do the unfaithful servant to possess a talent of gold if all he did was bury it in the sand? Take your book — your talent of gold — and invest it in people. Whether the Lord chooses to make it a best-seller or uses it to change the destiny of only a dozen people, you will know that what you wrote had a positive influence.

Do You Need a Literary Agent?

by Dennis E. Hensley

AGENTS CAN DO MUCH TO SAVE YOU TIME, and they can usually increase your income compared to a traditionally published author without one. Most agents take up to 15 percent (20 percent for international sales) of your advances, royalties, sales bonuses, spin-off earnings, and speaking fees. Most agents will also bill you separately for phone calls, mailing and copying expenses, and travel costs related to selling your manuscripts, unless you're bringing in an inordinate amount of business for the agency.

Most writers insist that agents' fees are worth it and that they make more money in the long run, but before you sign with an agent, know what you are getting into.

Agents don't make money unless you do, so it can be as hard to land an agent as it is to find a traditional publisher. The catch-22 is that while agents are looking for new talent, they're eager to sign experienced, already selling authors who can make them money from the start.

On the plus side, an experienced agent can serve you in many ways. The agent often sees possibilities in book ideas, offers focus on a project, and plays devil's advocate with you. Agents spot weak points in book proposals. They study publishers' catalogs to determine trends, needs, and desires of various companies. They look at publishers' ads in trade journals to determine the current emphasis of a house, and also to see who has the biggest promotional budgets.

They know when to approach a publishing house with a manuscript or when to hold an auction to pit one publisher against another to get the highest advance. In negotiating contracts, agents argue for the best terms related to subsidiary rights, foreign translation rights, serial rights, TV and movie and book club rights, ad budgets, advances and royalties, copyright ownership, and sometimes even matters related to book design. That's how agents bring added value.

Some agents are even getting into representing authors to self-publishing companies, taking their commissions out of the services the writer purchases in exchange for working through the details with the publisher.

An agent won't make any money on you unless he or she sells your book to a traditional publisher. (Agents don't bother marketing short stories or articles unless a writer is someone of staggering fame.) So agents are good at nagging editors to make a decision about a book submission.

Agents will serve as a writer's confidant, morale booster, and cheerleader when a project gets tedious or a writer begins to lose confidence. After a manuscript is sold and a book is published, agents also carefully review every royalty statement to be sure it's timely and accurate.

You will want an agent with accessibility, honesty, energy, savvy, experience, confidence, and a sense of humor.

You will want an agent with accessibility, honesty, energy, savvy, experience, creativity, enthusiasm, patience, vision, endurance, confidence, and a sense of humor. Ask people in your writers club whom they recommend. Check writers' guides. Go to writers conferences and make appointments with agents and evaluate their enthusiasm for your book ideas.

Judge a literary agent on the three Rs: reputation, rates, and reception. How well-respected is the agent? What does he or she charge? How excited is he or she about you and your manuscript?

Agents do not write your books for you. They don't copyedit them either. In fact, they will seldom help you write your proposals. You are the writer; the agent is the salesperson.

To land an agent, you need to prove you have the potential to earn money for that agent. So bring your portfolio when you meet. Show the agent your published articles, stories, columns, and anything else that demonstrates you are already a working writer. They'll want to know about the sales of your self-published projects and how you've promoted them.

Also, have a book proposal and a completed book manuscript. The manuscript needs to be completed not only to verify it is a good piece of writing, but also to show that you are capable of completing the project, for which they expect you to receive an advance

Come with a list of questions. If it's a good fit, close the deal. If not, seek someone else.

When you meet with an agent, don't feel intimidated. These people need authors so they can earn a living. Come with a list of questions. If it's a good fit, close a deal. If not, seek someone else.

If you are like most writers, you prefer to focus on the creative aspects of writing. But you'll never have a chance to engage in creative writing if you don't have the time for it or you are too strapped for cash. Review this material frequently and make its rules your guides for advancing your career.

Used by permission of the Jerry Jenkins Writers Guild.

PART 4

Support for Writers

8

Christian Writers Conferences and Workshops

(*) before a listing indicates unconfirmed or no information update.

(+) before a listing indicates it's a new listing this year.

ALABAMA

SOUTHERN CHRISTIAN WRITERS CONFERENCE. Tuscaloosa/First Baptist Church; early June. Contact: Joanne Sloan, SCWC, PO Box 1106, Northport AL 35476. (205) 333-8603. E-mail: SCWCworkshop@bellsouth.net. Website: www.scw-conference.com. Editors/agents in attendance. Attendance: 200+.

ARIZONA

AMERICAN CHRISTIAN WRITERS MENTORING RETREAT. Phoenix, Clarion Hotel; September 11-12, 2015; September 9-10, 2016. Contact: Reg A. Forder, PO Box 110390, Nashville TN 37222. Toll-free (800) 21-WRITE. E-mail: ACWriters@aol.com. Website: www.ACWriters.com. Offers full & partial scholarships. Attendance: 12-30.

ARKANSAS

SILOAM SPRINGS FALL WRITERS WORKSHOP. Siloam Springs; September 2015. Director: Margaret Weathers, 716 W. University Ave., Siloam Springs AR 72761. (479)524-6598. E-mail: rogeneo@centurylink.net. Offers a special track for teens & grades 1-12. Contest for poetry & prose. Attendance: 25.

CALIFORNIA

ACT ONE: WRITING PROGRAM. Hollywood. Contact: Terence Berry, 2690 N. Beachwood Dr., Hollywood CA 90068. (323) 464-0815. Fax (323) 468-0315. E-mail: information@actoneprogram.com. Website: www.ActOneProgram.com. Act One offers an intensive training program for screenwriters, taught by professionals working in Hollywood. We also offer a script consulting service and run a screenplay competition with a $5,000 cash prize. Courses available in late February, May, June, and June-August. Application fee $50; tuition $3,825. Payment plans available.

CASTRO VALLEY CHRISTIAN WRITERS SEMINAR. (see West Coast Christian Writers Conference)

CHAIRS (The Christian Authors, Illustrators, and Readers Society). Contact: Nancy I. Sanders, 6361 Prescott Court, Chino CA 91710. (909) 590-0226. E-mail: jeffandnancys@gmail.com. Website: www.nancyisanders.com. Occasional writer's mentor groups and classes for children's writers. Some events are free and some require registration and a fee. Contact for more information.

MOUNT HERMON CHRISTIAN WRITERS CONFERENCE. Mount Hermon (near Santa Cruz); March 26-31, 2015. Website: www.mounthermon.org/writers. (888) MH-CAMPS. Offering instruction for all levels of writers, professional to beginner (including special track for teen writers). Many well-known editors and agents in attendance. Offers partial scholarships on tuition only. Awards for a variety of writing genres. Mentoring clinic two days before writers conference, March 24-25. All details on website November 1 (no brochure). Faculty: 50. Writers: 400. Director: Mona Hodgson.

MOUNT HERMON HEAD-START MENTORING CLINIC. Mount Hermon; March 24-25, 2015. This mentoring session is held the two days prior to the regular spring conference. See the listing for Mount Hermon Christian Writers Conference for details or www.mounthermon.org.

ORANGE COUNTY CHRISTIAN WRITERS CONFERENCE. April 24-25, 2015. Contact: Antonio L. Crawford, dir.; PO Box 1458, National City CA 91951. (619) 791-5810. E-mail: ncwcsd@yahoo.com. Website: www.occwf.org. Held at Trinity Presbyterian Church. Consult with editors, agents, published authors. Offers special track for advanced writers and teens. Offers full scholarships. Agents & editors in attendance. Contest: WestBow Press Writing Contest. See website for list of faculty and conference details. Attendance: 200.

SAN DIEGO CHRISTIAN WRITER'S GUILD "WRITING FOR LIFE" FALL CONFERENCE. San Diego; October 2015. Contact: Jennie Gillespie, PO Box 270403, San Diego CA 92198. Phone/fax: (760) 294-3269. E-mail: info@sandiegocwg.org. Website: www.sandiegocwg.org. Speakers: Phillip Yancey, Ellie Kay. Offers an advanced track. Editors/agents in attendance. Contest: Unpublished manuscript contest (details on Website). Offers partial scholarships. Attendance: 200.

SANTA BARBARA CHRISTIAN WRITERS CONFERENCE. Westmont College. Spring 2015. Contact: Dr. Opal Mae Dailey, PO Box 40860, Santa Barbara CA 93140. (805) 252-9822. E-mail: info@cwgsb.com. Website: www.CWGSB.com. Editors in attendance. Attendance: 50-70.

+WEST COAST CHRISTIAN WRITERS CONFERENCE. Fremont; February 20-21, 2015. Contact: Susy Flory and Carrie Dameron. C/O Carrie Dameron, PO Box 11123, Pleasanton CA 94588. (925) (595-4311. E-mail: westcoastchristianwriters@gmail.com. Website: http://westcoastchristianwriters.com. Speakers: Kathi Lipp, Michele Cushatt, Bill Giovanetti, Suzanne Woods Fisher, Marci Seither. Editors in attendance. Partial scholarships. Contest: Ethel Herr Memorial Scholarship. Attendance: 200.

WRITER'S SYMPOSIUM BY THE SEA. San Diego/Point Loma Nazarene University; February 24–26, 2015. Contact: Dean Nelson, Professor, Journalism Dept., PLNU, 3900 Lomaland Dr., San Diego CA 92106. (619) 849-2592. Fax (619) 849-2566. E-mail: deannelson@pointloma.edu. Website: www.pointloma.edu/writers. Speakers, interviews, and workshops. Speakers: Joyce Carol Oates, Hanna Rosin, Lysley Tenorio. No scholarships. Attendance: 350 each night.

WRITE TO INSPIRE. Sacramento; October 2015. Contact: Elizabeth M. Thompson, PO Box 276794, Sacramento CA 95827-6794. (916) 607-7796. E-mail: inspirewriters@gmail.com. Website: www.inspirewriters.com. Editors/agent in attendance. Contests: Fiction, nonfiction, poetry, and children's. Information about the contests is available on Website. Offers full & partial scholarships. Attendance: 250.

COLORADO

COLORADO CHRISTIAN WRITERS CONFERENCE. Estes Park; May 13–16, 2015. Director: Marlene Bagnull, LittD, 951 Anders Rd., Lansdale PA 19446. Phone/fax (484) 991-8581. E-mail: mbagnull@aol.com. Website: http://colorado.writehisanswer.com. Conferees choose 6 hour-long workshops from 42 offered or a clinic—fiction, nonfiction, and speakers—by application) plus one six-hour continuing session from 8 offered. Four 15-minute one-on-one appointments, paid critiques, editors' panels, and general sessions. Early bird workshops Wednesday afternoon. Teens Write all day Saturday, plus teens are welcome to attend the entire conference at 60% off. Contest for published and not-yet-published writers (only open to conferees) awards two 50% discounts off 2016 conference registration fee. Editors & agents in attendance. Offers full & partial scholarships. Attendance: 210 conferees, 55 faculty.

+EVANGELICAL PRESS ASSOCIATION ANNUAL CONFERENCE. Westminster; April 8-10, 2015; Lancaster PA, April 6-8, 2016. Lamar Keener, Executive dir., PO Box 62400, Colorado Springs CO 80962. (719) 358-2322. Editors in attendance. No scholarships. Contest: Open to EPA members. Freelance writers, who join EPA as Associate Members, are eligible to enter the contest. Attendance: 175-200.

DISTRICT OF COLUMBIA

NATIONAL CHRISTIAN WRITERS CONFERENCE. Washington DC.; July 2015. Contact: Antonio L. Crawford, PO Box 1458, National City CA 91951-1458. (619) 791-5810. E-mail: ncwcsd@yahoo.com. Website: www.ncwcfr.com.

FLORIDA

AMERICAN CHRISTIAN WRITERS MENTORING RETREAT. Orlando, Ramada Gateway; November 20-21, 2015; November 18-19, 2016. Contact: Reg A. Forder, PO Box 110390, Nashville TN 37222. Toll-free (800) 21-WRITE. E-mail: ACWriters@aol.com. Website: www.ACWriters.com. Offers full & partial scholarships. Attendance: 12-30.

+BRANDON CHRISTIAN WRITERS/ACW CHAPTER. Brandon. Contact: Cheryl Johnson, pres., meets at St. Andrews United Methodist Church, 3315 Bryan Rd., Brandon FL 33511. (813) 763-3154. E-mail: info@brandonchristianwriters.com. Website: brandonchristianwriters.wordpress.com. Membership (35) open. Sponsors the Florida Inspirational Writers Retreat in October.

DEEP THINKERS RETREAT. February. Contact: Susan May Warren, PO Box 1290, Grand Marais MN 55604. E-mail: retreats@mybooktherapy.com. Website: http://deepthinkers.mybooktherapy.com. Offers an advanced track. This five-day retreat is for novelists who want to bring their writing to a new level, with deeper characterization, stronger wordsmithing, and a more compelling plot. Speakers: Susan May Warren, Rachel Hauck. No scholarships. Each retreat attendee receives a private consultation about his or her writing. If ready for advanced writing techniques, we teach that. Sponsors the My Book Therapy Frasier Contest. Attendance: 16.

FLORIDA CHRISTIAN WRITERS CONFERENCE. Lake Yale/Leesburg; February 25–March 1, 2015. Contact: Eva Marie Everson, 530 Lake Kathryn Circle, Casselberry FL 32707. (407) 615-4112. E-mail: FloridaCWC@aol.com. Website: www.FloridaCWC.net. Special classes for advanced writers and teens. Contest (see website). Keynote speakers/editors/agents. Keynote speaker: Davis Bunn. Offers full and partial scholarships.

Attendance: 250-300. Offers advanced track (15 hours of class time—by application only) and teen track hosted and led by Bryan Davis.

GEORGIA

AMERICAN CHRISTIAN WRITERS MENTORING RETREAT. Atlanta, Hotel Indigo; July 10-11, 2015; July 8-9, 2016. Contact: Reg Forder, Box 110390, Nashville TN 37222. Toll-free (800) 21-WRITE. E-mail: ACWriters@aol.com. Website: www. ACWriters.com. Offers full & partial scholarships. Attendance: 12-30.

CATCH THE WAVE WRITERS CONFERENCE. Atlanta; August 2015. Contact: Cynthia L. Simmons, PO Box 2673, Woodstock GA 30188. Phone/fax (770) 926-8627. E-mail: cynthia@christianauthorsguild.org. Website: www.christianauthorsguild. org. Offers beginning nonfiction and fiction. Also appropriate for teens. We aim other classes at advanced writers. Editors/agents in attendance. Full scholarships offered. Short story contest every year. Attendance: 50.

ILLINOIS

KARITOS CHRISTIAN ARTS CONFERENCE. The 22nd Annual Karitos Christian Arts Conference. Karitos is unique among conferences for Christian artists in that it brings all of the arts together. More information at www.karitos.com.

WRITE-TO-PUBLISH CONFERENCE. Wheaton (Chicago area); June 3-6, 2015. Contact: Lin Johnson, 9118 W. Elmwood Dr., Ste. 1G, Niles IL 60714-5820. (847) 296-3964. Fax (847) 296-0754. E-mail: lin@writetopublish.com. Website: www.write-topublish.com. Offers freelance career track (prerequisite: 1 published book). Majority of faculty are editors and agents. Offers full & partial scholarships. Attendance: 200.

INDIANA

+INDIANA FAITH & WRITING CONFERENCE. Anderson University, Anderson IN; October 30-31, 2015. E-Mail: IFWC@Anderson.Edu. Website: www.FaithandWriting. com. Provides publishing opportunities, mentoring for excellence in writing, and a community of literary Christians at a fantastic two-day conference on the university campus. Contest details on the Website.

MIDWEST WRITERS WORKSHOP. Muncie/Ball State University Alumni Center (always the last Thursday, Friday, and Saturday of July). Our 42nd summer workshop! Contact: Dept. of English, Ball State University, Muncie IN 47306-0484. Director: Jama Kehoe Bigger. (765) 282-1055. E-mail: midwestwriters@yahoo.com. Website: www.mid-westwriters.org. Sponsors a contest. Editors/agents in attendance. Attendance: 225.

KANSAS

CALLED TO WRITE. Pittsburg; April 9-11, 2015. Contact: Julane Hiebert, 350 Lake Rd., Council Grove KS 66846. (785) 561-0217. E-mail: julhiebert@gmail.com. Website: calledtowriteconference.blogspot.com. Contest for attendees only: adult fiction, nonfiction, poetry, devotionals, children. Speakers: Ramona Tucker (OakTara editor); Kathleen Y'Barbo (author); Jeane Wynn of Wynn Media (marketing). Editors in attendance. Offers full and partial scholarships. Attendance: 70-75.

KENTUCKY

KENTUCKY CHRISTIAN WRITERS CONFERENCE. Elizabethtown; June 25-27,

2015. Held at: Grace Heartland Church. Address: PO Box 2719, Elizabethtown KY 42702. (502) 330-2773 or (270) 683-5920. E-mail through Website: www.kychristian-writers.com. Keynote: Jesse Floria. Editors/agents in attendance. Offers scholarships. Contest: see website. Attendance 80-100.

MICHIGAN

AMERICAN CHRISTIAN WRITERS MENTORING RETREAT. Grand Rapids, Ramada Plaza Hotel; June 12-13, 2015; June 10-11, 2016. Contact: Reg Forder, PO Box 110390, Nashville TN 37222. Toll-free (800) 21-WRITE. E-mail: ACWriters@aol.com. Website: www.ACWriters.com. Offers full and partial scholarships. Attendance: 12-30.

BREATHE CHRISTIAN WRITERS CONFERENCE. Grand Rapids area; October 9-10. 2015. Contact: Ann Byle, 3148 Plainfield Ave. NE, Ste. 237, Grand Rapids MI 49525-3285. (616) 389-4436. E-mail: breathewritersconference@gmail.com. Website: www.breatheconference.com. We offer workshops appropriate for both beginning and advanced writers, plus 2-hour workshop intensives in several areas. 2015 features intensives in poetry, children's picture books, and public speaking. Special track for advanced writers. Editors/agents in attendance. Offers full scholarships. Attendance: 90.

FAITH WRITERS CONFERENCE. Faith Writers' 2015 International Writing Conference is the second weekend in August. Join us for a time of fellowship and teaching from Faith Writers' own skilled members. These conferences are known for being different—as much about support and encouragement as about writing facts and skills. US location to be announced. Check www.faithwriters.com/conference.php for more information.

FESTIVAL OF FAITH & WRITING. Grand Rapids; April 14-16, 2016 (held every other year). Contact: Shelly LeMahieu Dunn, 1795 Knollcrest Circle S.E., Grand Rapids MI 49546. (616) 526-6770. E-mail: ffw@calvin.edu. Website: http://festival.calvin.edu. Editors/agents in attendance; no scholarships. Attendance: 1,800.

MARANATHA CHRISTIAN WRITERS' CONFERENCE. Muskegon; located on the shore of Lake Michigan. September 2015. Contact: Cindy & Dave Lambert, Maranatha, 4759 Lake Harbor Rd., Muskegon MI 49441-5299. E-mail: info@maranathachristianwriters.com. Website: www.maranathachristianwriters.com. Check website for details and online registration. Website: www.WriteWithPurpose.org. Our experts offer contests, continuing courses, and a wide variety of elective workshops. Focus is on personal attention and up-to-date information to help you meet your goals. Consultations with agents, editors, and publishers included in tuition. Contest details on Website. Full scholarships available. Attendance: 200 max.

+YOUR TIME TO WRITE. Jackson Michigan area; spring & fall 2015. Contact: Mary Busha; 4054 Horton Rd., Jackson MI 49201. Phone/fax: (517) 416-0133. E-mail: yourtimetowrite@gmail.com. Our workshops offer a variety of sessions for beginning and advanced writers; we work with writers from book idea stage to final editing and publication.

MINNESOTA

AMERICAN CHRISTIAN WRITERS MENTORING RETREAT. Minneapolis, Country Inn & Suites; August 7-8, 2015; August 5-6, 2016. Contact: Reg Forder,

PO Box 110390, Nashville TN 37222. Toll-free (800) 21-WRITE. Website: www. ACWriters.com. Offers full & partial scholarships. Attendance: 12-30.

STORYCRAFTERS RETREAT. Minneapolis. Contact: Susan May Warren, PO Box 1290, Grand Marais MN 55604. (218) 387-2853. E-mail: retreats@mybooktherapy.com. Website: http://storycrafters.mybooktherapy.com. This private coaching retreat is for writers at all levels. We focus on storycrafting—starting with an idea and leaving with a plotted story. Sponsors the My Book Therapy Frasier Contest (winner attends retreat for free). Limit 16.

MISSOURI

HEART OF AMERICA CHRISTIAN WRITERS NETWORK CONFERENCES. Kansas City. Typically Thursday to Saturday of the second weekend of November. Check website for dates and additional events. Contact: Jeanette Littleton, 3706 N.E. Shady Lane Dr., Gladstone MO 64119. Phone/fax (816) 459-8016. E-mail: HACWN@ earthlink.net. Website: www.HACWN.org. Offers classes for new and advanced writers. Editors/agents in attendance. Contest details on brochure. Attendance: 125.

NEW MEXICO

CLASS CHRISTIAN WRITERS CONFERENCE. Albuquerque's First Baptist Church; Fall 2015 (see Website for date). Editors and agents in attendance. Contact: Linda Gilden, director, PO Box 36551, Albuquerque NM 87176. E-mail: linda@lindagilden. com. Website: www.classeminars.org. Scholarships may be available. Attendance: 150.

SOUTHWEST WRITERS MINI WORKSHOPS. Albuquerque; various times during the year (check website for dates). Contact: Conference Chair, 3200 Carlisle Blvd. NE, Ste. 114, Albuquerque NM 87110. (505) 830-6034. E-mail: swwriters@juno.com. Website: www.southwestwriters.com. General conference. Agents/editors in attendance. Attendance: 50.

NEW YORK

SOCIETY OF CHILDREN'S BOOK WRITERS & ILLUSTRATORS CONFERENCE IN CHILDREN'S LITERATURE. New York; February 6-8, 2015. Members $450; non-members $550. Contact: Sara Rutenberg, 8271 Beverly Blvd., Los Angeles CA 90048. (323) 782-1010. Fax (323) 782-1892. E-mail: sararutenberg@scbwi.org. Website: www. scbwi.org. Includes a track for professionals. Editors/agents in attendance. Attendance: 900.

NORTH CAROLINA

BLUE RIDGE MOUNTAINS CHRISTIAN WRITERS CONFERENCE. Lifeway Ridgecrest Conference Center; May 17-21, 2015. Contact: Alton Gansky, 4721 W. Princeton Ave., Fresno Ca 93722. (760) 220-1075. E-mail: alton@ganskycommunications.com. Website: www.brmcwc.com or http://ridgecrestconferencecenter.org/event/blueridgemountainchristianwritersconference. Offers an advanced track. Editors and agents in attendance. Sponsors three contests (details at www.brmcwc.com). Offers limited scholarships. Attendance: 350.

CHRISTIAN COMMUNICATORS CONFERENCE. August 2015 in Asheville NC. Attendance: limited to 30. Vonda Skelton, dir. 205 White Meadow Ct., Simpsonville SC 29681. (864)906-2256. Fax (864) 963-5892. E-mail: vondaskelton@gmail.com.

Website: www.ChristianCommunicators.com. Keynote speakers: Vonda Skelton, Carolyn Knefely. No editors or agents in attendance. Offers full and partial scholarships. The goal of this conference is to educate, validate, and launch women in their speaking ministries. Most of our attendees are also writers. After all, writing and speaking go hand-in-hand—and speaking sells books.

*WRITE2IGNITE. Conference for Christian Writers of Literature for Children and Young Adults. March 2015. Contact: Jean Hall, Director, PO Box 1101, Indian Trail NC 28079. (704) 238-0491. E-mail: write2ignite@jeanmatthewhall.com.

OHIO

+DAYTON BOOK EXPO. Dayton; April 25, 2015. Contact: Valerie J. Lewis Coleman, Pen of the Writer, 893 S. Main St., PMB 175, Englewood OH 45322. Phone/fax: (888) 802-1802. E-mail: info@daytonbookexpo.com. Website: www.DaytonBookExpo.com. Speakers: Valerie J. Lewis Coleman, LaTonya Branham. Editors in attendance. Attendance: 400+.

NORTHWEST OHIO CHRISTIAN WRITERS. Holland; a Saturday in October 2015. 26th Annual Seminar. Contact: Shelley R. Lee, Pres. (shelleyrlee@gmail.com), 12400 Jerry City Rd., Cygnet OH 43413. (419) 308-3615. Meets 5-6 times a year at St. Mark's Church, Bowling Green OH. Spring retreat and fall seminar with a nationally known author or editor. Meetings are free and open to public. More detail and full schedule found at www.nwocw.org. Attendance: 35.

PEN TO PAPER LITERARY SYMPOSIUM. Dayton; October 3, 2015. Contact: Valerie J. Lewis Coleman, Pen of the Writer, 893 S. Main St., PMB 175, Englewood OH 45322. Phone/fax: (888) 802-1802. E-mail: info@penofthewriter.com. Website: www.penofthewriter.com. Speakers: Valerie J. Lewis Coleman, Tenita C. Johnson, Dr. Karen M.R. Townsend. Editors in attendance. No scholarships. Attendance: 25.

+WRITE ON! WORKSHOP. Dayton; March 2015 (typically the last Saturday). Contact: Valerie J. Lewis Coleman, Pen of the Writer, 893 S. Main St., PMB 175, Englewood OH 45322. Phone/fax: (888) 802-1802. E-mail: info@penofthewriter.com. Website: www.penofthewriter.com. Speakers: Valerie J. Lewis Coleman, Tenita C. Johnson, Editors in attendance. No scholarships. Attendance: 25.

OKLAHOMA

+THE SUCCESSFUL WRITER CONFERENCE. Tulsa Bible Church; May 29-30, 2015. E-mail: marthajcurtis@yahoo.com. Website: www.TheSuccessfulWriterConference@wordpress.com. Schedule, pricing, and registration information available on the Website.

OREGON

OREGON CHRISTIAN WRITERS SUMMER COACHING CONFERENCE. Portland; August 10-13, 2015. Keynote speakers: Jane Kirkpatrick, Ed Underwood. Contact: Lindy Jacobs. Oregon Christian Writers, 1075 Willow Lake Rd. N, Keizer OR 97303. (541) 408-6306. E-mail: summerconference@oregonchristianwriters.org, or lindyj@bendcable.com. Website: www.OregonChristianWriters.org. Includes about 7 hours of training under a specific coach/topic and more than 30 hour-long afternoon workshops on a variety of writing-related topics. Editors/agents in attendance. Partial scholarships. Mentoring and manuscript reviews. Offers partial scholarships to members who apply.

Attendance: 250. OCW also offers 3 one-day Saturday conferences—winter in Salem, spring in Eugene, and fall in Portland. Check Website for information on all conferences.

PENNSYLVANIA

GREATER PHILADELPHIA CHRISTIAN WRITERS CONFERENCE. Cairn University, Langhorne; July 29–August 1. Founder and director: Marlene Bagnull, LittD, 951 Anders Rd., Lansdale PA 19446. Phone/fax (484) 991-8581. E-mail: mbagnull@aol.com. Website: www.writehisanswer.com/Philadelphia. Keynote speakers: Dr. Ted Baehr, Jim Watkins, and 3 more. Conferees choose 6 hour-long workshops from 60 offered or a clinic by application plus one six-hour continuing session from 8 offered. Four 15-minute one-on-one appointments, paid critiques, editors panels, and general sessions. Contest (registered conferees only) awards 50% off 2015 conference registration to a published and not-yet-published conferee. Especially encourages African American writers. Faculty of 50 authors, editors, and agents. Partial scholarships offered. Attendance: 250.

MONTROSE CHRISTIAN WRITERS CONFERENCE. Montrose; July 19-24, 2015. Contact: Jim Fahringer, Montrose Bible Conference, 218 Locust St., Montrose PA 18801-1473. (570) 278-1001. Fax (570) 278-3061. E-mail: mbc@montrosebible. org. Website: www.montrosebible.org. Tracks for beginners, advanced writers, and teens (some years). Editors/agents in attendance. Provides a few partial scholarships. Attendance: 100.

CECIL MURPHEY'S WRITER TO WRITER CONFERENCE. The Hershey Lodge, 325 University Drive, Hershey, PA 17033; February 5-7, 2016. (727) 596-7625. Fax: (727) 593-3523. E-mail: service@munce.com. Website: www.writertowriter.com. Keynote speaker: Cecil Murphey. Allows writers to go from "think to ink." The unique format makes it accessible in terms of cost, timing, and convenient venues. Offers workshops in four areas: nonfiction, fiction, publishing, and marketing. Contest: Called PUB Board: A Shark Tank-like experience; three conferees are selected in advance who will introduce their project to a star panel of conference faculty.

ST. DAVIDS CHRISTIAN WRITERS' CONFERENCE. Grove City College, Grove City; June 2015. Contact: Amy Mable, (724) 894-2522. E-mail: amymablesdcwa@ gmail.com. Website: www.stdavidswriters.com. Offers tracks for beginning and advanced writers, fiction, nonfiction, children's, poetry, and more. Contests for participants; information on website. Editors/agents in attendance. Offers partial scholarships. See website for information on their Writers' Colony. Attendance: 70.

SOUTH CAROLINA

CAROLINA CHRISTIAN WRITERS CONFERENCE. Spartanburg, First Baptist Church, 250 East Main Street, Spartanburg SC 29306. (864) 583-7245. March 2015. Editors and agents in attendance. Contact: Linda Gilden, director, PO Box 2928, Spartanburg SC 29304. E-mail: linda@lindagilden.com. Website: www.fbs.org/writers. Full scholarships available. Attendance: 100.

+WRITE2IGNITE! CONFERENCE FOR CHRISTIAN WRITERS OF LITERTURE FOR CHILDREN AND YOUNG ADULTS. North Greenville Univ., Tigerville SC; March 27-28, 2015. Contact: Jean Hall, PO Box 1101, Indian Trail, NC 28079. (704) 578-0858. E-mail: write2ignite@jeanmatthewhall.com. Website: www.write2ignite. com. For middle school and high school students we offer workshops presented by professional authors and editors, along with fun activities and participation in our general sessions alongside adult writers. Several writing contests are offered through the year on our blog at http://write2ignite.com/category/blog. Editors/agents in attendance. Full scholarships. Attendance: 100.

TENNESSEE

AMERICAN CHRISTIAN WRITERS MENTORING RETREAT. Nashville, Opryland Guest House; March 27-28, 2015; April 1-2, 2016. Contact: Reg Forder, PO Box 110390, Nashville TN 37222. Toll-free (800) 21-WRITE. E-mail: ACWriters@aol. com. Website: www.ACWriters.com. Offers full and partial scholarships. Attendance: 40-80.

+MID-SOUTH CHRISTIAN WRITERS CONFERENCE. Memphis, Collierville First Baptist Church; March 7, 2015. Keynote: Vonda Skelton. Choice of 9 workshops. Contact: April Carpenter, PO Box 586, Olive Branch MS 38654. E-mail: midsouthchristianwriters@gmail.com. Website: www.midsouthchristian writers.com. Attendance: 50-75.

+CECIL MURPHEY'S WRITER TO WRITER CONFERENCE. Murphreesboro; Embassy Suites, 1200 Conference Center Blvd., Murphressboro TN 37129; September 18-20, 2015. (727) 596-7625. Fax: (727) 593-3523. E-mail: service@munce.com. Website: www.writertowriter.com. Keynote speaker: Cecil Murphey. Allows writers to go from "think to ink." The unique format makes it accessible in terms of cost, timing, and convenient venues. Offers workshops in four areas: nonfiction, fiction, publishing, and marketing. Contest: Called PUB Board, a *Shark Tank*-like experience; three conferees are selected in advance who will introduce their project to a star panel of conference faculty.

TEXAS

+AMERICAN CHRISTIAN FICTION WRITERS (ACFW) NATIONAL CONFERENCE. Dallas; September 17-20, 2015. Contact: Robin Miller, dir., PO Box 101066, Palm Bay FL 32910-1066. E-mail: director@acfw.com. Website: www.acfw.com/conference. Continuing education sessions and workshop electives specifically geared for 5 levels of writer experience from beginner to advanced. Track for advanced writers. Editors/agent in attendance. Full scholarships. The Genesis Contest is for unpublished writers whose Christian fiction manuscript is completed. The Carol Awards honor the best of Christian fiction from the previous calendar year. Attendance: 650.

AMERICAN CHRISTIAN WRITERS MENTORING RETREATS. Dallas; April 10-11, 2015; April 22-23, 2016. Contact: Reg A. Forder, PO Box 110390, Nashville TN 37222. Toll free: (800) 21-WRITE. E-mail: acwriters@aol.com. Website: www.acwriters.com. Speakers include Jim Watkins, Dr. Dennis Hensley, Lin Johnson, Holly Miller, and others. Editors in attendance. Offers full & partial scholarships. Attendance: 12-30.

EAST TEXAS CHRISTIAN WRITERS CONFERENCE. Marshall; October 30-31, 2015. Contact: Dr. Jerry Hopkins, Professor of History, East Texas Baptist University, One Tiger Drive, Marshall TX 75670. (903) 923-2083. Fax (903) 923-2077. E-mail: jhopkins@etbu.edu. Website: www.etbu.edu/news/cwc. Offers an advanced and teen track. Beginning, intermediate, and advanced; youth are emphasized and encouraged. Special pricing for senior citizens, youth/students. Sponsors a writers contest in three categories:short story, poetry, essay (grand prize, 1st–3rd place winners; cash awards). Editors/agents in attendance. Partial scholarships. Attendance: 160.

TEXAS CHRISTIAN WRTERS CONFERENCE. August 1, 2015. Houston First Baptist Church in Houston. Contact Martha Rogers, 6038 Greenmont, Houston TX 77092-2332. (713) 686-7209. E-mail: MarthaRogers@sbcglobal.net. Website: www. centralhoustoniwa.com. Includes The Inspirational Writers Alive! Open Writing Competition, critiques, and workshops. (See competition details in Contest section.)

WASHINGTON

NORTHWEST CHRISTIAN WRITERS RENEWAL CONFERENCE. Redmond; May 15-16, 2015. Contact: Diana Savage, PO Box 2706, Woodinville WA 98072-2706. (425) 298-3699. E-mail: renewal@nwchristianwriters.org. Website: http://nwchristian-writers.org. Keynote speaker: Angela Hunt. Editors/agents in attendance. Offers full scholarships. Attendance: 150

WISCONSIN

GREEN LAKE CHRISTIAN WRITERS CONFERENCE. Green Lake; August 16-21, 2015. 67th year. Green Lake Conference Center, W2511 State Rd. 23, Green Lake WI 54941-9300. (920) 294-3323. Website: www.glcc.org. Contact Jan White Moon, dir., at (920) 229-2418, or janet.p.white@gmail.com. Classes in fiction, nonfiction, poetry. Seminars, writing contest, one-on-one with instructors, editors, critiquing. Editors in attendance. Partial scholarships. Attendance: 30-40.

WRITING WORKSHOPS & RETREATS. 920 Market St., La Crosse WI 54601; (608) 791-5295. E-mail: fscenter@fspa.org. Check Website for dates: www.FSCenter.org.

CANADA/FOREIGN

COMIX35, various international locations & dates. Contact: Nate Butler, PO Box 73706, Houston TX 77273-3706. E-mail: nate@comix35.org. Website: comix35.org. Editors in attendance. Tentative locations for 2015: Taiwan in April and Norway in September.

INSCRIBE CHRISTIAN WRITERS' FELLOWSHIP FALL CONFERENCE. Wetaskiwin AB, Canada; last weekend of September 2015. Contact: Gwen Mathieu, PO Box 6201, Wetaskiwin, AB T9A 2E9. (780) 352-4006. E-mail: mathieug@xplor-net.com. Website: www.inscribe.org/events/fall-conference Some editors in attendance. No agents. Hosted by Inscribe Christian Writer's Fellowship, a Canada-wide organiza-tion for Christians who write. Contests for members (see www.inscribe.org/contests/inscribe-fall-competition for details). Attendance: 100.

WRITE CANADA. Toronto, Ontario; Contact: The Word Guild, Ste. 226, 245 King George Rd., Brantford ON N3R 7N7, Canada. E-mail: writecanada@thewordguild. com. Website: www.the wordguild.com/events/write-canada. Annual conference hosted by The Word Guild, an association of Canadian writers and editors who are Christian. Offers a career track. Editors/agents in attendance. Fresh Ink Contest. Bursaries avail-able. Attendance: 250.

CONFERENCES THAT CHANGE LOCATIONS

ACT ONE: SCREENWRITING WEEKENDS. Two-day workshops; see Website for dates and locations. Contact: Conference Coordinator, 2690 Beachwood Dr., Lower Fl., Hollywood CA 90068. (323) 464-0815. Fax (323) 468-0315. E-mail: information@ActOneProgram.com. Website: www.ActOneProgram.com. Open to anyone who is interested in learning more about the craft of screenwriting. No editors/agents in attendance. Attendance: 75.

+AMERICAN CHRISTIAN FICTION WRITERS (ACFW) NATIONAL CONFERENCE. Dallas; September 17-20, 2015 (changes location every year). Contact: Robin Miller, dir., PO Box 101066, Palm Bay FL 32910-1066. E-mail: director@acfw.com. Website: www.acfw.com/conference. Continuing education sessions and workshop electives specifically geared for 5 levels of writer experience from beginner to advanced. Track for advanced writers. Editors/agent in attendance. Full scholarships. The Genesis Contest is for unpublished writers whose Christian fiction manuscript is completed. The Carol Awards honor the best of Christian fiction from the previous calendar year. Attendance: 650.

AMERICAN CHRISTIAN WRITERS MENTORING RETREATS. Various dates and locations (see individual states where held). Contact: Reg A. Forder, PO Box 110390, Nashville TN 37222. Toll-free (800) 21-WRITE. E-mail: ACWriters@aol.com. Website: www.ACWriters.com. Speakers include: Jim Watkins, Dennis Hensley, Lin Johnson, Holly Miller, and others. Editors in attendance. Offers full & partial scholarships. Attendance 12-30.

AUTHORIZEME. Various locations and dates; by invitation to locations. Contact: Sharon Elliott, PO Box 1519, Inglewood CA 90308-1519. Phone/fax: (310) 508-9860. E-mail: AuthorizeMe@sbcglobal.net. Website: www.AuthorizeMe.net. AuthorizeMe is a 12-hour, hands-on seminar that helps writers get their book ideas out of their heads, onto paper, and into a professional book proposal format ready to submit to an acquisitions editor. Seminars offered nationwide. For a list of scheduled seminars, or to sponsor a seminar in your area, check website. No editors or agents in attendance. Attendance: 10-50.

CHRISTIAN LEADERS AND SPEAKERS SEMINARS (The CLASSeminar). PO Box 36551, Albuquerque NM 87176. (702) 882-0638. Website: www.classeminars.org. Sponsors several seminars across the country each year. Check website for CLASSeminar dates and locations. For anyone who wants to improve his or her communication skills for either the spoken or written word, for professional or personal reasons. Speakers: Florence Littauer and others. Attendance: 75-100.

EVANGELICAL PRESS ASSOCIATION CONVENTION. Changes location every year. Westminster CO, April 8-10, 2015; Lancaster PA, April 6-8, 2016. Contact: Lamar Keener, Conv. Chairperson, PO Box 20198, El Cajon CA 92021. (888) 311-1731. E-mail: business@evangelicalpress.com. Website: www.evangelicalpress.com. Attendance: 175. Annual convention for editors of evangelical periodicals; freelance communicators welcome. Editors in attendance. Contest open to members only.

INTERNATIONAL CHRISTIAN RETAIL SHOW. (Held in a different location each year.) Contact: CBA Colorado Springs CO 80962-2000. Toll-free (800) 252-1950. (719) 265-9895. Fax (719) 272-3510. E-mail: info@cbaonline.org. Website: www.christianretailshow.com. Entrance badges available through CBA. Attendance: 5,000.

+NEW ENGLAND CHRISTIAN WRITERS RETREAT. City in New England (varies); fall 2015. Contact: Lauren Yarger, 2 Long Lott Rd., West Granby CT 06090. (860) 653-7733. E-mail: nechristianwritersretreat@yahoo.com. Website: www.newenglandchristianwritersretreat.com. Speakers: Tessa Afshar, Lucinda Secrest McDowell. No scholarships. Novice to multi-published authors attend. Retreat focuses on writing time. Attendance: 55.

"WRITE HIS ANSWER" SEMINARS & RETREATS. Various locations around US; dates throughout the year; a choice of focus on periodicals or books (includes indie publishing or mastering the craft). Contact: Marlene Bagnull, LittD, 951 Anders Rd., Lansdale PA 19446. (484) 991-8581. E-mail: mbagnull@aol.com. Website: www.write-hisanswer.com/seminars. Attendance: 20-60. One- and two-day seminars by the author of *Write His Answer: A Bible Study for Christian Writers.*

9

Area Christian Writers' Clubs, Fellowship Groups, and Critique Groups

(*) before a listing indicates unconfirmed or no information update.
(+) before a listing indicates it's a new listing this year.

ARIZONA

CHANDLER WRITERS GROUP/ACW CHAPTER. Chandler. Contact: Jenne Acevedo. (480) 510-0419. E-mail: jenneacevedo@cox.net. http://chandlerwriters. wordpress.com. Membership (20) open.

EAST VALLEY CHRISTIAN WRITERS. (EVCW). Mesa. Contact: Brenda Jackson. (480) 827-1545. E-mail: brendaattheranch@yahoo.com. Membership (3) open.

FOUNTAIN HILLS CHRISTIAN WRITERS' GROUP/ACW CHAPTER. Fountain Hills. Contact: Lenna Wyatt, 14223 N. Westminster Pl., Fountain Hills AZ 85268. (480) 836-8968. E-mail: tykeJ@juno.com. Membership (10-15) open. Occasionally we sponsor a conference; maybe once a year.

NORTHERN ARIZONA WORD WEAVERS. Cottonwood. Contact: Alice Klies, 235 S. Bull Dogger Cir., Cottonwood AZ 86326. (928) 300-9700. E-mail: alice.klies@ gmail.com. Website: www.word-weavers.com. Membership (30) open. Meeting time: Second Saturday, 9:30–noon. Meeting address: Spirit of Joy Lutheran Church, 330 Scenic Drive, Clarkdale AZ. We bring in special speakers the second Saturday in October each year for a small conference for writers in Northern Arizona, Phoenix, and surrounding areas.

ARKANSAS

*****SILOAM SPRINGS WRITERS.** Siloam Springs. Contact: Margaret Weathers, 716 University St., Siloam Springs AR 72761. (479) 524-6598. Members (21) open. Sponsors contest, open to non-members.

CALIFORNIA

AMADOR FICTION WRITERS. Ione. Contact: Kathy Boyd Fellure, PO Box 1209, Ione CA 95640-1209. (209) 274-0205. E-mail: kathyfellure2@juno.com. Website: www.amadorfictionwriters.com. Membership (15) open. Sponsors an annual literary read; October 3, 2015

AMADOR FICTION WRITERS GROUP. Fremont. Contact: Kathy Boyd Fellure, PO Box 1209, Ione CA 95640-1209. Website: www.amadorfictionwriters.com. Membership (10) open to experienced writers only.

INSPIRE CHRISTIAN WRITERS: Equipping Writers to Inspire the World. Meets in multiple locations nationwide and online. Contact: Elizabeth M. Thompson, PO

Box 276794, Elk Grove CA 95827. (916) 670-7796. E-mail: elizabeth mthompson@ comcast.net. Group e-mail: inspirewriters@gmail.com. Website: www.inspirewriters. com. Membership (200+) open. Hosts 2 annual Write to Inspire Conferences. Also host genre specific contests in conjunction with our conferences. Open to non-members. Check website for details.

SAN DIEGO COUNTY CHRISTIAN WRITERS GUILD. San Diego County. Contact: Jennie Gillespie, PO Box 270403, San Diego CA 92198. Phone/fax (760) 294-3269. E-mail: info@sandiegocwg.org. Website: www.sandiegocwg.org. Membership (200) open. To join their Internet newsgroup, e-mail your name and address to info@sandiegocwg.com. Sponsors 10 critique groups, fall seminar, and spring fellowship brunch. Sponsors a contest: Unpublished Manuscript Contest. Winner receives 15-minute private consultation with faculty member of their choice at fall conference.

+SUNRISE CHRISTIAN WRITERS. Fair Oaks. Contact: Sue Tornai, 8321 Greenback Ln., Fair Oaks CA 95628. (916)990-5728. E-mail: suetornai@comcast.com. Website: www.sunrisechristianwriters.blogspot.com. Membership (10) open.

*TEMECULA WRITERS CRITIQUE GROUP. Temecula. Contact: Rebecca Farnbach, 41403 Bitter Creek Ct., Temecula CA 92591. (951) 699-5148. E-mail: rfarnbach@hotmail.com. Membership (18) open. We meet at the above address on the 2nd Tuesday of each month at 7 p.m., except for December when it's the 1st Tuesday. Affiliated with San Diego Christian Writers Guild.

COLORADO

SPRINGS WRITERS. Woodmen Valley Chapel/Colorado Springs. Contact: Scoti Springfield Domeij, 5209 Del Paz Dr., Colorado Springs CO 80918. (719) 209-9066. E-mail: springswriters@gmail.com. Website: http://springswriters.wordpress.com. Membership (350) open. Offers ½ day mini-boot camps and 7 ½ hour boot camps throughout the calendar year and a monthly free conference-quality workshop taught by published authors, agents, and professionals working in the publishing industry or in journalism.

CONNECTICUT

WORD WEAVERS BERKSHIRES. Sherman. Contact: Carol Barnier, 6 Church Rd., Sherman CT 06784. (203) 702-7006. E-mail: carol@carolbarnier.com. Website: www. wordweaversberkshires.org. Membership (15) open.

DELAWARE

DELMARVA CHRISTIAN WRITERS' FELLOWSHIP. Georgetown. Contact: Candy Abbott, PO Box 777, Georgetown DE 19947-0777. (302) 856-6649. Fax (302) 856-7742. E-mail: info@delmarvawriters.com. Website: www.delmarvawriters.com. Membership (20+) open. Sponsors The Book Event, November 8, 2015. Crossroads Community Church, 20684 State Forest Rd., Georgetown DE 19947. Book sales by Christian authors (limited space). Judi Folmsbee, dir., info@JudiFolmsbee.com, (302) 684-3603.

FLORIDA

BRANDON CHRISTIAN WRITERS/ACW CHAPTER #3029. Contact: Cheryl Johnston, Pres., St. Andrews United Methodist Church, 3315 Bryan Rd., Brandon FL 33511. (813) 763-3154. E-mail: info@brandonchristianwriters.com. Membership

(30+) open. Meets 4th Thursdays monthly. Sponsors Florida Inspirational Writers Retreat (see conference listing).

PALM BEACH CHRISTIAN WRITERS/ACW CHAPTER. North Palm Beach. Contact: Aria Dunham, 11231 US Highway 1, PMB 231, North Palm Beach FL 33408. (561) 707-0757. E-mail: Aria@AriaDunham.com. Website: http://PalmBeachACW. wordpress.com. Membership (10) open. Meeting dates, times, and locations listed on the website.

PLATFORM-POWER LLC. Contact: Aria Dunham. 11231 US Highway 1, #231, North Palm Beach FL 33408. (561) 707-0757. E-mail: Aria@ariadunham.com. Website: www.ariadunham.com.com. Meeting dates, times, and locations listed on the website.

SUNCOAST CHRISTIAN WRITERS. Seminole. Contact: Elaine Creasman, 13014—106th Ave. N., Largo FL 33774-5602. Phone/fax (727) 595-8963. E-mail: emcreasman@aol.com. Membership (10-15) open.

WORD WEAVERS FIRST COAST. Contact: Samantha Koivistoe, acting chapter president. E-mail: koitoes@gmail.com. Website: www.word-weavers.com. Membership (15+) open. Meeting time is second Saturday each month, 10:00 a.m.–1:00 p.m. Meeting address: St. Augustine. Contact chapter president for address details.

WORD WEAVERS GAINESVILLE. Contact: Lori Roberts, chapter president. E-mail: llwroberts@cox.net. Website: www.word-weavers.com. Meets 2nd Sunday of the month, 2:00-4:30 p.m. Membership (10+) open.

+WORD WEAVERS NORTH JAX. Contact: Richard New, chapter president. E-mail: loco7mo@yahoo.com. Website: www.word-weavers.com. Membership: open. Meets the second Saturday each month, 10:00 a.m.- 1:00 p.m. Meeting address: North Jackson Baptist Church, Jacksonville FL Contact chapter president for address details, or chack: www.njbc.org.

WORD WEAVERS ORLANDO. Contact: Taryn Souders, chapter president. E-mail: tarynjoy@souders.net. Website: www.word-weavers.com. Meets 2nd Saturday of the month, 10:00-12:30 p.m. Membership (80+) open.

WORD WEAVERS SOUTH FLORIDA. Contact: Patricia Hartman, chapter president. E-mail: Patricia@PatriciaHartman.net. Website: www.word-weavers.com. Membership (25+) open.

WORD WEAVERS SPACE COAST. Contact: Evelyn Miracle, chapter president. E-mail: eveymiracle@gmail.com. Website: www.word-weavers.com. Membership (20+) open. Meeting time: Second Sunday, 2:00-4:30 p.m.

WORD WEAVERS TAMPA. Contact: Tina Yeager, chapter president. E-mail: humbleauthor@yahoo.com. Website: www.word-weavers.com. Membership (20+) open.

WORD WEAVERS TREASURE COAST. Contact: Loretta Beasley, chapter president. E-mail: ruhischild2@bellsouth.net. Website: www.word-weavers.com. Meets 1st Saturday of the month, 9:30-noon. Membership (20+) open.

WORD WEAVERS VOLUSIA COUNTY. Contact: Donna Collins Tinsley, chapter president. E-mail: ThornRose7@aol.com. Website: www.word-weavers.com. Membership (15+) open. Meeting time: First Monday, 7:00–9:00 p.m.

GEORGIA

CHRISTIAN AUTHORS GUILD. PO Box 2673, Woodstock GA 30188. (770) 735-3020. Fax: www.christianauthorsguild.org. Website: www.christianauthorsguild.org. The CAG meets twice monthly with guest authors/speakers, classes, and mentoring for aspiring writers and authors. The group hosts a half-day mini-conference outreach called Coffee & Quill in March and a larger, two-day Catch the Wave Writers Conference in August. Membership (70) open. Yearly dues $30.

EAST METRO ATLANTA CHRISTIAN WRITERS/ACW CHAPTER. Covington. Contact: Lisa Hetzel, 2584 King Louis Rd., Conyers, GA 30012. (404) 293-9011. E-mail: hetzellisa@gmail.com. Website: www.emacw.blogspot.org. Membership (20) open. Check website for monthly meetings and speakers.

WORD WEAVERS GREATER ATLANTA. Contact: Jorja Davis, chapter president. E-mail: jorja.davis@gmail.com. Website: www.word-weavers.com. Membership (10+) open. Meeting time: First and third Saturdays, 9:00 a.m.–11:30 a.m., and online. Mailing address: 2315 Rocky Mountain Road NE, Atlanta GA 30066-2113.

ILLINOIS

WORD WEAVERS AURORA. Aurora. Contact: Cindy Huff, pres. (630) 281-0337. E-mail: cindyshuff@comcast.net. Website: www.word-weavers.com. Membership (4) open. Meeting time: Second Saturday, 1-3 p.m. Meeting address: Hope Fellowship Church, 221 Locust St., Aurora IL 60506.

WORD WEAVERS LAND OF LINCOLN. Contact: Sarah Tierney, chapter president. E-mail: mpcc.counseling@gmail.com. Website: www.word-weavers.com. Membership (15+) open.

+WORD WEAVERS LISLE. Contact: Christy Brunke. E-mail: Christy@ChristyBrunke.com. (708) 805-3365. Meets 3rd Saturday of the month, 10:00-noon., at the Lisle Library District, 777 Front St., Lisle IL. Membership open.

IOWA

*IOWA SCRIBES. Contact: Ed Dickerson, 1764 62nd St., Garrison IA 52229-9628. (319) 477-3011. E-mail: edickers@netins.net. Facebook: www.facebook.com/kimngollnick#!/groups/215400341881935/. Website: www.kimn.net/scribes.htm. Membership (6-10) open.

MARYLAND

*BALTIMORE AREA CHRISTIAN WRITERS. Owings Mills. Contact: Theresa V. Wilson, MEd, PO Box 47182, Windsor Mill MD 21244-3571. (443) 622-4907. E-mail: writerseminar@aol.com. Social networking sites: www.twitter.com/WritersCoach21; www.facebook.com/writersinthemarketplaceupdates. Webinar conferencing. Focused on building author platform and publishing support. Membership (50) open.

MICHIGAN

FIRST FRIDAY'S WRITERS GROUP. Critique group meets the first Friday of each month. Davison Free Methodist Church, 502 Church Street, Davison MI 48423. Contact Arlene Knickerbocker for details. (810) 793-0316 or writer@thewritespot.org.

+KALAMAZOO CHRISTIAN WRITERS/ACW CHAPTER. Kalamazoo. Contact: Peter

DeHaan, Voyage Church, 6339 Atlantic Ave., Kalamazoo MI 49009. E-mail: dehaan, peterdehaan.com. Website: https://www.facebook.com/groups/343855935722455. Membership (8) open.

WORD WEAVERS WEST MICHIGAN. Groups meet in Grandville, Holland, Zeeland, North Grand Rapids, and Muskegon/Norton Shores. Contact: Anna Moore Bradfield, chapter president. E-mail: info@annamoorebradfield.com. Website: www. word-weavers.com. All groups meet on the 1st and 3rd Tuesdays. Membership (60+) open.

MISSISSIPPI

BYHALIA CHRISTIAN WRITERS/ACW CHAPTER. Contact: April Carpenter, Byhalia MS. (901) 378-0504. E-mail: bcwriters@gmail.com. Has BCW online Yahoo group. Has on-ground, online Yahoo group, and Facebook group. Membership (12-15) open. Sponsors the Mid-South Christian Writers Conference.

MISSOURI

HEART OF AMERICA CHRISTIAN WRITERS NETWORK. Kansas City metro area. Contact: Mark and Jeanette Littleton, 3706 N.E. Shady Lane Dr., Gladstone MO 64119. Phone/fax (816) 459-8016. E-mail: HACWN@earthlink.net. Website: www. HACWN.org. Membership (150) open. Sponsors monthly meetings, weekly critique groups, professional writers' fellowships, a contest (open to nonmembers), a newsletter, marketing e-mails, and a conference in November.

OZARKS CHAPTER OF AMERICAN CHRISTIAN WRITERS. Springfield. Meets monthly, Sept. to May. Contact: Jeanetta Chrystie, pres., OCACW, 5042 E. Cherry Hills Blvd., Springfield MO 65809-3301. (417) 832-8409. E-mail: DrChrystie@ mchsi.com. James Cole-Rous, newsletter ed. Submit articles to OzarksACW@yahoo. com. Guidelines on website: www.OzarksACW.org. Sponsors an annual contest (open to nonmembers); genre, dates, and guidelines on website. See website for other events. Membership (47) open. Newsletter-only subscriptions available.

NEBRASKA

MY THOUGHTS EXACTLY. Fremont. Contact: Cheryl Paden, PO Box 1073, Fremont NE 68025. (402) 727-6508. E-mail: cherylpaden@juno.com. Membership (7) open. Sponsors fall writers retreat in Red Cloud, NE. Retreat focuses on individual writing with writing prompts.

NEW JERSEY

NORTH JERSEY CHRISTIAN WRITERS GROUP. North Haledon NJ. Barbara Higby, leader. Contact: Susan Panzica, 681 High Mountain Rd., North Haledon NJ ot508. (201) 755-5730. E-mail: njcwgroup@gmail.com. Website: www.njcwg.blogspot. com. Membership (12) open.

NEW YORK

THE SCRIBBLERS/ACW CHAPTER. Riverhead. Contact: Bill Batcher, pres., c/o First Congregational Church, 103 First St., Riverhead NY 11901. E-mail: bbatcher@ optonline.net. Membership (12) open. Meets monthly and sponsors annual writing retreat on Long Island.

...IER CHRISTIAN WRITERS' FELLOWSHIP. Vestal. Contact: ...now Ave., Binghamton NY 13905-3810. (607) 797-5852. E-mail: ...nail.com. Membership (6-8) open.

...S WESTERN NEW YORK. Contact: Janet Erickson, chapter president. E-mail: JanEricks@aol.com. Website: www.word-weavers.com. Meets 2nd Tuesday, 6:30-9:00 p.m. Membership (10+) open.

NORTH CAROLINA

NEW COVENANT WRITERS. Lincolnton. Contact: Robert Redding, 3392 Hwy. 274, Cherryville NC 28021-9634. (704) 530-3380. E-mail: minwriter@yahoo.com. Membership (6) open.

OHIO

DAYTON CHRISTIAN SCRIBES. Kettering. Contact: Lois Pecce, 9909 Stephanie St., Dayton OH 45458-3709. (937) 433-6470. E-mail: epecce@compuserve.com. Membership (32) open. Publishes monthly newsletter for local and national membership.

MIDDLETOWN AREA CHRISTIAN WRITERS (MAC WRITERS). Franklin. Contact: Donna J. Shepherd. Healing Word Assembly of God, 5303 S. Dixie Hwy., Franklin OH 45005. (513) 423-1627. Fax (513) 424-1817. E-mail: donna.shepherd@ gmail.com. Website: http://.middletownwriters.blogspot.com. Membership (25) open. Sponsors Greater Harvest Workshops.

MOVING AHEAD ACW CHAPTER. Bowling Green. Contact: Shelley Lee, President, 12400 Jerry City Rd., Cygnet OH 43413. (419) 308-3615. E-mail: mlka@toast.net. Website: www.NWOCW.org. Members (40) open. ACW Chapter. Sponsors annual conference, October, Holland OH.

NW OHIO CHRISTIAN WRITERS. Holland; a Saturday in October 2015. 26th Annual Seminar. Contact: Shelley R. Lee, Pres. (shelleyrlee@gmail.com), 12400 Jerry City Rd., Cygnet OH 43413. (419) 308-3615. Meets 5-6 times a year at St. Mark's Church, Bowling Green OH. Spring retreat and fall seminar with a nationally known author or editor. Meetings are free and open to public. More detail and full schedule found at www.nwocw.org. Attendance: 35.

OKLAHOMA

FELLOWSHIP OF CHRISTIAN WRITERS. Tulsa. Contact: Elece Hollis, pres. Meets at Kirk of the Hills Presbyterian Church, 4102 E. 61st , Tulsa OK. (918) 733-2832. Website: http://fellowshipofchristianwriters.org. Membership (65) open. Sponsors and annual writers' conference.

OKC CHRISTIAN FICTION WRITERS (ACFW CHAPTER). Edmond/Oklahoma City. Contact: Susan Crawford. E-mail: ocfwchapter@gmail.com. Website: www.okc-christianfictionwriters.com. Meets 3rd Saturday, 1:00-3:00 p.m. Membership open; includes members-only discussion e-mail loop and discounted special events.

WORDWRIGHTS, OKLAHOMA CITY CHRISTIAN WRITERS. Edmond. Contact: Milton Smith, 6457 Sterling Dr., Oklahoma City OK 73132-6804. (405) 721-5026. E-mail: HisWordMatters@yahoo.com. Website: www.shadetreecreations.com. Membership (20+) open. Occasional contests for members only. Hosts an annual writers' conference with American Christian Writers, March 2015, in Oklahoma City. Send an SASE for information.

OREGON

OREGON CHRISTIAN WRITERS. Contact: president at president@oregonchristian-writers.org or business manager at business@oregonchristianwriters.org or write to 1075 Willow Lake Rd. N., Keizer OR 97303. Website: www.oregonchristianwriters. org. (503)393-3356. Meets for three all-day Saturday conferences annually: winter in Salem (February 28, 2015); spring in Eugene (May 16, 2015); and fall in Portland (October 17, 2015). Print newsletter published the month before each one-day conference, and monthly e-news sent to members. Annual four-day Summer Coaching Conference with editors and agents held mid to late summer (August 10-13, 2015) in Portland metro area. Multi-genre Cascade Writing Contest held in spring; finalists announced in June; award presentations made at the summer conference. Membership (350) open.

WORD WEAVERS PORTLAND EAST. Gresham. Contact: Terry Murphy, chapter president. E-mail: TerryMurphy.disciplespost.com. Website: www.word-weavers.com. Membership (10) open. Meeting time: third Tuesday, 9:30-11 a.m. Meeting address: please contact Terry for location.

WORDWRIGHTS. Gresham (near 182nd & Powell). Contact: Susan Thogerson Maas, 27526 S.E. Carl St., Gresham OR 97080-8215. (503) 663-7834. E-mail: susan. maas@frontier.com. Membership (4-5) open.

PENNSYLVANIA

*FIRST WRITES. Chambersburg. Contact: Dawn Hamsher. 225 S. Second Street, Chambersburg PA 17201. E-mail: 1stwrites@gmail.com. Website: www.1stwrites. blogspot.com. Membership open.

GREATER PHILADELPHIA CHRISTIAN WRITERS FELLOWSHIP. Lansdale. Contact: Marlene Bagnull, 951 Anders Rd., Lansdale PA 19446-5419. Phone/fax (484) 991-8581. E-mail: Mbagnull@aol.com. Website: http://writehisanswer.com/greater-philly christianwriters. Membership (10) open. No application or dues. Meets one Thursday morning a month, September–June in Marlene's Lansdale home. Sponsors annual writers' conference (July 29–August 1, 2015).

JOHNSTOWN CHRISTIAN WRITERS' GUILD. Contact: Betty Rosian, 102 Rustic Ave., Johnstown PA 15904-2122. (814) 255-4351. E-mail: wordsforall@hotmail.com. Membership (17) open.

LANCASTER CHRISTIAN WRITERS/ACW CHAPTER.   Lancaster Alliance Church, 210 Pitney Rd., Lancaster. Contact: Jeanette Windle. E-mail: jeanette@jeanettewindle.com. Website: http://.lancasterchristianwriterstoday.Blogspot. com. Membership (300+, monthly attendance 30-60) open. Sponsors a one-day conference in spring.

LANSDALE CHRISTIAN WRITERS FELLOWSHIP/CRITIQUE GROUP. Contact: Marlene Bagnull, 951 Anders Rd., Lansdale PA 19446-5419. (484) 991-8581. E-mail: mbagnull@aol.com. Membership (8) open. Women only.

SOUTH CAROLINA

*CAROLINA CHRISTIAN WRITERS, LOCAL CHAPTER OF ACFW. SC AND NC. Founded 2007. E-mail: carolinacfw@gmail.com. Website: www.carolinachris-tianwriters.com. Facebook: www.facebook.com/CarolinaChristianWriters. Twitter: @

carolinacfw. Membership (17). CCW normally meets the second Saturday in even-numbered months, requires an annual membership fee of $10 (in addition to membership in ACFW). Welcomes all ages. Consists of published and unpublished Christian authors in various genres, with the primary focus on writing Christian fiction.

PALMETTO CHRISTIAN WRITER'S NETWORK. Lexington. Contact: Linnette R. Mullin, 20 Longshadow Cir., Lexington SC 29072. E-mail: pcwn@live.com; Website: http://pcwn.blogspot.com. Twitter hashtag: #PCWN. Membership (18) open. PCWN meets monthly. No member fee at this time. Welcomes ages 18 and up. Consists of published and unpublished Christian authors, writers, magazine editors, columnists/journalists, freelance writers, and bloggers in various genres—fiction and nonfiction. We write for the glory of God. Linnette R. Mullin, author and freelance writer at www.LinnetteMullin.com.

WORD WEAVERS SUMMERVILLE. Contact: Kay Colon, chapter president. E-mail: kay_colon@hotmail.com. Website: www.word-weavers.com. Membership (10+) open. Meeting time: First Monday, 7:00-10:00 p.m. Meeting address: Summerville Presbyterian Church, 407 South Laurel St., Summerville SC 29483.

WRITE2IGNITE! TWO-4-ONE CRITIQUES. We offer two simultaneous written critiques from Write2Ignite! team members for one reasonable price. Specialize in manuscripts for children and young adults. Not an editing service. Details at www.write2ignite.com. Contact Jean Hall at write2ignite@jeanmatthewhall.com.

WRITING 4 HIM. Spartanburg. Contact: Linda Gilden, 1600 Reidville Rd., Spartanburg SC 29301. (863) 595-2626. E-mail: linda@lindagilden.com. Meets once a month. Membership (50) open. Supports the Carolina Christian Writers Conference.

TENNESSEE

COLLIERVILLE AMERICAN CHRISTIAN WRITERS. (CCWriters2)/ACW Chapter. Collierville. Contact: Susan Reichert, 2400 Linkenholt Dr., Collierville TN 38017-8822. (901) 853-4470. E-mail: tnlms44@aol.com. Membership (36) open.

TEXAS

CENTRAL HOUSTON INSPIRATIONAL WRITERS ALIVE! Houston. Contact: Martha Rogers, Houston's First Baptist Church, 7401 Katy Freeway, Houston TX 77024. (713) 686-7209. E-mail: marthalrogers@sbcglobal.net. Website: www.central-houston1wa.com. Membership (30) open. IWA Open Writing Competition: January 1 to May 15. Categories: Adult, YA, children's short stories, poetry, drama, articles, devotionals, book proposals. Contact: Pat Vance: patav@aol.com. Open to non-members. Sponsors Texas Christian Writers Conference.

CHRISTIAN WRITERS GROUP OF GREATER SAN ANTONIO. Universal City/San Antonio area (First Baptist Church of Universal City). Contact: Brenda Blanchard. (210) 945-4163. E-mail: brendablanchard1@aol.com. Meets every Monday from 6:30-8:30 p.m. at FBCUC in Faith Building, 1401 Pat Booker Rd., Universal City TX. Has quarterly guest speakers. Membership (40-50) open. Sponsors 3 conferences per year. March/June/October at First Baptist Church of Universal City.

CROSS REFERENCE WRITERS. Brazos Valley. E-mail: CrossRefWriters@yahoo.com. Website: http://sites.google.com/site/crossreferencewriters. Membership open.

DFW READY WRITERS/ACFW BRANCH. Colleyville. Contact: Lee Carver, president. E-mail: leecarver2@aol.com. Blog: www.dfwreadywriters.blogspot.com. Meets the second Saturday at 10:30 a.m. Membership open.

INSPIRATIONAL WRITERS ALIVE! Three chapters in Houston and one in Amarillo. Sponsors a one-day summer conference, Texas Christian Writers Conference on August 1, 2015, at Houston's First Baptist Church. Also sponsors an annual contest (January 1–May 15) open competition for all genres of writers. For contest information, contact Patricia Vance at patav@aol.com; for conference information contact Martha Rogers at marthalrogers@sbcglobal.net.

*INSPIRATIONAL WRITERS ALIVE!/AMARILLO CHAPTER. Contact: Jerry McClenagan, pres., 6808 Cloud Crest, Amarillo TX 79124. (806) 674-3504. E-mail: jerrydalemc@sbcglobal.net. Membership open. Sponsors a contest open to members, and a seminar the Saturday after Easter.

NORTH TEXAS CHRISTIAN WRITERS/ACW CHAPTERS. Meetings held in Argyle, Arlington, Burleson, Canton, Cedar Hill, Corinth, Crandall, Dallas, Denton, Double Oak, Flower Mound, Fort Worth, Frisco, Garden Valley, Granbury, Irving, Kilgore, Lake Worth, Lindale, N. Richland Hills, Plainview, and Plano. Contact: NTCW, PO Box 820802, Fort Worth TX 76182-0802. (817) 715-2597. E-mail: info@ntchristianwriters.com. Website: www.NTChristianWriters.com. Membership (250+) open. Sponsors an annual conference in June, evening classes, one-day seminars, and three-day mentoring clinics throughout the year.

PINEY WOODS CHRISTIAN WRITERS. Huntsville. Contact: Robin Bryce, chapter president. (936) 661-4285. E-mail: robin@robinbryce.com. Website: www.word-weavers.com. Membership open. Meeting time: second Monday, 6:30-9:00 p.m. Meeting address: Target Starbucks, 259 Interstate 45, Huntsville TX 77340.

ROCKWALL CHRISTIAN WRITERS GROUP. Rockwall. Contact: Leslie Wilson, 535 Cullins Rd., Rockwall TX 75032. (214) 505-5336. E-mail: leslieporterwilson@gmail.com. Website: www.rcwg.blogspot.com. Membership (20-25) open.

WRITERS ON THE STORM/ACW CHAPTER. The Woodlands. Contact: Linda P. Kozar, 7 South Chandler Creek Cir., The Woodlands TX 77381. (832) 797-7522. E-mail: zarcom1@aol.com. Blog: http://wotsacfw.blogspot.com. Membership (50-60) open. Contest: Writers on the Storm—Storming the Short Story Contest, June 1-30. Open to non-members. A writer's workshop in January.

VIRGINIA

CAPITAL CHRISTIAN WRITERS. Fairfax. Directors: Betsy Dill & Sarah Hamaker, PO Box 2332, Centreville VA 20122-0873. Phone/fax (703) 803-9447. E-mail: ccwriters@gmail.com. Website: www.CapitalChristianWriters.org. Meets second Monday of odd-numbered months. Speakers, website for authors, blog, occasional workshops. (Membership (25-35) open. Has occasional Saturday workshops.

+JOYWRITERS: An American Christian Writers Chapter, PO Box 342, Fancy Gap VA. (276) 237-7574. E-mail: vherlock@yahoo.com. On FaceBook under above name. Contact: Vie Herlocker. Open to Christians who write for the faith and general markets. Meetings are educational rather than critique oriented, and members are both published and not-yet-published.

NEW COVENANT WRITER'S GROUP. Newport News. Contact: Mary Tatem, 451 Summer Dr., Newport News VA 23606-2515. (757) 930-1700. E-mail: rwtatem@juno. com. Membership (8) open.

+ROANOKE VALLEY CHRISTIAN WRITERS/ACW CHAPTER. Roanoke. Contact: Barbara Baranowski, 6757 Waterstone Dr., Roanoke VA 24018. (540) 581-5117. E-mail: barbaramb@cox.net. Website: www.roanokevalleychristianwriters.org. Membership (20) open.

WASHINGTON

SPOKANE CHRISTIAN WRITERS' GROUP. Spokane. Contact: Ruth McHaney Danner, PO Box 18425, Spokane WA 99228-0425. (509) 328-3359. E-mail: ruth@ ruthdanner.com. Membership (15) open.

WALLA WALLA CHRISTIAN WRITERS. Walla Walla. Contact: Helen Heavirland, PO Box 146, College Place WA 99324-0146. Phone/fax: (541) 938-3838. E-mail: hlh@bmi.net. Membership (8) open.

WALLA WALLA VALLEY CHRISTIAN SCRIBES. College Place. Contact: Helen Heavirland, PO Box 146, College Place WA 99324-0146. Phone/fax: (541) 938-3838. E-mail: hlh@bmi.net. Membership (8) open.

WISCONSIN

LIGHTHOUSE CHRISTIAN WRITERS. Rotating in members' homes. Third Tuesdays, 10 a.m. Contact: Lois Wiederhoeft, 110 Oak St., Apt. #2, Peshtigo WI 54157. (715) 582-1024. E-mail: 2loisann@hotmail.com. Membership (12) open. Sponsors a conference every 3 yrs.

PENS OF PRAISE CHRISTIAN WRITERS. Manitowoc. Contact: Cofounders Becky McLafferty, 9225 Carstens Lake Rd., Manitowoc WI 54220. (920) 758-9196; or Sue Kinney, 4516 Laurie Ln., Two Rivers WI 54241. (920) 793-242-3631. E-mail: rebeccamclafferty@gmail.com, or susanmarlenekinney@gmail.com. Membership (8-12) open. Meets the third Monday of every month, 6:30 p.m.-8:30 p.m., at Faith Church, 2201 42nd St., Manitowoc WI 54220.

+WORD AND PEN CHRISTIAN WRITERS. Menasha. Contact: Chris Stratton, (920) 739-0752; e-mail: gcefsi@new.rr.com. Or Beth Ziarnik, (920) 235-0664, e-mail: bethz@new.rr.com. Meets monthly at St. Thomas Episcopal Church, 226 Washington St., Menasha WI 54952. Membership (14) open.

CANADIAN/FOREIGN

NEW ZEALAND CHRISTIAN WRITERS. Contact: Janet Fleming, PO Box 115, Kaeo 0448, New Zealand. E-mail: mjflamingos@xtra.co.nz. Website: www.nzchristianwriters.org. Workshops, (autumn and spring), biannual weekend retreat, local groups, contests for members, and bimonthly magazine.

SWAN VALLEY CHRISTIAN WRITERS GUILD. Swan River. Contact: Addy Oberlin, PO Box 132, Swan River MB R0L 1Z0, Canada. Phone/fax (204) 734-4269. E-mail: waltadio@mymts.net. Membership (8) open.

THE WORD GUILD. Contact: Jayne Self, administrator. E-mail: WriteCanada@ thewordguild.com. (800) 969-9010, ext. #2. An organization of Canadian writers and editors who are Christian. We meet in various cities and online. We sponsor an annual conference, now in Toronto, Ontario, Canada, in June. Write Canada: www.writecanada.org. We sponsor contests open to nonmembers who are Canadian citizens: http://canadianchristianwritingawards.com. Website: www.thewordguild.com. The Word Guild, 245 King George Rd., Brantford ON N3R 7N7, Canada.

WORD WEAVERS MISSISSAUGA. Contact: Ann Peachman Stewart, chapter president. E-mail: Peachie01@sympatico.ca. Website: www.word-weavers.com. Membership (15+) open. Meeting time: Second Tuesday, 7:00-9:00 p.m. Meeting address: Portico Community Church Room 213, 1814 Barbertown Rd., Mississauga ON L5M 2M5, Canada.

NATIONAL/INTERNATIONAL & ONLINE GROUPS (NO STATE LOCATION)

AMERICAN CHRISTIAN FICTION WRITERS. PO Box 101066, Palm Bay FL 32910. Robin Miller, exec. Dir. (director@acfw.com); and conference dir. (ct@acfw.com). Website: www.acfw.com. E-mail loop, online courses, critique groups, local chapters, and ACFW Journal magazine for members. Send membership inquiries to membership@acfw.com. Membership (2,600+) open. Sponsors contests for published and unpublished writers. Conducts largest fiction conference annually.

+CHRISTIAN SMALL PUBLISHERS ASSN. (CSPA). Internet based. Contact: Sarah Bolme, PO Box 481022, Charlotte NC 28269. (704) 277-7194. Fax: (704) 717-2928. E-mail: cspa@christianpublishers.net. Website: www.christianpublishers.net. Membership (130+) open. Sponsors Christian Small Publishers Book of the Year Award, open to non-members; www.bookoftheyear.net.

PEN-SOULS. (prayer and support group, not a critique group). Conducted entirely by e-mail. Contact: Janet Ann Collins, Grass Valley CA. E-mail: jan@janetanncollins.com. Membership (12) open by application.

WORD WEAVERS INTERNATIONAL, INC. President, Eva Marie Everson, 530 Lake Kathryn Circle, Casselberry FL. Vice President, Mark T. Hancock. (407) 615-4112. E-mail: WordWeaversInternational@aol.com. Website: www.Word-Weavers.com. Membership (500+) open, in over 30 chapters in US and Canada. Sponsors Florida Christian Writers Conference (see conferences) Feb/March annually. Sponsors both face-to-face groups and online groups.

WORDWEAVERS ONLINE GROUPS. Contact: Bruce Brady. E-mail: BCBrady01A@gmail.com. Website: www.word-weavers.com.

WRITE2IGNITE!/ACW CHAPTER. Online group. Contact: Jean Hall, PO Box 1101, Indian Trail NC 28079. (704) 578-0858. E-mail: write2ignite@jeanmatthewhall.com. Website: www.write2ignite.com. Membership: 10 on leadership team, plus about 85 conference attendees. Open to new members. Sponsors several contest yearly through our blog; open to non-members. Sponsors the Write2Ignite! Conference for Christian Writers of Literature for Children and Young Adults.

10

Editorial Services

It is often wise to have a professional editor critique or edit your manuscript before you submit it to an agent or publisher—some agents even require a written evaluation. The following people offer this kind of service. We recommend asking for references or samples of their work.

Abbreviations of work they offer:

B brochures
BCE book contract evaluation
CA coauthoring
GE general editing/manuscript evaluation
GH ghostwriting

LC line editing or copyediting
NL newsletters
PP PowerPoint
SP special projects
WS website development

Abbreviations of the types of material they evaluate:

A articles
BP book proposals
BS Bible studies
D devotionals
E essays
F fillers

GB gift books
JN juvenile novels
N novels
NB nonfiction books
P poetry
PB picture books

QL query letter
S scripts
SS short stories
TM technical material
YA young adults

ACKELSON LIGHTHOUSE EDITING. 13326 Community Rd., #11, Poway CA 92064-4754. (858) 748-9258. E-mail: Isaiah68LA@sbcglobal.net. Website: www.lighthouseedit.com. E-mail/write. GE/LC/GH/CA/B/NL/BCE. Edits: A/SS/N/NB/BP/QL/BS/E/D. Charges $35 for article/short-story critique; $60 for 3-chapter book proposal. Send SASE for full list of fees. Editor since 1981; senior editor 1984-2014.

ALL ABOUT WORDS/RENEE GRAY-WILBURN, 1820 Smoke Ridge Dr., Colorado Springs CO 80919. (719) 271-7076. E-mail: waywords@earthlink.net. E-mail contact. GE/LC/GH/CA/SP. Edits: A/SS/F/N/NB/QL/PB/BS/GB/TM/D. Over 15 years of writing, editing, and proofreading experience across many genres. Have authored 4 children's books and one adult nonfiction book, along with hundreds of magazine articles. Have nearly 10 years experience working as a freelance writer and editor for various ministries and independent authors. Open to coauthoring opportunities. I typically charge an hourly rate based on the type of work. May charge on a per project basis for book-length general editing or writing projects. Rates begin at $20/hr for proofreading.

AMERICAN CHRISTIAN WRITERS/REG A. FORDER, PO Box 110390, Nashville TN 37222. (800)-21-WRITE. E-mail: ACWriters@aol.com. Website: ACWriters.com. E-mail contact. GE/LC. Edits: A/SS/P/N/NB/BP/JN/BS/GB/D/S. 25 years of editing experience. Check /website or e-mail for price sheet. Very low prices.

AMI EDITING/ANNETTE M. IRBY, PO Box 7162, Covington WA 98042-7162. (425) 433-8676. E-mail: editor@AMIediting.com. Website: www.AMIediting.com.

E-mail contact; deposit amount depends on project. GE/LC. Edits: A/SS/N/D. Published author; an acquisitions editor for a Christian publisher and a freelance editor. She has worked with Summerside Press and Guideposts, including editing for Susan May Warren, Tricia Goyer, and several other CBA authors. See Website for testimonials. In-depth Critiquing Serve, first 5 pages $100. Full ms editing services: $30/hr (general) and $40/hr. (rush); deposit of $100 required to begin. Will offer a per page rate if client prefers, contact to begin. Payment is required in advance via PayPal or check. Quick Editing Help Question: $5.

ANCIENT PATHS ONLINE/SKYLAR HAMILTON BURRIS, Flower Mound TX. E-mail: skylarburris@yahoo.com. Website: www.editorskylar.com. E-mail contact. LC/B/NL/WS. Edits: A/SS/P/F/N/NB/BP/QL/JN/BS/TM/E/D. Primarily works with authors who are planning either to self-publish or to submit their work to traditional publishing houses and who have completed books that require line-by-line copy editing prior to final proofreading and publication. My freelance editing services have been employed by a diversity of authors and businesses. BA and MA in English. Over 14 years as a magazine editor; 15 years newsletter editing and design. Charges authors $2 and $3.50/double-spaced page for editing. Please send two sample pages from the middle of your work for a precise quote. I will also provide a free sample edit of these two pages. Charges $40/hr. for newsletter editing, writing, and design.

MARILYN A. ANDERSON EDITING, WRITING, PROOFREADING, TUTORING, 127 Sycamore Dr., Louisville KY 40223-2956. (502) 244-0751. Fax (502) 452-9260. E-mail: shelle12@aol.com, bethanyad@bellsouth.net, manderson@bethanylouisvulle. com. E-mail/$25 deposit. GE/LC/B/NL/SP/WS/writing coach. Edits: A/F/NB/BS/TM/E/D. Charges $15-20/hr. for proofreading, $25/hr. for extensive editing, or negotiable by the job or project. Holds an MA and a BA in English; former high school English teacher; freelance consultant since 1993. References available. Contributing member of The Christian PEN.

AMY BOEKE'S EDITING SERVICE, 2017 Rural St., Rockford IL 61107. E-mail: abboeke@gmail.com. E-mail contact. GE/LC/B/NL/SP/writing coach. Edits: A/SS/F/N/NB/BP/QL/JN/BS/GB/E/D. BA English Studies, magna cum laude; M.A.T. (Secondary English Education). Charges $40-100 for articles; $250-750 for books. Payment by check or PayPal preferred.

B. K. NELSON, INC./OBNITA K. NELSON, 1565 Paseo Vida, Palm Springs CA 92264. (760) 844-0444. Fax (760) 778-6242. E-mail: bknelson4@cs.com. Website: http://nelsonbookmovielecture.com. E-mail/deposit of $150. GE/BCE. Edits: NB/BP/QL/S/N/bios. Has been a literary agent for 22 years and has sold more than 3,000 books to royalty publishers. Edited extensively. Converts novels to scripts. We do not deal with self-publishing. Contact for rates. Charges flat rates.

CARLA'S MANUSCRIPT SERVICE/CARLA BRUCE, 10229 W. Andover Ave., Sun City AZ 85351-4509. (623) 876-4648. E-mail: Carlaabruce@cox.net. E-mail contact. GE/LC/GH/NL/writing coach. Edits: A/SS/P/F/N/NB/BP/QL/BS/E/D. Twenty-six years ghostwriting/editing; authored two contemporary Christian novels. Charges $25/hr.

CHRISTIAN COMMUNICATOR MANUSCRIPT CRITIQUE SERVICE/SUSAN TITUS OSBORN, 3133 Puente St., Fullerton CA 92835-1952. (714) 990-1532. E-mail: Susanosb@aol.com. Website: www.christiancommunicator.com. E-mail contact. Staff of 18 editors. GE/LC/GH/CA/BCE/writing coach. Edits: A/SS/P/F/N/NB/BP/JN/PB/QL/BS/GB/TM/E/D/S/screenplays. In business 28 years. $100 for stories/articles/picture books. Three-chapter book proposal $160 (up to 40 pgs.). Additional editing $40/hr.

+CHRISTIAN EDITOR CONNECTION/KATHY IDE. E-mail: kathyde@christianeditor.com. website: www.christianeditor.com. E-mail contact. Connects authors, editors, agent, and publishers with established, professional freelance editors who meet their specific needs. Members must pass tests to evaluate their skills in whatever services they wish to offer.

CHRISTIAN MANUSCRIPT SUBMISSIONS.COM, (408) 966-3998. E-mail: info@ christianmanuscriptsubmissions.com. Website: www.ChristianManuscriptSubmissions. com. An online manuscript submission service operated by the Evangelical Christian Publishers Association (ECPA). ChristianManuscriptSubmissions.com is the only manuscript service created by the top Christian publishers looking for unsolicited manuscripts in a traditional royalty-based relationship. It allows authors to submit their manuscript proposals in a secure, online format for review by editors from publishing houses that are members of the ECPA.

+THE CHRISTIAN PEN: PROOFREADERS AND EDITORS/KATHY IDE. E-mail: KathyIde@Christianeditor.com. Website: www.TheChristianPEN.com. E-mail contact. A professional support organization, open to active and aspiring freelancers, for the purpose of networking and sharing skills. The Website has helpful tips, tools, and articles. We have an e-mail discussion loop, online courses, a quarterly newsletter, and more. Contributing members get extra benefits such as discounts on the online courses, active job leads for self-published authors, book reviews and client shout-outs in the newsletter, and opportunities to write for the newsletter and teach online courses. They can also run ads for their services on the Website (for a small fee).

+CREATIVE ENTERPRISES STUDIO/MARY HOLLINGSWORTH, PO Box 224, Fort Worth TX 76095. (817)312-7393. Fax: (817) 685-7393. E-mail: AcreativeShop@aol.com. Website: CreativeEnterprisesStudio.com. E-mail contact. GE/LC. Edits: N/NB/BP/JN/PB/BS/GB/D. With 30 years experience in Christian publishing, our 20-member team works with traditional publishers, churches, ministries, companies, and individuals, providing top-quality editorial and publishing services in many different areas and genres. See "Credentials" on our Website for specifics. We provide custom estimates for each project, based on the client's needs and the specific work required.

+CREST PUBLISHER SERVICES/EDWARD BOLME, PO Box 481022, Charlotte NC 28269. (704) 995-6739. E-mail: info@crestpub.com. Website: crestpub.com. E-mail contact. GE/LC/GH/CA/B/NL/SP. Edits: A/SS/N/NB/JN/PB/BS/GB/ TM/E/D. Also does interior design and typesetting services. Provides everything from copy-editing to graphic design and typesetting for Christian and general authors and small presses. For ghostwriting, I have five published novels as well as dozens of user's guides to my credit. Partial deposit with the balance due upon satisfactory completion of the project.

CREWS AND COULTER EDITORIAL SERVICES/JANET K. CREWS/B. KAY COULTER, 806 Hopi Trl., Temple TX 76504-5008. (254) 778-6490 (Coulter) or (254) 939-1770 (Crews). E-mails: janetcrews@sbcglobal.net or bkcoulter@sbcglobal. net. Website: crewsandcoultereditorial.com. E-mail/deposit of half of estimated total. GE/LC/GH/CA. Edits: N/NB/BP/QL/JN/PB/BS/GB/D. Crews: 17 years experience; Coulter: 13 years experience. Charges $30/hr.; $100 minimum.

DEDICATED PUBLICATION SERVICES/TAMMY L. HENSEL, PO Box 382, College Station TX 77841-0382. (979) 204-0674. Fax (979) 823-6252. E-mail: tammylou. hensel@gmail.com. Website: DedicatedPublicationServices.com. E-mail. GE/LC/B/ NL/SP/WS/articles, press releases, ads, and other documents, writing coach. Edits: A/ SS/F/N/NB/BP/QL/JN/PB/BS/GB/TM/E/D/S/academic books/papers, depending on subject. Bachelor's degree in journalism and history from Baylor University, plus more than 25 years writing, editing, and public-relations experience in print media. Very strong writing, editing, and communication skills. Experienced in both content and line-by-line editing, page design, manuscript preparation, newsletters, proposals, advertising, and more. Proficient in use of *The Chicago Manual of Style, The AP Stylebook, APA Publication Manual,* and *The Christian Writer's Manual of Style.* Published works include newspaper and magazine features, devotions, and inspirational articles. Rates are determined by the individual needs of the project and based on those recommended by the Editorial Freelancers Association (www.the-efa.org/res/rates.php). A deposit is required for first project but may be waived on return business. Customary rates from magazine and book publishers are accepted if within industry standards.

EB WORD PRO/BARBARA WINSLOW ROBIDOUX, 127 Gelinas Dr., Chicopee MA 01020-4813. (413) 594-6567. E-mail: ebwordpro@aol.com. Call.. GE/LC. Edits: A/SS/N/NB/BP/QL/BS/GB/E/D. Book reviewer for several publications. On staff of Susan Osborn's Manuscript Critique Service. Editorial consultant for Rob Mitchell's award-winning bio Castaway Kid. Charges $15/hr.

EDITING SERVICES/SUSAN G. MATHIS, 945 Rangely Dr., Colorado Springs CO 80921. (719) 331-9352. E-mail: mathis.wordworks@gmail.com. Website: www. SusanGMathis.com. E-mail contact. GE/LC/GH/CA/SP/writing coach. Edits: A/SS/N/NB/BP/QL/PB/BS/D. Published author, nonfiction, fiction. Former editor of a dozen publications. 20+ years writing/editing experience. Rates determined after discussion with client.

EDITOR FOR YOU/MELANIE RIGNEY, 4201 Wilson Blvd., #110328, Arlington VA 22203-1859. (703) 863-3940. E-mail: melanie@melanierigney.com. E-mail contact. GE. Edits: N/NB/BP/D. Thirty years in communications, including five years as the editor of Writer's Digest Magazine, nine years with Advertising Age magazine, and time with Macmillan Computer Publishing and Thomson Financial Publishing. For rate sheet, go to: http://editorforyou.com/ratesheet.html.

+EDITORIAL SERVICES/JAMIE CHAVEZ, Murphreesboro TN. E-mail: jamie. chavez@comcast.net. Website: http://www.jamiechavez.com. E-mail contact. GE/LC/ CA. Edits: SS/N/NB/BP/JN/E. Eleven years with Thomas Nelson Publishers, currently 10 years as freelance editor. See Website for portfolio. Content edit: word count; line/copy edit: per hour; coauthor: negotiated.

+EDITORIAL SERVICES/CAROLE CUDNIK, 101 Rockywood Way, Niceville, FL 32578-2357. (850) 974-3392. E-mail: carle.cudnik@gmail.com. Website: www.carolecudnik.com. E-mail contact. GE/LC/NL/research assistance. Edits: A/SS/F/N/NB/BS/GB/D/Memoir. Thirty years experience in writing, reviewing, and editing for US government. AA Communications Applications Technology. Certificate in copy editing. Contributing member of The Christian PEN. Provides editing services to Christian authors, freelance writers, publishers, and ministries. Offers per page rates, hourly rates, and project rates. Complimentary 2-page sample edit offered. Payments accepted via PayPal. Payment plans available.

EDITORIAL SERVICE/STERLING DIMMICK, 311 Chemung St., Apt. 5, Waverly

NY 14892-1463. (607) 565-4247. E-mail: sdimmick311@gmail.com. Call. GE/LC/ GH/CA/SP. Edits: A/SS/P/F/N/NB/BP/QL/JN/PB/BS/GB/TM/E/D/S. Has an A.A.S. in Journalism; BA in Communication Studies. Charges $20/hr. or by the project.

EDITORIAL SERVICES/LISA HAINLINE, PO Box 1382, Running Springs CA 92382 (909) 939-0311. E-mail: info@lionsgatebookdesign.com Website: www.lionsgatebookdesign.com. Call/e-mail. Edits/evaluates: A/BP/NB/D/GE/GH/LC/NL. Editorial team specializes in nonfiction books by new and self-published authors. We provide manuscript critiques and all levels of editing. Submit 3 chapters for quote.

EDITORIAL SERVICES/JEANETTE HANSCOME, San Ramon CA. E-mail: jeanettehanscome@gmail.com. Website: http://jeanettehanscome.com. E-mail contact. GE/GH/CA/SP/writing coach. Edits: A/SS/F/N/NB/JN/BS/GB/E/D. Author of 3 YA books with Focus on the Family; editor for 10 years; 400+ published articles, devotions, and stories; teaches and critiques online, locally, and at writers' conferences. Charges $45-$50/hr; flat or per-project fees negotiable.

+EDITORIAL SERVICES/KATHERINE HARMS, 411 Walnut St. #4033, Green Cove Springs FL 32043. (443) 621-3110. E-mail: katherine@katherineharms.com. Website: http://katherineharms.com. "My objective is to help Christian writers flood the market with high quality books and other publications.".

EDITORIAL SERVICES/JOY P. GAGE. (928) 645-6534. E-mail: jnkwriters@swiftaz. net. Edits adult fiction and nonfiction. Charges $35/hr. Offers one-day writing workshops for groups (call for details).

EDITORIAL SERVICES/MELISSA JUVINALL, 5226 Ninebark Dr., Fitchburg WI 53711. (309) 452-8917. E-mail: kangaj1@hotmail.com. E-mail contact. GE/LC. Edits: A/N/NB/JN/PB/BS/GB/TM/E/D. Has a BA & MA in English; specializes in children's lit.; 9+ years editing experience; 8 years book award judge; 2 years editing in the workplace. Charges by the page for proofreading and copyediting; by the hour for content edit.

+EDITORIAL SERVICES/LESLIE L. MCKEE. E-mail: lmckeeediting@gmail.com. Website: http://lmckeeediting.wix.com/mckeeediting.

EDITORIAL SERVICES/REBECCA FLORENCE MILLER. E-mail: rmiller001@ luthersem.edu. Website: rebeccaflorencemiller.wordpress.com. E-mail contact. GE/ LC/B/NL/SP/WS/writing coach. Edits: A/SS/N/NB/BP/QL/JN/PB/BS/E/D/blog posts/email newsletters/Websites. Wrote feature articles for local and national publications. Degree in English/creative writing. Mdiv from Lutheran Seminary; currently a freelance writer, editor, and blogger. Member of Christian PEN. Testimonials and writing sample on Website. I offer a free sample edit for every new client. Each quote is different, based on the project's specific editing needs, but I almost always bill per page (not per hour). Payment plans available when needed.

EDITORIAL SERVICES/KIM PETERSON, 1114 Buxton Dr., Knoxville TN 37922. E-mail: petersk@BethelCollege.edu or peterskus@yahoo.com. E-mail. GE/LC/GH/ CA/B/NL/SP/WS/PP/mentoring/writing coach. Edits: A/SS/P/F/N/NB/BP/QL/ JN/PB/GB/TM/E/D. Freelance writer; college writing instructor; freelance editor; conference speaker. MA in print communication. Charges $28-36/hr.

EDITORIAL SERVICES/DIANE E. ROBERTSON, 6058 Arlene Way, Bradenton FL 34207. (941) 928-5302. E-mail: pswriter1@netzero.net. Website: dianerobertsonwriter.com. E-mail contact. GE/LC/writing coach. Edits: A/SS/N/NB. Has written a woman's fiction book, a children's book, a memoir, and 1 book on all types of creative writing, 200+ magazine articles, short stories, and children's stories; previously served as associate editor of 2 magazines; presently teaches short story, novel writing, magazine writing, writer's workshops, and memoir creative writing classes at several colleges and independent living centers. Charges $35/hr. Prefers half payment up front and remainder on delivery.

EDITORIAL SERVICES/LESLIE SANTAMARIA, 1024 Walnut Creek Cove, Winter Springs FL 32708. (407) 497-5365. E-mail: leslie@lesliesantamaria.com. Website: www.lesliesantamaria.com. E-mail contact. GE/LC/writing coach. Edits: A/SS/P/F/N/NB/BP/QL/JN/PB/BS/GB/TM/E/D/S. Published author and book reviewer with 20+ years book and magazine editing experience and a BA in English. Specializes in children's materials. Charges by the project after free initial consultation.

+EDITORIAL SERVICES/CATHY STREINER, 3123 Olde Sutton Parke Dr., Orange Park FL 32073. Phone/fax: (904) 527-8117. E-mail: Cathy@thecorporatepen.com. E-mail contact. GE/LC/CA/B/NL/SP/WS/writing coach. Experience includes writer coaching and more than 20 years of writing/editing, as well as a Christian novel. Pricing is per-page, per-project, hourly, or hourly with a maximum, depending on the situation. Please contact for special rates and a free initial consultation.

EDITORIAL SERVICES/KELLY K. TOMKIES, 36 N. Cassady Ave., Bexley OH 43209. (614) 732-4860. E-mail: kakwrite@aol.com. E-mail contact; deposit is 1/3 of total fee. GE/LC. Edits: A/SS/N/NB/BP/QL/BS/GB/TM/E/D/S. I have been a professional freelance editor for more than 15 years, working with individual authors, publishers, and publishing service companies. Prefers to negotiate a flat fee per project.

EDITORIAL SERVICES/BETTY L. WHITWORTH, 11740 S. Hwy. 259, Leitchfield KY 42754. (270) 257-2461. E-mail: Blwhit@bbtel.com. Call/e-mail. Editing for fiction and nonfiction books/articles and short stories. Retired English teacher, currently working as a newspaper columnist/journalist and independent editor. Worked with 50+ writers. Send 20 pages, SASE for return of ms with $25.00. Will give estimate for entire project after viewing those pages.

THE EDITORIAL SERVICE AGENCY/BRENDA WILBEE, 4959 Columbus Ave., Bellingham WA 98299. (360) 389-6895. E-mail: Brenda@brendawilbee.com. Website: BrendaWilbee.com. E-mail contact. GE/LC/B/NL/SP/W/writing coach. Edits: A/SS/F/N/NB/D. Offers graphic design services for brochures, bookmarks, websites. Has MA in professional writing; BA in creative writing; AA in graphic design; has taught college composition for 7 yrs.; author of 9 CBA books and 100s of articles; 17 yr. contributor to Daily Guideposts; and has freelanced as a writer, editor, and designer for 35 yrs. Award-winning author of 10 books. Will do book design, layout, and covers. Charges $50/hr. for all projects.

EDITOR WORLD, LLC/PATTI FISHER, PO Box 24, Newport VA 24128. (614) 500-3348. E-mail: info@editorworld.com. Website: www.editorworld.com. E-mail contact. GE. Edits: A/SS/N/NB/BP/QL/JN/BS/GB/TM/E/D/S. At Editor World we have a wide range of editors and services. Clients are charged per word.

EDIT RESOURCE, LLC/ERIC & ELISA STANFORD, 3578-E Hartsel Dr., #387, Colorado Springs CO 80920. (719) 290-0757. E-mail: info@editresource.com. Website: www.editresource.com. E-mail contact. GE/LC/GH/CA/writing coach. Edits A/SS/N/NB/BP/QL/JN/PB/BS/GB/D. Combined 35 years of professional editing experience. Rates determined after discussion with client.

EPISTLEWORKS CREATIONS/JOANN RENO WRAY, Helping Writers Reach Their High Call. Cheswick PA. (918) 695-4528. E-mail: epedit@epistleworks.com. Website: http://epistleworks.com. E-mail preferred. GE/LC/GH/CA/B/NL/SP/ Research. Edits: A/SS/P/F/N/NB/BP/D. Creates graphic art: covers, logos, cartoons, website design, site content management. PR materials: (static or animated) brochures, booklets, and web ads. Uses signed contracts with clients. Experienced writer, editor, and artist since 1974. Previous editor for two Tulsa OK monthly Christian newspapers, publisher/editor of an online magazine, business columnist, editing clients' work. Edited pastors' and ministers' newsletters, newspapers, and books. Speaker/teacher at national Christian writers' conferences. Over 3,300 published articles, stories, poem in print, periodicals. Articles in 18 compilation books. Charges start at $25/hr. Required $45 nonrefundable consulting fee (deducted from total). Binding estimates. Detailed time-clock report. Discounts available. Accepts checks, money orders, or PayPal. E-mail or see website for detailed information on services.

+EVERFAITH PRESS EDITORIAL SERVICES, 2373 NW 185th Ave. #510, Hillsboro OR 97124. (559) 744-3553. E-mail: getpublished@everfaithpress.com. Website: www. everfaithpress.com. E-mail contact. GE/LE/GH/CA/writing coach. Edits: SS/N/NB/ JN/GB/D. Imprint of award-winning publishing company, Ellechor Media. Our team has over 20 years of experience and have worked with a variety of authors to help them achieve their publishing dreams. We also provide relevant references upon request. Our pricing is available on our Website, but is primarily driven by word count and genre.

FAITHFULLY WRITE EDITING/DAWN KINZER, 25914—188th Ave. S.E., Covington WA 98042-6021. (253) 630-7617. E-mail: dawnkinzer@comcast.net. Website: www.faithfullywriteediting.com. E-mail contact. GE/LC. Edits: A/SS/N/ NB/D. Published writer with short stories, articles, and devotions. Experience in editing both fiction and nonfiction. Created and edited department newsletter for national telecommunications corporation. Serves as a judge for contests that award excellence in Christian fiction. Member of The Christian PEN, The Christian Editor Network, and American Christian Fiction Writers. Rates are by page and depend on type of work required. Payment is made in advance of each block of work being completed. Complimentary 2-page sample edit offered with initial contact.

FAITHWORKS EDITORIAL & WRITING, INC./NANETTE THORSEN-SNIPES, PO Box 1596, Buford, GA 30515. Phone/fax (770) 945-3093. E-mail: nsnipes@bell-south.net. Website: www.faithworkseditorial.com. Freelance editor, copyeditor/line editor, proofreader, work-for-hire projects. Edits memoirs, picture books, devotions, juvenile or adult nonfiction, articles, and business. Author of more than five hundred articles/ stories, with stories in more than sixty compilation books. Member: The Christian PEN (Proofreaders & Editors Network) and CEC (Christian Editor Connection). Proofreader for *Cross & Quill* newsletter (CWFI) for two years. Proofreader for corporate newsletters for past ten years. More than twenty-five years writing experience. Ten years editing experience. Edit for ghostwriters, children's fiction writers, and writers of adult nonfiction. Not only have my clients self-published, but some of my clients have published with houses such as Zondervan, Tyndale, and Revell.

FICTION FIX-IT SHOP/MEREDITH EFKEN, Grandville MI 49418. E-mail: editor@fictionfixitshop.com. Website: www.fictionfixitshop.com. E-mail. GE/LC/writing coach. Will edit N/BP/QL. We specialize in editing and coaching for adult and YA novels. We opened in 2006 and have worked for published authors, beginning writers, and publishers. All our editors are also multi-published novelists, so we understand fiction writers' needs. We charge a flat rate—either as listed on Website for smaller projects or a project quote for full or partial manuscripts based on length and type of work needed. We use PayPal.

ANNA FISHEL EDITORIAL CONSULTANT, 3416 Hunting Creek Dr., Pfafftown NC 27040. (336) 416-7463. E-mail: awfishel@triad.rr.com. E-mail contact. GE/LC/CA/writing coach. Edits A/SS/N/NB/QL/JN/GB/D. Estimates offered. A professional editor since 1988; published author of 6 children's books. Usually charges by the hour, but with larger jobs, I offer a package fee.

B. C. HARVEY EDITORIAL SERVICES, 309 Carriage Place Ct., Decatur GA 30033. (404) 580-9431. E-mail: Boncah@aol.com. Website: www.BonnieHarvey.com. E-mail contact/deposit amount negotiable. GE/LC/GH/writing coach. Will edit N/NB/JN. Ph.D, University teacher (English); 25 years editing experience, author of 23 books. Charges by word count, by the page, or overall project (novels or non-fiction mss).

DR. DENNIS E. HENSLEY, 6824 Kanata Ct., Fort Wayne IN 46815-6388. (765) 998-5590. Fax (260) 485-9891. E-mail: dnhensley@hotmail.com. Website: www. dochensley.com. E-mail contact. GE/LC. Edits: A/SS/P/F/N/NB/BP/QL/JN/E/D/ business texts/comedy/academic articles/editorials/Op-Ed pieces/columns/speeches/ interviews. PhD in English; Taylor University professor of professional writing. Author of 54 books and 3,500 articles and short stories. Charges by the project. Rate sheet for SASE or by e-mail.

HESTERMAN CREATIVE, V. L. HESTERMAN, PHD, PO Box 6788, San Diego CA 92166. E-mail: vhes@earthlink.net. E-mail contact. GE/CA/SP/writing coach. Edits: A/SS/N/NB/BP/QL/BS/GB/E/D. Twenty-five years experience as book editor, author, writing teacher and coach, journalist, curriculum developer, photographer. Edits/ develops nonfiction material, including books, essays, memoirs, and photo books; works with publishers, agents, and writers as coauthor, line editor, or in editorial development. Will do line edits of fiction. Standard editorial rates; actual price quote depends on services needed after seeing sample pages of project. E-mail her what services you need; include phone number for follow-up call. Will give binding quote with sample of writing and query/proposal.

KATHY IDE EDITING, Brea CA. E-mail: Kathy@kathyide.com. Website: www. kathyide.com. E-mail contact. GE/LC/GH/CA/B/NL/SP/writing coach. Edits: A/ SS/F/N/NB/BP/QL/JN/BS/GB/TM/E/D/S. As author of *Proofreading Secrets of Best-Selling Authors,* she has written books, articles, short stories, devotionals, play scripts, and Sunday school curriculum. She has ghostwritten 10 nonfiction books and a 5-book novel series. Kathy is a full-time freelance editor/proofreader/mentor for new writers, established authors, and book publishers. Charges by the hour. Mention this listing to get a $5/hr. discount.

IZZY'S OFFICE/DIANE STORTZ, PO Box 31239, Cincinnati OH 45231. (513) 602-6720. E-mail: diane.stortz@gmail.com. Website: www.dianestortz.com. E-mail contact. GE/LC. Edits: NB/JN/PB/BS/GB/D. 20+ years in-house editing experience, former editorial director, 8 years freelancing. See website for client list and partial list of projects. Customized quote based on project needs.

JOY MEDIA SERVICES/JULIE-ALLYSON IERON, PO Box 1099, Park Ridge IL 60068. E-mail: joy@joymediaservices.com. Website: http://joymediaservices.com. Contact by e-mail. GE/LC/GH/CA/B/NL/SP/WS/writing coach. Edits: A/F/N/NB/ BP/QL/BS/GB/D. Master's degree in journalism and 25+ yrs. experience in Christian publishing. Specializes in Christian living, memoirs, Bible teaching, devotional, and Bible study genres. Charges $40 per hour; negotiates for larger projects. Half of fee up front.

JRH EDITING/JENNIFER HAMILTON, Coaching, Mentoring, in-depth edits/ critiques. Email me at jennifer@jrhediting.com. To see editing examples visit www. jrhediting.com. JRH EDITING, Where "Your Work is My Heart."

*KMB COMMUNICATIONS INC./LAURAINE SNELLING, PO Box 1530, Tehachapi CA 93581. (661) 823-0669. Fax (661) 823-9427. E-mail: TLsnelling@yahoo.com. Website: www.LauraineSnelling.com. E-mail contact. GE. Edits: SS/N/JN. Charges $100/hr. with $100 deposit, or by the project after discussion with client. Award-winning author of 70 books (YA and adult fiction, 2 nonfiction); teacher at writing conferences.

C.S. LAKIN, COPYEDITOR AND WRITING COACH/SUSANNE LAKIN, 335 Casa Loma Rd., Morgan Hill CA 95037. (530) 200-5466. E-mail: cslakin@gmail. com. Website: www.livewritethrive.com. E-mail contact. GE/LC/writing coach. Edits: A/SS/P/N/NB/BP/QL/JN/PB/BS/GB/E/D. Has years of editing experience for the book publishing industry. Specializes in contemporary fiction, fantasy, and nonfiction books, including those on biblical topics. I critique more than 200 mss a year, and have written and published 14 novels in various genres. I charge $60/hr. For all editing services. All editing services provided (charged by the hour) and specializing in manuscript critiques (charged by the page). Rates for various packages and types of projects can be found at www.critiquemymanuscript.com.

LOGOS WORD DESIGNS, LLC./LINDA L. NATHAN, PO Box 735, Maple Falls WA 98266-0735. (360) 599-3429. Fax (360) 392-0216. E-mail: linda@logosword. com. Website: www.logosword.com. E-mail contact. GE/LC/GH/B/NL/SP/publishing consultation/writing assistance/writes proposals/manuscript submission services. Edits: A/BP/BS/TM/E/D/F/JN/N/NB/PB/QL/SS/TM/YA/BPE/academic/legal/ apologetics/conservative political/textbooks/traditional & self-publishing consultation. Over 30 years experience in wide variety of areas, including publicity, postdoctoral; BA Psychology/some MA. Member: Editorial Freelance Assn.; NW Independent Editors Guild; American Christian Fiction Writers. All manner of author support services: Let us move you from rough draft to publishing and promotion. Quote per project. See rates at bottom of http://logosword.com/editing-services.html.

+NEXT INDEX SERVICES/JESSICA MCCURDY CROOKS, 6703 NW 7th St., Kln 2614, Miami FL 33126. (954) 406-5426. E-mail: nextindexservices@gmail.com. Website: www.next-index.com. E-mail contact. LC/GH/WS/other. Edits: A/SS/N/ NB/BS/TM/D. Charges by the page, hourly, and by the project—depending on what is best. Provides indexing services.

NOBLE CREATIVE, LLC/SCOTT NOBLE, PO Box 131402, St. Paul MN 55113. (651) 494-4169. E-mail: snoble@noblecreative.com. Website: noblecreative.com. E-mail contact. GE/LC/GH/CA/B/NL/SP/WS/writing coach. Edits: A/F/N/NB/ BP/QL/BS/GB/E/D. Award-winning writer and editor with more than 15 years experience working with clients on a variety of communication projects. Former Assistant ed. at Decision magazine and current executive editor of Refreshed magazine. Masters degree in Theological Studies. Charges by the hour or the project.

KAREN O'CONNOR COMMUNICATIONS/KAREN O'CONNOR, 10 Pajaro Vista Ct., Watsonville CA 95076. (831) 768-7335. E-mail: karen@karenoconnor.com.

Website: www.karenoconnor.com. E-mail. GE/LC/writing coach. Book proposal commentary/editing. Edits: A/F/NB/BP/QL. Forty years of professional published writing; 30 years mentorng writers; was a mentor for the Christian Writers Guild; freelance editor for Believers Press. Half-hour free evaluation before project details are agreed upon; $90/hr. or flat fee depending on project.

PERFECT WORD EDITING SERVICES/LINDA HARRIS, 4912 Copper Springs View, #J104, Colorado Springs CO 80916. (719) 464-5189. E-mail: lharris@perfectwordediting.com. Website: www.perfectWordEditing.com. E-mail contact. GE/LC/B/NL/SP. Edits: A/SS/P/F/N/NB/BP/QL/JN/PB/BS/GB/E/D. Over 35yrs. experience. Member of The Christian PEN and Christian Editor Connection. Charges $4-$25/page for new clients.

PICKY, PICKY INK/SUE MIHOLER, 1075 Willow Lake Road N., Keizer OR 97303-5790. (503) 393-3356. E-mail: suemiholer@comcast.net. E-mail contact. LC/B/SP/NL. Edits: A/NB/BS/D/GB/F. Charges $35 an hour or $50 for first 10 pages of a longer work; writer will receive a firm completed-job quote based on the first 10 pages. Freelance editor for several book publishers since 1998. References available. My approach to editing is reflected in my company's name.

+PREMISE WEB/EUGENE CLINGMAN, RR 1 Box 1540, Winona MO 65588. (417) 280-0311. Fax: (417) 812-6667. E-mail: books@4hisname.com. Website: www.4hisname.com.

PWC EDITING/PAUL W. CONANT, 527 Bayshore Pl., Dallas TX 75217-7755. Cell (214) 289-3397. E-mail: pwcediting@gmail.com. Website: www.pwc-editing.com. E-mail contact. LC/B/NL/SP/proofreading. Edits: A/SS/F/N/NB/BP/JN/PB/BS/TM/E/D/dissertations/ case studies, theses, magazines, textbooks. I have 19 years experience mainly with nonfiction, about 80% by Christian authors; I get leads from Kathy Ide's editor network and Thumbtack.com, as well as repeat customers. Magazine editing goes back to 1995; textbook editing to 2000; dissertation editing to 2002; nonfiction editing to 1995; technical editing to 2004. I charge by the hour. But I require a sample to edit plus a word count, so I can determine the length of the edit time to provide an accurate estimate. The process usually requires processing time for the author and a second pass to ensure finalization of the manuscript.

REVISION EDITING AGENCY/KIMBERLY SHUMATE, PO Box 40974, Eugene OR 97404. E-mail: revisioneditingagency.shumate@gmail.com. Website: www.revisioneditingagency.wordpress.com. E-mail submissions only. Copyediting and critique services for sample chapters, full-length mss, cover letters, book proposals, magazine articles, blog entries, etc. Fiction or nonfiction. Details on website.

RIGHT PRICE EDITING/AMANDA PRICE, 795 CR236, Eureka Springs AR 72631. E-mail: rightpriceediting@gmail.com. Website: www.rightpriceediting.com. E-mail contact. GE/LC. Edits: A/SS/N/NB/JN/BS/GB/E/D. I have worked as an editor with a wide range of publishers and authors for nine years, both in house and as a freelancer. I charge by the word, and the rate depends on the level of editing needed. I do a free five-page sample edit to give a recommendation for the editing level.

SCRIBBLE COMMUNICATIONS/BRAD LEWIS, Colorado Springs CO. (719) 649-4478. Fax (866) 542-5165. E-mail: brad.lewis@scribblecommunications.com. Website: www.scribblecommunications.com. E-mail contact. GE/LC. Charges by project, mutually agreed upon with publisher or author, and stated in editor/author agreement.

ANDY SCHEER EDITORIAL SERVICES, 5074 Plumstead Dr., Colorado Springs CO 80920. (719) 282-3729. E-mail: Andy@AndyScheer.com. Website: http:// AndyScheer.com. Prefers e-mail. Offers copyediting, substantive editing, and developmental editing for book-length projects. 30 years experience in Christian writing, editing, and publishing. Former editor-in-chief of Christian Writers Guild. Has served as a judge for national fiction and nonfiction contests. Per page rates posted on website.

+SCRIVEN COMMUNICATIONS/KATHIE NEE SCRIVEN, 22 Ridge Rd., #220, Greenbelt MD 20770. (240) 542-4602. E-mail: kathiescriven@yahoo.com. Call/e-mail contact. GE/LC/GH/WS/rewriting. Edits: A/SS/NB/BP/QL/BS/D/commentaries. Over 48 Christian book editing assignments completed, mostly nonfiction. Former editor of three Christian publications, public speaking on prayer, BS in communication/ journalism from Towson University. Improving copy and rewriting problem areas are my specialties, along with helping authors with their marketing and publicity strategies. Prices vary depending on project and turn-around time desired, but generally $25/hr.

SHIRL'S EDITING SERVICES/SHIRL THOMAS, 9379 Tanager Ave., Fountain Valley CA 92708-6557. (714) 968-5726. E-mail: Shirlth@verizon.net. Website: shirlthomas.com. E-mail (preferred)/write, and send material with $100 deposit. GE/ LC/GH/SP/review/rewriting. Edits: A/SS/P/F/N/NB/BP/QL/GB/D/greeting cards/ synopses. Consultation, $75/hr.; evaluation/critique, $75/hr.; mechanical editing, $65/ hr.; content editing/rewriting, $75/hr.

SILVER CROSS/KATHERINE SWARTS, Houston TX. (832) 573-9501. E-mail: ks@ houstonfreelancewriter.com. Website: www.houstonfreeciallancewriter.com. E-mail contact. GH/CA/B/NL/SP/WS. Edits: A/NB/E/D/WS/blogs/social media materials. Over 150 articles published in periodicals, including *The Lookout* and *Focus on the Family Clubhouse.* Over six years of blogging and social media experience. Charges by the project.

SALLY STUART, 15935 S.W. Greens Way, Tigard OR 97224. Phone/fax (503) 642-9844. E-mail: stuartcwmg@aol.com. Website: www.stuartmarket.com. Blog: www. christianwritersmarketplace.blogspot.com. Call/e-mail. GE/BCE/agent contracts. Edits: A/SS/N/NB/BP/GB/JN. No poetry or picture books. For books, send a copy of your book proposal: cover letter, chapter-by-chapter synopsis for nonfiction (5-page overall synopsis for fiction), and the first three chapters, double-spaced. Comprehensive publishing contract evaluation $75-200. Author of 38 books (including 26 editions of *The Christian Writer's Market Guide*), and her newest, *The Writing World Defined: A to Z*, plus 45+ years experience as a writer, teacher, marketing expert. Charges $40/hr. for critique; $45/hr. for phone/personal consultations.

TWEEN WATERS EDITORIAL/TERRI KALFAS, PO Box 1233, Broken Arrow OK 74013-1233. (918) 346-7960. E-mail: terri@terrikalfas.com. E-mail contact. GE/LC/ GH/CA/NL/SP/BCE/writing coach. Edits: A/N/NB/JN/BS/GB/D/project management/book doctoring. Multiple editorial and freelance writing services. Over 25 years writing and publishing experience. Available as conference speaker and workshop teacher. Rates negotiated on a per project basis and are dependent on amount of work required.

PEN-SOULS. (prayer and support group, not a critique group). Conducted entirely by e-mail. Contact: Janet Ann Collins, Grass Valley CA. E-mail: jan@janetanncollins.com. Membership (12) open by application.

THE VERSATILE PEN/CHRISTY PHILLIPPE, 8816 S. 73rd East Ave, Tulsa OK 74133. (918) 284-7635. E-mail: christy6871@aol.com. Website: www.theversatilepen. com. Prefers e-mail contact. GE/LC/GH/B/NL. Edits: A/SS/N/NB/JN/BS/GB/D. Has 20+ years editing experience in the Christian publishing industry, as a freelancer, managing editor, senior editor, and editorial director. Many books edited or ghostwritten have been listed on the *New York Times* best-seller lists. Have experience ghostwriting Christian nonfiction and inspirational/gift books. Have edited both fiction and nonfiction. Have strong skills in back cover copy writing, as well as compilations and Bible study/curriculum development. Reasonable rates and fast turnaround!

LEE WARREN COMMUNICATIONS, Omaha NE. E-mail: leewarrenjr@outlook. com. Website: www.leewarren.info/editing. E-mail contact. GE/LC. Edits: A/F/N/ NB/BP/D. Has written 6 nonfiction royalty books and hundreds of articles in newspapers, magazines, and websites. Also edited and critiqued more than 100 fiction and nonfiction manuscripts for self-publishing company and edited/critiqued another 50 manuscripts or proposals for a manuscript-critique service. Charges by the hour.

JAMES WATKINS. E-mail: jim@jameswatkins.com. Website: www.jameswatkins. com. E-mail contact. GE/LC/GH/WS. Edits: A/NB/BP/QL/BS/D/S. Award-winning author of 16 books, 2,000+ articles, associate acquisitions editor with Wesleyan Publishing House; winner of four editing and 2 book awards. 30+ years experience. Charge $2/pg. for critique, market suggestions; $5/pg. for content editing; $15/pg. for rewriting/ghosting; $60/hr. for consulting.

WINGS UNLIMITED EDITORIAL SERVICES/CRISTINE BOLLEY, 712 N Sweet Gum Ave., Broken Arrow OK 74012-2156. (918) 250-9239. Fax (888) 446-1174. E-mail: WingsUnlimited@aol.com. E-mail contact. GE/writing coach. Edits: NB/D/ sermons to books and conceptual content design. Specializes in turning sermon series into books for classic libraries. Author/coauthor/ghostwriter of 30+ titles. Over 30 years experience in development of bestselling titles for major Christian publishing houses. All fees negotiated in advance: developmental edits (format/house-style/clarity) average $2,500/project. Additional ghostwriting fees are negotiable in advance of beginning the project.

WORDS FOR ALL REASONS/ELIZABETH ROSIAN, 102 Rustic Ave., Johnstown PA 15904-2122. (814) 255-4351. E-mail: louiserosian@gmail.com. Website: www. savingsense2.wordpress.com. GE/LC/GH/CA. Edits A/SS/P/F/N/NB/BP/QL/BS/ GB/E/D. More than 35 years experience writing, teaching, and editing; more than 1,000 published works, plus inspirational novel, how-to book, and 6 chapbooks. Rate sheet on website.

+WORDWISE MEDIA SERVICES, 4083 Avenue L, Suite 255, Lancaster CA, 93536. (866) 739-0440. E-mail: submit@wordwisemedia.com. Website: www.wordwisemedia. com. Copyediting or critique, any genre except poetry or picture books, ten years experience. More info on website.

THE WRITE EDITOR/ERIN K. BROWN, 1479 Summerdale Rd., Corvallis MT 59828. (406) 961-5546. E-mail: thewriteeditor@gmail.com. Website: www.write-editor.net. E-mail contact. GE/LC/B/NL/SP. Edits: A/SS/N/NB/BP/QL/JN/BS/ GB/E/D/curriculum. Offers e-book conversion, critiques. Professional freelance writer since 2001. Has a certificate in editorial practices: graduate school, USDA, Washington DC; Christy Award judge 2006–2013; member of American Christian Fiction Writers; The Christian PEN; coauthor of *The Lost Coin.* Fee depends on length of ms and level of edit. We offer a free sample edit, from which the author can evaluate the edit, and I can determine the level of edit required, length of turnaround time, and project fee.

WRITE HIS ANSWER MINISTRIES/MARLENE BAGNULL, LittD, 951 Anders Rd., Lansdale PA 19446. Phone/fax (484) 991-8581. E-mail: mbagnull@aol.com. Website: www.writehisanswer.com. E-mail contact. GE/LC. Edits: A/SS/N/NB/BP/BS/D. Author of 8 books, over 1,000 sales to Christian periodicals, 31 years directing Greater Philly Christian Writers Conference, 18 years directing Colorado Christian Writers Conference, honorary Litt.D for my work encouraging and equipping Christian writers. Charges by the hour or set fee for entire project.

WRITE NOW SERVICES/KAREN APPOLD, Macungie PA 18062 (610) 351-5400. Fax (917) 793-8609. E-mail: KAppold@msn.com. Website: www.writenowservices. com. E-mail. GE/LC/GH/CA/B/NL/SP/WS. Edits: A/SS/BP/QL/BS/TM/E/D/S/ write articles. I have worked in the editorial field since 1993, which included serving as the editor of a daily newspaper and editor of a home magazine. I have owned a full-time home-based editorial consulting business since 2003. Clients include an extensive range of non-profit organizations, businesses and media in the fields of medicine/health, management, career building, home remodeling, real estate investing and business. Rates determined after free evaluation of project/charges per hour, per project, or by word.

WRITER'S EDGE SERVICE, E-mail: info@writersedgeservice.com. Website: www. writersedgeservice.com. For over 20 years, the Writer's Edge Service has been a method of effective communication between writers and major traditional Christian publishers. Writer's Edge, utilizing professional editors with many years of experience in working with major Christian publishers, evaluate, screen, and expose potential books to traditional Christian publishing companies. Because most traditional publishers no longer accept unsolicited manuscripts and no longer sift through what used to be called the slush pile, new or relatively unknown writers have little chance to be seen by a traditional publisher unless they have a credible literary agent. Writer's Edge Service, in full cooperation with more than 75 traditional royalty-based Christian publishers, gives writers another option. The acquisition editors of these companies have agreed to view relevant manuscripts that make the cut at Writer's Edge because they know they have been carefully screened and evaluated before being passed to them for consideration. Over the years, hundreds of authors have been successfully published because of Writer's Edge Service. Standard Fee is $99. See website for instructions. *Note:* We no longer accept manuscripts by regular mail. All subscribers must go to the website, click on the "How to Submit a Book" and follow the step-by-step instructions.

THE WRITE SPOT/ARLENE KNICKERBOCKER, Where Quality and Economy Unite, 8470 N Henderson Rd., Davison MI 48423. (810) 793-0316. E-mail: writer@ thewritespot.org. Website: http://thewritespot.org. E-mail. GE/LC/B/NL/SP/classes and speaking/writing coach. Edits: A/SS/P/NB/BS/D. More than 100 published credits since 1996; taught writing classes for 13 years; have edited professionally for seven years. Charges by the hour; prices on website.

WRITER'S RELIEF, INC./RONNIE L. SMITH, 207 Hackensack Street, Wood-Ridge NJ 07075. (866) 405-3003. Fax (201) 641-1253. E-mail: info@wrelief.com. Website: www.WritersRelief.com. Call or e-mail. LC/NL/targeting submissions. Proofs: A/SS/P/F/N/NB/JN/E. Twenty years experience as an author's submission service. Subscribe to their e-publication, Submit Write Now!: Leads & Tips for Creative Writers. Contact for rates.

WRITE THE FIRST TIME EDITING SERVICE/CAROL E. SCOTT, PO Box 105, Niles OH 44446-0105. (330) 240-2313. E-mail: carolscotte@yahoo.com. Call/$50 deposit. GE/LC. Edits: A/SS/P/JN/BS/D. All material should be on a flash drive or CD. Retired teacher of 30 years. 10 years editing experience. Charges $5/page.

WRITING CAREER COACH/TIFFANY COLTER, 14665 Fike Rd., Riga MI 49276. (517) 936-5896. E-mail: Tiffcolter@gmail.com. Website: www.WritingCareerCoach. com. E-mail contact. GE/LC/GH/CA/SP/WS/writing coach. Edits: A/SS/N/NB/ QL/JN/BS/E/D/publishing plans/writing business plan consulting/time management coaching/consulting. I have been a content editor and writing coach for more than 7 years. My clients include award-winning writers, self-published and traditionally published novelists, as well as business consultants, speakers, teachers, and non-writers with a story to tell. I have judged for top writing contests across the country for published and unpublished writers. I served as judge for ACFW's writing contests for more than five years as well as the top contest in Christian fiction twice. In addition to fiction, I've judged poetry and essay contests. I graduated with my BA in 1998 with a summa cum laude distinction. References available upon request, or simply check my LinkedIn page for a large number of endorsements. I charge 1.2 cents/word for content edits or proofreads. $.07/word for rewriting. $.10/word for developmental editing. Phone coaching is $65/hr personalized. (All amounts in USD. I work with many intl. clients as well.)

YOUR TIME TO WRITE/MARY BUSHA, 4054 Horton Rd., Jackson MI 49201. (517)416-0133. E-mail: yourtimetowrite@gmail.com. E-mail contact. GE/LC/BCE/ writing coach. Edits: A/NB/BP/QL/BS/D. I offer workshops for beginner, intermediate, and experienced writers, specifically on what to do if they have book ideas and/or what to do once their mss are written. I have over 35 years experience in publishing, from small-town weekly newspaper to managing the editorial department of a daily newspaper. In book publishing, I have worked with hundreds of writers over the years, helping them to get their words in print, either as an editor, writing coach, publisher, or literary agent. I charge a page fee for reading and evaluating mss. I charge hourly for editing. E-mail me for rates.

CANADIAN/FOREIGN

AOTEAROA EDITORIAL SERVICES/VENNESSA NG, PO Box 228, Oamaru 9444, New Zealand. +64224346995. E-mail: editor@aotearoaeditorial.com. Website: www. aotearoaeditorial.com. E-mail contact. GE/LC/writing coach. Edits: SS/N. Ten+ years critiquing experience. Page rates vary depending on project: start from US $2/critique, $2/basic proofread, and $4/copyedit. (Rates are in US dollars and can be paid by PayPal or Western Union.)

AY'S EDIT/ALAN YOSHIOKA, PhD, PO Box 27586, Vancouver BC, Canada V5Z 4M4. (416) 531-1857. E-mail: ay1@aysedit.com. Website: www.aysedit.com. E-mail contact. GE/LC/B/NL/SP/WS. Edits: A/NB/TM/E/D. Certified proofreader and copy editor (Editors' Association of Canada since 1999). Recognized expertise in orthodox Christian responses to same-sex attraction. Charges hourly or by word count.

CHESTNUT LANE CREATIVE/ADELE SIMMONS, PO Box 116 Stn Main, Whitby ON L1N 5R7, Canada. (905) 263-4211. E-mail: ChrstnutLaneCreative@bell.net. Website: AdeleSimmons.WordPress.com. E-mail contact. GE/LC/CA/B/NL/SP/ substantive editing/rewriting/writing/writing coach. Edits: A/SS/P/F/NB/JN/PB/ BS/GB/TM/E/D/S/songwriting. Over 40 years experience in most genres, with focus on nonfiction, marketing, books. Shortlisted for the prestigious Tom Fairley Award of Excellence in Editing in Canada 2013. Charges hourly or by the project.

DARS CORRECTIONS/DARLENE OAKLEY, #1- 136 Page St., St. Catherines ON L2R 4A9, Canada. ((905) 397-8575. E-mail: darlene@darscorrections.com. Website: www.darscorrections.com. E-mail contact. GE/LC/NL/SP/writing coach. Edits: A/ SS/N/NB/BP/QL/BS/E/D. I charge per word. Specific rates are indicated on my Website. I offer payment-plan options as well for all my writers if that makes it easier for them to manage the cost of the edit.

DORSCH EDITORIAL/AUDREY DORSCH, 90 Ling Road, PH 302, Toronto ON M1E 4Y3, Canada. (416) 439-4320. E-mail: audrey@dorschedit.ca. Website: www. dorschedit.ca. E-mail contact. GE/LC. Will edit: N/NB. BRE, Honours Diploma in Journalism Administration. More than 35 years of experience, first in newspaper writing, then magazine and book editing, then freelance book editing. I look at each manuscript and prepare a project-specific quote.

EDITORIAL SERVICES/AIMEE REID, 1063 King St. W, Suite 301, Hamilton ON L8S 4S3, Canada. (905) 317-9234. E-mail: areid@aimeereid.com. Website: aimeereid. com, and aimeereidbooks.com. E-mail contact. GE/LC/SP/(developmental, substantive, stylistic editing). Edits: A/SS/NB/JN/PB/BS/D. B.A. In English; editor of curriculum for all ages for Mennonite Publishing Network and Brethren Press; freelance writer; children's writer published with Penguin Random House. I charge per hour and provide an estimate based on a sample of the writing.

WENDY SARGEANT, 21 Carinyan Dve, Birkdale, Queensland 4159, Australia. Phone: 0498026980. E-mail: wordfisher52@gmail.com. E-mail contact. GE/LC/GH/CA/ writing coach. Edits: A/SS/F/N/NB/BP/QL/JN/PB/BS/GB/TM/E/D/S. Copywriting. Special interests: technical material, business humor, children's books, educational books (primary, secondary, tertiary, and above), fiction, history, legal. Manuscript assessor and instructional designer with The Writing School. Award-winning author published in major newspapers and magazines. Editing educational manuals. Project officer and instructional designer for Global Education Project, United Nationals Assoc. Information specialist for Australian National University. Charges $20/hr.

11

Publicity Services

+CREATIVE ENTERPRISES STUDIO, PO Box 224, Fort Worth TX 76095. (817) 312-7393. Fax: (817) 685-7393. E-mail: ACreativeShop@aol.com. Website: http://CreativeEnterprisesStudio.com. Contact: Mary Hollingsworth.

+INSPIRED AUTHORS PRESS, LLC., 1000 Pearl Rd., Pleasantville TN 37033. (931) 593-2484. Fax: (931) 593-2494. E-mail: mel@inspiredauthorspress.com. Website: www.inspiredauthorspress.com. Details on website.

+LITFUSE PUBLICITY GROUP, 19011 – 8th Ave. NE, Shoreline WA 98155. (206) 947-3743. E-mail: info@litfusegroup.com. Website: www.litfusegroup.com. Contact: Amy Lathrup. Specializes in all genres of Christian fiction and nonfiction, including Christian living and devotionals. Fees vary by services: from a 3-week blog tour to a 6-month publicity campaign (we also do social media campaigns, Facebook parties, and webcasts). Previous clients include HarperCollins, David C. Cook, Focus on the Family, Moody, Revell, Tricia Goyer, Suzanne Woods Fisher, Cecil Murphey, and Cynthia Ruchti. Hits in *USA Today*, FOX News, CNN/HLN, *The Christian Post, 700 Club*, and *The Harvest Show*. Prefers e-mail contact.

+MCCLURE MUNTSINGER PUBLIC RELATIONS, PO Box 804, Franklin TN 37065. (615) 595-8321. Fax: (615)595-8322. E-mail: info@mmpublicrelations.com. Website: www.mmpublicrelations.com. Specializes in nonfiction, celebrity, sports, memoir, and multi-media. We work with debut authors, pastor-authors, routine bestsellers, national figures, but typically not self-published authors. Cost is tailored to each campaign and book. Former clients include all major publishers, including HarperCollins, David C. Cook, Tyndale, and Crossway. We specialize in knowing how to place religious books in both Christian media and general market media, traditional outlets and online. Contact by e-mail.

+MEDIA CONNECT, 301 E. 57th St., New York NY 10022. (212)593-6337. E-mail: SharonF@finnpartners.com. Contact: Sharon Farnell by e-mail. Specializes in a variety of nonfiction memoirs, Christian living, business, health, sports, cookbooks, interior design, family/parenting, etc. Also covers select fiction titles. We work with debut authors, as well as established writers and national figures and celebrities. We work with the Christian media as well as general-market media. We tailor cost to each campaign, depending on the services recommended/selected. Previous clients include Thomas Nelson, Zondervan, Bethany House, B&H Publishing, Col. Oliver North, Rebecca St. James, Sheila Walsh, Dr. Kevin Leman, Jenifer Sands, Wanda Brunstetter, and Anne Graham Lotz. Some hits include Fox News Channel, CNN, *Good Morning America, The Today Show,* various shows on ESPN, *Glenn Beck, Mark Levin, Dennis Miller, Hannity, 700 Club, USA Today, Scholastic Parent, Harvard Business Review, The Christian Post, HomeLife,* and *ParentLife.*

+ROCKY MOUNTAIN MEDIA GROUP. (719) 494-3389. E-mail: info@rm2g.com. Website: http://rm2g.com. Contact: Jeff or Julie Abel.

+ROUTE 1 MANUSCRIPTS AND PUBLICITY, 803 E. Sandusky Ave., Bellefontaine OH 43311. (937) 407-7983. E-mail: sharynkopf@gmail.com. Website: www.route1-manuscripts.com. Specializes in fiction and nonfiction. Open to author at any stage, but focusing on debut authors at this time. A la carte options starting at $500. Also does campaigns from 1–6 months at $1,500–$2,500/month. Longer commitments contracted on a retainer. We are a new business taking over for Kathy Carlton Willis of KCW Communications. Prefers contact by e-mail.

12

Christian Literary Agents

Asking editors and other writers is a great way to find a good, reliable agent. You might also want to visit www.agentresearch.com and www.sfwa.org/beware/agents for tips. For a database of more than 500 agencies, go to www.literaryagent.com.

The site for the Association of Authors' Representatives (www.aaronline.org) carries a list of agents who don't charge fees, except for office expenses. Their website will also provide information on how to receive a list of approved agents. Some listings below indicate which agents belong to the Association of Authors' Representatives, Inc. Those members have subscribed to a code of ethics. Lack of such a designation, however, does not indicate the agent is unethical; most Christian agents are not members.

(*) before a listing indicates unconfirmed or no information update.

(+) before a listing indicates it's a new listing this year.

ALIVE LITERARY AGENCY (formerly Alive Communications) 7680 Goddard St., Ste. 200, Colorado Springs CO 80920. (719) 260-7080. E-mail: bhaigh@alivecom.com. Agents: Rick Christian, Bryan Norman, Lisa Jackson, and Andrea Heinecke. Submit to: submissions@aliveliterary.com. Well known in the industry. Estab. 1989. Represents 125+ clients. Member of AAR. Handles adult novels and nonfiction, and crossover books. Nonfiction books 50%, novels 40%, juvenile books (and miscellaneous) 10%. Be advised that his agency works primarily with well-established, best-selling, and career authors. Always looking for a breakout, blockbuster author with genuine talent.

> **Contact:** By e-mail. No simultaneous submissions. Responds in 6-8 wks. to referrals only. May not respond to unsolicited submissions.
> **Sold to:** Many Christian publishers.
> **Commission:** 15%
> **Fees:** Only extraordinary costs with client's pre-approval; no review/reading fee.
> **Tips:** "Rewrite and polish until the words on the page shine. Endorsements and great connections may help, provided you can write with power and passion. Network with publishing professionals by making contacts, joining critique groups, and attending writer's conferences in order to make personal connections and to get feedback."

AMBASSADOR AGENCY, PO Box 50358, Nashville TN 37205. (615) 370-4700. E-mail: info@AmbassadorAgency.com. Website: www.AmbassadorAgency.com. Agent: Wes Yoder. Estab. 1973. Recognized in the industry. Represents 25-30 clients. Open to unpublished authors and new clients. Handles adult nonfiction and fiction, crossover books, and e-books. No sci-fi or medical. No extra fees.

> **Contact:** By e-mail. Responds in 4-6 wks.
> **Sold to:** All A-level publishers.
> **Commission:** 15%; foreign 15% plus expenses.

+BANNER SERVICES, LLC, PO Box 1828, Winter Park CO 80482. (719) 200-2580. E-mail: Mike@MikeLoomis.CO. Website: www.mikeloomis.CO. Agent:

Mike Loomis. Estab. 2009. Open to new clients; specializing in unpublished authors. Represents 12 clients. Handles Christian nonfiction, business nonfiction, and crossover books. Responds in 4 wks.

Contact: E-mail.
Commission: 15%
Fees: None for representation.
Tips: Especially open to new/aspiring authors.

BOOKS & SUCH LITERARY MANAGEMENT, 52 Mission Circle, Ste. 122, PMB 170, Santa Rosa CA 95409-5370. E-mail: representation@booksandsuch.com. Website: www.booksandsuch.com. Agents: Janet Kobobel Grant, founder and president; Wendy Lawton, vice president; Rachelle Gardner, agent; Rachel Kent, agent; Mary Keeley, agent. Well recognized in industry. Estab. 1996. Member of AAR, ACFW, CBA. Represents more than 250 clients. Open to new or unpublished authors (with recommendation only). Handles fiction and nonfiction for all ages except children's, and general market books.

Contact: e-query; no phone query. Accepts simultaneous submissions. Responds within 6 weeks, if interested.
Commission: 15%. Foreign 20%, if foreign rights agent is involved.
Sold to: 17 Christian publishers.
Fees: None.
Comment: "We have established a tight-knit community among our clients and offer them training in marketing, their careers, and the writing craft. Despite being one of the largest Christian literary agencies, we work hard to be nimble in an age of publishing disruption and to think long-term for our clients as we help to build their careers."
Tips: "We concentrate our efforts on adult manuscripts, but we represent a small number of authors who write teen materials and an even smaller number who write middle grade or children's. None of our agents represent speculative fiction."

CURTIS BROWN LTD., 10 Astor Pl., New York NY 10003-6935. (212) 473-5400. Website: www.curtisbrown.com. Agents: Maureen Walters, Laura Blake Peterson, and Ginger Knowlton. Member AAR. General agent; handles religious/inspirational novels for all ages, adult nonfiction, and crossover books. Guidelines at: www.curtisbrown. com/submissions.php.

Contact: Query with SASE; no fax/e-query. Submit outline or sample chapters. Responds in 6-8 wks. Fees: Charges for photocopying and some postage.

KEITH CARROLL, AGENT, PO Box 428, Newburg PA 17257. (717) 423-6621. Fax (717) 423-6944. E-mail: keith@christianliteraryagent.com. Website: www.christianlit-eraryagent.com. Estab. 2009, functioned as an author coach since 2000. Represents 94 clients. New clients welcome. Specializes in helping authors prepare for publication, as a coach. Handles adult and teen nonfiction, adult fiction, picture books, e-books, crossover books. Accepts simultaneous submissions. Responds in 5-8 weeks.

Contact: Phone and e-mail.
Commission: 10%
Fees: Small fee for introductory consultation with unpublished authors, which includes a review/analysis of author's material, a two-hour personal phone call to advise and recommend regarding publishability.

CREDO COMMUNICATIONS, 3148 Plainfield Ave. NE, Ste. 111, Grand Rapids MI 49525. (616) 363-2686. E-mail: connect@credocommunications.net. Website: www.

credocommunications.net. Agents: Timothy J. Beals, founder and pres. (tim@credo-communications.net), open to new clients; Ann Byle (ann@credocommunications.net), open to new clients; Karen E. Neumair (karen@credocommunications.net), open to new clients; David Sanford, not accepting new clients. Recognized in the industry. Estab. 2005. Represents 70 clients. Handles novels and nonfiction for all ages, picture books, e-books, crossover books. Have current contracts with 40+ publishers. New clients by referral only. Other services offered: coaching for self-published authors on production, marketing, sales, and distribution.

    Contact: E-mail connect@credocommunications.net. Accepts simultaneous submissions. Responds in 4 wks.

    Sold to: 26 Christian publishers.

    Commission: 15%; foreign varies.

    Fees: None.

    Tips: "Seeking creative fiction and thoughtful nonfiction by established authors.

THE BLYTHE DANIEL AGENCY INC., PO Box 64197, Colorado Springs CO 80962-4197. (719) 213-3427. E-mail: blythe@theblythedanielagency.com. jessica@theblythedanielagency.com. Website: www.theblythedanielagency.com. Agents: Blythe Daniel, Jessica Kirkland (fiction). Recognized in the industry. Estab. 2005. Represents 75+ clients. Open to unpublished authors with an established platform/network and previously published authors. Handles inspirational novels, adult nonfiction, young adult fiction/nonfiction, limited children's books, gift books, e-book, screenplays, TV/movie scripts, crossover books, secular books. Represents bestselling authors and ACFW awarded authors. Accepting all fiction except sci-fi, biblical, or mystery.

    Contact: By e-mail or mail. Accepts simultaneous submissions. Responds in 8 weeks.

    Commission: 15%; Foreign 15%

    Sold to: Most all of the CBA publishing houses and some general market publishers.

    Fees: None.

    Also: Provides publicity and marketing campaigns to clients as a separate service from literary representation.

    Tips: "Our agency looks for authors with more than one book potential in his or her category. We look to build career authors not just publish one book. We are acquiring books in Christian living, spiritual growth, current events, inspirational, business/leadership, church leadership, marriage, parenting, apologetics, political, social issues, women's issues, new voices, ministry leaders, pastors, journalists, and other professionals, and some gift and cookbooks."

DANIEL LITERARY GROUP, 1701 Kingsbury Dr., Ste. 100, Nashville TN 37215. No phone calls. E-mail: submissions@danielliterarygroup.com. Website: www.danielliterarygroup.com. Agent: Greg Daniel. Estab. 2007. Recognized in the industry. Represents 50 clients. Open to new clients. Handles adult nonfiction, gift books, crossover and secular books. Specializes in thoughtful nonfiction in both the CBA and general market.

    Contact: E-mail only. Accepts simultaneous submissions. Responds in 3-4 wks.

    Sold to: 16 Christian publishers.

    Commission: 15%; foreign 20% if sub-agent is used.

    Fees: None.

DYSTEL & GODERICH LITERARY MANAGEMENT INC., 1 Union Square W., Ste. 904, New York NY 10003. (212) 627-9100. Fax (212) 627-9313. E-mail: Miriam@

dystel.com. Website: www.dystel.com. Agents: Jane Dystel, Miriam Goderich, Stacey Glick, Michael Bourret, Jim McCarthy, Lauren Abramo, Jessica Papin, John Rudolph, Mike Hoogland, Rachel Stout, and Sharon Pelletier. Each agent has a separate e-mail address on Website. Prefers e-queries. Estab. 1994. Recognized in the industry. Represents 5-10 religious book clients. Open to unpublished authors and new clients. Handles fiction and nonfiction for adults, gift books, general books, crossover books. Member AAR. Submission guidelines at: http://www.dystel.com/submission-requirements.

   Contact: Query letter with bio. Brief e-query; no simultaneous queries.
   Responds to queries in 3-5 wks.; submissions in 2 mos.
   Commission: 15%; foreign 19%.
   Fees: Photocopying is author's responsibility.
   Tips: "Send a professional, well-written query to a specific agent."

FINE PRINT LITERARY MANAGEMENT, 115 W. 29th St., 3rd Fl., New York NY 10001. (212) 279-1282. Fax (212) 279-0927. E-mail: peter@fineprintlit.com. Website: www.fineprintlit.com. Agents: Peter Rubie, Stephany Evans, and 4 other agents. Open to unpublished authors and new clients. General agent. Handles adult religion/spirituality nonfiction for teens and adults.

   Contact: Query/SASE; accepts e-query. Responds in 2-3 mos.
   Commission: 15%; foreign 20%.

GARY D. FOSTER CONSULTING, 733 Virginia Ave., Van Wert OH 45891. (419) 238-4082. E-mail: gary@garydfoster.com. Website: www.garydfoster.com. Agent: Gary Foster. Estab. 1989. Represents 50+ clients. Recognized in the industry. Open to unpublished authors and frequently open to new clients. Handles religious/inspirational adult novels and nonfiction, teen/YA nonfiction, gift books, crossover books, teen/YA novels. Prefers overtly Christian content. Accepts simultaneous submissions.

   Contact: E-mail. Responds usually in 1-3 wks.
   Commission: 15%. Foreign varies.
   Fees: Charges a nominal fee upon signing of representation agreement.
   Sold to: 10 Christian publishers.
   Tip: "Open to talented first-time authors, CBA or ECPA."

SAMUEL FRENCH INC., 235 Park Ave. South, 5th Floor, New York NY 10003. (212) 206-8990. Fax (212) 206-1429. E-mail: publications@samuelfrench.com. Website: www.samuelfrench.com, www.bakersplays.com. Agent: Amy Rose Marsh. Estab. 1830. Open to new clients. Handles rights to some religious/inspirational stage plays. Owns a subsidiary company that also publishes religious plays.

   Contact: See website for full submission information. Accepts simultaneous submissions; responds in 10 wks.
   Commission: Varies.
   Fees: None.

GLOBAL TALENT REPS, INC., 125 Corsair Cir., Parker CO 80014. E-mail: Info@ globaltalentreps.com. Website: www.globaltalentreps.com. Agent: Andrew J. Whelchel III (a.whelchel@globaltalentreps.com). Estab. 2001. Open to unpublished authors and new clients. Represents 5 clients. Handles religious/inspirational novels for adults, nonfiction for adults, screenplays, TV/movie scripts, e-books, and crossover books. Please no romance. Seeking humor, parenting, edgy Christian fiction like "Cursebreaker," and low-budget scripts $5M and under.

Contact: Query by e-mail (use online form). Accepts simultaneous submissions; responds in 8 wks.
Commission: 10% film; 15% books; 5% scouting; foreign 10% plus foreign sales agents fees, if any.
Fees: None.

SANFORD J. GREENBURGER ASSOCIATES INC., 55 Fifth Ave., New York NY 10003. (212) 206-5600. Fax (212) 463-8718. Agents have their own e-mail addresses (on Website). Website: www.greenburger.com. Agents: Heide Lange, Dan Mandel, Matthew Bialer, Brenda Bowen, Faith Hamlin, Courtney Miller-Callihan, Nicholas Ellison, Chelsea Lindman, Lindsay Ribar, Rachael Dillon Fried, and Thomas Miller. Estab. 1945. Represents 500 clients. Open to unpublished authors and new clients. General agent; handles adult religious/inspirational nonfiction. Member of AAR.
Contact: Query/proposal/3 sample chapters by mail with SASE, or e-mail. Accepts simultaneous queries. Responds in 6-8 wks. to query; 2 mos. to ms.
Commission: 15%; foreign 20%.
Fees: Charges for photocopying and foreign submissions.

HARTLINE LITERARY AGENCY, 123 Queenston Dr., Pittsburgh PA 15235. (412) 829-2483. Fax (888) 279-6007. E-mail: joyce@hartlineliterary.com. Website: www. hartlineliterary.com. Blog: www.hartlineliteraryagency.blogspot.com. Agents: Joyce A. Hart, only authors met at conferences or referrals; Terry Burns, open to new clients (terry@heartlineliterary.com); Diana Flegal, only authors met at conferences or referrals (diana@hartlineliterary.com); Andy Scheer, not open to new clients (andy@hartline-literary.com); Linda Glaz, open to new clients (linda@hartlineliterary.com); Jim D. Hart, open to new clients; Recognized in industry. Estab. 1992. Represents 300 clients. Member of AAR. Handles teen/YA and adult nonfiction, teen/YA and adult novels, secular books, crossover books. No poetry, children's books, fantasy, or science fiction. If crossover or secular, they must be clean, family-friendly books, with no swearing or graphic sex.
Contact: E-mail/phone/fax/letter; e-mail preferred. Accepts simultaneous submissions; responds in 6-8 wks.
Sold to: 12 Christian publishers.
Commission: 15%; foreign 15%; films 20% and 25%.
Fees: None.
Tips: "Please look at our website before submitting. Guidelines are listed, along with detailed information about each agent. Be sure to include your biography and publishing history with your proposal. The author/agent relationship is a team effort. Working together we can make sure your manuscript gets the exposure and attention it deserves."

THE JEFF HERMAN AGENCY, LLC, PO Box 1522, 29 Park St., Stockbridge MA 01262. (413) 298-0077. E-mail: Jeff@jeffherman.com. Website: www.jeffherman.com. Agent: Jeff Herman. Estab. 1987. Recognized in the industry. Represents 20+ clients with religious books. Open to unpublished authors and new clients. Handles adult nonfiction, general books, crossover, e-books.
Contact: Query by mail/SASE, or by e-mail. Accepts simultaneous submissions and e-queries. Responds in 4 wks.
Commission: 15%; foreign 15% or 10% when sub-agent is used.
Fees: None.
Tips: "I love a good book from the heart. Let your mind follow your heart."

HIDDEN VALUE GROUP, 27758 Santa Margarita Pkwy., #361, Mission Viejo CA 92691. E-mail: njernigan@hiddenvaluegroup.com. Submit to: bookquery@hiddenvaluegroup.com. Website: www.HiddenValueGroup.com. Agents: Jeff Jernigan and Nancy Jernigan. Estab. 2001. Recognized in the industry. Represents 18 clients with religious books. Open to previously published authors only. Handles adult fiction and nonfiction, teen/YA nonfiction (few), picture books, gift books, e-books, and crossover books. No poetry, articles, or short stories.

> **Contact:** E-mail. Accepts simultaneous submissions. Responds in 4-6 wks.
> **Commission:** 15%; foreign 15%.
> **Fees:** None.
> **Tips:** "Looking for romance and suspense fiction projects as well as women's nonfiction. Make sure the proposal includes author bio, 2 sample chapters, and manuscript summary. Marketing plan to promote your project is a must."

HORNFISCHER LITERARY MANAGEMENT, PO Box 50544, Austin TX 78763. E-mail: queries@hornfischerlit.com or jim@hornfischerlit.com. Website: www.hornfischerlit.com. Agent: James D. Hornfischer. Estab. 2001. Represents 45 clients. Open to unpublished authors and new clients (with referrals from clients). Considers simultaneous submissions. Responds in 1 mo. General agent; handles adult religious/inspirational nonfiction. Submission guidelines at: http://www.hornfischerlit.com/Hornfischer_Literary_Management_LP/Submissions.html.

> **Contact:** E-query only for fiction; query or proposal for nonfiction (proposal package, outline, and 2 sample chapters). Considers simultaneous queries. Responds to queries in 5-6 wks.
> **Commission:** 15%; foreign 25%.

D. C. JACOBSON & ASSOCIATES, 3689 Carman Drive, Suite 200 C, Lake Oswego OR 97035. (503) 850-4800. Fax (503) 850-4805. E-mail: submissions@dcjacobson.com. Website: www.dcjacobson.com. Agents: Don Jacobson, Jenni Burke, Blair Jacobson, Heidi Mitchell, Tawny Johnson. Estab. 2006. Represents 100+ clients. Recognized in the industry (former owner of Multnomah Publishers; multiple best-selling books). Open to unpublished or self-published authors and new clients. Handles adult and teen religious/inspirational novels and nonfiction, memoirs, crossover books, children's books.

> **Contact:** Submissions and queries through website form only. Accepts simultaneous submissions; responds in 8 wks.
> **Commission:** 15%.
> **Fees:** No reading fees.
> **Tips:** "Looking for fresh writing that will redeem culture and renew the church. Please review our website thoroughly before submitting your proposal."

JELLINEK & MURRAY LITERARY AGENCY, 47—231 Kamakoi Rd., Kaneohe HI 96744. Phone/fax (808) 239-8451. E-mail: rgr.jellinek@gmail.com. Agent: Roger Jellinek. Estab. 1995. Represents a few Christian clients. Open to unpublished authors; new clients by personal reference (otherwise only June through December). Handles adult religious/inspirational nonfiction, crossover books, general books.

> **Contact:** E-mail only. Accepts simultaneous submissions; responds in 6 wks.
> **Commission:** 15%; foreign 20%.
> Fees: No, except for unusual travel or Express Mail

WILLIAM K. JENSEN LITERARY AGENCY, 119 Bampton Ct., Eugene OR 97404. Phone/fax (541) 688-1612. E-mail: queries@wkjagency.com. Website: www.wkjagency.

com. Agent: William K. Jensen. Estab. 2005. Recognized in the industry. Represents 38 clients. Open to unpublished authors and new clients. Handles adult fiction (no science fiction or fantasy), nonfiction for all ages, picture books, gift books, crossover books. 200-400 word description of your book. If no response in 4 weeks, assume they are not interested. Submission guidelines at: http://www.wkjagency.com/contact.php.

> **Contact:** E-mail only using online form; no phone queries. No attachments. Accepts simultaneous submissions. Responds in 12 wks.
> **Commission:** 15%.
> **Fees:** No fees.

NATASHA KERN LITERARY AGENCY INC., PO Box 1069, White Salmon WA 98672. Website: www.natashakern.com. Agent: Natasha Kern. Well-recognized member of Author's Guild, ACFW, RWA. Estab. 1987. Represents 36 religious clients. Currently closed to queries from unpublished writers. We cannot read unsolicited queries or proposals. We will continue to meet with writers at conferences.

K J LITERARY SERVICES, LLC, 1540 Margaret Ave., Grand Rapids MI 49507. (616) 551-9797. E-mail: kim@kjliteraryservices.com. Website: www.kjliteraryservices.com. Agent: Kim Zeilstra.

> **Contact:** E-query preferred; phone query OK.
> **Commission:** 15%.
> **Tips:** "Taking new authors by referral only."

THE STEVE LAUBE AGENCY, 5025 N. Central Ave., #635, Phoenix AZ 85012-1502. (602) 336-8910. E-mail: info@stevelaube.com. Website: www.stevelaube.com. Agents: Steve Laube (pres.), Tamela Hancock Murray, Karen Ball, and Dan Balow. Estab. 2004. Well recognized in the industry. Represents 200+ clients. Open to new and unpublished authors. Handles adult Christian fiction and nonfiction, theology, how-to, health, Christian living, and selected YA. No children's books, end-times literature, or poetry. Accepts simultaneous submissions. Responds in 6-8 wks.

> **Contact:** Please use guidelines on website: www.stevelaube.com/guidelines. If guidelines are not followed, the proposal will not receive a response.
> **Commission:** 15%; foreign 20%.
> **Fees:** No fees.
> **Tips:** "Looking for fresh and innovative ideas. Make sure your proposal contains an excellent presentation."

LEVINE GREENBERG ROSTAN LITERARY AGENCY INC., 307 Seventh Ave., Ste. 2407, New York NY 10001. (212) 337-0934. Fax (212) 337-0948. E-mail: submit@levinegreenberg.com. Website: www.levinegreenberg.com. Agents: James Levine and Arielle Eckstut. Estab. 1989. Represents 250 clients. Open to unpublished authors and new clients. General agent; handles adult religious/inspirational nonfiction. Member AAR.

> **Contact:** See guidelines/submission form on website; requires e-query; does not respond to mailed queries.
> **Commission:** 15%; foreign 20%.
> **Fees:** Office expenses.
> **Tips:** "Our specialties include spirituality and religion."

THE LITERARY GROUP INTL., 1357 Broadway, Ste. 316, New York NY 10018. (6212) 400-1494. E-mail: fweimann@theliterarygroup.com. Website: www.theliterarygroup.com. Agent: Frank Weimann. Recognized in the industry. Estab. 1986. Represents 300 clients (120 for religious books). Member of AAR. Open to new clients and unpublished authors. Handles adult novels, teen/young adult novels, picture books, adult nonfiction, teen/young adult nonfiction. Children's nonfiction, gift books, e-books, crossover. Submission guidelines at: http://www.theliterarygroup.com/index. php?option=com_content&view=article&id=175&Itemid=225.

Contact: E-mail; 2-page synopsis.
Commission: 15%; foreign 20%.
Fees: Expenses for overseas postage/FedEx/DHL/UPS.
Tips: Merged with Folio Literary Management, LLC in 2013.

LITERARY MANAGEMENT GROUP, LLC, PO Box 40965, Nashville TN 37204. (615) 812-4445. E-mail: brucebarbour@literarymanagementgroup.com. Website: www.literarymanagementgroup.com. Agents: Bruce R. Barbour; Karen A. Moore (karen@literarymanagementgrou.com, (614) 266-2876). Estab. 1995. Well recognized in the industry. Represents 100+ clients. No unpublished authors; open to new clients. Handles adult novels, teen/YA and adult nonfiction, screenplays, gift books, crossover books. Other services offered: book packaging and consulting.

Contact: E-mail preferred. Will review proposals, no unsolicited mss. Accepts simultaneous submissions; responds in 3-4 wks.
Commission: 15%; foreign 15%.
Sold to: Every major publisher of Christian books.
Fees: No fees or expenses on agented books.
Tips: "Follow guidelines, proposal outline, and submissions format on website. Use Microsoft Word. Study the market and know where your book will fit in."

LIVING WORD LITERARY AGENCY/KIMBERLY SHUMATE, PO Box 40974, Eugene OR 97401. E-mail: livingwordliterary@gmail.com. Website: livingwordliterary.wordpress.com. Agent: Kimberly Shumate. Estab. 2009. Recognized in the industry as a proud member of the ECPA. Represents 30 clients. Handles adult fiction and nonfiction (see agency website for genre exclusions). Not accepting autobiographies. Not interested in fantasy or science fiction. Looking for women's historical romance.

Contact: E-mail. No simultaneous or hard copy submissions; responds in wks.
Sold to: Zondervan, Charisma Media, Whitaker.
Commission: 15%; foreign 25%.
Fees: No fees.
Tips: "Looking for originality and unique voices."

STERLING LORD LITERISTIC INC., 65 Bleecker St., New York NY 10012. (213) 780-6050. Fax (212) 780-6095. E-mail: info@sll.com. Website: www.sll.com. Agent: Claudia Cross. Recognized in the industry. In addition to clients in the general market, she represents 10 clients with Christian/religious books. Open to unpublished clients with referrals and to new clients. Handles adult and teen Christian fiction, including women's fiction, romance novels, adult nonfiction exploring themes of spirituality, gift books, crossover books, general books. Submission guidelines at: http://www.sll.com/submissions.aspx.

Contact: E-query (with referral only). Accepts simultaneous submissions, if informed. Responds in 4-6 wks.
Commission: 15%; foreign 20%.
Fees: "We charge for photocopy costs for manuscripts or any costs above and beyond the usual cost of doing business."

MACGREGOR LITERARY, PO Box 1316, Manzanita OR 97124. E-mail: submissions@macgregorliterary.com or through Website: www.MacGregorLiterary.com.

Agents: Chip MacGregor, Sandra Bishop, Amanda Luedeke. Estab. 2006. Member of AAR. Recognized in the industry. Handles teen and adult religious/inspirational novels and nonfiction; crossover and secular books. Submission guidelines at: http://www.macgregorliterary.com/submission. Does not return unsolicited submissions, even if postage is included.

Contact: E-mail query. Accepts simultaneous submissions. Responds in 4 wks.
Commission: 15%; foreign 20%.
Fees: No fees or expenses.
Tips: "We are not looking to add unpublished authors except through conferences and referrals from current authors."

MANUS & ASSOCIATES LITERARY AGENCY, 425 Sherman Ave., Ste. 200, Palo Alto CA 94306. (650) 470-5151. Fax (650) 470-5159. E-mail: manuslit@manuslit.com. Website: www.manuslit.com. Agents: Jillian Manus, Janet Wilkens Manus, Penny Nelson, Dena Fischer, Stephanie Lee, and Jandy Nelson. Members AAR. Estab. 1994. Open to unpublished authors and new clients. Handles adult religious/inspirational novels and nonfiction, gift books, crossover and general books. Submission guidelines at: http://www.manuslit.com/flash/index.html.

Contact: Query by mail/fax/e-query (no attachments or phone calls). For fiction, send first 30 pages, bio, and SASE. For nonfiction, send proposal/sample chapters. Responds in 12 weeks, only if interested.
Commission: 15%; foreign 20-25%.

WILLIAM MORRIS LITERARY AGENCY, 1325 Avenue of the Americas, New York NY 10019. (212) 586-5100. Fax (212) 246-3583. E-mail: vs@wma.com. Website: www.wma.com. Agent: Valerie Summers. Recognized in the industry. Estab. 1898. Hundreds of clients with religious books. Not open to unpublished authors or new clients. Handles all types of material. Member AAR.

Contact: Send query/synopsis, publication history by mail/SASE. No fax/e-query. No unsolicited mss.
Commission: 15%; foreign 20%.
Fees: None.

NAPPALAND LITERARY AGENCY, 446 East 29th St. #1674, Loveland CO 80539. E-mail: literary@nappaland.com. Website: www.nappalandliterary.com. Division of Nappaland Communications Inc. Agent: Mike Nappa. We are committed to developing authors whose writing is: Authentic. Relevant. Eternal. Estab. 1995. Recognized in the industry. Represents 12 clients. Prefers published authors; prefers authors who are referred by a current Nappaland author or traditional publishing company professional. Handles secular books, adult nonfiction and novels. Does not handle memoirs, children's books, romance novels, screenplays, poetry, or anything about cats (no exceptions).

Contact: Query letter only by e-mail. Accepts simultaneous submissions; responds in 4 wks. Unsolicited queries are automatically rejected unless sent during "open submission" periods. If interested in seeing more, they will contact you.
Commission: 15% for literary representation; 15% for public-relations representation; 20% foreign.
Sold to: 25 Christian publishers.
Fees: None.
Tips: "Please do not send us a query that says, 'I know you don't usually represent this kind of book, but…' We will mock your obtuseness with heartless cruelty and then reject you anyway. And we won't even feel bad about it."

B. K. NELSON LITERARY AGENCY AND LECTURE BUREAU, 1565 Paseo Vida, Palm Springs CA 92264. (760) 778-8800. NY Office: (914) 741-1322. Websites: www. bknelson.com; bknelsonlecturebureau.com; bknelsoneditorialservices.com. Agent: B.K. Nelson, pres.; ed. Dir., John W. Benson. Incorporated in New York, Certificate of Qualification California. Notary License, Degree of Bachelors of Laws, Diploma in American Law and Procedure. Sold over 2,000 books. Represents adult and children's religious and inspirational fiction and nonfiction, self-help, how-to, movies. Member BBB. 80 clients.

NUNN COMMUNICATIONS INC., 1612 Ginger Dr., Carrollton TX 75007. (972) 394-6866. E-mail: info@nunncommunications.com. Website: www.nunncommunica-tions.com. Agent: Leslie Nunn Reed. Estab. 1995. Represents 20 clients. Recognized in the industry. Not open to unpublished authors. Handles adult nonfiction, gift books, crossover books, and general books.
  Contact: By e-mail. Responds in 4-6 wks.
  Commission: 15%.
  Fees: Charges office expenses if over $100.

KATHI J. PATON LITERARY AGENCY, PO Box 2236, Radio City Station, New York NY 10101-2236. (212) 265-6586. E-mail: KJPLitBiz@optonline.net. Website: www.PatonLiterary.com. Agent: Kathi Paton. Estab. 1987. Handles adult nonfiction: Christian life and issues.
  Contact: Prefers e-query.
  Commission: 15%; foreign 20%.
  Fees: For photocopying and postal submissions.

PATRICK-MEDBERRY ASSOCIATES, 567 W. Channel Islands Blvd. #179, Port Hueneme CA 93041. No phone calls please. E-mail: peggy@amarismedia.com. Website: www.amarismedia.com. Agents: Peggy Patrick Medberry and Chauncey J. Medberry. Not currently looking for new clients but will look at query letter or e-mail. Recognized in the industry. Estab. 2005. Management and production company special-izing in Christian writers, directors, and producers, as well as religious and inspirational novels, screenplays, TV/movie scripts, crossover books, general books, and screenplays.
  Contact: Query by letter or e-mail. Accepts simultaneous submissions.
  Commission: 15%; foreign 15%.
  Fees: None.
  Tips: "We are a management company. And unlike an agency we bring to and work with Amaris Media International as producers on products that interest us. We will respond only to projects that are potentially high concept and able to be produced on multiple platforms."

*THE QUADRIVIUM GROUP, 7512 Dr. Phillips Blvd., Ste. 50-229, Orlando FL 32819. Website: www.TheQuadriviumGroup.com. Agents: Steve Blount (SteveBlount@ TheQuadriviumGroup.com); Susan Blount (SusanBlount@TheQuadriviumGroup. com). Estab. 2006. Represents 20-30 clients. Recognized in the industry. Open to a limited number of unpublished authors (with credentials, platform, compelling story/ idea) and to new clients (mostly by referral). General agent. Handles Christian and general fiction and nonfiction for all ages, gift books, crossover books. Other services offered: consulting on book sales and distribution.
  Contact: E-mail preferred; responds in 2-4 wks.
  Commission: 15%; foreign 20%.
  Fees: Only extraordinary costs with client's permission.

RED WRITING HOOD INK, 2075 Attala Rd. 1990, Kosciusko MS 39090. (662) 582-1191. Fax (662) 796-3161. E-mail: redwritinghoodink@gmail.com. Website: http://redwritinghoodink.net. Agent: Sheri Williams. Estab. 1997. Clients with Christian books: 50%. Recognized in the industry. Open to unpublished authors with strong platform; open to new clients. Handles novels and nonfiction for MG, YA, adult, crossover books. No children's younger than MG.

    Contact: E-mail/letter. Accepts simultaneous submissions noted as such; responds in 1-6 weeks to e-mail; no postal submissions accepted or acknowledged.

    Commission: 15%; foreign 20%.

    Tips: "Beta readers are priceless. Research is essential to a compelling story where readers connect with your characters. Unless specifically stated in our response, we will not accept another query on the same project once we have passed."

ROSS YOON LITERARY AGENCY, 1666 Connecticut Ave. N.W., Ste. 500, Washington DC 20009. (202) 328-3282. Website: www.rossyoon.com. Agent: Gail Ross (gail@rossyoon.com); Howard Yoon (howard@rossyoon.com; Anna Sproul-Latimer (anna@rossyoon.com). Recognized in the industry. Estab. 1987. Represents many clients. Member of AAR. General agent; handles adult religious/inspirational nonfiction.

    Contact: No mailed queries; e-queries only. Accepts simultaneous queries.

    Commission: 15%; foreign 25%.

    Fees: Office expenses.

SCHIAVONE LITERARY AGENCY, INC., 236 Trails End, West Palm Beach FL 33413-2135. Phone/fax (561) 966-9294. E-mail: profschia@aol.com. Website: www.publishersmarketplace.com/members/profschia. Agent: Francine Edelman (FrancineEdelman@aol.com). Recognized in the industry. Estab. 1996. Represents 6 clients. Open to published authors only. Handles adult, teen/YA nonfiction; teen/YA novels, secular books.

    Contact: E-mail only; one-page e-query (no attachments). Accepts simultaneous submissions. Responds in 4-6 wks.

    Sold to: 5 religious publishes, and all major NYC houses.

    Commission: 15%; foreign 20%.

    Fees: None.

    Tips: "We are highly selective. We prefer submissions from authors published by major houses. One-page e-queries only. We do not accept postal queries. No phone calls."

SUSAN SCHULMAN LITERARY AGENCY, 454 W. 44th St., New York NY 10036. (212) 713-1633. Fax (212) 581-8830. E-mail: schulman@aol.com. Website: www.susanschulmanagency.com. Agents: Susan Schulman; Linda Migalti (schulmanagency@yahoo.com); Christine LeBlond (CleBlond@schulmanagency.com. Recognized in the industry. Estab. 1982. Represents 6 clients. Member of AAR. Open to unpublished authors and new clients. Handles adult and teen/YA religious/inspirational novels; children's, teen/YA and adult nonfiction; picture books.

    Contact: E-query. Accepts simultaneous submissions. Responds in 2 wks.

    Commission: 15%; foreign 10% + 10% to co-agent, if used.

    Sold to: Thomas Nelson and Zondervan.

    Fees: None.

SERENDIPITY LITERARY AGENCY, LLC, 1633 Broadway, New York NY 10019. E-mail: rbrooks@serendipitylit.com. Website: www.serendipitylit.com. Agents: Karen Thomas (karen@serendipitylit.com; Dawn Michelle Hardy (dawn@serendipitylit.com); Nadeen Gayle (nadeen@serendipity.com); Chelcee Johns (chelsee@serendipitylit.com); Siobahn McBride (siobahn@serendipity.com). Not yet recognized in the industry. Member AAR. Estab. 2000. Represents 50 clients; 3 with religious books. Open to unpublished authors and new clients. General agent; handles fiction and nonfiction for all ages, gift books, crossover books, general books, poetry books, e-books. No science fiction.

> **Contact:** By e-mail. Accepts simultaneous submissions. Responds in 4 wks.
> **Commission:** 15%; foreign 20%.
> **Fees:** None.

THE SEYMOUR AGENCY, 475 Miner Street Rd., Canton NY 13617. (315) 386-1831. E-mail: marysue@theseymouragency.com. Website: www.theseymouragency.com. Agents: Mary Sue Seymour, and Nichole Resciniti (nicole@theseymouragency.com). Handles all types of Christian books, including YA. Recognized in the industry. Estab. 1992. Member of AAR. Accepts simultaneous submissions. Represents 30 religious clients. Open to unpublished authors and new clients (prefers published authors). Handles secular books, adult nonfiction and novels.

> **Contact:** Query letter or e-mail with first 50 pages of ms. For nonfiction, send proposal with chapter 1. Simultaneous query OK. Responds in 1 mo. for queries and 2-3 mos. for mss.
> **Commission:** 15%; foreign 20%.
> **Sold to:** 10 Christian publishers.
> **Fees:** None.
> **Tips:** "We have multi-book sales to Zondervan, Thomas Nelson, Harvest House, Cook Communications, Abingdon Press, Bethany House, Guideposts, and HarperOne."

KEN SHERMAN & ASSOCIATES, 1275 N. Hayworth, Ste. 103, Los Angeles CA 90046. (310) 273-3840. Fax (310) 271-2875. E-mail: ken@kenshermanassociates.com. Agent: Ken Sherman. Estab. 1989. Represents 50 clients. Open to unpublished authors and new clients. Handles adult religious/inspirational novels, nonfiction, screenplays, and TV/movie scripts.

> **Contact:** By referral only. Responds in 1 mo.
> **Commission:** 15%; foreign 20%; dramatic rights 15%.
> **Fees:** Charges office expenses and other negotiable expenses.

WENDY SHERMAN ASSOCIATES, 27 W. 24th St., Ste. 700B, New York NY 10110. (212) 279-9027. Fax (212) 279-8863. E-mail: submissions@wsherman.com. Website: www.wsherman.com. Agents: Wendy Sherman, Kimberly Perel. Open to unpublished authors and new clients. General agents. Handle adult spiritual nonfiction.

> **Contact:** Contact: Query by e-mail only. Guidelines on website.
> **Commission:** 15%; foreign 25%.

MICHAEL SNELL LITERARY AGENCY, PO Box 1206, Truro MA 02666-1206. (508) 349-3718. E-mail: snell.patricia@gmail.com. Website: http://michaelsnellagency.com. Agents: Michael and Patricia Snell. Estab. 1978. Represents 200 clients. Open to unpublished authors and new clients. General agent: handles adult religious. Proposal guidelines at: http://michaelsnellagency.com/ftp___michaelsnellagency.com/Proposal_Guidelines.html.

Contact: E-mailed, or mailed query with SASE. Accepts simultaneous queries, but not simultaneous submissions. Responds in 1-2 wks.
Commission: 15%; foreign 15%.

SPENCERHILL ASSOCIATES, LTD./KAREN SOLEM, Sarasota FL. (941) 677-0142. E-mail: submissions@spencerhillassociates.com. Website: www.spencerhillassociates. com. Agent: Karen Solem. Member of AAR. Recognized in the industry. Estab. 2001. Represents 15-25 clients with religious books. Not currently open to unpublished authors; very selective of new clients. Primarily handles adult Christian fiction; no YA, children's, or nonfiction.
Contact: By e-mail.
Commission: 15%; foreign 20%.
Fees: Photocopying and Express Mail charges only.
Tips: "Check website for latest information and needs and how to submit. No nonfiction."

LESLIE H. STOBBE LITERARY AGENCY, 300 Doubleday Rd., Tryon NC 28782. (828) 808-7127. E-mail: lhstobbe123@gmail.com. Website: www.stobbeliterary.com. Agents: Les Stobbe is looking for professional-level adult fiction and nonfiction by writers with significant platform; Sally Apokedak is looking for YA fiction and nonfiction appealing to contemporary youth and children's fiction and non-fiction (see separate listing). No board books. Especially interested in literature with Christian values appealing to a secular market. Well recognized in the industry. Estab. 1993. Represents 80 clients. Open to unpublished authors and new clients. Handles adult fiction and nonfiction, teen/YA fiction and nonfiction, picture books, children's novels and nonfiction, e-books, crossover books.
Contact: By e-mail. Considers simultaneous submissions; responds within 10 weeks.
Commission: 15%.
Fees: None.
Sold to: 20 Christian publishers.
Comment: "Our preference are books imbued with Christian values. We will not take on books with which we disagree, either because of theological perspective or style of expression."
Tip: "Because of the intense competition for the few slots open to debut authors, it is wise to use a professional editor to polish your final version."

+LES STOBBE LITERARY AGENCY/SALLY APOKEDAK, AGENT. E-mail: sally@ sally-apokedak.com. Website: http://sally-apokedak.com/blog-literary-agents-sally-apokedak. Agent: Sally Apokedak, open to submissions. Recognized in the industry. Estab. 1993. Represents 1 client. Handles children's, teen/YA, adult novels; nonfiction for children, teen/YA, adult; picture books, gift books, e-books, crossover and secular books. In picture books, author/illustrators only. Guidelines: http://sally-apokedak. com/submission-guidelines-2.
Contact: By e-mail. Accepts simultaneous submissions. Responds in 30 days, only if interested.
Commission: 15%; foreign 10%.
Sold to: Harper Collins Christian.
Fees: None
Tips: "Eager to find YA and middle grade books for the general market, that are

also written from a Christian worldview. A great voice and a fresh premise are both vital if you want Sally to represent you."

SUITE A MANAGEMENT TALENT & LITERARY AGENCY, 120 El Camino Dr.; Ste. 202, Beverly Hills CA 90212. (310) 278-0801. Fax (310) 278-0807 (limit 2 pg. query). E-mail: suite-a@juno.com. Agent: Lloyd D. Robinson. Recognized in the industry. Estab. 1990. Represents 10 clients. Open to new and unpublished clients (if published in other media). Handles novels for children, teen/YA, and adults; screenplays; TV/movie scripts; secular books. Specializes in screenplays and novels for adaptation to TV movies.

> **Contact:** By e-mail. Initial query should be limited to: a 1-page resume/bio, including educational background, list of published credits, and list of contest awards. One-page synopsis should include: title, W.G.A. registration or US copyright number, logline, and 3 paragraphs including beginning, middle, and ending; not a pitch sheet.
> **Commission:** 10%, foreign 10%.
> **Fees:** "For authors without recognized publishing credits, I attach first as a Publishing Consultant with a one-time fee of $3,500. Upon publication, I attach as a Talent Agent (10%) with credit for P.C. Fee. As a talent agent I then submit for adaptation for film or television MOW.
> **Comments:** Representation limited to adaptation of novels and true-life stories for film and television development. Work must have been published for consideration.

MARK SWEENEY & ASSOCIATES, 28540 Altessa Way, Ste. 201, Bonita Springs FL 34135. (239) 594-1957. E-mail: sweeney2@comcast.net. Agents: Mark Sweeney; Janet Sweeney. Recognized in the industry. Estab. 2003. Open to new clients, but very selective. Represents 120 clients. Handles teen/YA and adult religious/inspirational nonfiction, crossover books, gift books, e-books, secular books; no fiction at this time.

> **Contact:** E-mail. Accepts simultaneous submissions. Responds in 1 week.
> **Sold to:** All Christian book publishers.
> **Commission:** 15%; foreign 15%.
> **Fees:** None.
> **Tips:** "Most of our consulting business and new author acquisitions are by referral."

TALCOTT NOTCH LITERARY SERVICES, 276 Forest Rd., Milford CT 06461. (203) 877-1146. Fax (203) 876-9517. Website: www.talcottnotch.net. Agents: Gina Panettieri (gpanettieri@talcottnotch.net), Paula Munier, Rachael Dugas, Jessica Negron, and Saba Sulaiman. Building a Christian presence in the industry. Estab. 2003. Represents 25 clients (3 with religious books). Open to unpublished authors and new clients. Handles nonfiction and fiction, crossover and general market books for all ages.

> **Contact:** Prefers e-queries (editorial@talcottnotch.net), but accepts hard copies. Accepts simultaneous submissions; responds in 8 wks.
> **Commission:** 15%; foreign or with co-agent 20%.
> **Fees:** None.
> **Tips:** "While Christian and religious books are not our main focus, we are open to unique and thought-provoking works from all writers. We specifically seek nonfiction in areas of parenting, health, women's issues, arts and crafts, self-help, and current events. We are open to academic/scholarly work as well as commercial projects."

3 SEAS LITERARY AGENCY, PO Box 8571, Madison WI 53708. (608) 221-4306. E-mail: queries@threeseaslit.com. Website: www.threeseaslit.com. Agents: Michelle Grajkowski and Cori Deyou. Estab. 2000. Represents 40 clients. Open to unpublished authors and new clients. General agent; handles adult religious/inspirational novels and nonfiction. Submission guidelines at: http://threeseasagency.com/submissions. html#genres.

> **Contact:** E-query only with synopsis and 1 chapter (queries@threeseaslit.com). No attachments. Considers simultaneous submissions. Responds in 2-3 mos.
> **Commission:** 15%; foreign 20%.

TRIDENT MEDIA GROUP, LLC, 41 Madison Ave., 36th Fl., New York NY 10010. (212) 333-1511. Fax (212) 262-4849. E-mail: info@tridentmediagroup.com. Website: www.tridentmediagroup.com. Agent: Don Fehr. Open to unpublished authors and new clients. Unpublished authors use submission form on the Website. General agent. Handles adult religious nonfiction. Submission guidelines at: http://www.tridentmediagroup.com/contact-us.

> **Contact:** No unsolicited mss. Query/SASE first; send outline and sample chapters on request. Responds to queries in 3 wks.; mss in 6 wks.
> **Commission:** 15%.

VAN DIEST LITERARY AGENCY, 34947 SE Brooks Rd., Boring OR 97009. (503) 676-8009. E-mail: david@christianliteraryagency.com. Website: www.ChristianLiterary Agency.com. Agent: David Van Diest, open to additional clients. Estab. 2003. Represents 25 clients. Open to unpublished authors. Recognized in the industry. Handles teen/YA and adult novels, nonfiction for all ages, and children's novels. Charges no fees.

> **Contact:** By e-mail. Use online form. Responds in 6 wks.
> Commission: 15%; 15% foreign.

WATERSIDE PRODUCTIONS INC., 2055 Oxford Ave., Cardiff CA 92007. (760) 632-9190. Fax (760) 632-9295. E-mail: admin@waterside.com. Website: www.waterside.com. Agent listed on Website with their specialties. Estab. 1982. Interested in handling Christian books or books that otherwise challenge and engage readers from a Judeo-Christian perspective. Prefers nonfiction, but will look at fiction (the bar is very high). In addition to spiritually oriented books, devotions, theology, chick lit, and mom lit, list includes business books: leadership, marketing, sales, business development. Submission guidelines at: http://www.waterside.com/submission-form.

> **Contact:** Query via online form (see website). Considers simultaneous submissions.
> **Commission:** 15%; foreign 25%.

WINTERS & KING, INC., 2448 E. 81st St., Ste. 5900, Tulsa OK 74137-4259. (918) 494-6868. Fax (918) 491-6297. E-mail: dboyd@wintersking.com. Website: www.wintersking.com. Agent: Thomas J. Winters. Estab. 1983. Represents 100+ clients. Recognized in the industry. Rarely open to unpublished authors; open to qualified new clients with a significant sales history/platform. Handles adult religious/inspirational novels & nonfiction for all ages, gift books, e-books, crossover books, general w/underlying Christian theme.

> **Contact:** By fax (918) 491-6297. No more than 10 pages.
> **Commission:** 15%; foreign 15%.
> **Fees:** None.
> **Tips:** "Unsolicited proposals/manuscripts will not be acknowledged, considered, or returned. Solicited proposals/outlines/samples/manuscripts that are not

in proper format will not be reviewed or considered for representation. No handwritten submissions."

WOLGEMUTH & ASSOCIATES, 8600 Crestgate Cir., Orlando FL 32819. (407) 909-9445. E-mail: info@wolgemuthandassociates.com. Website: www.wolgemuthand associates.com. Agents: Robert Wolgemuth; Andrew D. Wolgemuth; Erik S. Wolgemuth; Austin Wilson. Well recognized in the industry. Estab. 1992. Number of clients not disclosed. Member of AAR. Handles teen/YA and adult nonfiction.

    Contact: By e-mail. Accepts simultaneous submissions.

    Sold to: all CBA publishers.

    Commission: 15%.

    Fees: None.

    Tips: "We work with authors who are either bestselling authors or potentially bestselling authors. Consequently, we want to represent clients with broad market appeal. Please refer to our Website for submission guidelines."

WORDSERVE LITERARY GROUP, 7061 S. University Blvd., Centennial CO 80122. (303) 471-6675. Fax (303) 471-1297. E-mail: greg@wordserveliterary.com ("Query" in subject line). Website: www.wordserveliterary.com. Agents: Greg Johnson, (admin@ wordserveliterary.com) adds only a few clients a year; Alice Crider (alice@wordserveliterary.com), open to new clients, and Sarah Freese (sarah@wordserveliterary.com) open to new clients. WordServe is also partnered with www.faithhappenings.com to promote their authors and books in all of their ministry and PR endeavors. Recognized in the industry. Estab. 2003. Represents 150+ clients. Recognized in the industry. Open to new clients. Handles novels and nonfiction for all ages, gift books, picture books, crossover books, general books (memoir, military, self-help, adult fiction), e-books. No screenplays or poetry. Accepts simultaneous submissions. No extra fees.

    Contact: By e-mail. Visit website for submission guidelines. Responds in 4-8 wks.

    Sold to: More than 60 publishers and imprints.

    Commission: 15%; foreign 20-30% (depending on how many co-agents are involved).

    Fees: None.

    Tips: "Nonfiction: First impressions count. Make sure your proposal answers all the questions on competition, outline, audience, felt need, etc. Fiction: Make sure your novel is completed before you submit a proposal (synopsis, plus 5 chapters)."

+WORDWISE MEDIA SERVICES, 4083 Avenue L, Suite 255, Lancaster, CA, 93536. (866) 739-0440. Fax: (866)501-4280. E-mail: steve@wordwisemedia.com (for general inquiries only, not submissions).Website: www.wordwisemedia.com. Agents: Steven Hutson, Dave Fessenden, Dr. Jim Lance. Recognized in the industry. Estab. 2005 as a freelance editing service; literary agency since 2011. Represents 45 clients, twelve with religious books. Open to unpublished authors, prefers referrals. Handles fiction and nonfiction for adults and children, both Christian and secular market; no poetry, short stories, or picture books.

    Contact: Phone, fax, email. Responds in 30 days, OK to nudge afterward.

    Commission: 15% for books; more for foreign or motion picture projects, if shared with another agent.

    Fees: Postage and printing (at cost) for mailed ms (very rare).

    Tips: For submissions, download query form and follow website instructions carefully. Specify the agent's name in the e-mail subject line, if you have a preference.

WRITERS HOUSE,   21 W. 26th St., New York NY 10010. (212) 685-2400. Fax (212) 685-1781. E-mail: dlazar@writershouse.com. Rebecca Sherman, Sr. Agent, juvenile and young adult. E-mail: rsherman@writershouse.com. Website: www.writershouse. com. Agent: Dan Lazar. Founded 1974. Represents trade books of all types, fiction and nonfiction, including all rights. Handles film and TV rights. No screenplays, teleplays, or software. No unsolicited mss, query first with an intelligent two-page letter stating what's wonderful about the book, what it's about, and what background and experience you, as an author, bring to it. Queries generally responded to within 6 weeks and mss within 8 weeks. No reading fee. Submission guidelines at: http://www.writershouse. com/content/submissions.asp.

YATES & YATES, 1551 N. Tustin Ave., Ste. 710, Santa Ana CA 92705. (714) 480-4000. Fax (714) 480-4001. E-mail: email@yates2.com. Website: www.yates2.com. Agents: Sealy Yates, Matt Yates, Curtis Yates, Mike Salisbury. Estab. 1989. Recognized in the industry. Represents 50+ clients. No unpublished authors. Handles adult nonfiction.
   Contact: E-mail.
   Commission: Negotiable.

ZACHARY SHUSTER HARMSWORTH LITERARY AND ENTERTAINMENT AGENCY, 1776 Broadway, Ste. 1405, New York NY 10019. (212) 765-6900. Fax (212) 765-6490. Or 535 Boylston St., Ste. 1103, Boston MA 02116. (617) 262-2400. Fax (617) 262-2460. E-mail: mchappell@zshliterary.com. Website: www.zshliterary.com. Agent: Mary Beth Chappell (Boston office). Recognized in the industry. Represents 15-30 religious clients. Open to unpublished authors and new clients. Handles adult religious/inspirational novels and adult nonfiction, crossover books, general books.
   Contact: E-mail with online form only; no unsolicited submissions.
   Commission: 15%; foreign and film 20%.
   Fees: Office expenses only.
   Tips: "We are looking for inspirational fiction, Christian nonfiction, especially that focuses on the emerging/emergent church or that which would appeal to readers in their 20s and 30s, and teen/YA series.

13

Contests

A listing here does not guarantee legitimacy. For guidelines on evaluating contests, go to http://www.sfwa.org/other-resources/for-authors/writer-beware/contests.

CHILDREN/YOUNG-ADULTS

THE CHILDREN'S WRITER CONTESTS. Offers a number of contests for children's writers. Website: www.childrenswriter.com.

HIGHLIGHTS FOR CHILDREN FICTION CONTEST. (570) 253-1080. Website: www.highlights.com. Offers 3 prizes of $1,000 each for stories up to 800 words for children; for beginning readers up to 500 words. See website for guidelines and current topic. (To find contest info put "Contest" in search field.) No crime, violence, or derogatory humor. No entry fee or form required. Entries must be postmarked between January 1 and January 31.

CORETTA SCOTT KING BOOK AWARD. Coretta Scott King Task Force, American Library Assn. Toll-free (800) 545-2433. E-mail: olos@ala.org. Website: www.ala.org. Annual award for children's books by African American authors and/or illustrators published the previous year. Books must fit one of these categories: preschool to grade 4; grades 5–8; grades 9–12. Deadline: December 1 each year. Guidelines on website (click on "Awards & Grants"/click on contest name on list). Prizes: a plaque, a set of encyclopedias, and $1,000 cash. Recipients are authors and illustrators of African descent whose distinguished books promote an understanding and appreciation of the "American Dream."

MILKWEED PRIZE FOR CHILDREN'S LITERATURE. Milkweed Editions. (612) 332-3192. E-mail: editor@milkweed.org. Website: www.milkweed.org. Annual prize for unpublished novel intended for readers 8–13; 90–200 pgs. Prize: $10,000 advance against royalties and publication. Guidelines on website (Click on "Submissions Guidelines & Prizes").

POCKETS WRITING CONTEST. (615) 340-7333. Fax (615) 340-7267. E-mail: pockets@upperroom.org. Website: www.pockets.org. United Methodist. Lynn W. Gilliam, ed. Devotional magazine for children (6–11 yrs.). Fiction-writing contest; submit between March 1 and August 15 every yr. Prize: $500 and publication in Pockets. Length: 750–1,000 words. Must be unpublished and not historical fiction. Previous winners not eligible. Send to Pockets Fiction Contest at above address, designating "Fiction Contest" on outside of envelope. Send SASE for return and response. Details on website (click on "Breaking News"/"Annual Fiction Contest").

SOCIETY OF CHILDREN'S BOOK WRITERS & ILLUSTRATORS GOLDEN KITE AWARDS. Website: www.scbwi.org. Details on website (click on "Awards & Grants"/"Golden Kite Awards").

FICTION CONTESTS

AMAZON BREAKTHROUGH NOVEL AWARD. In cooperation with Penguin and Hewlett-Packard. Penguin will publish winning novel with a $25,000 advance. November deadline.

AMERICAN CHRISTIAN FICTION WRITERS CONTESTS. Fax (866) 714-1281. E-mail: genesis@ACFW.com, carolawards@acfw.com, impress@acfw.com, or contests@acfw.com. . Website: www.acfw.com/contests. Sponsors 2 fiction contests for unpublished writers and the Carol Awards for published authors. See website for current contests and rules under the "Contests" tab.

ATHANATOS CHRISTIAN MINISTRIES BOOK LENGTH NOVEL CONTEST. (202) 697-4623. E-mail: director@athanatosministries.org. Website: www.christianwritingcontest.com. Novel 40,000–90,000 words. Prizes: 1st prize: $1,500 and a possible book contract; 2nd prize: $1,000 and a possible book contract. Entry fee: $69.95. Deadline: September 1.

BARD FICTION PRIZE. Awarded annually to a promising, emerging young writer of fiction, age 39 years or younger. Entries must be previously published. Deadline: July 15. No entry fee. Prizes: $30,000 and appointment as writer-in-residence for one semester at Bard College, Annandale-on-Hudson NY. E-mail: bfp@bard.edu. Website: www.bard.edu/bfp.

BOSTON REVIEW SHORT STORY CONTEST. *Boston Review.* Website: www.bostonreview.net. Prize: $1,500 (plus publication) for an unpublished short story up to 4,000 words. Entry fee: $20. Deadline: October 1. Details on website (click on "About"/ scroll down to "Contest"/"Aura Estrada Short Story Contest").

BULWER-LYTTON FICTION CONTEST. For the worst opening line to a novel. Deadline: April 15. Website: www.bulwer-lytton.com. Rules on website.

CANADIAN WRITER'S JOURNAL SHORT FICTION CONTEST. White Mountain Publications, PO Box 1178, New Liskeard ON P0J 1P0, Canada. (705) 647-5424. Canada-wide toll-free (800) 258-5451. E-mail: cwc-calendar@cwj.ca. Website: www.cwj.ca. Sponsors semiannual short fiction contests. Deadline: April 30. Length: to 1,500 words. Entry fee: $5. Prizes: $150, $100, $50. All fiction needs for CWJ are filled by this contest. Click on "CWJ Short Fiction Contest."

ALEXANDER PATTERSON CAPPON PRIZE FOR FICTION. New Letters, UMKC, University House, 5101 Rockhill Rd., Kansas City MO 64110. (816) 235-1168. E-mail: newletters@umkc.edu. Website: www.newletters.org. Deadline: May 18. Entry fee: $15. Prize: $1,500. Click on "Awards for Writers."

THE CHRISTY AWARDS. Phone/fax (734) 663-7931. E-mail: CA2000DK@aol.com. Website: www.christyawards.com. Awards in 9 fiction genres for excellence in Christian fiction. Nominations made by publishers, not authors. For submission guidelines and other information, see website (click on "Forms"/"Official Guidelines"). Awards are presented at an annual Christy Awards Banquet held Friday prior to the annual ICRS convention in July.

+CHRISTIAN ADVENTURE/ROMANCE FICTION CONTEST, Diana Perry Books, P. O. Box 1001, Reynoldsburg, Ohio, 43068. Contact: Diana Perry. Tell an exciting story in action-adventure genre while weaving a passionate romantic subplot to show that Christians can wait for marriage and yet be very passionate and loving. Rules on website. Max: 20 pages/5000 words. Prizes: 1st Place: $300, trophy, mention on website,

DianaPerryBooks T-shirt, press releases in your local newspapers. 2nd Place: $200, trophy, mention on website, T-shirt, local press releases. 3rd Place: $100, trophy, mention on website, T-shirt, local press releases. 4th/5th Places: $50/$25, plaque, mention on website, T-shirt, local press releases. We also list names of next 25 honorable mention on website. Contest guidelines and entry form on DianaPerryBooks.com. Check website for guest judges. Mail entry form, your story and a $15 money order only to Christian Adventure/Romance Fiction Contest at above address postmarked no later than end of November. Winners announced on website and via mail January 1st. Prizes mailed within 10 days of announcement.

JACK DYER FICTION PRIZE. Crab Orchard Review, Fiction Contest, Dept. of English, Mail Code 4503, Southern Illinois University–Carbondale, 1000 Faner Dr., Carbondale IL 62901. (618) 453-5321. Website: www.siuc.edu/~crborchd. Entry fee: $10. Prize: $1,500. Deadline: submit between March 1 and May 10 (may vary). Submit fiction up to 6,000 words. See website for guidelines.

GLIMMER TRAIN PRESS FICTION CONTESTS. Glimmer Train Press. Website: www.glimmertrain.com. Sponsors a number of contests. Check website for current contests (click on "Writers' Guidelines").

JAMES JONES FIRST NOVEL FELLOWSHIP. (570) 408-4547. E-mail: cwriting@ wilkes.edu. Website: www.wilkes.edu/pages/1159.asp. Deadline: March 15. Entry fee: $30. Prizes: $10,000 first prize; $1,000 for two runners-up. Submit a 2-page outline and the first 50 pages of an unpublished novel. Guidelines on website.

SERENA MCDONALD KENNEDY AWARD. Snake Nation Press. Website: www. snakenationpress.org. Novellas up to 50,000 words or short-story collection up to 200 pgs (published or unpublished). Deadline: July 30 (check website to verify). Entry fee: $25. Prize: $1,000 and publication. Guidelines on website (click on "Contests").

NATIONAL WRITERS ASSOCIATION NOVEL-WRITING CONTEST. The National Writers Assn., 10940 S. Parker Rd., #508, Parker CO 80134. (303) 841-0246. Website: www.nationalwriters.com. Check website for current contests and guidelines (click on "Contests"/then name of contest).

NATIONAL WRITERS ASSOCIATION SHORT-STORY CONTEST. The National Writers Assn. (303) 841-0246. Website: www.nationalwriters.com. Check website for current contest and guidelines (click on "Contests"/then name of contest).

THE FLANNERY O'CONNOR AWARD FOR SHORT FICTION. University of Georgia Press. Website: www.ugapress.uga.edu. For collections of short fiction, 50,000–75,000 wds. Prize: $1,000, plus publication under royalty book contract. Entry fee: $25. Deadline: between April 1 and May 31 (postmark). Guidelines on website (click on "About Us"/"For Prospective Authors"/"Flannery O'Connor Award for Short Fiction").

GRACE PALEY PRIZE FOR SHORT FICTION. (703) 993-4301. E-mail: awp@awp-writer.org. Website: www.awpwriter.org. Prize: $4,000 and publication. Entry fee: $25. Deadline: Postmarked between January 1 and February 28.

KATHERINE ANNE PORTER PRIZE FOR FICTION. Literary Contest/Fiction, Nimrod Journal, University of Tulsa. (918) 631-3080. E-mail: nimrod@utulsa.edu. Website: www.utulsa.edu/nimrod/awards.html. Quality prose and fiction by emerging writers of contemporary literature, unpublished. Deadline: submit between January 1 and April 30. Entry fee: $20. Prizes: $2,000 and publication; $1,000 and publication. Guidelines on website (click on "Nimrod Literary Awards").

SILVER QUILL BEST SHORT FICTION CONTEST. E-mail: storytellermag1@ yahoo.com. Website: www.thestorytellermagazine.com. 3,000 wds. max. Entry fee: $5. Deadine: September 25 annually. Prizes: 1st place: $50, 2nd place: $25, 3rd place: $15, 4th place: $10. Open genre contest. Writers may enter as often as they wish, but entry fee must accompany each entry. Name, address, phone, e-mail, title of story, and word count should be on cover page. Name should not appear anywhere else on ms. No pornography, graphic anything, New Age, or children's stories. Mail entries to: *The Storyteller*, 2441 Washington Rd., Maynard AR 72444.

TOBIAS WOLFF AWARD IN FICTION. Western Washington University, Bellingham WA. E-mail: bhreview@cc.wwu.edu. Website: www.bhreview.org. Short story or novel excerpt up to 8,000 words. Deadline: postmarked between December 1 and March 15. Entry fee: $18 for first story/chapter; $10 each additional. Prize: $1,000, plus publication. Details on website.

WRITER'S JOURNAL ANNUAL FICTION CONTEST. E-mail: writersjournal@ writersjournal.com. Website: www.writersjournal.com. Sponsors several contests; see website (click on "Contests"/scroll down to "Contest Entry Manuscript Format").

WRITE TO INSPIRE. July deadline. Elk Grove CA. Contact Elizabeth Thompson. Inspire Christian Writers, PO Box 276794, Sacramento, CA 95827. (916) 607-7796. Limited to writers unpublished by traditional publishers or published only in anthologies, compilations, or periodicals.

NONFICTION CONTESTS

AMY WRITING AWARDS. Cosponsored by The Amy Foundation and WORLD News Group. The awards are designed to recognize creative, skillful journalism that applies biblical principles to stories about issues and lives. The goal is for non-Christian readers to see the relevance of biblical truth and for Christian readers to become disciples. First prize is $10,000 with a total of $34,000 given annually (additional prizes of $1,000–5,000). To be eligible, a .pdf of your article, as published, must be submitted using an online submission form. Deadline for submitting entries published in the first six months is July 15. Deadline for submitting entries published in the second six months is January 15. You may make both first-half and second-half submissions, but the total number of entries for the year cannot exceed 10. Visit www.worldmag.com/ amyawards for an online submission form and to see the judging rubric. Submitted articles must be published in a secular journalistic outlet and must be reinforced with at least one passage of Scripture. Winners are notified by May 1. For questions contact via e-mail at amyawards@worldmag.com. Website: www.worldmag.com/amyawards.

AWP CREATIVE NONFICTION PRIZE. Assoc. of Writers and Writing programs, George Mason University, Fairfax VA. E-mail: awp@awpwriter.org. Website: www. awpwriter.org. For authors of book-length manuscripts; submit only 150–300 pgs. Deadline: February 28. Entry fee: $15 for members; $30 for nonmembers. Prize: $2,000. Guidelines on website (click on "Contests"/"AWP Award Series").

THE BECHTEL PRIZE. T*eachers and Writers Magazine* contest. E-mail: info@twc. org. Website: www.twc.org/publications/bechtel-prize. Contemporary writing articles (unpublished) to 3,500 words. Deadline: June 30 (varies). Entry fee: $20. Prize: $1,000, plus publication.

DOROTHY CHURCHILL CAPON PRIZE FOR ESSAY. New Letters, UMKC, University House. (816) 235-1168. E-mail: newletters@umkc.edu. Website: www.

newletters.org. Deadline: May. Entry fee: $15. Prize: $1,500. Guidelines on website (scroll down and click on "New Letters Writing Contests").

ANNIE DILLARD AWARD IN CREATIVE NONFICTION. Essays on any subject to 8,000 words. Deadline: between December 1 and March 15. Entry fee: $18 for first; $10 each additional. First prize: $1,000. Unpublished works only, up to 8,000 words. E-mail: bhreview@cc.wwu.edu. Website: www.wwu.edu/~bhreview. Details on website (click on "Contests"/"Contest Submission Guidelines").

EVENT CREATIVE NONFICTION CONTEST. Deadline: mid-April, annually. $1,500 in prizes. Judges reserve the right to award either two prizes valued at $750 or three at $500. Plus winners get published in Event. Must be creative nonfiction and must not exceed the 5,000-word limit. Entry fee is $34.95, including a one-year subscription to Event. See http://www.eventmagazine.ca/contest-nf for details.

GRAYWOLF PRESS NONFICTION PRIZE. (651) 641-0036. Website: www.gray-wolfpress.org/graywolf-press-nonfiction-prize. For the best literary nonfiction book by a writer not yet established in the genre. Deadline: between June 1 & June 30 (varies). Entry fee: none. Prize: $12,000 advance and publication. Guidelines on website (click on "Submission Guidelines").

GUIDEPOSTS CONTEST. Website: www.guideposts.org. Interfaith. Writers Workshop Contest held on even years, with a late June deadline. True, first-person stories (yours or someone else's), 1,500 words. Needs one spiritual message, with scenes, drama, and characters. Winners attend a weeklong seminar in New York (all expenses paid) on how to write for *Guideposts*.

HALO MAGAZINE WRITING CONTEST. Deadline July 31. Maximum of 1,000 wds. on topic of "How I Found Jesus." $25 entry fee. 1st prize: $150, 2nd prize: $100, 3rd prize: $50. All participants receive a one-year subscription. Send submissions to Halo Magazine Writing Contest, 1643 Pinnacle Dr. SW, Wyoming MI 49519. All entries become property of *Halo Magazine* and may be used in future issues.

RICHARD J. MARGOLIS AWARD. Blue Mountain Center, Margolis & Assocs. E-mail: hsm@margolis.com. Website: www.award.margolis.com. Given annually to a promising young journalist or essayist whose work combines warmth, humor, wisdom, and concern with social justice. Deadline: July 1. Prize: $5,000. Guidelines on website.

MASTER BOOKS SCHOLARSHIP ESSAY CONTEST. PO Box 726, Green Forest AR 72638. (870) 438-5288. Fax (870) 438-5120. E-mail: mbscholarship@newleaf-press.net. Essay contest; $3,000 college scholarship; website: www.nlpg.com/scholar-ship. Details on website.

WRITE TO INSPIRE. July deadline. Elk Grove CA. Contact Elizabeth Thompson. Inspire Christian Writers, PO Box 276794, Sacramento, CA 95827. (916) 607-7796. Limited to writers unpublished by traditional publishers, or published only in anthologies, compilations, or periodicals.

PLAY/SCRIPTWRITING/SCREENWRITING CONTESTS

ACADEMY NICHOLL FELLOWSHIPS IN SCREENWRITING. (310) 247-3010. E-mail: nicholl@oscars.org. Website: www.oscars.org/nicholl/index.html. International contest held annually, open to any writer who has not optioned or sold a treatment, teleplay, or screenplay for more than $25,000. Up to five $35,000 fellowships offered each year to promising authors. Deadline: May 1. Entry fee: $35 for early-bird deadline;

$50 for regular deadlines; and $65 for late deadline. Guidelines/rules/FAQ can be found online.

AMERICAN ZOETROPE SCREENPLAY CONTEST. E-mail: contests@zoetrope. com. Website: www.zoetrope.com/contests. Deadline: August 1 (early), September 6 (final). Entry fees: $35 (early), $50 (final). Prizes: First prize $5,000. That winner and 10 finalists will be considered for film option and development.

AUSTIN FILM FESTIVAL SCREENWRITERS COMPETITION. (512) 478-4795. Fax (512) 4786205. E-mail: matt@austinfilmfestival.com. Website: www.austinfilm-festival.com or www.OnStory.tv. Offers a number of contest categories for screenplays. See current details on website.

BAKER'S PLAYS HIGH SCHOOL PLAYWRITING COMPETITION. Plays may be about any subject and any length as long as the play can be reasonably produced by high school students on a high school stage. Deadline: January 30. Prizes: $500, $250, and $100. Guidelines on website: www.bakersplays.com (go to "Information" box & click on "Contests & Festivals").

+CHRONOS PRIZE FOR INSPIRING SCREENPLAYS BY ESTABLISHED FILM-MAKERS. John Templeton Foundation. E-mail: contact@chronoprize.com. Website: www.chronoprize.com. Annual contest. For established writers with a religious message. Prize: $50,000.

KAIROS PRIZE FOR SPIRITUALLY UPLIFTING SCREENPLAYS. John Templeton Foundation. E-mail: contact@kairosprize.com. Website: www.kairosprize.com. Annual. For first-time screenwriters with a religious message. Prizes: $25,000, $15,000, $10,000. Guidelines on website (click on "Guidelines").

MOONDANCE INTERNATIONAL FILM FESTIVAL COMPETITION. E-mail: director@moondancefilmfestival.com. Website: www.moondancefilmfestival.com. Open to films, screenplays, and features. Deadline: May 30. Entry fees: $50–100. Prize: winning entries screened at festival. Details on website.

MILDRED & ALBERT PANOWSKI PLAYWRITING AWARD. Award Coordinator, Forest Roberts Theatre, Northern Michigan University, Marquette MI. Website: www. nmu.edu/theatre. Unpublished, unproduced, full-length plays. Deadline: September 1. Prizes: $2,000, a summer workshop, a fully mounted production, and transportation to Marquette. Guidelines on website (click on "Playwriting Award").

SCRIPTAPALOOZA ANNUAL INTERNATIONAL SCREENPLAY COMPETITION. (323) 654-5809. E-mail: info@scriptapalooza.com. Website: www.scriptapalooza.com. Over $25,000 in prizes and over 90 producers reading all the entries. Entry fees are from $45–60, plus you can get feedback on your entry now. Deadlines: January 5, March 2, and April 22 final.

POETRY CONTESTS

ANHINGA PRIZE FOR POETRY. E-mail: info@anhinga.org. Website: www.anhinga. org. A $2,000 prize for original poetry book in English. Winning manuscript published by Anhinga Press. For poets trying to publish a first or second book of poetry. Submissions: 48–80 pgs. Number pages and include $25 reading fee. Deadline: between February 15 and May 1 each year. Details on website (click on contest name).

MURIEL CRAFT BAILEY MEMORIAL POETRY AWARD. E-mail: poetry@comstockreview.org. Awarded annually. Deadline: July 1. Prizes: $100 to $1,000. Finalists published in the *Comstock Review*. Unpublished poems up to 40 lines. Entry fee: $5 for each poem (no limit on number of submissions). Details on website: www.comstockreview.org.

BALTIMORE REVIEW POETRY CONTEST. All styles and forms of poetry. April 1–July 1. Entry fee: $10. Prizes: $300 and publication; $150; $50; plus publication in the *Baltimore Review*. Details on website: www.baltimorereview.org. Click on "Contests" on main menu.

BLUE MOUNTAIN ARTS POETRY CARD CONTEST. (303) 449-0536. E-mail: poetrycontest@sps.com. Website: www.sps.com. Biannual contest. Next deadlines: June 30, December 31. Use online form for submissions. Rhymed or unrhymed original poetry (unrhymed preferred). Poems also considered for greeting cards or anthologies. Prizes: $300, $150, $50. Details on website ("Poetry Contest").

BOSTON REVIEW ANNUAL POETRY CONTEST. Deadline: June 1. First prize: $1,500, plus publication. Submit up to 5 unpublished poems. Entry fee: $20 (includes a subscription to *Boston Review*). Submit manuscripts in duplicate with cover note. Website: www.bostonreview.net. Details on website (click on "About"/"Contests"/name of contest).

CAVE CANEM POETRY PRIZE. Supports the work of African American poets with excellent manuscripts who have not found a publisher for their first book. Deadline: April 30 (varies). Prize: $1,000, publication by a national press, and 15 copies of the book. Entry fee: $15. Details on website: www.cavecanempoets.org (click on "Book Awards"/click on name of contest/scroll down and click on "Competition Guidelines").

49TH PARALLEL POETRY AWARD. Mail Stop 9053, Western Washington University, Bellingham WA. (360) 650-4863. E-mail: bhreview@cc.wwu.edu. Website: www.wwu.edu/~bhreview. Poems in any style or on any subject. Deadline: submit between December 1 and March 15. Entry fee: $18 for first entry; $10 for each additional entry. First prize: $1,000 and publication. Details on website.

FLO GAULT STUDENT POETRY COMPETITION. Sarabande Books. E-mail: info@sarabandebooks.org. Website: www.sarabandebooks.org. Prize: $500. Submit up to 3 poems. Deadline: October 30. Details on website (click on "Student Poetry Prize").

GRIFFIN POETRY PRIZE. (905) 618-0420. E-mail: info@griffinpoetryprize.com. Website: www.griffinpoetryprize.com. Prizes: two $65,000 awards (one to a Canadian and one to a poet from anywhere in the world) for a collection of poetry published in English during the preceding year; plus additional prizes ($200,000 in prizes total). All submissions must come from publishers. Deadline: December 31. Details on website.

TOM HOWARD/JOHN H. REID POETRY CONTEST. Website: www.winningwriters.com/tompoetry.htm. Deadline: between December 15 and September 30. Poetry in any style or genre. Published poetry accepted. Entry fee: $7 for every 25 lines. Prizes: $3,000 first prize; total of $5,550 in cash prizes. Details on website.

THE JAMES LAUGHLIN AWARD/ACADEMY OF AMERICAN POETS. 75 Maiden Ln. Ste. 901, New York NY 10038; (212) 274-0343x13. E-mail: pguzman@poet.org. Website: www.poets.org. The nation's only second-book award for poetry that is given annually and is open to all poets who are citizens of the United States. Beginning in 2015, recipients of the award will receive an all-expense-paid weekend at The Betsy's Writer's Room in Miami Beach FL. Recipients receive $5,000, and copies of the winning book are purchased and distributed to approximately 1,000 members of the Academy. Submissions will be accepted between January 1 and May 15. See Website for additional contests.

BARBARA MANDIGO KELLY PEACE POETRY AWARDS. Nuclear Age Peace Foundation. (805) 965-3443. E-mail: wagingpeace@napf.org. Website: www.wagingpeace.org. Annual series of awards to encourage poets to explore and illuminate positive visions of peace and the human spirit. Deadline: July 1. Prizes: $1,000 for Adult; $200 for Youth 13–18 years; and $200 for Youth ages 12 and under. Adult entry fee: $15 for up to 3 poems; $5 for youth; no fee for 12 and under. Details on website (see right-hand column).

NEW LETTERS PRIZE FOR POETRY. New Letters, UMKC. (816) 235-1168. E-mail: newletters@umkc.edu. Website: www.newletters.org. Deadline: May 18. Entry fee: $15 for first entry; $10 ea. for additional. Prize: $1,500 for best group of 3 to 6 poems.

PEARL POETRY PRIZE. Pearl Editions. Website: www.pearlmag.com. Deadline: submit between May 1 and June 30. Entry fee: $20. Prizes: $1,000 and publication in *Pearl Editions.*

RICHARD PETERSON POETRY PRIZE. *Crab Orchard Review,* Poetry Contest, Dept. of English, Mail Code 4503, Southern Illinois University–Carbondale, 1000 Faner Dr., Carbondale IL 62901. (618) 453-5321. Website: www.siuc.edu/~crborchd. Entry fee: $15. Prize: $1,500. Deadline: submit between March 1 and May 10 (may vary). Submit up to 3 poems; 100-line limit.

POETRY SOCIETY OF VIRGINIA POETRY CONTESTS. Website: www.poetrysocietyofvirginia.org. Categories for adults and students. Prizes: $20–$250. Entry fee per poem for nonmembers: $4. Deadline: March 15. List of contests on website.

SLIPSTREAM ANNUAL POETRY CHAPBOOK COMPETITION. Website: www.slipstreampress.org/contest.html. Prize: $1,000, plus 50 copies of chapbook. Deadline: December 1. Send up to 40 pages of poetry. Reading fee: $20. Guidelines on website.

SOUL-MAKING KEATS LITERARY COMPETITION. Categories: poetry, flash fiction, memoir vignette, short story, humor, novel excepts, intercultural essay, literary nonfiction, religious essay, young adult poetry and prose,. Low entry fees, cash prizes. E-mail: SoulKeats@mail.com. Website: www.soulmakingcontest.us. Sponsored by National League of American Pen Women. Deadline: November 30.

HOLLIS SUMMERS POETRY PRIZE. Ohio University Press. (740) 593-1155. E-mail: oupress@ohio.edu. For unpublished collection of original poems, 60–95 pgs. Entry fee: $25. Deadline: October 31. Prize: $1,000, plus publication in book form. Details on website: www.ohioswallow.com/poetry_prize (scroll down to "About OU Press" and click on "Poetry Prize").

SUMMERTIME BLUES POETRY CONTEST. E-mail: storytellermag1@yahoo.com. Website: www.thestorytellermagazine.com. Entry fee $5 per 1–3 poems. Deadline: August 31 annually. Prizes: 1st place: $25; 2nd place: $15; 3rd place: $10. Any style poem is acceptable. Writers may enter as often as they wish, but entry fee must accompany each entry. Name, address, phone, e-mail, title of poem, and word count should be on cover page. You may include only one cover page per 3 poems. Name should not appear anywhere else on ms. No pornography, graphic anything, New Age, or children's poetry will be accepted. Mail entries to: *The Storyteller,* 2441 Washington Rd., Maynard AR 72444.

THE MAY SWENSON POETRY AWARD. Utah State University Press. (435) 797-1362. Website: www.usu.edu/usupress. Collections of original poetry, 50–100 pgs. Deadline: September 30. Prize: $1,000, publication, and royalties. Reading fee: $25. Details on website ("Swenson Poetry Award").

KATE TUFTS DISCOVERY AWARD. Claremont Graduate University. (909) 621-8974. E-mail: tufts@cgu.edu. Presented annually for a first or very early work by a poet of genuine promise. Prize: $10,000. Deadline: September 15. Details and entry form on website: www.cgu.edu/tufts.

KINGSLEY TUFTS POETRY AWARD. Claremont Graduate University. (909) 621-8974. E-mail: tufts@cgu.edu. Presented annually for a published book of poetry by a midcareer poet. Prize: $100,000. Deadline: July 1. Details and entry form on website: www.cgu.edu/tufts.

UTMOST NOVICE CHRISTIAN POETRY CONTEST. Utmost Christian Writers Foundation, Canada. E-mail: nnharms@telusplanet.net. Website: www.utmostchristianwriters.com/poetry-contest/poetry-contest-rules.php. Nathan Harms. Entry fee: $10/poem. Prizes: $500, $300, $200; Best Rhyming Poem $150. Deadline: August 31. Details and entry form on website.

MULTIPLE-GENRE CONTESTS

BAKELESS LITERARY PUBLICATION PRIZES. Bread Loaf Writers' Conference, Middlebury College. E-mail: bakelessprize@middlebury.edu. Website: www.bakelessprize.org. Book series competition for new authors of literary works of poetry, fiction, and nonfiction. Entry fee: $10. Deadline: between September 15 and November 1. Details on website.

BEST NEW CANADIAN CHRISTIAN WRITING AWARDS. The Word Guild, Canada. E-mail: admin@thewordguild.com. Website: www.thewordguild.com. Sponsors a number of contests annually. Check website for any current contests and guidelines (click on "Awards"/"Contests").

BLUE RIDGE CONFERENCE WRITING CONTEST. (760) 220-1075. E-mail: alton@gansky-communications.com. Website: http://brmcwc.com. Sponsors three book contests. First prize: a trophy plus $200 scholarship toward conference. Fiction or nonfiction. Unpublished Writers, Director's Choice, and the industrywide Selah Awards. See website for information.

CHRISTIAN SMALL PUBLISHER BOOK OF THE YEAR. Website: www.bookoftheyear.net. Christian Small Publisher Book of the Year Award is designed to promote small publishers in the Christian marketplace as well as to bring recognition to outstanding Christian books from small publishers. Publishers and authors nominate titles for the award and Christian readers vote to determine the winners.

COLUMBIA FICTION/POETRY/NONFICTION CONTEST. Website: www.columbiajournal.org/contests.htm. Length: 20 double-spaced pgs. or up to 5 poems. Prize: $500 in each category, plus publication. Deadline: January 15 (varies). Details on website.

ECPA CHRISTIAN BOOK AWARD. (480) 966-3998. E-mail: awards@ecpa.org. Website: www.ChristianBookAwards.com. The Christian Book Award program recognizes the highest quality in Christian books and is among the oldest and most prestigious award programs in the religious publishing industry. Finalists and awards are selected in seven categories: Bibles, Fiction, Children, Inspiration, Bible Reference,

Nonfiction, and New Author. Sponsored by ECPA and major retail and media partners (www.ECPA.org).

EVANGELICAL PRESS ASSOCIATION ANNUAL CONTEST. PO Box 20198, El Cajon CA 92021. (888) 311-1731. E-mail: director@evangelicalpress.com. Website: www.evangelicalpress.com. Sponsors annual contest for member publications. Deadline: early January.

WILLIAM FAULKNER–WILLIAM WISDOM CREATIVE WRITING COMPETITION. Offers significant cash prizes in seven categories: Novel, Novella, Novel-in-Progress, Short Story, Essay, Poem, and Short Story by a High School Student. For details, visit www.wordsandmusic.org and download guidelines and entry form. Or e-mail the Society at Faulkhouse@aol.com.

FRESH INK CONTEST. (for nonpublished writers). Website: https://thewordguild.com/contests/fresh-ink. Prizes awarded in two age categories: ages 18 to 29 and 30 and over. Grand prize: $100; Second prize: $50.

ERIC HOFFER AWARD. *Best New Writing.* E-mail: info@hofferaward.com. Website: www.HofferAward.com. Submit books via mail; register online. Submit prose online only. The prose category is for creative fiction and nonfiction less than 10,000 words. Annual award for books features 17 categories including e-books and older books. Pays $250–2,000. Guidelines at www.hofferAward.com. Book deadline: January 21; prose deadline: March 31.

INSCRIBE CHRISTIAN WRITERS' CONTEST. Edmonton AB, Canada. (780) 542-7950. Fax (780) 514-3702. Website: www.inscribe.org. Sponsors contests open to non-members; details on website.

INSIGHT WRITING CONTEST. (301) 393-4038. Fax (301) 393-4055. E-mail: insight@rhpa.org. Website: www.insightmagazine.org. Review and Herald/Seventh-day Adventist. A magazine of positive Christian living for Seventh-day Adventist high-schoolers. Sponsors short story and poetry contests; includes a category for students 22 or under. Prizes: $50–250. Deadline: June 1. Submit by e-mail. Details on website (click on "Writing Contest").

+INSPIRATIONAL WRITERS ALIVE! OPEN WRITING COMPETITION. Categories: Short Story-Fiction (adults/young adults), Short Story-Fiction (children/teens), Article, Poetry, Devotional, Nonfiction Book Proposal, and Drama. Limit of two entries per category. Deadline: May 15, 2015. Entry fee: $5–$15 per entry, depending on category and member/nonmember status. Prizes: 1st place: $30, 2nd place: $20, 3rd place: $15. Contact: Martha Rogers, 6038 Greenmont, Houston TX 77092-2332, (713) 686-7209. E-mail: marthalrogers@sbcglobal.net.

GRACE IRWIN AWARD. Website: https://thewordguild.com/contests/grace-irwin-prize. All shortlisted finalists in fiction and nonfiction book categories in The Word Guild Canadian Christian Writing Awards will contend for the Grace Irwin Award. Prize $5,000. A separate round of independent judging will determine the prizewinner.

MINISTRY & LITURGY VISUAL ARTS AWARDS. (408) 286-8505. Fax (408) 287-8748. E-mail: vaa@rpinet.com. Website: www.rpinet.com/vaaentry.pdf. Visual Arts Awards held in 4 categories throughout the year. Best in each category wins $100. Entry fee: $30. Different deadline for each category (see website).

NARRATIVE MAGAZINE SPRING 2015 STORY CONTEST. Website: www.NarrativeMagazine.com. Fiction and nonfiction. Submission fee: $22. Prizes $2,500/$1,000/

$500, plus 10 finalists at $100 each. Also sponsors a fall contest. Complete guidelines on website.

NARRATIVE MAGAZINE 30 BELOW CONTEST-2015. www.NarrativeMagazine. com. Fiction, nonfiction, poetry, graphic novels, graphic art, audio, video, and photography. Submission fee: $22. Prizes $1,500; $750; $300, plus 10 finalists will receive $100 each. Complete guidelines on website.

NARRATIVE MAGAZINE WINTER 2015 STORY CONTEST. Website: www.Narrative Magazine.com. Fiction and nonfiction. Submission fee: $22. Prizes $2,500/$1,000/$500, plus 10 finalists will receive $100 each. Also sponsors a spring contest. Complete guidelines on website.

NEW MILLENNIUM AWARDS. Website: www.newmillenniumwritings.com/awards. html. Prizes: $1,000 award for each category. Best Poem, Best Fiction, Best Nonfiction, Best Short-Short Fiction (fiction and nonfiction 6,000 words; short-short fiction up to 1,000 words; 3 poems to 5 pgs. total). Entry fee: $17 each. Deadline: June 17. Guidelines on website.

NEW MILLENNIUM WRITINGS SEMIANNUAL WRITING CONTESTS. Contact: Steve Petty (stevepetty@live.com). Website: www.newmillenniumwritings.com. Includes fiction, short-short fiction, poetry, and creative nonfiction. Entry fee: $17. Prizes: $1,000 in each category. Deadlines: June 17 & November 30.

ONCE WRITTEN CONTESTS. Fiction and poetry contests. Website: www.oncewritten.com.

OREGON CHRISTIAN WRITERS CASCADE WRITING CONTEST. Sponsors a multiple genre contest for both published and unpublished works (fiction, nonfiction, young adult, poetry, children's, and short entries: columns, stories, and devotionals). E-mail cascades@oregonchristianwriters.org. Guidelines on website: www.oregonchristianwriters.org. Cascade Awards presented at annual OCW summer conference August 10–13, 2015, Portland. Deadline: April 30.

THE EUPLE RINEY MEMORIAL AWARD. E-mail: storytellermag1@yahoo.com. Website: www.thestorytellermagazine.com. 3,000 wds. max. Entry fee $5/story. Deadline postmark: June 30 annually. Prizes: 1st place: $50; 2nd place: $25; 3rd place: $15; 4th place: $10. Plus an Editor's Choice Award. Open genre contest, but must be about family—good or bad. Can be fiction or nonfiction (indicate which). Writers may enter as often as they wish, but entry fee must accompany each entry. Name, address, phone, e-mail, title of story, and word count should be on cover page. Name should not appear anywhere else on ms. No pornography, graphic anything, New Age, or children's stories will be accepted. Mail entries to: The Storyteller, 2441 Washington Rd., Maynard AR 72444.

MONA SCHREIBER PRIZE FOR HUMOROUS FICTION AND NONFICTION. E-mail: brad.schreiber@att.net. Website: www.brashcyber.com or www.bradschreiber. com. Humorous fiction and nonfiction to 750 words. Prizes: $500, $250, and $100. Entry fee: $5 per entry. Foreign entries, please include US currency. Deadline: December 1. Details on website (click on contest name at bottom of illustration).

SOUL-MAKING KEATS LITERARY COMPETITION. Entering its twentieth year, Soul-Making Keats Literary Competition consists of thirteen categories with cash prizes awarded to first, second, and third place in each. Annual deadline is November 30 (postmarked), and winners and honorable mentions are invited to read at the Awards Event at the Koret Auditorium, San Francisco Mail Library, Civic Center. Complete details are available at the website: www.soulmakingcontest.us or via an SASE to The Webhallow House, 1544 Sweetwood Dr., Broadmoor Vlg., CA 94015.

TICKLED BY THUNDER CONTESTS. Canada. (604) 591-6095. E-mail: info@tickledbythunder.com. Website: www.tickledbythunder.com. Sponsors several writing contests each year in various genres. Entry fee $10 for nonsubscribers. Prizes: Based on point system. See website for details.

THE WORD GUILD CANADIAN CHRISTIAN WRITING AWARDS. (For published writers.) Thirty-five awards, encompassing 19 book categories and 16 article/short piece categories, including song lyrics, scripts or screenplays, and blog posts. Round One deadline is September 30 and Round Two deadline is December 31. The fee structure is available on the website for members and non-members. Categories of books and articles, etc., can be found on the website: https://thewordguild.com/contests/the-word-awards.

WRITER'S DIGEST COMPETITIONS. (715) 445-4612, ext. 13430. E-mail: WritersDigestWritingCompetition@fwmedia.com. Website: www.writersdigest.com. Sponsors annual contests for articles, short stories (multiple genres), poetry, children's and young adult fiction, inspirational writing, memoirs/personal essays, self-published books, and scripts (categories vary). Deadlines: vary according to contest. Prizes: up to $3,000 for each contest. Some contests also offer a trip to the annual Writer's Digest Conference in New York City. See website for current contests and rules.

WRITERS-EDITORS NETWORK ANNUAL WRITING COMPETITION. E-mail: editor@writers-editors.com. Website: www.writers-editors.com. Open to all writers. Deadline: March 15. Nonfiction, fiction, children's, poetry. Prizes: $100, $75, $50. Details on website (see right-hand column).

WRITERS' UNION OF CANADA AWARDS & COMPETITIONS. Canada. (416) 703-8982. Fax (416) 504-9090. E-mail: info@writersunion.ca. Website: www.writersunion.ca. Sponsors the Short Prose Competition for Developing Writers. Deadline: March 1; entry fee $29/story; maximum word count 2,500. First prize: $2,500. Details on website.

RESOURCES FOR CONTESTS

ADDITIONAL CONTESTS. You will find some additional contests sponsored by local groups and conferences that are open to nonmembers. See individual listings in those sections.

FREELANCE WRITING: WEBSITE FOR TODAY'S WORKING WRITER. Website: www.freelancewriting.com/writingcontests.php.

OZARK CREATIVE WRITERS CONTESTS. E-mail submissions only: ozarkcreativewriters@earthlink.net. Website: www.ozarkcreativewriters.org. Multiple contests listed on website.

THE WRITE PLACE BY KIMN SWENSON GOLLNICK. Contest listings. Website: www.KIMN.net/contests.htm.

THE WRITER CONTEST. *The Writer* magazine. (262) 796-8776. E-mail: editor@writermag.com. Website: www.writermag.com. General. How-to for writers. Occasionally sponsors a contest and lists multiple contests. Check website.

MAJOR LITERARY AWARDS

AUDIES: www.audiopub.org

CALDECOTT MEDAL: www.ala.org

CAROL AWARDS: www.acfw.com/carol

EDGAR: www.mysterywriters.org

HEMINGWAY FOUNDATION/PEN AWARD: www.pen-ne.org

HUGO: http://worldcon.org/hugos.html

NATIONAL BOOK AWARD: www.nationalbook.org

NATIONAL BOOK CRITICS CIRCLE AWARD: www.bookcritics.org

NEBULA: http://dpsinfo.com/awardweb/nebulas

NEWBERY: www.ala.org/alsc/awardsgrants/bookmedia/newberymedal/newberymedal

NOBEL PRIZE FOR LITERATURE: www.nobelprize.org

PEN/FAULKNER AWARD: www.penfaulkner.org

PULITZER PRIZE: www.pulitzer.org

RITA: www.rwanational.org/cs/contests_and_awards

14

Denominational
Book Publishers and Periodicals

ASSEMBLIES OF GOD
Book Publisher
My Healthy Church

Periodicals
Enrichment Journal
For Every Woman
God's Word for Today
Live
Pentecostal Evangel
Take Five Plus
Testimony

BAPTIST, FREE WILL
Book Publisher
Randall House

Periodicals
Treasure

BAPTIST, SOUTHERN
Book Publisher
B&H Publishing
New Hope Publishers

Periodicals
Baptist Press
Mature Living
On Mission
Point
Founders Journal
ParentLife

BAPTIST (OTHER)
Book Publisher
Earthen Vessel
    Publishing
Judson Press (American)

Periodicals
Baptist Bulletin
    (Regular)
The Baptist Standard
Common Call

Secret Place (American)
Word & Way

CATHOLIC
Book Publisher
American Catholic
    Press
Canticle Books
Catholic Univ. of
    America Press
Franciscan Media
HarperOne (Cath. bks.)
Loyola Press
Oregon Catholic Press
Our Sunday Visitor
Pauline Books
Pauline Kids & Teens
St. Catherine of Siena
    Press

Periodicals
America
Arlington Catholic
    Herald
Catechist
Catholic Digest
Catholic New York
Catholic Sentinel
CGA World
Columbia
Eureka Street
Every Day With the
    Word
Leaves
Our Sunday Visitor
Parish Liturgy
Prairie Messenger
Priest, The
Share
St. Anthony Messenger
Today's Catholic Teacher
U.S. Catholic

CHRISTIAN CHURCH/
CHURCH OF CHRIST
Book Publisher
CrossLink Publishing

Periodicals
Christian Chronicle
Christian Standard

CHURCH OF GOD
(HOLINESS)
Periodicals
Church Herald and
    Holiness Banner
Gems of Truth

CHURCH OF GOD
(OTHER)
Book Publisher
Warner Press (Anderson
    IN)

Periodicals
Bible Advocate
    (Seventh-day)
Church of God Evangel
    (Clevelnd TN)
Now What?
    (Seventh-day)
Pentecostal Messenger
    (Pentecostal)

EPISCOPAL
Book Publisher
Forward Movement

Periodicals
Church of England
    Newspaper
Encompass
Forward Day by Day

LUTHERAN
Book Publisher
Concordia

Concordia Academic
  Press
Kirk House Publishers
Langmarc Publishing
Lutheran University
  Press
Lutheran Voices

Periodicals
  Canada Lutheran
    (ELCC)
  Canadian Lutheran
  L Magazine
  Lutheran Digest
  Lutheran forum
  Lutheran Journal
  Lutheran Witness

MENNONITE
Periodicals
  The Messenger
  Canadian Mennonite
  Christian Leader
  Purpose
  Rejoice!

METHODIST, FREE
Periodicals
  Evangel
  Light and Life

METHODIST, UNITED
Book Publisher
  Abingdon Press

Periodicals
  Good News (NY)
  Mature Years
  Methodist History
  Pockets
  Upper Room

NONDENOMINATIONAL
Book Publisher
  AMG Publishers
  Christian Writers Ebook
    Net
  Group Publishing
  Meriwether Publishing
  Port Hole Publications

Subsidy Publisher
  Healthy Life Press

Periodicals
  Believer's Bay
  Joyful Living
  Sparkle

PRESBYTERIAN
Periodicals
  ARP Magazine
  byFaith
  Presbyterians Today
  These Days

QUAKER/FRIENDS
Book Publisher
  Friends United Press

Periodicals
  Friends Journal
  Quaker Life

REFORMED
Periodicals
  The Banner
  The Banner Online
  Christian Courier
  Perspectives
  Reformed Worship

SEVENTH-DAY
ADVENTIST
Book Publisher
  Pacific Press

Periodicals
  Guide Magazine
  Insight
  Jour. of Adventist
    Education
  Kid's Ministry Ideas
  Ministry Magazine
  Our Little Friend
  Primary Treasure
  Vibrant Life
  A Virtuous Woman

WESLEYAN CHURCH
Book Publisher
  Wesleyan Publishing
    House

Periodicals
  Light from the Word
  Wesleyan Life Online

MISCELLANEOUS
DENOMINATIONS
**Anglican Church of
Canada**
  Anglican Journal

Antiochian Orthodox
  Ancient Faith Publishing

Brethren in Christ Church
  In Part

Churches of God
  The Gem

Evangelical Covenant
  The Covenant Companion

**Evangelical Fellowship of
Canada**
  Anglican Journal

Evangelical Free Church
  EFCA Today

Grace Brethren Churches
  BMH Books
  GraceConnect

**Intl. Pentecostal Holiness
Church**
  The Experience

Nazarene Church
  Holiness Today

**Open Bible Standard
Churches**
  Message of the Open Bible
    & Online

United Church of Canada
  United Church Observer

BONUS SECTION

Writer's Helps

Winning Fiction

Knowing Enough About Your Characters

by Dave Lambert

MOST NOVELISTS ARE GUILTY OF NOT KNOWING ENOUGH about their characters — inventing just enough as they go to get by, but never developing the depth of understanding of their characters to bring authenticity to their depiction.

The surest way to force yourself to delve deeply enough into the lives of your characters is to write detailed biographies of them. Those biographies may never show up in the finished novel, although portions are likely to show up here and there. But they give you the knowledge to create characters whose actions and words resonate with your reader.

When, in your novel, Millie can't keep her fingers from fiddling with any small, loose object in arm's reach, there's a reason: She stopped smoking just three months ago, and her fingers are still reaching for a cigarette. In fact, she often brings those objects to her lips and nibbles on them. But only because you know that she recently stopped smoking did it occur to you to give her that nervous habit.

Her eagerness to please comes from her flawed relationship with her harsh, disapproving father. That's also why country music (the kind he listened to) makes her nervous. Because her family was poor and there was never enough food, Millie now eats too much and tends to hoard food in her spotless apartment — spotless because Millie's mother equated sloppiness with sin.

Where did Millie go to school? How many schools did she attend? What kind of teachers did she have? What did she enjoy studying, if anything, and what relationship does that interest have, if any, with the profession she finally chose? Or did she choose it? Maybe she fell into her job by accident.

Has she been in love? Is there anyone she's in love with now, whether he knows it or not? What types of food does she enjoy most? Does she enjoy cooking, and is she good at it? What's her favorite restaurant? How does she feel about spending money on eating out?

What is her attitude toward clothes? How does she feel about her appearance — what part of her body is she most self-conscious about? What would she change about herself, if she could? Does she play the lottery? How is she at handling money? Is she a "pet person"? What childhood pets touched her life?

If Millie is a Christian, how long has she been one? Did her parents believe? Did they go to church? How many siblings did Millie have, and are they still living? What was her relationship with them like when she was young, and what is it like now? Where do they live? How does she get along with her neighbors? Is she an introvert or an extrovert? A thinker or a feeler?

How can you write convincingly about a character without knowing such things?

How can you write convincingly about a character without knowing such things? You can't.

Five writers each invented a teenage character, then collaborated on a series of novels about that group of friends. The novelist who had invented each character wrote a novel from that character's point of view. But since all of the characters were included in each novel, we had to provide each other with detailed information sheets about our character. They included several pages of mundane but essential data — height, weight, and so on — as well as the more distinctive. We could not have written the novels without those clues into our characters' lives. You may want to create your own personal data sheets for each of your characters.

What are some things you need to know about your characters? Here's a partial list, intended to spark your own efforts:

- The nature of their childhood
- Fears
- What they love and what they hate
- General temperament
- Dreams and longings
- Vices
- Quirks
- Relationships: with family, friends, parents, lovers, co-workers, boss, employees, church family, neighbors
- Tastes in food, music, clothes, friends, entertainment, recreation, transportation, vacations
- Education and career
- Appearance, health, disabilities
- Secrets
- Details of their history
- Gifts and talents
- Verbal habits
- Relationship to God or lack thereof
- Mental and emotional habits and health
- Where they live, and why, and how they feel about it

That list could be much longer. And every item opens a world of questions. Take career. Knowing what your character does for a living is just the beginning. You need to know how good she is at it and how long she's been doing it. Is she frustrated in her job or fulfilled? Does she feel she's underworked or overworked? What is her work environment like, and how does she feel about it?

Or take appearance. You need to know not only how your characters look, but also how they feel about how they look. Do they have body issues? How do they feel about their hair? Why do they dress as they do?

Though most of the background you create for your characters will be implied on the page rather than expressed directly, you still need to communicate enough to your readers that they understand the people in your story.

Used by permission of the Jerry Jenkins Writers Guild.

What Your
Characters Must Do

by Dave Lambert

IF YOUR FICTION IS TO WORK, your characters must be in conflict. They must grow and develop through the course of the story. They must be active, not passive. They must be adequately and believably motivated. And at least a few of them must be fully developed, with depth, complexity, and internal struggles and contradictions.

They Must Be in Conflict

Every significant character in your fiction must be someone in conflict. Without conflict, there is no story. Without conflict, there can be no growth.

The various classifications of conflict, such as man versus nature, are sometimes useful. But especially for Christian novelists, it's more useful to remember something once said by William Faulkner: In the best fiction, all meaning comes from "the heart in conflict with itself ... ." All other conflicts, whether with other humans, nature, or God, point to that central conflict. The cry of fiction's strongest characters is the same as that of Paul:

> I do not understand what I do. For what I want to do I do not do, but what I hate I do. ... For I have the desire to do what is good, but I cannot carry it out. For what I do is not the good I want to do; no, the evil I do not want to do — this I keep on doing. ... What a wretched man I am! Who will rescue me from this body of death?
> — Rom. 7:15, 18, 19, 24 NIV

They Must Grow

Each of us changes as we go through life. We learn things. We may become hardened because of bitterness, anger, sin, or greed. We may learn to stop living selfishly and place others before ourselves. Our goals change. We sink into despair, we find our true calling, or we are transformed by love. But we all change. We all grow. And the characters in your fiction have to change and grow in the same ways.

They Must Act

Your characters must not merely be acted upon. They must be agents, making decisions and shaping their environment. Novelists are sometimes tempted to turn their characters into victims in an attempt to gain reader sympathy. It generally has the opposite effect.

One enduring idea that comes to us from the ancient Greek playwrights is that the hero's ultimate victory or downfall has to be predicated on his own actions and decisions, not imposed or bestowed on him from outside. Even the most passive of protagonists must, in the end, choose something and do it.

They Must Be Consistent and Adequately Motivated

The last thing a novelist wants is for a reader to stop halfway through and say, "Wait, this character would never do this. She would never say this." When your readers think that, two things happen. First, your story loses credibility. It no longer rings true. Above all, Christian novelists should desire to write fiction that is "true." Second, your readers are bounced out of the fictional dream. No longer immersed in the world you've created; they're aware they are sitting and reading a novel — and a not skillfully crafted one.

You want your readers to believe that when your characters speak or act, that is exactly how they would speak or act in that situation. The only way to accomplish that is first to know your characters well enough to know how they will speak and act and, second, to ask yourself constantly as you write, "How will this character behave now?"

Two observations. First, it's dangerous for you as a writer to start a story by figuring out how you want it to end — and then trying to write to that ending. When you do that, you're not asking as you write, "How would this character behave in this situation?" Instead you're asking, "What should I make this character do next to get to the ending I want?" The too-common result is that you make your characters behave in a way that isn't true to them. In my years an editor of fiction, this is one of the most common reasons

I have to question an author about inconsistent characterization.

Writing to a preconceived ending seems a particular temptation for Christians. I suspect that many of us start a novel with a sense of what we want the point of the sermon to be — the spiritual "takeaway" — and then we write to that point. That's a good way to concoct a sermon, but not a good way to write fiction.

Your characters have to behave like real people, not like pawns you move to have the story come out just the way you want.

"True fiction" has to be true to the human condition. That means your characters have to behave like real people in real situations, not like pawns you move to have the story come out just the way you want.

A better choice is to let your cast of characters take over the story by behaving in ways consistent to their character as you've created it — and reluctantly rethink the ending you wanted. The result will be a novel that's much more satisfying to your readers.

Even though you want your characters to be consistent throughout your novel, you also want them capable of occasionally surprising your readers. Novels without surprises are dull. The secret is to make even those surprises consistent with the characters you've created. If your characters are complex enough, that should be possible. Real people often behave in surprising ways, but at some level even those surprises are consistent with that person's emotional, spiritual, and psychological makeup. And that leads us to the need for fully rounded characters.

You Need Both Round and Flat Characters

E. M. Forster, in his book *Aspects of the Novel*, distinguishes between round and flat characters:

> Flat characters … in their purest form … are constructed round a single idea or quality: when there is more than one factor in them, we get the beginning of the curve towards the round. The really flat characters can be expressed in one sentence such as, "I will never desert Mr. Micawber." There is Mrs. Micawber — she says she won't desert Mr. Micawber; she doesn't, and there she is. … The test of a round character is whether it is capable of surprising in a convincing way. If it never surprises, it is flat.

A novel that contains only flat characters, those with no complexity, surprises, or internal contradictions (that internal struggle Paul expressed so eloquently in Romans 7), will be a novel without surprises or insight into the mysteries of life.

Plot-driven fiction often contains only flat characters. They're much easier to maneuver through a complex, pulse-pounding plot. They don't ask embarrassing questions, let their conscience get in the way, or suffer angst or depression. Ultimately, though, fiction that doesn't include fully complex, rounded characters reveals less about the human condition — and therefore reveals less about our relationship with God — and is less likely to remain in the readers' mind, nagging them toward greater self-understanding.

Used by permission of the Jerry Jenkins Writers Guild.

To Outline or Not

by Dave Lambert

WHAT ABOUT OUTLINING? Don't many novelists work up an outline before they write their first draft, sometimes even a detailed plan for each scene? Yes, some do — and claim they can't write a novel any other way.

Katherine Anne Porter said she would never write the first page of a short story until she knew what the last page would say. Dostoyevsky wrote eight successive outlines of *The Idiot*, changing his conception of the story dramatically. Henry James wrote detailed scenarios of his novels before he began his first drafts; his scenario for *The Ambassadors* ran 20,000 words. Agatha Christie forced herself to chart her works-in-progress in great detail, from beginning to end.

Other writers couldn't come up with such an outline to save their lives — and couldn't write from it even if they did. For them, the first draft is the way they discover the story. Here's mystery novelist Raymond Chandler:

> I have never plotted anything on paper. I do my plotting in my head as I go along, and usually I do it wrong and have to do it all over again. I know there are writers who plot their stories in great detail before they begin to write them, but I am not one of that group. With me, plots are not made, they grow. And if they refuse to grow, you throw the stuff away and start over again.

If you've already written a novel or two, you probably know how you work best. But if you're reading this in preparation for your first novel, attempt an outline first. I suggest this partly as a way of managing the work and making the monumental task of writing a novel less daunting. It may be easier to begin the journey if you have at least some notion of where you're headed.

I suggest an outline of at least a dozen pages and possibly two or three dozen. In that outline, you'll make a lot of guesses. Even the plot is just a guess; you may make major plot changes in your first draft and your revisions. You may add or subtract characters and change the nature of the conflict, and you very likely will change the ending (at least I hope you'll let yourself make such changes).

The scenes you sketch in your outline, if you work at that level of detail, will almost certainly be juggled, re-ordered, dropped, and added. That's as it should be. Think of that outline as a map at the beginning of a long journey. It would be too frightening to begin with no map at all. But once you've begun, as you gain confidence and get used to the road, you begin to think of the map as just a general guide. You give yourself permission to explore side routes, visit unfamiliar stops, change the order of the trip, and follow your whims. The outline helps you get started, but shouldn't make you its slave.

Novelists work in different ways, but all novelists have ways in which they work best. One of the most important tasks for all writers of fiction is to find the system, the place, the tools, the atmosphere, the approach, and the mood that foster their greatest creativity — and then reproduce those conditions as nearly as possible each time they approach their fiction. The creative impulse is a precious, even sacred thing. Nourish and cherish it.

The Power of Surprise

by Dave Lambert

WE CHRISTIANS SOMETIMES HAVE A HARD TIME trusting the creative act — the process through which something that didn't exist before (a character, a story) comes into existence. Yet those who believe that God spoke the world into existence should certainly trust the creative process. They should be thrilled to participate with God in creating our own world of story.

Too often, we Christians are obsessed by control. And tight control stifles the creative impulse. If we have turned our lives over to Christ and asked Him to take control of everything, then perhaps we should learn to trust some of the things He might do through us when we release some of that control — even if the result is surprising. Or especially if the result is surprising.

The Principle of Surprise

All good writing is surprising. It should be as surprising for us as we create it as it is for others when they read it. One great joy of writing fiction is being surprised by our characters and what they do and say.

In fact, if you don't find your characters doing things you had not anticipated, if you don't find yourself saying as you write, "Where did this come from?" you face the danger that your readers will find your story too predictable. In Hollywood, scriptwriters call such writing "on the nose." If you're not being surprised as you write, your readers likely won't be either. This is true even if you first outline your story.

If you're not being surprised as you write, your readers likely won't be either.

To many Christians, the unconscious mind seems threatening. How do we know it's not revealing something sinful about ourselves? Worse, how do we know it's not influenced negatively by something outside ourselves?

But there's no reason to assume the right-side functions of our brain can't honor God. To become powerful writers of fiction, we sometimes have to let the right side of our brains lead us. Later the analytical side will have the opportunity to revise and shape everything the creative side comes up with.

Nowhere is the creative side more crucial than in producing that all-important first draft. Why is the first draft so important? It's not important in deciding what words actually end up on the page. By the time you finish revising, few of the words you scribble in your first draft may remain. It's not even important in determining what scenes end up in the final version or the story's final shape. All those may change during revision.

Your first draft, however, is key in deciding how much freedom you'll allow yourself in exploring the story and the characters. Are you going to hold to some plan so tightly, you don't allow yourself to explore what you learn about the characters and the story as you go? If so, you risk never discovering what your story truly is.

The Principle of Discovery

Good writing is the process of discovering what you believe. At the same time, good writing is discovering what you want to say.

You may respond, "That's backwards. First you figure out what you believe, then you figure out how you want to say it, then you write."

That makes perfect sense — except to those who've learned one of the great secrets of creative expression. The act of creative expression forces you to explore your subject matter, your beliefs, and your assumptions in a way and at a depth you've never done before.

Unless you've forced yourself to re-think your message, you've missed a precious opportunity.

In the process of writing you encounter your faulty assumptions, your prejudices, and your blind spots with a rigor you may never have brought to them before. When that happens, you may have to rethink the direction you had in mind. In fact, unless you've forced yourself to re-think your message, you've missed a precious opportunity for growth and self-discovery.

The language leads, and the wise writer follows.

What are the techniques that will allow you to give yourself the scope and creativity to let your story find its course? One is free writing. In its simplest form it consists of simply getting words on paper (or the computer screen) as quickly as possible, without engaging your brain's critical function. No second guessing, no looking back. Only forward motion. Try it.

Once you master this technique, there's no reason to have writer's block again. Typically, writers experience writer's block because they're trying to write well. *In Bird by Bird,* Anne Lamott suggests we give ourselves permission to write badly. Easier said than done, but she's right. It's important to give our creativity the latitude to explore and create the story we're searching for. Learn to write badly at first — so you can write brilliantly in the end.

Used by permission of the Jerry Jenkins Writers Guild.

Establishing a Fictional Dream

by Dave Lambert

THE NOTION OF THE FICTIONAL DREAM can guide us in knowing what works and what doesn't in a story, in deciding what stays and what goes, and in deciding how to shape a scene or a plot or how to develop a character. In *The Art of Fiction,* John Gardner says:

> One of the chief mistakes a writer can make is to allow or force the reader's mind to be distracted, even momentarily, from the fictional dream .... The writer distracts the reader — breaks the film, if you will — when by some slip of technique or egoistic intrusion he allows or forces the reader to stop thinking about the story (stop 'seeing' the story) and think about something else.

We've all had the experience of immersing ourselves in a short story or novel so completely, we're not even aware of holding a book. Then blam! We stumble across some awkward exposition, clumsy bit of dialogue, or poorly motivated action. Immediately, we're aware that we're reading a book. The author went to great lengths to put us in a fictional dream world, and then blew it.

How does a novelist create the fictional dream? By doing well all the things a novelist must do: creating believable, interesting, memorable characters; putting credible, economic dialogue in their mouths; moving smoothly from one well-crafted scene to the next; handling deftly the complexities of plot; giving the reader enough detail to envision your setting; and so on.

Like learning to play the piano, learning to write fiction is not a matter of memorizing a set of rules. It's a matter of mastering a set of techniques. The artist — and fiction writers are artists — who desires to excel at fiction must dedicate himself to mastering them.

As you've heard it said: How does one learn to write? By writing and writing and writing. That's because the writing itself is your practice. Every page of fictional narrative you write is like that half-hour at the piano keys, honing your skills.

The essential techniques of fiction — the disciplines that allow a novelist to create a vivid and continuous fictional dream — are the subject of the next articles.

Three Things Readers Expect

by Dave Lambert

THE FIRST PAGE OF A NOVEL, or the first sentence of a short story, constitutes an implied agreement between you and your reader. Each wants something from the other, and each promises something to get what he wants.

You want continuation — for your reader to read to the end. You want intensity, too; not simply reading casually with one eye on the TV, but for the reader to pay attention to your scenes and characters, noticing even subtle things.

You also want assent, sometimes called a *willing suspension of disbelief* — to receive the benefit of the doubt to stay with the story rather than constantly gauging how likely its events are.

Finally, you want your reader to understand what he's reading.

But the reader doesn't have to give you any of those. You have to earn them by keeping your end of that implied contract.

The first thing the contract promises is that there will be a story — not just philosophy or a sermon. Things will happen and there will be tension to be resolved — a *story*.

Second, you promise the story will be told in terms of people. True, you can dress those people in rabbit skins, as Richard Adams did in *Watership Down,* or in hobbit skins, as Tolkien did in his famous trilogy. But if you've read those books, you know that Adams's rabbits were people and so were Tolkien's hobbits. They thought like people, they acted like people. The story wouldn't have meant anything to us if they hadn't.

Third, you promise that the story will have an end — as well as a beginning and a middle. Why mention the end first? One of the greatest frustrations in reading a story is getting to the end and saying, "That's it?"

> *Your readers need you to bring the main conflicts to some sort of conclusion.*

A piece of fiction needs a satisfying ending. That doesn't mean everything has to be resolved; the best, most satisfying fiction often leaves some things open. But your readers need you to bring the main conflicts to some sort of conclusion. They need, in the book's language and rhythm, a strong sense of finality.

You can't expect your reader to stick with your story unless you uphold your end of the bargain. If, ten pages into your novel, a reader realizes you don't know what you're doing and won't offer a pleasant reading experience, why bother? There isn't enough time in life to read all the good books, so why waste time on bad ones?

Learn to see your fiction as your readers will.

Used by permission of the Jerry Jenkins Writers Guild.

Tools for Creating Character

by Dave Lambert

THE MOST EFFECTIVE TOOL for conveying and developing character in fiction is showing characters in action (showing rather than telling).

In life if you want to learn who people really are, watch what they say and do. If you want your readers to get a feel for who your characters really are, show it through dialogue and action.

Still, every novelist sometimes finds it necessary to convey character through weaker but still effective means: summary (telling rather than showing). But let's talk about the more effective means first.

Action

Does your protagonist lunge toward people, enthusiastically greeting everyone she meets, making everyone feel like the most important person in her life at that moment? Or does she shrink from contact, rarely meeting anyone's eyes, escaping from conversations as quickly as she can? Does she rush to the phone or let it ring? These tell you much about her relationships and her personality.

Does the assailant in your story attack people in the heat of anger — violent only for a moment, then rush from the scene in remorse? Or does he initiate the conflict coldly, just for the enjoyment of inflicting pain, and then linger over the assault?

The way your characters drive, eat, kiss, shake hands, walk, dance, discipline their children — their tics, their laughter, gestures, mannerisms, and habits — all are effective tools for creating character.

But you can use actions to develop character in other ways. It's also significant how other characters in the novel act around the one you're trying to describe. Do co-workers and friends avoid your character? What does their body language communicate? Do those of the opposite sex seem romantically interested in your character? If so, do their approaches imply either looseness or aloofness on the part of your character? The responses and reactions of others to your character say a great deal about him.

Dialogue

In life we reveal much about ourselves by what we say and how we say it. In fiction that is even more true, because the dialogue is shaped by a novelist who intends it to reveal character.

Your characters reveal information about themselves through dialogue in several ways. For one, they can intentionally give information:

> Delores shivered in the night air. "What was that? That sound?"
>
> Anthony looked out across the twilit hills, listened as one more yipping call echoed, and said, "Coyotes. They're not as close as they sound, though. And don't worry; they won't bother us."
>
> "How do you know so much about coyotes?"
>
> "I lived on a ranch in eastern Oregon for a few years."
>
> "Really? When was that?"
>
> "Oh, when I was a teenager. Didn't get along too well with my parents, and my dad packed me off to live with my uncle and aunt. He thought it was a punishment, but to tell you the truth, I liked it a lot better than living with my parents. I would have stayed out there, I think."

"Why didn't you?"

"My uncle died. Aunt Betty couldn't keep the place going by herself, so she sold it."

For another, they can unintentionally reveal information:

"Did she sell it to someone in the family?"

"No. No, there wasn't anybody else in the family who still lived out West. She had it on the market for a year or more, and then she ended up selling it for a lot less than it was worth to a couple of slopeheads."

"To — who?"

"Uh — you know. Orientals."

"You called them …"

"That was just what my uncle called 'em."

"Oh."

Dialogue can also convey character information when two characters talk about a third:

"He called them what?"

Delores shook her head. "I know, Agnes, it sounds horrible, doesn't it? I guess it never occurred to me that he might be prejudiced."

"But he's from the West. Aren't they supposed to be more open-minded out there?"

"Well, for one thing, he didn't live his whole life out West. He was born in Baltimore, and his family lived near Washington D.C. until he went to live with his uncle in Oregon. But I didn't even tell you the worst yet."

"Oh, no."

"He's been in jail."

"In jail? For what?"

"Assault. On a Hispanic man."

Dialogue is an incredibly versatile tool for characterization. It often cuts two ways. When Character A says something about Character B, he reveals not only information about Character B, but also about himself: attitudes, emotions, fears, hostility, and so on.

Dialogue reveals a great deal about relationships when you compare, for instance, the haughty, distant way Edward talks to Henry with the warm, even deferential way he speaks to Louis.

Writing With a Full Palette of Emotions

by Dave Lambert

UNLESS YOU DISCIPLINE YOURSELF TO DEFINE PRECISELY what emotion your character is feeling, how do you know how your character will act? What your character will say? How do you describe the room, the day, or an event from that character's point of view?

There is a long list of emotions any novelist needs to be familiar with. Just as a painter needs access to thousands of colors, a novelist needs access to all human emotions, and needs to know how to express them.

Consider anger. Imagine you're writing a scene in which your protagonist is angry. Do you know enough to write that scene? I don't think so. Let's parse that more finely. What are the various faces of anger, the emotions that fall into that same family? Consider these:

- Frustration
- Rage
- Hate
- Hostility
- Irritation
- Jealousy
- Revenge
- Suspicion

There's a big difference between hate and irritation, between suspicion and frustration. Before you can create that character's emotional state convincingly, you've got to define it precisely. It's not just anger — it's something more specific. Depending on how you define it, your character will speak, act, think, and feel in different ways.

Let's make another list. What are various colors of sadness? Here are just a few:

- Sorrow
- Disappointment
- Loneliness
- Despair
- Regret
- Grief
- Unhappiness

Again, great differences. Your character may be unhappy simply because the cappuccino machine is broken and he can't get his coffee. But he wouldn't grieve over it (unless he's emotionally unbalanced, which is a possibility you'll want to use only rarely).

Let's go to the other extreme. What are some emotions in the same family as happiness?

- Relief
- Ecstasy
- Pleasure
- Joy
- Hope
- Contentment

- Satisfaction
- Giddiness
- Sense of accomplishment
- Excitement
- Gratitude

There are vast differences in the ways your characters would express these emotions. Someone who is quietly content might walk through a room and fluff up the flowers in a bouquet. Someone excited about the imminent arrival of a long-absent family member might not even notice the flowers.

We could list all the colors of love, fear, apathy, desire, surprise, or curiosity. But the principle is clear: Emotions are complex. Until we define our characters' emotions specifically and accurately, we'll be inexact in describing them. And they will all begin to sound the same.

Used by permission of the Jerry Jenkins Writers Guild.

Selecting Scenes

by Dave Lambert

THERE IS NO ONE RIGHT WAY TO SELECT and write the scenes that will make a story. The sequence that would be right for one writer would be awkward and ineffective for another. You are the writer; you must decide what scenes, and in what order, work best for your story and your characters.

When do you make that selection? It doesn't happen in your first draft. At that point, you're simply trying to get the story down in some form, any form.

When at long last you complete that first draft and read through it, you might find sections of narrative summary that are really just sketches of scenes — important ones you'll go back later and flesh out so your readers can experience them along with the characters.

Undoubtedly, you will also find a lot of scenes, summaries, and descriptions that will never make it into the next draft. Even though you may have needed to write those for your own sake as you explored the characters and the story, they aren't crucial to the story.

Writers who outline may think through some of their scene selection as they're outlining. Still, it's almost inevitable that some of those decisions will change as they compose their first draft.

At some point you have to decide which scenes stay, which get the ax, and where you may need additional scenes.

Whether you write that first draft with or without the help of an outline, at some point you are going to have to decide which scenes stay, which get the ax, and where you may need additional scenes. How do you make those decisions?

First, *you need to know what the novel is about* — what is its central conflict. How can you decide what scenes go in without knowing what job they have in the grand scheme?

Second, *you need to know what happens in the book.* The action in chapter ten may require that the scene in chapter four be left in. If the scene in chapter seven has no relation to anything that follows, it probably should be cut.

Third, *you need to determine the purposes of each scene.* I say purposes, plural, because even in a sprawling novel you don't have the luxury of writing scenes that do just one thing.

In your revision you should begin revising and combining scenes to make them perform more than one task. Advancing the plot, characterization, exposition, foreshadowing, establishing voice or tone — the same scenes can and should accomplish these and many other tasks.

Varying Your Scenes

by Dave Lambert

YOU WOULD NEVER WRITE A PAGE with all the sentences the same length and structure. The same goes for scenes. To keep the rhythm of your fiction lively and intriguing, vary your scenes.

As an editor of fiction, I see a lot of manuscripts with the scenes maddeningly uniform in length and intensity. I recently edited a novel in which (before the author rewrote it) scene after scene contained just two characters. Two characters — just enough for a conversation. The next scene would have two different characters, and another conversation.

Readers might not recognize this pattern repeated ad nauseum, but they would know after a couple of dozen pages that the novel was flat and boring. Vary the personnel in your scenes: solo scenes, duo scenes, small ensemble scenes, crowd scenes. Vary the setting: indoor scenes, outdoor scenes, estate scenes, ghetto scenes, shopping mall scenes, airplane scenes.

Another common mistake is to make all the scenes about the same length. Again, your readers might not know the novel's rhythm makes it predictable and boring, but they will know it is. Vary the length of your scenes.

Imagine a movie in which every scene has the same level of emotional intensity or the same pace. Give readers variety: some scenes so intense their knuckles will turn white from gripping the book — followed by other scenes far less intense. Give them some scenes filled with action, others consisting simply of two or three people sitting and talking. Vary the pace of the scenes — some with things happening quickly, others leisurely.

Even a series of fast-paced, emotionally intense scenes with lots of action can get boring if there's no break.

Build gradually to those scenes, then break to something not so breathless.

Will you recognize, as you're writing your first draft, that you're getting into a rut? Probably not — nor should you. Your goal at that point is just to get the story down in rough form. As you're revising you'll flag scenes that need to be re-cast or put in different order.

Tasks for A Scene's First Lines
by Dave Lambert

THERE WILL BE NO HARDER-WORKING SENTENCES in your novel or short story than these. If those sentences don't handle their job well, your reader will flounder.

One of a novelist's biggest tasks is creating a vivid and continuous fictional dream. Lack of clarity in the first few lines of a scene risks bouncing your reader out of that dream. When your readers aren't clear what's happening, they're suddenly aware they've encountered a novelist who got sloppy.

Here are things opening lines must do well:

Establish Point of View

Every novel is a mystery novel — people read novels to discover what's going to happen. But while it's desirable to have readers unsure what will happen next, it's neither fair nor wise to have them unsure what's happening at the moment.

Your readers should never doubt which character's eyes they're seeing the scene through. So the first few lines of every scene must establish, clearly and without confusion, the point of view.

When the entire novel is written in a single point of view, as with most first-person novels, this isn't a problem. But in a multiple-viewpoint novel, your readers know that any particular scene might be experienced through the eyes of any of a cast of characters. They have no way of knowing which until you tell them.

If the point of view remains vague until several lines into a scene, your reader will stay disoriented until you finally establish a clear viewpoint. Nothing you try to communicate up to that point will be effective.

Even in a carelessly written scene, the point of view eventually becomes clear. Your goal is to make it clear from the beginning

Establish a Clear Sense of Place

Your reader should also have no doubt, after the first few lines, where the scene is taking place. Yet such lack of clarity is common in unedited manuscripts. Writers who love dialogue often try to convey a sense of headlong rush in a fast-paced scene by writing in dialogue only.

Fiction works by stimulating a reader's imagination to envision a scene.

But fiction works by stimulating a reader's imagination to envision a scene. You don't want your reader simply hearing the scene — you want it scrolling through your reader's imagination with appeal to all senses: hearing, sight, smell, touch, even taste. That makes the novelist responsible to provide enough description of the setting so the reader can supply the rest of the details.

It's not enough to know the scene between Grace and her daughter, Melody, takes place indoors. Are they at Grace's home, Melody's, someone else's? Are they in the kitchen, living room, or a bedroom? Is it an executive home or a fixer-upper? Clean or messy? Newly redecorated or past its prime?

Two dangers in not adequately setting a scene in the first few lines: First, the scene loses clarity, intensity, and power. Second, readers can make wrong assumptions. A scene's setting can do much to add emotional power, convey mood, and add strength to characterization. If you don't establish the setting quickly, you forfeit your opportunity to benefit from the power of a strong sense of place.

If all your reader knows in the first few lines is that Grace and Melody are sitting talking quietly, she will probably assume they are talking in a quiet place. A page later your reader will be puzzled to discover Melody and Grace are in a crowded bus station. If the scene is presented from one of their viewpoints, why didn't it convey a sense of what that character was so annoyingly aware of?

Such a lack of care on the author's part will bounce readers out of the fictional dream.

Establish a Clear Sense of Time

Those first few lines should also make clear aspects concerning time. In most cases you want to communicate how much time has passed since the last scene. That may be simple, depending on how you've set the scene in the previous one. If it ended with a married couple dashing around to get ready for a dinner party at the ambassador's house, and the next scene begins with the husband and wife at a formal party with the ambassador, your readers will assume the scene begins an hour or two later. If such clues aren't present, find some device to set the scene on the novel's calendar.

In most cases you want to communicate how much time has passed since the last scene.

As with any fiction technique, there are exceptions. An obvious one, usually at the beginning of chapters, is when considerable time has passed — and the amount of time is not immediately significant. For instance, a chapter ends with a businessman, whose children are grown and whose wife recently died, realizing one afternoon that the world of business no longer appeals to him. He really wants to become a fishing guide. He turns off his computer, tells his secretary and his boss good-bye, and walks out.

The next chapter begins with him in his canoe, gliding down a small river in Montana, searching for trout. Your reader will assume the businessman has made good on his resolution. But since time in your character's new life moves at a more leisurely pace, it isn't immediately important if it's three months later or nine. At some point you'll need to communicate how long it's been — but you can do that when it's convenient and necessary.

It is significant, though, to clarify whether it's just after daybreak, with dew still suspended on the spider webs along the bank and wisps of fog drifting through the trees; or noon, with mosquitoes buzzing around your protagonist's sweating face and turtles sunning themselves on the rocks; or sunset, with the treetops glowing orange, deer moving cautiously through the forest, and a hatch of mayflies dancing on the water's surface, attracting trout.

The novelist has to communicate time of day early in every scene. I can't tell you how many times I've been editing a novel and started working through a scene I assumed was set in the daytime, only to find three pages into the scene some reference to stars or moonlight or headlights. Those surprises disorient your readers. At the beginning of each scene, make clear when it is taking place.

Used by permission of the Jerry Jenkins Writers Guild.

Only One Point of View

by Dave Lambert

WHEN YOU CHOOSE A POINT OF VIEW, you are choosing the means by which your reader will perceive the story. You are choosing the character your readers will be as they experience your story.

Among the things a writer expects from readers are intensity and continuity — that they will keep reading to the end, and that they will engage with the characters and story. But if you handle point of view carelessly or constantly hop from one character's mind to another, you hinder your readers' ability (and motivation) to engage with your characters. As William Sloane puts it in *The Craft of Writing:*

> All the scenes of our individual lives are perceived by us singly and separately. All of us are persons who have never been anybody but ourselves, and if a writer can tell his story in terms of only one vicarious self the reader can become submerged deeper in the story than if he has to surface to change age, condition, and even sex. Life deals out to each of us one, and only one, means of perception.

Imagine you're reading a story narrated — or so you think — in the third-person point of view of a middle-aged, unhappily married banker. You've been identifying with that banker for several pages, and you're starting to understand how he thinks and feels.

Without warning, in the middle of a conversation, you find yourself thrown into the mind of his 16-year-old daughter. You try to adjust, try to begin thinking like the daughter — until a dozen lines later when the author throws you back into the mind of the banker.

But that lasts only a page, when you find yourself seeing the story through the eyes of a neighbor who comes to the door — a younger man about whom you know nothing. How are you supposed to know how to think and feel?

Regardless whether you think this kind of jumping from viewpoint character to viewpoint character is allowed, how does this affect your reading experience? A scene in which the author bounces from one character's consciousness to another's prevents you from submerging yourself as deeply and intensely into the character and the scene as would one narrated from the point of view of one character only. You are forced, instead, to read at the surface.

Refusing to pick a point of view and stick to it prevents the reader from experiencing the very thing the novelist desires. This is why William Sloane says in *The Craft of Writing:* "With rare and tricky exceptions, there is in successful fiction one and only one means of perception to a scene."

What limitations does the writer accept when he chooses to stay in just one character's viewpoint for a scene? For one, he must set limits on how he handles dialogue. Sloane again:

> It is a temptation for the writer to hop into one mind after another as his characters talk. To write successful dialogue the author must have access to the minds of all his characters, but the reader must not perceive any more than he would in real life. We all hear conversations with our own ears only.

In other words, restrict what you communicate in the scene to what the viewpoint character would know. If two detectives are questioning a suspect (Alice), and the scene is presented from the point of view of Larry, one of the detectives, it isn't kosher to throw in a line like, "But Frank strongly suspected that Alice was not telling everything she knew." (That's telling rather than showing, which means it's weaker writing.) If we're in Larry's head, the only way we can know what Frank suspects is by what Larry hears or observes.

If Frank's suspicions are important to your story, there are ways to communicate that:

> "Come on," Frank snarled.
> "What!" Alice said, near tears.
> "You think we don't know all this already? There's a whole lot you know that you aren't tellin' us, and if you want to cop a plea, you better give us somethin' good."

Describing Your Characters
by Dave Lambert

IF YOU'RE RESTRICTED to the awareness of a single character, how do you handle descriptions of that character? Have them step in front of a mirror? Possible — but it, too, has been overdone to the point of cliché.

It's also awkward to have a character focus too much on her own appearance, unless she is dressing for an important interview. Outside of such circumstances, most of us don't walk around thinking about our height, weight, complexion, body type, and manner of dress — the very things you need to convey in a character's physical description. If your characters aren't thinking about it, how do you fit it into their narration?

If your novel is written in multiple viewpoints, that problem is easily resolved. If chapter one is written from Jack's point of view, have him describe his wife, Evelyn, when she walks into the room.

The trick is to give him a credible reason for mentioning how she looks. Maybe he's proud of her appearance and dwells on it. Maybe he's disgusted with her appearance. Maybe she's wearing a new outfit or has a new hairdo. Either way, it shouldn't be hard to fit in a basic description of Evelyn. If chapter two is written from Evelyn's point of view, she can return the favor.

Every novelist should develop the skill to accomplish everything required in a novel through dialogue and action. It's not that hard to work partial descriptions in here and there in the course of the scene. For instance, your protagonist and first-person narrator is a college student rushing to class:

> I amazed myself by sliding into my seat a good thirty seconds before the clock struck eleven. Lateesha looked up at me and did a double-take.
> "Holy cow," she whispered, then giggled. "What did you do to yourself? Your hair — "
> "I was in a hurry," I said. Did she think I had hours to spend in front of the mirror?
> "Well, OK, girl, but you look like a blonde troll doll. Couldn't you brush in the car?"
> "I ride a bike."
> "Then throw a handkerchief over it or something. Here, use mine." She handed me a pink-and-lavender one, exactly wrong for my green-and-navy outfit. "And you've got jam or somethin' on your cheek."
> I wiped with my finger. Yuck. From that stupid Pop-Tart while I rode.

You're not likely to create a complete character description that way, but you can at least provide clues.

And when it comes to character description, a few clues are all your readers need; their imagination will supply the rest.

Or how about:

> As Alice stumbled through her story, Larry found himself watching his partner.
> Frank's jaw tightened rhythmically, and he snorted every now and then.
> Larry held up a hand, silencing Alice. "What're you thinkin' Frank?"
> Frank looked back at him, then squinted at Alice. "We'll talk about it later."

Unless you're using an omniscient narrator, you can be in the head of only one character at a time. Any dialogue must be experienced through the awareness of only one viewpoint character. You can't tell the motivations of other participants in that conversation (unless they confess those motivations) although you can certainly imply them. You can't tell their hidden agendas — but you can certainly give your readers clues to what's going on behind the dialogue.

Except for your viewpoint character, characters' emotions have to be revealed by what they say and by their actions and appearance — by how those emotions are perceived by the character who is acting as our means of perception.

Limiting yourself to one character's viewpoint means you can't directly express foreknowledge. That requires omniscience. Those "little did he know" statements immediately bounce your reader out of the head of your character. If he doesn't know, and we're in his head, then who's telling us about it?

At times the skillful novelist can express foreknowledge. One is when an omniscient narrator is telling the story, but that's rare in contemporary fiction. Another is in first-person narration. Readers usually assume the narrator is relating these events after they are all over. We assume the narrator knows how it turned out, even though we don't. That enables first-person narrators to get away with statements like, "If I'd known then what I know now …" But use that sparingly, as it can quickly become clichéd.

Used by permission of the Jerry Jenkins Writers Guild.

The Illusion of Real Speech

by Dave Lambert

HAVE YOU EVER READ A COURT TRANSCRIPT? They're barely intelligible. Most people speak in awkward, halting, ungrammatical, and unclear speech — especially under pressure. We also augment our words with facial expressions and gestures. Without those, the meaning is often lost.

That's one reason that, when we discuss dialogue, we're not talking about real speech. We're talking about an approximation of it.

Fictional dialogue, like everything else in fiction, is an illusion. But it has to be convincing. Though it's far more clear, direct, complete, and intentional than normal speech, it has to seem like the way people really talk. That's the reason the court transcript is surprising. Both speaker and hearer forget the awkwardness, the halting, and the repetition, selectively hearing only the important stuff.

Fictional dialogue should read the way people *think* they sound.

Common Mistakes in Fictional Dialogue

A friend who taught high-school English liked to distinguish between formal English and what he called kitchen English.

"Most of us don't use formal English that often," he said. "We might in writing a letter to our congressman or when we have to give a speech. In normal conversations we speak informally, even casually, and often in incomplete sentences or thoughts. We say just enough to get the idea across and leave it to our listeners to fill in the grammatical or logical blanks."

In the fictional dialogue I edit, I often find unnatural, stilted, and too wordy language. That comes from trying to impose the rhythms and word choice of formal English on situations that call for kitchen English.

How do you give the illusion of informal English in dialogue?

If you listen to people in conversation, you'll notice they often trip over each other's comments, sometimes all speaking at once. Yet in dialogue, the only effective way to indicate that is to show characters stepping all over each other's comments, not allowing others to complete a thought, so that much of the dialogue ends mid-sentence:

> "But why would they even listen to us?" Alan said. "What right do we have to expect —"
>
> "Alan, listen to me," I said, trying to stay calm.
>
> "No, you listen! After everything we've pulled, when we walk in there tonight —"
>
> "Alan —"
>
> "When they see us come waltzing in like nothing happened —"
>
> "What do you think did happen?" I said. Alan's theatrics were getting old. "Good grief, you make it sound like somebody died. We're only talking about a few —"
>
> "Scott, you have no idea who we're dealing with! Do you realize what people like that do to people like us when we foul up?"

"But when I handle dialogue that way," you might say, "I may never find a convenient place to go back and complete the thought of the previous speaker." True. But in conversation we often don't always get to complete our thoughts. Someone interrupts us, the conversation moves on, and the moment — and the point — are lost. "But if that's true in fictional dialogue," you say, "then won't those conversations contain a lot of incomplete thoughts?" Yes. That's part of the illusion.

Your job is to make sure the thoughts left incomplete are ones the fictional character was trying to make — not points you needed to establish in that scene.

When you want to give the impression of a lively discussion, you can begin a sentence for no other reason than to have another character interrupt it. This can also heighten suspense. Just as the character is about to reveal something, have her dialogue interrupted by an impatient antagonist. Then, a few pages or a chapter or two later, lead your character back to this subject to reveal a little more.

Consider this approach. As your character walks away from that frustrating conversation, have her mentally express regret she didn't get to finish the thought. She then can do so in her head. It may not matter if the other characters hear it, as long as your readers do.

Another distinction: In fictional dialogue, you can choose words carefully. Spoken

Four Tasks of Dialogue
by Dave Lambert

BECAUSE FICTION IS AN ECONOMICAL medium, dialogue must accomplish several things at once:

Character Development
Dialogue must develop and establish your characters. The things each character says help your reader understand more about that character. So craft dialogue carefully to reveal the things you want revealed.

Plot Development
One primary use of dialogue is developing the plot. Our readers hear characters speaking of events as they unfold, hear them speculate about their meaning and importance, notice the tension developing among characters in increasingly uneasy conversations, and hear what they're revealing and choosing not to reveal. Gradually the plot unfolds — much of it through words our characters say.

Description
Dialogue can describe conflicts, settings, and other characters, as well as bring the reader up-to-date.

But isn't dialogue static when it goes on at length accomplishing nothing but description? Yes. But that should never become a problem because you should always be doing several things with your dialogue. While you're describing the setting and what's going on off-stage, you're also giving information about the characters and increasing the tension between them.

Exposition
Using dialogue for exposition is tricky. Clumsily done, it can damage the dialogue's credibility or bog down your story. We've all read fiction where the dialogue contains too much exposition.

When that happens, the reader may think, *These characters would never say that. Why would they be telling one another what they all already know?*

In nineteenth century plays, initial exposition would often be handled by two maids who would come out with their feather dusters and say, "Oh, hurry! We have to get ready for the master's grand ball tonight. I've heard the duchess is coming!" Playgoers may be willing to suspend their disbelief about unrealistic dialogue to convey exposition. But readers are less likely to excuse clumsy dialogue.

The writer of fiction has other tools for handling exposition, such as interior monologue or narrative summary.

conversation takes place in real time, often at a rapid pace. We may wish we could choose just the right words, but we blurt out the first word that occurs to us or stumble around only to come up with a word we realize wasn't quite what we meant.

In fictional dialogue you have time during your revision for reconsideration. There's no reason not to come up with exactly the right word — as long as you realize the right word is one that preserves the illusion of real speech, with all its false starts and inexactness. It must faithfully represent the speech of your characters, with their limitations and faults.

Even within those constraints, it's a great satisfaction for novelists sometimes to grant themselves the privilege of saying exactly the right thing at the right time.

In fiction, dialogue always has a point. But it's risky to make that point too obvious. Most fictional conversations take place among normal people. So they should often seem to wander around the point before finally leading back to it.

That's all part of the illusion. In real life, dialogue rarely moves in a straight line. Novelist and fiction editing guru Sol Stein calls this "indirect dialogue," where a character ignores a question or answers one he has not been asked.

> "What are you doing here, Jim?" she said.
> "Have you seen George?" Jim said.
> "*Why* are you here?"
> "George is not going to be happy when he hears what I've got to say."

Another part of the illusion is that your characters need to speak differently from each other. Next time you're in a crowd or in a discussion with a large group, listen to the speech patterns. Some people are quiet, others dominate. Some ask questions, others want to talk only about themselves. There are people who speak with an extensive vocabulary and others who grunt one-syllable responses. Some speak in complete sentences with impeccable grammar, others speak in fragments, or with grammar that suggests a limited education. Some are assertive and confrontive, others conciliatory and reassuring.

Does your character like to shock others by what she says? Does she say more than she should simply because she doesn't know when to shut up?

To know how your characters speak, you must know about their education, cultural background, home life, personal history, personality type, and so on. As you create an identity for your characters, consider how that affects their speech.

When I find a story where all the characters speak alike, I can usually tell how the author speaks. It's a common failing of beginning novelists to make each character speak with the novelist's own voice.

A character won't always use the same vocabulary. Do you speak the same way with your boss, your spouse, your pastor, your fishing buddies, your kids, and your siblings? Not likely.

We speak one way when interviewing for a job and another when we're the one doing the interviewing. One way when we're lecturing our kids and another when firing an employee. One way when teaching a Sunday school class and another when arguing with a neighbor.

Our voices are unique, but not all our conversations sound the same. That should also be true of your characters.

Ways to Create and Manage Suspense

by Dave Lambert

EVERY NOVEL IS A MYSTERY NOVEL. The reader continues reading to find out something. Usually when you ask people in the middle of the novel why they want to finish the book, they answer, "To find out what happens." If you give away too much of your plot too soon, don't introduce enough tension, or fail to foreshadow enough complications, you reduce readers' motivation.

There are many techniques to create and manage suspense. We'll look at four: delay, long lines and short lines of conflict, foreshadowing, and the ticking clock.

Delay

In some ways, suspense is a form of teasing the reader. Think of your novel's plot reduced to a paragraph:

> Brad returns from Europe after WWII to learn his sweetheart, Laura (like Brad, a gymnast) and his idolized older brother have disappeared. Townspeople tell Brad that Laura changed her mind about their engagement and couldn't face him, so she left for New York, and that his brother moved to California without leaving a forwarding address. But that story doesn't ring true. Confused and grief stricken, Brad launches his own investigation, despite pleas of the townspeople to let things lie. His anger toward the pair builds as evidence mounts that they fell in love and ran off together. But anger turns to horror as his painstaking detective work reveals the truth. His brother, in the throes of paranoid schizophrenia, first stalked and then shot Laura before being shot in turn by the sheriff. Her spine severed and unwilling to face Brad as a paraplegic, Laura moved to a distant city, insisting no one tell Brad. But Brad finds and claims her, undaunted by her wheelchair.

If that's the story in a nutshell, why not just give your reader the nutshell and save many hours of reading, not to mention many months of writing? The enjoyment for the reader comes not in knowing how the story ends, but in the journey itself — reading for the enjoyment of getting to know the characters and watching as the story unfolds layer by layer, clue by clue, frustration by frustration, obstacle by obstacle, revelation by revelation. A reader expects the resolution to be delayed by a series of complications.

The subtle, skillful, and fitting use of delay increases the reader's identification with the characters.

Novelists intentionally build in delay after delay in revealing plot developments. The more obvious of those devices — such as irrelevant distraction or a string of transparent and silly red herrings — annoy and frustrate the reader.

Even so, the subtle, skillful, and fitting use of delay increases the suspense and tension and also increases the reader's identification with the characters as he vicariously shares their experiences.

You can hardly go wrong by remembering this adage, referring to your readers: Make them wait.

Long Lines and Short Lines

The strands of tension in a novel come in both long and short versions. The long ones — the big conflicts that won't be resolved until the end — are either revealed or hinted at early in the novel to capture the reader's interest. If not actual matters of life and death, these conflicts at least seem that important to the characters. They usually involve a choice of some kind — at best, a moral choice.

"All true suspense," John Gardner says in *The Art of Fiction*, "is a dramatic representation of the anguish of moral choice." These are the book's major themes.

If you think of your novel as a net to capture the reader, the long strands are the ones that weave from one end to the other. The shorter strands weave in and out of the longer ones, keeping everything tightly connected and filling otherwise empty spaces.

The shorter strands could be subplots, some which needn't appear until later and some of which may be resolved long before the climax. The shorter strands could also be red herrings that are investigated by the protagonist and discarded. The shorter strands are the book's minor themes.

As Vincent McHugh points out in *Primer of the Novel*, a novel that contains primarily long strands without enough short strands may cause the reader to skip ahead to see how things turn out. A novel that emphasizes shorter strands, but lacks overarching themes, might seem like a collection of short stories — entertaining in places, but not worth finishing.

Foreshadowing

The first line of Hemingway's novel *A Farewell to Arms* is often cited as an example of foreshadowing: "The leaves fell early that year." However subtly, it foretells an early death.

Most foreshadowing by beginning novelists is neither subtle nor effective. "If only Delores had known what horror awaited her in California, she never would have gone." Besides the point-of-view violations in such a line, it's clumsy. The most effective foreshadowing occurs when characters themselves are aware something is about to happen — when the farmer notices geese flying south early and feels an uneasiness about the coming winter, or when the old man wakes with a twinge and says, "Last time my knees felt this way was before that big storm in '61."

Think of every scene as pointing the reader toward developments further in the novel.

The best approach to foreshadowing — rather than trying to stick some in every now and then — is to think of every scene as pointing the reader toward developments further in the novel. Each scene somehow foreshadows what comes after. As you write (or rewrite) each, think of what later parts of the plot this scene points toward. Write the scene to prepare the reader for that later development.

The Ticking Clock

You've seen this principle in movies. The protagonist has only limited time to complete his task before the bomb goes off, or the kidnappers kill his wife, or the tide rises so high his father, trapped between two rocks, is drowned. He works diligently at first, but as the clock ticks and danger looms, tension mounts and he works more quickly, more desperately, discarding one plan after another as they prove ineffective. There are shouts, sweat, frantic racing from one place to another —always with one eye on the clock.

Not every novel needs a ticking clock. Romance novels or other relationship-oriented novels often don't need one because the tension comes from elsewhere. But nearly all suspense novels need one.

When much is at stake, the tension is heightened when the good guys must not only do the impossible, but also do it in a small window of disappearing time. Some novelists even call attention to this with chapter headings that keep track of elapsing time:

Sunday, April 22, 8:06 A.M.
Twelve hours, 32 minutes before impact

Those are handy for building tension in a plot-driven novel, but unnecessary if the prose itself keeps a close eye on the clock.

If the tension in your novel isn't growing adequately as the climax nears, ask yourself: Where's the ticking clock?

Keys to Effective Conflict

by Dave Lambert

WITHOUT CONFLICT THERE IS NO STORY

Think of any story that has stood the test of time, and without much thought you'll be able to identify the driving conflict.

"The Three Little Pigs" has two primary conflicts: the pigs against the wolf and the two foolish pigs against their own slothful natures. In *Robinson Crusoe* it's Crusoe against nature as he struggles to survive on a remote island. In *The Wizard of Oz,* Dorothy's desire to return to Kansas is thwarted again and again as she and her faithful helpers strive to satisfy the demands of the wizard while avoiding the wicked witch and her winged monkeys. In the Bible's account of David and Goliath, the small but fearless shepherd must prevail over the giant warrior to save his family and his nation.

In any story — whether plot-driven, character-driven, literary, fairy tale, Christian, secular, romance, western, or mainstream — the reader keeps reading to find out what happens, to find out how the conflict is resolved. It's up to the writer to keep those conflicts, and their tantalizingly slow resolution, always before the reader.

Conflict and Confrontation

Confrontation is not the same as conflict. Sometimes confrontation can reduce tension, as when you arrange a confrontation to "get this out in the open" or "to clear the air."

Confrontation is also not a substitute for conflict. Just because two characters yell at each other doesn't mean there's a clearly defined conflict between them. Far better to have a strongly felt conflict simmering beneath the surface than to have only lots of hollering and running around. Substance is better than noise.

As the novel progresses, you want the overall level of tension to build.

In fiction, tension may wax and wane, but it should never disappear. As the novel progresses, you want the overall level of tension to build. Confrontation is simply one tool you use to manage conflict development.

Conflicts Must be Personal

Several years ago I worked on a novel of political suspense with an author who had a great deal of political experience. The things that interested this author about life in Washington were the political infighting and intrigue.

"That's great," I kept saying, "but this novel has to be about more than who wins the election. The stakes don't just have to be high, they have to be personal. Unless your protagonists are experiencing personal conflict about some matter crucial to them, your readers won't care who wins the election."

He agreed — and pointed out that his protagonist was beginning, in the early parts of the book, to develop a romantic interest in another staffer. "That's good," I said. "Develop that and tie their romance in some significant way to the resolution of the political problem."

While professional conflicts may have some importance to us in practical terms, they count in fiction only if they have strong personal implications.

If the businessman in the novel sets a goal of acquiring five new companies in the next twelve months, we yawn. If we discover the man who owns one of those companies had an affair with his wife last year, and that the businessman intends to dismantle and destroy his rival's company, we take notice. How will that act of vengeance affect the businessman and his wife?

Conflict Has to Hurt Your Characters

Many writers get so close to their characters, they're afraid to make things too hard for them.

But a compelling plot requires conflict. The bigger and more daunting and stubborn the conflict, the better. Aren't the most satisfying novels those in which, just when you think the protagonist is about to overcome his adversary, wham! Here comes some complication, and he's right back where he started or worse? How can he get out of this one? And when he finally claws his way to where he has some hope, here comes another disaster.

If you resolve your conflicts too easily and quickly, you drain the tension.

Those rising and falling fortunes of your protagonist are what keep your readers going. If you resolve your conflicts too easily and quickly, you drain the tension out of your book. If you resolve your protagonist's problems halfway through so you can show her enjoying the fruits of her struggle, there's really no reason to keep reading.

When you get to "They lived happily ever after," that's the end of the story. The conflict has ended, the curtain comes down, the audience stands and goes home. The end.

Don't frustrate your readers by giving your characters too-easy conflicts and letting them resolve them too soon. Torture your characters until the end. Any moments of peace your characters enjoy are just temporary respites to lull them into a false sense of security before the other shoe drops.

Used by permission of the Jerry Jenkins Writers Guild.

Don't Make These Plot Mistakes

by Dave Lambert

Taking Too Long To Get to the Conflict

The primary conflict in your novel should emerge within the first chapter or two, at least in implication.

If we don't know the primary conflict until chapter seven, your novel has structural problems. What have you been up to? Six chapters of exposition make pretty deadly reading. Your subplots, intriguing as they may be, probably lack the thematic weight to keep your reader's interest that long.

It's that primary conflict, the life-and-death concern of your protagonist — and the reader's desire to see how your characters resolve it — that makes your novel readable to the end. Your reader needs to see that conflict developing, sense its importance, and be intrigued by it from the beginning.

Giving Away Too Much Too Soon

If you give away the solution in chapter five, your reader has no reason to keep reading. Identify those things your reader is curious to find out. Make a list if you have to. Then parcel out a little information every chapter or so, giving readers both some satisfaction in discovering something about the mystery and a greater sense of hunger to find out the rest.

Only in the final chapter should your reader learn the solution to the mystery. Even if you plan to make your final chapter an emotional resolution to the mystery that was solved in the previous chapter, keep a few things hidden until the end.

The Episodic Plot

In life many things happen at once. But you can give your reader only one scene at a time. The illusion of fiction is that your plot is unfolding much like life — except, to paraphrase Mark Twain, making more sense. This means that in your plot, everything is connected to everything else, and everything is moving toward a coherent, inclusive resolution.

In your plot, everything is connected to everything else, and moving toward a coherent resolution.

But what about a plot that contains one loosely related episode after another, like a collection of short stories that shares the same cast? It will feel like just a series of episodes.

An example would be *All Things Bright and Beautiful* by James Herriot (not a novel, but more of a memoir). Each chapter is a short story — entertaining, fun to read, but still a self-contained short story.

It may have no relation to the rest of the stories other than occurring in the same place and having the same protagonist. Certain threads run through the book, but those long strands are loose and relatively minor. We read not so much to see how they turn out, but because we're captivated by Herriot's writing and the charming world he creates.

But that's not a good structure for a novel. Those long threads of plot have to be strung much more dominantly throughout so that every chapter hangs on them and takes its shape from them.

You don't have the luxury in a novel of throwing in a cute story about a cat or about kids swimming in the river who emerge to discover someone has stolen their clothes. Those chapters, if included, have to relate to the overall conflict and the continuing story and push it toward resolution.

Resolving Things Too Completely

Though fiction gives only an illusion of real life, you want that illusion as convincing as possible. In real life, things don't get wrapped up neatly and completely at the end. Some things never get resolved. Many things that are resolved aren't resolved happily.

At the end of your novel, if there are no loose ends and everything falls wonderfully into place, the reader shakes her head. That isn't life as we know it.

John Gardner explains it this way in his discussion in *The Art of Fiction* of the difference between the "perfect" plots of the short story and novella and the deliberately "imperfect" plot of the sprawling novel:

> The "perfect" novel lacks the richness and raggedness of the best long fictions. ... The novel ... makes some pretense of imitating the world in all its complexity; we not only look closely at various characters, we hear rumors of distant wars and marriages, we glimpse characters whom, like people on the subway, we will never see again. As a result, too much neatness in a novel kills the novel's fundamental effect.

Authors of short stories and novellas can allow themselves a tidy resolution in which the intentionally limited subject matter is wrapped up with a bow. But to attempt the same neatness in a novel gives a clear impression of unreality.

Don't let your novel become too loose and baggy, but as it ends, your reader should sense that life, in all its complexity, will continue for these characters beyond the final word of the book — and that much remains unsettled in their lives.

Used by permission of the Jerry Jenkins Writers Guild.

Double Check Your Dialogue

by Dave Lambert

THE BEST EXERCISE FOR IMPROVING YOUR DIALOGUE is to read it aloud. If possible, have someone else, whose ear you trust, listen as you read.

Identify all of those places where it just doesn't sound natural. If it sounds forced, too formal, or colloquial; if your attempt at dialect falls flat (as it almost always does); or if the rhythm, word choice, or timing doesn't sound like what someone would normally say, then flag it for revision. (You can probably revise as you read. Just speak the line the way it sounds most natural, then write it down.) Once you're revised it — read it aloud again.

Be careful in your use of dialogue tags such as "he said," "she explained," or "John asked."

Simpler is better. The last thing you want your reader to notice are dialogue tags — to be aware she's reading them. They should be nearly invisible signposts enabling the reader to know who's saying what.

Dialogue tags are of almost no value in letting your reader know how things were said — "he stuttered," "she protested." Using dialogue tags to get that information across is a clear case of telling rather than showing. Too often they are redundant:

> "Stop it!" she ordered.
> "I wasn't even there!" he protested.
> "Where are you going?" he asked.

In each case, "said" would have worked as well or better.

Some novelists even avoid the use of "asked" following a question, rightly deducing that it is redundant.

> "Why?" she said.

Avoid long exchanges of dialogue in which there are no or very few tags. Your reader will lose track of who's saying what. Not surprisingly, in editing novels I often find that in those long, unattributed exchanges the novelist also has lost track.

Avoid, whenever possible (nearly always) the pairing of adverbs with dialogue tags: "he whispered softly," "she said imploringly," "they shouted angrily." The adverb is usually redundant; how else can you whisper? In nearly every case, it's a shortcut to avoid describing the actions much more powerfully:

> "They shouted, their faces twisted in rage as they threw whatever was handy at the line of policemen."

As Michael Seidman says in *The Complete Guide to Editing Your Fiction*, "Adverbs are like a good spice: They have to be used delicately. Whenever I see them in dialogue, I know the author has missed an opportunity to show, not tell."

Throughout *Self-Editing for Fiction Writers* Browne and King investigate the use of what they call *beats* — those short interruptions of dialogue to describe what the characters are doing, what's going on around them, or where it's taking place. I've italicized the beats in this example:

Edna sipped her tea, then set the cup down deliberately. "Come now, Roger. You can't expect me to believe that."

He raised an eyebrow. "It's all the same to me whether you believe it or not." *He glanced out the window, then back again, pausing briefly before he continued.* "It's not my job to make you believe it."

"It's not me you have to convince," she said, *her voice taking on a harder edge.* "It's the police."

Notice how a good beat shows rather than tells. Here are a few suggestions they give for making effective use of beats:

- *How many beats do you have?* (It may be time to get out the highlighters yet again and mark all your beats.) How often do you interrupt your dialogue?
- *What are your beats describing?* Familiar, everyday actions (such as dialing a telephone or buying groceries)? How often do you repeat a beat? Are your characters always looking out of windows or lighting cigarettes? (Garrison Keillor said of his first novel, "My characters smoked cigarettes the way some people use semicolons.")

15

Resources for Writers

Jerry B. Jenkins does not endorse the following organizations, websites, articles, or services, but we hope this listing will be a good starting place as you develop your writing as well as your platform.

Helpful Websites (Christian and General Markets)
These are a sampling of the variety of sites of potential interest to you as a writer looking to develop a platform. A Google search for the specific topic on which you need guidance will provide additional options. Some of these are not geared toward the Christian market.

Bestseller Labs: Practical Advice on How To Get Published and Grow Your Readership: http://bestsellerlabs.com/how-to-find-readers-on-twitter/

eBook-Pub.com: e-publish today!: http://www.ebook-pub.com/

Writer's Relief: Author's Submission Service: http://www.writersrelief.com/

Christian Fiction Blog Alliance: Where People Come Together to Further the Lord's Kingdom by Supporting Christian Fiction: http://www.christianfictionblogalliance.com/

The Savvy Book Marketer: The Tools You Need to Sell More Books: http://bookmarketingmaven.typepad.com/resources/2009/11/book-marketingresources.html

Body and Soul Publishing: http://www.bodyandsoulpublishing.com/advertising-for-christian-authors/ (Offers a section where authors can post their books for free to get reviews. Other advertising opportunities available.)

Grammar Girl: Quick and Dirty Tips for Better Writing: http://grammar.quickanddirtytips.com/

The Writer: http://www.writermag.com/

Poets & Writers: http://www.pw.org/magazine

Jonathan Gunson, Bestseller Labs: http://bestsellerlabs.com/7-free-photo-libraries/

eBook-Pub.com: http://www.ebook-pub.com/

Jeff Goins: http://goinswriter.com/resources/

Blogs (Christian and General Markets)
These are a sampling of current writers' blogs. A Google search for the specific topic on which you need guidance will provide other options.

Michael Hyatt, Intentional Leadership: http://michaelhyatt.com/

Rob Eagar, WildFire Marketing: http://www.startawildfire.com/blog

Dan Blank: http://wegrowmedia.com/blog/

Author Media: Growing Your Platform Online: http://www.authormedia.com/blog/

Where Writers Win: Marketing, Websites, Training and Tools for Emerging Authors: http://writerswin.com/blog/#axzz2KfJ5InsG

Rachelle Gardner: http://www.rachellegardner.com/category/popular-posts/

The Quick and Dirty: The Latest From Your Experts: http://blog.quickanddirtytips.com/

Godly Writers: http://www.godlywriters.com/tag/social-media-2/

Sally Stuart's Blog: http://christianwritersmarketplace.blogspot.com/

Facebook Pages
There are many pages and groups on Facebook for writers of various genres and levels. Search for these and other pages to find ones that best fit your needs. Also, search for your favorite authors and join their Facebook pages so you can watch how they use this social media option.

Christian Speakers Services

Blogging Bistro, LLC: A full menu of Social Media Services

Inspire Christian Writers

Ebookmybook

Online Articles
These are a small sampling of how-to and advice articles geared toward developing your platform.

How to Build your Author Platform (Writer's Digest): http://www.writersdigest.com/writing-articles/by-writing-goal/get-published-sell-my-work/how-to-build-your-author-platform

The Basics of Building a Writer's Platform (Writer's Digest): http://www.writersdigest.com/writing-articles/by-writing-goal/build-a-platform-start-blogging/building-a-writers-platform

Book Publicity: A Labor of Love (Christian Fiction Online Magazine): http://www.christianfictiononlinemagazine.com/aug-08-buzz_publicity.html

Are You Social Media Savvy or Social Media Awkward?: http://altongansky.typepad.com/writersconferences/2013/01/are-you-social-media-savvy-or-social-media-awkward.html

Social Media and Christian Authors: http://keikihendrix.com/social-media-etiquette-and-christian-authors/

Books
Note: Some of these are not specifically geared to the Christian market.
General Titles

Bird by Bird by Anne Lamott (Doubleday Anchor Books, 1994)

Culture Making: Recovering our Creative Calling by Andy Crouch (IVP, 2008)

How to Write What You Love and Make a Living at It by Dennis E. Hensley, PhD (Shaw/Random House, 2000)

I Know What You're Thinking by Lillian Glass, PhD (John Wiley & Sons, 2002)

No Mentor but Myself: A Collection of Articles, Essays, Reviews, and Letters by Jack London on Writing and Writers edited by Dale L. Walker (Kennikat Press, 1979)

On Writing Well (30th Anniversary Edition) by William Zinsser (Harper Perennial, 2006)

Scribbling in the Sand by Michael Card (IVP, 2002)

Stein on Writing by Sol Stein (St. Martins, 1995)

The Craft of Writing by William Sloane (Norton, 1979)

The Creative Call by Janice Elsheimer (Waterbrook Press, 2001)

The Synonym Finder by J. I. Rodale (Rodale Press, 1986)

The Write Way by Richard Lederer and Richard Dowis (Simon & Schuster Pocket Books, 1995)

The Writer's Little Helper by Jim Smith (Writer's Digest Books, 2012)

Word Painting by Rebecca McClanahan (Writer's Digest Books, 1999)

Writers on Writing edited by James N. Watkins (Wesleyan Publishing House, 2005)

Writing for the Soul by Jerry B. Jenkins (Writer's Digest Books, 2006)

Writing World Defined: A to Z by Sally E. Stuart (Bold Vision 2015)

Children's Books

Writing Books for Children by Jane Yolen (The Writer, Inc., 1973)

Fiction

Characters, Emotion, and Viewpoint by Nancy Kress (Writer's Digest Books, 2005)

Characters & Viewpoint by Orson Scott Card (Writer's Digest Books, 1988)

Dialogue by Gloria Kempton (Writer's Digest Books, 2004)

Dynamic Characters by Nancy Kress (Writer's Digest Books, 2004)

Elements of Fiction Writing: Conflict and Suspense by James Scott Bell (Writer's Digest Books, 2012)

Fiction Attack! by James Scott Bell (Compendium Press, 2012)

Fiction Writing Demystified by Thomas Sawyer (Ashleywilde, Inc., 2003)

Getting into Character by Brandilyn Collins (John Wiley & Sons, 2002)

Goal, Motivation, and Conflict by Debra Dixon (Gryphon Books for Writers, 1996)

How Fiction Works by Oakley Hall (Writer's Digest Books, 2003)

How to Grow a Novel by Sol Stein (St. Martin's Griffin, 1999)

Mastering Point of View by Sherri Szeman (Story Press, 2001)

On Writing by Stephen King (Scribner, 2010)

On Writing Romance: How to Craft a Novel That Sells by Leigh Michaels (Writer's Digest Books, 2007)

Plot and Structure by James Scott Bell (Writer's Digest Books, 2004)

Revision and Self-Editing by James Scott Bell (Writer's Digest Books, 2012)

Self-Editing for Fiction Writers by Renni Browne and Dave King (William Morrow, 2004)

Spider, Spin Me a Web by Lawrence Block (William Morrow, 1996)

Story by Robert McKee (ReganBooks, 1997)

Techniques of the Selling Writer by Dwight Swain (University of Oklahoma Press, 1982)

Telling Lies for Fun and Profit by Lawrence Block (William Morrow, 1994)

The Art of Character by David Corbett (Penguin Books, 2013)

The Art of War for Writers by James Scott Bell (Writer's Digest Books, 2009)

The Dance of Character and Plot by DiAnn Mills (Bold Vision Books, 2013)

The Emotion Thesaurus by Becca Puglisi and Angela Ackerman (CreateSpace Independent Publishing Platform, 2012)

The Fire in Fiction by Donald Maass (Writer's Digest Books, 2009)

The First 50 Pages by Jeff Gerke (Writer's Digest Books, 2011)

The Liar's Bible by Lawrence Block (Open Road Media, 2011)

The Moral Premise by Stanley D. Williams (Michael Wiese Productions, 2006)

The Power of Body Language by Tonya Reiman (Gallery Books, Reprint Edition 2008)

The Scene Book by Sandra Scofield (Penguin Books, 2007)

Writing Dialogue by Tom Chiarella (Story Press, 1998)

Writing the Breakout Novel by Donald Maass (Writer's Digest Books, 2002)

Writing the Breakout Novel Workbook by Donald Maass (Writer's Digest Books, 2004)

Grammar and Style

Formatting & Submitting Your Manuscript by Cynthia Laufenberg and the editors of Writer's Digest (Writer's Digest Books, 2004)

Garner's Modern American Usage (3rd Edition) by Bryan A. Garner (Oxford, 2009)

Grammar Girl's Quick and Dirty Tips for Better Writing by Mignon Fogarty (Holt, 2008)

Nitty-Gritty Grammar by Edith H. Fine and Judith P. Josephson (Ten Speed Press, 1998)

Punctuate It Right by Harry Shaw (HarperCollins Reference Library, 2010)

The Associated Press Stylebook and Briefing on Media Law (46th Edition) (Associated Press, 2013)

The Chicago Manual of Style by the University of Chicago Press Staff (University of Chicago Press, 2010)

The Christian Writer's Manual of Style (Updated and Expanded Edition) edited by Robert Hudson (Zondervan, 2004)

The Elements of Style by William Strunk, Jr. and E. B. White (Macmillan, 2009)

Woe Is I (3rd Edition) by Patricia T. O'Conner (Riverhead Books, 2009)

Marketing

Book Proposals That Sell by W. Terry Whalin (Write Now Publications-ACW Press, 2005)

Create Your Writer Platform: The Key to Building an Audience, Selling More Books, and Finding Success as an Author by Chuck Sambuchino (Writer's Digest Books, 2012)

Get into Bed with Google by Jon Smith (The Infinite Ideas Company, 2008)

Get Known Before the Book Deal: Use Your Personal Strengths to Grow an Author Platform by Christina Katz (Writer's Digest Books, 2008)

Guerrilla Marketing for Writers: 100 No-Cost, Low-Cost Weapons for Selling Your Work by Jay Levinson, Rick Frishman, Michael Larsen, and David L. Hancock (Morgan James Publishing, 2010)

Guerrilla Social Media Marketing: 100+ Weapons to Grow Your Online Influence, Attract Customers, and Drive Profits by Jay Levinson and Shane Gibson (Jere L. Calmes, Publisher, 2010)

How to Write a Book Proposal by Michael Larsen (Writer's Digest Books, 2004)

Internet Marketing Made Easy by Jo-Anne Vandermeulen (The Laurus Company, 2012)

Platform: Get Noticed in a Noisy World by Michael Hyatt (Thomas Nelson, 2012)

Premium Promotional Tips for Writers by Jo-Anne Vandermeulen (The Laurus Company, 2009)

Promote Your Book: Over 250 Proven, Low-Cost Tips and Techniques for the Enterprising Author by Patricia Fry (Allworth Press, 2011)

Sell More Books by J. Steve Miller and Cherie K. Miller (Wisdom Creek Press, 2011)

Sell Your Book Like Wildfire: The Writer's Guide to Marketing and Publicity by Rob Eagar (Writer's Digest Books, 2012)

Shameless Self Promotion and Networking for Christian Creatives by Paula K. Parker, Mike Parker, and Torry Martin (WordCrafts Press, 2011)

Small Time Operator: How to Start Your Own Business, Keep Your Books, Pay Your Taxes, and Stay Out of Trouble by Bernard B. Kamoroff (Taylor Trade Publishing, 2013)

Social Media Just for Writers: The Best Online Marketing Tips for Selling Your Books by Frances Caballo (ACT Communications, 2012)

The Christian Writer's Market Guide by Jerry B. Jenkins (2015)

The Sell Your Novel Tool Kit by Elizabeth Lyon (Penguin Books, 2002)

The Social Media Bible: Tactics, Tools, and Strategies for Business Success by Lon Safko

The Ultimate Guide to Marketing Your Business with Pinterest by Gabriela Taylor (CreateSpace Independent Publishing Platform, 2013)

Periodicals

Effective Magazine Writing by Robert C. Palms (WaterBrook Press, 2000)

Feature & Magazine Writing: Action, Angle and Anecdotes (2nd edition) by David E. Sumner and Holly G. Miller (Wiley-Blackwell, 2009)

Writer's Digest Handbook of Magazine Article Writing (2nd edition) edited by Michelle Ruberg (Writer's Digest Books, 2005)

Writing Articles from the Heart: How to Write and Sell Your Life Experiences by Marjorie Holmes (Writer's Digest Books, 1993)

Science Fiction

World-Building by Stephen L. Gillet (Writer's Digest Books, 1996)

E-Books

Secrets to E-book Publishing Success (Kindle edition) by Mark Coker (Smashwords Guides, 2013)

Magazines

Christian Communicator by American Christian Writers (monthly)

Writer's Digest by F&W Publications (monthly)

DVDs

Grabbing the Reader in the First 10 Pages (audio CD) by Michael Hauge and James Mercurio (Producer) (2005)

The Hero's 2 Journeys by Michael Hauge and Christopher Vogler (Writer's Audioship, 2001)

Organizations and Services

These can help you develop your craft and establish your platform.

Advanced Writers and Speakers Association: http://www.awsa.com/

Somersault Group: http://somersaultgroup.com/home

Constant Contact (E-mail Marketing Service): http://www.constantcontact.com/index.jsp

Readership: http://bestsellerlabs.com/how-to-find-readers-on-twitter/

Glossary

Advance: Money a publisher pays to an author up front, against future royalties. The amount varies greatly from publisher to publisher and is often paid in two or three installments (on signing contract, on delivery of manuscript, and on publication).

All rights: An outright sale of your material. Author has no further control over it.

Anecdote: A short, poignant, real-life story, usually used to illustrate a single thought. Need not be humorous.

Assignment: When an editor asks a writer to create a specific piece for an agreed-upon price.

As-told-to story: A true story you write as a first-person account, but about someone else.

Audiobooks: Books available on CDs or in other digital formats.

Avant-garde: Experimental; ahead of the times.

Backlist: A publisher's previously published books that are still in print a year after publication.

B & W: Abbreviation for a black-and-white photograph.

Bar code: Identification code and price on the back of a book read by a scanner at checkout counters.

Bible versions: AMP—Amplified Bible; ASV—American Standard Version; CEV—Contemporary English Version; ESV—English Standard Version; GNB—Good News Bible; HCSB—Holman Christian Standard Bible; ICB—International Children's Bible; KJV—King James Version; MEV—Modern English Version; MSG—The Message; NAB—New American Bible; NAS—New American Standard; NEB—New English Bible; NIrV—New International Reader's Version; NIV—New International Version; NJB—New Jerusalem Bible; NKJV—New King James Version; NLT—New Living Translation; NRSV—New Revised Standard Version; RSV—Revised Standard Version; TLB—*The Living Bible;* TNIV—Today's New International Version.

Bimonthly: Every two months.

Bio sketch: Information about the author.

Biweekly: Every two weeks.

Bluelines: Printer's proofs used to catch errors before a book is printed.

Book proposal: Submission of a book idea to an agent or editor; usually includes a cover letter, thesis statement, chapter-by-chapter or story synopsis, marketing and promotion information, and 1–3 sample chapters.

Byline: Author's name printed just below the title of a story, article, etc.

Camera-ready copy: The text and artwork for a book that are ready for the press.

Chapbook: A small book or pamphlet containing poetry, religious readings, etc.

Circulation: The number of copies sold or distributed of each issue of a publication.

Clips: See "Published clips."

Column: A regularly appearing feature, section, or department in a periodical using the same heading; written by the same person or a different freelancer each time.

Concept statement: A 50- to 150-word summary of your proposed book.

Contributor's copy: Copy of an issue of a periodical sent to an author whose work appears in it.

Copyright: Legal protection of an author's work.

Cover letter: A letter that accompanies some manuscript submissions. Usually needed only if you have to tell the editor something specific or to give your credentials for writing a piece of a technical nature. Also used to remind the editor that a manuscript was requested or expected.

Credits, list of: A listing of your previously published works.

Critique: An evaluation of a piece of writing.

Defamation: A written or spoken injury to the reputation of a living person or organization. If what is said is true, it cannot be defamatory.

Derivative work: A work derived from another work, such as a condensation or abridgment. Contact copyright owner for permission before doing the abridgment and be prepared to pay that owner a fee or royalty.

Devotional: A short piece that shares a personal spiritual discovery, inspires to worship, challenges to commitment or action, or encourages.

Editorial guidelines: See "Writers' guidelines."

Electronic submission: The submission of a proposal or article to an editor by electronic means, such as by e-mail or on disk.

Endorsements: Flattering comments about a book; usually carried on the back cover or in promotional material.

EPA/Evangelical Press Assn.: A professional trade organization for periodical publishers and associate members.

E-proposals: Proposals sent via e-mail.

E-queries: Queries sent via e-mail.

Eschatology: The branch of theology that is concerned with the last things, such as death, judgment, heaven, and hell.

Essay: A short composition usually expressing the author's opinion on a specific subject.

Evangelical: A person who believes that one receives God's forgiveness for sins through Jesus Christ, and believes the Bible is an authoritative guide for daily living.

Exegesis: Interpretation of the Scripture.

Feature article: In-depth coverage of a subject, usually focusing on a person, an event, a process, an organization, a movement, a trend or issue; written to explain, encourage, help, analyze, challenge, motivate, warn, or entertain as well as to inform.

Filler: A short item used to "fill" out the page of a periodical. It could be a timeless news item, joke, anecdote, light verse or short humor, puzzle, game, etc.

First rights: Editor buys the right to publish a piece that has never before appeared.

Foreign rights: Selling or giving permission to translate or reprint published material in another country.

Foreword: Opening remarks in a book introducing the book and its author.

Freelance: As in 50% freelance: means that half of the material printed in the publication is supplied by freelance writers.

Freelancer or freelance writer: A writer who is not on salary but sells his or her material to a number of different publishers.

Free verse: Poetry that flows without any set pattern.

Galley proof: A typeset copy of a book used to detect and correct errors before the print run.

General market: What we used to refer to as the secular market.

Genre: Refers to type or classification, as in fiction or poetry. Such types as westerns, romances, mysteries, etc., are referred to as genre fiction.

Glossy: A photo with a shiny, rather than matte, finish. Also, a publication printed on such paper.

Go-ahead: When a publisher tells you to proceed and write or submit your article.

Haiku: A Japanese lyric poem of a fixed 17-syllable form.

Hard copy: A physical manuscript, as opposed to one on disk or via e-mail.

Holiday/seasonal: A story, article, filler, etc., that has to do with a specific holiday or season. This material must reach the publisher the stated number of months prior to the holiday/season.

Homiletics: The art of preaching.

Honorarium: If a publisher indicates they pay an honorarium, it means they pay a small flat fee, as opposed to a set amount per word.

Humor: The amusing or comical aspects of life that add warmth and color to an article or story.

Interdenominational: Distributed to a number of different denominations.

International Postal Reply Coupon: See "IRC."

Interview article: An article based on an interview with a person of interest to a specific readership.

IRC or IPRC: International Postal Reply Coupon: can be purchased at a local post office and should be enclosed with a physical manuscript sent to a foreign publisher.

ISBN: International Standard Book Number; an identification code needed for every version of a book.

Journal: A periodical presenting news in a particular area.

Kill fee: A fee paid for a completed article done on assignment that is subsequently not published. Amount is usually 25–50% of original payment.

Libel: To defame someone by an opinion or a misquote that puts his or her reputation in jeopardy.

Light verse: Simple, lighthearted poetry.

Little/Literary: Small-circulation publications whose focus is providing a forum for the literary writer, rather than on making money. Often do not pay, or pay in copies.

Mainstream fiction: Other than genre fiction, such as romance, mystery, or science fiction. Stories of people and their conflicts handled on a deeper level.

Mass market: Books intended for a wide, general market, rather than a specialized market. These books are produced in a smaller format, usually with smaller type, and are sold at a lower price. The expectation is that their sales will be higher.

Ms: Abbreviation for manuscript.

Mss: Abbreviation for more than one manuscript.

Multiple submissions: Submitting more than one piece at a time to the same publisher, usually reserved for poetry, greeting cards, or fillers — not articles. Also see "Simultaneous submissions."

NASR: Abbreviation for North American Serial Rights; permission for a periodical targeting readers in the US and Canada to publish a piece.

New Adult Fiction: A developing fiction genre with protagonists in the 18–25 age range.

Newsbreak: A newsworthy event or item sent to a publisher who might be interested in publishing it because it would be of interest to his readership.

Nondenominational: Not associated with a particular denomination.

Not copyrighted: Publication of your piece in such a publication will put it into the public domain, meaning it is not then protected. Ask that the publisher carry your copyright notice on your piece.

Novella: A short novel, usually 20,000–35,000 words. Length varies from publisher to publisher.

On acceptance: Periodical or publisher pays a writer at the time the manuscript is accepted for publication.

On assignment: Writing a piece at the specific request of an editor.

Onetime rights: Selling the right to publish a story one time to any number of publications (usually refers to publishing for a non-overlapping readership).

On publication: Publisher pays a writer when his or her manuscript is published.

On speculation/On spec: Writing something for an editor with the agreement that the editor will buy it only if he or she likes it.

Overrun: The extra copies of a book printed during the initial print run.

Over the transom: Unsolicited manuscripts that arrive at a publisher's office.

Payment on acceptance: See "On acceptance."

Payment on publication: See "On publication."

Pen name/pseudonym: Using a name other than your legal name on an article or book to protect your identity or that of people included, or when the author wishes to remain anonymous. Put the pen name in the byline under the title, and your real name in the upper, left-hand corner.

Permissions: Asking permission to use text or art from a copyrighted source.

Personal experience story: An account based on a real-life experience.

Personality profile: A feature article that highlights a specific person's life or accomplishments.

Piracy: To take the writings of others just as they were written and put your name on them as the author.

Plagiarism: To steal and use the ideas or writings of another as your own, rewriting them to make them sound like your own.

Press kit: A compilation of promotional materials on a particular book or author, usually organized in a folder, used to publicize a book.

Print-on-Demand (POD): A printing process where books are printed one at a time or in small groups instead of in quantity. The production cost per book is higher, but no warehousing is necessary. Bookstores have traditionally not carried self-published POD books.

Public domain: Work that has never been copyrighted, or for which the copyright has expired. Copyright laws vary from country to country, but in the US, work published before 1923 has entered the public domain. Work published between 1923 and 1963 may still be protected if the copyright has been renewed.

Published clips: Copies of articles you have had published, from newspapers or magazines.

Quarterly: Every three months.

Query letter: A letter sent to an editor about an article you propose to write and asking if he or she is interested in seeing it.

Reporting time: The number of weeks or months it takes an editor to get back to you about a query, proposal, or manuscript you have sent.

Reprint rights: Selling the right to reprint an article that has already been published. You must have sold only first or onetime rights originally, and wait until it has been published the first time.

Review copies: Books given to reviewers or buyers for chains

Royalty: The percentage an author is paid by a publisher on the sale of each copy of a book.

SAE: Self-addressed envelope (without stamps).

SAN: Standard Account Number, used to identify libraries, book dealers, or schools.

SASE: Self-addressed, stamped envelope. Should always be sent with a hard-copy manuscript or query letter.

SASP: Self-addressed, stamped postcard. May be sent with a hard-copy manuscript submission to be returned by publisher indicating it arrived safely.

Satire: Ridicule that aims at reform.

Second serial rights: See "Reprint rights."

Secular market: An outdated term for the non-Christian publishing market.

Semiannual: Issued twice a year.

Serial: Refers to publication in a periodical (such as first serial rights).

Sidebar: A short feature that accompanies an article and either elaborates on the human interest side of the story or gives additional information on the topic. It is often set apart by appearing within a box or border.

Simultaneous rights: Selling the rights to the same piece to several publishers simultaneously. Be sure everyone is aware that you are doing so.

Simultaneous submissions: Sending the same manuscript to more than one publisher at the same time. Usually done with non-overlapping markets (such as denominational or newspapers) or when you are writing on a timely subject. Be sure to state in a cover letter that it is a simultaneous submission and why.

Slander: The verbal act of defamation.

Slanting: Writing an article so that it meets the needs of a particular market.

Slush pile: The stack of unsolicited manuscripts that have arrived at a publisher's office.

Speculation: See "On speculation."

Staff-written material: Material written by the members of a magazine staff.

Subsidiary rights: All those rights, other than book rights, included in a book contract such as paperback, book club, movie, etc.

Subsidy publisher: A book publisher who charges the author to publish his or her book, as opposed to a royalty publisher who pays the author.

Synopsis: A brief summary of a work; ranges from one paragraph to several pages.

Tabloid: A newspaper-format publication about half the size of a regular newspaper.

Take-home paper: A periodical sent home from Sunday school each week (usually) with Sunday school students, children through adults.

Think piece: A magazine article that has an intellectual, philosophical, or provocative approach to a subject.

Third world: Reference to underdeveloped countries of Asia and Africa.

Trade magazine: A magazine whose audience is in a particular trade or business.

Traditional verse: One or more verses with an established pattern that is repeated throughout the poem.

Transparencies: Positive color slides, not color prints. Now generally replaced by high-resolution digital photos.

Unsolicited manuscript: A manuscript an editor didn't specifically ask to see.

Vanity publisher: See "Subsidy publisher."

Vignette: A short, descriptive literary sketch of a brief scene or incident.

Vitae/Vita: An outline of one's personal history and experience.

Work-for-hire: Signing a contract with a publisher stating that a piece of writing you are creating is with the understanding that in return for the agreed payment, you grant the publisher full ownership and control of the material.

Writers' guidelines: Information provided by a publisher that gives specific guidance for writing for the publication. If the information is not offered online, send an SASE with your request for printed guidelines.

ELECTRONIC FILE TYPES ALL WRITERS SHOULD KNOW

Until recent decades, there was only one file type: ink on paper. These days, most writers type on a computer keyboard, and the variety of software can cause confusion.

Sending an editor an incompatible file can delay or complicate the process — the computer equivalent of expecting them to decipher something in a foreign language.

What's a 'File Extension'?

Every computer document carries a three- or four-letter designation. It not only identifies the file type, but also points to the kinds of computer programs that can open the document. No matter what program you write in, know how to export (or save-as) to other formats.

Word-Processing Files

.doc and *.docx* — Microsoft Word ranks by far as the most common word processor. Most editors request files be sent in this format.

.rtf — One of the earliest file types, the Rich Text Format is straightforward and accessible. Some publishers request submissions in *.rtf* because: 1) any computer with a text-editing program can open it and 2) the format is too rudimentary to spread viruses.

.pages — This type of file is automatically created by the word-processing program Pages, which comes with most new Apple computers. But it can be opened only by Pages users. Before sending a document created in this program, convert it to another file type. *Note:* Many Macs also have Microsoft Word installed. If you're unsure what program you're using, open one of your manuscripts and look for the *app title,* written in bold letters in the top left corner.

.wps — Microsoft Works, now discontinued, saves files in this type, as do some versions of Kingsoft Writer (a free alternative to Word). Any current version of Word can open *.wps* files, but some companies may not be up-to-date. Be in the habit of exporting *.wps* files to *.rtf* or *.doc* format.

.odf and *.odt* — The free word-processing programs OpenOffice and LibreOffice automatically save files in this format. Microsoft Word cannot open these

documents, so convert files created by these programs to *.doc* or *.rtf.*

Files for Photos

For good reproduction in print, publishers need photos with 300 dpi (dots per inch) resolution. A cell phone picture typically does not measure up — either in sharp focus or 300 dpi resolution. If you're submitting images from old photos, it's best to scan the original negative (at 2,400 dpi) rather than scan a print.

.jpg **or** *.jpeg* — Most digital cameras save images in this format. It offers a good compromise between quality and file size. Photos can come in many other formats, including *.raw, .tiff, .gif,* and *.bmp.* Unless the editor asks otherwise, send photo files as a *.jpg.*

About the Contributors

Dennis E. Hensley, PhD, is the author of 54 books, the most recent being *Jesus in the 9 to 5* (AMG Publishers). He is director of the professional writing major at Taylor University and a columnist for *Christian Communicator*. His 3,000 published freelance articles have appeared in national magazines and leading newspapers.

Jerry B. Jenkins is the best-selling author of more than 180 books, with sales of more than 70 million copies, including the best-selling Left Behind series. He is former vice president for publishing and currently chairman of the board of trustees for the Moody Bible Institute of Chicago. Twenty of his books have reached the New York Times best-seller list. His latest novel, the sequel to *I, Saul* from Worthy Publishing, is *Empire's End*.

Virelle Kidder, a full time writer and conference speaker, is the author of six books including *The Best Life Ain't Easy*. Widely published in national magazines, she served for many years as a contributing writer for *Today's Christian Woman* and as a mentor with the Jerry B. Jenkins Christian Writers Guild. Visit her at www.VirelleKidder.com.

Dave Lambert is the owner of Lambert Editorial and the editorial director for the Somersault Group. The author of ten books, he has served as senior fiction editor at Howard Publishing, a division of Simon & Schuster; executive editor for fiction at Zondervan; and a member of the Editorial Board for the Jerry B. Jenkins Christian Writers Guild.

Les Stobbe has worked in Christian publishing as an editor, consultant, and literary agent for more than 50 years. Les has authored or co-authored 14 books and more than 500 feature articles. He served the Jerry B. Jenkins Christian Writers Guild as Executive Editor and a member of its Editorial Board.

Index

This index includes book publishers, periodicals, distributors, greeting cards/specialty markets, and agents, as well as some of the organizations/resources you may need to find quickly. Conferences and groups are listed alphabetically by state in those sections.